THE ROUTLEDGE HANDBOOK OF INSURGENCY AND COUNTERINSURGENCY

This new handbook provides a wide-ranging overview of the current state of academic analysis and debate on insurgency and counterinsurgency, as well as an up-to-date survey of contemporary insurgent movements and counterinsurgencies.

In recent years, and more specifically since the insurgency in Iraq from 2003, academic interest in insurgency and counterinsurgency has substantially increased. These topics have become dominant themes on the security agenda, replacing peacekeeping, humanitarian operations and terrorism as key concepts. The aim of this volume is to showcase the rich thinking that is available in the area of insurgency and counterinsurgency studies and act as a further guide for study and research.

In order to contain this wide-ranging topic within an accessible and informative framework, the editors have divided the text into three key parts:

* Part I: Theoretical and analytical issues
* Part II: Insurgent movements
* Part III: Counterinsurgency cases

The Routledge Handbook of Insurgency and Counterinsurgency will be of great interest to all students of insurgency and small wars, terrorism/counter-terrorism, strategic studies, security studies and IR in general, as well as professional military colleges and policymakers.

Paul B. Rich is co-editor of the journal *Small Wars & Insurgencies* and author/editor of ten books.

Isabelle Duyvesteyn is Special Chair in Strategic Studies at Leiden University, the Netherlands, Senior Lecturer at the Department of History of International Relations at the Institute of History, Utrecht University, the Netherlands, and author/editor of three books.

THE ROUTLEDGE HANDBOOK OF INSURGENCY AND COUNTERINSURGENCY

Edited by Paul B. Rich and Isabelle Duyvesteyn

Routledge
Taylor & Francis Group

LONDON AND NEW YORK

First published in paperback 2014
First published 2012
by Routledge
2 Park Square, Milton Park, Abingdon, Oxon OX14 4RN

Simultaneously published in the USA and Canada
by Routledge
711 Third Avenue, New York, NY 10017

Routledge is an imprint of the Taylor & Francis Group, an informa business

Typeset in Bembo by
Wearset Ltd, Boldon, Tyne and Wear

British Library Cataloguing in Publication Data
A catalogue record for this book is available from the British Library

Library of Congress Cataloging-in-Publication Data
The Routledge handbook of insurgency and counterinsurgency / edited by Paul B.
Rich and Isabelle Duyvesteyn.
p. cm.
Includes bibliographical references and index.
1. Insurgency–Handbooks, manuals, etc. 2. Insurgency–Case studies. 3. Guerrillas–
History. 4. Counterinsurgency–Handbooks, manuals, etc. 5. Counterinsurgency–Case
studies. I. Rich, Paul B., 1950– II. Duyvesteyn, Isabelle, 1972– III. Title: handbook of
insurgency and counterinsurgency.
U240.R69 2012
355.02'18–dc23
2011032272

ISBN: 978-0-415-56733-6 (hbk)
ISBN: 978-0-415-74753-0 (pbk)
ISBN: 978-0-203-13260-9 (ebk)

CONTENTS

Contents

Contents

ILLUSTRATIONS

Figures

Tables

CONTRIBUTORS

Ian Beckett is Professor of Military History at the University of Kent. A Fellow of the Royal Historical Society, he has held chairs in both the United States and UK, and has published widely on counterinsurgency.

David J. Betz is a senior lecturer in the War Studies Department at King's College London. He is the head of the Insurgency Research Group there as well as the academic director of MA War in the Modern World. He is a Senior Fellow of the Foreign Policy Research Institute. He has written on information warfare, the future of land forces, the virtual dimension of insurgency, propaganda of the deed, and British counterinsurgency.

Thijs Brocades Zaalberg is a researcher at the Netherlands Institute for Military History (NIMH) in The Hague, where he focuses on peacekeeping, counterinsurgency and civil–military co-operation. His dissertation *Soldiers and Civil Power* earned him his PhD in history from the University of Amsterdam in 2005. His most recent book on Dutch military operations in Iraq was published in September 2010.

Robert J. Bunker is a Distinguished Visiting Professor and Minerva Chair, Strategic Studies Institute, U.S. Army War College, Carlisle, PA. He holds degrees in Political Science, Government, Behavioral Science, Anthropology/Geography, Social Science and History. His research specializations include non-state threats and counter-terrorism.

Sergio Catignani is a Senior Lecturer in Security and Strategic Studies in the Strategy and Security Institute and Senior Research Fellow at the Institute of Arab and Islamic Studies at the University of Exeter. He is the author of *Israeli Counter-Insurgency and the Intifadas* (Routledge, 2008) and co-editor of *Israel and Hizbollah: An asymmetric conflict in historical and comparative perspective* (Routledge, 2009).

Warren Chin is a senior lecturer in the Defence Studies Department in King's College London and teaches at the Royal College of Defence Studies and the Joint Services Command and Staff College. He specializes in the study of defence, war and strategy.

Lawrence E. Cline is an Adjunct Professor with Troy University. He also is a contract instructor for counter-terrorism with the Center for Civil-Military Relations, Naval Postgraduate School. He is a retired US Army Military Intelligence officer with service in Lebanon, El Salvador, Desert Storm, Somalia and Iraq.

Christopher Coker is Professor of International Relations at the London School of Economics and Political Science. He is the author of numerous books including *Barbarous Philosophers: Reflections on the Nature of War from Heraclitus to Heisenberg* (Hurst, 2010); *Ethics and War in the Twenty-first Century* (London: Routledge, 2009) and many others.

Isabelle Duyvesteyn is Special Chair in Strategic Studies at Leiden University and Senior Lecturer at the Department of History of International Relaat Utrecht University in the Netherlands. Her most recent publications include a special issue of *The Journal of Strategic Studies*, 'The Escalation and De-escalation of Irregular War', Vol. 35, No. 5 (2012) and 'The Irrelevance of the Security Dilemma for Civil Wars', *Civil Wars* (forthcoming 2014).

Abel Esterhuyse is a lecturer at the Faculty of Military Science of Stellenbosch University at the South African Military Academy. He holds a PhD from Stellenbosch University and an MSS from Pretoria University. Before joining the Faculty of Military Science, Dr Esterhuyse served as a lieutenant colonel in the South African Army. At present, Dr Esterhuyse leads a team of international researchers commissioned to investigate the military and institutional culture of the army.

David P. Fidler is the James Louis Calamaras Professor of Law at the Indiana University Maurer School of Law. He is co-editor with Sumit Ganguly of *India and Counterinsurgency: Lessons Learned* (Routledge, 2009).

Sumit Ganguly is the Rabindranath Tagore Chair in Indian Cultures and Civilizations, Director of the India Studies Program, and Professor of Political Science at Indiana University. He is co-editor with David Fidler of *India and Counterinsurgency: Lessons Learned* (Routledge, 2009).

Antonio Giustozzi is an independent researcher associated with the Crisis States Research Centre (LSE). He is the author of several articles and papers on Afghanistan, as well as of three books, *War, Politics and Society in Afghanistan, 1978–1992, Koran, Kalashnikov and Laptop: The Neo-Taliban Insurgency, 2002–7* and *Empires of Mud: War and Warlords in Afghanistan*. He also edited a volume on the Taliban, *Decoding the New Taliban*, featuring contributions by specialists from different backgrounds.

Namrata Goswami is Research Fellow at the Institute for Defence Studies and Analyses, New Delhi. She specializes in ethnic conflicts, conflict prevention, management and resolution, and international relations theory. Dr Goswami was a Senior Fellow at the United States Institute of Peace (USIP), Washington, DC from October 2012 to June 2013, Visiting Fellow at the South Asia Institute, University of Heidelberg (November–December 2010), the International Peace Research Institute, Oslo (PRIO), August 2006 to July 2010 and a Visiting Fellow at the Centre for Dialogue, La Trobe University, Melbourne, from April to August 2009. She is also a recipient of the Fulbright-Nehru Senior Research Fellowship, 2012–2013.

Judith Palmer Harik was associate professor of comparative politics at the American University of Beirut from 1982 until 2003 when she became president of Lebanon's Matn University. She is the author of *Hezbollah: The Changing Face of Terrorism* (London: I.B. Tauris, 2004) and has numerous works on that subject as well as on post-civil war and contemporary politics in Lebanon.

Ahmed Hashim is Associate Professor in Strategic Studies, RSIS, Nanyang Technological University, Singapore.

Alice Hills is Professor of Conflict Studies at Durham University, UK, where her research addresses the nature of sub-state security. Her research focuses on why public police evolve as they do, and what explains their interaction with governments, militaries and societies.

Geraint Hughes is a lecturer at the Defence Studies Department, King's College London, and is at present teaching at the Joint Services Command and Staff College, Shrivenham, UK. His research interests include land warfare since 1945 and counterinsurgency, and he is currently working on his second book, on the topic of proxy warfare.

Margret Johannsen is a political scientist and works as Senior Research Fellow at the Institute for Peace Research and Security Policy at the University of Hamburg (IFSH). She is lecturer in the postgraduate programme 'Peace and Security Studies' at Hamburg University and co-editor of the annual German 'Peace Report'. She has authored numerous publications on arms control, the Israeli–Palestinian conflict, the Middle East peace process, and European and US Middle East policy.

David Kilcullen is an author, former professional soldier and diplomat. His academic background is in the political anthropology of insurgency in traditional societies. He is the author of numerous scholarly articles and books, including *The Accidental Guerrilla* (2009), *Counterinsurgency* (2010) and *Out of the Mountains* (2013).

David Lewis is Senior Lecturer in Politics at the Department of Politics at the University of Exeter. He has research interests in the areas of security, peacebuilding, political change and conflict, and has considerable field experience in Central Asia, the Caucasus and South Asia.

Steven Metz is the Director of Research at the US Army War College Strategic Studies Institute and writes a weekly column called "Strategic Horizons" for *World Policy Review*.

Thomas R. Mockaitis is Professor of History at DePaul University. He is the author of *Iraq and the Challenge of Counterinsurgency*, *British Counterinsurgency in the Post-Imperial Era* and *British Counterinsurgency: 1919–1960*. He has taught at the Royal Military Academy of the Netherlands, the Center for Civil-Military Relations at the Naval Post-Graduate School, the NATO School, the US Marine Corps Command and Staff College and the Canadian Forces Staff College.

Shehzad H. Qazi is a Fellow at the Institute for Social Policy and Understanding and a Pollster at Charney Research where he conducts research in crisis and transitional countries. He is also a Contributing Analyst at Wikistrat.

William Reno is a Professor of Political Science and Director of the Program of African Studies at Northwestern University in Chicago. He is the author of *Corruption and State Politics in Sierra Leone* (Cambridge University Press, 1995), *Warlord Politics and African States* (Lynne Rienner, 1998) and *Warfare in Independent Africa* (Cambridge University Press, 2011). He has written extensively on the organization and behaviour of armed groups in Africa.

Paul B. Rich is a researcher and editor of the journal *Small Wars and Insurgencies*. He has taught at the Universities of Warwick, Bristol and Melbourne. His publications include *State Power and Black Politics in South Africa* (1996), *The Counter-Insurgent State* (co-editor) (1997), *Warlords in International Relations* (1999) and *Crisis in the Caucasus: Russia, Georgia and the West* (2009). He is currently working on a study of literature, the media and depictions of terrorism.

Julian Schofield (PhD Columbia) is an associate professor of political science at Concordia University, and is the author of *Militarization and War* (Palgrave Macmillan, 2007). His articles have appeared in *Armed Forces & Society*, the *Journal of Strategic Studies*, *International Relations*, and others. He has conducted extensive fieldwork in Pakistan, India and Bangladesh, as well as Southeast Asia and the Middle East. His current research focuses on security relations in South Asia, counterinsurgency theory and strategic implications of trade.

David E. Spencer is a Professor of Counter Terrorism at the William J. Perry Center for Hemispheric Defense Studies in Washington, DC, one of the Department of Defense's five regional centers that provides defense education to students from allied and partner nations around the globe. He completed his PhD dissertation on insurgent logistics in Latin America at George Washington University. He has published extensively on terrorism and insurgent movements in Latin America.

David H. Ucko is Associate Professor at the College for International Security Affairs, National Defense University and an adjunct fellow at the Department of War Studies, King's College London. He is the author of *Counterinsurgency in Crisis: Britain and the Challenges of Modern Warfare* (Columbia University Press, 2013), *The New Counterinsurgency Era: Transforming the U.S. Military for Modern Wars* (Georgetown University Press, 2009) and co-editor of *Reintegrating Armed Groups After Conflict: Politics, Violence and Transition* (Routledge, 2009).

Martin I. Wayne is the China Security Fellow at the National Defense University's Institute for National Strategic Studies. In 2005, Dr Wayne conducted extensive fieldwork in Xinjiang. He is the author of *China's War on Terrorism: Counter-Insurgency, Politics and Internal Security* (Routledge, 2008).

Yuri M. Zhukov is a Fellow with the National Security Studies Program at the Weatherhead Center for International Affairs, and a PhD Candidate in the Department of Government at Harvard University. His research interests include epidemiological models of insurgency and counterinsurgency, wargaming and simulation, with an empirical focus on Russia and Eurasia. Mr Zhukov previously worked in a variety of civilian and contractor positions at the Department of Defense.

PREFACE AND ACKNOWLEDGEMENTS

This volume of research papers seeks to provide a general guide to the current state of academic thinking in the field of insurgency and counterinsurgency. It started as a project initially proposed to us by Andrew Humphrys, senior editor of Military, Strategic and Security Studies at Routledge in early 2009. The volume brings together a group of renowned international experts as well as some noted younger scholars in the fields of insurgency, counterinsurgency and strategic studies. There is of course an extensive literature on these topics in the areas of politics, history international relations and strategic and military studies. This literature grows rapidly year on year and is often bewildering to students and researchers, especially those quite new to the field. The compendium's aim therefore is to bring together a collection of analyses into one accessible source. The volume seeks to present a comprehensive global picture of insurgency and counterinsurgency as well as expose readers to the broader themes of analytical and scholarly debate.

The process of producing this book was eventful. It reflected life in more than one way. There were inevitable delays, due to illnesses but also happier events such as the arrival of a little baby girl. The editors would like in particular to thank Andrew Humphrys, Rebecca Brennan and Annabelle Harris at Routledge and Phillippa Nichol, Gail Welsh, Allie Waite and Amy Ekins at Wearset. The maps of Sri Lanka and Pakistan have been reprinted with kind permission of the United Nations Cartography Department. Also Ian Beckett, Mark T. Berger, Daniel Castro, Tom Durrell Young, Tom Marks, John Nagl, Kevin O'Brien, John Russell, Erin Simpson and Jeff Sluka, deserve our thanks for their consideration, input, reading and commenting on draft manuscripts as well as all the contributors of this volume. Without their inspiration and hard work this volume would not have seen the light of day.

Paul B. Rich and Isabelle Duyvesteyn

1

THE STUDY OF INSURGENCY AND COUNTERINSURGENCY

Paul B. Rich and Isabelle Duyvesteyn

The interest in the topics of insurgency and counterinsurgency has been far from consistent. Several times insurgency has been declared dead and buried; Steven Metz wrote in 1995 that '[t]he insurgents of the world are sleeping' (Metz 1995: 1). Walter Laqueur concluded in 1998 that '[g]uerrilla war may not entirely disappear but, seen in historical perspective, it is on the decline' (Laqueur 1998). The interest in counterinsurgency has suffered a similar fate. Preferably forgotten after the Vietnam War, after the recent spike in interest, it has now again been declared beyond its peak and even useless for explaining current violence.

Not only has the interest in the topics come and gone, the level and content of debate has also been subject of harsh criticism. David Kilcullen, who is a contributor to this volume, has contended that '[c]lassical counterinsurgency ... constitutes a dominant paradigm through which practitioners approach today's conflicts – often via the prescriptive application of "received wisdom" derived by exegesis from the classics' (Kilcullen 2006–7: 111). Moreover the distinguished military historian Martin van Creveld rejected the whole notion of counterinsurgency which, he argues, amounts to little on the grounds that since 99 per cent of it has been written by the losing side it is of little real value (van Creveld 2006: 268; Peters 2007; Duyvesteyn 2011).

This unsteady interest in and harsh criticism of insurgency and counterinsurgency studies is in many respects surprising. Not only do we know that the majority of wars in the international system since 1815 are of an intra-state, as opposed to an inter-state, variety; importantly, these wars have often been fought in an irregular manner (Kalyvas 2007). After the end of the Cold War, the many conflicts that emerged, such as in the Balkans, East and West Africa, were all fought predominantly using indirect strategies of attack. The most notable exception has been the confrontation between Ethiopia and Eritrea between 1998 and 2000, where trench warfare occurred (repeating a pattern set in the Iran–Iraq War in the 1980s).

Given this background, the study of insurgency and counterinsurgency in the academic fields of military and strategic studies has been a rather marginal enterprise. There is hardly a consistent body of scholarship devoted to these topics. Roughly since Clausewitzean times until the 1960s, guerrilla warfare and insurgencies were often viewed as peripheral to mainstream military conflict, which was centred around conventional inter-state war in which military assets were mobilised in pursuit of political objectives by rival states in an anarchic international system. During the period of the Cold War insurgencies were viewed by many analysts as dark, even exotic phenomena which did not fit easily into strategic classification centred on theories of nuclear deterrence.[1] At the same time the body of strategic thought forged during the Cold War era became increasingly abstract and ahistorical and imprisoned by a technological determinism. By the time the Cold War came to an end, nothing short of an 'existential crisis', in the words of Hew Strachan, had emerged within strategic studies. It was out of this crisis that insurgency (which now replaced the rather dated term 'low intensity conflict') became subsequently cata-pulted onto the central plane of strategic studies as many Western states found themselves involved in a range of military conflicts around the world resulting from ethnic and clan conflicts in weak or 'failing' states (Strachan 2008). While devising answers to these security challenges, most states involved largely overlooked the relevance of insurgency and counterinsurgency thought.

In recent years, however, and more specifically since the insurgency in Iraq from 2003, aca-demic interest in insurgency and counterinsurgency has substantially increased. These topics have become dominant themes on the security agenda, replacing peacekeeping, humanitarian opera-tions and terrorism as key concepts. Apparently, 'more has been written on [counterinsurgency] ... in the last four years than in the last four decades' (Kilcullen 2006–7: 111). In these last few years, a growing body of strategic theorists has recognised that insurgencies are an inextricable part of mainstream strategic studies. In 1999 Colin Gray observed in a major textbook that 'small wars and other savage violence' are 'part of the same empirical and intellectual universe which includes Western strategic experience' (Gray 1999: 293; Strachan 2008).[2] Since the operations in Afghani-stan and Iraq started to provide unforeseen challenges, the discussion about insurgency and coun-terinsurgency re-emerged with force. Not only for its historical notoriety but also because of its academic significance and necessity, this fickle attention for the topics seems unjust. The aim of this volume is to demonstrate the rich thinking that is available in the area of insurgency and coun-terinsurgency studies and act as a further guide for study and research.

The historical evolution of 'people's war', guerrilla and insurgency

The general analytical surveys of insurgency usually emphasise both the range and diversity of these conflicts and the relatively small number that have succeeded on their own in overthrow-ing state power and achieving any form of major political transformation. Stretching back to guerrilla conflicts in the Ancient World such as those of the Jewish guerrillas against Roman rule in Judea or the Gallic guerrillas against Caesar in Gaul, most guerrillas failed in the end to over-throw states on their own and required help in some form from external regular forces (Ellis 1995).[3] Guerrilla conflict has tended to wax and wane in its political and strategic saliency, in part because – for long periods of ancient and early modern history – the exact differences between regular and irregular military formations were not especially clear and on occasions blurred. With the end of the Ancient World for instance the gap between regular uniformed armies and those of guerrilla narrowed in the European Middle Ages as the armed forces of medieval monarchical states and those of irregular military formations was not especially wide. With the 'military revolution' of the seventeenth and eighteenth centuries this gap proceeded to increase once more as the seventeenth-century nation-states' armies underwent what J.R. Hale has termed a 'military reformation' in the terms of increased technological sophistication; by the following century, this would be accompanied by growing professionalism in terms of organisation, drill, uniforms and structures of command (Hale 1985; see also Arnold 2002; Ellis 1995; Anderson 1988; Duffy 1987).

In the nineteenth century a considerable number of guerrilla struggles were waged on the borders and frontiers of European colonial empires. The very term 'small wars' only really entered into general strategic parlance through the writings of Colonel Charles Callwell in the 1880s and 1890s, especially his book published by the British War Office in 1896: *Small Wars: Their Principles and Practice*. The term had actually been used much earlier in European military writing in the eighteenth and nineteenth centuries but this debate did not have much impact on wider military and strategic thinking – perhaps because of the very negative effect of the guerrilla in Spain against the French occupying force between 1808 and 1813 from which the word *guerrilla* (Spanish for 'small war') derives (Laqueur 1977: 100).[4]

The Spanish guerrillas or *partidas* proved highly ill disciplined and were prone as much to banditry as attacking the French. Though they did help to tie down French occupying forces they helped to undermine the Spanish regular army as many troops deserted to the *partidas* (Esdaile 1988: 250–80). They hardly served as a major model for insurgency in the nineteenth century and Callwell's book focused more on colonial rebellions that had emerged in various parts of the European colonial empires in the years following the Indian 'Mutiny' of 1857. His book was especially notable for focusing on principles of mobile warfare which would soon be tested in campaigns by Britain in South Africa against the Boers between 1899 and 1902 and by the United States in Cuba and the Philippines between 1895 and 1902 (Beckett 2001: 35–7).[5]

Callwell's conceptualisation of 'small war' however lacked any really dynamic features. He failed to see it as expanding to a conventional level and he preferred to make a rather more static three-fold classification of 'small wars' into: (1) campaigns of conquest and annexation; (2) campaigns for the suppression of insurrection and lawlessness; and (3) campaigns to avenge a 'wrong' or to 'overthrow a dangerous enemy' (Callwell 2010: 21–5). This static dimension to his discussion was in part a product of the fact that he set himself the relatively limited task of providing a 'tactical textbook' as well as the fact that he wrote at a time when neither the legitimacy nor durability of European imperial power was in any serious doubt. The book though was useful for the way it pointed to the problems presented to incumbent forces by the difficulties of terrain and climate which in effect acted as a form of force multiplier for indigenous guerrilla forces; in turn they made offensive action essential in order to secure a decisive military victory. Callwell had no real grasp of 'protracted war' by guerrilla forces which he felt were always liable to rapid collapse should their leaders or 'chiefs' be removed or incapacitated (Callwell 2010: 88).

The onset of two world wars in the first half of the twentieth century ensured that this marginalisation of debate on insurgency would continue well into the 1950s when the onset of 'wars of national liberation' began to exercise the minds of strategic planners and military theorists in various Western states. By this time some major developments had occurred in the very conceptualisation of insurgency by the expansion of guerrilla conflict in various parts of what would become known as the developing world in the decades after the First World War.

Before the twentieth century guerrilla conflict was often linked to reactionary or even counter-revolutionary movements – as in the case of the revolt in the Vendée in the 1790s – and did not have anything like the same meaning as 'people's war' (Joes 1998; Laqueur 1977: 22–9).[6] This latter term evolved only slowly in the course of the nineteenth century since it was avoided by many of that century's most notable revolutionary thinkers such as Marx and Engels who were sceptical that there could be anything like a proper 'people's war' in industrialised Europe. Both revolutionaries effectively started with Clausewitz's argument that guerrilla should at best be seen as an adjunct to conventional war, leading them to emphasise the idea of mass revolutionary insurrection on the French revolutionary model in order to ensure the moral rather than the military collapse of state power (Beckett 2001: 14; Ibrahim 2004: 114).

Indeed there were only a few scattered efforts before 1914 to link guerrilla warfare to revolution. In Italy the Piedmontese and Italian nationalist Giuseppe Mazzini saw guerrilla conflict as aiding an insurrection against Habsburg rule but the most sophisticated treatment of this idea was probably by the lesser known figure of Carlo Bianco, an Italian revolutionary who rather misleadingly interpreted the guerrilla conflict in Spain against Napoleon as a model for insurrectionary warfare against the Habsburgs. Bianco envisaged small guerrilla units of 10–50 rebels in the early stages of this struggle, gradually widening to encompass a popular insurrection that would eventually include flying columns and a regular revolutionary army (Ibrahim 2004: 116). These ideas did not get far in the middle years of the nineteenth century when the Piedmontese state was wary of using even small bands of popular militias and Mazzini preferred to leave the whole issue of social revolution until after Italian unification (which would not occur through an insurgent people's war as Garibaldi and his followers had hoped).

So the idea of 'people's war' really had to wait until the twentieth century before it could become part of strategic parlance. There are some surprising features to this, since the concept of popular sovereignty and the very invention of the idea or fiction of the people as a decisive political force stemmed from the English revolution of the 1640s. In a rather more attenuated form it had been embodied in the revolutionary settlement in America in the 1780s so that, as a political concept, popular sovereignty was hardly new by the mid to late nineteenth century (Morgan 1989). However, outside the Atlantic littoral of the English-speaking proto-democracies the term was still an unfamiliar one that threatened established and hierarchical elites resting on traditional forms of dynastic power, especially following the demise of radical liberalism in the decades after the Napoleonic wars. The nineteenth century has often been rather inaccurately termed an 'age of revolutions', for most of the revolutions that did occur during this period such as those of 1830 and 1848 failed to achieve long-term political transformation of states and certainly failed to secure the wide-ranging social revolutions that would occur in Mexico after 1910, Russia after 1917 and China after 1949. To this extent the real turning point for revolutionary 'people's war' was the end of the First World War when the collapse of four empires in Europe created the opening and opportunities within international politics for revolutionaries to seize and hold power (Hobsbawm 1994: 54–84; Hall 1996: 67–110). Even then, though, 'people's war' did not make that many advances in the interwar period with perhaps the most notable insurgent achievement being the liberation of southern Ireland in the early 1920s from British rule while elsewhere rebellions in North Africa, the Middle East and India were crushed. Even in China Mao Zedong was largely unsuccessful in the 1930s in implementing his guerrilla war theories and it would not be until the Japanese invasion after 1937 and the advent of the Second World War that the real break came in the evolution of Maoist protracted war (Porch 2001: 199–201).

We should in any case be wary of allowing the concept of 'people's war' to be completely dominated by Maoist concepts of protracted guerrilla warfare which some recent scholars of insurgencies and 'post Maoism' have been inclined to do (Ellis 1995: 11; Taber 1970; Clapham 1998: 2; Mackinlay 2009. See also Rich 2010 for criticisms of this approach). This will be further discussed below. Historians of insurgencies have paid far too little attention to the trinitarian features of military conflict originally identified by Clausewitz: people, state and army (Duyvesteyn 2005). The term 'people's war' tends to obfuscate this division and leads to the rather false assumption that the 'people' have in some way become mobilised into a popular mass army operating against in many cases a foreign or colonial regime.

This mobilisation obviously depended upon different kinds of political processes in the societies concerned, rendering periodisation and generalisation difficult, not least because the wars concerned were subject to varying degrees of external intervention by other states (Laqueur 1977: 279). There has been a tendency in some historical writing on insurgency (such as those of Walter Laqueur) to resist any serious generalisation and to ascribe guerrilla war to the combination of a number of chance factors.

However, there is still a considerable need in this area for the application of an historical sociology that can begin to unravel differing political responses to processes of modernisation and economic transformation resulting from the increasing integration of these societies into a global market economy. The study of the various examples of 'people's war' such as Mexico in the early twentieth century following the revolution of 1910, China under Mao in the 1930s and 1940s, Vietnam from the 1950s through to the mid 1970s, Cuba with the Castro revolution of 1959 and Algeria during the war against the French from 1954 to 1962 suggests a varying pattern of conflict in which the 'the people' may become mobilised into a revolutionary political party operating alongside of, or in some cases in competition with, an army. The model of the revolutionary party took a number of differing forms but it was strongly shaped in the decades after 1917 by that of the Soviet model forged by Lenin and later Stalin: more re-evaluation of this model is needed though by a closer examination of the military ideas of Trotsky and the mobilisation of the Red Guards by the Bolsheviks in what was really a military *coup d'état* in October 1917 (see in particular Nelson 1988).

In some senses a process of evolutionary mutation had occurred within revolutionary theory leading to a shift from a dominant 'Parisian paradigm' of the nineteenth century anchored in the French revolution to a 'Comintern paradigm' following the Russian revolution of 1917 to a 'guerrilla' or 'people's war paradigm' following the 1949 Chinese Communist revolution (Johnson 1973: 111). The 'guerrilla paradigm' actually had quite a short life since by the late 1960s it was evident that not all revolutions would be based on people's war while attempted 'people's war' did not in all cases lead to revolution. In addition a more hard-nosed realist view indicated that the 'people's war' discourse was in a very real sense a cover for China's own efforts to impact on international politics and which declined as these objectives became increasingly pragmatic in the 1970s following the Nixon visit (Johnson 1973: 103).

Moreover the number of successful cases of 'people's war' has proved rather slim. Looking from the early twentieth century onwards it is evident that in some cases, such as that of Mexico, the peasant rebellions led by Zapata and Pancho Villa failed to lead to the creation of a successful revolutionary party and ended up as an anachronistic rebellion overridden by urban political machines controlled by the middle class. Likewise in Algeria the counterinsurgency waged by the French succeeded in isolating the exiled Front de Libération Nationale (FLN) revolutionary party leadership from support at the local level and left it weak by the time of independence in 1962, leading within three years to a coup that secured military control of the new postcolonial state (Wolf 1971: 276–302).

It is really the examples of China and Vietnam which have provided the strongest examples for 'people's war' directed by a revolutionary party that maintained close links with the different peasant groups in the countryside – with Mao emphasising in particular the centrality of the 'middle' and 'poor' peasantry in the building of a revolutionary party to confront both the rival Kuomintang and, after 1937, the invading Japanese army. The three-phased model of Maoist 'protracted war' went on to become something of an ideological icon for radical guerrilla theorists in the 1960s and 1970s (Ranger 1985). Indeed some analysts detected a distinct 'model' of guerrilla warfare centred on basic Maoist precepts of peasant support, protracted war, national appeal, leadership, organisation and the breakdown of the opposing regime. Such a model could, it was predicted, be extended on a global basis even if it did not always come accompanied by a 'Communist' label (Girling 1969).

The Maoist model looked as follows: the insurgent uses guerrilla terrorism and other tactics as the main means to wage a political-strategic battle aimed at the political leadership of a state. Mao Zedong conceptualised an insurgency strategy, or revolutionary war, as he termed it, as a three-stage process (Mao 2005). In the first stage, a small dedicated group of fighters carries out short and sharp hit-and-run actions to create liberated areas in the countryside where government control is absent. By provoking the government to strike back hard, the fighters hope to win supporters and by using propaganda tools they aim to increase their numerical strength. In the second phase the liberated areas should be extended into liberated zones, which can be linked up. In the last and final phase, a conventional confrontation should be sought with the remaining government forces to defeat them on the battlefield.

Subsequently, two important deviations were proposed. First, Che Guevara stated that a small dedicated cadre could compensate for the long-drawn-out process of political and military mobilisation of the peasant masses (Guevara 1969). The theory was broadly derived from the Cuban guerrilla experience of fighting against the forces of the corrupt Batista regime in Havana between 1954 and 1959 (Debray 1980; Debray *et al*. 1969).[7] Even before its popular theorisation by Regis Debray, it is evident from Guevara's own popular book on the subject that the guerrilla 'column' would undergo some form of inevitable expansion as it gained new followers – a process Guevara metaphorically compared to a beehive releasing a new queen after its has reached a certain size to form a new colony (Guevara 1969: 22). Debray's *foco* strategy was based on effectively reversing the relationship between peasants and revolutionary party as the guerrilla army itself now took on a 'vanguard' role in political mobilisation. The *foco* concept appealed to Guevara as a means of speeding up peasant-based insurgencies throughout Latin America and the Third World as part of a global strategy of promoting social revolution against Western influence and control.

Guevara's ideas on guerrilla acquired mythical status amongst some discussion on insurgency and revolution in the 1960s and early 1970s. In one short book, for instance, published as part of popular student series by Fontana in 1970, Andrew Sinclair rather foolishly claimed that Guevara's *Guerrilla Warfare* was more immediately influential than Marx's *Communist Manifesto* and that Guevara himself was 'the Garibaldi of his age, the most admired and loved revolutionary of his time' (Sinclair 1970: 44, 92).[8] The problem with this assessment was that it confused Western student admiration for a romantic figure (whose picture often adorned campus dormitories) for real political and strategic influence at the local level in Third World insurgencies.

Guevara, in the initial stages of the Cuban revolution, called for a guerrilla army to be the foundation for an 'armed democracy'. Guevara himself along with Regis Debray was largely responsible for forging a myth of a peasant-based revolution at a time when this was beginning to run into conflict with the dominant line in the Popular Socialist Party (PSP) in Cuba which was one of 'unity' and 'mass action' that involved the urban population as well (Suarez 1967: 41–2). Guevara's concept of peasant based revolution contained strongly romantic features that linked it with Maoist guerrilla ideas in its rejection of cities as terrains for insurgent struggle. The approach reflected deeper divisions within Marxist and radical thought over the nature of peasantries and rural peoples who had been traditionally dismissed by Marx, Engels and Lenin as backward and superstitious. In reaction to this and to the perceived failures of the Soviet system, a newer body of left-wing thought veered in the 1960s back towards glamorising the rural peasantry at a time when they were fast being eclipsed in many developing states by rapid urbanisation and a drift of the rural poor and landless into urban shanty towns (Oppenheimer 1969: 36–49). In any event, the Guevarist and *foco* model of insurgency proved to be relatively short-lived given Guevara's own disastrous expedition and death in his Bolivian adventure in 1967. The same year a similar *foco* concept was applied by the Sandinista (FSLN) rebels in the northern Pancasan mountains of Nicaragua with similarly disastrous results. The Nicaragua debacle prompted a political debate within the FSLN and a gradual shift towards a more popularly based strategy of urban insurrection which would eventually lead to the overthrow of the Somoza dictatorship in 1979 (Zimmermann 2000: 99–100, *passim*).

The second deviation from the Maoist model was proposed by two South American theorists of urban guerrilla warfare, Carlos Marighella and Abraham Guillén, who argued that in states where the majority of the population lived in cities the central focus of revolutionary people's war had to lie in urban guerrilla warfare. As Matthew Carr has recently argued, there was a strongly romantic tone to this approach from theorists who had a rather poor understanding of the problems that accompanied urban insurgent warfare. Marighella was a long-standing Brazilian revolutionary activist who finally broke with the Communist Party in 1967 before being cornered and killed by the police. His mini manual showed a poor understanding of just how far states in South America could go in isolating urban guerrillas (Marighella 2002). Guillén, by contrast, could at least claim to have rather more strategic expertise being a veteran of the Spanish Civil War of the 1930s, though he recognised that urban guerrilla warfare would be different to the sieges of cities like Stalingrad, Warsaw and Berlin in the Second World War. He focused instead on the need for urban guerrilla formations to be highly mobile and to strike at the government's fixed positions and then melt away into the urban metropolis: a prognosis that has been to a considerable degree borne out by warfare in cities such as Mogadishu and Baghdad with only a few cities being subject to full-scale conventional bombardment such as Grozny by the Russian army in the Second Chechen War of 1999–2000 (and still employing a doctrine indeed derived from the Second World War experience).

One of the central problems in any case with urban insurgency has been its high propensity to lapse into either random terrorism or gangland warfare. In the case of the former urban guerrilla warfare really ends up as an extension of the old anarchist 'propaganda by deed' concept of the late nineteenth century. It is not surprising that most major strategic theorists have never rated urban insurgency very highly as a major strategy of revolutionary overthrow of states (Oppenheimer 1969). Marighella imagined that urban insurgency would provoke the establishment to use repression which would create a support base for the cause of the activists.[9] He still saw urban insurgency as subordinate to rural guerrilla warfare though he was not averse to the use of terrorism in order to sustain it: a perception that was well brought out in the urban terrorist campaign waged by the FLN in the so-called 'Battle of Algiers' in 1957 which would in the end be decisively defeated by the French Paras under General Massu – a struggle that would be captured in the epic film by Gillo Pontecorvo in 1966, *The Battle of Algiers*. The same pattern would be demonstrated on an even more dramatic scale in Uruguay in the early 1970s as the constitution of a liberal democratic state was suspended as the Uruguayan state resorted to a ruthless counterinsurgency strategy to isolate and defeat the urban insurgency of the *Tupamaros* guerrillas (Carr 2011: 143–55).

It is fair to conclude that there is a high propensity for campaigns of urban guerrilla warfare to regress into terrorist movements given the difficulties of sustaining an insurgent network in the highly policed urban terrain. Few of the insurgent campaigns that are examined in this volume really fit into a specifically urban form of insurgency and most are still pivoted upon military action in a rural terrain, with urban insurgent activity in a supporting role. As Andy Mack has pointed out 'urban guerrilla warfare' as a whole remains a shadowy military construct based on an essential 'non strategy' that is often fatally orientated towards challenging its enemy at his strongest rather than weakest points (Mack 1974). As a distinct 'strategy' moreover it has been generally eclipsed in the last two decades by the emergence of two other forces that have emerged in the post-Cold War global order: globalised insurgency which has often chosen to hide terrorist networks within urban locations and international drug gangs which have also taken on many of the features of urban insurgent formations. The latter type of formations deserve in particular much more serious analysis as the Chapter 4 by Robert Bunker in this volume indicates.

Returning to the theme of the Maoist domination of guerrilla insurgencies in the twentieth century it was clear that by the middle 1970s, in the case of Vietnam, basic Maoist precepts were partially followed as the war escalated in many areas to a conventional level, leading to huge losses for both the NLF National Liberation Front and the North Vietnamese Army under Giap in the 1968 Tet Offensive and the 1975 invasion of the South leading to the collapse of the South Vietnamese regime. Maoist guerrilla theory had been forged at a time when the insurgency in China had been a largely localised affair despite the Japanese invasion in 1937 and later Soviet intervention in Manchuria in 1945. By the late 1960s Maoist-type insurgencies appeared to be increasingly on the decline in what had by then come to be called the 'Third World'. Modernisation and urbanisation had in many cases led to an undermining of the peasantry while in other cases various models of land reform took the heat out of Maoist precepts of peasant-based protracted war. Only in rather more remote terrains such as the highlands of Peru or the mountainous regions of Nepal would Maoist warfare still form the guiding political ideology of rural insurgency, while Maoism as a general force in international politics underwent a serious decline following the political transformation in China in the late 1970s following the rise of Deng Xiaoping.

The radical identification with peasant based insurgency did not in any case survive for much longer, with its last real testing grounds being Southern Africa in the course of the 1970s as the surviving European colonial regimes of Mozambique, Angola and Rhodesia – together with the more complicated case of South Africa – came under growing pressure from a variety of guerrilla formations with a range of political ideologies. Significantly none adopted any form of *foco* model and the guerrilla insurgencies such as FRELIMO in Mozambique, the rival UNITA and MPLA movements in Angola and ZAPU and ZANU-PF in Rhodesia in the 1970s can now be seen as the last phase of rural insurgency geared to promoting an anti-colonial social revolution. The insurgencies did much to hasten the demise of the colonial regimes in the region though it is hard to see them following any specifically Maoist strategy in the process. As Terence Ranger has pointed out in one of the best studies of this pattern of insurgency in Rhodesia, much of the insurgency was fomented by a radicalisation of peasant consciousness in response to the settler expropriation of land that stretched back in many instances to the 1940s (Ranger 1985).

The transfer of power in Rhodesia in 1980 following the election victory of Robert Mugabe's ZANU-PF thus marks a major watershed in the rural insurgencies, though one that was not really recognised as such at the time. Rhodesia was really among the last major rural anti-colonial insurgencies and thereafter any such rural insurgencies became increasingly disconnected from the concept of revolutionary warfare. Indeed with the beginning of Mujahideen resistance (with CIA and Pakistani ISI support) in the early 1980s to the Soviet invasion of Afghanistan in late 1979 it is possible to see the emergence of a different pattern of rural insurgency driven by an Islamist ideology which rejected the Western revolutionary tradition from 1789 and sought a reactionary restoration of a medieval social order rooted in an imagined Islamic golden age set in the past.

However, following the withdrawal of the United States from South Vietnam (and the collapse of that state two years later) there was a temporary lull. Apart from engagement in the El Salvadorian insurgency in the mid 1980s, the United States resumed its active engagement in 'low intensity conflict' with its short-lived and rather disastrous engagement in Somalia at the 'Battle of Mogadishu' in 1993. Since the beginning of the twenty-first century, there has been a renewed intensification of insurgency warfare across the globe in a more complex international environment that is no longer marked by earlier superpower rivalries of the Cold War or the anti-colonial insurgencies within declining European empires.

The rise of counterinsurgency

Like insurgency, the strategy behind counterinsurgency also has deep roots in military and strategic thought and practice, though one that has been rather more closely linked to individual 'national' traditions. For traditional militaries it has always been a form of war which has been seen as difficult and complex.

In a general sense occupying armies or militaries that are faced with sporadic small-scale attacks from guerrilla formations have a series of basic choices. At the crudest level they can seek to dry up any local or popular support for these guerrillas by massacring the populations or driving them into enclaves where they can be more closely monitored or controlled. However, most imperial armies of occupation discover that there are limits to such a strategy if they are going to need this population to make the land under their control economically productive or the basis for a colonial society. Thus from the time of the Romans some form of political deals or treaties have been brokered with the leaders of the subjugated population in order to neutralise the insurgency by political rather than straightforward military means. This is a broad historical consideration that needs to be taken into account when measuring the success of liberal democratic regimes in exiting out of insurgent conflicts through pacted deals with insurgent groups compared to more authoritarian regimes which might often end up being able to do the same thing. Clearly not all of the latter can easily do so – as evidenced by the desperate desire by the Salazarist regime in Portugal to hang on to its colonies in Mozambique, Guinea Bissau and Angola in the 1960s when any serious military assessment would have told it that they were lost. But many others will (such as the authoritarian powers taken by the new Fifth French Republic under de Gaulle to exit out of Algeria in 1962) suggesting that analysts need to avoid any simple linkage between a domestic democratic political culture and an adroit management of foreign insurgent conflicts

One of the most intensely political forms of counterinsurgency in the post-1945 period was that defined by the counterinsurgent French strategists as *guerre revolutionnaire*. It was heavily shaped by the experience of the French army following its defeat in 1940 and again at Dien Bien Phu in 1954. The linkage of guerrilla warfare with social revolution had emerged in China in the 1930s and been termed 'revolutionary warfare' by Mao Zedong in 1936. The concept of warfare being pursued to attain a new social order was taken up by the Vietminh in Vietnam after 1945 and in turn was picked up by French officers captured by the Vietminh after 1949: these officers were able, on their return to France, in the early 1950s, to make it a central part of French strategic vocabulary in a manner that stood in marked contrast to the less politicised approach of British and American strategic theorists (Fall 2005: 370).[10] The French approach would be taken to its extremes in the debacle of Algeria over the period 1954–61 in which the French Fourth Republic would itself collapse following a coup by a group of French officers willing to sacrifice French democracy for the preservation of *L'Algerie Française*.

Post-1945 French theorists such as Beaufre, Trinquier and Galula were not, it has to be said, the sole originators of French counterinsurgency strategy: this had roots almost as deep as those of the British in the form of the tache d'huile or 'oil spot' strategy of great colonial pacifiers such as Lyautey and Gallieni in the nineteenth century. The concept of 'pacification' was always very prominent in French counterinsurgency theory, reversing the conventional strategic assumption that military conquest brings political concessions or surrender by the conquered party. Here pacification through political support gained by administrative work at the local level secures successes at the tactical military level (de Durand 2010: 13).

By contrast, the British approach has remained dominated since the 1950s insurgencies in colonial arenas such as Malaya and Kenya by the idea of 'minimum force' and reliance where possible on conventional civil and policing structures. The approach is taken by some analysts to describe more or less at face value the operation of British contemporary counterinsurgent doctrine based on the 2001 army manual *Counterinsurgency Operations* (Alderson 2010: 29). The minimum force 'philosophy' has roots in the Victorian reverence for English common law and can also be traced to a Protestant and Church of England championing of individual liberty against the power of the state. For some writers such as Tom Mockaitis the minimum force concept has demonstrated the comparative successes of British counterinsurgency to that of the United States which, with the notable exception of the campaign against the Huk guerrillas in the Philippines, became bogged down in a counterinsurgent war in Vietnam marked by continuous military escalation in the late 1960s and early 1970s in an apparent bid to drive the North Vietnamese enemy to the negotiating table and where none of the basic precepts of minimum force applied (Mockaitis 1990).

Critics of the minimum force approach, however, have pointed to several examples where the philosophy was clearly abandoned, such as the Amritsar Massacre of 13 April 1919 in the Jallianwala Bagh where a party of unarmed Sikhs, including women and children, were shot down by Indian army soldiers led by Brigadier General Rex Dyer (Lloyd 2010). At best the term 'minimum' in 'minimum force' is a relative concept and can be interpreted in a multitude of different ways by local commanders. Overall it was part of a Victorian mythology of empire and made general sense when running such a vast and disparate edifice as the British empire in the nineteenth century when the actual forces to hand to quell any insurrection were often only tiny (Lloyd 2010; Marshall 2010). It has come to mean rather less in the course of the twentieth century with the retreat from empire and the lurch into more modern forms of counterinsurgent campaign with increasingly sophisticated military technology. Moreover the British government in the period after 1945 chose to exclude the operation of international law from colonial counterinsurgencies and this in some cases encouraged random acts of torture, murder and beatings of prisoners which did much to undermine the strict enforcement of minimum force (Thornton 2004, 2009; Bennett 2007; Elkins 2005).

It is possible to investigate the comparative importance of these various historical legacies of the various national traditions in insurgency and counterinsurgency: it seems from this sort of exercise for instance that there is now relatively little to find from the French tradition of *guerre revolutionnaire* on contemporary French thinking. Though the writings of the French officer David Gallula, especially in his book *Counterinsurgency Warfare*, may be considered far more influential in the way they emphasised that the 'rules' of revolutionary war favoured the insurgents and counterinsurgents had to be prepared to do a variety of 'non military' tasks in order to win over the broad bulk of the civilian population to their cause.

In time, this approach, together with the work of other British military strategists such as Robert Thompson and Frank Kitson, would exert some influence on US strategic debate in the decades after the Vietnam debacle. At a general strategic level, however, the US military withdrew from any engagement in insurgent conflicts in the decade after the defeat in Vietnam in 1975, though this did not stop thinking continuing at the academy level and in military colleges. As John Nagl has graphically argued in his *Learning to Eat Soup with a Knife* there were powerful constraints against developing an organisational learning culture that would engage with lessons learned from the Vietnam conflict. Such learning could only really develop within a new educational culture that, Nagl argued, needed to be fostered to engage with new ideas and values that would be confronted in a new post-Cold War era (Nagl 2005). These issues would become increasingly pertinent by the 1990s as the end of the Cold War saw the emergence of a range of insurgent conflicts in the developing world, as well as in parts of Europe such as the Balkans as the state of Yugoslavia disintegrated into violent civil war. These conflicts fuelled a new set of debates both within military and academic circles which have had a major impact on the way insurgent and counterinsurgent conflicts can be understood.

Concepts and recent debate

Insurgency and counterinsurgency can, and have been, conceptualised in many different ways. Insurgency can be seen as a tactic of warfare – where it is often used synonymously with guerrilla – or alternatively, it is seen as a type of strategy to conduct war. These approaches differ based on the level of strategy on which it is placed. Generally seen, over the course of modern history insurgency has been elevated from a tactic to a strategy. More recently, a reverse development seems to be taking place, where insurgency is stripped of its strategic dimension and reduced to a tactic, as will be elaborated in several contributions in this volume.

When conceptualising insurgency as a tactic, the activity has an extremely long pedigree in warfare. Guerrilla methods are aimed at striking the opponent where he least expects it. The main idea behind it is to avoid the enemy strengths and concentrate on his weaknesses. An ideal type insurgency struggle would look, in the words of Stathis Kalyvas, as follows:

> The state (or *incumbents*) fields regular troops and is able to control urban and accessible terrain; while seeking to militarily engage its opponents in peripheral and rugged terrain; challengers (rebels or *insurgents*) hide and rely on harassment and surprise. Such wars often turn into wars of attrition, with insurgents seeking to win by not losing while imposing unbearable costs on their opponent.
>
> *(Kalyvas 2007: 428, italics in original)*

When insurgency is conceptualised as strategy, the relevant history is more recent. When guerrilla tactics developed into a more comprehensive strategic approach at the start of the twentieth century, the term insurgency has been applied. Mao Zedong is generally credited as the *auctor intellectualis* of this development. The strategic approach to insurgency can currently be found in the American *Counterinsurgency Field Manual FM 3–24*, which defines the concept as

> an organized movement aimed at the overthrow of a constituted government through the use of subversion and armed conflict … [in other words] an organized protracted politico-military struggle designed to weaken the control and legitimacy of an established government, occupying power, or other political authority while increasing insurgent control.
>
> *(US Army and Marine Corps 2007: 2)*

There has been large scale debate, which will be further elaborated on in this volume, about the development of insurgency and insurgency thinking over the course of the twentieth and twenty-first centuries. Steven Metz and Bard O'Neill, among others, have previously suggested that in order to understand modern insurgency we have to take a closer look at the changing nature of the actors, the issues of contention and the instruments used in these struggles (Metz 2007–8; O'Neill 2005; Metz and Millen 2004; Mackinlay 2009, 2002; Clapham 1998; Metz 1994).

The actors have not only changed in shape but also in number. No longer does an insurgent fit the typology of an independence movement in the context of a decolonisation struggle. Other actors, such as non-governmental organisations, diaspora groups, criminal gangs and virtual audiences complicate the picture these conflicts present. Most of these actors are argued to not be bound by territory (Mackinlay 2009). Some actors work pragmatically together in so-called 'federated insurgent complexes' to describe the overlapping and unclear nature of the actor(s) (Brennan 2005).

Motivations are argued to have shifted from nationalism, decolonisation, liberation and revolution to, most importantly, the Salafist jihad. Bard O'Neill has proposed the most elaborate list of possible motivations of insurgency campaigns: anarchist, egalitarian, traditionalist, plural-ist, apocalyptic–utopian, secessionist, reformist, preservationist and commercialist (O'Neill 2005). More recently, John Mackinlay has introduced the concept of post-Maoist insurgency. He shares with David Kilcullen the idea that insurgency has morphed from purely national struggles into a global undertaking (Mackinlay 2009, 2002; Kilcullen 2005; Hoffman 2007). While Maoist insurgencies were characterised, among others, by a clear ideology, a national state being the target of violence, with a binary view of the audiences involved, post-Maoism relies on multiple audiences, a multiplicity of actors and a proliferation of communications and virtual communities (Mackinlay 2009). Global insurgency does not display a centre of gravity that can be targeted by military and political instruments as such.

Apart from motivation, the means have also been argued to differ to such an extent that past insurgency campaigns have become incomparable. First, mobilisation is said to occur largely through the Internet, the so-called cyber-mobilisation or electronic '*lévee en masse*' (Kurth Cronin 2006: 77). The Internet in this regard provides a virtual base area, where the insurgent can group, develop and plan actions. Second, the role of the media and the influence it exerts on the multiple audiences involved has changed (Norris *et al.* 2003). While the media is an indispensable tool in both insurgency and counterinsurgency, the all-pervasiveness of the modern media has given this kind of struggle a whole new quality. Third, a popular instrument these days to fight insurgency in such conflicts as Iraq, Afghanistan and the Palestinian territories has been the suicide bomb (Pape 2005; Bloom 2005; Atran 2006). This coincides with a reluc-tance to accept casualties in Western states. Jeffrey Record even talks about 'Force-Protection Fetishism' (Record 2000; Freedman 2006; Luttwak 1995). Fourth, another means which fea-tures prominently on the security agenda is the category of nuclear, bacteriological, chemical and radiological weapons.

The context is certainly also subject to change. First, several scholars stress the transnational nature of modern insurgencies as a significantly new feature; traditionally 'each movement oper-ated in its own country, emulation typically happened after the event, and direct cooperation between movements was rare' (Kilcullen 2006–7: 114). Nowadays, the transnational nature of insurgency is a constituent component of insurgency. Second, the social context of insurgency has been interpreted more widely. While 'insurgency does have an important political compo-nent … [it] is only part of the picture. Insurgency also fulfils the economic and psychological needs of the insurgents' (Metz 2007). There is increasing overlap between insurgency and crim-inal activity. Third, the geographical context differs from past experiences, the urban backdrop as opposed to a rural one is now dominant (Kilcullen 2006–7: 114; cf. Kalyvas 2004). As Frank Hoffman argues, 'distance is exchanged for density. Urbanisation presents an environment with populations and infrastructures so dense that law enforcement, intelligence, and conventional military assets may not be as effective' (Hoffman 2007: 76). This development is not surprising. The population, as is claimed in key counterinsurgency texts, forms the centre of gravity and today the majority of the world's population lives in urban centres.

A note of caution is warranted at this stage. All these claims to insurgency being completely different from the past disregard important continuities but also the fact that not only insurgency has changed but also the world around us. Increased international communication, for example, not only influences insurgency struggles but has brought a new quality to daily life. In other words, it would be highly surprising if insurgents had not adopted this feature of twenty-first century society (Duyvesteyn 2004). There is important continuity in regard to the essence of these conflicts.

Similarly, in order to conduct counterinsurgency, the political nature of the insurgency challenge remains a dominant theme. The nation state, as central building block in international affairs, continues to form an important focal point. In the words of Sarah Sewall: 'There are important differences in the analogy between counterinsurgency and an effort to defeat Al Qaeda and its allies, but the overall strategic problem is uncannily parallel: sustaining the statist norm in the face of radical and violent revolutionaries' (2007: xlii).[11]

Commensurate with discussions about insurgency, counterinsurgency can also be defined as a set of tactical tools or alternatively as an overarching strategy to defeat an opponent. The American *Field Manual FM 3–24* describes counterinsurgency as 'military, paramilitary, political, economic, psychological, and civic actions taken by a government to defeat an insurgency'. By listing all the instruments of state it seems to imply a technique rather than a strategy but the overall *Field Manual* follows the strategic approach.

Alternatively, experts have conceptualised counterinsurgency as a tactic or technique of warfare. An optimal mixture is sought of coercive and conciliatory means, most often according to a prescriptive list. David Ucko argues in this volume (Chapter 6) that

> counterinsurgency, like insurgency, is not a strategy, but a description of a strategic end-point, either to mount or defeat a threat to the established authorities. A list of prescriptions can be used as a guide to develop a case specific answer to the mounted challenge.

Counterinsurgency thinking is largely a product of the era of decolonisation, when concepts and ideas were developed on how to deal with political challenges by independence movements. David Kilcullen, in Chapter 11 of this volume, even claims to be able to pinpoint the exact date of inception of this classical counterinsurgency thinking in a RAND symposium in the spring of 1962. This classical thought is plagued by two serious but little recognised shortcomings. First, the empirical base of the insights is extremely small, using and referring to only a handful of cases. Second, the prescriptions that were derived from this limited foundation seem to be ideologically charged. The prescription of the hearts and minds ideas – we need to entice the population as the key to strategic success – go against the large body of historical evidence of coercion being the instrument of choice.

From 2006 onwards the classical counterinsurgency thinking experienced a renaissance. Neo-classical thinkers, such as John Nagl, went back to the works of David Galula and Robert Thompson to derive inspiration for the armed challenges in Iraq and Afghanistan (Nagl 2005). Harking back to these trusted concepts of the colonial counterinsurgency repertoire, they tried to apply the recipes in early twenty-first century exigencies. Apart from the school of neo-classical counterinsurgency thinkers, David Martin Jones and M.L.R. Smith identified a second school of counterinsurgency thought (Jones and Smith 2010). The second school of global counterinsurgency or post-classical counterinsurgency, among whom are counted John Mackinlay and David Kilcullen, look at a worldwide counterinsurgency struggle fought in distant battle theatres as much as on home soil (Mackinlay 2009; Kilcullen 2005). These thinkers point to differences in the strategic environment which, they argue, provide a qualitative change warranting a new approach. Kilcullen introduces the concept of 'accelerated counterinsurgency'. While pointing to the time constraints of foreign military operations, he makes an argument for quick and forceful action against violent irreconcilables and making political overtures to the reconcilables. It is not counterinsurgency in its classical or neo-classical guise that is being applied in Afghanistan, rather it is a mixture of kinetic peace enforcement together with war termination measures that is making a difference (Chapter 11, this volume).

Jones and Smith dissect that there are serious problems with both sets of ideas (Jones and Smith 2010). The neo-counterinsurgency thinkers run the risk of reducing counterinsurgency to a tactical toolkit readily available to be applied when necessary. The global counterinsurgency thinkers have a tendency to downplay the ideological content of the struggle and reduce it to an 'accidental guerrilla' syndrome, where especially local grievances need addressing (Kilcullen 2009).

Apart from debate about (counter-)insurgency concepts, ideas and theories, there is also an important development in counterinsurgency doctrine. The publication of the American *Field Manual 3–24* in December 2006 holds special importance. A product of the American Army and Marine Corps, it was developed to fill a void during the Iraq campaign after the fall of the Hussein regime. While intended specifically for the Army and Marine Corps it now holds such stature that in practice it overrides NATO counterinsurgency doctrine, which should inform the NATO operations in Afghanistan. In fact, the lack of strategic vision of the coalition partners in Afghanistan has now led to a situation in which the doctrine has become 'a panacea for what continues to remain a dangerous strategic vacuum' (Marshall 2010: 244; Strachan 2010). Strachan argues that

> [i]t is very easy, in the continuing absence of strategy – of political goals to which the military efforts is to be adapted – for counter-insurgency doctrine to fill the gap, for operations to double as strategy. Crudely put, Field Manual 3–24 took the place of a coalition strategy for Iraq in 2007.
>
> *(2010: 168)*

This rather worrying trend, which has continued in Afghanistan, underlines the importance and significance of the scholarship in this area.

It is clear that there is no universally agreed set of definitions for the study and practice of insurgency and counterinsurgency – and we did not set one for this volume either. Defining concepts is an act essential to any academic endeavour but also an act where the academic is at complete liberty. As an ultimate consequence we have to accept that this leaves open the possibility of concluding, as David Ucko will do in Chapter 6 of this volume, that these fundamental questions lead to a potentially obsolete debate. Along similar lines, David Kilcullen will argue in Chapter 11 that the focus on faulty counterinsurgency concepts leads us completely astray.

The outline of this volume

The volume has been structured into three separate parts: the first part will deal with general analytical and theoretical issues which have emerged in debates on insurgency and counterinsurgency since the end of the Cold War; the second part will deal with insurgent movements and the third part will focus on counterinsurgency campaigns. The purpose is to provide the reader with an overview of what is available in this field of study and where the challenges lie. The book does not provide new research, although several authors have used the opportunity to present some innovative and refreshing insights. Rather this book is intended as both an introduction to and synthesis of this research field.

In Part I, Ian Beckett starts off with an overview of the historiography of insurgency, concluding among others that there is a lot more room for detailed case study analysis. Steven Metz follows by looking at the strategic nature of insurgency. Robert Bunker, in Chapter 4, provides an argument, trying to push the boundaries of the concept of insurgency. David Betz subsequently looks at the link between insurgency and the technological revolution. Chapter 6 shifts attention to counterinsurgency. David Ucko opens the debate about counterinsurgency by dissecting both the concept and its current application, concluding that there are serious problems with both. Thijs Brocades Zaalberg follows the conceptual discussion with a treatment of the wider intellectual quagmire of counterinsurgency, peace operations and the comprehensive approach. Are there any differences between these concepts and their practical application or are they all just euphemisms for good old counterinsurgency? Alice Hills concludes in Chapter 8 that the often heard mantra of police forces as key to effective counterinsurgency is not met with an equal amount of scholarship. Geraint Hughes also looks at the practical application of counterinsurgency on the ground focusing on intelligence gathering and special operations as constitutive elements of effective counterinsurgency. The use of these instruments is not without problems and repercussions. This moral and ethical angle is further taken up by Christopher Coker who argues that common humanity should inform counterinsurgency practices in order to be able to terminate the conflict with the best prospects for peace. David Kilcullen's contribution completes this first part of the volume with a critical look at the current counterinsurgency paradigm and its critics. Kilcullen especially points to the narrow range of colonial models that were drawn in the original development of counterinsurgency doctrine in the early 1960s and suggests that modern counterinsurgency has now moved away from what can easily be attacked as a straw man. He points to a much deeper and more sophisticated development of counterinsurgency centred around the four concepts of effectiveness, appropriateness, ethics and policy.

The second part of the volume is exclusively devoted to insurgency case studies, where Africa is discussed by William Reno, Iraq by Ahmed Hashim, Hamas and Hezbollah by Judith Palmer Harik and Margret Johannsen, Southeast Asia by Larry Cline, India by Namrata Goswami, Afghanistan by Antonio Giustozzi and Pakistan by Shehzad Qazi and Latin America by David E. Spencer. By no means exhaustive, this part is intended to provide some insights into the scholarship in this area. The limited number of case studies can, in some way, be seen as indicative of the large room that is still available for good quality case study analysis in this area. This unfortunate state of affairs is also brought forward by Beckett and Esterhuyse in this volume (Chapters 2 and 28).

Part III turns to counterinsurgency cases, looking at the United States (Thomas Mockaitis), Israel (Sergio Catignani), the United Kingdom (Warren Chin), Russia (Yuri Zhukov), India (David Fidler and Sumit Ganguly), Sri Lanka (David Lewis), Pakistan (Julian Schofield), China (Martin I. Wayne) and South Africa (Abel Esterhuyse). Despite the present emphasis on the more tempered approach to counterinsurgency, the case studies point to a prevalence of the harsher forms of dealing with political violence. This is representative for the available case study material. These points will be taken up in the concluding chapter of the volume, which will provide an overall summary and some indications on where the editors see future research going.

Notes

1 Even with the upsurge of interest in insurgencies there was still however a tendency for some analysts to view them as exotic. J. Bowyer Bell for instance saw insurgencies as examples of quasi-demonic 'dragon wars' fought in the shadows by gunmen operating in an expanding terrain of weak states and state breakdown (Bowyer Bell 1999; Kaplan 2000).
2 Gray in an earlier study published just before the end of the Cold War ignored the whole question of guerrilla insurgency and concentrated instead on the centrality of nuclear strategy (Gray 1990). As recently as 1998 the British military writer John Keegan in his Reith lectures that year on war completely ignored the whole question of insurgent warfare (Keegan 1999).

3 At a more general level work is only really beginning in reinterpreting many periods of European pre-modern history in terms of insurgencies and counterinsurgencies. For one recent example that examines the Christian resistance in Spain to the Arab invasion of AD 711, see Widdowson (2009).

4 Laqueur is at a loss to explain exactly why these writings did not have a wider impact. Best has suggested that the Spanish struggle came to be viewed by military historians and international jurists as a 'cautionary example of what war should *not* be like' (Best 1982: 175). A more general historical assessment of the military dimensions of the Peninsula War is urgently needed. Napoleon's invading army had no real doctrine or strategy to meet insurrectional warfare. Overplaying its hand by the brutal suppression of the uprising in Madrid on 2 May 1808 (graphically captured in Goya's painting) led to a national rebellion and the humiliating defeat of the French army at Bailen in July. By the end of the year Napoleon had 250,000 troops in Spain fighting arguably one of the first real modern counter-guerrilla campaigns. This destroyed the myth of Napoleon as 'liberator' and forced him to meet the Russian Tsar at Erfurt to consolidate the agreement at the Treaty of Tilsit. It still did not prevent the Spanish model being emulated in later conflicts in the Tirol, Germany and later Russia in 1812. The loss of this prestige in turn forced Napoleon into a strategy of escalation in Spain which led eventually to a total of 350,000 French troops being deployed. They still could not suppress the insurrection except on the central plains where the decisive role of the French cavalry came into play. All these themes need detailed evaluation in order to flesh out a fuller picture of the historical emergence of guerrilla warfare in the nineteenth century.

5 Beckett has described Callwell as making 'the only distinctive contribution by any British soldier to the development of military thought in the nineteenth century' (Beckett 2001: 35).

6 Laqueur points out that the very isolation of the Vendean revolt makes it one of the 'purest' forms of guerrilla 'specimens'. It is thus questionable whether most insurgencies in the nineteenth century can really be described as 'people's war' in the way Best chooses to do (Best 1982: 168–83, 265–72).

7 Debray first visited Cuba as a philosophy student in 1961. He appears to have had relatively minimal impact on Guevara and he really became an agent run by Cuban intelligence in the early 1960s who saw him as a useful means to influence a wider radical audience in the West. Guevara indeed was not especially keen for Debray to even be on the last ill-fated attempt at a *foco* in Bolivia in 1966–7 following disastrous earlier attempts in Argentina in 1963–4 and in the Congo in 1966 where Guevara himself led a Cuban contingent supporting Laurent Kabila (Beckett 2001: 170).

8 The romantic image of Che is rather undermined by the brief portrait painted by Pablo Neruda who on a visit to Cuba met Che when he was still a minister in Castro's regime. The romantic hero emerges more as a warrior with a lust for conflict. 'War … war … war', he exclaimed to the shocked Neruda. 'We are always against war, but once we have fought in a war, we can't live without it. We want to go back to it all the time' (Neruda 1982: 323).

9 The differences between terrorism and urban guerrilla become very fuzzy here. It leads Walter Laqueur to conclude that 'The normal use of "urban guerrilla" is a euphemism for urban terrorism which has a negative public relations image' (Laqueur 1977: 403). Overall, the effectiveness of urban campaigns has been seriously questioned (Morrison-Taw and Hoffman 1994).

10 For the extension of the Maoist revolutionary war concept to the Vietminh see Pike (1966: 31–43).

11 Kilcullen challenges this reasoning and maintains that 'insurgency today follows state failure, and is not directed at taking over a functioning body politic, but at dismembering or scavenging its carcass, or contesting an "ungoverned space"' (2006–7: 112; Hoffman 2007: 81).

References

Alderson, Alexander (2010) 'Britain', in Thomas Rid and Thomas Keaney (eds), *Understanding Counterinsurgency: Doctrine, Operations and Challenges*. London and New York: Routledge: 28–40.

Anderson, M.S. (1988) *War and Society in Europe of the Old Regime, 1618–1789*. London: Sutton.

Arnold, Thomas (2002) *The Renaissance at War*. London: Cassell.

Atran, Scott (2006) 'The Moral Logic and Growth of Suicide Terrorism', *The Washington Quarterly*, 29 (2): 121–48.

Beckett, Ian F.W. (2001) *Modern Insurgencies and Counter Insurgencies*. London and New York: Routledge.

Bennett, Huw (2007) 'The Other Side of COIN: Minimum and Exemplary Force in British Counterinsurgency in Kenya', *Small Wars and Insurgencies*, 18 (4): 638–64.

Best, Geoffrey (1982) *War and Society in Revolutionary Europe, 1770–1870*. London: Fontana.

Bloom, Mia (2005) *Dying to Kill: The Allure of Suicide Terror*. New York: Columbia University Press.

Bowyer Bell, J. (1999) *Dragonwars: Armed Struggle & the Conventions of Modern War*. London: Transaction.

Brennan, Rick (2005) *Future Insurgent Threats*. Santa Monica: RAND.

Callwell, Charles E. (2010) *Small Wars: A Tactical Textbook for Imperial Soldiers*. London: Greenhill.

Clapham, Christopher (1998) 'Introduction: Analysing African Insurgencies', in Christopher Clapham (ed.), *African Guerrillas*. Oxford: James Currey: 1–18.

Creveld, Martin van (2006) *The Changing Face of War; Lessons of Combat from the Marne to Iraq*. New York: Ballantine.

de Durand, Etienne (2010) 'France', in Thomas Rid and Thomas Keaney (eds), *Understanding Counterinsurgency: Doctrine, Operations and Challenges*. London and New York: Routledge: 11–28.

Debray, Regis (1980) *Revolution in the Revolution*. London: Greenwood Press.

Debray, Regis, Leo Huberman and Paul Sweezy (1969) *Regis Debray and the Latin American Revolution*. New York: Monthly Review Press.

Duffy, Christopher (1987) *The Military Experience of the Age of Reason*. London: Routledge.

Duyvesteyn, Isabelle (2004) 'How New is the New Terrorism', *Studies in Conflict and Terrorism*, 27 (5): 439–54.

Duyvesteyn, Isabelle (2005) *Clausewitz and African War; Politics and Strategy in Liberia and Somalia*. London: Frank Cass.

Duyvesteyn, Isabelle (2011) 'Hearts and Minds, Cultural Awareness and Good Intelligence: The Blue Print for Successful Counterinsurgency?', *Intelligence and National Security*, 26 (4): 445–59.

Elkins, Caroline (2005) *Imperial Reckoning; The Untold Story of Britain's Gulag in Kenya*. New York: Henri Hold.

Ellis, John (1995) *From the Barrel of a Gun: A History of Guerrilla, Revolutionary and Counter-Insurgency War from the Romans to the Present*. London: Greenhill Books.

Esdaile, Charles, (1988) 'Heroes or Villains? The Spanish Guerrillas in the Peninsula War', *History Today*, April: 29–36.

Fall, Bernard (2005) *Street without Joy: The French Debacle in Indochina*. Mechanicsburg: Stackpole.

Freedman, Lawrence (2006) *The Transformation of Strategic Affairs*, Adelphi Paper 379. London: Routledge.

Girling, J.L.S. (1969) *People's War: The Conditions and Consequences in China and in South East Asia*. London: Allen & Unwin.

Gray, Colin S. (1990) *War, Peace and Victory*. New York: Touchstone.

Gray, Colin S. (1999) *Modern Strategy*. Oxford: Oxford University Press.

Guevara, Che (1969) *Guerrilla Warfare*. London: Penguin.

Hale, J.R. (1985) *War and Society in Renaissance Europe, 1450–1620*. London: Sutton.

Hall, John A. (1996) *International Orders*. Cambridge: Polity Press.

Hobsbawm, Eric (1994) *The Age of Extremes*. London: Michael Joseph.

Hoffman, Frank (2007) 'Neo-Classical Counterinsurgency?', *Parameters*, Summer: 71–87.

Ibrahim, Azeem (2004) 'Conceptualisation of Guerrilla Warfare', *Small Wars and Insurgencies*, 15 (3): 112–23.

Joes, Anthony James (1998) 'Insurgency and Genocide: La Vendee', *Small Wars and Insurgencies*, 9 (3): 17–40.

Johnson, Chalmers (1973) *Autopsy on Peoples War*. Berkeley and London: University of California Press.

Jones, David Martin and M.L.R. Smith (2010) 'Whose Hearts and Whose Minds? The Curious Case of Global Counter-Insurgency', *Journal of Strategic Studies*, 33 (1): 81–121.

Kalyvas, Stathis (2004) 'The Urban Bias in Research on Civil Wars', *Security Studies*, 13 (3): 160–90.

Kalyvas, Stathis (2007) 'Civil Wars', in Carles Boix and Susan S. Stokes (eds), *The Oxford Handbook of Comparative Politics*. Oxford: Oxford University Press, pp. 416–34.

Kaplan, Robert D. (2000) *The Coming Anarchy: Shattering the Dreams of the Post War World*. New York: Vintage.

Keegan, John (1999) *War and Our World*. London: Hutchison.

Kilcullen, David (2005) 'Countering Global Insurgency', *Journal of Strategic Studies*, 28: 597–617.

Kilcullen, David (2006–7) 'Counterinsurgency Redux', *Survival*, 48 (4): 111–30.

Kilcullen, David (2009) *The Accidental Guerrilla*. London: Hurst.

Kurth Cronin, Audrey (2006) 'Cyber-Mobilization: The New *Levée en Masse*', *Parameters*, Summer: 77–87.

Laqueur, Walter (1977) *Guerrilla: A Historical and Critical Study*. London: Weidenfeld & Nicolson.

Laqueur, Walter (1998) *Guerrilla Warfare; A Historical and Critical Study*. New Brunswick: Transaction.

Lloyd, Nick (2010) 'The Amritsar Massacre and the Minimum Force Debate', *Small Wars and Insurgencies*, 21 (2): 382–403.

Luttwak, Edward (1995) 'Towards Post Heroic Warfare', *Foreign Affairs*, 74 (3): 109–22.

Mack, Andrew (1974) 'The Non Strategy of Urban Guerrilla Warfare', in Johan Niezing (ed.), *Urban Guerrilla*. Brussels: Rotterdam University Press, pp. 22–45.

Mackinlay, John (2002) *Globalisation and Insurgency*, Adelphi Paper 352. New York: International Institute of Strategic Studies.

Mackinlay, John (2009) *The Insurgent Archipelago*. London: Hurst.

Mao Zedong (2005) *On Guerrilla Warfare*, trans. Samuel Griffith. New York: Dover.

Marighella, Carlos (2002) *The Mini-Manual of the Urban Guerrilla*. Toronto: Abraham Guillen Press. Also available at: www.marxists.org/archive/marighella-carlos/1969/06/minimanual-urban-guerrilla (last accessed 28 January 2011).

Marshall, Alex (2010) 'Imperial Nostalgia, the Liberal Lie, and the Perils of Postmodern Counterinsurgency', *Small Wars and Insurgencies*, 21 (2): 233–51.

Metz, Steven (2007–8) 'New Challenges and Old Concepts: Understanding 21st Century Insurgency', *Parameters*, 37 (4): 20–32.

Metz, Steven and Raymond Millen (1994) 'Insurgency after the Cold War', *Small Wars and Insurgencies*, 5 (2): 63–82.

Metz, Steven and Raymond Millen (1995) *Counterinsurgency: Strategy and the Phoenix of American Capability*. U.S. Army War College, Strategic Studies Institute.

Metz, Steven and Raymond Millen (2004) *Insurgency and Counterinsurgency in the 21s Century: Reconceptualizing Threat and Response*. Carlisle, PA: Strategic Studies Institute.

Mockaitis, Thomas (1990) *British Counterinsurgency, 1919–1960*. London: Macmillan.

Morgan, Edmund S. (1989) *Inventing the People: The Rise of Popular Sovereignty in England and America*. New York and London: Norton.

Morrison-Taw, Jennifer and Bruce Hoffman (1994) *The Urbanization of Insurgency*. Santa Monica: RAND.

Nagl, John A. (2005) *Learning to Eat Soup with a Knife: Counterinsurgency Lessons from Vietnam and Malaya*. Chicago and London: University of Chicago Press.

Nelson, Harold (1988) *Leon Trotsky and the Art of Insurrection, 1905–1917*. London: Frank Cass.

Neruda, Pablo (1982) *Memoirs*. Harmondsworth: Penguin.

Norris, Pippa, Montague Kern and Marion Just (eds) (2003) *Framing Terrorism: The News Media, the Government and the Public*. New York: Routledge.

O'Neill, Bard (2005) *Insurgency and Terrorism: From Revolution to Apocalypse*. Washington, DC: Potomac Books.

Oppenheimer, Martin (1969) *Urban Guerrilla*. Harmondsworth: Penguin.

Pape, Robert A. (2005) *Dying to Win: The Strategic Logic of Suicide Terrorism*. New York: Random House.

Peters, Ralph (2007) 'Progress and Peril; New Counterinsurgency Manual Cheats on the History Exam', *Armed Forces Journal International*, 144. www.armedforcesjournal.com/2007/02/2456854.

Pike, Douglas (1966) *Vietcong*. Cambridge, MA: MIT Press.

Porch, Douglas (2001) *Wars of the Empire*. London: Cassell.

Ranger, Terence (1985) *Peasant Consciousness and Guerrilla War in Zimbabwe*. London: James Currey.

Record, Jeffrey (2000) 'Force-Protection Fetishism: Sources, Consequences, and Solutions', *Aerospacce Power Journal*, 14 (2): 4–11.

Rich, Paul B. (2010) 'Counterinsurgency or a War on Terror? The War in Afghanistan and the Debate on Western Strategy', *Small Wars and Insurgencies*, 21 (2): 414–27.

Sewall, Sarah (2007) 'Introduction to the University of Chicago Press Edition: A Radical Field Manual', in US Army and Marine Corps, *Counterinsurgency Field Manual: U.S. Army Field Manual No. 3–24*. Chicago: University of Chicago Press, pp. xxi–xliii.

Sinclair, Andrew (1970) *Guevara*. London: Fontana.

Strachan, Hew (2008) 'Strategy and the Limitation of War', *Survival*, 50, 3, 31–54.

Strachan, Hew (2010) 'Strategy or Alibi? Obama, McChrystal and the Operational Level of War', *Survival*, 52 (5): 157–82.

Suarez, Andres (1967) *Cuba: Castro and Communism 1959–1966*. Cambridge, MA: MIT.

Taber, Robert (1970) *The War of the Flea: A Study of Guerrilla Warfare Theory and Practice*. London: Paladin.

Thornton, Rod (2004) 'The British Army and the Origins of its Minimum Force Philosophy', *Small Wars and Insurgencies*, 15 (1): 83–106.

Thornton, Rod (2009) '"Minimum Force": A Reply to Huw Bennett', *Small Wars and Insurgencies*, 20 (1): 215–24.

US Army and Marine Corps (2007) *Counterinsurgency Field Manual: U.S. Army Field Manual No. 3–24*. Chicago: University of Chicago Press.

Widdowson, Mark (2009) 'The Early Christian Insurgency in Islamic Spain', *Small Wars and Insurgencies*, 20 (3–4): 478–506.

Wolf, Eric R. (1971) *Peasant Wars of the Twentieth Century*. London: Faber & Faber.

Zimmermann, Matilda (2000) *Sandinista: Carlos Fonseca and the Nicaraguan Revolution*. Durham, NC and London: Duke University Press.

Part I

Theoretical and analytical issues

2

THE HISTORIOGRAPHY OF INSURGENCY

Ian Beckett

The academic study of insurgency and counterinsurgency is a relatively modern development, and even its professional military study was often neglected in the past.

Insurgency is usually taken to refer to the means by which, increasingly through the twentieth century, the traditional methods associated with the long history of guerrilla and irregular warfare became revolutionary in both intent and practice. Social, economic, psychological and, especially, political elements were grafted on to traditional hit-and-run tactics in order to radically alter the structure of a state by force.

Clearly, as well as a pre-history of insurgency, there was also a pre-history of writing upon irregular warfare. In so far as this was undertaken, however, it was mostly by military practitioners with the first real texts emerging in the late eighteenth century from two Hessian officers, Johann von Ewald and Andreas Emmerich, who had served in North America with the British army, and by the Prussian, Georg Wilhelm von Valentini. Similarly, the experience of the French Revolutionary and Napoleonic Wars stimulated others to record their impressions in the course of the 1820s, including the Prussian, Carol von Decker; the Russian, Denis Davidov; and the Frenchman, Le Mière de Corvey. Most major military theorists, however, such as Antoine-Henri Jomini and Carl von Clausewitz eschewed any form of 'people's war' as something to be avoided at all costs. Indeed, only revolutionary nationalists such as the Italians, Giuseppe Mazzini, Giuseppe Garibaldi and Carlo Bianco; and the Poles, Wojciech Chrzanowski, Karol Stolzman and Józef Bem, identified 'people's war' as a viable means of asserting a national consciousness in a liberation struggle. Though they made an effort to understand it, Marx and Engels did not produce any coherent theoretical position on guerrilla warfare, believing that there was little scope for it within a rapidly industrialising Europe.

The expansion of European colonial empires, with increasing exposure to 'savage' warfare in Africa and Asia, led a few soldiers to produce theoretical works on the nature of irregular warfare and the appropriate response to it. These included the Dutchman, Klaas van der Maaten, and most prominently, the British soldier, Charles Callwell, whose classic study, *Small Wars: Their Principles and Practice*, was first published in 1896. Following the First World War, other such works appeared, including Charles Gwynn's *Imperial Policing* (1934), and from the US Marine Corps, *Small Wars Manual* (1940), largely the work of Harold Utley. The increasing possibilities of guerrilla warfare were also recognised by T.E. Lawrence, whose *Seven Pillars of Wisdom* (1935) and contribution to the *Encyclopaedia Britannica* in 1927, based on his role in the

Arab Revolt against the Ottoman Turks during the war, proved an elegant and influential exposition of its potential when waged in a political cause. Yet, few soldiers or academic writers had any real interest in irregular warfare, and this long remained the case. To illustrate the point, comparison can be made between the two editions of the well-known *Makers of Modern Strategy*, published respectively in 1943 and 1986.

The first, edited by Edward Gordon Meade, comprised 547 pages of main text and had 20 separate chapters on the development of military theory from Machiavelli to Hitler. Just one chapter of 25 pages by Jean Gottman discussed the nineteenth-century French counterinsurgency theorists, Bugeaud, Gallieni and Lyautey. No other form of insurgency or counterinsurgency was mentioned. The second edition, edited by Peter Paret, specifically claimed to take a boarder view than the original, its 28 chapters now running to 871 pages. Yet, apart from Douglas Porch's updated version of Gottman's chapter, only one new chapter of 47 pages by John Shy and T.W. Collier was devoted to 'revolutionary war'. It was included on the grounds that, what had not been presumed to exist in 1943, was now a significant, but conceivably short-lived factor in warfare through the decline of European colonial empires, and of conflict between nation-states. Moreover, Shy and Collier had only six pages on counterinsurgency. Six paragraphs were devoted to American counterinsurgency efforts, two to the French 1950s concept of *guerre révolutionnaire*, and one uninformative paragraph to the extensive British experience.

It would appear by the 1950s and 1960s then that little had changed in over 40 years in the perception of insurgency and especially counterinsurgency as a legitimate subject for study. Most other standard histories of warfare or military thought at the time were equally dismissive of all forms of what might be termed low-intensity conflict. No reference at all was included in Preston *et al.*'s *Men in Arms*, first published in 1956, until the fifth edition in 1991, which finally included a single chapter of 32 pages (out of 292) on the subject. Curiously, the Algerian and Vietnam Wars were briefly discussed in a previous chapter on *conventional* warfare. There was no mention at all in J.F.C. Fuller's *The Conduct of War* (1961), Theodore Ropp's *War in the Modern World* (1973), or even the first edition of Michael Howard's *War in European History* (1976). Archer Jones' *The Art of War in the Western World* (1988) had a number of references in his 723 pages to 'raiding strategy', but these included examples from antiquity, and only two pages were devoted to nineteenth-century colonial warfare. Even works specifically devoted to modern war since 1945 such as Laurence Martin, *Arms and Strategy* (1973) and Lawrence Freedman, *Atlas of Global Strategy* (1985) barely mentioned insurgency or counterinsurgency. What was then a standard student text, Baylis *et al.*'s *Contemporary Strategy* had 19 pages out of 312 devoted to revolutionary warfare in its original 1975 edition: the much extended two-volume edition in 1987 was not much better with just 23 pages (out of 518). Within this, the section on counterinsurgency had increased from two to four pages, largely through the addition of a discussion of the then Soviet intervention in Afghanistan.

Such neglect of insurgency and counterinsurgency would now be unthinkable. New ideological, political and commercial imperatives encouraging intra-state conflict and insurgency were already beginning to emerge in the 1980s, amid the breakdown of the international bipolar political system, and the emergence of identity politics and of many more non-state actors. Thus, there was beginning to be a corrective to the neglect of insurgency and counterinsurgency. Perhaps surprisingly, as long ago as 1961, Cyril Falls had an 11-page chapter on 'small wars' in his *The Art of War*, though Falls chose to describe what those he termed 'partisans' as having exerted less influence on history than 'commonly asserted'. Hew Strachan, *European Armies and the Conduct of War* (1983) included a full chapter on colonial warfare in his survey of the development of warfare between 1700 and 1945, while the essays edited by Colin McInnes and Gary Sheffield, *Warfare in the Twentieth Century* (1988) included one on colonial warfare between 1900 and 1939, and another on insurgency and counterinsurgency since 1945. There had also been some 'popular' histories of guerrilla warfare published such as John Ellis, *A Short History of Guerrilla Warfare* (1975), and Robert Asprey, *War in the Shadows* (1975), to which could be added more academic studies, L.H. Gann, *Guerrillas in History* (1971), Sam Sarkesian, *Revolutionary Guerrilla Warfare* (1975) and Walter Laqueur, *Guerrilla* (1977).

The neglect of insurgency and counterinsurgency was the more surprising when low-intensity conflict was already the most prevalent form of conflict. Notwithstanding two world wars, this had been so throughout the twentieth century, if not before. In the case of the British experience of warfare, the instances of conventional warfare as opposed to some form of low-intensity conflict since 1945 were especially few, amounting to 35 months of the Korean War, in which no more than five battalions were deployed at any one time, ten days at Suez in 1956, and 25 days of the land campaign of the Falklands in 1982. Only 14 out of 94 separate British operational commitments between 1945 and 1982 were not in the form of low-intensity conflict of some kind, and only 1968 had seen no British soldier killed on active service in that same period. For understandable reasons, military professionals have long tended to perceive themselves as existing primarily to wage conventional warfare, whatever the actual experience. It was not just a matter of institutional conservatism and a preconceived concept of what constituted 'real' war, but a reflection of the unglamorous and uncomfortable nature of irregular warfare, in which results might not be obtained quickly, in which success could not be measured in conventional military terms, and in which soldiers were confronted with political and social pressures to a far greater extent than most other forms of conflict.

Just as some soldiers in the past such as Gallieni, Lyautey, Utley, Callwell and Gwynn had recognised the reality of routine colonial soldiering, so there had been those who had attempted to analyse the emerging pattern of insurgency after 1945. Studies such as Roger Trinquier, *La Guerre Moderne* (1964); David Galula, *Counterinsurgency Warfare* (1964); John Pushtay, *Counterinsurgency* (1965); John McCuen, *The Art of Counterrevolutionary Warfare* (1966); George Tanham, *Communist Revolutionary Warfare* (1962); and the analysis of the British success in the Malayan Emergency of 1948–60 in Robert Thompson's influential *Defeating Communist Insurgency* (1966), were essentially responses to the perceived significance of the prevalence of Maoist methods of revolutionary warfare following Mao's victory in the Chinese Civil War in 1949, and the transmission of such methods to Malaya, French Indochina, and the Philippines. Equally, Castro's success on Cuba in 1959 had reputedly led the US armed forces to buy up much of the first edition of *The War of the Flea* (1965) by the American left-wing journalist, Robert Taber. The work of revolutionaries such as Vo Nguyen Giap, *People's War, People's Army* (1962); Mao, *Selected Military Writings* (1963); Che Guevara's *Guerrilla Warfare* (1969) and *Reminiscences of the Cuban Revolutionary War* (1968); Amilcar Cabral, *Revolution in Guinea* (1969); and Carlos Marighela, *For the Liberation of Brazil* (1971) became generally available in English. Two insurgent leaders had also published useful accounts, namely Menachem Begin, *The Revolt* (1951), and George Grivas, *Guerrilla Warfare and EOKA's Struggle* (1964). There were also some early analyses such as Samuel Griffith, *Mao Tse-tung on Guerrilla Warfare* (1965); Richard Gott, *Guerrilla Movements in Latin America* (1970); D.C. Hughes, *The Philosophy of the Urban Guerrilla* (1973); Robert Moss, *Urban Guerrillas* (1972); and A.C. Porzecanski, *Uruguay's Tupamaros* (1973). The emphasis upon Latin America's urban guerrilla groups was understandable in terms of the apparent threat to US interests, but the phenomenon was short-lived.

Then, in 1971, another practitioner, Frank Kitson famously challenged the assumptions underpinning Robert Thompson's approach to counterinsurgency in *Low-intensity Operations*. Kitson called for British soldiers not only to consider the practical requirements of counterinsurgency, but also to look beyond the Malayan example. It was in the spirit of Kitson's challenge that the late John Pimlott and Ian Beckett introduced counterinsurgency as a special subject for study at the Royal Military Academy, Sandhurst in the early 1980s. It gave rise to *Armed Forces and Modern Counter-insurgency* (1985), the intention being to arrive at a general framework for analysis that could then be applied to a variety of different campaigns. Ronald Haycock had edited a rather discursive collection of essays, *Regular Armies and Insurgency* (1979) that, while similarly organised as a series of case studies, did not require individual authors to try to conform to such a analytical framework as was envisaged. Subsequently, the case study approach has remained popular as in David Charters and Maurice Tugwell, *Armies in Low-intensity Conflict* (1989); Max Manwaring, *Uncomfortable Wars* (1991); and Daniel Marston and Carter Malkasian, *Counterinsurgency in Modern Warfare* (2008). Subsequent to *Armed Forces and Modern Counter-insurgency*, a similar methodology of analysis was used in Ian Beckett's edited collection, *The Roots of Counter-insurgency* (1988).

In the case of the United States, it was the experience of Vietnam that stimulated a new interest in insurgency and counterinsurgency. Of course, it has continued to generate an enormous amount of new scholarship. Early important work included D.S. Blaufarb, *The Counterinsurgency Era* (1977); Andrew Krepinivich, *The Army and Vietnam* (1986); Larry Cable, *Conflict of Myths* (1986); and D. Michael Shafer, *Deadly Paradigms* (1990). Representative of the continuing work in this area is Eric Bergerud, *The Dynamics of Defeat* (1991); Michael Hennessy, *Strategy in Vietnam* (1997); Richard Hunt, *Pacification* (1995); and John Nagl, *Learning to Eat Soup with a Knife* (2005). As Nagl's work suggests, comparisons between Malaya and Vietnam are still popular, as shown by Donald Hamilton, *The Art of Insurgency* (1998) and Sam Sarkesian, *Unconventional Conflicts in a New Security Era* (1993). The continued relevance of the comparison, however, is doubtful.

Armed Forcers and Modern Counter-insurgency was able to draw upon some early analyses of individual campaigns. These included for the British experience, J. Bowyer Bell, *Terror Out of Zion* (1977); Anthony Clayton, *Counter-Insurgency in Kenya, 1952–60* (1976); Richard Clutterbuck, *The Long, Long War: The Emergency in Malaya, 1948–60* (1966); Julian Paget, *Counter-insurgency Campaigning* (1967) and *Last Post* (1969); and Anthony Short, *The Communist Insurrection in Malaya* (1975). For the French experience, there was A.A. Heggoy, *Insurgency and Counterinsurgency in Algeria* (1972); Alistair Horne, *A Savage War of Peace: Algeria* (1977); Peter Paret, *French Revolutionary Warfare from Indochina to Algeria* (1964); and John Talbott, *The War Without a Name* (1981). The formative American experience in the Philippines had also been covered in N.D. Valeriano and C.T.R. Bohannan, *Counter-Guerrilla Operations* (1962).

As interest in counterinsurgency has grown appreciably, so more and more individual studies have appeared. In the British case, knowledge of campaigns has been extended by Susan Carruthers, *Winning Hearts and Minds* (1995); David Charters, *The British Army and Jewish Insurgency in Palestine, 1945–47* (1989); John Coates, *Suppressing Insurgency* (1992); David Easter, *Britain and the Confrontation with Indonesia* (2004); Raffi Gregorian, *The British Army, the Gurkhas and Cold War Strategy in the Far East* (2002); Robert Holland, *Britain and the Revolt in Cyprus* (1998); Tim Jones, *Post-war Counter-insurgency and the SAS* (2001) and *SAS: The First Secret Wars* (2005); J.E. Petersen, *Oman's Insurgencies* (2007); Richard Stubbs, *Hearts and Minds in Guerrilla Warfare* (1988); and Jonathan Walker, *Aden Insurgency* (2004). There are also valuable overviews by Thomas Mockaitis, *British Counter-insurgency, 1919–60* (1990) and *British Counter-insurgency in the Post-imperial Era* (1995); John Newsinger, *British Counter-insurgency: From Palestine to Northern Ireland* (2002); and Charles Townshend, *Britain's Civil Wars: Counterinsurgency in the Twentieth Century* (1986). Surprisingly, perhaps, there is still no adequate monograph on the long-running British campaign in Northern Ireland between 1969 and 1998.

One aspect of British counterinsurgency that has aroused particular controversy is the issue of 'minimum force'. Initially, it was suggested by John Newsinger's questioning of the concept in the context of the Mau Mau insurgency in Kenya between 1952 and 1959. Newsinger and Mockaitis debated the issue in the journal *Small Wars and Insurgencies* in 1992 and the matter has been debated again most recently in the same journal by Huw Bennett and Rod Thornton. In passing, it might be noted that *Small Wars and Insurgencies* itself, first published in 1990, was a real indication of the growing academic interest in the subject. Subsequently, books by David Anderson, *Histories of the Hanged* (2005) and Caroline Elkins, *Imperial Reckoning* (2005) have revived the controversy. There has also been further critical appraisal of the notion of the exceptionalism of British minimum force in the inter-war period. In this latter regard, it should be noted in passing that there has been an increasing interest in the pre-history of insurgency and counterinsurgency prior to 1945, with many excellent monographs. Unfortunately, space precludes any coverage here of this particular area of research and writing.

Equally, knowledge of the French experience, particularly in Algeria, has been greatly extended by Martin Alexander *et al.*, *The Algerian War and the French Army* (2002); Martin Alexander and John Keiger, *France and the Algerian War* (2002); and Tony Clayton, *The Wars of French Decolonisation* (1994) and *Frontiersmen* (1999). There has been less on Portuguese, Rhodesian and South African campaigns. For Rhodesia, there is J.K. Cilliers, *Counter-insurgency in Rhodesia* (1985); Paul Moorcraft and Peter McLaughlin, *Chimurenga* (1982), which has been republished in an updated version as *Counter-insurgency in Rhodesia* (1985); and Peter Godwin and Ian Hancock, *Rhodesians Never Die* (1993). For the Portuguese experience, there is the important analysis in John Cann, *Counterinsurgency in Africa* (1997) and his edited collection, *Memories of Portugal's African Wars* (1998).

Elsewhere, Maoist ideology as motivation survived in some areas such as Peru, Thailand and Nepal. Tom Marks examined the phenomenon as a whole in *Maoist Insurgency since Vietnam* (1996), while the particular case of the 'Shining Path' in Peru was studied in David Scott Palmer, *The Shining Path of Peru* (1992). The vestiges of the Cold War in Central America were depicted in J. Dunkerley, *The Long War: Dictatorship and Revolution in El Salvador* (1982); Hugh Byrne, *El Salvador's Civil War* (1996); William Robinson and Kent Norsworthy, *David and Goliath: Washington's War against Nicaragua* (1987); R. Pardo-Maurer, *The Contras* (1990); and Jorge Osterling, *Democracy in Colombia* (1989). Colombia has remained a focus for insurgency, as examined in Claire Metelits, *Inside Insurgency* (2010). Almost the last of the Cold War campaigns was that waged by the Soviets in Afghanistan, as studied by David Isby, *War in a Distant Country* (1989); Mark Galeotti, *Afghanistan* (1995); and Lester Grau in *The Bear Went Over the Mountain* (1998) and *The Soviet-Afghan War* (2002).

While the end of the process of European decolonisation and of the Cold War and its concomitant ideological competition has removed many earlier motivational impulses behind insurgency, insurgency remains just as prevalent. If anything, while globalisation has decreased the likelihood of states being able to sustain inter-state conflict unilaterally, intra-state conflict has increased where state systems remain underdeveloped, as in parts of Africa, Asia and Latin America. Moreover, in some cases, the distinction between war and organised crime has become increasingly blurred. It is not possible to encompass all the writing on ongoing insurgencies in Africa, Asia and the Middle East, but monographs include Martin Smith, *Burma* (1991); Ram Mohan, *Sri Lanka* (1989); Christopher Clapham's edited collection, *African Guerrillas* (1998); Ruth Iyob, *The Eritrean Struggle for Independence* (1995); Paul Richards, *Fighting for the Rain Forest* (1996); and Bard O'Neill, *Armed Struggle in Palestine* (1978).

The wealth of new research is reflected in Ian Beckett, *Modern Insurgencies and Counterinsurgencies* (2001), while some of the key journal articles were reproduced in Ian Beckett,

Modern Counter-insurgency (2007). Similarly, other general studies have appeared including Anthony James Joes, *Guerrilla Warfare* (1996), *Guerrilla Conflict before the Cold War* (1996), *Resisting Rebellion* (2004), and *Victorious Insurgencies* (2010); Edwin Corr *et al.*, *Uncomfortable Wars Revisited* (2008); and Mark Moyar, *A Question of Command* (2009). Ironically, many former insurgent movements once in power have themselves faced insurgency, as examined by Paul Rich and Richard Stubbs, *The Counter-insurgent State* (1997). More theoretical works had also appeared such as Bard O'Neill, *Insurgency and Terrorism* (1990) and J. Bowyer Bell, *The Dynamics of Armed Struggle* (1998).

Perhaps inevitably, events in Iraq and Afghanistan since 2001 have not only re-focused military minds on insurgency and counterinsurgency but stimulated further academic studies. It is also the case, however, that much of this work must remain provisional in nature given the continuing conflict. With respect to Iraq, the most useful monographs thus far are Ahmed Hashim, *Insurgency and Counter-insurgency in Iraq* (2006); David Kilcullen, *The Accidental Guerrilla* (2009); Thomas Mahnken and Thomas Keaney, *War in Iraq* (2007); Thomas Ricks, *The Gamble* (2007); and Bing West, *The Strongest Tribe* (2008). On Afghanistan, there is Peter Marsden, *The Taliban* (1998) and Hy Rothstein, *Afghanistan and the Troubled Future of Unconventional Warfare* (2006).

Writing on insurgency and counterinsurgency has come a long way from the first tentative attempts by military practitioners to understand the emerging patterns of irregular warfare in the eighteenth century, and its subsequent examination by those confronting opposition to colonial rule. Just as its study was something of a minority interest among military professionals, so its consideration by academe was also slow to develop. Serious academic study of insurgency and counterinsurgency has only really emerged since the mid 1980s and, even then, its growth as a subject has not always been one of uniform progression. Indeed, its recent currency as an issue of immediate contemporary relevance has given writing on the subject new emphasis after arguably another downturn in interest. The frequent recurrence of the 'poor man's war' should long ago have encouraged continued examination of insurgency and counterinsurgency but, then, as in so many counterinsurgency campaigns since 1945, lessons seemingly have to be constantly relearned.

Recommended readings

Asprey, Robert (1975) *War in the Shadows*. London: Macdonald.
Beckett, Ian (2001) *Modern Insurgencies and Counter-insurgencies*. London: Routledge.
Joes, Anthony (1996) *Guerrilla Conflict before the Cold War*. Westport: Greenwood Press.
O'Neill, Bard (1990) *Insurgency and Terrorism*. Washington, DC: Brassey's Defence Publishers.

References

Alexander, Martin and Keiger, John (eds) (2002) *France and the Algerian War*. London: Frank Cass.
Alexander, Martin, Evans, Martin and Keiger, John (eds) (2002) *The Algerian War and the French Army, 1954–62*. Basingstoke: Palgrave.
Anderson, David (2005) *Histories of the Hanged*. London: Weidenfeld & Nicolson.
Asprey, Robert (1975) *War in the Shadows*. London: Macdonald.
Baylis, John, Booth, Ken, Garnett, John and Williams, P. (1975) *Contemporary Strategy*. London: Croom Helm.
Beckett, Ian (ed.) (1988) *The Roots of Counter-insurgency: Armies and Guerrilla Warfare, 1900–45*. London: Blandford Press.
Beckett, Ian (2001) *Modern Insurgencies and Counter-insurgencies: Guerrillas and their Opponents since 1750*. London: Routledge.

Beckett, Ian (ed.) (2007) *Modern Counterinsurgency*. Aldershot: Ashgate.

Beckett, Ian and Pimlott, John (eds) (1985) *Armed Forces and Modern Counter-insurgency*. London: Croom Helm.

Begin, Menachem (1951) *The Revolt: The Story of the Irgun*. London: W.H. Allen.

Bergerud, Eric (1991) *The Dynamics of Defeat*. Boulder: Westview Press.

Blaufarb, D.S. (1977) *The Counterinsurgency Era: US Doctrine and Performance*. New York: Free Press.

Bowyer Bell, J. (1977) *Terror Out of Zion: Irgun, Lehi and the Palestine Underground, 1929–49*. New York: St Martin's Press.

Bowyer Bell, J. (1998) *The Dynamics of Armed Struggle*. London: Routledge.

Byrne, Hugh (1996) *El Salvador's Civil War: A Study of Revolution*. Boulder: Westview Press.

Cable, Larry (1986) *Conflict of Myths: The Development of American Counter-insurgency Doctrine and the Vietnam War*. New York: New York University Press.

Cabral, Amilcar (1969) *Revolution in Guinea*. New York: Monthly Review Press.

Callwell, Charles (1896) *Small Wars: Their Principles and Practice*. London: HMSO.

Cann, John (1997) *Counterinsurgency in Africa: The Portuguese Way of War, 1961–74*. Westport: Greenwood Press.

Cann, John (ed.) (1998) *Memories of Portugal's African Wars, 1961–74*. Quantico: Marine Corps Association.

Carruthers, Susan (1995) *Winning Hearts and Minds: British Governments, the Media and Colonial Counter-insurgency, 1944–60*. Leicester: Leicester University Press.

Charters, David (1989) *The British Army and Jewish Insurgency in Palestine, 1945–47*. London: Macmillan.

Charters, David. and Tugwell, Maurice (eds) (1989) *Armies in Low-intensity Conflict: A Comparative Analysis*. Toronto: Brassey's Defence Publishers.

Cilliers, J.K. (1985) *Counter-insurgency in Rhodesia*. London: Croom Helm.

Clapham, Christopher (ed.) (1998) *African Guerrillas*. Oxford: James Currey Ltd.

Clayton, Anthony (1976) *Counter-Insurgency in Kenya, 1952–60*. Nairobi: Transafrica.

Clayton, Anthony (1994) *The Wars of French Decolonisation*. London: Longman.

Clayton, Anthony (1999) *Frontiersmen: Warfare in Africa since 1950*. London: Routledge.

Clutterbuck, Richard (1966) *The Long, Long War: The Emergency in Malaya, 1948–60*. London: Cassell & Co.

Coates, John (1992) *Suppressing Insurgency: An Analysis of the Malayan Emergency, 1948–60*. Boulder: West-view Press.

Corr, Edwin, Fishel, John and Manwaring, Max (eds) (2008) *Uncomfortable Wars Revisited*. Norman: University of Oklahoma Press.

Dunkerley, J. (1982) *The Long War: Dictatorship and Revolution in El Salvador*. London: Junction Books.

Easter, David (2004) *Britain and the Confrontation with Indonesia, 1960–66*. London: I.B. Tauris.

Elkins, Caroline (2005) *Imperial Reckoning*. New York: Henry Holt & Co.

Ellis, John (1975) *A Short History of Guerrilla Warfare*. London: Littlehampton Books.

Falls, Cyril (1961) *The Art of War*. Oxford: Oxford University Press.

Freedman, Lawrence (1985) *Atlas of Global Strategy*. London: Macmillan.

Fuller, J.F.C. (1961) *The Conduct of War*. London: Methuen.

Galeotti, Mark (1995) *Afghanistan: The Soviet Union's Last War*. London: Routledge.

Galula, David (1964) *Counterinsurgency Warfare: Theory and Practice*. New York: Praeger.

Gann, L.H. (1971) *Guerrillas in History*. Stanford: Hoover Institution Press.

Giap, Vo Nguyen (1962) *People's War, People's Army*. New York: Praeger.

Godwin, Peter and Hancock, Ian (1993) *Rhodesians Never Die: The Impact of War and Political Change on White Rhodesia, 1970–80*. Oxford: Oxford University Press.

Gott, Richard (1970) *Guerrilla Movements in Latin America*. London: Nelson.

Grau, Lester (1998) *The Bear Went Over the Mountain: Soviet Combat Tactics in Afghanistan*. London: Routledge.

Grau, Lester (2002) *The Soviet-Afghan War: How a Superpower Fought and Lost*. Lawrence: University Press of Kansas.

Gregorian, Raffi (2002) *The British Army, the Gurkhas and Cold War Strategy in the Far East, 1947–54*. Basingstoke: Palgrave.

Griffith, Samuel (1965) *Mao Tse-tung on Guerrilla Warfare*. New York: Praeger.

Grivas, George (1964) *Guerrilla Warfare and EOKA's Struggle: A Politico-Military Struggle*. London: Long-mans Green and Co.

Guevara, Che (1968) *Reminiscences of the Cuban Revolutionary War*. London: Allen & Unwin.

Guevara, Che (1969) *Guerrilla Warfare*. Harmondsworth: Penguin.

Gwynn, Charles (1934) *Imperial Policing*. London: Macmillan.

Hamilton, Donald (1998) *The Art of Insurgency: American Military Policy and the Future of Strategy in Southeast Asia*. Westport: Greenwood Press.

Hashim, Ahmed (2006) *Insurgency and Counter-insurgency in Iraq*. London: Hurst & Co.

Haycock, Ronald (ed.) (1979) *Regular Armies and Insurgency*. London: Croom Helm.

Heggoy, A.A. (1972) *Insurgency and Counterinsurgency in Algeria*. Bloomington: Indiana University Press.

Hennessy, Michael (1997) *Strategy in Vietnam: The Marines and Revolutionary Warfare in I Corps, 1965–72*. Westport: Greenwood Press.

Holland, Robert (1998) *Britain and the Revolt in Cyprus, 1954–59*. Oxford: Clarendon Press.

Horne, Alistair (1977) *A Savage War of Peace: Algeria, 1954–62*. London: Macmillan.

Howard, Michael (1976) *War in European History*. Oxford: Oxford University Press.

Hughes, D.C. (1973) *The Philosophy of the Urban Guerrilla*. New York: William Morrow.

Hunt, Richard (1995) *Pacification: The American Struggle for Vietnam's Hearts and Minds*. Boulder: Westview Press.

Isby, David (1989) *War in a Distant Country: Afghanistan, Invasion and Resistance*. London: Weidenfeld.

Iyob, Ruth (1995) *The Eritrean Struggle for Independence: Domination, Resistance, Nationalism*. Cambridge: Cambridge University Press.

Joes, Anthony (1996) *Guerrilla Warfare: A Historical, Biographical and Bibliographical Source Book*. Westport: Greenwood Press.

Joes, Anthony (1996) *Guerrilla Conflict before the Cold War*. Westport: Greenwood Press.

Joes, Anthony (2004) *Resisting Rebellion*. Lexington: University Press of Kentucky.

Joes, Anthony (2010) *Victorious Insurgencies*. Lexington: University Press of Kentucky.

Jones, Archer (1988) *The Art of War in the Western World*. London: Harrap.

Jones, Tim (2001) *Post-war Counter-insurgency and the SAS, 1945–52*. London: Routledge.

Jones, Tim (2005) *SAS: The First Secret Wars*. London: I.B. Tauris.

Kilcullen, David (2009) *The Accidental Guerrilla: Fighting Small Wars in the Midst of a Big One*. London: Hurst & Co.

Kitson, Frank (1971) *Low-intensity Operations*. London: Faber & Faber.

Krepinevich, Andrew (1986) *The Army and Vietnam*. Baltimore: Johns Hopkins University Press.

Laqueur, Walter (1977) *Guerrilla: A Historical and Critical Study*. London: Weidenfeld & Nicolson.

Lawrence, T.E. (1935 edn) *Seven Pillars of Wisdom*. London: Amereon Ltd.

McCuen, John (1966) *The Art of Counterrevolutionary Warfare*. London: Faber & Faber.

McInnes, Colin and Sheffield, Gary (eds) (1988) *Warfare in the Twentieth Century*. London: Unwin Hyman.

Mahnken, Thomas and Keaney, Thomas (eds) (2007) *War in Iraq*. London: Routledge.

Manwaring, Max (ed.) (1991) *Uncomfortable Wars: Toward a New Paradigm of Low Intensity Conflict*. Boulder: Westview Press.

Mao Tse-tung (1963) *Selected Military Writings*. Beijing: Foreign Languages Press.

Marighela, Carlos (1971) *For the Liberation of Brazil*. Harmondsworth: Penguin.

Marks, Tom (1996) *Maoist Insurgency since Vietnam*. London: Routledge.

Marsden, Peter (1998) *The Taliban: War, Religion and the New Order in Afghanistan*. London: Zed Books.

Marston, Daniel and Malkasian, Carter (eds) (2008) *Counterinsurgency in Modern Warfare*. London: Osprey.

Martin, Laurence (1973) *Arms and Strategy*. London: Weidenfeld & Nicolson.

Mead, Edward Gordon (ed.) (1943) *Makers of Modern Strategy*. Princeton: Princeton University Press.

Metelits, Claire (2010) *Inside Insurgency: Violence, Civilians, and Revolutionary Group Behaviour*. New York: New York University Press.

Mockaitis, Thomas (1990) *British Counter-insurgency, 1919–60*. London: Macmillan.

Mockaitis, Thomas (1995) *British Counter-insurgency in the Post-imperial Era*. Manchester: Manchester University Press.

Mohan, Ram (1989) *Sri Lanka: The Fractured Island*. Harmondsworth: Penguin.

Moorcraft, Paul and McLaughlin, Peter (1982) *Chimurenga: The War in Rhodesia*. Marshalltown: Sygma-Collins.

Moss, Robert (1972) *Urban Guerrillas*. London: Temple Smith.

Moyar, Mark (2009) *Question of Command: Counterinsurgency from the Civil War to Iraq*. New Haven: Yale University Press.

Nagl, John (2005) *Learning to Eat Soup with a Knife: Counter-insurgency Lessons from Malaya and Vietnam*. Chicago: Chicago University Press.

Newsinger, John (2002) *British Counter-insurgency: From Palestine to Northern Ireland*. Basingstoke: Palgrave.

O'Neill, Bard (1978) *Armed Struggle in Palestine*. Boulder: Westview Press.

O'Neill, Bard (1990) *Insurgency and Terrorism: Inside Modern Revolutionary Warfare*. Washington, DC: Brassey's Defence Publishers.

Osterling, Jorge (1989) *Democracy in Colombia: Clientist Politics and Guerrilla Warfare*. New Brunswick: Transaction Publishers.

Palmer, David Scott (1992) *The Shining Path of Peru*. Basingstoke: Palgrave.

Paget, Julian (1967) *Counterinsurgency Campaigning*. London: Faber & Faber.

Paget, Julian (1969) *Last Post: Aden, 1964–67*. London: Faber & Faber.

Paret, Peter (1964) *French Revolutionary Warfare from Indochina to Algeria: The Analysis of a Political and Military Doctrine*. London: Pall Mall Press.

Paret, Peter (ed.) (1986) *Makers of Modern Strategy*. Princeton: Princeton University Press.

Pardo-Maurer, R. (1990) *The Contras, 1980–89: A Special Kind of Politics*. New York: Greenwood Press.

Petersen, J.E. (2007) *Oman's Insurgencies*. London: SAQI.

Porzecanski, A.C. (1973) *Uruguay's Tupamaros: The Urban Guerrilla*. New York: Praeger.

Preston, A. Wise, S.F. and Warner, H. (1956) *Men in Arms*. London: Atlantic Press.

Pushtay, John (1965) *Counter-insurgency Warfare*. New York: The Free Press.

Rich, Paul and Stubbs, Richard (eds) (1997) *The Counter-insurgent State*. Basingstoke: Palgrave.

Richards, Paul (1996) *Fighting for the Rain Forest: War, Youth and Resources in Sierra Leone*. Oxford: James Currey Ltd.

Ricks, Thomas (2007) *The Gamble: General David Petraeus and the American Military Adventure in Iraq*. London: Allen Lane.

Robinson, William and Nosworthy, Kent (1987) *David and Goliath: Washington's War against Nicaragua*. London: Monthly Review Press.

Ropp, Theodore (1973) *War in the Modern World*. New York: Collier.

Rothstein, Hy (2006) *Afghanistan and the Troubled Future of Unconventional Warfare*. Annapolis: Naval Institute Press.

Sarkesian, Sam (1975) *Revolutionary Guerrilla Warfare*. Chicago: Precedent.

Sarkesian, Sam (1993) *Unconventional Conflicts in a New Security Era: Lessons from Malaya and Vietnam*. Westport: Greenwood Press.

Shafer, D. Michael (1990) *Deadly Paradigms*. Leicester: Leicester University Press.

Short, Anthony (1975) *The Communist Insurrection in Malaya, 1948–60*. London: Frederick Muller.

Smith, Martin (1991) *Burma: Insurgency and the Politics of Ethnicity*. London: Zed Books.

Strachan, Hew (1983) *European Armies and the Conduct of War*. London: Allen & Unwin.

Stubbs, Richard (1988) *Hearts and Minds in Guerrilla Warfare: The Malayan Emergency, 1948–60*. Singapore: Oxford University Press.

Taber, Robert (1965 edn) *The War of the Flea*, London: L. Stuart.

Talbott, John. (1981) *The War Without a Name: France in Algeria, 1954–62*, London: Faber & Faber.

Tanham, George. (1962) *Communist Revolutionary Warfare*, London: Methuen.

Thompson, Robert. (1966) *Defeating Communist Insurgency*, London: Chatto & Windus.

Townshend, Charles (1986) *Britain's Civil Wars: Counterinsurgency in the Twentieth Century*. London: Faber.

Trinquier, Roger (1964) *Modern Warfare*. London: Pall Mall Press.

US Marine Corps (1940 edn) *Small Wars Manual*. Manhattan, KS: Sunflower University Press.

Valeriano, N.D. and Bohannan, C.T.R. (1962) *Counter-Guerrilla Operations: The Philippine Experience*. New York: Praeger.

Walker, Jonathan (2004) *Aden Insurgency: The Savage War in South Arabia, 1964–67*. Stroud: History Press.

West, Bing (2008) *The Strongest Tribe: War, Politics and the Endgame in Iraq*. New York: Random House.

3

RETHINKING INSURGENCY

Steven Metz

Insurgency has existed as long as people have used violence to resist states and empires but its strategic significance has ebbed and flowed throughout history, increasing when conventional war between great powers was unlikely and states were ineffective at defeating it. During the Cold War, nuclear weapons diminished the probability of direct warfare between the superpowers, leading them towards proxy conflict. Combined with the crumbling of European colonial empires and the political mobilization of the peasantry in many parts of the world, this increased the strategic significance of insurgency. The refinement of insurgent methods by the Chinese, Vietnamese, Algerians and others led to its 'golden age'. A type of conflict that previously festered at the periphery of global statecraft then moved to the fore.

One result was the emergence of an insurgency industry in the West, centred not only in militaries, government agencies and intelligence services, but also in segments of academia, journalism, research institutes and, to some extent, security-related corporations.[1] This first appeared in European nations involved with anti-colonial insurgencies, particularly the United Kingdom and France. But once decolonization was complete, the United States dominated. This industry shaped not only the way that states and their militaries undertook counterinsurgency, but also the way insurgency was understood in the academic world and among the wider public. And because American and European ideas about insurgency were considered 'modern', they influenced non-Western nations, particularly those keen to obtain outside support. Many of them sent their best officers to the United States and Europe for professional education, allowing them to absorb Western ideas about insurgency.

In the 1990s a number of nations in South America and Asia remained involved in insurgency-based conflicts but the insurgency industry collapsed in Europe and North America. In the United States, particularly within the military, involvement in counterinsurgency was considered unlikely. If it did happen, thinking went, the United States would only provide limited advice and support, primarily by the small US Army Special Forces community. No new doctrine emerged; insurgency faded from the curriculum in the military's professional education system. A generation of officers gave it little thought. Research institutes and defence contractors abandoned counterinsurgency and instead embraced multinational peacekeeping and humanitarian intervention, both elevated from strategic insignificance to significance by conflict in the Balkans and sub-Saharan Africa. Interest among academics also faded.[2] Insurgency persisted in Colombia, Sri Lanka, Indonesia, Peru, Burma, the Philippines, Nepal, Uganda, Sierra

Leone, Liberia, South Africa, India, Chechnya and, perhaps most importantly, Palestine. But, for the West, these were the death throes of the old security system, anachronisms which did not merit new thinking and serious attention. In most cases, the states confronting the insurgents were happy to have it that way.

Then Iraq and Afghanistan rocketed insurgency back to a position of strategic significance for the West. In short order, the insurgency industry was reborn. Academics and think tank analysts rediscovered the topic. It exploded in the military educational systems. New – or apparently new – concepts and doctrine blossomed. This process followed the normal pattern for reviving dormant topics: just as the European Renaissance of the fifteenth and sixteenth centuries was based on classical learning, the insurgency industry dusted off old theories, models and concepts from the Cold War, and applied them with only modest revision. Cold War-era thinkers such as the French officer David Galula, US Army colonel John McCuen, Central Intelligence Agency official Douglas Blaufarb and British officer Robert Thompson were once again all the rage (Galula 2006; McCuen 1966; Blaufarb 1977; Thompson 1978). Even new analysis relied largely on Cold War case studies (Nagl 2005).

The problem is that the basic conceptualization of insurgency – the stock-in-trade of the industry – arose from and reflected the Western tradition as applied through colonialism. It is based on a model of politics and development which is culture specific and – importantly – only partly applicable to those parts of the world susceptible to insurgency. It demanded a re-engineering of the political, economic, security and even social systems that was possible only through colonialism, at least in nations not part of Western culture. Thus the orthodox conceptualization may not be wholly inapplicable in the contemporary security environment, but does not fully reflect reality in conflict-prone regions. In one sense it is correct: insurgency is a symptom of deeper social, economic and political shortcomings. The problem comes from assuming that encouraging a state to emulate the Western political model is the cure, or that insurgency is distinct from other dimensions of the deeper pathology. The solution is a broad reconceptualization of insurgency.

The orthodox conceptualization

The dominant Western conceptualization of insurgency – call it the orthodoxy – reflects more general Western notions of politics and history. It was shaped by colonial attitudes and conflicts, forged and refined in Cold War conflicts, and adopted very nearly intact to twenty-first century conflicts. It was based on ideas about civil society and politics born of the European Enlightenment. These hold that government should be 'of the people', with the 'the people' defined by citizenship in a nation. A 'legitimate' government is, from this perspective, one that seeks the best interests of a majority of its citizens. When a government does not represent the interests of 'the people', conflict and violence may occur. Political and economic systems should distribute rewards based on individual merit rather than affinity and affiliation. A legitimate government establishes rules and laws to assure that this happens and then executes them. If it does not, it loses legitimacy and becomes prone to instability and conflict. Governments which reflect these principles are stable, offering no political space for organized violence to coalesce.

The idea arose from the European Enlightenment that the logical and inevitable path of development is from parasitic political systems where the state is simply a tool by which an aristocracy or elite controls the peasantry and extracts resources from them to a 'modern' political system based on a social contract. States which govern in the public interest and provide services (including security) equitably and according to formal rules are legitimate. The population accepts the state's authority and its monopoly on the exercise of force since this is done for the general benefit. Conflict – which can, under some circumstances, take the form of insurgency – occurs when states do not evolve in this direction, do not evolve fast enough to satisfy the demands of the politically mobilized segments of society, or threaten to disempower a particular group such as those based on a particular ethnicity or a traditional elite. This suggests that counterinsurgency must deal both with insurgents directly through military and police actions and undertake reform to better reflect the Western notion of legitimacy. The curative to insurgency, in the orthodox conceptualization, is controlled and correctly paced modernization – defined as the institutionalization of the values, ideas and institutions that emerged from the European Enlightenment (Marshall 2010).

Because the advantages – the correctness – of a system based on these values, ideas and institutions was so evident, opposition to it was attributed to evil or at least misguided people. The solution was to eradicate the evil and educate the misguided. This was the core of counterinsurgency. Hence to Westerners who became involved in counterinsurgency or counterinsurgency support,[3] it was both war – the use of violence to destroy or disempower those with opposing ideas – and programmes to win over misguided people who had been beguiled by the evil through a combination of psychological action and good deeds, particularly the provision of goods, services and infrastructure. At least that was the theory.

Following the Second World War, insurgency emerged from the combination of nationalism and anti-colonialism, peasant unrest, leftist or communist ideologies which exploited and organized this discontent, and, in come cultures, a tradition of banditry and raiding. There were two main currents: conflicts based on opposition to outside rulers, particularly the European colonial powers, and class based conflicts (some with ethnicity elements) against local elites. The latter were most common in Latin America and the Philippines (where the power system still reflected the Spanish colonial tradition). Of the colonial counterinsurgents, the British, Dutch, Belgians and, somewhat later, Spanish and Portuguese developed approaches reflecting imperial stabilization. Policing was central; local issues and grievances were paramount. The French understanding of insurgency-based conflict was the most holistic, stressing its revolutionary nature. The theorists of *guerre revolutionaire* 'assumed a flexible, fanatic opponent who had outmaneuvered an army that was both naive in the ways of subversive war and received insufficient backing from the government and people back home' (Paret 1964: 7).

The emphasis on 'an army' was important. Where the British saw counterinsurgency as akin to colonial policing and thus stressed the synthesis of police and military efforts, the French (and later the Americans) considered it to be more like war than policing. Eventually this perspective dominated. Even non-colonial states facing insurgency adopted it. This made sense: being the victim or target of war did not imply that a state was flawed or culpable. Facing rebellion did. Eventually insurgency came to be understood within the Western conceptualization of war which, as articulated by the nineteenth-century Prussian theorist Clausewitz, is viewed as purposeful behaviour with a rational, policy-focused dimension intermixed with passion and chance. For instance, Roger Trinquier, one of the primary French writers on *guerre revolutionaire*, called it 'a new form of warfare' which included 'an interlocking system of actions – political, economic, psychological, military – that aims at the *overthrow of the established authority in a country and its replacement by another regime*' (Trinquier 2006: 5, italics in original). Traditional armed forces, Trinquier continued, 'no longer enjoy their accustomed decisive role. Victory no longer depends on one battle over a given terrain. Military operations, as combat actions carried out against opposing armed forces, are of only limited importance and never the total conflict' (Trinquier 2006: 5) This idea persists – the first sentence of chapter 1 of current British counterinsurgency doctrine states, 'Counterinsurgency is warfare' (British Army 2010: 1–1).

The idea that insurgency was a variant of war dominated American thinking. President John Kennedy, who initiated US efforts in counterinsurgency, called it

> another type of war, new in its intensity, ancient in its origin – war by guerrillas, subversives, insurgents, assassins, war by ambush instead of combat; by infiltration instead of aggression, seeking victory by eroding and exhausting the enemy instead of engaging him.[4]

Seeing insurgency this way allowed American presidents to mobilize domestic support for involvement by portraying it as an act of aggression by evil people but it hindered US effectiveness at counterinsurgency. The American strategic culture traditionally considers war an episodic and unusual condition. When it occurs, military efforts move to the fore. The objective is the decisive defeat of the enemy and a return to normalcy – 'not war'. The conflict is, in current terminology, 'enemy centric' rather than condition centric. This left the United States psychologically and organizationally ill equipped for protracted and ambiguous conflicts, particularly those involving insurgency. Since war in American strategic culture was caused by evil people rather than the behaviour of those who were attacked, it was difficult to grapple with the idea that insurgency reflected deep systemic and even cultural flaws. American counterinsurgents understood the importance of systemic re-engineering but remained most comfortable with defeating the enemy. The thinking was that the local elite and political leaders would undertake the re-engineering.

While most Western nations have clung to the notion that insurgency is war of a peculiar variant, this idea has not been universal. Some strategic theorists such as Ralph Peters, Edward Luttwak, Martin van Creveld and Michael Scheurer argue that it is more like war than not, and hence the objective is the use of force to defeat the enemy (Luttwak 2007; Peters 2006; Scheuer 2008; van Creveld 2006).[5] This follows a long tradition. Throughout history, many practitioners of counterinsurgency, from Rome to the Soviet Union and contemporary Sri Lanka, took this track, treating insurgency as an enemy–centric conflict where decisive military victory was attainable (so long as one was not squeamish about the application of force). From this perspective, the appropriate response is force directed at insurgents and their supporters – to 'out terrorize the terrorists'. It also suggests that it is primarily a military activity, and that decisive defeat of the insurgents should be the goal. Despite the logic of this idea the norm, as codified in Western doctrine, has been to attempt an uneasy blend of war and political and economic (but not social and cultural) re-engineering. This addresses the symptoms of pathological systems but largely leaves the foundation of the conflict intact.

The difference between conventional war and counterinsurgency arose from the triangular nature of the conflict. Conventional war sought to destroy the enemy's armed forces or at least render them ineffective. At times, this was done indirectly by eroding the armed forces' support, whether psychologically by crushing the will of the enemy population (e.g. strategic bombing) or physically, by destroying the enemy's industry and agriculture. But even actions directed at something other than the enemy's armed forces were undertaken because of the effect on the armed forces. The assumption was that the enemy population supported its armed forces. This support could only be shattered by force or the threat of force.

In the orthodox conceptualization of insurgency, the population – or at least most of it – was seen as 'swayable'. It might support the insurgents either willingly or under duress, but could be enticed to end this support by the provision of goods and services including political and economic opportunities, security and physical infrastructure. This reflected the market logic of Western political theory which saw politics as rational, value optimizing activity. In the historical context which gave rise to the orthodox conceptualization, this made some sense. Throughout what was then known as the 'Third World', previously quiescent segments of the population, particularly the rural peasantry, were awakening during the twentieth century. Their loyalty was up for grabs. Insurgent leaders capitalized on this and attempted, with mixed results, to use popular support to compensate for their weaknesses in numbers, money and arms. The orthodox conceptualization thus saw insurgency as a violent competition for public support in a political market where leaders and ideas competed for support. 'At the heart of any counterinsurgency (COIN) campaign', according to a paper written to augment British counterinsurgency doctrine, 'lies one basic requirement – the population of the territory concerned should form the perception that the government offers a better deal than do the insurgents' (Crawshaw 2009). As befits the Western tradition, it was all a matter of rational choice and optimizing outcomes, reflecting the idea that politics, like the economy, should reflect a moderated but open market. As is often true, French theorists took the point even further. Trinquier, for instance, contended that victory in counterinsurgency (or 'modern warfare') required 'the unconditional support of a population' – something that no government on earth has ever or will ever attain (Trinquier 2006: 6).

The official definitions of insurgency used by Western nations reflect their broader political ideas: it is a form of war used by insurgents in pursuit of political objectives, often to seize state power and become the state (and thus attain a monopoly on sanctioned violence). The leftist revolutionary insurgencies of the twentieth century were considered paradigmatic. In an important 2008 study from the RAND Corporation, for instance, David Gompert and John Gordon characterized insurgency as 'war by other means' composed of 'organized movements to overthrow existing ruling structures by a combination of force and popular appeal' (Gompert and Gordon 2008: xxix). Such ideas also permeated official thinking. The US military's first post-Vietnam counterinsurgency doctrine defined insurgency as 'an organized, armed political struggle whose goal may be the seizure of power through revolutionary takeover and replacement of the existing government' (US Army 1990).[6] Current US Army counterinsurgency doctrine – written in response to the conflict in Iraq – states that 'Political power is the central issue in insurgencies and counterinsurgencies; each side aims to get the people to accept its governance or authority as legitimate' (US Army 2006: 1–1). Joint US doctrine defines insurgency as 'the organized use of subversion and violence by a group or movement that seeks to overthrow or force change of a governing authority' (US Army 2009: I-1). Australian doctrine defines it as an 'organised, violent and politically motivated activity conducted by non-state actors and sustained over a protracted period that typically utilises a number of methods, such as subversion, guerrilla warfare and terrorism, in an attempt to achieve change within a state' (Australian Army 2008: 2–1). The Indian military considers it 'an organised armed struggle by a section of the local population against the State, usually with foreign support' (Indian Army 2004: 16).

Conceptualizing insurgency as a variant of war (albeit with a few different features than conventional state-on-state war) propels strategy and policy in a particular direction. For instance, it makes the response primarily or, at least, heavily military. While the United States, at least, has sometimes used the word 'war' euphemistically (the 'war on poverty', the 'war on drugs'), it has always been more literal in the realm of insurgency and counterinsurgency. Logically, if insurgency is war, then the military should be the leading organization. And since the military's organizational ethos remains, despite efforts to alter it, enemy centric, few if any counterinsurgency campaigns have transcended this notion. For Western nations and those influenced by Western ideas, conceptualizing insurgency as a variant of war also focused efforts to counter it on the national state. As many scholars have noted, the modern territorial nation state became the dominant type of political organization in large part because of its effectiveness at war (Tilly 1992; van Creveld 1999). Treating insurgency as a form of war meant that the solution was strengthening the national state, to include augmenting national security forces, both military and police. And treating it as war meant that 'victory' – defined as the destruction of the enemy – was the goal. Systemic factors which allowed the emergence of conflict might be addressed (as began to happen with conventional wars in the twentieth century), but this was to follow the defeat of the enemy or be part of such a defeat.

Ultimately the orthodox conceptualization of insurgency, arising out of Western political concepts and twentieth-century anti-colonial and leftist insurgencies, reflected an array of assumptions:

- insurgents want to become the state or to split a nation and become the state in some part of it;
- insurgency is caused by bad people willing to pursue their political goals outside the existing political and legal system;
- because they are weaker than the state, the insurgents need popular support;
- popular support is up for grabs; the public acts according to the Western notion of rational choice – seeking to maximize benefits; they will support the side that offers the best deal;
- legitimacy is based on a market logic – assumes that 'the people' expect the state to provide goods and services;
- the 'people' as a whole are politically salient; the side that gets the most support wins (as in an election);
- the solution to insurgency is for the state facing it to become more 'developed', defined as more Western-like.

As interest in insurgency revived in the early twenty-first century, there was little effort to re-examine these assumptions.

The counter-orthodox conceptualization

The principles which emerged from the European Enlightenment are not the norm in much of the world. Nor are they likely to be in the near term. Instead politics and political economy are a spoils system. Rewards are distributed based on control of the state and affinity or affiliation with those who control it. Elites use the political system to extract the maximum resources. The concept of 'the people' as it emerged from the European Enlightenment – defined by national citizenship – is weak or absent. The elites do not seek a revolutionary transformation of the political and economic systems even though this might result in less conflict. Conflict is simply a business expense – the cost of sustaining the system. Instead elites seek the perpetuation of systems that benefits them and their clients, undertaking only the degree of reform necessary to prevent the collapse of the system and, if possible, keep outside assistance flowing. There is, then, a need to transcend the orthodox conceptualization of insurgency which considers it a form of traditional war caused by variance from the political and economic model which emerged from the European Enlightenment. This would have two tracks: a redefinition of insurgency and a different conceptualization of its context.

One way to avoid common (and largely useless) debates over whether a particular organization or a particular conflict is or is not an insurgency and to move beyond the notion that anything which does not replicate the state-centric, revolutionary conflicts of the twentieth century is not insurgency, is to think of it as a *type of strategy* that can be used in many types of conflicts by many types of organizations (Duyvesteyn and Fumerton 2009). This avoids many of the common distinctions which encumber the orthodox conceptualization. Analysts often debate whether an organization is an insurgency or a terrorist movement. For instance, Namrata Goswami illustrates the common thinking when she distinguishes the two by arguing that insurgents desire to control a given area and terrorists do not, instead using violence against non-combatants 'for political signaling' (Goswami 2009: 69). It is more accurate to treat terrorism as a tactic or operational method which can be used in a variety of strategies, including a strategy of insurgency. 'Pure' terrorist movements are nearly always ones which are incapable of implementing a full scale strategy of insurgency. Insurgents often use terrorism heavily in the initial stages of their strategy, hoping that it will gain attention and draw support which can then be used in a more general campaign using a strategy of insurgency. It is to 'awaken' potential supporters.

Another distinction sometimes used by both scholars and military or government officials is between insurgency and civil war. A civil war is simply a violent conflict within a nation – the antagonists share a citizenship. If there is a significant asymmetry between the antagonists, the weaker may resort to a strategy of insurgency. Often they do so because they lack the power to undertake a strategy based on conventional combat. But an insurgency is not analytically distinct from a civil war. One concept deals with how an organization uses its resources; the other with the identification of the antagonists.

As a strategy, insurgency is adopted by a weak organization against a power structure and the organizations which dominate it. It is most often used by a non-state organization against a state but may also be used by a non-state organization against a transnational power structure (e.g. al-Qaeda), or by a nation (e.g. Iran). The weak organization may seek specific political objectives or, in some cases, control of and a total transformation of the power structure. The strategy of insurgency uses or threatens the use of violence. Non-violent movements may adopt a strategy which has some of the characteristics of insurgency but is not actually insurgency.

Within the strategy of insurgency, the weak organization seeks to postpone resolution of the conflict while it adjusts the power balance in its favour. Thus the strategy deliberately seeks to extend the conflict. An organization using insurgency assumes that postponing resolution will lead to a shift in the power balance in its favour because it has superior will, coherence and sense of purpose. Some of the most effective movements using insurgency have a teleological ethos, believing that the laws of history or divine will are on their side and will eventually remedy their weakness. Insurgency involves diminishing the importance of realms of conflict or 'battlespaces' where the weak organization is inferior, particularly the conventional military one, and emphasizing ones where its inferiority is less, such as the psychological realm. Phrased differently, the strategy seeks to make the conventional military realm non-decisive. This is one of the most important points on which insurgency can differ from traditional war. In addition to surviving and taking actions which weaken the power structure or state, a strategy of insurgency entails actions and activities designed to augment the strength of the movement or organization using it – again as part of shifting the power balance. This may involve building alliances or partnerships or directly augmenting the strength of the movement or organization by recruitment, fund raising, acquiring weapons or other tools, training, and developing more effective organizations and operational methods.

Organizations and movements can attempt the strategy of insurgency anywhere but it takes roots and, on rare occasions, succeeds in certain types of political-economic systems. States vulnerable to insurgency tend to be ones where the key prizes – the things which determine control of the nation – are the capital and regions which produce the resources which fuel the modern sector of the economy, often by exports. The modern sector of the economy seldom dominates the daily life for most people. Vulnerable states always have a modern sector along with grey or black economies and informal sectors which are larger in terms of their impact on the population. So long as the state controls the national capital, other major cities and the resource-producing regions, it is willing to tolerate limited or even no control over the hinterlands, urban slums, and the informal or grey and black economies.

Patronage is the lifeblood of politics in these systems, as also discussed in the contribution by William Reno in this volume (Chapter 12). Elites which dominate the state and the modern sector of the economy develop a web of patron/client relationships, sometimes based purely on personality but often with an overlay of family, clan, ethnicity or sect. Political power takes the form of concentric circles. The inner ring is the national leader and his closest patrons – often family. The rings consist of others with declining affinity the further from the core. The fusion of political and economic power means that the patronage of the state is lucrative and used to buy support or, at least, political passivity. Patronage based systems do not focus their attention on the population as a whole, but on individuals or groups who could pose a challenge to the system. These are bought off or, if necessary, repressed. Potential opponents of the system are played against each other.

Most states throughout history have followed this model, as do many, probably most, nations today. Citizens or occupants of the state did not expect extensive services from the state other than some degree of protection from invaders or bandits and, in some societies, maintenance of infrastructure, often having to do with waterways and irrigation.[7] The social contract which serves as the foundation of legitimacy is much more limited than the type that emerged from the European Enlightenment. More importantly, the notion that development invariably moves towards an Enlightenment-style social contract may not be totally false, but evidence suggests that it is very different than the sort of linear progression which many Western theorists – including some contemporary ones – expected. There is a social contract of sorts with those with the power to challenge the system or those geographically close to the capital or resource-producing regions. But the further removed from power or sources of power, the weaker the social contract.

Such systems are brittle and prone to conflict. Rulers misjudge threats. They may not be able to extract enough resources to fuel the patronage system. Elites do not care about conflict by people or places removed from the centres of power. Thus rebellion, secession and organized banditry are common. But, for the elite, they are tolerable unless they threaten the core of the system. Most of the time, the conflict in such systems does not take the form of insurgency. But in the twentieth century a number of factors gave rise to politically based conflicts based on insurgency. One was the political awakening of previously apolitical segments of societies, particularly rural peasants. While history is replete with peasant revolts, this awakening melded with an ideology, developed and refined by non-elite urban intellectuals, based on socialism and anti-colonialism. Like the nationalist and anti-feudal revolts of the late eighteenth, nineteenth and early twentieth centuries, this gave the discontent of excluded but mobilized segments of society a focus other than purely local grievances, thus making it more powerful and dangerous. Anti-colonialism blended with new forms of political discourse on the left in the Western world and the organization of anti-authoritarian politics among the youth to glamorize political insurgency. Western college students did not wear T-shirts with a picture of bandits or leaders of localized peasant revolts, but did sport the image of insurgents like Che Guevara. Within the nations where insurgency-based conflict occurred, to be an insurgent was seen as noble, a gesture of self-sacrifice, thus appealing to the idealism which was particularly powerful among the youth as they looked for new frameworks of identity and order to replace traditional ones crumbling in the face of urbanization, increased communication, expanded education and wider economic change. It was a perfect storm of factors spawning a golden age of insurgencies.

Global politics amplified this trend by making the means of insurgency – particularly weapons and knowledge – readily available. In part this was a result of the massive amount of armaments and military expertise left over from the Second World War. But, more importantly, it was the result of the Cold War, as the two ideological blocs, constrained from direct military confrontation by nuclear weapons, turned to proxy conflict. Initially the Soviets, their allies and the Chinese armed and trained insurgents while the United States and other Western powers armed and trained counterinsurgents. By the 1980s, both sides aided friendly insurgents and counterinsurgents. The United States saw Nicaragua and, especially, Afghanistan as strategic successes arising from support for insurgents.

The key point is that systems based on patronage rather than on a permeable market for talent and ambition are prone to pathologies, whether political violence or other forms such as organized crime. Youth bulges, urbanization and the breakdown of old methods of order – and the accompanying anomie – amplify the problem. In any society, the weaker the system for distracting and disciplining the youth, particularly young males, the greater for violence of all kinds, including the political. If the pathologies are not organized politically using a strategy of insurgency, they will simply manifest in some other form, at least in the absence of systemic re-engineering and a major change in the political and economic culture. This is sustained because those with the power to re-engineer the system have a vested interest in it. Their objective is to preserve the system as much as possible while staving off challenges that might destroy it and their ability to extract reward from it. Often the optimal situation is a controlled, isolated or contained insurgency-based conflict which is organized around an ideology capable of attracting support from outsiders for the state and the elite.

The idea that a fragile or challenged elite benefits from political violence is important. Organized violence has always played an important role in creating nations and in legitimizing a system which avoids defeat. The psychologically liberating effect of political violence has been a recurring theme among French thinkers like Georges Sorel and Frantz Fanon (Sorel 1961; Fanon 1963). The United States, as Michael Vlahos notes, was created and re-created by its Revolutionary War, Civil War and participation in the world wars of the twentieth century (Vlahos 2009; Wilson 1966). In the modern security environment, few states can undertake a traditional war against another state so sub-national violence serves as a surrogate, justifying the regime and the system.

Finally, war economies become an important part of insurgency-based conflicts. Internal wars 'frequently involve the emergence of another alternative system of profit, power, and protection in which conflict serves the political and economic interests of a variety of groups' (Berdal and Keen 1997: 797). Hence the insurgents, criminals, militias or even the regime have a greater interest in sustaining a controlled conflict than in attaining victory. As Paul Collier notes:

> various identifiable groups will 'do well out of the war'. They are opportunistic businessmen, criminals, traders, and the rebel organizations themselves. The rebels will do well through predation on primary commodity exports, traders do well through the widened margins on the goods they sell to consumers, criminals will do well through theft, and opportunistic businessmen will do well at the expense of those businesses that are constrained to honest conduct.

(Collier 2000: 103–4)

Within this context, movements or organizations which utilize a strategy of insurgency vary in three dimensions. The first is their functional focus. All such movements simultaneously generate resources (people, money, arms, information), they undertake violence and they pursue political goals. Their priority among these varies according to both conditions and strategic choices. An insurgent movement which feels that time is against it or the balance of power between it and the state has shifted in its favour will focus on violence and political objectives. A movement which feels that time is on its side or is still too weak to directly attain its political objectives will focus on resource generation. A common pattern is for insurgency-based movements to eventually lower their emphasis on both violence and political objectives and concentrate on resource generation. They become, in effect, criminal enterprises with a veneer of politics.

A second dimension is organizational coherence. Movements using a strategy of insurgency fall along a continuum. At one pole are formal organizations with internal specialization and a command hierarchy. They evince strategic behaviour – balancing ways, ends and means, and adjusting the strategy as conditions change. In many ways, they emulate the state and may administer areas they control in a state-like way. Insurgencies using a Maoist approach see the progression towards such formality as the logical evolution of their movement. At the other end of the continuum, insurgencies are informal. They are composed of semi-autonomous cells or bands, sometimes with a loose degree of cooperation among them (but not formal command). Their armed actions take the form of swarming. Such movements are less likely to become state-like, but are more survivable than formal ones since there are no critical nodes or centres of gravity which can cause the movement to collapse if destroyed. The point, though, is that formality and informality are not binaries. A movement is not one or the other. Rather, insurgencies fall somewhere between formality and informality, and may shift along the continuum during their lifespan and the duration of a conflict.

The third dimension is objective. Again, this is best conceptualized as a continuum. At one end is simple survival; at the other are teleological objectives such as replacing the state or even sparking a transnational revolution which alters the balance of power across a region or many regions. While the orthodox conceptualization of insurgency, with its roots in the Maoist movements of the twentieth century, is based on the idea that all insurgencies want to replace the state, in the modern context many want the power of the state but not the responsibility. In other words, they seek only to augment their ability to extract resources, including both power and money. They seek to alter the players in a parasitic or patronage-based system, but not the system itself. Many of the insurgency-based movements in sub-Saharan Africa take this form. For example the Lord's Resistance Army in northern Uganda gives little indication of wanting to assume administrative responsibility for their region, much less the country as a whole, but instead to be a more effective parasite (Vinci 2005). Under such conditions, the Western notion of legitimacy, which undergirds the orthodox conceptualization of insurgency, is nearly meaningless.

A key part of an insurgency-based conflict is the struggle by the antagonists to portray what is taking place. The more that the insurgent movement can make the conflict about affinity, identity and justice, the greater the advantage for them. Involvement by outsiders which support the state facilitates this. The state, by contrast, gains by portraying the conflict in terms of legality versus illegality, or as external aggression. Ultimately the battle of portrayal is not, in itself, decisive, but it is very important for the outcome of an insurgency-based conflict.

Implications

Because the Western notion of counterinsurgency is derived from the Western authored, orthodox conceptualization of insurgency, it concentrates on strengthening the state which exists in a patronage-based, often parasitic, political context. Thus it seldom leads to a decisive outcome in terms of permanently stabilizing the system, instead simply making the state more effective at fending off challenges, distributing patronage and extracting resources. Afghanistan under Hamid Karzai is a perfect illustration. At times the Western style of counterinsurgency does help quell an insurgency – Iraq for instance. But so long as the system remains deeply flawed, the pathology simply takes other forms. The insurgency in El Salvador ended in the 1990s but today that nation is nearly paralysed by organized crime and gang activity. Often entities other than the national state remain the primary providers of security and justice; the economy remains divided into a formal sector which does not serve most of the population and an informal sector which does. For outsiders involved in counterinsurgency support, this may be enough: the conflict moved from the front page of the newspaper to an afterthought. But this is not victory if it is defined as creating a stable national state with a near monopoly of force. Like health problems in a society or crime, the violence may be controlled or pushed into a less destructive form, but it persists.

States vulnerable to insurgency are those which fall into a grey area. They are patronage-based, parasitic and closed but not fully effective at repression. Patronage-based, parasitic closed systems which *are* effective at repression like North Korea, Iraq under Saddam Hussein, Iran, China and Syria do not allow the space for insurgency to coalesce and strengthen. Only when such systems begin to lose their ability or willingness to repress does the space exist for insurgency to form. In the spring of 2011, Libya seems to be such a state; Zimbabwe may become one.

In the contemporary security environment, the resources for insurgency-based conflict – arms, money and information – remain available. The only question is whether the motivation also persists. During the twentieth century insurgency sometimes appealed to individuals and organizations excluded from power in patronage or parasitic systems or ones ruled by outsiders because it seemed to offer a feasible and appealing method for the weak to confront or vanquish the strong. Today interconnectedness and information technology help provide alternative methods as the wave of popular rebellions that swept the Arab world in 2011 showed. If a dictator can be overthrown relatively quickly by 'people power', there is little incentive to undertake the arduous and dangerous insurgency approach. Egypt is a perfect illustration: insurgency failed there in the 1990s while popular uprising worked in 2011. At the same time, the insurgencies in Iraq, Afghanistan, Sri Lanka and dozens of other places have not succeeded, at least in the way their architects intended. All of this suggests that insurgency-based conflict may again be ebbing. Certainly patronage-based, parasitic systems will continue to experience high levels of violence but it is likely to take other forms – perhaps the criminal warfare of Mexico – rather than traditional political insurgency. As insurgency ebbs, it will flow again in the future. When this happens viewing it as a strategy and reconceptualizing its dynamics and context will help scholars and governments better understand it.

Notes

1 I do not use the word 'industry' in a value-laden, pejorative sense (a tendency derived from the Marxist intellectual tradition) but simply to mean a range of organizations and individuals filling the demand for counterinsurgency analysis and actions.
2 I was typical, writing nothing on insurgency or counterinsurgency between 1995 and 2004, instead focusing on what was called the 'revolution in military affairs'.
3 A foreign state undertakes counterinsurgency *support* when the primary counterinsurgent force is local. For instance, the United States and the United Kingdom undertook counterinsurgency in Iraq through 2004, and then shifted to counterinsurgency support.

4 President John F. Kennedy, Remarks at West Point to the Graduating Class of the US Military Academy, 6 June 1962.
5 It is no coincidence that all of these works appeared during the height of frustration over the conflict in Iraq.
6 In part, the admission that insurgencies may have aims more limited than taking over the state was a result of the fact that the United States was itself supporting or had recently supported insurgencies in Nicaragua, Angola and Afghanistan while the doctrine was being written.
7 The pioneering work on 'hydraulic' states or empires was Wittfogel (1957).

Recommended readings

Berdal, Mats and David M. Malone (eds) (2000) *Greed and Grievance: Economic Agendas in Civil Wars*. Boulder: Lynne Rienner.
Joes, Anthony James (2004) *Resisting Rebellion: The History and Politics of Counterinsurgency*. Lexington: University Press of Kentucky.
Kalyvas, Stathis N. (2006) *The Logic of Violence in Civil War*. Cambridge: Cambridge University Press.
Metelits, Claire (2010) *Inside Insurgency: Violence, Civilians, and Revolutionary Group Behavior*. New York: New York University Press.
Metz, Steven (2007) *Rethinking Insurgency*. Carlisle Barracks: US Army War College Strategic Studies Institute.
Ucko, David H. (2009) *The New Counterinsurgency Era: Transforming the U.S. Military for Modern Wars*. Washington, DC: Georgetown University Press.
Weinstein, Jeremy M. (2007) *Inside Rebellion: The Politics of Insurgent Violence*. Cambridge: Cambridge University Press.

References

Australian Army (2008) Land Warfare Doctrine 3–0–1, *Counterinsurgency*.
Berdal, Mats and David Keen (1997) 'Violence and Economic Agendas in Civil Wars: Some Policy Implications', *Millennium*, 26 (3): 795–818.
Blaufarb, Douglas S. (1977) *The Counterinsurgency Era: U.S. Doctrine and Performance*. New York: Free Press.
British Army (2010) Army Field Manual, Volume 1, Part 10: *Countering Insurgency*, January.
Collier, Paul (2000) 'Doing Well Out of War: An Economic Perspective', in Mats Berdal and David M. Malone (eds), *Greed and Grievance: Economic Agendas in Civil Wars*. Boulder: Lynne Rienner, pp. 91–112.
Crawshaw, Colonel (retd) Michael (2009) 'The Evolution of British COIN', supporting document for Joint Doctrine Publication (JDP) 3–40: *Security and Stabilisation: The Military Contribution*. London: Ministry of Defence.
Creveld, Martin van (1999) *The Rise and Decline of the State*. Cambridge: Cambridge University Press.
Creveld, Martin van (2006) *The Changing Face of War: Lessons of Combat, from the Marne to Iraq*. New York: Ballantine.
Duyvesteyn, Isabelle (2007) 'The Paradoxes of the Strategy of Terrorism', in Jan Angstrom and Isabelle Duyvesteyn (eds), *Understanding Victory and Defeat in Contemporary War*. London: Frank Cass, pp. 117–41.
Duyvesteyn, Isabelle and Mario Fumerton (2009) 'Insurgency and Terrorism: Is there a Difference?', in Caroline Holmqvist-Jonsater and Christopher Coker (eds), *The Character of War in the 21st Century*. London: Routledge, pp. 27–41.
Fanon, Frantz (1963) *The Wretched of the Earth*. New York: Grove.
Galula, David (2006) *Pacification in Algeria, 1956–1958*. Santa Monica: RAND Corporation.
Gompert, David C. and John Gordon IV (2008) *War by Other Means: Building Complete and Balanced Capabilities for Counterinsurgency*. Santa Monica: RAND.
Goswami, Namrata (2009) 'India's Counter-Insurgency Experience: The "Trust and Nurture" Strategy', *Small Wars and Insurgencies*, 20 (1): 66–86.
Indian Army (2004) *Doctrine, Part 1*, December.
Luttwak, Edward N. (2007) 'Dead End: Counterinsurgency Warfare as Military Malpractice', *Harpers*, February: 33–42.

McCuen, John J. (1966) *The Art of Counter-Revolutionary War*. Mechanicsburg: Stackpole.

Marshall, Alex (2010) 'Imperial Nostalgia, the Liberal Lie, and the Perils of Postmodern Counterinsurgency', *Small Wars and Insurgencies*, 21 (2): 233–58.

Nagl, John A. (2005) *Learning to Eat Soup With a Knife: Counterinsurgency Lessons From Malaya and Vietnam*. Chicago: University of Chicago Press.

Paret, Peter (1964) *French Revolutionary Warfare From Indochina to Algeria: The Analysis of a Political and Military Doctrine*. New York: Praeger.

Peters, Ralph (2006) *Never Quit the Fight*. Mechanicsburg: Stackpole.

Scheuer, Michael (2008) *Marching Toward Hell: America and Islam After Iraq*. New York: Free Press.

Sorel, Georges (1961) *Reflections on Violence*. New York: Collier.

Thompson, Robert (1978) *Defeating Communist Insurgency: Experiences From Malaya and Vietnam*. London: Palgrave Macmillan.

Tilly, Charles (1992) *Coercion, Capital and European States: AD 990–1992*. Malden: Wiley-Blackwell.

Trinquier, Roger (2006) *Modern Warfare: A French View of Counterinsurgency*. Westport: Praeger.

US Army (1990) Field Manual 100–20, U.S. Air Force Pamphlet 3–20, *Military Operations in Low Intensity Conflict*, December.

US Army (2006) Field Manual 3–24/Marine Corps Warfighting Publication 3–33.5, *Counterinsurgency*, December.

US Army (2009) Joint Publication 3–24, *Counterinsurgency Operations*, October.

Vinci, Anthony (2005) 'The Strategic Use of Fear by the Lord's Resistance Army', *Small Wars and Insurgencies*, 16 (3): 360–81.

Vlahos, Michael (2009) *Fighting Identity: Sacred War and World Change*. Westport: Praeger.

Wilson, Edmund (1966) *Patriotic Gore*. Oxford: Oxford University Press.

Wittfogel, Karl (1957) *Oriental Despotism: A Comparative Study of Total Power*. New York: Random House.

4

CHANGING FORMS OF INSURGENCY

Pirates, narco gangs and failed states

Robert J. Bunker

The primarily bipolar world that helped to characterize the decades long Cold War has begun to realign itself. The information revolution, increasing globalization, the ongoing expansion of transnational terrorist and insurgent networks, and many other elements of this systemic level change have continued to take place into the early twenty-first century. Within the context of this large-scale shift in human and state relations, one question that has often been asked by analysts is whether changing forms of insurgency are taking place. If this is so, these changing forms of insurgency would be distinct from the currently dominant political form of insurgency found in the revolutionary, and at times nationalistic, writings of Mao Zedong, Giap, Thai, Guevara, Marighella, Urbano, Bayo and others. Almost all of our current understanding of insurgency theory is derived from this dominant form that reached its zenith in the decades following the Second World War.

Such changing forms of insurgency challenge in fact our modern definition of political insurgency by incorporating both pre-modern and post-modern constructs. Concepts of 'private warfare' – waged by individuals such as warlords – and 'privatized warfare' – waged by mercenary and free companies and corporations – very much help to define both very old and newly emergent forms of conflict. So too do the concepts of religious crusade and jihad once embraced by the Christian and Islamic religions during their early expansionist periods and now again being promoted by the extremist fringes of both these religions and newer religious cults. 'RAHOWA' (racial holy war promoted by white supremacists), 'Jihad' (holy warfare to expand and defend an Islamic state) and 'Divine Justice' (God's will carried out by La Familia Michoacana) are but a few examples of the war cries of these holy warriors.

The dominant political form of insurgency current in contemporary analysis, on the other hand, is one which usually seeks to create a shadow government which will ultimately replace the pre-existing government of a state through a phased process of resistance such as that defined by strategic defence, stalemate and eventual strategic offence. Tools of the trade include targeted killings (assassinations and executions), hit-and-run tactics, booby traps and IEDs, propaganda, re-education camps, and psychological warfare and terrorism. The defined end state is the replacement of the government of a nation-state by a different governmental structure. The nature of the state ultimately remains the same with only its political leadership and structure changing. The basis of the insurgency itself is thus political in nature and exists within the paradigm of the Westphalian state system established in 1648 and which continues to define the modern world order.

New forms of insurgency, contrastingly, would conceivably be drawn initially from non-political elements derived either from combinations of criminality and illicit profit or spirituality and religion. Early thinking influencing the new economic insurgency perceptions can be attributed to Steve Metz, with his concepts of 'commercial insurgency', and John P. Sullivan, with his later concepts of 'criminal insurgency'. Metz has also been notable for examining the way that insurgencies have a 'spiritual' dimension and this approach has gained increasing acceptance by other scholars. Secular criminals and holy warriors would thus represent the extreme ends of a new insurgent spectrum with many combinations found along the continuum. While the political element, at least within the context of the Westphalian nation-state, is not a component of these changing forms of insurgency, it would at some point come into play as pre-existing governments are challenged and their authority usurped.

Thus parallel shadow governments do emerge. However, they are criminal and/or religious in nature and thereby defy older revolutionary warfare derived insurgency patterns. The political element is simply not recognized as such because no separation of the legitimate (legal) and illegitimate (criminal) or the church (religious) and the state (political) exist within the new social order promoted by the insurgents in control of the territory they have now seized. Such expanses can range in size from a few streets, to a section of a town or entire city, all the way up to the territories of once sovereign states.

It is enlightening to look at two recent types of conflicts that have been held up as potential examples of those changing forms of insurgency – the rise of pirates in Somalia and the proliferation of narco gangs, primarily in Latin America. Of these two potentially incipient forms of insurgency, piracy is still relatively immature and questionable in its nature as such. The narco gang phenomenon, on the other hand, is far more mature in nature as an insurgent form and makes an ideal case study in portraying how these insurgency forms can change over time. For these reasons, piracy will be addressed first and in a more limited manner than narco gangs which this author feels better supports the contention that the nature of insurgency itself is changing.

Pirates

The state of knowledge concerning the acts and institution of piracy goes well back to the age of Classical city-states – Rhodes, Crete, Athens, and the early Roman republic – and throughout the non-Western world in the various littoral seas, ocean coastal areas and other bodies of water wherever maritime commerce arose. Piracy is derived from criminal acts such as robbery, hijacking, plunder, ransom and hostage-taking directed at boats and ships, their crew and passengers, and the material cargo that they contain. Acts of piracy also extend to the historical plundering of seacoast towns and cities by marauding fleets of seaborne criminals. Low levels of piracy always exist, as does basic criminal activity on the land, and will in the vacuum of strong political authority and policing measures rise in both the frequency and severity of the criminal acts involved. Imperial Rome, the Ming Dynasty and the British Empire all engaged in successful anti-piracy campaigns that extended imperial and sovereign control over their seas and oceans of influence.

Where state and empire weakness exists, however, such as during times of civil and extended wars and transitions in human history between state forms, piracy flourishes as both a criminal activity, organized and unorganized, and as a form of state policy based on privateering (e.g. a commission provided by a state which provides legal justification to attack, seize and destroy opposing enemy ships and other properties). Hence, golden ages of piracy have come and gone over the course of many eras with the most celebrated recent period – known for such flamboyant personages as Henry Moran, Captain Kidd and Blackbeard – taking place from the mid-seventeenth to the early eighteenth centuries.

Historically, however, piracy is not normally linked to the concept of insurgency which itself is a modern construct and, consequently, accepted positions or schools of thought on such linkages simply do not exist. This does not mean that relationships and synergies between pirates and insurgents are non-existent but rather that few, if any, scholars have attempted to analyse such potentials. Acts of piracy in the modern era have been steadily increasing since the early 1990s with principal areas of recent criminal activity including the Malacca Strait, the West African coast, and off the coast of Somalia. For statistics on such acts, the International Maritime Bureau (IMB; see www.icc-ccs.org), which established the Piracy Reporting Centre in 1992, provides the most comprehensive dataset available. Recent worldwide statistics show that 406 acts of piracy took place in 2009 as opposed to 239 acts taking place in 2006 with increases noted in both 2007 and 2008. Within the wider literature, these acts of piracy become blurred with acts of air piracy, maritime terrorism and smuggling, especially that of narcotics trafficking, along with the location where the acts took place – whether within the territorial jurisdiction of a nation-state or international seas – further complicating legal and academic interpretations of just what represents an act of piracy. In some instances, these problems of interpretation can have very detrimental governmental consequences. For example, in August 2010, a domestic US court deemed that Somali 'pirate defendants' who engaged in a failed attempt at piracy against the warship *U.S.S. Ashland* were immune to prosecution due to legal statute problems. Because they failed in their piracy attempt, they were legally determined not to be actual pirates since Supreme Court case law, dating back to 1820, states that one must be successful in the commission of piracy to fit the criteria of a bona fide pirate!

The most likely setting for potentially linking modern piracy to acts of insurgency is the rampant piracy taking place off the coast of Somalia extending out into the littoral Red Sea, the Gulf of Aden, and much further out into the Indian Ocean and the Arabian Sea now over 1,000 nautical miles from Somalia per International Maritime Bureau (IMB) reports. The IMB states:

> The total number of incidents [in 2009] attributed to the Somali pirates stands at 217 with 47 vessels hijacked and 867 crewmembers taken hostage. Somalia accounts for more than half of the 2009 figures, with the attacks continuing to remain opportunistic in nature.[1]

Somalia can be considered the modern poster child of the failed state phenomena and has existed without a functioning central government since the 1990s. The United Nations and the United States attempted to engage in humanitarian and peace operations in the 1992–6 period via United Nations Operation in Somalia I & II (UNOSOM I & II)/Operation RESTORE HOPE, but both eventually pulled out in disgust and exhaustion and also in partial humiliation at the futility of their efforts. The territories of that former state now represent a patchwork of overlapping enclaves and fortified zones controlled by gangs and warring clans, criminal groups, Islamic insurgents and terrorists, local warlords, a small governmental pocket in Mogadishu of very questionable legitimacy, some foreign African troops via the African Union Mission in Somalia (AMISOM), and of course many coastal villages containing pirate bases. Weak states with limited central governmental authority and marginal economic and military resources provide fertile ground for insurgent activities. Still, the Somali pirates themselves should not be considered insurgents because, at this point, they are solely criminally focused and no direct economic links on their part to insurgency exist. The question then becomes whether piracy supports insurgents in any tangential fashion. The linkages to insurgency that are of most interest would focus on the economic, military and political activities between the Somali pirates and the actual insurgent forces.

From an economic perspective, piracy could provide much needed hard currency to insurgents through reselling the cargo of the ships seized, and even more importantly, securing ransom payments for hostages and the ships themselves. Multimillion dollar ransoms delivered in cash to the pirates to release cargo and tanker ships have taken place on a number of occasions. Where this linkage breaks down is that the al-Qaeda affiliated insurgents, such as the Islamic Courts whom are the major insurgent force in Somalia, do not appear from news sources to be directly involved in piracy. In fact, they have gone after some of the pirate bases – though they may have done so because taxes that they may have imposed on the pirates were not paid.

On the military side, piracy is based on the deployment of small boarding craft containing criminals carrying infantry small arms – principally Russian assault rifles and rocket propelled grenades (RPGs). Mother ships increasingly exist which have extended the range of these small craft and allow for multiple boarding craft to be deployed against a targeted vessel. Since opposing political structures are not being targeted, active assassinations are not taking place, and kidnapping is for economic purposes, as opposed to political re-education (indoctrination) or execution purposes, no military attributes of an insurgency can be said to be taking place. Additionally, bribery and co-option of governmental officials, as seen with some of the newer forms of insurgency, is not an attribute of Somali pirate activities.

Lastly, from a political perspective, it could be argued that piracy represents the extension (or projection) of a failed state environment from the land onto the sea and ocean. The rule of law is thus replaced by anarchy and crime not only within the territorial jurisdiction of a nation-state but also within the international seas. The international legal structure is thus challenged but not to the extent that a competing legal structure is being promoted by some sort of organized insurgent navy. The response to the anarchy and crime being projected by the Somali pirates onto the seas has been individual sovereign and multilateral task forces of warships sent to patrol the threatened international waters and, in some cases, the institution of the convoy system for cargo and tanker ships which traverse the greater Horn of Africa region. Attacks on individual cruise ships have also taken place with the institution of such countermeasures as avoiding Somali coast regions, placing non-lethal acoustic devices, and even hiring extra private security guards with heavier weapons to protect some of these craft. The response of sovereign states and private cruise lines to Somali piracy focuses on anti-criminal rather than anti-insurgency protocols. In no way is an 'insurgency at sea' considered to be taking place or for that matter even contemplated as a potential threat at this time.

From this above analysis, the pressing issues and potentials pertaining to piracy vis-à-vis evolving forms of insurgency would appear to be:

- At what point could an insurgent group conceivably, such as the Islamic Courts movement, create a naval arm for the purpose of raising capital via the pursuit of piracy? If such activities were promoted, would Sharia law then de facto be implemented on the high seas as a challenge to conventional international law? While such potentials may currently sound far fetched, they would be no different than what is currently taking place in a number of territories where the local laws of a sovereign state are being challenged on land with Sharia law being imposed by insurgent groups in such locales as Iraq, Afghanistan, Pakistan and of course Somalia where hundreds acts of piracy are currently taking place on a yearly basis.
- At a micro-level, would a local clan leader or warlord with political authority who engages in piracy be considered a 'post-modern insurgent' if in fact they are creating a criminally based governmental structure which derives its economic foundation from trading in illicit goods, such as narcotics and slaves, and criminal pursuits such as ransoming cargo ships and

their crews? Such a governmental structure would be in variance to nation-state legal norms and the Westphalian state system of international laws. Such a pirate clan leader or pirate warlord would represent a de-evolution of the current international system where the pre-modern and post-modern have come full circle and from a social and political perspective are anathema to the values of our modern age.

- At a macro-level, do increasing levels of piracy foretell the beginning of a new golden age of piracy emerging during this transition from the modern to the post-modern world? As the Westphalian state comes under increasing pressure as a state form archetype by challenging organizational entities such as city states, market states, regional states and criminal transnational federations (ghost states), will some of these new entities utilize piracy as an economic strategy to help fuel the 'political organizational insurgency' that is being directed against the Westphalian state form and the international system that it has erected over the last 500 years?

Narco gangs

Modern narco gangs are a relatively recent phenomena with their origins in Colombia dating back to the late 1970s and early 1980s. Mexico, since late 2006, has fallen into a state of open warfare between the federal government and the competing drug trafficking organizations and between the narco gangs and various cartels themselves. Prior to 2006, the Mexican state and the drug traffickers, for the most part, mostly benefited from the drug trade as a by-product of the systemic corruption upon which the Mexican political system has been built since the 1920s. The interrelationship between the Mexican elite tied into one-party PRI (Partido Revolucionario Institucional) rule and the drug trade goes back to the 1970s when the initial cartels emerged along federal policing regions found within that country. With major electoral challenges to the PRI via the PAN (Partido Acción Nacional) party in 2000, and the later rise of the reformist Calderón government, the old system of drug trafficking collusion broke down. This is not unexpected given that, with their growing levels of wealth, a shift in power was already underway in the direction of the cartels. Symptoms of this trend were increasing levels of corruption taking place within Mexico, which its political system and society could not sustain. (See also Chapter 11 by David E. Spencer in this volume.)

Major Mexican drug trafficking organizations have risen and fallen in power over the decades with Sinaloa, Gulf, Los Zetas, Juarez, Tijuana and La Familia representative of the more dominant cartels of today. Networks of street and criminal gangs in Mexico, the United States, Central America and increasingly South America support these groups. In the United States alone, over 50,000 Sureños gang members, such as Mara Salvatrucha and 18th Street, are tied into these networks. Additionally, former Mexican special forces personnel, Los Zetas, and former military personnel from Guatemala and other countries have become cartel enforcers. Since 2006, over 28,000 people have been killed in the criminal insurgencies in Mexico with military small arms and body armour now common cartel weaponry. Mexican law enforcement, at all levels, has long been corrupted by the cartels, as have been the courts, with the Mexican military now deployed to suppress cartel activity in hot spots throughout the country. Most of these hot spots are drug transshipment points and other major cartel zones of control. Torture and beheadings, the increasing use of improvised explosive devices (IEDs) and the assassination of reporters covering cartel activity in Mexico are ongoing. Additionally, the first reported car bombing in Mexico took place in Ciudad Juárez in July 2010 against Mexican Federal police with additional car bombings now taking place.

Newer perspectives on narco gangs view them as major components of 'criminal insurgencies' taking place in Mexico and increasingly in Central America and other regions of the globe, such as West Africa. Many of these perceptions are drawn from lessons learned from earlier cartel activity in Colombia. At a minimum, these criminal insurgencies are creating failed communities and sovereign-free zones and/or, as in the case of Mexico, what are known as 'zones of impunity'. Such zones, now found in hundreds of geographic regions in Mexico alone, have become defensive gang and cartel bastions ruled by fear, intimidation and the well-known insurgent technique of giving an individual the choice between *¿Plata O Plomo?* – either accepting our silver or being filled with our lead. The magnitude of this problem has become clear to President Calderón who in August 2010 publicly stated that the drug gangs are now attempting to replace the government in parts of Mexico.[2] What began as primarily an illicit commercial endeavour based on drug trafficking has morphed into full-blown criminal insurgencies, each with their own unique political agenda. These political agendas are very different from that found in revolutionary and nationalistic warfare writings.

A major component of the insurgency paradigm discussed in this chapter is the traditional school of thought concerning policing and law enforcement, heavily influenced by American and European perspectives. These perspectives are derived from clearly delineated law enforcement and military roles and do not recognize an intra-state security environment where crime and war has blurred. In fact, this well-entrenched school of thought has long considered such narco gangs and drug trafficking organizations (DTOs) to be solely engaging in a form of criminal activity. At best, DTOs, mafias and the more sophisticated narco gangs (which may include some prison, street and outlaw motorcycle gangs) have generally been placed into the more threatening category of organized crime, which is a federal and international policing (INTERPOL) concern. Still, this form of organized crime derived from narcotics trafficking is, in worst case scenarios, viewed as attempting to create a symbiotic and parasitic relationship with a host state so that it can freely engage in its illicit activities and no more.

This view on policing and law enforcement is dominant because the older forms of organized crime groups that have existed in Italy, the United States, Chechnya, China and Japan for many centuries have never sought to replace the government of their respective host nations. The traditional school has increasingly been challenged by newer political and military perspectives on intra-state conflict, blurred operational environments – where criminal and military activities become grey and in some instances merge, and societal warfare concerns over future state organizational forms.

Even more threatening insurgency concerns, then, focus on the assorted narco gangs, cartels and their mercenary foot soldiers representing the vanguard in the formation of new criminally-based patterns of state social and political organization. This would result in a shift in human values to non-traditional Westphalian norms and open the way to patterns of living such as those conceivably derived from illicit narcotics use, killing for sport and pleasure, and even Santa Muerte (Saint Death) spirituality increasingly linked to human sacrifice. These rather dark components of emerging criminal norms and behaviours cannot be understated. From this perspective, *¿Plata O Plomo?* takes on a rather profound almost religious significance, that is, join us in our criminality and become one of us or die. Rather than age-old religious conversion by the sword, we are now witnessing post-modern criminal conversion by the bullet.

Drug trafficking organizations can be thus viewed as a direct threat to state sovereignty and, ultimately in the more extreme threat scenarios, state survival and, as a result, direct military intercession into these conflicts is not only warranted but imperative. The traditional school response to these newer perspectives is to propose that a spectrum of criminal activity now exists in regard to narcotics trafficking. Less sophisticated narco gang operations would fall into the category of low intensity crime while the more sophisticated and threatening operations, such as those conducted by the more prominent Mexican drug cartels, would fall into the category of high intensity crime. Such high intensity crime, it is argued, would continue to be the sole purview of federal and international law enforcement response and currently defines the position taken by transnational organized and global crime scholars and even some military scholars on this debate. As a result, the de facto position of this school of thought holds that narco gangs and cartels have not arisen to the level of a direct threat to a state's sovereignty and survival and do not require any form of direct military intercession.

The differing positions taken by the traditional school and newer perspectives over the meaning of narco-terrorism are also of interest. Traditional views of cartel violence consider narco-terrorism to be an inaccurate term because such cartel activities are devoid of a political component and therefore are not actual terrorism. Beheadings, torture and bombings, at best, are a manageable law enforcement problem and are simply treated as organized criminal acts between competing drug trafficking entities and between some of those entities and a government and no more. Alternative perspectives concerning narco-terrorism view it as a component of insurgency techniques, especially attacks on police, judges and governmental personnel, and as examples of psychological warfare being waged against the citizens of a country such as Colombia or Mexico. Therefore, drug cartels and narco gangs actively engage in acts of domestic and international terrorism and require specialized military support in order to combat them. These groups' viewpoints are far less divergent when al-Qaeda, Taliban and Hizbollah narcotics related activities are considered since both schools of thought readily considered them terrorist groups. Since political terrorism as a threat is typically considered dominant to narco-terrorism, radical Islamic violence – even if it is somehow associated with drug trafficking – is normally only viewed as a political challenge.[3]

The two regions where major narco insurgencies have been and are taking place are Colombia and Mexico with some spillover into surrounding areas such as Guatemala, Honduras and neighbouring states. Colombia is an interesting study of an early narco gang insurgency against a sovereign state as it occurred back in the 1980s. Pablo Escobar and his Medellin cartel clumsily attempted to gain influence over Colombian society and government by means of corruption and political positioning – at one point, Escobar was elected as a senator and attempted to create his own political party. When this failed, his cartel declared open war on the state and engaged in a campaign of kidnappings, assassinations and even car bombings before he was eventually hunted down and killed and his cartel dismantled. Conflicting trends in Colombia over the last few decades, with both the decentralization and recentralization of drug cartel activities have since taken place. This can be seen with the elimination of the larger cartels, the Medellin and Cali organizations, and subsequent rise of dozens of baby cartels while at the same time the leftist FARC (Fuerzas Armadas Revolucionarias de Colombia) and the ELN (Ejército de Liberación Nacional), along with the right-wing AUC (Autodefensas Unidas de Colombia) have become, to varying degrees, de facto major drug trafficking organizations. Profiteering is subsuming the leftist and right-wing ideologies of these insurgent and self-defence groups. They are becoming hybrid criminal-political organizations more in line with the warlords found in Africa and other regions of the world. Colombia had in the past attempted to trade large regions of land with these drug funded insurgent groups in return for peace, which is in some ways reminiscent of a medieval France that ceded its sovereign rule of Normandy over to the Vikings.

A number of pressing issues and challenges are currently the subject of ongoing debate with regard to narco gangs and their interrelationship with both insurgents and the role that they play in actual insurgencies:

- Heated debates are raging over the security of the southern United States border with Mexico. Actual cartel and gang violence is considered by some to be less of a threat than that of corruption of federal, state and local agents and other public servants though corruption works best when it is utilized as part of the *plata o plomo* technique. Arguments for and against cartel violence and corruption penetrating into US territory continue as do questions relating to whether penetrations are representative of criminal insurgencies taking place along the border. So far violence levels in US border cities are fairly low, as opposed to Mexico border *plazas* (drug shipment cities), though levels of corruption in the Border Patrol and other agencies is increasing. Strong anti-illegal immigration laws recently passed in Arizona, the construction of the new border fence, and other issues, such as armed private groups patrolling the border, are adding layers of complexity and divisiveness to these debates.

- It is becoming increasingly recognized by scholars that some form of convergence between cartels, terrorists, gangs, mafias, private armies and insurgents is taking place. As these groups mutate and merge and evolve and devolve, they readily come in contact with and influence each other. Early work on evolutionary patterns (gang generations and cartel phases) exists but remains immature. Still, each re-formation of these groups is viewed as getting more sophisticated and threatening than their earlier organizational forms. Little of these processes are understood yet they are commonly viewed as a byproduct of globalization, maturing networks of criminal activity and hyper-competitive illicit economic environments which have resulted in higher levels of intra-state conflict taking place between diverse non-state groups. Ongoing conflict has become a process of criminal group evolution with newer groups, such as Los Zetas, representing a true firebreak in narco foot soldier tactical and operational capabilities.

- The extension of narco operations into other illicit money making operations – human trafficking, street extortion and taxation, kidnapping, commodities and bulk theft, slavery, and illicit organ harvesting – in addition to narcotics trafficking, is providing new economic opportunities for narco gangs and their networks. As these groups increase their relative wealth compared to smaller and weaker states, it is being debated if they will be satisfied with subordinating themselves to such states or if they will seek to fully co-opt them via new criminal insurgencies. Of real concern is the rise of actual criminal and narco states and the increasing growth of their networks via a process of Neo (narco)-imperialism.

Conclusions

This chapter suggests that insurgency itself is changing with a shift from a political basis to one initially based on criminal and spiritual foundations. These new bases of insurgency, however, ultimately become political in nature. The type of political action pursued by these newer forms of insurgency extends beyond the boundaries of the Westphalian sovereign state and is both pre- and post-modern in nature. Since it is insurgency which leads to new and competing social and political organizational forms it is thus viewed as a challenge to the traditional nation-state system. The discussion and analysis of piracy and its relationship to such a new form of insurgency is at best hypothetical in nature – no clear empirical linkages currently exist. The more in-depth treatment and review of the narco gangs in Latin America are, however, an entirely different matter. A strong case can be made that such gangs, especially those threatening the integrity and national security of Mexico, are waging active criminal insurgencies against its federal government. If this analysis is correct, then our understanding of what constitutes an insurgency will dramatically shift in the decades to come as the war over social and political organization continues to expand with new warmaking entities such as narco gangs, potentially pirate confederations and legions of holy warriors, and the associated mercenaries supporting them, creating shadow governments that seek to challenge and ultimately replace the authority of the Westphalian state form.

Notes

1 '2009 Worldwide Piracy Figures Surpass 400', *International Maritime Bureau*, 14 January 2010. Available at: www.icc–ccs.org/index.php?option=com_content&view=article&id=385:2009-worldwide-piracy-figures-surpass-400&catid=60:news&Itemid=51.
2 'Calderon: Mexico Drug Gangs Seeking to Replace State', *BBC News*, 5 August 2010. Available at: www.bbc.co.uk/news/world-latin-america-10877156.
3 Even this perception is somewhat problematic – since a religious basis of insurgency exists – but Islamic insurgencies are outside the scope of this chapter and will not be further commented upon.

Recommended readings

Brands, H. (May 2009) *Mexico's Narco-Insurgency and U.S. Counter-Drug Policy*. Carlisle Barracks, PA: Strategic Studies Institute, US Army War College. Available at: www.strategicstudiesinstitute.army.mil/pubs.

Bunker, R.J. (ed.) (2010) *Narcos Over the Border: Gangs, Cartels and Mercenaries*. London: Routledge.

Bunker, R.J. and Bunker, P.L. (November 2007) *Subject Bibliography: Piracy and Maritime Terrorism*. Quantico: FBI Academy Library. Available at: http://fbilibrary.fbiacademy.edu/bibliographypage.htm.

Bunker, R.J. and Bunker, P.L. (January 2010) *Subject Bibliography: Mexican and Colombian Drug Cartels*. Quantico: FBI Academy Library. Available at: http://fbilibrary.fbiacademy.edu/bibliographypage.htm.

Gottschalk, J.A. and Flanagan, B.P. (2000) *Jolly Roger with an Uzi: The Rise and Threat of Modern Piracy*. Annapolis: Naval Institute Press.

Lehr, P. (ed.) (2007) *Violence at Sea: Piracy in the Age of Global Terrorism*. New York: Taylor & Francis.

Metz, S. (June 2007) *Rethinking Insurgency*. Carlisle, PA: Strategic Studies Institute, U.S. Army War College.

Murphy, M.N. (2009) *Small Boats, Weak States, Dirty Money: Piracy and Maritime Terrorism in the Modern World*. New York: Columbia University Press.

5

CYBERSPACE AND INSURGENCY

David J. Betz

Cyberspace is an 'emergent phenomenon'[1] of the Information Age at the beginning of which, for better or worse, humanity now finds itself. No good historian would yet attempt to write a history of its impact upon human society because it is still too early to tell. Nevertheless we implicitly understand that it is very large because cyberspace already touches so many aspects of daily life. Individuals, groups, corporations and governments are investing enormous amounts of time and money in cyberspace. It is transforming the way we do all sorts of things from the ways in which we make money and govern ourselves to the ways in which we maintain friendships and find spiritual and intellectual sustenance. It is also changing the way that we fight wars of all sorts, including insurgency.

Insurgency is also an emergent phenomenon. As John Mackinlay (2009: 5) explains, amongst its most salient features is that it naturally reflects the society from which it emerges:

> the techniques of an insurgency evolve with the societies from which it arises. Since the Cold War the pace of social change has accelerated dramatically, not just in the rich, secure nations of the northern hemisphere, but also in developing countries as they have become gripped by global change. Just as the structures of these societies have altered out of all recognition, so it is possible that an insurgency arising from them can take on unforeseen characteristics. Furthermore, if the communications revolution has given birth to global communities and global movements, so too can it herald a form of insurgent energy that is de-territorialised and globally connected.

That is what has driven its evolution from one form to another over the ages. The changes of human society in accordance with technological, social and environment developments cause changes in insurgency, the quintessentially bottom-up form of warfare. This chapter is about the interaction of these two emergent phenomena: how cyberspace is exploited by 'global insurgents' in order to achieve a reach, sophistication and virulence which they otherwise would not have; how insurgency is being shaped by cyberspace, shifting the centre of gravity in such conflicts from populations defined by territory to the 'virtual dimension' where identities are more fluid and transnational; and how both, possibly, are shaping the global political economy in which we all live causing consternation in the defence establishments of the world about the utility of conventional forces.

Holding onto reality: information and human history

In order to understand the form of insurgency which inhabits and preys upon the digital 'Information Society' (Drucker 1969; Bell 1974; Masuda 1981; Castells 2010) we need to start with an understanding of the precepts which govern that society. It is worthwhile considering this in long perspective because one of the troubles with much of the literature on cyberspace is that it tends to begin with the invention of the microchip, or the World Wide Web, and as a result tends to overemphasize recent change over longer historical continuity. That said, neither should one underestimate the magnitude of the developments which have occurred in just the last two decades.

There are three basic things which can be done with information: it can be transmitted (communicated); it can be stored; and it can be processed for analysis for manipulation. In all human history from the time we acquired language until today there have been just five 'information eras'. In each of these the archetypal forms and sophistication of information processes produced different patterns of politics, culture, science, religion, economy and war. Let us review them briefly.

Before literacy all information was transmitted by voice, communication was 'one-to-one' or very few. The range of communication was limited to that of the human voice and the only means of information storage was human memory. About 100,000 years ago we learned to 'tally' – to record the quantity of things with beads, notches on a bone, or knots in a string (Schmandt-Besserat 1998: 158–61), and about 5,000 years ago primitive account-ants learned how to record both the quantity and type of things by the use of clay tablets on which data was inscribed by means of pressing the cut end of a reed into wet mud in a pat-terned manner – logographic writing, literacy as we know it, was born (Schmandt-Besserat 1998: 192).

But for approximately the next 6,500 years until the invention of the mechanical printing press in the mid-fifteenth century only a small elite enjoyed the fruits of written knowledge. The range of transmission in this era was as far as a letter could be carried (at no more than the speed of a fast horse or ship). Information was stored in semi-durable form in semi-organized libraries but information processing was rudimentary as knowledge tended to be esoteric and fragmentary, scattered as it was in handwritten texts guarded jealously by 'craft' scholars and clergymen who very largely constituted the literate class.

Mass literacy was not an immediate impact of the invention of mechanical print – it was more a development of the Industrial Revolution, which began over 200 years later. In fact what was initially important about mechanical print as opposed to craft script was its relative orderliness and uniformity.[2] Print media has no inherent superiority over handwritten script in terms of range or velocity of communication either, but it could be produced in huge volume (although the cost of initial typesetting was formidable) which caused a vast expansion in the sum of overall knowledge; moreover, coincident developments in cataloguing, indexing and other aids to data analysis made possible more complex information processing.

Print, therefore, tended to have a bridging and unifying effect in science; but in socio-politics and religion, by contrast, its impact was divisive and fragmenting, 'making possible pamphlet wars and doctrinal polarization' (Kaestle 1985: 19). It is no coincidence that scholars such as Hobsbawm dubbed the era which coincided with mass literacy the 'Age of Revolution' because mass conflicts over ideas and beliefs are practically impossible to conduct without mass media. Thus we see that while history is peppered with insurrections from the biblical period onward, insurgency in the sense of guerrilla tactics *plus* mass political subversion is essentially a modern concept.[3]

People often associate mass communication with radio and television. This is, however, incorrect. After all in 1830, according to Stephens, 100 years before radio's 'Golden Age' *The Times* of London was already hitting a mass audience, selling 10,000 copies a day in a city of two million. The actual significance of electronic media relative to machine print is not so much in relative audience size as it is in fidelity of transmission – sounds and especially images have much greater emotional impact than text because they convey a functional facsimile of reality as opposed to a mere description.[4]

It is hard to overstate the importance of this in the history of insurgency: revolution needs icons and symbols – images that 'embody a sense of universality of blight and at the same time innocence', in the words of an Iranian writer quoted by Ravitz on the image of the death of Neda Soltan, a young woman murdered by a pro-government *Basiji* militiaman in June 2009 while protesting the disputed Iranian elections. Images are particularly potent icons; in consequence they have huge potential propaganda power; moreover, the velocity of electronic communication is potentially instantaneous and global, allowing a large audience to experience an event anywhere in the world in real- or near real-time – further heightening its potential shock effect.[5]

Much ink has been devoted to the study of traditional media and insurgency and war; nonetheless, it is worth outlining the main findings of that literature as explained by Livingston, particularly as it relates to expeditionary counterinsurgency campaigns, before going on to look at the impact of digital 'new media' (Livingston 1997). First, it is understood that the media acts as an *accelerant* of events, contracting decision-making time in a crisis. Second, it is often regarded as an *impediment* to the exertion of force over a long period by democratic states, because by injecting emotional content in coverage it gradually undermines public support and political will. And third, it is thought to have a main role in *agenda setting* potentially leading to the reordering of foreign policy priorities by spotlighting a particular crisis.

In the counterinsurgency literature there is a wide consensus that this matters because it is believed by theorists such as Mack and Arreguin-Toft that 'big nations lose small wars' not because their forces are defeated in the field but because their domestic will becomes exhausted by the perception conveyed (whether accurately or inaccurately) by the media that the conflict is 'unwinnable' or 'not worth it'. This is the master narrative of American failure in Vietnam (Rid 2007) and French failure in Algeria (Horne 1977), for instance – and is rapidly becoming the leitmotif of the NATO campaign in Afghanistan; the basic effect, however, was pithily encapsulated by Colin Powell (quoted in Livingston 1997: 5):

> [The American people] ... are prepared to take casualties. Even if they see them on live television, as long as they believe it's for ... a cause that is understandable ... They will not understand it, if it can't be explained.

Insurgents quickly realized the power of media spectacle to rocket a cause onto the international agenda. Before 9/11 there is no better example of this than the attack on the 1972 Munich Olympic Games by the Palestinian terror group Black September which killed 11 Israeli athletes. The attacks were widely decried – even by the Palestine Liberation Organization which feared that the Palestinian cause had been damaged by the atrocity – yet they were also hugely successful. As Black September (quoted in Hoffman, B. 2006: 70) boasted: 'A bomb in the White House, a mine in the Vatican, the death of Mao Tse-Tung, an earthquake in Paris could not have echoed through the consciousness of every man in the world like the operation at Munich.' Recognition that the main function of insurgent operations is the attraction of the media spotlight, rather than death and destruction per se, is readily apparent in Carlos Marighela's famous *Minimanual of the Urban Guerrilla*. And it is evident as well, shows Aust, in the operations of European anarcho-communist terror groups such as the Baader-Meinhof Gang who were very skilful propagandists; indeed, Ulrike Meinhof was a noteworthy journalist who had written for the influential German leftist magazine *Konkret* before founding the gang with Andreas Baader and Gudrun Ensslin. British Prime Minister Margaret Thatcher was not wrong to say at the height of the 'Troubles' in Northern Ireland that, publicity was the 'oxygen' of terrorism:

> In this evil strategy, the actions of the media are all important. For newspapers and television, acts of terrorism inevitably make good copy and compelling viewing. The hijacker and the terrorist thrive on publicity: without it, their activities and their influence are sharply curtailed. There is a fearful progression, which the terrorists exploit to the full. They see how acts of violence and horror dominate the newspaper columns and television screens of the free world. They see how that coverage creates a natural wave of sympathy for the victims and pressure to end their plight no matter what the consequence. And the terrorists exploit it. Violence and atrocity command attention.

Which brings us to the present day in which it is said that information on digital networks – stories, innovations and data on practically every subject imaginable – has replaced labour and fixed capital as the central organizing principle of society. Whereas modern industrial society was relatively ordered, unitary and centralized, the *post-modern* information society has quite different characteristics. While information society theorists might differ on detail or emphasis most would agree that they include intangibility (Rifkin 2000: 55), miscellaneousness (Weinberg 2008), horizontality and self-organization, anonymity, digital ubiquity and societal fluidity (Hassan 2008; Borgmann 1999; Kallinikos 2006).

Consider the impact of digitization on the three things which can be done with information. Twenty years ago just a handful of countries could afford colossally expensive secure and instantaneous global communications, now anyone with a laptop and a network connection can:

*   *transmit* information whether 'one-to-one' or 'one-to-many', effectively globally and instantaneously in a variety of forms from text to video;
*   *process* information (i.e. copy, cross-reference, cross-check, combine or manipulate it) easily and cheaply with standard commercial software;[6] and
*   *store* information in vast quantities almost indefinitely on cheap, miniature and portable digital devices, or indeed in the 'cloud' independent of any particular device.

We live in an 'information ecology' (whether or not we wish it) which is denser, more ever-present and pervasive than has existed before. Manuel Castells (2009), one of the most prominent scholars mapping the contours of the new Information Society, calls the communications paradigm of this new era 'mass *self*-communication'. It is a profoundly important development – at least as important as the invention of print and perhaps as much as literacy itself – with significant impact on all aspects of social life, including insurgency and war.

In media studies, Marshall McLuhan's aphorism 'the medium is the message' (McLuhan and Fiore 1997) holds something of the same position as does Clausewitz's famous maxim 'war is the extension of politics by other means' to students of war. In the 1960s McLuhan discerned the emergence of what he called a 'global village' as a result of the rise of global communications. War, he argued, in this situation would take the form of a 'war of icons' in which the belligerents would seek to defeat their rivals by the erosion of their 'collective countenance' with 'electric persuasion ... dunking entire populations in new imagery' (McLuhan 2001: 370). He was ahead of his time, but not by much; what McLuhan saw building in the early 1960s is now a self-evident reality – just look around, according to the United Nations the chances are now one in two, *wherever* you are in the world, that the person next to you will own a mobile communications device – in the Western world 'personal electronic devices' (i.e. all the things you are asked to turn off on airplanes on take-off and landing) outnumber people by a wide margin.

Increasingly scholars and statesmen speak of 'mediatized' wars while commanders apprehend that the centre of gravity of the wars they are in exists more in the virtual dimension than the physical one, in the perception of the conflict more so than its material actuality. No one has captured this more eloquently than the British general Rupert Smith who has written that 'we are conducting operations now as though we are on stage, in an amphitheatre or Roman arena' and who describes the role of the theatre commander in this sort of war as akin that of a theatre or film 'producer' (Smith 2006: 284–5).

Some analysts, Castells most importantly, argue that de-territorialized insurgency is the paradigmatic conflict type of the Information Age. 'The conflicts of our time', he writes, 'are fought by networked social actors aiming to reach their constituencies and target audiences through the decisive switch to multimedia communication networks' (2009: 49). Before dismissing such claims as academic fancy it is worth noting that senior officers on either side of the Atlantic have said similar things. For instance, Britain's Chief of Defence Staff, General Sir David Richards argued recently in a speech to the International Institute for Strategic Studies, 'Conflict today, especially because so much of it is effectively fought through the medium of the Communications Revolution, is principally about and for People – hearts and minds on a mass scale'.

The massive concern of defence and foreign policy establishments on either side of the Atlantic with 'strategic communications', 'information operations', 'public diplomacy' and other variations on propaganda (to give it its proper name, see Taylor 2006) also reflects and reinforces Castells' point. What better confirmation of the relevance of his thesis than the words of both the current and previous US defence secretaries that we are not only in a media war but losing it? Said Donald Rumsfeld in a 2006 speech, 'Our enemies have skilfully adapted to fighting wars in today's media age, but for the most part we—our country—our government, has not adapted'; while according to Robert Gates in 2007:

> It is just plain embarrassing that al-Qaeda is better at communicating its message on the internet than America. As one foreign diplomat asked a couple of years ago, 'How has one man in a cave managed to out-communicate the world's greatest communication society?'.

Thus far we have seen no conflict which might be described as insurgency *in* cyberspace – that is to say insurgency in an entirely 'virtual community'; such a thing is theoretically possible, perhaps it is even inevitable once (if) the digital environment evolves polities worth subverting and overthrowing; for the time being, however, insurgency in cyberspace is science fiction. What is real, however, is the way that cyberspace has infused conflict of all types, bringing on a dimension of rhetorical conflict which is no less consequential for being intangible. To quote al-Qaeda's number two Ayman al-Zawahiri, 'I say to you that we are in a battle, and that more than half of this battle is taking place in the battlefield of the media'.

Also it has given insurgency tools which lend it a global reach, sophistication and capacity for strategic impact which it did not have previously. Let us turn now to that development.

The arsenal of insurgency

'We must be the great arsenal of democracy', said President Franklin Delano Roosevelt in a famous speech on 29 December 1940 enjoining America to gird itself for the challenge of the Second World War. According to Lind and subsequently Hammes, the Second World War II – the quintessential *industrial* war, war based on mass of men and machines – has been superseded by a new type, 'Fourth Generation Warfare' (4GW). The gist of 4GW theory is that for a number of reasons, largely technological but also political, economic and cultural, war can be categorized according to four types:

- first-generation warfare – the sort waged by Napoleon involving muzzle-loading artillery, muskets, and columns and lines of infantry and cavalry;
- second-generation warfare – as seen during much of the First World War, conducted with massive formations employing indirect firepower and quick-firing infantry weapons;
- third-generation warfare – which began with the German light infantry tactics of 1918, developed a theory of all-arms coordination including armour and aircraft in the interwar period, and reached a sort of apotheosis with the German 'Blitzkrieg' in 1940 (with limited repeats in the Six-Day War in 1967 and the Gulf War in 1991); and,
- fourth-generation warfare – largely a post-Second World War development, which is said to combine guerrilla tactics, or civil disobedience, with disinformation campaigns and political activity exploiting 'soft networks' to directly attack enemy political will, as opposed to regular military forces.

According to Hammes (2005: 190), 4GW 'uses all available networks ... to convince the enemy's political decision-makers that their strategic goals are either unachievable or too costly for the perceived benefit'. The resemblance of 4GW to insurgency is readily apparent; indeed much of the criticism of 4GW focuses on its lack of novelty (Van Creveld 2005), also its dubious historical grounding (Freedman 2005). Yet even so the concept deserves contemplation for two reasons. First, because 4GW theorists were amongst the first to talk about the *socio-technological* changes which have been transforming warfare, as opposed to the merely technological ones which so enthralled enthusiasts of the so-called 'Revolution in Military Affairs' for most of the 1990s (Hoffman, F. 2006; Betz 2006, 2007, 2008; also McMaster 2008).

> Socially, the world is dramatically smaller. In 1945, the vast majority of people in the world knew only their own village. Even in developed nations, most knew only what they read in their newspapers and had little or no contact with people of other nations. Today, citizens of developed nations communicate with and travel freely around the globe. Small generators and satellite TV have delivered the world to even isolated, primitive villages.
>
> *(Hammes 2005: 196)*

In other words, even before the advent of the World Wide Web had really gathered a head of steam 4GW was beginning to describe the power of connectivity to shift the centre of gravity of insurgency from the local to the global – and subsequently, as we shall see, to the virtual. Second, 4GW observed a development which has become perhaps the central problem of contemporary counter-terrorism:

> 4GW practitioners are making more and more use of materials made available by the society they are attacking. This allows them to take a very different strategic approach.

> It relieves the 4GW practitioner of the strategic necessity of defending core production assets, leaving them free to focus on offence rather than defence. It also relieves them of the logistics burden of moving supplies long distances. Instead, they have to move only money and ideas—both of which can be digitized and moved instantly.
>
> *(Hammes 2005: 207)*

The 9/11 attacks remain the exemplar of this type of attack in scale if not sophistication but there are numerous instances of it both before (such as the bombings of the Marine Barracks in Beirut, Khobar Towers in Saudi Arabia and US embassies in Africa) and after (notably the bombings in Bali, Madrid and London). The November 2008 attacks in Mumbai which killed at least 173 people, wounded more than 300, and shut down a major world city for three days represent a worrisome harbinger of what death, destruction and disruption can be achieved with a combination of low-cost civilian systems and highly motivated personnel using basic infantry tactics and weapons. The attackers' equipment consisted of AK-74 assault rifles, ammunition, home-made hand grenades, energy bars, mobile phones (the supply of which they replenished from their victims) and a hijacked civilian fishing boat, all of which (including the weapons) are readily available anywhere in the world, with the possible exception of totalitarian 'securocracies' such as North Korea.

To date, no terror or insurgent group has combined a physical attack with a simultaneous cyber-attack, for instance to disrupt emergency response systems, although analysts such as Professor Peter Somers of the London School of Economics quoted by the *Daily India* have raised expectations that ultimately they will do so – most likely around the London 2012 Olympics; nor have there been any attempts at cyber-terror, although hacking by state and non-state groups for espionage and profit is increasingly prevalent (Michael 2010). But the search for examples of 'pure' cyber-terror or cyber-insurgency misses a larger point: as Seymour Goodman *et al.* (2007) put it, 'cyberspace always touches ground somewhere', and the 9/11 attacks, the Bali bombing, London's 7/7 bombings and the massacre in Mumbai *are* examples of cyberspace touching the ground; al-Qaeda's mode of operation, the whole concept of 'global insurgency' makes no sense without the dense web of interconnectivity which is cyberspace; without it there would be no global forum into which to transmit their narrative of repression and resistance through propaganda of the deed (Betz 2008; Bolt and Betz 2008), no secure global communications capability for planning, recruitment and financing of their organizations, and no open-source intelligence and analysis network in the form of the World Wide Web which is integral to their functioning.

'History will not portray Osama bin Laden as a mere terrorist', wrote Berkowitz (2003: 17), 'Rather instructors at West Point and Annapolis will cite him as one of the first military commanders to use a new kind of combat organization in a successful operation'. No one has explored the operational concept of this 'new kind of combat organization' further than John Robb, a software entrepreneur cum strategist who describes it as 'open-source warfare' drawing a parallel with the open-source movement in software development. The gist of Robb's argument, that war is being transformed from a predominantly closed and state-centred affair to a more open one in which non-state groups can challenge nations and win, rests on two bases:

- 'Superempowerment' – an idea which holds that the digital technologies which collectively are bringing on the Information Age also enable insurgent groups to organize themselves in flexible, non-hierarchical networks which can work collaboratively on tasks of mutual interest, arm and educate themselves, gather intelligence, and plan and pursue strategies which they could not have done otherwise.

- 'Systems disruption' – essentially an Information Age relabeling of the time-honoured guerrilla tactic of exhausting one's adversary through attacks on their societal infrastructure (physical, economic or political) as opposed to their organized military forces, except enhanced by the fact that in digitizing so many aspects of their critical societal infrastructure advanced states have created potentially vast new vulnerabilities.

As with 4GW, to which 'open-source warfare' acknowledges a significant intellectual debt, a criticism which may be aimed at Robb's thesis is that it is hardly novel – after all Van Creveld's *Transformation of War* declared the end of state-centred war more than 20 years ago, Mary Kaldor's *New and Old Wars* claimed to distinguish a whole new non-state war type almost 15 years ago, and it has been over a decade since Robert Kaplan's *Atlantic* article 'The Coming Anarchy' was reworked into a book with similar predictions (Van Creveld 1991; Kaldor 1998; Kaplan 2001). Nevertheless, though he might not have been the first to voice them, Robb's ideas are increasingly empirically confirmed by the research of other scholars.

Historically, insurgencies have been forced to make trade-offs in optimal structure between that which lends the greatest capacity and that which provides the most resiliency. Traditional hierarchical groups have good military capacity, strong political organization and subversive potential; but they are also rigid, relatively easily infiltrated and can be dealt a death blow if their leadership is decapitated. By contrast, horizontally-networked groups operating in the manner of a grassroots social movement are more fluid, difficult to penetrate and less vulnerable to catastrophic collapse upon the death of a leader; the trouble with them is that their offensive capability rests upon only a handful of individual operators. 'Superempowerment' makes these trade-offs less stark: 'leaderless jihad' – networked insurgent groups able to act in a cohesive and purposeful manner despite an apparent lack of organizational structure – becomes possible (Sageman 2008).

The main problem with Robb's 'global guerrillas' thesis is its fixation with tactics.[7] To be sure the factors which underlie the Information Age, i.e. intangibility, anonymity, digital ubiquity, etc., do have malignant effects, super-empowering small groups who aim to pull the whole system down using the tools of civilization against it; but while the tactical opportunities for such groups to cause 'system-disruption' are fascinating (and frightening) it is not really clear how this technique is supposed to lead to the achievement of actual political ends. For that we need to turn to another group of scholars who are looking at global insurgency more strategically.

The insurgent blogipelago

Two scholars are particularly noteworthy, David Kilcullen and John Mackinlay, both of whom have attempted to define 'global insurgency' and explain its operational method; their thinking has much in common, perhaps most importantly they share a degree of iconoclasm. According to Kilcullen (2006: 11), the rise of global insurgency means 'a traditional counterinsurgency paradigm will not work for the present war: instead, a fundamental reappraisal of counterinsurgency is needed'. In similar vein, Mackinlay (2009) likes to refer to 'Maoism', by which he means classical insurgency (i.e. in the pattern of Mao Zedong's successful insurgency in China and of his Cold War era successors and emulators), and 'post-Maoism' by which he means the form of insurgency which prevails today ('Bin Ladenism' has not taken off as a descriptor).

Global insurgency, as they describe it, is a popular social movement which feeds on local grievances, integrating them into broader ideologies and linking disparate conflicts through globalized communications; its aim is to change the (global) status quo through an admixture of propaganda of the deed, subversion and open warfare; both are keen to delink analytically the wider social movement which is Islamism from any specific terror group such as al-Qaeda; and at the centre of both analyses is the de-territorialized essence of the phenomenon, the *networked* nature of global insurgency which allows it to act in a concerted manner despite the apparent lack of structure.

Mackinlay's theory is perhaps bolder and more thoroughly developed. He delineates Maoism from post-Maoism across a range of categories. For example: Maoist insurgent objectives are national, whereas post-Maoist objectives are global; the population involved in Maoist insurgency is local and singular, whereas the multiple populations involved in post-Maoist insurgency are dispersed and unmanageable; therefore the centre of gravity in Maoist insurgency is local, whereas in post-Maoist insurgency it is multiple and possibly irrelevant; the all-important subversion process in Maoist insurgency is top-down, whereas in post-Maoist insurgency it is bottom-up; Maoist insurgent organization is vertical and structured, whereas in post-Maoism it is an unstructured network; and whereas Maoist insurgency takes place in a real and territorial context, the post-Maoist variant's vital operational environment is virtual (Mackinlay 2009; also Betz 2008). His starkest finding is that the expeditionary campaigns of the War on Terror have essentially missed the point, achieving nothing at best or actively harming the West's security at worst because,

> The communities which are the heartlands of the insurgent energy, the energy that has attacked our cities and our populations, live and act on a different plane. They stretch around the world in an archipelago of individuals, cells and communities; they have no territory, they exist in isolated but interconnected groups that are horizontally-related rather than vertically ordered, and their shared sense of outrage is regenerated by the exertions and the visibility of the campaign. In these wispy, informal patterns, without territory and without formal command structures they are not easily touched by the kinetic blows of a formal military campaign.
>
> *(Mackinlay 2009: 6)*

In other words the impact of cyberspace on insurgency is neither mysterious nor confined to a purely digital sphere. In actuality, just as cyberspace 'touches the ground' in our daily lives producing different forms of economic, social and political organization and modes of activity, so too is it exploited by new forms of insurgent groups which seek to challenge the status quo in new ways.

Some insurgents have been significantly empowered by this process. It is important to bear in mind, however, the mechanism by which such groups operate in order to understand the nature of the threat they represent. In future, it may be the case that some of these groups obtain and employ some form of weapon of mass destruction – indeed there is a certain frightful inevitability to current technological and social trends which seem likely to intersect at some point in a truly massive terror attack, beyond the point of which it is even more difficult than usual to make predictions. In the meantime, however, the strategic operating concept of global insurgency is the propaganda of the deed event.

The most significant work on this nineteenth-century phenomenon, updated by twenty-first century insurgency, has been done by Neville Bolt. According to Bolt, propaganda of the deed 'acts as a lightning rod for collective memory'; it is a communications tool designed to unlock a set of assumptions in the target population – it is akin to political marketing or, as Smith might have put it, 'theatre'. The major difference between propaganda of the deed in the past and propaganda of the deed now is not its essence as a communicative act, after all that is long established. As Jan Schreiber (1978: 113; see also Crelinsten 1989) wrote over 30 years ago:

> The more one considers terrorism as a phenomenon, the less it resembles other forms of violence and the more it looks like a form of communication. There is a 'speaker' (the terrorist), an 'audience' (the primary victim and all the other onlookers in the world), and a 'language' (the threat of violence against an innocent party).

Rather, the difference is the existence now of a truly global, sensory-rich, dense, immersive and interactive digital 'mediascape', conveyed in part if not largely, by cyberspace – an Information Society, in short – in which the resonant aftershock of the propaganda of the deed event can propagate, triggering associations with societal memories in an 'archipelago of violence'. Global insurgency is a virus of this emerging system; unfortunately, it is not at all clear yet what is the appropriate antibody.

Conclusion

The 9/11 attacks changed attitudes towards the study of insurgency: not just because the exigencies of Iraq and Afghanistan forced reluctant armies to once again contemplate countering it, but because the norm of 'regular' conflict in the opinion of a number of prominent strategists looks decidedly irregular (Evans 2003; Gray 2005). Of course there is debate over how long this will last and what to do about it (Gentile 2008; Nagl 2008; also Betz 2007). In this chapter it has been argued that the shift is profound and lasting, not that other forms of conflict are obviated by the new one, but that inevitably as the organizing principles of human society have changed with technological development, above all in the range, forms and velocity of communications, so too has changed the pattern of warfare generally and the character of insurgency specifically. In many ways insurgency, when understood in the sense of an ideational conflict conducted largely by non-violent means through propaganda and persuasion (although punctuated with sharp conflict), has become mainstream.

The study of insurgency too after many years of being regarded as a niche area, despite the fact that this has been the most prevalent form of conflict since 1945 (Holsti 1996), has also entered the mainstream. Along the way it has become vastly more vibrant, polyglot, multidisciplinary and generally heterogeneous than it was in the past. Mackinlay's and Kilcullen's work are the best available syntheses of a number of important themes from diverse fields. These include: examination of global insurgency as Islamic activism, defined as the 'mobilization of contention to support Muslim causes', using social movement theory (Wiktorowicz 2004); analyses of the concept of 'globalized Islam' and the 'virtual Ummah' (Roy 1994, 2006; Kepel 2004, 2006), the de-territorialized population which is the prize of global insurgency, and of its relationship with the process of radicalization, particularly of Muslims in European countries which increasingly face what are essentially domestic counterinsurgencies amongst a significant non-integrating minority (Stevens and Neumann 2009); and the updating of the concept of propaganda of the deed for the twenty-first century (Bolt and Betz 2008). If anything unifies these diverse studies it is a preoccupation with the new 'virtual territories of the mind', as Mackinlay calls it, or 'cyberspace' as it is more colloquially known, which contemporary insurgency haunts.

Notes

1 Emergent phenomena occur when simple entities operating in accordance with basic rules exhibit complex behaviours collectively. They tend to arise when a complex system possesses a high degree of diversity, organization and connectivity. Complex behaviours of a collective are not easily deduced

from behaviour of the individual entities that make it up. Examples of emergence are legion, including the flocking of birds and fish, ant colonies and slime moulds, traffic patterns, urban development, the stock market, weather systems and human consciousness (Holland 1998; Johnson 2001).

2 Lavishly embellished, handwritten translations of ancient texts were one-offs – each more or less different from one another. A mechanically printed book, on the other hand, was always the same and once disseminated could become an authoritative text (i.e. the same whether you read it in Rome or Riga).

3 Dozens of examples of popular insurrection ranging from Quintus Servorius' revolt against Roman rule in Spain from 81 to 72 BCE to William Wallace's against the English King Edward I in Scotland at the end of the thirteenth century are to be found in the first four or five chapters of Asprey's comprehensive two-volume work *War in the Shadows: The Guerrilla in History*. These required deft political skills, generally in order to unify diverse and fractious tribes against an encroaching imperial power; but the only plausible example of mass subversion in this era is Christianity's penetration of the late Roman Empire – not covered by Asprey but clearly Edward Gibbon (1789) saw it in roughly these terms in his masterwork *The Decline and Fall of the Roman Empire* although he did not use the terms insurrection or insurgency.

4 Consider the difference between the written score to Beethoven's 'Ode to Joy', for instance, as opposed to a tape recording of the same. Both are in a sense recordings, the former marked out with ink on paper, the latter in modulations on a long ribbon of magnetized material; one, however, requires the mind of a trained musician to interpret while the other, given a tape player, is in effect the symphony itself.

5 Numerous examples of iconic photos which produced enormous effect on the perception of conflict exist: Vietnamese girl screaming in fear and pain fleeing a napalm strike; summary execution in the street of a Viet Cong guerrilla by the Saigon police commander; young woman wailing over the body of a student shot by National Guardsmen at Kent State University; these are just a few images seared into the collective consciousness, easily recalled and requiring no captionation.

6 So cheaply that online retailers and search engines do this in microseconds every time a user performs a search, gradually building an ever-more sophisticated profile of each individual with each interaction.

7 'Global Guerrillas' is the title of his blog: http://globalguerrillas.typepad.com.

Recommended readings

Betz, D.J. (2008) 'The Virtual Dimension of Contemporary Insurgency and Counterinsurgency', *Small Wars and Insurgencies*, 19 (4): 513–43.
Castells, M. (2009) *Communication Power*. Oxford: Oxford University Press.
Kilcullen, D. (2009) *The Accidental Guerrilla: Fighting Small Wars in the Midst of a Big One*. London: Hurst.
Mackinlay, J. (2009) *The Insurgent Archipelago*. London: Hurst.
Smith, R. (2006) *The Utility of Force: The Art of War in the Modern World*. London: Penguin.

References

Daily India (2010) '2012 Olympics Could Face "Blended" Physical, Cyber Attack: Security Expert', 3 March. Available at: www.dailyindia.com/show/366067.php.
Al-Zawahiri, A. (2005) Letter to Abu Musab Al-Zarqawi dated 9 July 2005, translated by the Office of the Director of National Intelligence, News Release No. 205, 11 October. Available at: www.dni.gov/press_releases/20051011_release.htm.
Arreguín-Toft, I. (2005) *How the Weak Win Wars: A Theory of Asymmetric Conflict*. Cambridge: Cambridge University Press.
Asprey, R. (2002) *War in the Shadows: The Guerrilla in History*, 2 vols. Lincoln: iUniverse.
Aust, S. (2008) *The Baader Meinhof Complex*. London: The Bodley Head, Ltd.
Beckett, I. (2001) *Modern Insurgencies and Counterinsurgencies*. Abingdon: Routledge.
Bell, D. (1974) *The Coming of Post-Industrial Society*. New York: Harper.
Berkowitz, B. (2003) *The New Face of War*. New York: The Free Press.
Betz, D.J. (2006) 'The More You Know, The Less You Understand: The Problem with Information Warfare', *Journal of Strategic Studies*, 29 (3): 505–33.
Betz, D.J. (2007) 'Redesigning Land Forces for Wars Amongst the People', *Contemporary Security Policy*, 28 (2): 221–43.

Betz, D.J. (2008) 'The Virtual Dimension of Contemporary Insurgency and Counterinsurgency', *Small Wars and Insurgencies*, 19 (4): 513–43.

Bolt, N. and Betz, D.J. (2008) *Propaganda of the Deed 2008: Understanding the Phenomenon*. London: RUSI.

Borgmann, A. (1999) *Holding on to Reality*. Chicago: University of Chicago Press.

Castells, M. (2009) *Communication Power*. Oxford: Oxford University Press.

Castells, M. (2010) *The Information Age: Economy, Society and Culture*, vols 1–3, 2nd edn. London: Blackwell.

Crelinsten, R. (1989) 'Terrorism and the Media: Problems, Solutions, and Counter-problems', *Political Communication and Persuasion*, 6: 311–39.

Drucker, P. (1969) *The Age of Discontinuity*. New York: HarperCollins.

Evans, M. (2003) 'From Kadesh to Kandahar: Military Theory and the Future of War', *Naval War College Review*, 16 (3): 132–50.

Freedman, L. (2005) 'War Evolves into the Fourth Generation: A Comment on Thomas X. Hammes', *Contemporary Security Policy*, 26 (2): 254–63.

Gates, R. (2007) Landon Lecture, Kansas State University, 26 November 2007. Available at: www.defense.gov/speeches/speech.aspx?speechid=1199.

Gentile, G. (2008) 'Let's Build an Army to Win All Wars', *Joint Force Quarterly*, 52: 27–33.

Gibbon, E. (1789) *The Decline and Fall of the Roman Empire*. Petersburg (FLO): Red and Black Pub.

Goodman, S.E., Kirk, J.C. and Kirk, M.H. (2007) 'Cyberspace as a Medium for Terrorists', *Technological Forecasting and Social Change*, 74 (2): 193–210.

Gray, C. (2005) *Another Bloody Century*. London: Weidenfeld & Nicolson.

Hammes, T.X. (2005) 'War Evolves into the Fourth Generation', *Contemporary Security Policy*, 26 (2): 189–221.

Hassan, R. (2008) *The Information Society*. Cambridge: Polity Press.

Hobsbawm, E. (1988) *The Age of Revolution: 1789–1848*. London: Abacus.

Hoffman, B. (2006) *Inside Terrorism*. New York: Columbia University Press.

Hoffman, F. (2006) 'Complex Irregular Warfare: The Next Revolution in Military Affairs', *Orbis*, 50 (3): 395–411.

Holland, J. (1998) *Emergence from Chaos to Order*. Oxford: Oxford University Press.

Holsti, K.J. (1996) *The State, War and the State of War*. Cambridge: Cambridge University Press.

Horne, A. (1977) *A Savage War of Peace*. New York: Viking.

Johnson, S. (2001) *Emergence*. London: Penguin.

Kaestle, C.F. (1985) 'The History of Literacy and the History of Readers', *Review of Research in Education*, 12: 11–53.

Kaldor, M. (1998) *New and Old Wars*. Cambridge: Polity Press.

Kallinikos, J. (2006) *The Consequences of Information*. Cheltenham: Edward Elgar Publishing.

Kaplan, R. (2001) *The Coming Anarchy*. New York: Vintage Books.

Kepel, G. (2004) *The War for Muslim Minds*. Cambridge, MA: Harvard University Press.

Kepel, G. (2006) *Jihad: The Trail of Political Islam*. London: I.B. Tauris.

Kilcullen, D. (2005) 'Countering Global Insurgency', *Journal of Strategic Studies*, 28 (4): 597–617.

Kilcullen, D. (2006) 'Counter-insurgency Redux', *Survival*, 48 (4): 111–30.

Kilcullen, D. (2009) *The Accidental Guerrilla: Fighting Small Wars in the Midst of a Big One*. London: Hurst.

Lind, M. (1989) 'The Changing Face of War: Into the Fourth Generation', *Marine Corps Gazette*, October: 22–6.

Livingston, S. (1997) 'Clarifying the CNN Effect', Shorenstein Centre, Harvard University, Research Paper R-18.

Mack, A. (1975) 'Why Big Nations Lose Small Wars', in K. Knorr (ed.), *Power Strategy and Security: A World Politics Reader*. Princeton: Princeton University Press, pp. 126–51.

Mackinlay, J. (2002) *Globalisation and Insurgency*, Adelphi Paper 352. London: International Institute for Strategic Studies.

Mackinlay, J. (2009) *The Insurgent Archipelago*. London: Hurst.

McLuhan, M. (2001) *Understanding Media*. Abingdon: Routledge.

McLuhan, M. and Fiore, Q. (1997) *War and Peace in the Global Village*. New York: Hardwired.

McMaster, H.R. (2008) 'Learning from Contemporary Conflicts to Prepare for Future War', *Orbis*, 52 (4): 564–84.

Marighela, C. (2008) *Minimanual of the Urban Guerrilla*. Petersburg (FLO): Red and Black Pub.

Masuda, Y. (1981) *The Information Society as Post-Industrial Society*. Bethesda: World Future Society.

Merom, G. (2003) *How Democracies Lose Small Wars*. Cambridge: Cambridge University Press.

Michael, A. (2010) *Cyber Probing: The Politicization of Virtual Attack*, Defence Academy of the United Kingdom, 10–12. Available at: www.da.mod.uk/colleges/arag/document-listings/special/Special%20Series_10_12%20(WEB).pdf/view.

Nagl, J. (2008) 'Let's Win the Wars We're In', *Joint Force Quarterly*, 52: 20–6.

Ravitz, J. (2009) 'Neda: Latest Iconic Image to Inspire', CNN International, 24 June 2009. Available at: http://edition.cnn.com/2009/WORLD/meast/06/24/neda.iconic.images/index.html.

Richards, General Sir D. (2010) 'Future Conflict and its Prevention: People and the Information Age', speech at the International Institute for Strategic Studies, 18 January. Available at: www.iiss.org/recent-key-addresses/general-sir-david-richards-address.

Rid, T. (2007) *War and Media Operations*. London: Routledge.

Rifkin, J. (2000) *The Age of Access*. London: Penguin.

Robb, J. (2007) *Brave New War*. Hoboken: John Wiley and Sons, Inc.

Roosevelt, F.D. (1940) 'Arsenal of Democracy' speech, radio address, 29 December. Available at: www.mtholyoke.edu/acad/intrel/WorldWar2/arsenal.htm.

Roy, O. (1994) *The Failure of Political Islam*. New York: Columbia University Press.

Roy, O. (2006) *Globalized Islam: The Search for a New Ummah*. New York: Columbia University Press.

Rumsfeld, D. (2006) 'New Realities in the Media Age', Council on Foreign Relations speech, 17 February. Available at: www.cfr.org/publication/9900/new_realities_in_the_media_age.html.

Sageman, M. (2004) *Understanding Terror Networks*. Philadelphia: University of Philadelphia Press.

Sageman, M. (2008) *Leaderless Jihad: Terror Networks in the Twenty-First Century*. Philadelphia: University of Philadelphia Press.

Schmandt-Besserat, D. (1998) *Before Writing*. Austin: University of Texas Press.

Schreiber, J. (1978) *Terrorists and World Order*. New York: Morrow and Co.

Smith, R. (2006) *The Utility of Force: The Art of War in the Modern World*. London: Penguin.

Stephens, M. 'History of Radio' in *Collier's Encyclopaedia*. Available at: www.nyu.edu/classes/stephens/Collier's%20page.htm.

Stevens, T. and Neumann, P. (2009) 'Countering Online Radicalization: A Strategy for Action', London: International Centre for the Study of Radicalization and Political Violence. Available at: www.icsr.info/publications/papers/1236768491ICSROnlineRadicalisationReport.pdf.

Taylor, P.M. (2006) *Munitions of the Mind*. Manchester: Manchester University Press.

Thatcher, M. (1985) Speech to the American Bar Association, 15 July. Available at: www.margaretthatcher.org/document/106096.

United Nations, Global ICT Developments, www.itu.int/ITU-D/ict/statistics/ict/index.html.

Van Creveld, M. (1991) *The Transformation of War*. New York: Free Press.

Van Creveld, M. (2005) 'It Will Continue to Conquer and Spread', *Contemporary Security Policy*, 26 (2): 229–32.

Weinberg, D. (2008) *Everything is Miscellaneous*. New York: Holt.

Wiktorowicz, Q. (2004) *Islamic Activism: A Social Movement Theory Approach*. Bloomington: Indiana University Press.

6

WHITHER COUNTERINSURGENCY

The rise and fall of a divisive concept

David H. Ucko[1]

Since its encounter with political violence in Iraq and Afghanistan, the US military has taken significant steps to improve its understanding of counterinsurgency. Faced with operational demands for which they had little preparation, its troops adapted quickly, on the fly, and while under fire. Nearly ten years on, the outcome of these campaigns still hangs in the balance, but the sustained operational experience has already had a profound effect on the US military as an institution. During this period its priorities have shifted, from a near-exclusive focus on major combat operations to a greater emphasis on the types of missions encountered in theatre, be they termed 'counterinsurgencies', 'stability operations' or, somewhat perversely, 'small wars'. As part of the reorientation, US military thinking now reflects greater awareness of war's political essence, its unpredictability, and of what it means to intervene in foreign polities. The rate of institutional change has in many ways been impressive, given the United States' fraught relation to counterinsurgency since the Vietnam War.

The process of change is not limited to the United States, though it is here that it has been the swiftest and most apparent. It was not until 2010, four years after the US Army and Marine Corps published their seminal counterinsurgency manual, that the French armed forces followed suit; NATO, meanwhile, has yet to ratify its 'Allied Joint Publication for Counterinsurgency', despite being engaged in Afghanistan since 2003.[2] Even so, change is occurring, prompted by repeated military tours in Afghanistan and Iraq. Counterinsurgency has thus moved from being a marginal concern, indelibly (and ill-fatedly) associated with the Vietnam War, to a prime preoccupation among the armed forces of several European countries. Whereas the United Kingdom and France have long traditions of counterinsurgency and old manuals that could be dusted off and updated, several other European nations are pondering this term for the first time and are, in many cases, finding that its nature and requirements differ significantly from those of previous experiences with peacekeeping and humanitarian operations.

For proponents of this learning process, the progress made represents the hopeful first few steps of a much longer and sorely needed transformation. Yet the rise of counterinsurgency has also confronted a backlash, and resistance to the idea is rapidly spreading – in part because of its perceived failure to bring results in Afghanistan. Most of those who follow the debate will attest to counterinsurgency's gradual 'falling out of grace', whereby a concept perceived as necessary and innovative only a few years ago is now deeply unpopular and in danger of being flushed out before even taking root. NATO forces will undoubtedly retain a presence in Afghanistan for years to come, as will US forces in Iraq, but there is little enthusiasm for the *concept* of counterinsurgency or hope that its associated lessons and principles may help, either in ongoing operations or elsewhere. Indeed, references to counterinsurgency are increasingly likely to draw tired sighs or outright hostility, as if the concept were a big con, conceived out of sheer naivety, or worse, with an intention to deceive.

A crossroad has thus been reached, where what has been learned over the last decade is either rejected or consolidated. To some, the opportunity to come to grips with counterinsurgency is matched in magnitude only by the cost of failing to do so, yet to detractors the concept is based on poor scholarship and distracts the armed forces from their 'true' calling. The two camps are engaged in a tug-of-war, but it is unclear where either team stands or whether they are pulling at the same rope. This is therefore a good point at which to ask some pressing questions: is counterinsurgency theory truly bogus, or is it the soil in which this seed is planted that is unsupportive of its germination and growth? If the critics of counterinsurgency are right, is there nonetheless something to this concept that ought to be saved? If the critics are wrong, what are the benefits of retaining and promoting counterinsurgency as a military priority today?

Counterinsurgency as a thesis

The first and most basic problem in assessing counterinsurgency as a concept is that it lacks any agreed definition or meaning, which complicates its status as a 'thesis'. The most common definition is derived from US military doctrine, which defines counterinsurgency as 'those military, paramilitary, political, economic, psychological, and civic actions taken by a government to defeat insurgency' (US Department of the Army and US Marine Corps 2006: 1:1). Yet this definition is too broad, as it fails to exclude from its remit *any* action ostensibly taken to counter an insurgency. Counterinsurgency is therefore given neither form nor substance; it is simply the label used to describe the totality of actions aimed at defeating irregular forces. Even the *effectiveness* of such action is irrelevant to the use of the term, as the definition centres on the *intent* to defeat the insurgency rather than the *success* in doing so. Beyond this intent, there is nothing to help distinguish counterinsurgency from any other type of operations, as any action 'taken by a government to defeat an insurgency' is by definition and by that very fact 'counterinsurgency'.

This is a conundrum for those interested in counterinsurgency and who operate with an implicit and much narrower understanding of what is meant by this term. One attempt to get around this conundrum was through the introduction of terms like 'population-centred' and 'enemy-centred' counterinsurgency, to distinguish between competing views of how these operations should be understood and conducted (US Department of Defense 2006: 4). Analytically speaking, these terms are awkward and highly unsatisfying: most successful counterinsurgency campaigns are concerned with both the population *and* the enemy – facets that are difficult to separate – and are, in any case, 'strategy-centric'. Elsewhere, there has been a temptation to talk of 'good' and of 'comprehensive' counterinsurgency so as to differentiate between those who 'get it' and those who do not. The vagueness inherent to these statements is testament to the lack of specificity in the discussion as a whole.

The reason there is no better definition is because counterinsurgency is a fluid concept that is dependent on circumstance. As David Kilcullen (2009: 183) points out, 'there is no such thing as a "standard" counterinsurgency ... the set of counterinsurgency measures adopted depends on the character of the insurgency'. Yet this is also unsatisfactory, particularly when counterinsurgency experts and scholars are asked to define their terms. 'Counterinsurgency' then emerges as a useful shorthand label employed to describe something that is impossible to define, and it is then simply hoped that those who talk about it all mean the same thing. This can provide for a very ambiguous and unproductive conversation.

The alternative to this endemic vagueness would be to laden the definition with more content, plausibly by leaning on the characteristics shared by previous and current campaigns. But this would appear to be both an unending and thankless task, as for every two counterinsurgency analysts there tends to be three views of what characteristics matter the most. Efforts to substantiate the term also risk inviting a form of conceptual navel-gazing that abstracts the discussion from the full diversity of counterinsurgency campaigns throughout history. Indeed, between the near-impossibility of finding differentiated terms to describe a messy reality, and the political process that invariably accompanies such an effort, it is necessary to ask whether clearer semantics or more structured definitions could in fact capture the essence of counterinsurgency any better than the loosely-defined terms used to date. At some point, it may be wiser to take the approach of historian Hugh Seton-Watson, who in the introduction to one of his books notes that while his effort to make sense of his chosen subject 'undoubtedly lacks neatness', this is 'inevitable because the subject itself is not neat' (as cited in Berdal 2009: 27).

Theory or practice

In the absence of an agreed-to definition, counterinsurgency tends to be understood according to its implementation. But because there is no set criteria of what constitutes a genuine counterinsurgency operation, it is also difficult to establish a shared practice to point towards as a valid representation of theory. In turn, any operation conducted in Afghanistan, Iraq or elsewhere, against insurgents, is said to be counterinsurgency, and the concept is judged according to all or any of these experiences.

In these conditions, counterinsurgency rarely shines. Instead, the somewhat predictable outcome is that the concept undergoes a decline for the very same reason that it was initially introduced: the very difficult problem of overcoming insurgency. While the initial interest in counterinsurgency tends to stem from unanticipated adversity in combating 'rebel', 'guerrilla' or other 'non-state armed groups', once fully engaged in what are typically protracted, challenging and costly campaigns, these initial reasons for re-discovering this approach to operations are lost, or rather drowned out: by heartfelt exhortations to withdraw, to abandon the imperial pretensions of 'nation-building' and to return the military to its traditional duties. A similar trend is apparent today. Whereas instability in post-invasion Iraq prompted the US military's initial rediscovery of counterinsurgency, the eventual demise of the concept is likely to spring from its perceived failure, in Afghanistan, to manage the problem it is ostensibly intended to address – or to do so at an acceptable cost.

Judging counterinsurgency in this manner makes sense, intuitively. By this logic, counterinsurgency emerges as nothing but a myth, periodically restored from the historical wastebasket, promoted by a new generation of naive enthusiasts, and returned back to the basket from whence it came once it is found to bring nothing but despair, exhaustion and disappointment, all at a terrible price. This is a temptingly simple conclusion, but it is also too hasty, suffering as it does from three serious shortcomings.

First, there is a need to differentiate between counterinsurgency theory and its implementation. The term may lack a set definition, but greater awareness of the scholarly literature and military doctrine reveals a distinct divergence between how these operations are conceived of in theory and conducted in practice. Both in Iraq and Afghanistan, troop numbers have been a constant concern; the needed cultural, political and linguistic awareness has been patchy;

civil–military coordination has been found wanting; host-nation partners have typically been less than cooperative; and broadly speaking, these large-scale interventions have also lacked a unified strategy or clearly defined end-state. In Iraq, the US-led coalition shifted to a counter-insurgency-informed strategy four years into the campaign with the so-called 'surge', a short-lived affair by the standard of past counterinsurgency campaigns. This effort was tremendously helped by the 'turning' of local Sunni insurgent groups, something the surge itself in some cases provoked, yet even then the political end-result remains highly contested and sustained stability is far from guaranteed. In Afghanistan, what can only be described as 'counterinsurgency lite' has fared less well, and now confronts the limited time-lines that most troop-contributing countries have imposed on their participation in the campaign. Beyond the difficulties of raising troops for the mission, of controlling the country's borders or of eliminating havens, the campaign is further undercut by the illegitimacy and unaccountability of NATO's host-nation partners and by the lack of clarity as to the campaign's overall objective, which tends to shift between state-building, counter-terrorism, saving NATO's reputation and keeping the United States happy (a prime concern among European troop contributors).

Of course, it is impossible to intervene only when the perfect conditions are already in place, and any assessment of counterinsurgency that relied on such best-case scenarios would be both self-fulfilling and worthless. At the same time, given the demands and risks of these endeavours, it is also important not to enter into them with scant planning or preparation for the aftermath, as was the case in both Iraq and Afghanistan, and then to hope for immediate returns. Indeed, given the naivety with which they were launched, the ill-advised improvisational approach to the initial escalation of violence, and the subsequent hurry to get out, perhaps these campaigns are not the model counterinsurgencies on which this concept ought to be judged. Instead, the case could be made that the US military and its NATO allies are simply ill-structured and ill-prepared for these ambitious efforts, which is reason enough for further institutional change and for greater caution when considering future interventions.

There is certainly a need to disaggregate theory and practice, but it is also important not to render the theory beyond reproach. Already, defenders of counterinsurgency theory have been compared to die-hard Marxists, in that both insist on the infallibility of their cherished doctrine, while blindly ascribing its highly problematic track record to poor implementation. It is a powerful charge: a concept or ideology that survives only on paper, or that is unworkable, has very limited worth, particularly when its attempted application causes lives to be needlessly lost. The redeeming point about counterinsurgency is that its theory has shown practical value, albeit typically on an operational and tactical rather than strategic level. Indeed, virtually all Western land-based campaigns against insurgents, guerrillas and other non-state armed actors have reaffirmed the general validity of what are often referred to as 'counterinsurgency principles': these touch upon the importance of achieving a nuanced political understanding of the campaign, operating under unified command, using intelligence to guide operations, isolating insurgents from the population, using the minimum amount of force necessary to achieve set objectives, and assuring and maintaining the perceived legitimacy of the counterinsurgency effort in the eyes of the populace. Most important, perhaps, is the exhortation to adapt and arrive at a tailored response rather than to fall back on template solutions (see Thompson 1966; Kitson 1977: 284–90; Cohen *et al.* 2006).

That these principles have practical utility is not wholly surprising, as they are also in large part commonsensical. For instance, there is nothing militarily controversial about linking good intelligence to effective strike operations, and it is also clear that in a foreign environment where adversary and civilian look alike, obtaining good intelligence will require a special understanding of and working with the local population. Similarly, it is difficult to find fault with the notion that a greater understanding of the environment, its people and structures, will present external actors with more and better options, or that controlling and influencing key populations will first require that they are adequately isolated from the intimidation, threats and coercion of others. As a political and military contest for control, counterinsurgency is concerned with combining coercion with co-option, which leads logically to the emphasis on fostering legitimacy for the intervention itself and for the actors it seeks to support. The validity of these premises is such that they have also been found relevant to other types of operations conducted to help stabilise war-torn lands, be they termed stabilisation missions, pacification or 'robust' peacekeeping. Indeed, in his survey of two decades of 'post-conflict peace-building', Mats Berdal (2009: 95–6) identifies 'three broad priority tasks' for outside forces: 'providing a secure environment; stabilising governing structures; and ensuring the uninterrupted flow of basic, life-sustaining services' – a familiar list of priorities for anyone well versed in counterinsurgency doctrine.

Yet, as Berdal (2009: 96) also adds, while these priorities appear self-evident when stated in such broad and abstract terms, each 'raises new and more searching questions and the answers to these … have proved anything but clear-cut'. This relates to a second problem with gauging counterinsurgency as a concept on the basis of its implementation: conducting counterinsurgency successfully is notoriously difficult. Thus, while a quick survey of past campaigns reveals the *general* validity of a number of broad principles, the campaigns themselves were not always successful. Intuitively, this high level of frustration should force a rejection of counterinsurgency as a failed concept. Yet while this may seem a logical recourse, the operational difficulties associated with counterinsurgency are unlikely to disappear and we would then need a new concept to grapple with these endemic challenges. Refusing to study and prepare for counterinsurgency will not reduce the need for the associated skills and capabilities and the desire to avoid counterinsurgency should not be confused with a ready ability to do so.

Operational or strategic

This leads to a third point: counterinsurgency, like insurgency, is not a strategy, but a description of a strategic end-point, either to mount or defeat a threat to the established authorities. The more difficult questions of whether to embark on such a campaign, or how to prosecute it, are strategic-level questions that counterinsurgency doctrine – operationally oriented as it is – cannot answer. A close reading of the theory reveals that it never encourages foolhardy campaigns to stabilise war-torn countries or to defeat insurgencies wherever they may rear their head; if anything, a note of caution regarding the requirements of such interventions can be parsed from the field manuals and main texts. More commonly, it has been the lack of awareness of such doctrine and texts that have necessitated their rediscovery: witness the gradual introduction of counterinsurgency principles and practices following the invasions of Afghanistan in 2001, of Iraq in 2003, but also following the initial failures to grapple with incipient insurgencies in the Philippines at the turn of the twentieth century, in Malaya and Algeria in the 1950s, in Vietnam in the 1960s and 1970s, and in El Salvador in the 1980s. When, as in these cases, a commitment is made to assist an insurgency-threatened government, the theory and principles of counterinsurgency can provide useful guidance in meeting this strategic end, but the latter is always decided upon and defined at a higher level and will itself be more or less realistic.

Even when the commitment has been made to engage in a protracted counterinsurgency campaign, the relevant doctrine still offers no roadmap or silver bullet, but merely a collection of tentative lessons learned. Such guidance may be very helpful in the design and execution of an effective *campaign plan*, but that plan must itself, as the theory clearly states, be adapted to specific circumstances; certainly, it must be closely tailored to the causative factors of violence, which will in each case be unique. As Hew Strachan (2008: 51) has cautioned:

> Strategy uses theoretical insights to question real events in a bid to shape them according to the needs of policy, but as soon as strategy allows the expectations of theory to lessen its grasp of what is really happening it has allowed theory to be its master rather than its tool.

This last point is frequently missed in current discussions of counterinsurgency. Because of the overbearing backdrop of the Afghanistan campaign, counterinsurgency is commonly judged on its ability to achieve the *strategic* aims set for this particular campaign. This is an odd and inauspicious test for the concept, not only because of the difficulties of conducting 'state-building' in Afghanistan, but because the link between the stated strategic objectives there (to 'disrupt, dismantle and defeat al-Qaeda') and the operational tenets of counterinsurgency is very difficult to discern. The country's terrain, size, geo-strategic location and past make foreign occupation a fraught endeavour and, even then, al-Qaeda is constrained neither to Afghanistan, nor to Pakistan, but would subsist even if the counterinsurgency campaign were successful and the region radically transformed. To many observers, 'counterinsurgency' is therefore an ill-suited and overly grandiose response to the problem of al-Qaeda and is judged accordingly, as a bad policy option for Afghanistan, rather than as a collection of principles and best practices, detached from any one campaign and operating below the realm of strategy.

This tendency is in part the result of an unfortunate conflation between the operational and strategic levels of war, one that relates intimately to a common misunderstanding of counterinsurgency today. The absence of a clear and viable strategy, more obvious in Afghanistan, but arguable also in the case of Iraq, has resulted in counterinsurgency, an operational concept, being leaned upon as strategy in its own right (Strachan 2010: 168). This has also been the tendency of some proponents of counterinsurgency, who confuse its related principles (population security, governance, legitimacy) as strategic ends in themselves, and try to pursue them all at once, with no clear vision of the desired end-state. Missed in this all-too-often hurried embrace of newly rediscovered theory is the need to adapt its premises and principles to the specific political goals being pursued. 'Strategy', Eliot Cohen writes,

> is the art of choice that binds means with objectives. It is the highest level of thinking about war, and it involves priorities (we will devote resources here, even if that means starving operations there), sequencing (we will do this first, then that) and a theory of victory (we will succeed for the following reasons).[3]

Plainly, a counterinsurgency field manual is unable to address these difficult questions or resolve the attendant trade-offs, though, importantly, it may provide valuable guidance and insight when it comes to tying carefully defined strategic aims to the design of operations.

Counterinsurgency as an antithesis

By scaling back the expectations of what 'counterinsurgency' as a concept can do, its value may be more fully appreciated. Counterinsurgency does not advocate or allow for painless foreign interventions, it does not provide a formulaic solution to the problem of political violence, nor does it constitute a comprehensible *strategy* with which to tackle insurgencies, al-Qaeda or the threat of global terrorism. Finally, to value the theory and doctrine of counterinsurgency is not necessarily to see wisdom in NATO's counterinsurgency campaign in Afghanistan, or to support similar interventions elsewhere.

What, then, does the theory of 'counterinsurgency' do? If the theory is only 'useful guidance', much of which is commonsensical, what is its worth? The key lies partly in what precedes counterinsurgency dialectically, the thesis to which counterinsurgency provides the antithesis. In the last half-century, what counterinsurgency principles have done is to illustrate the unique logic of political warfare and its distinctiveness from the 'conventional' types of military campaigns for which most Western armed forces are structured and trained. In the US context, this pattern is particularly clear: interest in counterinsurgency has tended to peak when senior civilian and/or military leaders realise the limitations of 'conventional' military force in managing the security problems of the day. In the early 1960s, President John F. Kennedy grew concerned that the dominant US policy of 'massive retaliation' was too inflexible to address the rising threat of political subversion (then seen as a Soviet Union-orchestrated phenomenon). Reacting to the ascendance of communism in Vietnam and in Laos, the instability of decolonisation in Africa and elsewhere and the successful communist revolution in Cuba, Kennedy pushed the US armed forces to adapt and to learn the basic principles and practices of 'counter-guerrilla' warfare (McClintock 1992: ch. 6). In the following few years, the US military developed new tactics and training exercises, expanded its special operations capacity, and its understanding of counterinsurgency.

This was, in Douglas Blaufarb's words (1977), a 'counterinsurgency era' for the US military, though the reforms were often all too limited and superficial to have a sustained effect. In either case, this was also an era that came to an abrupt and unhappy end in Vietnam – another case of a traumatic operational experience torpedoing a still incomplete leaning process. In the aftermath of US withdrawal from Vietnam, counterinsurgency was deliberately eliminated from US military doctrine, as the armed forces turned their attention to the Central Front and the prospect of an armoured confrontation with the Soviet Union. There were good reasons to concentrate on Europe, but that this shift comprised a simultaneous and total neglect of counterinsurgency was a direct result of the US military's particular reading of its experience in Vietnam and its view of counterinsurgency. Generally, the senior US military staff felt that in Vietnam 'the Army had lost a generation's worth of technical modernization while gaining a generation's worth of nearly irrelevant combat experience' (quoted in Herbert 1988).

The deliberate neglect of counterinsurgency following Vietnam meant that the concept needed to be 'rediscovered' in the 1980s, when the United States again grew concerned about instability in the Third World. As it happened, the late 1970s did not feature the anticipated showdown in Europe against the Soviet Union. Instead, the United States witnessed the ascendance of left-learning regimes in several countries, including many former US client states: Ethiopia (1974), Mozambique (1975), Angola (1976), Grenada (1979) and Nicaragua (1979). The Soviet invasion of Afghanistan in 1979, the Iranian revolution that same year, and the subsequent hostage crisis further demonstrated the volatility of international order and the vulnerability of US partners without its support. As in the 1960s these developments were perceived through the lens of the Cold War and as offering opportunities to the Soviet Union. The conclusion drawn within the US government was that the Cold War would be fought globally, requiring greater worldwide deployability and the capability to conduct 'low-intensity' operations, a new term for counterinsurgency and other types of 'irregular' operations (Downie 1988). In the 1980s, therefore, the US military again began to 'learn counterinsurgency': it issued new doctrine, adapted training exercises, and opened new centres and commands (notably the Special Operations Command). The activity was such that some spoke of the 1980s having once more 'ushered in a new counterinsurgency era' (Sarkesian 1986: 38). This time, the new knowledge was put into practice in El Salvador, a testing-ground for a vicarious form of counterinsurgency, fought with advisers rather than combat troops.

The US military's most recent 'counterinsurgency era', which began following the invasion of Iraq in 2003, was also motivated by a previous failure to grapple with the political complexities of war. Throughout the 1990s, a highly conventional and apolitical understanding of war marked US military thinking, as epitomised by the transformation programmes of Secretary of Defence Donald Rumsfeld. Resistance to the peacekeeping operations of the Clinton-era dovetailed perfectly with a growing fascination with information technology and precision strike capabilities. The future of war lay not with the infantry, rotating in and out of seemingly endless peace operations, but with airstrikes, drones, computer and satellites, dispensing force swiftly, precisely and decisively. 'Military operations other than war' (MOOTW), as they were termed, did not feature in the literature on transformation or were presented as amenable to the precision-strike toolkit offered through the 'information revolution' (Ucko 2009: 49–53).

It was against this backdrop that counterinsurgency experienced its most recent peak. Having deposed the Saddam Hussein regime and triggered by an insurgency against the government installed in its place, the US military reached out to counterinsurgency theory as a means of understanding and responding to the instability in Iraq. Meanwhile, this theory also dismantled the assumptions that had held sway during the 1990s, broadening the US military's mindset and culture, and its understanding of war. In that sense, the study of counterinsurgency again brought a welcome departure from prior misconceptions: it was a much-needed antithesis to a thesis that had not withstood its encounter with practice. Specifically, the concept instilled the idea that while wars are easy to begin, they are difficult to end, and that doing so requires a firm understanding of what causes violence to begin with. In reaffirming the political essence of war, it also forced a greater understanding of the local population and social context, which in turn brought concepts such as as legitimacy and population control to the fore.

Beyond counterinsurgency

The (re)discovery of counterinsurgency was a step forward from the 'transformation'-fuelled narrow-mindedness of the 1990s, but today counterinsurgency is no longer the antithesis, but itself the thesis. Its function as a reaction to muddy thinking is still being served, but it is also being held up in its own right and subjected to critical scrutiny. Such scrutiny is often sorely needed: the assumptions, the historical cases leaned upon, and the modern relevance of counterinsurgency theory are all areas that scream out for further research.

The problem with counterinsurgency scholarship is that it often gets too caught up in the specificities of theory, as if endless conceptual navel-gazing will reveal the answer to the problem of political violence. Part of the problem is the tendency, as counterinsurgency became a mainstream topic in strategic studies, for analysts and scholars to follow suit, eager to have their own say on this important topic. In the rush to get to the ball first, much of the ensuing scholarship lacks the firm anchoring in history or rigorous and time-consuming research needed to understand specific cases. There are only a handful of studies based on first-hand experience with the insurgency group being examined, and fieldwork and language skills are too often lacking. Inadequate attention has been given to area studies, regional experts and anthropological data; instead much of the research is self-referential and inward looking. In other cases, there is a tendency to want to be the one to crack the code, to overthrow 'conventional wisdom', or to find that particularly catchy acronym that explains it all. Within the ensuing deluge of counterinsurgency-related articles and books, there has been both wheat and chaff.

As the field gets overcrowded and the theory at times dangerously abstruse, there comes a point where it may be better to drop the term 'counterinsurgency' altogether: to recognise that it is too divisive, is readily misunderstood and that it at any rate is almost impossible to define. Indeed, given these attributes, and the nature of the discussion today, the longevity of 'counterinsurgency' as a military priority appears limited. Dropping counterinsurgency, however, would be to forfeit the functions that the term plays, first in grouping nominally similar types of operations into one helpful category, for insight, comparison and analysis, and second, in providing an oft-needed antithesis to the 'conventional' type of thinking on war that has tended to dominate within Western militaries.

The first, 'grouping' function can be useful but is probably dispensable. Certainly, there are as many risks and dangers as there are benefits in bringing together operations from different epochs and geographical settings just because they share the epithet 'counterinsurgency', a term whose meaning has evolved over time. Furthermore, the selection of operations for inclusion in this category is somewhat arbitrary, and excludes from consideration many interventions and armed campaigns that have relevant traits but were referred to by a different name: 'revolutions', 'civil wars', 'stability operations', 'small wars', 'robust peacekeeping' or 'post-conflict peace-building', to name but a few. Better to study past and current campaigns based on their shared characteristics rather than by what they were called.

It is less certain whether the term's second function, as a useful antithesis, has been fully served. For that reason, abandoning 'counterinsurgency' would need to be done with two critical caveats in mind. First, this should in no way signify a return to the understanding of war that preceded the ascendance of counterinsurgency in the first place, to wit, an understanding of war as 'conventional'. This idea of 'conventional war' has become an entrenched archetype within military thinking, in part due to a grossly simplified recollection of a limited number of conflicts that disproportionately shape the Western understanding of the phenomenon, primarily the Second World War and the imagined, yet ultimately averted, armoured confrontation on the Central Front. Yet on closer scrutiny, the notion of military confrontation on an isolated, unpopulated battlefield, in which the defeat of one side's forces brings decisive victory for the other, is patently suspect, more so today than ever before.

This relates intimately to the *nature* and *purpose* of war. On the former, it is historically typical for the termination of one phase of war to give way to new sources of uncertainty and instability. Indeed, the term 'post-conflict' is in this context highly misleading, as it suggests a clean break from war to peace, with little continuity between the two. It is more common for one conflict, upon its conclusion, to fuse into a new competition over resources, power and security, one that, unless carefully managed, will often take violent forms. As to the *purpose* of war, it is to consolidate a political compact that is preferable to the *status quo ante* and that is also sustainable. What this means is that even predominantly conventional wars will usually precede an 'unconventional' phase, because the gains made in combat require consolidation through stabilisation, political support, capacity-building or reconstruction. These realities of war are commonly missed in favour of neat theoretical distinctions and heuristic dividing lines.

Instead of returning to 'conventional war' as an alternative to 'counterinsurgency', the point would be to arrive at a more integrated understanding of 'war', informed by the experiences and campaigns of recent years, but without the divisive and vague jargon that they have provoked. This would also put an end to the bifurcation of wars as either 'conventional' or 'irregular'. At first sight, this bifurcation is helpful, as it rightly frames stabilisation and counterinsurgency as problems that require a different mindset and skills than pure combat, and that deserve independent study. At the same time, the neat theoretical dichotomy also encourages an unspoken belief that the two forms of war at either extremity have rarefied equivalents in practice. In so doing, it suggests that states have a choice between fighting conventional or irregular wars and that their forces can be tailored accordingly. Missed here is an appreciation of war as a complex political phenomenon, one that typically encompasses both irregular and conventional challenges and whose operating environment is rarely static but instead very difficult to control.

To reach a more fundamental understanding of war as a political phenomenon, it helps to consider some deeper questions about the requirements for true military effectiveness and the nature of the contemporary operating environment. First, what makes the use of military force effective? In a number of addresses in the mid 1990s, General Rupert Smith gave voice to this very question, suggesting a disconcerting lack of clarity on 'what is it we expect the use of force or forces to *achieve* as opposed to do' (as cited in Berdal 2000: 55). With this distinction in mind, what are armed forces expected to achieve and how are they best configured and supported to carry out the associated tasks? A second series of questions put the emphasis on the operational level: what are the features of the contemporary operating environment; what skill-sets and capabilities are required to meet these challenges; and which of these should reside within the armed forces?

These types of question talk neither of 'conventional' nor of 'counterinsurgency' operations, but rely on a broader conception of war based on its political purpose and likely challenges. However, in seeking to answer these questions, it quickly becomes clear that many of the lessons learned in recent counterinsurgency campaigns have a far broader relevance and should therefore not be forgotten. This raises the second caveat that must be fully taken onboard before 'counterinsurgency' is dismissed: eschewing the term does not mean that the operational challenges most closely associated with it will be avoided. Importantly, this remains the case even if we do not see another 'counterinsurgency campaign' or 'stability operation' in the near future. The bitter truth is that future land-based operations, whatever character they may take, are likely to involve a similar range of tasks as seen in today's campaigns. If territory is to be seized, stabilisation of that territory will be an unavoidable requirement. If the global trend of urbanisation continues, future operations will likely be conducted in built-up environments, where the local population cannot be ignored but more often must be co-opted and even protected against attack. Given the persistent attraction and apparent effectiveness of asymmetric tactics against militarily inferior adversaries; the frequency of operations aimed at building local capacity; and the continued threat of ungoverned spaces acting as potential havens for terrorist groups, expeditionary land forces are also likely to confront insurgents, militia and other 'irregular' threats in future land-based operations. Couple all this with the near-inevitability of operating within a local culture and population with whom the foreign forces will enjoy at best transient legitimacy, and the broader relevance of experiences in Iraq and Afghanistan becomes very clear indeed.

From here springs the imperative to retain the lessons learned in recent counterinsurgency operations, even if, conceptually, we move beyond the artificial dividing line between 'conventional' and 'irregular' campaigns. This would also be a major opportunity to export the principles commonly associated with counterinsurgency to the broader realm of warfare, where they are often equally applicable.[4] For example, while it is true that counterinsurgency is primarily 'political', the same holds true for all types of military operations. Similarly, the exhortation in counterinsurgency theory to understand your local environment is equally critical in wars of territorial conquest – though what it means to understand the terrain will naturally depend on its dominant features, one of which is the absence or presence of civilian populations. As to the emphasis in counterinsurgency theory on the requirements for effective interventions, this is something with far broader validity, touching upon the need to resource wars properly to meet set objectives. Finally, the emphasis on the local population as a potential partner or adversary should not be a concern lodged exclusively within the domain of counterinsurgency, much as the need to adapt and learn faster than your enemy is a cardinal requirement for all warfare, not just ones conducted against 'irregular adversaries'.

Conclusion

In the two months following its online publication in December 2006, the US Army and Marine Corps counterinsurgency manual was downloaded over two million times (Sewall 2007: xxi). At the time, against the backdrop of a raging civil war in Iraq and the gradual resurgence of the Taliban in Afghanistan, the new doctrine represented a milestone in the American military's learning of counterinsurgency, an approach to warfare that it was hoped would bring some sort of salvation to the two ongoing campaigns. As lead author of the manual and then commander of Multinational Forces – Iraq, Gen. David Petraeus was able to put some of its principles and practices into effect. The successes of the 'surge' in Iraq added credibility to the idea of counterinsurgency and elevated those most closely associated with it. Yet as the United States turned to Afghanistan, the new concept soon lost its shine. Contested from the outset by a vocal guard of sceptics, the backlash against counterinsurgency gained momentum as its attempted implementation in Afghanistan stuttered and, to many observers, failed. As a US military priority, the future of counterinsurgency now looks bleak, and what happens in the United States will no doubt seal its fate across much of Europe, where the embrace of counterinsurgency has from the outset been far more tentative.

Counterinsurgency deserves close and critical scrutiny. It is a divisive concept, one that is difficult to define, and whose implementation causes the loss of life. Furthermore, it is a highly unattractive form of warfare, and understandably there is no real appetite to repeat the types of engagements seen in Iraq and Afghanistan. Among critics, counterinsurgency is too ambitious, even presumptuous and arrogant, encouraging the idea that if equipped with the right doctrine, military forces can achieve social and political change in a foreign society that they do not understand. More discreet operations, carried out by local forces, and assisted by special forces, are seen as a less provocative, costly and fateful means of exerting influence as and when needed.

The criticism of counterinsurgency is often valid, but it also tends to ignore two points. First, counterinsurgency theory does not necessarily lead to calls for ambitious interventions in foreign countries, but provides guidelines and principles that have worked in similar settings and that may today be leaned upon in the construction of a campaign plan. Careful study and research is needed to determine how best to apply these principles to ongoing operations, and it is fair to say that the theory is better at raising the right questions than in providing the answers. Second, counterinsurgencies are rarely optional and are therefore likely to reappear, even after the operations in Afghanistan and Iraq draw down. This is not to say that future operations should be entered into carelessly, or that they would take the form of a 'counterinsurgency' or 'stability operation' per se. Instead, given the nature of the contemporary operating environment, an expeditionary land force is likely to encounter a similar set of challenges as in today's campaigns: that of operating in an urban environment, in the midst of a civilian population, in a different language and culture, all the while countering irregular adversaries. In the face of this enduring complexity, the principles and doctrine of counterinsurgency still have a role to play.

After years of operational involvement in counterinsurgency, many of these principles may seem commonsensical, if extremely difficult to honour in practice. Even so, they still appear necessary in illustrating the unique logic of counterinsurgency and its distinctiveness from the conventional types of campaigns for which most Western militaries train and prepare. This touches upon the second function of counterinsurgency doctrine: its use as a powerful corrective to the unhelpful tendency in the US military, but also elsewhere in the West, to divorce military affairs from political considerations, and to treat war as an elaborate targeting drill.

It is on these grounds that the decline of counterinsurgency would be regrettable, if through this process the associated knowledge and learning of the last few years is also forgotten. The one good reason to abandon the term, one that merits careful consideration, would be precisely because of its divisive and distorting connotations; the aim would then be to talk more plainly about the nature of war and of war-to-peace transitions. This in itself would be a step forward, away from artificial delineations between 'conventional' and 'irregular' operations and towards a defence posture based on the purposes of war and the likely features of tomorrow's operating environment. It would signify the intent, at long last, to understand and study war on its own terms. At the same time, to abandon counterinsurgency on this basis presumes that the operational and strategic lessons of recent years have been sufficiently internalised that the term has lost its utility as a necessary antithesis. It may be that we are not quite there yet.

Notes

1 Research for this chapter was conducted during his time as Transatlantic Fellow at the Stiftung Wissenschaft und Politik, in 2009–10.
2 For the US and French manuals, see, respectively, US Department of the Army and US Marine Corps, FM 3–24/MCWP 3–33.5. *Counterinsurgency* (Washington, DC: US Army, 2006) and Centre Interarmées de Concepts, de Doctrines et d'Expérimentations, DIA 3.4.4 *Contre-Insurrection (COIN)* (CICDE, November 2010).
3 Eliot Cohen, 'Obama's COIN Toss', *Washington Post*, 6 December 2009.
4 I am grateful to William F. Owen for this insight.

References

Berdal, Mats (2000) 'Lessons Not Learned: The Use of Force in "Peace Operations" in the 1990s', *International Peacekeeping*, 7 (4).

Berdal, Mats (2009) *Building Peace After War*. Abingdon: Routledge.

Blaufarb, Douglas (1977) *The Counterinsurgency Era: US Doctrine and Performance 1950 to the Present*. New York: Free Press.

Cohen, Eliot, Conrad Crane, Jan Horvath and John Nagl (2006) 'Principles, Imperatives, and Paradoxes of Counterinsurgency', *Military Review*, 86 (2).

Downie, Richard Duncan (1988) *Learning from Conflict: The U.S. Military in Vietnam, El Salvador, and the Drug War*. Westport, CT: Praeger.

Herbert, Paul (1988) 'Deciding What Has to Be Done: General William E. DePuy and the 1976 Edition of FM 100–5, Operations', *Leavenworth Papers*, 16. Ft. Leavenworth, KS: US Army Command and General Staff College.

Kilcullen, David (2009) *The Accidental Guerrilla: Fighting Small Wars in the Midst of a Big One*. New York: Oxford University Press.

Kitson, Frank (1977) *Bunch of Five*. London: Faber & Faber.

McClintock, Michael (1992) *Instruments of Statecraft: U.S. Guerrilla Warfare, Counterinsurgency, and Counterterrorism, 1940–1990*. New York: Pantheon Books.

Sarkesian, Sam C. (1986) 'Commentary on "Low Intensity Warfare": Threat and Military Response', in *Proceedings of the Low-Intensity Conference*. Ft. McNair. Washington, DC: Department of Defense, 14–15 January.

Sewall, Sarah (2007) 'A Radical Field Manual', introductory note to *The U.S. Army/Marine Corps Counterinsurgency Field Manual*. Chicago: University of Chicago Press.

Strachan, Hew (2008) 'Strategy and the Limitation of War', *Survival*, 50 (1).

Strachan, Hew (2010) 'Strategy or Alibi? Obama, McChrystal and the Operational Level of War', *Survival*, 52 (5).

Thompson, Robert (1966) *Defeating Communist Insurgency: The Lessons of Malaya and Vietnam*. New York: Frederick A. Praeger Publishers.

Ucko, David (2009) *The New Counterinsurgency Era: Transforming the US Military for Modern Wars*. Washington, DC: Georgetown University Press.

US Department of Defense, Office of the Under Secretary of Defense for Policy (2006) *Interim Progress Report on DoD Directive 3000.05: Military Support for Stability, Security, Transition, and Reconstruction (SSTR) Operations*. Washington, DC: Department of Defense.

US Department of the Army and US Marine Corps (2006) FM 3–24/MCWP 3–33.5. *Counterinsurgency*. Washington, DC: US Army.

7

COUNTERINSURGENCY AND PEACE OPERATIONS

Thijs Brocades Zaalberg[1]

In the wake of the events of 9/11, the thin line that divided peacekeeping from counterinsurgency seemed to blur at an accelerated pace. The American-led offensives in Afghanistan and Iraq resulted in different Western troop contributing nations using the two denominators for similar military activities under unified command. In the decade that followed the toppling of the Taliban regime, the US-led 'counter-terrorist' operation Enduring Freedom and the European-dominated International Security and Assistance Force (ISAF) 'peacekeeping' mission evolved and gradually fused into a campaign that currently defines the popular perception of counterinsurgency.

However, the close connection between fighting insurgencies and keeping the peace is certainly no twenty-first century phenomenon. History is littered with examples of quasi impartial (international) military forces trying to monitor peace agreements or to contain a conflict, only to end up fighting insurgent or separatist movements (Schmidl 2000). Well-known modern examples are the UN peacekeepers who fought Katangan secessionist forces in post-colonial Congo in the early 1960s and the British troops deploying in Northern Ireland in 1969 as 'peacekeepers' to halt sectarian violence, but soon finding themselves countering an insurgency led by the Provisional Irish Republican Army. During the 1990s, when UN(-authorized) peacekeeping in its many configurations temporarily became the dominant form of military operations for Western powers, the parallel occasionally popped up in the operational realm. The low-intensity conflict that erupted in Somalia after the 1992 international 'humanitarian' intervention, bore some resemblance to counterinsurgency and triggered memories of the Congo experience within the UN community. At approximately the same time, halfway around the world in the Cambodian jungle, Dutch marines operating as peacekeepers under UN-command relied on the British Army's counterinsurgency doctrine while performing 'duties in aid to the civil power' − public security tasks that were never part of their original UN-peacekeeping mandate (Brocades Zaalberg 2006: 109). Also British troops within NATO's Implementation Force (IFOR) in Bosnia in 1996 referred to counterinsurgency procedures that, according to the visiting British conflict analyst John Mackinlay, had proved effective in the past, but were officially set aside in the 1990s 'in favour of peacekeeping' (2009: 2).

In his thought-provoking book *The Insurgent Archipelago*, Mackinlay argued in 2009 that the similarities between insurgencies and the new internal wars on the one hand, and peacekeeping and counterinsurgency on the other hand, had always been quite obvious. He criticizes Western doctrine writers, UN officials and fellow conflict analysts for ignoring the parallel and creating a conceptual blur. He quite frankly admits that, as a United Nations researcher in that period, he did not at the time see himself as 'being on a journey through the evolutionary stages of insurgency', but Mackinlay is nevertheless harsh on his expert colleagues. Allegedly, they contributed to the terribly slow and inadequate response to the new internal wars that erupted at the Cold War's end by missing the opportunity to husband existing knowledge on insurgency and counterinsurgency – instead introducing a wide range of vague terminology for 'so-called peace support operations' in response to 'complex emergencies'. Mackinlay ascribes the lack of fundamental debate on the conceptual overlap and the applicability of counterinsurgency lessons and theory during peace operations to the 'excommunication' in the 1990s of the established circle of counterinsurgency experts and doctrine writers (2009: 2–3).[2] Only after the invasion of Afghanistan and Iraq, Mackinlay added, could it any longer be denied that 'confronting complex emergencies was simply counterinsurgency by another name' (2009: 89).

Mackinlay's claim, which he makes in the margins of a much broader argument on so-called globalized insurgency, while not altogether untrue, is certainly inaccurate. Overall, it is correct that relatively few scholars and no doctrine writers have entered this conceptual minefield. But nevertheless, in the academic realm, the parallels between counterinsurgency and peace operations have been both embraced and denounced by conflict analysts since the early 1990s. This chapter seeks to explain why the idea of a fundamental overlap between counterinsurgency and peacekeeping was not always obvious, but nevertheless embraced, denounced and reinvented by a select group of scholars. It does so by first addressing the key difference between the broad and narrow definitions of both peacekeeping and counterinsurgency. Subsequently, it deals with the arguments of the most important enthusiasts and sceptics, the crucial distinction between tactical similarities and politico-strategic differences and the importance of conceptual and operational development in time.

The chapter concludes by addressing the question whether recent experience in complex operations such as in Afghanistan and Iraq has proved the enthusiasts' argument correct. Have complex peace operations, particularly those that include (the ability to engage in) peace enforcement, always shown fundamental similarities with counterinsurgency? If yes, what are the key elements connecting them? Or is it safer to say that the notion of peace operations has come so far adrift during the previous two decades that many Western powers – for political reasons – have for a long time been able to present missions such as ISAF as peacekeeping rather than counterinsurgency? Has peacekeeping become a euphemism or have we entered, as some US counterinsurgency theorists have argued, the era of 'hybrid-warfare', wherein counterinsurgency, peace operations, state-building and fighting terrorism all blend into one?[3]

At opposite ends

Following Mackinlay's suggestion, it is hardly surprising that policy-makers, military leaders and conflict analysts treated peace operations and counterinsurgency as two separate and distinct campaign themes in the early post-Cold War years. At the time, the two disciplines appeared to be at opposing ends of the spectrum of conflict types that during the 1970s and 1980s had been lumped together under the now largely redundant term 'low-intensity operations'.[4] Moreover, whereas counterinsurgency seemed to have become a stale euphemism for violent suppression of popular resistance movements abroad, peacekeeping brought the promise of upholding what President George H.W. Bush called 'The New World Order' in a non-violent way. The parallel – if recognized – would be neither logical nor welcome under the conditions prevailing at Cold War's end.

The tendency of peacekeeping experts to ignore counterinsurgency was understandable considering its track record. Especially outside intervention on the side of the counterinsurgent did not 'inspire much enthusiasm for the prospects of success' (Snow 1996: 62). This certainly does not imply that insurgencies are predestined to succeed. However, by the early 1990s those lessons from successful counterinsurgency that had been learned by the European colonial powers and by the United States in Vietnam two decades before, were mostly forgotten or deliberately 'unlearned' within the Western military establishment. The Israeli military analyst Martin van Creveld wrote about the preceding episode in history:

> When the last colonies—those of Portugal—were freed in 1975, many people felt that an era in warfare had come to an end. Having suffered one defeat after another, the most important armed forces of the 'developed' world in particular heaved a sigh of relief; gratefully, they felt that they could return to 'ordinary' soldiering, by which they meant preparing for wars against armed organizations similar to themselves on the other side of the Iron Curtain.
>
> *(Van Creveld 2000)*

The aversion of the post-Cold War peacekeepers to latch on to counterinsurgency theory and tactics was even more obvious when considering war-torn countries such as Namibia, Cambodia and El Salvador in the late 1980s. These bloody conflicts were in essence insurgencies, wherein the superpowers supported either the rebels or the governments under attack in a counterinsurgency.[5] Peacekeeping was a means of putting an end to these proxy wars through the deployment of neutral, lightly armed, blue-helmeted soldiers. These 'knights in white armour' (Bellamy 1996) were certainly not deployed to defeat insurgent movements and therefore unlikely to dwell on counter-revolutionary warfare theory. Counterinsurgency violated the fundamental principles of classical United Nations peacekeeping and therefore, from an early post-Cold War perspective, there was little reason positively to connect the two disciplines.

Broad and narrow definitions

Before addressing the conceptual overlap or the lack thereof, it is crucial to understand the dual meaning of both peacekeeping and counterinsurgency. They are on the one hand catch-all phrases referring to a broad category of military and civilian activities, while on the other hand referring to a very specific concept or type of operation. Obviously, the fluidity of both concepts seriously complicated their comparison.

Peacekeeping in a traditional and narrow sense is used for situations where parties to a conflict, typically two states, agree to the interposition of UN troops in order to uphold a ceasefire.[6] Although the term is conspicuously absent from the UN Charter, this type of 'classic' or 'traditional' peacekeeping evolved from military observer missions to monitor truce agreements in the late 1940s into the UN's response to the Suez Crisis of 1956. Under Chapter VI of the UN Charter the 6,000-strong United Nations Emergency Force (UNEF) became the mother of all 'thin blue line' peacekeeping missions. UNEF allowed the intervening French and British forces to withdraw and then patrolled the armistice line between Egypt and Israel. Similar UN interposition-missions were established on Cyprus (from 1974), on the Golan Heights (also from 1974) and – under far more complex conditions – in Southern Lebanon (from 1979). The traditional principles of peacekeeping were thoroughly anchored in consent of the local parties involved, impartiality and the use of force restricted to self-defence by lightly armed forces.

Peacekeeping operations involving permanent members of the Security Council were mostly created outside the UN system.[7] Peacekeeping was mainly about manning buffer zones between armies and monitoring military adversaries. It was predominantly limited to the military domain and allowed for little civil–military interaction on the part of peacekeepers. Although there have been notable exceptions, such as the broadly mandated and violent *Opérations des Nations Unies au Congo* (ONUC), the majority of all peace operations initiated during the Cold War fell into this narrow peacekeeping category.

After 1989, the UN continued to use the term peacekeeping as a 'catch-all' phrase when both the scope and the number of new missions mushroomed. In order to meet the new post-Cold War challenges the development of peacekeeping doctrine centred on interventions in intra-state conflict (civil wars) instead of conventional warfare between states. In 1992, UN secretary general Boutros Boutros-Ghali made a categorization for future multinational interventions in *An Agenda for Peace*. The paper provided an analysis of and recommendations to the Security Council for ways to improve the UN's capacity to establish peace. *An Agenda for Peace* combined older peacekeeping principles and more recent experiences such as in Namibia (1989–90), where an integrated civil–military mission consisting of 4,500 troops, 1,500 police and 2,000 other civilians ensured Namibian independence from South Africa. This resulted in the definition of four more or less consecutive phases of international action to prevent or control armed conflict: preventive diplomacy, peacekeeping, peacemaking – including the possibility of peace enforcement when consent of one or more of the warring parties was lacking – and post-conflict peace building. This division in linear stages found its way into the doctrines of most Western armies, and would remain the prevailing conceptual framework for peacekeeping in its broad sense.[8]

Peacekeeping and post-conflict peace building proved relatively effective tools for controlling governments and former insurgent groups in a rather benign environment such as in Namibia, Mozambique, El Salvador and – to a lesser extent – Cambodia. The end to superpower rivalry and war-weariness facilitated solutions in these long-lasting internal conflicts. However, the end of superpower interference at the end of the Cold War also unleashed other powers, mainly ethnic nationalism, that would create new internal wars in the Balkans and elsewhere. In Somalia, Rwanda and Bosnia 'peacekeepers' were injected into a combat zone without a solid peace agreement to implement and with no peace to keep. These operations would criss-cross diagonally across the consecutive doctrinal phases and categories distinguished in *An Agenda for Peace* – while simultaneously combining elements of them all – as these missions inevitably moved beyond their limited, but vaguely defined humanitarian goals.

In some cases, peacekeepers found themselves confronted with an insurgent-like adversary who thwarted their humanitarian mission or obstructed the (local) peace agreement they were trying to uphold. Throughout the 1990s, responses to such challenges – the use or non-use of force – dominated the peacekeeping debate, especially after UN operations in Somalia (1993–5) and Bosnia (1992–5) slowly went down the road of peace enforcement. When 18 American soldiers died in Mogadishu after a raid on warlord Mohamed Aidid, the Somalia operation went awry and became a peacekeeper's doom scenario. It led the first British commander of UN forces in Bosnia, General Sir Michael Rose, to coin the phrase 'crossing the Mogadishu-line' between neutral peacekeeping and forceful intervention against one of the parties in a conflict. In the United States this incident created a strong aversion to peace operations amongst political and military leaders, many of whom already saw peacekeeping as an unwelcome diversion from the preparation for major conventional warfare. In most European capitals, the failure of enforcement measures in Somalia led to the questionable conclusion that they were on the right course by trying to stick as much as possible to a neutral position in Bosnia (Clarke and Herbst 1997:

70). Simplistic historical analogies between Bosnia and the Vietnam 'quagmire' were used extensively by those warning against more forceful intervention (Ten Cate 2007). In short, peacekeeping did not degenerate into counterinsurgency, with its implication of partiality and armed intervention in an internal conflict.

Counterinsurgency, like peacekeeping, is also used in both a narrow and a broad sense. It is a relatively recent label, introduced in the 1960s, for the military, paramilitary, political, economic, psychological and civic actions taken by a government and its foreign supporters to defeat insurgency, with an insurgency being an organized movement aimed at the overthrow of a government through use of subversion and armed conflict. Neither the definition of insurgency nor that of counterinsurgency therefore excludes conventional combat operations. However, in doctrine, popular debate and academic discourse, the term insurgency is almost exclusively reserved for subversion and irregular warfare, particularly the use of guerrilla and terrorist tactics. Similarly, the term counterinsurgency is used for any set of measures taken by a government and its foreign supporters to defeat an irregular opponent.

Used in a broad sense, counterinsurgency may include a fully militarized and violent 'enemy centric' suppression of popular resistance movements. It may also include exemplary force and terrorizing the population into withdrawing its support for the insurgents. However, counterinsurgency is often regarded as synonymous with a more enlightened and subtle 'population centric' approach to defeating insurgencies. This 'classic' counterinsurgency doctrine is best known from the semi-theoretical handbook *Defeating Communist Insurgency*, written by Sir Robert Thompson after his experience as an administrator in Malaya and an adviser in Vietnam. It was the result of decades of British experience in colonial policing culminating in Thompson's famous five principles (Thompson 1966). With communist revolutions sparking all over the world in the age of decolonization, this and other works of the time had a clear purpose: the defeat of Maoist-style, predominantly rural insurgent movements. French counterinsurgency practitioner and theorist David Galula had released a similar thesis two years earlier, propagating an approach aimed at protecting and winning over the people (1966). However, French counterinsurgency only worked on a tactical level in Algeria – which featured as Galula's primary case – because of the massive resources used and the often brutal methods applied. It ultimately failed on a political and strategic level because the French sought to maintain direct rule, as they had in Indochina. The French thus violated principle number one of classic counterinsurgency doctrine, which was to have a viable political goal. This is not to say that the British – who *did* accept decolonization as inevitable – were always subtle in their ways. Even during what is often considered the 'model campaign' in Malaya in the 1950s, the colonial power had effectively created a police state, albeit 'a police state with a conscience' (Beckett 2001: 92; see also Bennett 2007, 2009; Marshall 2010). The British typically avoided over-reliance on military means and the use of force and tended to see addressing the legitimate grievances on which an insurgency fed as their centre of gravity. They were able to do so because they managed to create a rather sophisticated and balanced civil–military system to counter insurgent threats (Kitson 1971). Current Western counterinsurgency doctrine is still predominantly based on the classic British and French theorists, although a recent school of 'global counterinsurgency' thinkers has tried to take the concept beyond its geographically limited 'neo-classic' parameters (Jones and Smith 2010).

Obviously, a debate on the parallels between peacekeeping and counterinsurgency is only relevant if the broad and narrow definitions are clearly distinguished. The comparison between the brutal suppression of popular resistance movements with the neutral interposition by unarmed peacekeepers in an observer's role is of course fruitless. The more likely comparison is that between the more enlightened 'population centric' version of counterinsurgency and what has become known as complex peace operations. The latter term refers to a combination of peacekeeping, peace building or state building and humanitarian action, performed by troops capable of enforcing the peace in cooperation with a host of civilian actors during or after intra-state conflict. In order to distinguish between the broad and the narrow definition of the term, the terms 'classic counterinsurgency (theory)' and 'classic peacekeeping' will be used to refer to the narrow versions. Counterinsurgency and peace operations refer to the broader concepts.

Reinventing the wheel?

During the 1990s, several counterinsurgency specialists argued that Western powers needed to draw on classic counterinsurgency lessons and theory when trying to impose peace in war-torn Somalia, Bosnia and future intra-state conflicts. As we have seen, their argument went largely unnoticed as the peacekeeping specialists who reigned supreme in the years of Cold War trium-phalism ignored counterinsurgency theory. However, this leaves the question whether the arguments brought forward by these counterinsurgency 'enthusiasts' were actually sound.

Larry Cable was amongst the first to draw the parallel when he argued in an article in the journal *Small Wars and Insurgencies* that American political leaders needed to 'reinvent the round wheel' in the post-Cold War order by embracing lessons from fighting insurgencies (1993). Remarkably, he actually put little effort into comparing counterinsurgency and peacekeeping or peace enforcement conceptually. As an authority on the development of US counterinsurgency doctrine in relation to the Vietnam War he simply defined peace operations in such a broad way that they virtually fitted the definition of counterinsurgency. According to Cable, peacekeepers needed to show the ability and the will to use the minimum necessary deadly force in the accomplishment of their mission. As witnessed during UN operations in Cambodia, Rwanda and Bosnia, this view was hardly accepted in peacekeeping circles at the time. But Cable was inspired by more forceful US-led interventions in northern Iraq and Somalia and argued that the insurgent, the counterinsurgent, the peace enforcer and the peacekeeper were operating under the same dynamics and all shared the same goal, namely political authority over a specified population in a defined geographical area. He even saw their basic tools of popular perception of legitimacy and a credible capacity to coerce as being essentially identical (1993: 229, 249, 255–6).

However for the sake of clarity (and contrary to Cable's claims) controlling and protecting territory and populations was hardly considered a peacekeeper's task at the time, not even during the massive US-led humanitarian operation in Somalia in 1992–3. But although Cable was inaccurate as far as peace operations in the early 1990s were concerned, his point was valid in view of later, more broadly mandated peace operations. In the latter half of the 1990s in Bosnia, Kosovo and East Timor, peacekeepers wearing green helmets would indeed come better prepared, equipped and mandated, allowing them to move to peace enforcement if nec-essary. Meanwhile, protection of the population gradually became a central and formal part of peacekeeping mandates in this period (Brahimi 2000).

Both Cable's inaccurateness *and* his prescience resulted from what seemed to be his lack of interest in UN peacekeeping as such. Instead, he was taking a broad historical perspective and pleaded for a more interventionist US foreign policy in a period when the Vietnam experience made the United States exceptionally wary of getting involved in 'other people's wars'. The United States had a long legacy of fighting small wars in the Philippines and Central America and had been successful in what Cable self-servingly called 'peacekeeping' during coercive interventions such as in Lebanon in 1958 and the Dominican Republic in 1964. However, the mantra 'no more Vietnams' had resulted in the rigid Weinberger-Powell doctrine in the mid-1980s. By embracing this doctrine the world's sole remaining superpower seemed to shun all but conventional warfare in support of major national security threats.[9] Fighting communist-inspired insurgencies was reduced to military advice and material support and renamed Foreign Internal Defence. Involvement of US tactical ground forces in this type of conflict in the Cold War's 'hot' regions such as Central America was commonly avoided. According to Cable, the concept of 'limited war' in support of policy had regrettably become 'a mystery to most Americans' (1993: 259). But as Cable's article was being published in the autumn of 1993, urban gun battles raged between US forces and Somali fighters in the streets of Mogadishu. With the painful Somalia experience reinforcing the lingering American 'Vietnam syndrome', Cable's call for a revival of counterinsurgency methods to quell the internal wars of the 1990s generated very few followers in the United States or elsewhere.

The tragic cases of Somalia and Bosnia heavily influenced Donald Snow when he argued quite the opposite of Cable in his book *Uncivil Wars* (1996). In contrast to Cable, Snow, as an American political scientist, took the nature of internal conflict rather than the kind of the intervention as his point of departure. This led him to conclude that insurgency and classic counterinsurgency practice and theories from the Cold War years held limited applicability to what he called 'new internal wars'. Apart from Snow's claim that outside military involvement in counterinsurgency – particularly physical intervention on the side of the government such as in Vietnam – had failed rather miserably, intervening forces in the 1990s were faced with a totally different type of conflict from the so-called wars of national liberation (1996: 85; see also Gent 2005). Central to Snow's argument was the fact that the lynchpin tying together Cold War insurgency and counterinsurgency – the assumed moderating impact of the struggle for popular support ('a common centre of gravity') – was sadly missing in places such as Somalia, Rwanda and Bosnia. The 'new combatants' narrowed their appeal to their own specific ethnic group. The conversion of other population groups by winning their 'hearts and minds', through the use of ideology, politics and good government, seemed not even an afterthought amongst the warring parties. Moreover, their ideological and political objectives were mostly vague and they seemed less interested in the installation of a new government than in the profit they could derive from continuing instability and lawlessness (Snow 1996: 107).[10]

Snow therefore strongly warned against 'dusting off Vietnam-era notions of insurgency and counterinsurgency', which he claimed – in sharp contrast to Mackinlay – 'was largely being done' in order to understand and solve these situations (1996: 7). However, he failed to clarify who in policy, military or academic circles was actively using this important historical and theoretical knowledge to inform peacekeeping initiatives. Considering that so little experience and doctrine from irregular warfare was actually used at the time, his advice seems superfluous. Nevertheless, Snow was willing to admit that from a peacekeeper's perspective there was some overlap in the activity involved. A more coercive form of intervention in an internal war like NATO's Implementation Force (IFOR) in Bosnia, which he called 'peace imposition', had 'almost all of the characteristics of intervention in a counterinsurgency'. Indeed, 'the closest correlation between traditional insurgency-counterinsurgency and new internal war is found at this level' (Snow 1996: 152).[11]

Thomas Mockaitis also approached the comparison from this angle despite reaching a different conclusion. Being a true believer in the classic British counterinsurgency model and military culture, he became the most passionate advocate of the strong link. Mockaitis was an American historian who was an expert on the British colonial and post-colonial experience and had much more faith in the lessons from colonial policing and fighting Maoist-style insurgencies than Snow and most other contemporaries (Mockaitis 1990, 1995a, 1995b). When first introducing the connection in the margins of an article on peacekeeping in intra-state conflict in 1995,

Mockaitis cautiously avoided using the term counterinsurgency. Instead, he referred to the British concept of 'aid to the civil power' as a framework for future operations falling between peacekeeping and peace enforcement, concluding that 'the British approach to handling unrest is eminently compatible with the UN Charter'. British soldiers had been constantly reminded that their tasks was 'not the annihilation of an enemy but the suppression of a temporary disorder', using a minimum of force. Meanwhile, the British had long understood that civil unrest was not primarily a military problem and therefore 'winning the hearts and minds', civil–military cooperation, state-building and internal security operations had always gone hand-in-hand in the empire (Mockaitis 1995a: 122–3).

Three years later Mockaitis took this argument further when he stressed that intervention to end civil conflict 'more closely resembles counterinsurgency than it does any other form of military conflict' (1998: 43). On the basis of the same Somalia and Bosnia cases, but now augmented by the recently rediscovered UN mission in Congo in the 1960s, he suggested that peace enforcement, which he essentially defined as intervention in an active conflict, was simply 'a new name for an old game'. Therefore, instead of building on classic peacekeeping, robust peace operations needed to be reconfigured on the basis of counterinsurgency operations. Heavy-handed American, French and Soviet-Russian practice needed to be avoided, but from an analysis of the British experience in fighting insurgencies there 'might emerge a new model for peace operations to end civil conflict' (1998: 43). Mockaitis' conclusion was persuasive and he and others recycled similar arguments several times,[12] but his analysis had some weak points. It paid little attention to the fact that the British approach and its success was as much about control and coercion as it was about 'winning the hearts and minds' and 'minimum use of force'.[13] Moreover, Mockaitis hardly measured the three cases against the criteria of what actually constituted counterinsurgency, its definition and its 'classic' principles. Most of all, his article lacked a thorough treatment of the crucial issue of impartiality and consent, which is at the heart of any peacekeeping debate.

The end of impartiality?

Peace operations and counterinsurgency were both about ending civil unrest and armed conflict. Much of the military activity involved was formally about 'establishing a safe and secure environment'. However, a counterinsurgent could, by definition, not be impartial as defeating an insurgency remained his strategic objective. Even if he chose to address the legitimate grievances on which it feeds as his centre of gravity, this remained a means to an end – and one that even the British hardly attained without causing heavy attrition amongst enemy forces.

The renowned counterinsurgency practitioner and theorist Frank Kitson, who had actually been the first to establish the link between counterinsurgency and UN-style peacekeeping in his seminal book *Low Intensity Operations: Subversion, Insurgency and Peace-keeping* (1971), was also the first to draw attention to this fundamental difference. Although he saw 'a surprising similarity in the outward forms of many of the techniques involved', the essential dissimilarity was that

> the peace-keeping force acts on behalf of both parties to a dispute, at the invitation of them both, and therefore must as far as possible carry out its task without having recourse to warlike action against either of them ... If the body [sponsoring the force] is responsible for the government of one of the sides the operation becomes one of ordinary war.
>
> *(1971: 25, 144, 146)*

A veteran of campaigns in Malaya, Kenya and Northern Ireland, Kitson warned that despite outward similarities, UN-type peacekeeping was a totally different activity from what used to be known within the British empire as 'keeping the peace or duties in aid of the civil power'. Both these tasks were concerned with operating on behalf of a government against people who wanted to upset its authority. In other words, 'keeping the peace and duties in aid of the civil power were polite terms used to describe mild forms of countering subversion' (1971: 25).

Impartiality became even more challenging during the 1990s (Duyvesteyn 2005). Peace enforcement doctrine held that force could be applied impartially if it served to ensure compliance with a mandate based on a UN Security Council Resolution, but such mandates were always open to different interpretations (Berdal 2000: 62). Moreover, whereas there was formally no enemy to defeat on a strategic level, the 'surprising similarities' mentioned by Kitson were primarily noticeable on the tactical level, where the notion of impartiality often had different implications for the peacekeepers on the ground. The proverbial 'strategic corporal' involved in a 'three block war' in Mogadishu in 1993 might indeed experience intensive fighting, even if the overall mission to which he contributed was about creating a safe environment for the impartial delivery of humanitarian aid (Krulak 1999). During other operations, local warlords who felt excluded from a peace deal or who, because of their loose attachment to the formal warring parties did not feel the urge to comply, could well act as enemies of the peace.

The end of impartiality seemed to come in sight in the Balkans in 1995 when American military assistance and training to the Croatian army combined with NATO airstrikes against Bosnian Serb targets were used to tilt the balance of power in favour of the Bosnian Croats and Muslims. However, even in Bosnia the cursor was only temporarily shifted towards explicit partiality. The forceful intervention at the expense of the strongest party mainly served to facilitate the signing of the Dayton Peace Accords in December that same year. The subsequent implementation of this peace agreement was overall impartial. It nevertheless proved a gruelling process for the peacekeepers involved. The formerly warring parties overtly complied with the military part of the peace agreement, but those who opposed the agreement's political implications shifted their subversive and sometimes insurgent-type efforts into the civilian sphere in 1996. Bosnian Serbs and Bosnian Croats did not obstruct the reintegration of the ethnically cleansed Bosnian state – one of the primary goals of the peace agreement – in the military sphere. Here, 60,000 IFOR peacekeepers armed with tanks and artillery keeping watch. Instead it was obstructed primarily by their police forces and civil administrators, often themselves former warriors who tried to maintain control and keep communities segregated. These 'anti-Dayton power structures' used subversive and even insurgency-like methods when they found the international community's weak spot: the large gap that emerged between military and civilian implementation of the peace agreement (Brocades Zaalberg 2006: 245–63).

The most important element of Mockaitis' argument in 1998 was therefore his call for a 'Malayan Emergency-style' comprehensive, fully integrated civil–military approach (Mockaitis 1998: 54). He could have gone further than referring to historical precedents by addressing the causes and effects of the emerging gap between military and civilian (police and administrative) capabilities in Bosnia. This would have strengthened a pivotal argument at a time when NATO was trying to limit its peacekeeping role to military activity. Particularly in the United States, the straightjacket of the Weinberger-Powell doctrine drove political and military leaders to keep civil and military efforts segregated by pressing upon their heavily armed peacekeepers that their mission was limited to stopping the fighting, thereby providing a shield behind which civilian peace- or state-building activities could occur. All other activity, such as policing or police monitoring, arresting war criminals and generous support to civilian implementation of the Dayton Peace Accords was denigrated as 'mission creep', the real or perceived progression of the military role beyond its original military parameters. NATO's primary mission became a complete success, but a weak civilian component and the lack of an effectively coordinated civil–military effort caused the peace process as a whole to stagnate. The large specialized military units that deployed to conduct Civil-Military Cooperation (CIMIC) NATO-style proved little more than a fig leaf for the civil–military gap (Brocades Zaalberg 2006: 275–84). The Stabilisation Force (SFOR) that succeeded IFOR only slowly changed its role to more active support for the understaffed and poorly organized international civilian effort to reintegrate the divided state. However, NATO's failure to do so at an earlier stage, when the formerly warring parties were still awed by its display of power and had not yet discovered the force's weak spot, had a devastating long-term effect on the viability of Bosnia as a state.

As in classic counterinsurgency theory, the need for a comprehensive approach had surfaced during several successful UN operations. But with NATO taking over the military side of peacekeeping in Bosnia – the world's 'peace-building laboratory' of the time – Western military forces weary of donning the blue helmet had rapidly unlearned this crucial lesson.[14] They had initially latched on to what they knew best – the principles of conventional warfare and the idea that military affairs could be divorced from civilian matters – and tried to project them onto robust peacekeeping missions. Now they gradually accepted that focusing on strictly military objectives was counter-productive and complex peace operations required a combination of police, administrative, social, economic and military measures. A better understanding of classic counterinsurgency theory would certainly have sped up this learning process and possibly the integration of the war-torn state. Nevertheless, despite its failings, NATO had played a crucial role in at least controlling the explosive situation in Bosnia and managed to do so for a large part because it remained more or less true to the peacekeeper's impartial role.

Closing the civil–military gap: towards a comprehensive approach

At the close of the twentieth century, the counterinsurgency parallel became even more relevant during the powerful international peace operations in Kosovo and East Timor. Mockaitis' claim that peace operations should be all about 'aid to the civil power' became reality in the course of these trusteeship-like experiences. After a short de facto military interregnum in both theatres in 1999, where soldiers entered a complete power vacuum and more or less substituted for civil authorities, the key task of military peacekeepers became one of supporting a UN-mandated international interim administration and its executive police. Peacekeepers became the military cork on which these two massive state-building exercises by civilian international organizations floated. Soldiers temporarily became governors and engaged in reconstruction on a limited scale, but their primary tasks became protecting the international civilian interim government against what were often called 'spoilers' (Stedman 1997). This was a polite term often used at the time for the insurgent-style operators in both Kosovo and East Timor that were undermining the peace settlement in similar ways to those used in Bosnia.

Both missions suffered from a very weak civilian component in their early stages, but much improved civil–military cooperation prevented them from failing at an early stage. Lieutenant General Sir Mike Jackson, the first NATO Kosovo Force (KFOR) commander in 1999, cooperated intensively with his civilian counterparts in the United Nations Mission in Kosovo (UNMIK) to prevent the Albanian anti-Serb guerrillas from the Kosovo Liberation Army (KLA) redirecting their insurgency against the international interim government that had not delivered what they had fought for: full independence from Serbia. KFOR and UNMIK only just succeeded, but could not prevent the Serb minority that dominated northern Kosovo from subverting the peace agreement by establishing an effectively autonomous Serbian zone. As a veteran from Northern Ireland who, as a division commander in Bosnia in 1996 had been troubled by IFOR's exaggerated fear of 'mission creep', Jackson clearly used counterinsurgency terminology when formulating the commander's intent. He wrote to his subordinate NATO brigade and battalion commanders:

> I seek a 'hearts and minds' campaign at low level, creating trust and mutual understanding. As relationships build, so will the flow of information allowing KFOR to pre-empt conflict … It is an operation amongst the people, whose perception is the Centre of Gravity: that all inhabitants of Kosovo are better off with the United Nations Mission in Kosovo and KFOR than without, that we jointly offer a better future.
>
> *(Brocades Zaalberg 2006: 332)*

In his book *The Accidental Guerrilla*, David Kilcullen suggests that the UN-mandated peace operation International Force East Timor (INTERFET) could also have generated an immediate backlash leading to an insurgency had law and order not been quickly established in the wake of the collapsed regime by an impartial and culturally sensitive force. Kilcullen carefully avoids calling the Australian-led peace operation – in which he served as a company commander – a counterinsurgency operation, which it was not. Instead he embraced another term that became increasingly popular to bridge the ever narrower gap between the two concepts when he wrote that '[d]espite some unrest after independence, INTERFET has been seen as a model for stabilization operations' (Kilcullen 2009: 196–7).

Whereas peace operations in Kosovo and East Timor appeared to be on the road to counterinsurgency at the turn of the century, the connection still did not attract much attention. Counterinsurgency remained a rather obscure campaign theme and the dominant international security debate of the time was focused on 'humanitarian intervention', the active intervention to relieve human suffering without consent or in absence of the sovereign state. The prevailing debate within peacekeeping circles concerned the duty to protect civilians and therefore came to share a crucial theme with counterinsurgency (Brahimi 2000). But even the British armed forces, despite the experience of men like General Jackson, witnessed a clear lack of interest for counterinsurgency in the course of the 1990s. With the end of the 'Troubles' in Northern Ireland in 1995 and new conflicts in the Balkans creating the assumption that the future mostly lay in peacekeeping, attention instead turned to what the British came to call 'peace support operations' (Alderson 2009).

Around the turn of the century, the tendency to segregate rather than integrate the two themes in doctrine and academic discourse continued to be explicable. Whereas impartiality may have been precarious, especially in the Kosovo crisis when NATO waged a prolonged air campaign against the Serbs, the actual operations on the ground were essentially impartial affairs. In both cases, peacekeepers were implementing Security Council resolutions based on peace agreements between warring parties – a crucial element missing in counterinsurgency. Peacekeepers had actually fired very few shots in anger as consent of the parties on the strategic level was maintained. Moreover, peace operations and counterinsurgency required a different mix of external and indigenous capability. 'Nation-building' specialist James Dobbins was the first to point out this crucial dissimilarity. Whereas the restoration of peace in a society that has lost the capacity to secure itself required the deployment of foreign forces, '[o]utside forces have a much harder time suppressing a well-entrenched local insurgency, and can seldom succeed unless they are acting in support of an increasingly capable and legitimate indigenous ally' (Dobbins 2008: 12). Peacekeeping was by definition an outsider's job, while counterinsurgency was essentially about the local government.

However, one dominant development made the two concepts increasingly hard to distinguish in future operations. The broad definition of peacekeeping allowed it to function like a sponge, absorbing an ever wider range of activities the post-conflict environment in the Balkans, East Timor and various African states. In the early 1990s, ambitions had expanded to promoting democratic governance systems and market-oriented economic growth, reforming and rebuilding the judicial sector and police as well as the armed forces and reconciliation efforts (Paris 2010). Around the turn of the century, peacekeeping increasingly took place in a power vacuum left by collapsed or retreating governments, making state-building its essence. In close cooperation with military peacekeepers, the predominantly civilian 'post-conflict peace builders' adopted a broad-based inter-agency response in an attempt to address the underlying political, economic and social problems. The increasing importance of this comprehensive approach to post-conflict operations obviously had much in common with Thompson's call for a coordinated government machinery in order to implement a comprehensive plan along civilian and military lines of operation. However, compared to the 'coordinated government machinery' of colonial days, its modern variant proved infinitely more complex as it took place in a multi-agency, multinational and – on the level of the many individual national contributors – whole of government environment (Brocades Zaalberg 2008). A substantial difference also remained between foreign soldiers supporting a UN-mandated international interim government and active (military) support to a colonial or indigenous government beset by an insurgency. Nevertheless, the comprehensive approach emerged as a crucial binding factor.

Peacekeeping as a euphemism?

After 9/11, the connection between peace operations and counterinsurgency grew in significance in the operational realm. As part of the so-called 'Global War on Terror' US and coalition forces first ousted the Afghan Taliban regime in 2001 with support of local opposition groups and then successfully took on the Baath regime in Iraq in 2003. Rapid offensive success was followed by what in colonial days would have been called protracted 'pacification campaigns' in both countries. The unpopular notion of counterinsurgency was initially not invoked in either theatre and was notably missing from the discussion (Mackinlay 2009: 3). In the early twenty-first century the descriptive terms such as 'stabilization operations' or 'stability and reconstruction' became accepted for this type of mission that fell somewhere between occupation duty, peace operations, state-building, counter-terrorism and counterinsurgency, but often combining elements of them all.

The case of Afghanistan shows an interesting evolutionary process. Two separate operations, one launched by the United States as counter-terrorism and the other by European NATO partners under the guise of peacekeeping and post-conflict reconstruction, evolved along two very different tracks from 2001 onwards. Only after 2005 did they gradually fuse into what was first and foremost an extremely complex counterinsurgency campaign, a reality that was grudgingly and belatedly accepted in the capitals of most European troops-contributing nations.

After the forceful removal of the Taliban regime four years earlier, the United States continued to search for its leaders and al-Qaeda fighters as part of Operation Enduring Freedom (OEF). With southern and eastern Afghanistan as its primary 'hunting ground', the US-dominated counter-terrorist operation took a predominantly enemy-centric approach. When this yielded little effect, American troops gradually incorporated tactical level counterinsurgency methods (Wright 2010). For instance, the development of the Provincial Reconstruction Team (PRT) model was aimed at spreading the influence of the Afghan government. These small, integrated civil–military teams engaged in capacity building and conducted 'hearts and minds' projects aimed at removing the causes for conflict and support to insurgents. Nevertheless, searching and destroying the Taliban leadership and their foreign jihadist allies remained the primary US focus (Jakobsen 2005). Meanwhile, the ambitious international state-building enterprise in Afghanistan lacked unity of effort and suffered from a serious lack of personnel and funds, partly because the United States had shifted its attention and resources to the upcoming war in Iraq in the course of 2002.

In Afghanistan, the small European-dominated International Security Assistance Force (ISAF) deployed under a UN mandate to Kabul in order to support and protect the new Afghan government headed by Interim President Hamid Karzai. Whereas the task to separate, monitor and demobilize armed factions was still a modest element of the ISAF mission, military support to the state, its civil administration and security forces, was its essence. This was no impartial mission, as only consent of the new Western-backed authorities was sought. However, with the notion of peacekeeping stretched to the limit in the course of the 1990s, it took NATO little effort to present ISAF as a peace operation when it assumed command of the operation in 2003. As long as armed opposition against the Western-backed Karzai government in Kabul was minimal and the job of the average NATO 'peacekeeper' on patrol in the capital differed little from that in Kosovo, the misuse of the term went largely unnoticed. Similarly, the British and Dutch governments got away with casting their role in the occupation of southern Iraq in the light of peace support and stabilization as long as they were not confronted with serious civil unrest and armed revolt. For the Dutch battlegroup operating in the relatively benign province Al Muthanna until its withdrawal in 2005 this was more or less possible, but the British forces in Basra and Maysan could hardly disguise after 2003 that their so-called stabilization operation was in fact an occupation turned into a counterinsurgency campaign (Brocades Zaalberg and Ten Cate 2011).

This trend towards increasingly outward similarities between peace support and counterinsurgency especially bothered the Canadian post-conflict researcher Ronald Paris. In reaction to a wave of criticism and cynicism surrounding peace-building – Paris argued that multinational peace operations had become carelessly conflated with the US-led Global War on Terror. Efforts to stabilize Iraq after the invasion bore some resemblance to liberal peace-building strategies pursued elsewhere by the UN, but this certainly did not put them on an equal footing (Paris 2010: 347–8). Paris based most of his argument on the comparison with the more controversial Iraqi case, but he may well have accentuated the gradual expansion of ISAF's mission and geographical scope. Under a broadened UN mandate, the NATO-led force expanded its operations through the deployment of PRTs to the north and the west of Afghanistan in order to allow the central government to exert its authority. Here, as in Kabul, these small and lightly armed military units, often augmented with some civilian staff, met with little resistance from former warlords, other 'local power brokers' or remnants of the Taliban. Only when NATO gradually took over from OEF and started to move a substantial force of over 10,000 heavily armed troops into the heartland of the revitalized Taliban movement in the south in the course of 2006, did Alliance troops become openly involved in sustained fighting with the Islamic fundamentalist insurgents. Nevertheless, the British, Canadian and Dutch governments – who were the main troop-contributors in the southern provinces – tended to present their mission as peace support or stabilization operations in search of a reconstruction effort centred on their PRTs. Their failure to present the extended ISAF operation in more realistic terms – the notions of insurgency and counterinsurgency continued to be avoided in order to ensure political and public support – proved particularly injudicious when the Taliban launched a ferocious offensive against NATO forces in the spring and summer of 2006 (Alderson 2009; Dimitru and De Graaf 2010).

Whereas most other European troops contributors continued to view ISAF in peacekeeping terms, the political and military leaders of the countries fighting in the south slowly and sometimes grudgingly came to accept the mission as a counterinsurgency. Luckily, their tactical commanders on the ground had mostly preceded them.[15] Meanwhile, the US government had started to shift its main effort in Afghanistan from an enemy-centric counter-terrorist approach to a broader population-centric counterinsurgency strategy under the flag of both OEF and ISAF.

When the Americans adapted in a similar, but much more fundamental way, in Iraq and injected extra troops and civilian capacity, their qualified yet remarkable success in 2007 and 2008 helped rid counterinsurgency of most of its negative colonial and Vietnam-era connotation on both sides of the Atlantic (see also Chapter 6 in this volume). 'The Surge' was clearly not the only factor in stopping the downward spiral of violence in Iraq since the occupation of 2003–4, but it is safe to say that the methods introduced and broadly promoted by a new generation of counterinsurgency thinkers and practitioners successfully built on classic doctrine and theory. Particularly the writings of Galula influenced this group, some of whom were on the editorial team of the highly praised US Army and Marine Corps Counterinsurgency Field Manual (FM 3–24).

Afghanistan became the next testing ground for this neo-classical counterinsurgency handbook (Jones and Smith 2010). Under the umbrella of ISAF, European coalition partners that had rapidly 'upscaled' from a peacekeeping mindset and accepted the counterinsurgency mission merged with a rapidly expanding US military force that was 'scaling down' from its fighting mentality. Strategic success – which had not yet been secured in Iraq – seemed illusive for ISAF whose mission remained to support a dysfunctional Afghan government. Nonetheless, as counterinsurgency quickly regained its former status as an important campaign theme, there was a prevailing tendency – particularly amongst newcomers to the field of irregular warfare – to embrace the earlier mentioned, somewhat naive notion of the concept as being predominantly about 'winning the hearts and minds' and 'minimum use of force'.[16] FM 3–24, as a major restatement of doctrine, however, often ended up being confused with historical practice.

Only against the background of this revived, positivist and at times historically selective conception of counterinsurgency, can we understand the latest contribution on the conceptual overlap with peace operations. Karsten Friis has been the first peacekeeping specialist to argue on the basis of a structural comparison that the two concepts 'are converging on each other' (2010: 50). While consciously steering away from mandates and political motivations, he compared the UN Department of Peacekeeping Operations capstone doctrine and FM 3–24 as well as operations. He correctly concluded that the doctrines shared commonalities in their practical focus on civilian solutions, the protection of civilians, civil–military and international unity of effort, host-nation ownership, intelligence and their acknowledgement of the limitations of the use of force. However, Friis overemphasized the soft side of counterinsurgency doctrine and operations. He showed little awareness of classic counterinsurgency writings and left out any reference to the key role of coercion, harsh emergency legislation, rigorous population-control measures and what British doctrine still calls 'neutralizing the insurgent' in defeating insurgencies. Like many contemporaries, he stripped counterinsurgency from its raw components, thereby making the parallels with peacekeeping highly visible, yet not entirely convincing. The similarities tended to lose their relevance without the context of both historical practice and what actually happened during recent conflicts.

Friis made an important contribution to the debate, but his analysis seemed to fall victim to what he himself rightfully called the tendency amongst students of the two disciplines 'to stay analytically within separate circles, contributing to different literatures and publishing in different journals' (2010: 49). This may also explain his claim that the two concepts have rarely been compared and the similarities are 'often ignored'. As we have seen, this is only partly true, but like the few scholars who actually did enter the comparative minefield before him in the previous two decades, Friis failed to either notice or to mention their work. He missed the opportunity to build on previous findings and actually engage in academic discourse. Without any reference to these earlier writings and little attention paid to the actual operational experience of peacekeepers and counterinsurgents, conflict analysts – like the policy-makers, military leaders and doctrine writers they often criticize – continued to reinvent the wheel.

Conclusion

Mackinlay has been correct in arguing that counterinsurgency theory and doctrine could have helped shape a more realistic approach to peace operations in the 1990s. The heady optimism that followed the end of superpower rivalry had unleashed tremendous international political ambitions in peace operations that mostly surpassed the existing conceptual thinking in the area of war and peace studies. It created both historical amnesia and doctrinal myopia that led to the neglect of counterinsurgency theory and doctrine. But his suggestion that the two had always been interchangeable and that this was only accepted after Afghanistan and Iraq has been shown to be incorrect. Instead, the two campaign themes that seemed so distant in the early 1990s gradually expanded into each other's spheres.

This rapprochement has been primarily the result of three prevailing trends. First, peacekeeping forces in their various forms started to operate under ever more robust mandates to put an end to internal conflicts. Their military capabilities increasingly allowed them to threaten with, or resort to, the use of force against non-compliant parties in a conflict area. Subsequently, counterinsurgency seemingly developed in the opposite direction as the neo-classic counterinsurgency theory tended to promote 'the softer side of COIN' and a too rosy view of what had been the key to strategic success in this type of conflict came to prevail. Second, the expanding role of peacekeepers and counterinsurgents in state-building drove them ever closer, especially in the wake of the 'Global War on Terror'. As both disciplines became married to these mostly civilian-led state-building enterprises, demands for the often heralded, but often poorly implemented comprehensive approach increased. It is against the background of this development that counterinsurgency specialist David Ucko wrote in 2010 about Mats Berdal's book on two decades of post-conflict peace building that, although it mentioned counterinsurgency only once, it nonetheless said more good things on this topic than many books with counterinsurgency in their title.[17]

This brings us to the final trend, which simultaneously functions as an important qualifier for the actual amount of overlap between peacekeeping and counterinsurgency. Even the post-'9/11' developments did not prove the argument of 'enthusiasts' like Mackinlay entirely right. The conceptual blur that occurred in this period was created by the often euphemistic and opportunistic use of the term 'peacekeeping', which – even in its more forceful incarnations – should formally have been reserved for missions deployed at the request of local parties after the negotiation of peace settlements to (civil) wars. The 'Global War on Terror' and 'Regime Change' resulted in two external invasions aimed at toppling governments, policies that revitalized the internal armed conflict in Afghanistan and generated an insurgency and a civil war in Iraq. These 'conditions of birth' were important, as the task of picking up the pieces and putting the two countries back together again through an explosive combination of state-building, peace support, counterinsurgency and counter-terrorism – or what has become known as hybrid warfare – was certainly no impartial affair. Therefore, despite the substantial convergence in methods and means, complex peace operations should still be treated as a different category from counterinsurgency.

Notes

1 The author wishes to thank Isabelle Duyvesteyn, Gijs Rommelse and Richard van Gils for helpful comments on an earlier version of this chapter.

2 Mackinlay wisely avoids directly claiming that the catastrophes in Somalia, Bosnia and Rwanda could have been averted if the UN and NATO had embraced a counterinsurgency approach, but the suggestion is nevertheless there.

3 Kilcullen ascribed the concept of hybrid warfare to Erin Simpson and Frank Hoffman.

4 During the 1990s, peace operations and counterinsurgency would be incorporated in the similarly generic concept Military Operation Other Than War (MOOTW).

5 In countries such as South Africa, former insurgents and counterinsurgents even merged into one national fighting force. Together with the post-1990 political environment this resulted in a strict anti-counterinsurgency position that, according to Anita Grossman, has seriously hampered South African National Defence Force's ability to perform peace operations in otherwise insurgent conflicts in Africa (Grossmann 2008).

6 There is no formal definition of peacekeeping or peace operations, as both terms are absent from the UN Charter and the UN Department of Peacekeeping Operations (UNDPKO) only provides a categorization of five 'peace and security activities': conflict prevention, peacemaking, peacekeeping, peace enforcement and peacebuilding (Bellamy and Williams 2010: 14–15).

7 For example the highly successful 'Multinational Force and Observers' (MFO) for the Sinai was established under US leadership in the 1980s, while the better-known, but ill-fated 'Multinational Forces' (MNF) in Lebanon (1982–4) was a combined American-British-French-Italian initiative.

8 See: *US Army Field Manual 100–23: Peace Operations* (December 1994) 2; British Army, *Wider Peacekeeping* (London: Ministry of Defence, 1994); The Royal Netherlands Army, *Landmacht Doctrine Publicatie III: Vredesoperaties* (1999).

9 Named after Casper Weinberger, Secretary of Defence during the Reagan administration, and Chairman of the Joint Chiefs of Staff General Colin Powell during the administrations of George H.W. Bush and Bill Clinton.

10 Snow's argument fits in with the 'new wars' thesis, which held that this mode of warfare drew on both guerrilla and counterinsurgency techniques, 'though the main target for attack is usually the civilian population and not other militia groups or government forces' (see also Kaldor 1999; Münkler 2005; Van Creveld 1991).

11 Regrettably, Snow hardly went into the practical details of tactical level peacekeeping to prove this point.

12 For instance Richard Lovelock underwrote the call for lessons from counterinsurgency experience to inform current practice in 2002. He stated that the Kosovo experience suggests that the comprehensive civil–military of the British counterinsurgency approach is 'fundamental to contemporary peace support operations' (Lovelock 2002; see also Ellis 2004; Mockaitis 1999).

13 A similar argument on the British Army's minimum force philosophy triggered a heated debate on the actual British methods in the late colonial period (see Bennett 2009; Thornton 2009).

14 Examples of relatively successful integrated UN civil–military peace-building operations are its mission in Cambodia, Eastern Slavonia and more recently in Liberia. The latter mission, according to a recent report commissioned by a Dutch NGO, represents 'the most developed version of UN reform as an integrated peace support mission' (Frerks *et al.* 2006). For 'peacebuilding laboratory' see Berdal (2009: 12).

15 The Dutch government initially avoided all reference to COIN and emphasized post-war reconstruction instead. Whereas the first Dutch ISAF Regional Command South Commander Major-General Ton van Loon avoided using the term counterinsurgency in the Netherlands, he freely used the term counterinsurgency in the United States in 2007. Two years later, the second Dutchman in this position, Major-General Mart de Kruif, did not feel constrained when he discussed the Afghan counterinsurgency campaign in the Netherlands and even the Dutch minister of defence would occasionally refer to the mission as counterinsurngency (see Brocades Zaalberg and Ten Cate 2011; Dimitru and De Graaf 2010).

16 I have to admit that as a newcomer to the field in 2004, I sometimes fell into this trap when writing a chapter on counterinsurgency for my dissertation *Soldiers and Civil Power* (see also Hack 2009).

17 David Ucko, 'Is "Counterinsurgency" an Empty Concept? Can we do better?', contribution to the weblog *Kings of War*, 26 March 2010 (www.kingsofwar.org.uk).

Recommended readings

Cable, Larry (1993) 'Reinventing the Round Wheel: Insurgency, Counterinsurgency and Peacekeeping Post Cold War', *Small Wars and Insurgencies*, 4 (2): 228–62.

Friis, Karsten (2010) 'Peacekeeping and Counter-Insurgency – Two of a Kind?', *International Peacekeeping*, 17 (1): 19–66.

Kilcullen, David (2009) *The Accidental Guerrilla: Fighting Small Wars in the Midst of a Big One*. London: Hurst and Company.

Kitson, Frank (1971) *Low Intensity Operations: Subversion, Insurgency and Peacekeeping*. London: Faber & Faber.

Mackinlay, J. (2009) *The Insurgent Archipelago: From Mao to Bin Laden*. London: Hurst and Company.

Mockaitis, Thomas R. (1995) 'Peacekeeping and Intra-State Conflict', *Small Wars and Insurgencies*, 6 (1): 112–25.

Mockaitis, Thomas R. (1998) 'From Counterinsurgency to Peace Enforcement: New Names for Old Games?', *Small Wars and Insurgencies*, 10 (2): 40–57.

Paris, Ronald (2010) 'Saving Liberal Peacebuilding', *Review of International Studies*, 36: 337–65.

Snow, Donald M. (1996) *Uncivil Wars: International Security and the New International Conflicts*. Boulder and London: Lynne Rienner.

References

Alderson, Alex (2009) *The Validity of British Army Counterinsurgency Doctrine after the War in Iraq*, Unpublished PhD Thesis, Cranfield University.

Beckett, Ian F.W. (2001) *Modern Insurgencies and Counter-insurgencies: Guerrillas and their Opponents since 1750*. London: Routledge.

Bellamy, Alex J. and Paul D. Williams (2010) *Understanding Peacekeeping*. Cambridge and Malden: Polity Press.

Bellamy, Christopher (1996) *Knights in White Armour: The New Art of War and Peace*. London Random House.

Bennett, Huw (2007) 'The Other Side of the COIN: Minimum Force and Exemplary Force in British Army Counterinsurgency in Kenya', *Small Wars & Insurgencies*, 18 (4): 638–64.

Bennett, Huw (2009) '"A very Salutary Effect": The Counter-Terror Strategy in the Early Malayan Emergency, June 1948 to December 1949', *The Journal of Strategic Studies*, 32 (3): 415–44.

Berdal, Mats (2000) 'Lessons not Learned: The Use of Force in "Peace Operations in the 1990s"', *International Peacekeeping*, 7 (2): 55–74.

Berdal, Mats (2009) *Building Peace after War*, Adephi Series.

The Brahimi Report (formally known as *Report of the UN Panel on Peace Operations*, October 2000, UN doc. A/55/305).

Brocades Zaalberg, Thijs (2006) *Soldiers and Civil Power: Supporting or Substituting Civil Authorities in Modern Peace Operations*. Amsterdam: Amsterdam University Press.

Brocades Zaalberg, Thijs (2008) 'The Historical Origins of Civil-Military Cooperation', in Sebastiaan J.H. Rietjens and Myriame T.I.B. Bollen (eds), *Managing Civil-Military Cooperation, A 24/7 Joint Effort for Stability*. Aldershot and Burlington: Ashgate.

Brocades Zaalberg, Thijs and Arthur ten Cate (2010) *Missie in Al Muthanna: De Nederlandse Krijgsmacht in Irak, 2003–2005*. Amsterdam: Boom Publishers.

Brocades Zaalberg, Thijs and Arthur ten Cate (2012) 'A Gentile Occupation: Unravelling the Dutch Approach in Iraq, 2003–2005', *Small Wars and Insurgencies*, 23 (1) (forthcoming).

Cable, Larry (1993) 'Reinventing the Round Wheel: Insurgency, Counterinsurgency and Peacekeeping Post Cold War', *Small Wars and Insurgencies*, 4 (2): 228–62.

Cate, Arthur ten (2007) *Sterven voor Bosnië. Een Historische Analyse van het Interventiedebat in Nederland, 1992–1995*. Amsterdam: Boom Publishers.

Clarke, Walter and Jeffrey Herbst (1996) 'Somalia and the Future of Humanitarian Intervention', *Foreign Affairs*, March–April.

Creveld, Martin van (1991) *The Transformation of War*. New York: Free Press.

Creveld, Martin van (2000) 'Through a Glass, Darkly: Some Reflections on the Future of War', *Naval War College Review*, Autumn.

Dimitru, George and Beatrice de Graaf (2010) 'The Dutch COIN Approach: Three Years in Uruzgan, 2006–2009', *Small Wars and Insurgencies*, 21 (3): 429–58.

Dobbins, James F. (2008) *Nation-building and Counterinsurgency after Iraq*. New York: A Century Foundation Report.

Duyvesteyn, Isabelle (2005) *Clausewitz and African War: Politics and Strategy in Liberia and Somalia*. New York: Taylor & Francis.

Ellis, Brent (2004) 'Back to the Future: The Lessons of Counterinsurgency for Contemporary Peace Operations?', *E-merge – A Student Journal of International Affairs*, 5: 21–52.

Frerks, G., B. Klem, S. van Laar and M. van Klingeren (2006) *Principles and Pragmatism: Civil-Military Action in Afghanistan and Liberia*. The Hague: Cordaid.

Friis, Karsten (2010) 'Peacekeeping and Counter-Insurgency – Two of a Kind?', *International Peacekeeping*, 17 (1): 19–66.

Galula, David (1966) *Counterinsurgency Warfare: Theory and Practise*. Westport: Praeger.

Grossmann, Anita M. (2008) 'Lost in Transition: the South African Military and Counterinsurgency', *Small Wars and Insurgencies*, 19 (4): 541–72.

Hack, Karl (2009) 'The Malayan Emergency as Counter-Insurgency Paradigm', *Journal of Strategic Studies*, 32 (3): 383–414.

Jakobsen, Peter Viggo (2000) 'The Emerging Consensus on Grey Area Peace Operations Doctrine: Will it Last and Enhance Operational Effectiveness?', *International Peacekeeping*, 7 (3): 36–56.

Jakobsen, Peter Viggo (2005) 'PRTs in Afghanistan: Successful but not Sufficient', DIIS Report.

Jones, David M. and Mike M.L.R. Smith (2010) 'Whose Hearts and Whose Minds? The Curious Case of Global Counter-Insurgency', *Journal of Strategic Studies*, 33 (1): 81–121.

Kaldor, Mary (1999) *New and Old Wars*. Cambridge: Polity.

Kilcullen, David (2009) *The Accidental Guerrilla: Fighting Small Wars in the Midst of a Big One*. London: Hurst and Company.

Kitson, Frank (1971) *Low Intensity Operations: Subversion, Insurgency and Peacekeeping*. London: Faber & Faber.

Krulak, Charles C. (1999) 'The Strategic Corporal: Leadership in the Three Block War', *Marines Magazine*, January.

Lovelock, Richard (2002) 'The Evolution of Peace Operations Doctrine', *Joint Forces Quarterly*, Spring.

Mackinlay, J. (2009) *The Insurgent Archipelago: From Mao to Bin Laden*. London: Hurst and Company.

Marshall, Alexander G. (2010) 'Imperial Nostalgia, the Liberal Lie, and the Perils of Postmodern Counter-insurgency', *Small Wars and Insurgencies*, 21 (2): 233–58.

Mockaitis, Thomas R. (1990) *British Counterinsurgency, 1919–1960*. New York: St. Martin's Press.

Mockaitis, Thomas R. (1995a) 'Peacekeeping and Intra-State Conflict', *Small Wars and Insurgencies*, 6 (1): 112–25.

Mockaitis, Thomas R. (1995b) *British Counterinsurgency in the Post-Imperial Era*. Manchester and New York: Manchester University Press.

Mockaitis, Thomas R. (1998) 'From Counterinsurgency to Peace Enforcement: New Names for Old Games?', *Small Wars and Insurgencies*, 10 (2): 40–57.

Mockaitis, Thomas R. (1999) *Peace Operations and Intrastate Conflict: The Sword and the Olive Branch?* Westport and London: Praeger.

Münkler, H. (2005) *The New Wars*. Cambridge: Polity.

Paris, Ronald (2010) 'Saving Liberal Peacebuilding', *Review of International Studies*, 36: 337–65.

Schmidl, Erwin (2000) 'The Evolution of Peace Operations from the Nineteenth Century', in Erwin Schmidl (ed.), *Peace Operations between War and Peace*. London and Portland: Frank Cass.

Snow, Donald M. (1996) *Uncivil Wars: International Security and the New International Conflicts*. Boulder and London: Lynne Rienner.

Thompson, Robert (1966) *Defeating Communist Insurgency: The Lessons of Malaya and Vietnam*. New York: Praeger.

Thornton, Rod (2000) 'Peace Support Operations and the Military Organization: The Role of Doctrine', *International Peacekeeping*, 7 (2): 41–62.

Thornton, Rod (2004) 'The British Army and the Origins of its Minimum Force Philosophy', *Small Wars and Insurgencies*, 15 (1): 83–106.

Thornton, Rod (2009) ' "Minimum Force": a Reply to Huw Bennett', *Small Wars and Insurgencies*, 20 (1): 215–26.

Wright, Donald P. *et al.* (2010) *A Different Kind of War: The US Army in Operation Enduring Freedom, October 2001 – September 2005*. Fort Leavenworth: Combat Studies Institute Press.

8

INSURGENCY, COUNTERINSURGENCY AND POLICING

Alice Hills

In Iraq in the summer of 2007, Sunni insurgents began a systematic campaign to kill police chiefs in their homes, policemen at road checkpoints, and would-be officers at recruiting posts, as they had done throughout the insurgency (*Australian*, 27 August 2007); in 2005 alone, 1,497 officers were killed and 3,256 wounded (*New York Times*, 16 January 2006). Thai and Yemeni police are similarly targeted, as are police in India where, in April 2010, Naxalite insurgents ambushed paramilitary police in the eastern state of Chattisgarh, killing 74 officers sent to reinforce the inexperienced local police (*Financial Times*, 7 April 2010). Meanwhile international forces in Afghanistan rely on indigenous police to distract attention from their troops or to provide the local security that will enable them to leave. Hence three-quarters of the US$14.2 billion requested in 2010 for Afghanistan's reconstruction is intended for training, equipping and mentoring the Afghan National Police (ANP) and army (Special Inspector, 2010).

This chapter addresses the issues raised by police and policing in insurgency and counterinsurgency. Police refers to the public or statutory police whose significance results from the political objectives it symbolises, the power relationships it reflects, and its close engagement with local populations. In counterinsurgency, police refers to indigenous officers and to the international civilian or paramilitary volunteer officers advising or mentoring them; it may also refer to retired officers contracted by international private security companies to train local police. In contrast, policing is a descriptive term alluding to the problem-solving, regulatory, enforcement and coercive activities of statutory and non-statutory (or customary) security groups.

The police role in insurgency is relatively straightforward. Local police play a negative role in insurgency because they reproduce the political order that insurgents challenge; their functions usually include regime representation and regulatory activities so they are targeted. In the early days of an insurgency police may attempt to police, but once violence reaches certain levels they either support the insurgents, or they disappear or they are killed. This is notably so in rural areas where police are rarely present. In contrast, the police role in counterinsurgency is multifaceted and assertive. International, national and local police are used in combination with troops to contain or crush insurgency, as in Iraq or Chechnya, or, more rarely, to address its root causes, as in Northern Ireland. Increasingly, as in Afghanistan, police are seen as an enabling element in non-military security operations involving Western forces (though all counterinsurgency is predicated on coercion), and are accordingly regarded as key local actors.

Understanding of the police role is, however, limited. Specifically, there is a fundamental lack of knowledge concerning the role and culture of the non-Western police on which strategic success in international operations rests.

The discussion that follows, which focuses on the police's role in counterinsurgency involving international forces, is organised in four sections. First, it offers an overview of the state of knowledge concerning the police role. Second, it notes topics currently the subject of debate. Third, it identifies the challenges and pressing questions confronting scholars and analysts before, fourth, drawing brief conclusions.

Current state of knowledge

It is sometimes claimed that there is an international consensus about counterinsurgency (e.g. Bayley and Perito 2010: 55), but the accuracy of this assumption is questionable. There may be general recognition of the principles thought to underpin contemporary Western counterinsurgency, but each campaign must still be understood in its historical and regional context. Thus to say that the 'support of the people' is 'essential for success' (Ellis quoted in Bayley and Perito 2010: 55) may be true as far as liberal democracies are concerned; it may even be 'the fundamental premise of the contemporary COIN consensus'. But consensus is often temporary, and support may be achieved by coercion, rather than conviction; activities such as 'hearts-and-mind' operations have always concerned control requirements, rather than beliefs.

Similarly, although US forces in the vanguard of counterinsurgency currently promote protection of the populace, this is not necessarily proof of the term's accuracy or abiding truth. Indeed, it took seven years of campaigning before a US commander of the International Security Assistance Force (ISAF) in Afghanistan (General McCrystal) admitted that 'our strategy cannot be focused on seizing terrain or destroying insurgent forces; our objective must be the population' (*JDW*, 30 June 2010: 21). Further, while counterinsurgency forces around the world follow US developments, they do so in order to exploit or anticipate, rather than emulate. Few are under any illusions as to the operational and political challenges of counterinsurgency, and many (e.g. India, Indonesia, Israel and the Russian Federation) have more experience. Even so, most conventional militaries agree that counterinsurgency is best avoided, especially in cities where population density and media presence exacerbate the political challenges of conducting operations.

The current state of knowledge is fragmented, especially in relation to police. This is not to suggest that the orthodoxies associated with international and/or regionally-located policy-makers, practitioners and scholars are analytically separate. Rather it is to emphasise that while there is an established literature covering the role of conventional militaries, consensus is usually temporary and localised; officials focus on time-urgent political and legal challenges, practitioners are aware of counterinsurgency's technical constraints, while scholars are influenced by academic and policy-relevant debates. Lessons from past operations remain influential, and the enduring challenge of translating military achievement into political success means that the writings of men such as Galula and Thompson are periodically rediscovered. But the resultant literature focuses on the military role, and policing and police are addressed only in so far as they affect military concerns. That few Western practitioners, officials and scholars attempt to understand the role and culture of indigenous police exacerbates divisions between rhetoric and reality.

There is no coherent or comprehensive orthodoxy regarding the police role in counterinsurgency, and consensus is offset by contingencies, political calculations, and national and institutional differences. Even so, certain strands and perspectives coalesce around the need for a police presence, and commonalities can be identified. Western assumptions are evident from policy, and are supported (and in some cases contradicted or undermined) by the knowledge of practitioners and scholars.

Policy-relevant approaches

International understanding reflects Western (i.e. US) responses to an amalgam of experience, political objectives and time-urgent problems that rarely, if ever, amounts to a long-term strategy. Thus officials in Washington, London and Brussels focus on reforming or reconstructing indigenous police because democratic-style policing is believed to be inherently desirable, and because transforming local police into a 'professional' police service offers their troops an exit strategy. Police are the favoured providers of local security because their use emphasises the commitment of governments to desirable goals such as the rule of law, lessens the chances of coups, and reinforces perceptions of insurgents as criminals rather than freedom fighters. Indeed, insurgents are usually criminalised, making them a police or (as in the case of Russian Federation forces in Chechnya) an internal security problem. This is understandable because counterinsurgency requires police work in the sense of identification, and regulatory and (for many liberal democracies) evidence-related activities. Also, insurgents' fund raising is often linked to transnational organised crime (Williams 2009). But beyond this divisions appear.

Western democracies prefer to police using civilian or gendarmerie officers, rather than troops, but opinions differ according to contingencies, national traditions and political calculations. In 2003–4, for example, insurgents in Iraq forced the Pentagon to reconsider its approach to policing: US warfighting troops did not want to police cities such as Baghdad, international civilian police officers were incapable of doing so, and the new Iraqi Police Service was not trained or equipped for counterinsurgency. The acrimonious nature of the debate that ensued between the departments of defence and state is evidence of the contested nature of even national orthodoxy. The UK's Chilcott Enquiry into the UK's involvement in Iraq, 2003–9, suggests that a similar situation existed in London as the ministries for defence, foreign affairs and development pursued their own sometimes contradictory and often obstructive agendas. Indeed, the Chilcott Enquiry is particularly instructive because it emphasises how UK ministries, like their international peers, recognised the police's potential but were unwilling to resource it adequately. This is evident from the testimony of Douglas Brand, the UK's chief police adviser in Iraq, 2003–4, who notes that while the US training system for a new Iraqi army involved 400 individuals and a big budget under a two-star general, there was nothing for police: 'There seemed to be ... [the] expectation that the police would ... rise like a phoenix and just get on with things' (Brand 2010a: 15).

Unrealistic expectations are intensified by analytical opaqueness, which is exacerbated by the Western tendency to conflate the police's counterinsurgency role with security sector reform (SSR) and peacekeeping (Kernaghan 2010a: 84). Despite the dramatically different levels of violence involved, officials tend to see the police role as part of an all-purpose kit for stabilising and reconstructing fragile or post-conflict countries. Indeed, the US government explicitly endorses the concept of SSR as a component of stabilisation and, by extension, counterinsurgency (Meharg *et al.*, 2009; US Army Field Manual 3–07 2008). There is an equally strong tendency to see the police role as peacekeeping. Witness a UK chief police adviser in Iraq arguing in 2006 that the UK's police task was covered by its UN police mission statement: 'to assist in the development of an efficient, effective, credible and community supported police service' (Smith 2010a: 3). In consequence, similar models tend to be adopted regardless of context; the version of SSR implemented in Baghdad in 2005 was that used in Bosnia Herzegovina and Kosovo (Smith 2010b: 12).

Practitioner perspectives

Brand and his colleagues share a perspective that is common amongst Western officers. There is no liberal consensus enshrined in a police equivalent to *FM 3–24* (which discusses police in counterinsurgency primarily in relation to host-nation support), but there is broad support for the view that successful counterinsurgency requires a multi-agent approach to supporting the local population and host-nation government, and that 'the police is the most important actor in counterinsurgency. Local police provide the first line of defense in COIN ... accurate intelligence, and efficient police and law enforcement are the key capabilities to defeat an insurgency early' (RAND 2008: 186).

Consensus is underpinned by the widespread conviction that responsibility for social order is primarily the police's (Neocleous 2000). Accordingly, counterinsurgency requires a police presence because it aims at facilitating or imposing a new form of order, and because developing a police is conventionally seen as ensuring justice and the security (i.e. well-being) of a populace. Additionally, Western advisers often believe that complex policing issues can be viewed in the light of the basic police principles and occupational commonalities that they take for granted. But this is to downplay the differences between counterinsurgency policing and policing in more benign environments (Kilcullen 2009: 61), and between different cultures. There are occupational commonalities shared by police (O'Neil *et al.* 2007) – organisations such as INTERPOL could not otherwise function – but local culture, norms and practices invariably influence what is understood as appropriate, and international advisers reform or rebuild local police in the light of their national or professional experience. This is notably so regarding issues such as the status of a police vis-à-vis military forces. Brand's opinion that the police function is to maintain order by providing a police presence, and that the resultant interaction is best managed through criminal justice processes may be orthodox among UK practitioners who believe that the military does not have the skills or training to keep order (their purpose is to disperse or repress disorder), but an officer from Italy's Carabinieri (which is a branch of the armed forces) may disagree.

Context matters, and while the elements of a Western policy-relevant orthodoxy can be identified, they reflect contingencies, rather than enduring truths. As the writings of strategists such as Trinqier remind us, attitudes and perspectives shift over the years; so does the case of the Thai police, which in the 1960s refused to play a role in counterinsurgency (Blaufarb 1977: 194–6). Arguably, it is the role of the academy to place policy-relevant and functional knowledge in its broader context, but in practice the scholarly record is even more uneven.

Academic knowledge

There are few if any accounts of police and policing in counterinsurgency written by scholars with expertise in comparative policing and counterinsurgency. Those with a police studies background (Bayley is the most eminent) focus on Western policy problems and generic liberal solutions even as they acknowledge that 'police activity is affected in predictable ways by social environment' (contrast Bayley 1977: 7). In contrast, the most insightful and influential analyses of counterinsurgency come from soldier-strategists (e.g. Kilcullen 2009), historians (Horne 1977), political figures (Thompson 1966) or regional specialists who acknowledge the police role, though do not analyse it in depth. Few explore the implications of ethnographic accounts of insurgencies in rural Africa, which is where most insurgencies occur, and where a conventional police presence is essentially irrelevant (Bøås and Dunn 2007).

Admittedly, many scholars working on counterinsurgency discuss policing, but the term usually refers to regulatory, investigative or public security activities by military forces during post-conflict or peacekeeping operations. Policing is understood as control measures that shift into preliminary or holding measures until responsibility can be handed over to a police, and is often spoken of as a security gap. This term came to prominence with the publication in 1998 of the Washington-based National Defense University's *Policing the New World Disorder* (Oakley *et al.* 1998: 8–15). Prompted by the US experience in Somalia and the Balkans, the term offers a conceptual tool for analysing developments during, for example, the early weeks of the Iraq insurgency when local police forces proved incapable of providing law and order, US military forces were neither trained nor equipped to do so, and the international gendarmerie forces capable of operating in such an environment were few in number.

As this implies, the police role in counterinsurgency is invariably analysed in terms of Anglo-American beliefs about what police should do, or are supposed to be, and what forms of social control are appropriate: there are few if any systematic and rigorous analyses of the role and perspectives of the indigenous police from which so much is expected. To paraphrase the anthropologist Marshall Sahlins, we do not know how 'natives' think (Sahlins 1995).

The foundations for a better understanding exist, but are as yet undeveloped. Findlay and Zvekić's 1993 analysis of alternative policing styles is suggestive of the possibilities, though it does not address counterinsurgency as such. For it argues that policing is best approached as a process of interaction of interests and powers within a specific environment: 'the particular interactions of interest, power and authority which distinguish the structures and functions of police work should be viewed as constructed around expectations of policing within a given cultural, political and situational context' (Findlay and Zvekić 1993: 6). Their work emphasises the localised and specific nature of police, policing and security in such a way as to challenge conventional priorities such as crime prevention (counterinsurgency related policing tends to be specific whereas crime control is more diffuse). But for now, knowledge of policing and the police in counterinsurgency is partial in both senses of the word.

Current debates

Current debate is shaped by the uneven record of US-led counterinsurgency operations in Iraq and Afghanistan. It relates to the question of who should provide policing, but focuses on police reform as a solution to operational and strategic challenges, and is judged in relation to military and political requirements. Two issues have broad relevance.

Types of police and policing

Counterinsurgency is a violent and brutal business, and policing in counterinsurgency is not the same as peacetime policing. Even so, international policy-makers expect military and police to perform miracles. In 2003, for example, the British troops who took Basra were expected to fill the gap left by the 16,000 Iraqi policemen who had formerly kept order in the city. Three years later, a 24-strong team of British police advisers, supported by 70 civilian private security staff employed by Armor Holdings, were expected to reform and/or train Basra's increasingly sectarian police forces even though their influence over them was negligible. The question therefore arises as to the type of police that can – or should – provide policing, what its relationship with military forces should be, and at what point police should take responsibility for local security. Police and military roles are widely seen as separate and distinct, and it is generally agreed that police should not be used (as has been the case in Afghanistan) as 'little soldiers'. The point at which transition should take place – and the skills required to handle it – is a matter for professional judgement, but also it is politically critical for governments wishing to drawdown troops. The timing of handovers is therefore the subject of debate.

Militaries are used for policing in multinational counterinsurgency operations because they are present, capable and well-resourced whereas police (international and indigenous) are absent, under-resourced, ineffective or sectarian. Perhaps for this reason, a military's choice of policing activities is selective. Depending on their remit, policing ranges from high-profile 'arrests' of war criminals to providing police with specialised weapons training. In between are house-to-house searches conducted in order to seize weapons, capture suspects, create a security cordon, and support or monitor local forces. Identification and intelligence are key objectives. Overall, the military approach to policing is shaped by specific problems, vested interests and fears of mission creep. Troops are not trained, equipped or recruited to police, and their response to disorder tends to involve dispersal or repression. That an intermediate stage between the two often arises adds a layer of ambiguity.

The critical variable affecting the type of police and the style of policing employed is the level of violence in the locality concerned. Combat troops were used in the early days of the Iraq insurgency, but there were never enough of them to police big cities, they were not trained for such work, they often used inappropriate tactics, and their reliance on technology intensified, rather than alleviated, the problems presented by operating in the midst of a population (Hills 2010: 45). Civilian police cannot operate in such circumstances, so the choice appears to be that either combat troops provide policing when there is no alternative, or that they (or other troops) are organised with policing duties in mind, or that some type of paramilitary force specialising in this work should be developed. A number of options were discussed at the time.

One possibility entailed the creation of a designated force that could carry out security missions, operating within the body of combat troops. Standing paramilitary forces such as Carabinieri and Gendarmerie Nationale, which share the characteristics of military and police, offer one model. They can fight as light infantry, but also they are trained as police and equipped to maintain public order, conduct investigations, make arrests and direct traffic. They can deploy quickly and were used successfully in the Balkans in the form of Multinational Specialised Units (MSU) and Special Police Units (SPUs). The UN's formed police units (FPUs) are another possibility. Indeed, the first all-female Indian FPU in Liberia in 2007 had seen service in Kashmir. Even the UK military favoured a Carabinieri-style police for Basra, as did Paul Kernaghan, the international policing representative to the UK's Association of Chief Police Officers, who argued that in order to police a locality police needed to be able to protect themselves; only then could they protect the populace (Kernaghan 2010a: 22). Other British advisers disagreed, however, and their views proved more influential (e.g. Smith 2010b: 15–17).

In fact, the discussion prompted by Iraq was merely the latest iteration of a long-running debate, which had, for example, been strong in US defence circles in the aftermath of the 1989 invasion of Panama as practitioners and analysts sought to share the policing task, or to shift it to organisations other than the US Army (e.g. Beaumont 1995; Field and Perito 2002; RAND 2008). But Iraq introduced a further tension as the United States' increasing reliance on commercial contractors led to companies such as DynCorp International providing the officers needed for police training. US domestic police structures mean that Washington has little choice to using contractors, but the costs are high, and the value of sending US officers from small towns to teach handcuffing and traffic duties to ANP recruits working in war zones is controversial (DOD 2010).

Police reform

Western counterinsurgency operations are currently predicated on protecting the populace; i.e. on providing local security in order to win the acquiescence or toleration of the host population – which includes policemen and their families and neighbours. Achieving this will, it is argued, allow international forces to exit. It is also thought to require the creation of a relatively reliable, effective and incorrupt police. In other words, successful counterinsurgency depends to some extent on police reform. But police reform is notoriously problematic (and expensive) even in benign circumstances. Not only is the police institution superbly resistant to change, but also officers live and work alone in their home neighbourhoods, and are susceptible to intimidation by local power brokers and sectarian interests. Most are notoriously ineffective, untrained, corrupt or brutal, and must therefore be trained, equipped and persuaded or coerced into adopting practices less likely to alienate local people. This is thought necessary because a second international goal is to enhance the legitimacy of not only the police, but also the governments concerned. In the Iraqi city of Tal Afar, for example, reform involved recruiting officers from a broader range of residents. They were then trained in a police academy (US forces and the Iraqi Army also trained police in military skills). Corrupt or brutal police were dismissed or prosecuted by the local and provincial government, and new senior officers from outside the locality were appointed (US Army Field Manual 3–24 2010: 5–23). But this picture glosses over the superficial and temporary nature of such projects.

Police reform is arguably the most significant – and intractable – of current debates because it raises fundamental questions about not only the West's understanding of policing realities in countries such as Iraq and Afghanistan, but also its comprehension of the dynamics underpinning counterinsurgency. Given several years, it is usually possible to retrain or reconstruct a police such as the ANP, but the chances of reforming it on democratic lines are minimal, especially when reform is not in the interests of the indigenous government. Counterinsurgency based on the utility of indigenous police and policing is for such reasons problematic. That there appears to be no real alternative makes the challenges even more pressing. Hence, perhaps, the banner Colin Smith saw when he attended the launch of '2006 – Year of the Police' at Baghdad Police College: 'Just enough is good enough' (Smith 2010a: 4–5). As he comments, this was, while realistic, 'not particularly encouraging'.

Challenges and pressing questions

The functional challenges associated with developing suitable local forces relate to resources, leadership, exercising power and organisational structures (US Army Field Manual 3–24 2009: Chapter 6), but those associated with comprehension are equally demanding.

The reality behind FM 3–24's headings is evident from Mark Etherington's account of his time as head of a small Coalition Political Authority (CPA) team in al-Kut, a provincial capital to the southeast of Baghdad. On arrival he found:

> Police clustered in small groups on the steps of their stations and nearby fences like crows. There appeared to be thousands of them, in almost comical disarray. The police had no infrastructure, rules, leadership or staff worth the name; most had no weapons and few officers appeared to do any work though it was clear that many were directly implicated in widespread and systematic corruption if not criminal activity.
>
> *(Etherington 2005: 27)*

Addressing this situation was problematic because equipment and clothing were distributed according to status and hierarchy, and morale was undermined by fears of retribution, assassination and mutiny (Etherington 2005: 217, 288). Later, the police in al-Kut sought protection by joining sectarian militia, just as they did in cities such as Basra. Those that did not hid behind the blast walls of the stations in which they were besieged. But this was understandable, as the case of Kirkuk in 2009 showed: 'The police chief had survived several assassination attempts, but since 2004, 680 police men had been killed in action in and around Kirkuk, with more than twice that number seriously injured' (*FT Magazine*, 13–14 June 2009). There was no possibility of developing the police intelligence capacity (i.e. special branch) that received wisdom recommends.

There is nothing novel or unexpected about this situation, yet the knowledge and experience associated with it has yet to be integrated into a coherent or inclusive understanding. Regarding comprehension, three points are noteworthy.

First, although the notion of an international consensus is promoted by IGOs such as the UN, and seemingly evidenced by the influence US doctrine and practice exerts on governments and security forces around the world, this actually reflects the tendency of Western policymakers, practitioners and scholars to universalise on the basis of specific cases while neglecting the social and political conditions that make them possible; contextual realities are neglected, as is the logic of practice embedded within them. This is notably so with counterinsurgency strategies reliant on a reformed police. Hence Stewart's observation from his time as a governorate co-ordinator in Iraq in 2003 that too many international police advisers fail to question the transferability of their usual practices (Stewart 2007: 87).

Assessing accurately the potential contribution of local police is a major challenge. Not only has southern police culture yet to be analysed, but also the gulf between international expectations and local realities is deepened by the extent to which international assessment teams draw on previous operational experience, and are subject to political pressure. For example, in the summer of 2003, Coalition advisers in Iraq based their plans for policing on what had worked in Kosovo and Haiti, where restructuring had been part of a stabilisation programme. Their goal was to recruit, train and equip primarily in order to increase police numbers. But judging success by the numbers of recruits usually results in the recruitment of unfit, illiterate or inappropriate individuals, thereby undermining the aim of establishing a professional police. Further, the programme's 18-month timeframe was dictated by the timing of the 2004 US presidential elections, and by military pressure, for the military could not withdraw from policing operations until the number of police was considered sufficient for local control (Brand 2010b).

Second, the operational challenges of counterinsurgency are pressing, but the need for strategic clarity is even more so. And it is usually missing, as is analytical clarity.

International forces must to strike a balance between the short-term needs of conducting COIN effectively and the long-term goal of establishing a sustainable police reflecting Western norms and procedures, but the two tend to be conflated. Confusion is then made worse by failure to develop a policing strategy. As Paul Kernaghan told the Chilcott Enquiry, there were plans for policing (though they usually proved incapable of responding to changes in the operational environment), but there was no 'clear, comprehensive, realistic strategic plan in Iraq' (Kernaghan 2010b: 4). Further, training projects were often mistaken for a strategy, with Coalition authorities judging success according to quantitative measures that were all too often meaningless. As General Martin Dempsey told the US House Armed Services Committee in 2007, more than 32,000 of Iraq's 188,000 police officers in the IPS (the largest Ministry of Interior force, with a presence in every province and district) were no longer working as police; 8–10,000 had been killed in action, 6–8,000 had been wounded, and some 5,000 had deserted. But

7–8,000 were unaccounted for, and he did not know how many had joined the insurgents (*JDW*, 20 June 2007: 5).

Third, despite the rhetoric attributing value to police and policing, international and local militaries alike regard policing – and police – as in some way inferior, and this is reflected in the political attention and resources policing receives. Just as Massu's paratroopers hated policing Algiers because it was a 'flic's job', so US Marines or British Army troops see their job as fighting, rather than collecting evidence or investigating kidnappings. This can affect the levels of security, logistical support, travel and accommodation offered to police officers who cannot operate without the support or protection of their military colleagues. The situation is made worse by the difficulty of recruiting good international officers (the numbers of those that volunteer is small) and technically proficient indigenous officers capable of providing leadership.

Police forces are, despite their enabling role, of secondary status, and military concerns take priority. This may reflect the degree of insecurity prevailing, or it may be more the result of institutional rivalry. In Iraq in 2003, for example, UK attempts to develop a strategic aim delivering 'an efficient, effective, credible and community-based, accountable police service' were quickly subsumed into military operational and logistic plans capable of dealing with the burgeoning insurgency. But status also reflects the small numbers of police advisers as compared to military forces. In practice, 'he who pays the piper calls the tune' (Smith 2010a: 4), and in Iraq this was the US military. Similar considerations apply to the relationship between local police and local militaries, which is easily upset by international interventions.

Significantly, the secondary status of police is mirrored in the academy where, with the exception of police studies (which has yet to address police in the context of COIN systematically), and international peacekeeping (which focuses on UNPOL and SSR), the police role is neglected. Counterinsurgency is emerging from military history to become an aspect of critical security studies (e.g. Bell and Evans 2010), but police and policing remains on the penumbra of conventional security studies.

Conclusions

There is an international consensus that police can play an enabling role in counterinsurgency, but the nature and purpose of their role is debated. Authoritarian regimes use paramilitary police to support military forces in internal security operations, while the United States and its allies (and IGOs such as the UN, NATO and EU) provide international police advisers to reform, mentor and/or train indigenous police on the basis that they can provide the local security required to win the support of the populace, enhance the legitimacy of the host government, and facilitate the exit of international militaries. Some commentators go even further, arguing that 'a well-trained, professional police force dedicated to upholding the rule of law and trusted by the population is essential to fighting … insurgency … and creating stability' (Thruelsen 2010: 80).

Despite decades of experience to the contrary, most Western policy-makers, advisers and scholars assume that local police culture and practice can be manipulated to accommodate international goals. The development of realistic plans for using police in counterinsurgency is accordingly rare. Most international campaigns are conducted without a clear police strategy – training is not a strategy – and are based on aspiration and the lack of viable alternatives, rather than policing realities. Not only are police in many countries predatory, but even where Western (and Westphalian) models are accepted, multiple tensions underpin the police role. Thus the use of local police can ensure the local security essential for strategically successful counterinsurgency, or it can trap local people, forcing them to take sides and risk punishment. The desirability of using indigenous police to provide local security is taken for granted, yet their role is typically limited by corruption, brutality, ineffectiveness and sectarianism, and by the knowledge that international counterinsurgency forces will leave. Similarly, local police are well-placed to gain the intelligence at the heart of efficient counterinsurgency, yet intelligence gathering is all too often influenced by the police's need to satisfy local power brokers or the government of the day. There is often no alternative to using police, but their potential is rarely assessed accurately; poorly paid and inadequately trained men in battered trucks cannot contain an insurgency.

Recommended readings

NB There are no texts rigorously and systematically analysing police and policing in COIN. Further, most contemporary texts address the topic primarily in the light of current US policy challenges.

Bayley, D. and Perito, R. (2010) *The Police at War*. Boulder: Lynne Rienner.

Hodes, C. and Sedra, M. (2007) *The Search for Security in Post-Taliban Afghanistan*, Adelphi Paper 391. Oxford: Oxford University Press.

Iraq Enquiry (2010) See the testimony and statements from Brand, Kernaghan and Smith. Available at: www.iraqinquiry.org.uk/transcripts/writtenevidence-bydate.aspx.

Kilcullen, D. (2009) *The Accidental Guerrilla: Fighting Small Wars in the Midst of a Big One*. London: Hurst.

Ucko, D. (2010) 'Lessons from Basra: The Future of British Counterinsurgency', *Survival*, 52 (4): 131–58.

References

Australian (2007) 'Police Targeted in Iraqi Blasts'.

Bayley, D. (ed.) (1977) *Police and Society*. London: Sage.

Bayley, D. and Perito, R. (2010) *The Police at War*. Boulder: Lynne Rienner.

Beaumont, R. (1995) 'Constabulary or Fire Brigade? The Army National Guard', *Parameters*, XXV (Summer): 73–81.

Bell, C. and Evans, B. (2010) 'From Terrorism to Insurgency: Re-mapping the Post-Interventionary Security Terrain', *Journal of Intervention and Statebuilding*, 4 (4) Forthcoming.

Blaufarb, D. (1977) *The Counterinsurgency Era: U.S. Doctrine and Performance, 1950 to the Present*. New York: Free Press.

Bøås, M. and Dunn, K. (eds) (2007) *African Guerrillas: Raging Against the Machine*. Boulder: Lynne Rienner.

Brand, D. (2010a) 'Transcript of Douglas Brand OBE Hearing. Iraq Enquiry', 29 June. Available at: www.iraqinquiry.org.uk/media/46386/20100629am-brand.pdf.

Brand, D. (2010b) 'Statement by Deputy Chief Constable (retired) Douglas Brand OBE, UK Chief Police Adviser to the Ministry of Interior, Baghdad, 2003–4', 29 June. Available at: www.iraqinquiry.org.uk/media/46150/brand-statement-final.pdf.

Department of Defense Office of Inspector General (2010) *DOD Obligations and Expenditures of Funds Provided to the Department of State for the Training and Mentoring of the Afghan National Police*. Available at: www.dodig.mil/audit/reports/fy10/10–042.pdf.

Etherington, M. (2005) *Revolt on the Tigris: The Al-Sadr Uprising and the Governing of Iraq*. London: Hurst.

Field, K. and Perito, R. (2002–3) 'Creating a Force for Peace Operations: Ensuring Stability with Justice', *Parameters*, XXX (11): 77–87.

Financial Times (2010) 'India Rebel Attack Kills 74 Police'.

Findlay, M. and Zvekić, U. (eds) (1993) *Alternative Policing Styles: Cross-Cultural Perspectives*. Deventer: UNICRI and Kluwer.

FT Magazine (2009) '"Manhunt": How can Poor Local Police Solve the Problems?'.

Gompert, D., Gordon, J. *et al.* (2008) *War by Other Means: Building Complete and Balanced Capabilities for Counterinsurgency*. Washington, DC: RAND.

Hills, A. (2010) *Policing Post-conflict Cities*. London: Zed.

Hodes, C. and Sedra, M. (2007) *The Search for Security in Post-Taliban Afghanistan*, Adelphi Paper 391. Oxford: Oxford University Press.

Horne, A. (1977) *A Savage War of Peace: Algeria, 1954–1962*. London: Macmillan.

Jane's Defence Weekly (JDW) (2007) 'US General Warns on Leadership Shortage for Iraqi Security Forces'.

JDW (2010) 'Afghan Sitrep', pp. 20–7.

Kernaghan, P. (2010a) 'Paul Kernaghan Transcript', 23 July. Available at: www.iraqinquiry.org.uk/media/48590/20100723am-kernaghan.pdf.

Kernaghan, P. (2010b) 'Statement by Chief Constable (retired) Paul Kernaghan', 23 July. Available at: www.iraqinquiry.org.uk/media/46162/kernaghan-statement-final.pdf.

Kilcullen, D. (2009) *The Accidental Guerrilla: Fighting Small Wars in the Midst of a Big One*. London: Hurst.

Meharg, S., Arnusch, A. and Merrill, S. (2009) *Security Sector Reform: A Case Study Approach to Transition and Capacity Building*. Carlisle, PA: Strategic Studies Institute. Available at: www.strategicstudiesinstitute.army.mil/pubs/display.cfm?pubID=960.

Neocleous, M. (2000) *The Fabrication of Social Order: A Critical Theory of Police Power*. London: Pluto.

New York Times (2006) '2,000 More MPs Will Help Train the Iraqi Police'.

Oakley, R., Dziedzic. M. and Goldberg, E. (1998) *Policing the New World Disorder: Peace Operations and Public Security*. Washington, DC: National Defense University.

O'Neill, M., Marks, M. and Singh, A.-M. (eds) (2007) *Police Occupational Culture: New Debates and Directions*. Oxford: Elsevier.

Sahlins, M. (1995) *How 'Natives' Think: About Captain Cook, for Example*. Chicago: University of Chicago Press.

Smith, C. (2010a) 'Statement of Colin FW Smith QPM, Assistant Chief Constable (Ret'd) to the Iraq Inquiry', 21 July. Available at: www.iraqinquiry.org.uk/media/46534/smith-statement.pdf.

Smith, C. (2010b) 'Colin Smith Transcript', 21 July. Available at: www.iraqinquiry.org.uk/media/49232/20100721-smith-final.pdf.

Special Inspector General For Afghanistan Reconstruction (2010) *Quarterly Report to the United States Congress, April*. Available at: www.humansecuritygateway.com/documents/SIGAR_QuarterlyReport_30April2010.pdf.

Stewart, R. (2007) *Occupational Hazards*. London: Picador.

Thompson, R. (1966) *Defeating Communist Insurgency: Experiences from Malaya and Vietnam*. London: Chatto & Windus.

Thruelsen, P. (2010) 'Striking the Right Balance: How to Rebuild the Afghan National Police', *International Peacekeeping*, 17 (1): 80–92.

US Army Field Manual 3–07 (2008) *Stability Operations*. Available at: http://usacac.army.mil/cac2/repository/FM307/FM3–07.pdf.

US Army Field Manual 3–24/MCWP 3–33.5 (2006) *Counter Insurgency*. Available at: www.fas.org/irp/doddir/army/fm3–24.pdf.

Williams, P. (2009) *Criminals, Militias, and Insurgents: Organized Crime in Iraq*. Carlisle, PA: Strategic Studies Institute. Available at: www.strategicstudiesinstitute.army.mil/pubs/display.cfm?pubID=930.

9

INTELLIGENCE-GATHERING, SPECIAL OPERATIONS AND AIR STRIKES IN MODERN COUNTERINSURGENCY[1]

Geraint Hughes

> Getting government forces into the same element as the insurgent is rather like trying to deal with a tomcat in an alley. It is no good inserting a large, fierce dog. The dog may not find the tomcat; if he does, the tomcat will escape up a tree; the dog will then chase the female cats in the alley. The answer is to put in a fiercer tomcat. The two cannot fail to meet because they are both in exactly the same element and have exactly the same purpose in life. The weaker will be eliminated.
>
> *(Thompson 1972: 119–20)*

On the night of 1 May 2011, four helicopters containing a task force of SEAL (US Navy special forces) commandos flew from Afghanistan to raid a compound in the Pakistani city of Abbottabad, 71 miles from the capital, Islamabad. At around 1 a.m. on the morning of 2 May the raiders stormed their target, killing the leader of al-Qaeda, Osama bin Laden. The outcome of the raid was hailed by US President Barack Obama as a major success, as the individual responsible for authorising 9/11 and other terrorist atrocities worldwide had finally been eliminated. But bin Laden's death has also been a source of controversy, concerning not only the legitimacy of what critics term an extra-judicial killing, but also the question of whether the Pakistani authorities knew that the founder and former leader of al-Qaeda was hiding in a city that houses their own military academy, and which also is a popular residence for senior military and security force personnel (Drehle 2011; *The Economist* 2011b).

The opening quote from Sir Robert Thompson's *Defeating Communist Insurgency* alludes to three important points relevant to any state, or coalition of states, involved in counterinsurgency (COIN) and counter-terrorism. The first is that regular armed forces configured for combat against equivalent formations from adversarial states are at a disadvantage in internal wars, where insurgents and terrorists mingle with the civilian population. The second is that military and security forces involved in such conflicts – whether at home or in an intervention operation overseas – require accurate intelligence on their enemies in order to combat them effectively (Kitson 1991: 95–6). The third, which is of particular importance for liberal democracies, is to ensure that irregular adversaries should be fought in a manner that minimises civilian casualties, as the killing and maiming of non-combatants is not only ethically abhorrent but politically counterproductive (Sheehan 1990: 317). This chapter will be mainly concerned with the second of Thompson's points, namely intelligence in relation to the successful prosecution of COIN although the discussion will also focus on the use of special forces and air strikes by counterinsurgent forces

Theorists and practitioners of COIN debate the respective merits of *enemy-* and *population-centric* approaches. In the former, the state focuses on the physical destruction of insurgents and terrorists, while in the latter the government side concentrates on protecting the population against violence and alleviating the political and socio-economic grievances which its adversaries have exploited (Kilcullen 2009: 180–1; US Army/USMC 2007: 41). However, efforts to persuade insurgents to lay down their arms or change sides have their limits, as in successive campaigns ending in a government victory a hard-core of the state's adversaries has fought to the bitter end, requiring government forces to eliminate, capture or expel them (Hughes 2009: 274–5, 285–6). As this chapter shows, there are both practical and normative problems inherent in both the generation of human intelligence (HUMINT) on an adversary, and the use of special forces and air power to combat insurgents.

Methodological challenges

The principal problem for any researcher working in this aspect of COIN is official secrecy. With exceptions such as Operation Neptune Spear (the killing of bin Laden), even democratic governments are loath to disclose information on the operations of their intelligence services and elite military units (Hughes 2010: 564). To complicate matters, insurgents and their sympathisers can accuse their enemies of carrying out 'false-flag' attacks. Such claims can be made to provide alibis for acts of violence which kill or maim large numbers of civilians, and can also be used to undermine the government's reputation amongst its citizens (Barclay 2010: 21–2; Wright 2010: 15).

A further methodological issue concerns the superficial glamour attached to elite units. In Britain's case, the mystique surrounding 22SAS can be seen in the popularity of memoirs written by veterans such as 'Andy McNab' and Chris Ryan. Units like 22SAS are also guaranteed media coverage and also interest from authors keen to publicise – if not glamorise – its exploits (Urban 2010). An added problem is the tendency of fantasists to produce spurious accounts which acquire a veneer of credibility thanks to gullible journalists or publishers. A prime example is that of the fake SAS veteran 'Paul Bruce', who published a bogus account of his activities in a British Army death squad in Northern Ireland in 1996 (Hughes 2010: 564–5).

Special forces operations in COIN

From both a historical and a contemporary perspective these can be subdivided into the following categories:

- plain-clothes operations to gather HUMINT;
- the targeted killing of key individuals within an insurgent/terrorist group;
- pre-emptive intervention missions;
- the organisation of indigenous counter-gangs and pseudo-gangs;
- irregular warfare against non-state adversaries.

In several COIN campaigns specialised military units have undertaken clandestine patrolling missions disguised as civilians, in order to track their adversaries, and to locate safe-houses, weapons caches, hideouts and other parts of an insurgency's support structure. The British Army raised such formations on an ad hoc basis in Palestine (1945–7), Aden (1962–7) and Northern Ireland (1969–98), and the Special Reconnaissance Regiment (SRR) has its origins in 14 Intelligence Company, which was established in January 1973 to provide British forces in Ulster with an undercover surveillance capability. Around five years later the British established the Force Research Unit (FRU) to operate in Northern Ireland, and its operatives recruited agents within both Republican and Loyalist terrorist groups (Hughes 2010: 565–6, 571–9). The work of the FRU remains a source of intense controversy. Depending upon which account of its operations one relies on, it either saved untold numbers of lives by infiltrating terrorist organisations and thwarting several of their plots, or it was complicit in a 'dirty war' in which civilians were callously sacrificed by the British Army (Ingram and Harkin 2004; Lewis 1999).

Other armed forces have established similar formations. The US Army founded the Intelligence Support Activity (ISA) in 1980 (Richelson 1999), while the French, Turkish and Indian militaries have also used plain-clothes squads to gather HUMINT in (respectively) Algeria in 1961–2, Turkish Kurdistan and Kashmir (Hughes 2010: 566). In the second case the clandestine intelligence unit of the Turkish gendarmerie (JITEM) went rogue, and its members were not only involved in running death squads against the PKK, but were also suspected of involvement in arms and drug trafficking (Jenkins 2008).

Targeted killing missions have been conducted by the Israeli Defence Forces (IDF) against its Palestinian adversaries since the early 1950s, when the IDF launched punitive raids into Egypt in response to *fedayeen* attacks against Israel. Since the outbreak of the second *intifada* in October 2000, the IDF have used uniformed and plain-clothes (*Mista-Aravim*) troops to eliminate cadres from Hamas, Islamic Jihad and other Palestinian groups in the Gaza Strip and West Bank. These are combined with air strikes (one of which killed Hamas' founder, Sheikh Ahmed Yassin, on 22 March 2004), and Mossad operations to assassinate terrorists in third countries, as demonstrated by the killing of Mahmoud al-Mabhouh in Dubai on 20 January 2010 (David 2010; Giladi 2010; Jones 2010: 126–43).

Pre-emptive intervention missions are theoretically distinct from target killings, as the declared objective of the governments and armed forces concerned is to capture suspected insurgents and terrorists if possible, and also to thwart atrocities while they are still being planned. Such missions may actually end with special forces operatives killing their adversaries, while the Israelis assert that their targeted killings save civilian lives by disrupting planned Palestinian attacks. Furthermore, insurgents and their sympathisers can claim that the government is operating a 'shoot-to-kill' policy, as Sinn Fein (the political wing of the Provisional IRA) did whenever Republican terrorists were shot dead by either the British Army or the Royal Ulster Constabulary (Taylor 2002: 270–85). As insurgent violence and sectarian killings intensified in Iraq after 2004–5, Coalition special forces attached to Task Force 145 conducted a series of 'kill or capture' missions directed against al-Qaeda in Iraq (AQI) and other insurgent groups in Baghdad and across the country. General David Petraeus, the commander of Coalition forces in Iraq in 2007–8, later described the activity of the US Delta Force, 22SAS and other elite formations as a vital complement to the 'surge' of regular US military forces which took place during his tenure of command (Hastings 2010; Rayment 2008; Smith 2007).

Elite military units have also raised 'counter' and 'pseudo-gangs' in a series of COIN conflicts. The former consist of a mixture of military personnel and locally-recruited fighters, who can include ex-insurgents who have been 'turned' (persuaded or coerced into changing sides). Examples include the Special Night Squads during the Arab revolt in Palestine (1937–9, consisting of British soldiers and Jewish volunteers), Kikuyu gangs run by the British Army and the colonial police in Kenya to fight the Mau Mau (1952–7), the 'Q-patrols' raised by the British against EOKA in Cyprus (1955–9) the *flechas* recruited by the Portuguese during their war in

Angola (1961–74), and the Provisional Reconnaissance Units operating with the US military and CIA in South Vietnam (from 1969 to 1972). Pseudo-gangs are formations that pose as insurgents in a long-term deception role, to either infiltrate an insurgency or to commit false-flag atrocities intended to sow discord within its ranks and discredit its cause. Due to their inherently covert nature, firm evidence of pseudo-gang activity is hard to acquire, yet it is evident that the Soviets employed them in a series of COIN campaigns from the Baltic States and Ukraine in the late 1940s to Afghanistan during the 1980s, where the KGB and its Afghan counterpart (KHAD) used fake *mujahidin* groups to exacerbate inter-mural feuds within the resistance. The Selous Scouts run by the Rhodesian military and security services between 1973 and 1979 are another notorious example. Pseudo-operations are not only ethically abhorrent, but they have also undermined the legal foundations of the state which use them, fulfilling the insurgent's objective of discrediting the government's cause (Melshen 1995; Hughes and Tripodi 2009: 16–22).

Finally, special forces units can fight insurgents and other irregular formations by leading or supporting equivalent indigenous forces in combat against them. During the latter phase of the Dhofar war in Oman (June 1970 to December 1975) teams from 22SAS raised local tribal militias, known as *firqat* forces, against the Marxist-Leninist PFLOAG (Jeapes 2005). In Afghanistan during the first three months of Operation Enduring Freedom US and other Coalition elite units coordinated the Northern Alliance and other anti-Taliban forces in their operations against al-Qaeda and Mullah Omar's regime (Finlan 2003: 92–108). However, with the revival of the Taliban insurgency in Afghanistan from 2005 onwards (Chin 2007: 216–18), American and allied special forces are now concentrating on missions aimed at decapitating the insurgency's leadership, which are similar in character to those Task Force 145 conducted against AQI (Grey 2010).

Precision air strikes

Since their adoption in warfare during the 1910s, aircraft have been continually employed by states fighting insurgents, providing close air support to ground forces, bombing and strafing suspected base areas and supply routes, transporting troops and supplies, and also providing what Western militaries currently call ISTAR – Intelligence, Surveillance, Target Acquisition and Reconnaissance (Corum and Johnson 2003). For Third World states involved in COIN campaigns ISTAR assets are often lacking in indigenous militaries, and Western states can often fill this capability gap for host-nation air forces (Marshall 2007: 78). Air power can have a devastating effect upon insurgents, particularly if the latter confronts their foes on terms favourable to the latter, as the Taliban did in a series of pitched battles against NATO forces in southern Afghanistan in 2005–6. However, in repeated conflicts air strikes have also aroused hostility from the local populace towards the government and its external supporters, because of the casualties that usually ensue. In Afghanistan since 2001 Coalition air attacks have repeated killed substantial numbers of civilians, one example being a strike on two hijacked fuel tankers near Kunduz on 4 September 2009 which left 142 dead, causing national outrage and protests from Hamid Karzai's government (Pritchard and Smith 2010: 72, 81; Girard 2009).

Technological advantages such as the introduction of precision-guided munitions (PGMs) in 1972 and subsequently Unmanned Aerial Vehicles (UAVs) have given Western militaries an enhanced ability both to gather intelligence and to strike insurgent targets with greater accuracy. Examples include the killing of the AQI leader Abu Musab al-Zarqawi in a US air raid on 7 June 2006 (Bowden 2007), the Israeli Air Force's (IAF) destruction of a convoy carrying the Hezbollah leader Sheikh Abas Musavi in southern Lebanon in February 1992 (Corum and

Johnson 2003: 414), and a suspected IAF strike against an arms caravan in Sudan in March 2009, reportedly carrying weapons from Iran to Hamas (*The Economist* 2009). Other states have also conducted similar attacks. During the first war in Chechnya (December 1994 to September 1996) the Chechen leader General Dzhokhar Dudayev met his death in a Russian air strike on 21 April 1996 – Russian signals intelligence (SIGINT) apparently acquired Dudayev's satellite phone signal, and an SU25 ground-attack jet fired a homing missile which killed him alongside members of his entourage (German 2003: 145). The Colombian armed forces have managed to eliminate senior FARC commanders through air strikes; notably Raul Reyes in late February 2008, and Mono Jojoy on 22 September 2010 (Waisberg 2009: 476; *The Economist* 2010). The success of such precision air strikes depends in all cases on accurate intelligence, whether from SIGINT, ISTAR, or from tip-offs provided either by informants amongst the civilian population or agents recruited within the insurgency. It is therefore unsurprising that insurgents and terrorists are demoralised by any indication that they have spies within their midst, and even a hint of treachery can often set off a debilitating 'mole-hunt', as was the case with the Abu Nidal organisation during the late 1980s (Freedman 2006: 90–1).

On 21 August 1998 the United States launched cruise missiles against terrorist training camps in Taliban-ruled Afghanistan (Operation Infinite Reach), in retaliation for al-Qaeda's bomb attacks against the US embassies in Nairobi and Dar-es-Salaam. Infinite Reach achieved modest results, and was interpreted both by officials in Washington and al-Qaeda propagandists as a pin-prick (Benjamin and Simon 2003: 153, 261; Clarke 2004: 190). The problem with cruise missiles launched from naval vessels (both surface ships and submarines) was that once 'actionable intelligence' on the location of bin Laden and other senior al-Qaeda figures was acquired, policy-makers in Washington DC authorised an attack, and the US Navy prepared its Tomahawks for firing, the opportunity to strike them had passed. The *Predator* UAVs developed jointly by the US Air Force (USAF) and the CIA since the mid 1990s offered a better option for policy-makers; unmanned drones could loiter over their targets while transmitting 'real-time' intelligence on their location. After 9/11 the CIA and USAF accelerated their efforts to introduce the larger *Predator-B* (subsequently dubbed *Reaper*) into service. *Reaper* can carry PGMs, including a *Hellfire* air-to-ground missile or a *Paveway* laser-guided bomb. Press reports state that the CIA runs UAV strikes in Pakistan, while the USAF is in charge of drone operations over Afghanistan and Iraq. However, *Reaper*'s limited payload means that manned jets and helicopters have been tasked to hit insurgent targets picked up by UAV sensors; in 2007 and 2008 *Reaper* flew 10,949 missions over Afghan and Iraqi air space, but was only directly involved in 244 attacks (Coll 2005: 445–7, 527–36, 548–9, 581; Drew 2009).

Implications

Political leaders and scholars alike may regard the methods described above as a means of achieving an immediate and decisive effect against an irregular adversary. Such thinking is evident with the current US Vice-President, Joseph Biden, and American analysts such as Andrew Bacevich, Edward Luttwak and Austin Long, all of whom favour a 'counter-terrorist strategy' in Afghanistan as an alternative to the troop reinforcements President Barack Obama ordered in December 2009. The 'counter-terrorist' approach abandons any efforts at nation-building, and advocates a campaign of attrition against the Taliban and al-Qaeda, using UAVs, special forces and air strikes, and local proxies (Boyle 2010: 335; Long 2010; Luttwak 2010). Yet the activities discussed in this chapter all have potentially negative consequences which can undermine any campaign – unilateral or multilateral – to defeat an insurgency.

One consequence of 9/11 was an increase in the US Department of Defense's capacity to conduct covert operations, defined by US law as actions intended 'to influence political, economic, or military conditions abroad, where it is intended that the role of the United States Government will not be apparent or acknowledged publicly' (Kibbe 2010: 569). The then-Secretary of Defense Donald Rumsfeld made Special Operations Command (SOCOM) a 'supported command', which gave it the capacity to plan its own missions, and after the spring of 2004 President George W. Bush gave SOCOM the task of attacking al-Qaeda across the globe, being given free rein to conduct missions in Yemen, Pakistan, Syria, Somalia and other states with which the United States was formally at peace. The potential diplomatic implications of this decision were demonstrated after one American raid across the Afghan-Pakistan border into South Waziristan on 3 September 2008. This incursion caused a furious reaction in Pakistan, leading its Chief of the General Staff to assert that his forces would defend their country's sovereignty 'at all costs' (Kibbe 2010: 569, 578–81; Pantucci 2009: 73). Prior to May 2011, the United States avoided special forces raids into Pakistan, and the operation to kill bin Laden was greeted with ill-disguised fury by the country's military elite. For its part, the Obama administration did not give the Pakistanis advance notification of Neptune Spear, and it is clear that US officials implicitly suspect that elements within Pakistan's military and intelligence service (the ISI) were complicit in sheltering the al-Qaeda leader (*The Economist* 2011a; Wright 2011).

A further criticism is that SOCOM's personnel are ill-employed in 'hunter-killer' missions to arrest or eliminate insurgents and terrorists (whether in Iraq, Afghanistan, Pakistan, Somalia or Yemen), and should be employed in their traditional tasks in COIN. These include training host-nation security forces, civil affairs (or 'hearts and minds') work to improve the socio-economic conditions of indigenous societies, and also mediation both with and between local political and tribal leaders. These activities arguably do more to bolster a host-nation government and to stabilise a weak state beset by insurgency than anti-terrorist 'man-hunts' (Kibbe 2010: 589; Kilcullen 2009: 299).

One contentious question concerns the efficacy of 'decapitation', of defeating an insurgency by eliminating its leaders. In October 2010 NATO officials claimed that the Taliban had been weakened by a series of air strikes and ground operations across southern Afghanistan, which have killed key commanders and left the movement as a whole on the verge of collapse (Kilcullen 2010; Loyd 2010). To sceptics, such pronouncements appear reminiscent of the 'light at the end of the tunnel' rhetoric of US officials in Vietnam. The Israeli-Palestinian conflict offers a direct contrast, as repeated IDF efforts to eliminate militant leaders only lead to the emergence of more intransigent successors. In this case, the IDF has achieved short-term gains in temporarily reducing the number of Palestinian terrorist attacks against Israeli citizens over the past decade, but it has not been able to force adversaries such as Hamas to abandon their goal of eliminating the 'Zionist entity' (Catignani 2008: 184; Jones 2010: 134).

Specialist operations such as clandestine patrolling and pre-emptive intervention rely very much on what British military doctrine calls 'framework operations' by regular troops (British Army 2006). From Northern Ireland to Baghdad during the surge, the presence of thousands of soldiers engaged in extensive and constant patrolling activity is required if special forces are to operate effectively; to use Thompson's analogy, the tame tomcat still needs a guard dog to help him flush out his quarry. In situations where the counterinsurgent lacks the military means to physically dominate the ground, special forces find it difficult to operate, particularly if local security forces are either too weak to preserve law and order, or are infiltrated by insurgents or militiamen. This became apparent in Basra in September 2005, when renegade Iraqi policemen took two operatives from 22SAS prisoner, forcing the British Army to launch a rescue mission which ended in a public confrontation with the police and local rioters (Hughes 2010: 580).

In cases where elite military units engage local surrogates to help them fight irregular adversaries, the consequences for state stability can be grave. US and allied special forces weakened Karzai's government in Afghanistan by using militias against al-Qaeda, thereby empowering warlords involved in destabilising and unsavoury activities such as drugs trafficking. Furthermore, surrogate forces may prove unreliable. The Pashtun militias hired by the Americans to trap bin Laden and the remnants of al-Qaeda at Tora Bora (December 2001) were bribed to let their quarry go, and the Pakistani journalist Ahmed Rashid has reported on cases where NATO has conducted air strikes against villages on the basis of false tip-offs from warlords (Rashid 2009: 106, 128–31). The manipulation of Western military power to settle tribal feuds reinforces the public criticism of the NATO intelligence effort in Afghanistan by three senior US officials, who argue that HUMINT is needed not on the Taliban's order of battle but the cultural characteristics, social structure and mentalities of the local civilian populace in each individual district (Flynn *et al.* 2010).

Targeted killings (whether by UAVs or specialist military units) are a source of inevitable controversy in liberal democracies; even in Israel human rights groups such as B'Tselem reject the official argument that the state faces an existential threat from its Palestinian foes which justifies the use of lethal force (Giladi 2010). In the case of the United States the deliberate targeting of individuals was explicitly banned by American law prior to 9/11, although a minority of officials such as Duane Clarridge (the former head of the CIA's Counterterrorist Center) railed against legal and ethical criticisms – '[why] is an expensive military raid with heavy collateral damage to our allies and to innocent civilians okay – more morally acceptable than a bullet to the head?' (Coll 2005: 144). In the aftermath of 9/11 repeated UAV strikes – most notably in the Federally Administered Tribal Areas (FATA) of northwest Pakistan – show that US officials now have fewer qualms about ordering drone attacks to kill militants such as Baitullah Mehsud (who died in a strike on 5 August 2009). Obama has inherited this aspect of his predecessor's counter-terrorist policy, and has in fact intensified the rate of UAV raids in the FATA (BBC 2010).

These attacks have aroused a furore within Pakistan, where there is widespread resentment concerning the US violation of national sovereignty and the casualties these strikes cause. Given the strength of militancy within the FATA, it is impossible to gain an independent and authoritative account which lists civilian as well as al-Qaeda, Pakistani Taliban and other insurgent/terrorist losses. The Pakistani researcher Farhat Taj argues that there is a contrast between public protest and private attitudes in the FATA, and her findings show that many tribesmen approve of the elimination of radical Islamists (notably Arabs, Chechens, Uzbeks and other foreigners) that have alienated the local community by their brutality. However, one consequence of UAV strikes is increasing anti-Americanism across Pakistan as a whole, and embarrassment for the government in Islamabad, which actually provides base rights for CIA drones and their crews. An additional and disturbing trend is the increase in suicide bombings and other terrorist atrocities in Pakistan, due to the fact that militant formations consider the authorities complicit in UAV raids against them. According to the BBC, drone strikes and terrorist attacks have respectively killed 700 and 1,800 people between January 2009 and June 2010 (BBC 2010; Pantucci 2009: 72–6; Sloggett 2010: 14–18; Taj 2010). Shortly after Neptune Spear a Frontier Corps base near Peshawar was hit by two suicide bombers, killing up to 80 people; the Pakistani Taliban's claim that this attack was intended to avenge bin Laden's death highlights the fact that Pakistan itself pays a heavy price for being in the frontline of the US-led 'long war' against al-Qaeda and affiliated militant organisations (Walsh 2011).

In conclusion, all of the activities discussed in this chapter can have a limited effect, and the ability of the counterinsurgent to eliminate key adversaries does not necessarily guarantee strategic success. Over three months after a Russian air strike killed General Dudayev Chechen fighters stormed Grozny and recaptured the city, humiliating the Russian military and forcing the federal government to negotiate peace terms with his successor, Aslan Maskhadov (German 2003: 146–7). The killing of Musavi did nothing to weaken Hezbollah, whose guerrilla attacks eventually led to the IDF's withdrawal from southern Lebanon in May 2000 (Bergman 2008: 239–53). There is also the fundamental dilemma which is of relevance to any government and any foreign supporters looking for a political resolution to the insurgency they are confronting. Near the end of the Cyprus 'emergency' in February 1959 the British Prime Minister Harold Macmillan cancelled a military operation which was likely to either capture or kill the EOKA leader Colonel George Grivas, due to concerns that it would undermine negotiations to resolve the Cypriot problem peacefully (Dimitrakos 2008: 389). In COIN and counter-terrorism – as opposed to chess – checkmate does not necessarily lead to victory, and it remains to be seen whether bin Laden's death in May 2011 has a lasting effect on al-Qaeda, and whether Neptune Spear is anything more than a tactical and temporary success in the 'long war'.

Note

1 The analysis, opinions and conclusions expressed or implied in this chapter are those of the author and do not necessarily represent the views of the JSCSC, the Defence Academy, the Ministry of Defence (MOD) or any other UK government agency.

Recommended readings

Due to the methodological problems discussed in this chapter, the literature on special operations and precision air strikes in COIN is sparse, aside from the sources noted in the bibliography. The fact that the conflicts in Afghanistan, Iraq, Pakistan and Israel-Palestine are ongoing means that it is also difficult to produce empirically-based research analysing the strategic utility of precision air-power and special forces operations. The author's forthcoming book *The Military's Role in Counter-Terrorism: Examples and Implications for Liberal Democracies* (Carlisle PA: Strategic Studies Institute/US Army War College 2010) discusses the utility and consequences of such military activity in greater detail.

References

Barclay, J. (2010) 'Collateral Damage. Propaganda Defends Muslim Casualties', *Jane's Intelligence Review*, 22 (5): 20–5.

BBC (2010) 'Mapping US Drone and Islamic Militant Attacks in Pakistan', 22 July 2010. Available at www.bbc.co.uk/news/world-south-asia-10648909 (accessed 26 October 2010).

Benjamin, D. and Simon, S. (2003) *The Age of Sacred Terror*. New York: Random House.

Bergman, R. (2008) *The Secret War With Iran: The 30-Year Covert Struggle for Control of a 'Rogue' State*. Oxford: Oneworld Publications.

Bowden, M. (2007) 'The Ploy', *The Atlantic Monthly*, May.

Boyle, M. (2010) 'Do Counterterrorism and Counterinsurgency go Together?', *International Affairs*, 86 (2): 333–53.

British Army (2006) *Operation Banner. An Analysis of Military Operations in Northern Ireland*. London: Ministry of Defence.

Catignani, S. (2008) *Israeli Counter-Insurgency and the Intifadas: Dilemmas of a Conventional Army*. Abingdon: Routledge.

Chin, W. (2007) 'British Counter-Insurgency in Afghanistan', *Defense & Security Analysis*, 23 (2): 201–25.

Clarke, R. (2004) *Against All Enemies: Inside America's War on Terror*. London: Free Press.

Coll, S. (2005) *Ghost Wars. The Secret History of the CIA, Afghanistan, and bin Laden, from the Soviet invasion to September 10, 2001*. London: Penguin.

Corum, J. and Johnson, W. (2003) *Airpower in Small Wars. Fighting Insurgents and Terrorists*. Lawrence: University Press of Kansas.

David, A. (2010) 'Spy Games. Mossad Returns to Form', *Jane's Intelligence Review*, 22 (5): 26–31.

Dimitrakos, P. (2008) 'British Intelligence and the Cyprus Insurgency, 1955–1959', *Journal of Intelligence and Counterintelligence*, 21 (2): 375–94.

Drehle, D. (2011) 'Killing bin Laden: How the US Finally Got its Man', *Time Magazine*, 20 April.

Drew, C. (2009) 'Drones are US Weapons of Choice in Fighting [al-]Qaeda', *New York Times*, 16 March.

The Economist (2009) 'A Battle Between Two Long Arms', 3 April.

The Economist (2010) 'The Beginning of the End', 2 October.

The Economist (2011a) 'They Got Him', 7 May.

The Economist (2011b) 'Humiliation of the Military Men', 14 May.

Finlan, A. (2003) 'Warfare by Other Means: Special Forces, Terrorism and Grand Strategy', *Small Wars and Insurgencies*, 14 (1): 92–108.

Flynn, P., Pottinger, M. and Batchelor, P. (2010) *Fixing Intel: A Blueprint for Making Intelligence Relevant in Afghanistan*. Washington, DC: Center for a New American Security.

Freedman, L. (2006). *The Transformation of Strategic Affairs*. Routledge/International Institute for Strategic Studies: Adelphi Paper No. 379.

German, T. (2003) *Russia's Chechen War*. London: Routledge Curzon.

Giladi, R. (2010) 'Out of Context: "Undercover" Operations and IHL [International Human Rights] Advocacy in the Occupied Palestinian Territories', *Journal of Conflict & Security Law*, 14 (3): 393–439.

Girard, R. (2009) 'Karzai: "Je ne serai pas une marionnette des Etas Unis"', *Le Figaro*, 7 September.

Grey, S. (2010) 'Capturing the Taliban: Afghan Covert War', 17 February. Available at: www.stephen-grey.com/2010/02/capturing-the-taliban-afghan-covert-war (accessed 26 October 2010).

Hastings, M. (2010) 'The Runaway General', *Rolling Stone*, 22 July.

Hughes, G. (2009) 'A "Model Campaign" Reappraised: The Counter-Insurgency War in Dhofar, Oman, 1965–1975', *Journal of Strategic Studies*, 32 (2): 271–305.

Hughes, G. (2010) 'The Use of Undercover Military Units in Counter-terrorist Operations: A Historical Analysis with Reference to Contemporary Anti-terrorism', *Small Wars & Insurgencies*, 21 (4): 561–90.

Hughes, G. and Tripodi, C. (2009) 'Anatomy of a Surrogate: Historical Precedents and Implications for Contemporary Counter-insurgency and Counter-terrorism', *Small Wars & Insurgencies*, 20 (1): 1–35.

Ingram, M. and Harkin, G. (2004) *Stakeknife. Britain's Secret Agents in Northern Ireland*. Dublin: The O'Brien Press.

Jeapes, T. (2005) *SAS Secret War*. London: Greenhill Books.

Jenkins, G. (2008) 'Susurluk and the Legacy of Turkey's Dirty War', *Jamestown Foundation Terrorism and Security Monitor*, 6 (9), 1 May.

Jones, C. (2010) 'Israel and the al-Aqsa intifada. The *Conceptzia* of Terror', in A. Siniver (ed.), *International Terrorism Post-9/11. Comparative Dynamics and Responses*. Routledge, pp. 126–43.

Kibbe, J. (2010) 'Covert Action, Pentagon Style', in L. Johnson (ed.), *The Oxford Handbook of National Security Intelligence*. Oxford: Oxford University Press, pp. 569–86.

Kilcullen, D. (2009) *The Accidental Guerrilla: Fighting Small Wars in the Midst of a Big One*. London: C. Hurst & Co.

Kilcullen, D. (2010) 'Unless We Beat Corruption All This Is For Nothing', *The Times*, 30 October.

Kitson, F. (1991) *Low Intensity Operations*. London: Faber & Faber.

Lewis, R. (1999) *Fishers of Men*. London: Hodder & Stoughton.

Long, A. (2010) 'Small is Beautiful: The Counterterrorism Option in Afghanistan', *Orbis*, 54 (2): 199–214.

Loyd, A. (2010) 'Taliban on Verge of Collapse, NATO and Afghan Officials Believe', *The Australian*, 8 October.

Luttwak, E. (2010) 'What would Byzantium do?', *Prospect Magazine*, 167, 27 January.

Marshall, A. (2007) 'Managing Withdrawal: Afghanistan as the Forgotten Example in Attempting Conflict Resolution and State Reconstruction', *Small Wars & Insurgencies*, 18 (1): 68–89.

Melshen, P. (1995) *Pseudo Operations: The Use by British and American Forces of Deception in Counter-Insurgencies*, Cambridge, unpublished PhD thesis.

Pantucci, R. (2009) 'Deep Impact: The Effect of Drone Attacks on British Counter-terrorism', *RUSI Journal*, 154 (5): 72–6.

Pritchard, J. and Smith, M. (2010) 'Thompson in Helmand: Comparing Theory to Practice in British Counter-insurgency Operations in Afghanistan', *Civil Wars*, 12 (1–2): 65–90.

Rashid, A. (2009) *Descent into Chaos: How the War against Islamic Extremism is being Lost in Pakistan, Afghanistan and Central Asia*. London: Penguin.

Rayment, S. (2008) 'SAS Kills Hundreds of Terrorists in "Secret War" against al-Qaeda in Iraq', *Daily Telegraph*, 30 August.

Richelson, J. (1999) '"Truth Conquers all Chains": The US Army's Intelligence Support Activity, 1981–1989', *International Journal of Intelligence and Counterintelligence*, 12 (2): 168–200.

Sheehan, N. (1990) *A Bright Shining Lie. John Paul Vann and America in Vietnam*. London: Picador.

Sloggett, D. (2010) 'Attack of the Drones: The Utility of UAVs in Fighting Terrorism', *Jane's Intelligence Review*, 22 (8): 14–18.

Smith, M. (2007) 'Secret War of the SAS', *The Sunday Times*, 16 September.

Taj, F (2010) 'Drone Attacks: Pakistan's Policy and the Tribesmen's Perspective', *Jamestown Foundation Terrorism and Security Monitor*, 23 (10), 11 March.

Taylor, P. (2002) *Brits*. London: Bloomsbury.

Thompson, R. (1972) *Defeating Communist Insurgency: Experiences from Malaya and Vietnam*. London: Chatto & Windus.

Urban, Mark (2010) *Task Force Black: The Explosive Story of the SAS and the Secret War in Iraq*. London: Little Brown and Co.

US Army/US Marine Corps (2007) *FM3–24 Counterinsurgency Field Manual*. Washington, DC and Chicago: Department of Defense/University of Chicago Press.

Waisberg, T. (2009) 'The Colombia–Ecuador Armed Crisis of March 2008: The Practice of Targeted Killing and Incursions against Non-State Actors Harbored at Terrorist Safe Havens in a Third Party State', *Studies in Conflict & Terrorism*, 32 (6): 476–88.

Walsh, D. (2011) 'Osama bin Laden "Revenge" Attack Kills Scores in Pakistan', *Guardian*, 13 May.

Wright, J. (2010) 'Urban Planning: The Campaign for Kandahar', *Jane's Intelligence Review*, 22 (10): 14–17.

10

ETHICS OF COUNTERINSURGENCY

Christopher Coker

Ethics of war courses traditionally revolve around two main claims. The first is that ethical practices inhere in the practice of war itself. The second is that we are bound by moral duty – whether required of us by God, humanity or natural law, to act honourably to those with whom we engage in battle. For the most part, most tend to agree with Kant that we have no way of inferring causal relationships outside experience. We cannot infer from a causal order of nature to a God who is the author of nature. There may well be an intelligent designer at work in the world, but if there is we cannot prove it. We cannot infer from the injunctions of God any moral obligations to behave well. We derive those from the experience in dealing with each other.

Let us take a central tenet of Kant's *Perpetual Peace*, the only book of his that is likely to be found on the syllabus of an ethics course in a military academy or college: 'No state at war with another shall permit such acts of hostility as would make mutual confidence impossible during a future time of peace' (Kant 1983: 96). The Kantian injunction cited above is to do nothing in war that makes peace impossible. It is really at one with his most famous formulation, the Second Categorical Imperative: we are all rational beings and therefore should be treated as ends in ourselves, not merely as means or building blocks to the ends of others. If peace is the only reason for going to war, then we must wage it in a way that does nothing that makes it unattainable – by treating our enemies, for example, as a means to some ill-defined greater end. Kant's views are embodied in the *Declaration of the Rights of Man* (1789) which grounded right behaviour in reason and social contract theory, though we can find similar sentiments in Cicero's *De Officiis*.

Indeed, Cicero's work is particularly interesting because of the absence of social contract theory in the ancient world. In Cicero's day humanity was the prerogative of the aristocracy – when mercy was shown at all it had to be earned, usually in combat. It was rarely shown to commoners (who did not extend it to aristocrats in turn). Mercy was a gift that might be expected but not demanded. It might have a political pay-off but it was largely part of a warrior's existential identity – it often marked a disdain for the world of instrumental ends.

Cicero could have left the argument there – he could have dealt himself out of the game but instead he dealt himself in. In the *De Officiis* he leaves the reader in no doubt about his message. 'Let us remember that justice must be maintained even towards the lowliest' (Cicero 1991: 39). Cicero did not say that cruelty to one's own kind is wrong; he counsels us to avoid being cruel even to the lowliest of our enemies. He accepts the common humanity of both the well-born and the low-born which was more than they tended to grant each other. He accepted that in war both find themselves in the same community of fate. He was intelligent enough to recognise that restraint from cruelty need not be the product of fellow feeling; it is a demand of war. Cicero's counsel against cruelty was grounded on the understanding that we have escaped the state of nature into a state of reason. It is our ability to perceive the consequences of our actions that sets us apart from more primitive people. Cruelty always put one at risk of regressing into warfare: as Thucydides had warned it can deprive people of the ability to satisfy their needs and reduce them to the level of their circumstances. When a soldier is stripped of all his socially acquired virtues and left in a moral vacuum he is in danger of returning to the primal state. His reason for reaching this conclusion carries with it a real insight. 'There is no military power so great that it can last for long under the weight of fear' (Cicero 1991: 2.26). For fear can beget fearfulness – to inspire fear and appear fearful at the same time is usually ruinous – it is likely to provoke a defeated people to revolt.

In short, Kant's injunction is not new. It inheres in the practice of war itself. It is merely expressed in a language with which we are more familiar: that of rights and duties. Indeed, when we look back at the Western battlefield over the last 500 years we see a remarkable consistency of practice. The laws of war rely on a mixture of natural law, military law, common custom and self-interest, and not much has changed. All that has happened is that in the course of the modern era natural law as part of international law has gone 'positivist' for the first time: the customs of war (the precedents created by the conduct of war itself) have remained much the same, but they have been gradually embodied in legal conventions negotiated by states. This should not be allowed to obscure the fact that the conventions that have been transformed into laws such as honouring surrenders, sparing the wounded, or respecting flags of truce – the social conventions that have reduced the danger and chaos of conflict for all combatants – have been observed for centuries. They can be seen as 'contractual etiquettes' which provide each party with a vital framework of expectations concerning the conduct of the other. We situate these rights in conventions, or laws of war. But a 'convention', as the word suggests, is the institution-alisation of a common practice and the practice is independent of its judicial formulation (i.e. enforcement in a court of law). As a modern thinker, Kant preferred the word 'responsibility': we are responsible for the soldiers we capture, or the women and children who fall into our hands. And that responsibility inheres in the dialectic between war and peace. What is important is not to stop, but to stop short: to prevent limited war from becoming unlimited.

Since Kant's day that responsibility has extended even further. So has the law of war. We have added what Michael Walzer calls the *ius post bellum*, the law of war after formal hostilities have ceased between two states, but during the continuation of military operations against non-state actors including in particular insurgents. As Hans Jonas reminds us, the concept of responsibility nowhere played a central role either in the moral systems of the past, or most philosophical theories of ethics. Nor did the feeling of responsibility appear as the affective moment in the formation of the moral will. Quite different feelings such as love or reverence were assigned this office. And that was largely because responsibility is a function of power and knowledge and until recently both were constrained. Today, by contrast, we have immense power, and greater knowledge though not alas greater wisdom. We are always having to relearn the lessons of history as we are doing in Afghanistan and Iraq.

Jonas and the new ethicists maintain that unlike traditional ethics which reckoned only with non-cumulative behaviour, we have to deal with uncertainties for which there is no historical precedent. We have to deal with the unanticipated consequences of our own actions. The military even coined a term for this in the 1990s; effects-based operations. In our networked world we pile up cumulative effects faster than ever before. Consequences can snowball. Our risk societies deal with probabilities not certainties; they are always estimating, measuring and anticipating the consequences of their actions, the better to manage them as best they can. We live in a world of perceptions, predictions and scenarios. Our actions are based on assumptions, projections and statistical probabilities. At this stage in history this is the shape of our ethical universe.

Finally, we no longer live in the stable world of the past. Once ethics was associated with continuity, its main concern was that the state should survive; hence the importance of prudence (not exceeding one's grasp), as well as moderation (not demanding a Carthaginian peace which could stoke up resentment followed by a wish for revenge). Our world, by contrast, is dynamic. Nothing is stable. Everything is in flux. We are future-oriented for this reason. Responsibility, insists Jonas, is a correlate of power, and the scope and the degree of power we enjoy must determine the scope of our responsibility. What morality restores to an increasingly uncertain world is the idea of responsibility – that what we do severally and collectively makes a difference and that as a consequence the future lies in our hands (Jonas 1999: 5).

Counterinsurgency operations clearly present a very demanding ethical challenge. We do not enter into contracts with insurgents, and they certainly have not signed up to the Geneva Convention. But most ethicists would argue that a state is bound to honour its own customs and conventions even so. The US Supreme Court ruled to this effect in 1967 when the US government asked the judges whether the Vietcong (VC) were owed the same rights as guerrilla fighters as the United States was bound to grant any regular combatant it found itself fighting (Bourke 1999: 197). We are bound for *prudential* reasons to act in good faith. The same ethics of war must apply in a counterinsurgency as they do in a conventional war.

The second approach to ethics insists that we are bound to act correctly according to the dictates of conscience or religious faith. Even Kant invokes a metaphysical concept: a Categorical Imperative. At which point, his critics would contend, he asks too much of us. First, he places far too much faith in reason. Reason for Kant is what it was for Plato – who also saw it as the necessary context of Man's deepest aspirations and ambitions, though Kant by contrast saw it as a mark of our common humanity (which can be seen as a nobler concept than Plato's). This fused at a critical moment with the French Revolution which Kant believed had opened a supreme historical window of opportunity for humanity to realise its own freedom in concrete political action – such as the *Declaration of the Rights of Man*.

Of course, today we have far less confidence in reason. We do not spell it with the upper case. And our ability to act unreasonably out of purely rational ends is unlimited as the revolutionary Terror in France later showed. Ethical rules are a manifestation of the Zeitgeist. And the spirit of the times can be murderous as the poet W.B. Yeats recognised in his poem, *The Second Coming*. Its most famous line is 'the centre cannot hold'. But there is another which is even more telling: 'Mere anarchy is loosed upon the world'. What he meant was not disorder or anarchy as such; he meant licensed killing. Twentieth-century states licensed their soldiers to kill in the name of abstract principles, those great 'alibis of aggression', Gay calls them, which allowed them to kill with a good conscience, and to kill on a large scale. One of the books whose insights I find especially invaluable is *The Cultivation of Hatred*, one of the volumes which comprise Peter Gay's monumental study of the bourgeois experience in nineteenth-century Europe. The Victorians engaged in continuous debates about the moral nature of aggression. These were particularly intense when nation clashed with nation, or class with class. The modern age was always trying to master nature, geography or the 'other' and ultimately, of course, 'self'. And it produced alibis of aggression which helped to identify the outsider who was to be bullied, ridiculed or exterminated at will. All this amounts to 'cultivated' hatred in both senses of the term – at once fostering and restraining hatred at the same time (Gay 1993).

In his writings on the war in the Caucasus, Tolstoy had shown how quickly civilised men can revert back to their natural state, how war can revert very quickly to warfare or indiscriminate violence when they see their enemy – as the Nazis saw the Slavs as little better than savages. In 1942 Ernst Junger in his *Caucasus Notebook* invoked Tolstoy by name, though he attributed the barbarism he witnessed at the Front to the new Dark Age in which he lived. 'Things like that belong to the style of the times' (James 2007: 338). *Zeitstil* is the word in German. The point is that barbarism inheres not just in our natures, but in the tendency of war to revert back to its origins, especially when discipline breaks down. The state of nature from which we have fled is one to which we can return quickly enough. 'War' is the distance we place not between ourselves and our nature, but between ourselves and the state of nature. The soldier must feed on war from a distance and the discipline of war (the warrior's honour) is precisely the distance he must maintain.

Unfortunately, the Germans, although largely adhering in the West to the laws of war which were later to be enshrined in the Geneva Conventions, refused to acknowledge they had any responsibilities in the East where they engaged in a war of extermination against an allegedly barbaric people. And the mentality – the spirit of the time – the *Zeitgeist* – was not just a reflection of Nazi indoctrination. It was also to be found in the upper reaches of the German army whose senior offices liked to pride themselves that they had managed to retain their honour by wearing a uniform unsullied by the doctrines of national socialism. In the winter of 1941, as the German offensive stalled in front of Moscow, it was decided to let Russian POWs freeze to death by taking away their winter clothing including their overcoats and felt boots. The decision to give them to German soldiers was in defiance of German military law, not to mention the laws of war. Admiral Canaris, the Head of German Military Intelligence, added in a memorandum on the legality of the war that this was not just a rejection of the Hague Conventions, it was a rejection of the entire core of customary law that had defined European behaviour in war for the past 200 years, including the belief that soldiers that have surrendered have a normative right to life (Kassimeris 2004: 86).

Kant's critics level another charge against him; they claim he drew an unhelpful distinction between the Categorical and Hypothetical imperatives which encourage us to treat prisoners of war well because of what might happen if we do not. This is the hypothetical imperative of prudence. The Categorical Imperative is limited to no such consideration; it is an absolute duty that we owe each other. When we have discerned a Categorical Imperative we discover a rule which admits no exception. It does, of course, have particular uses. The main one is that of individual responsibility: we are agents, not only actors. We are responsible to our conscience for our actions. The Categorical Imperative absolves us of the need to follow orders. But it does not help much in telling us what we should do; it only tells us what we should not. It is problematic in that it detaches the notion of duty from the notion of ends, purposes and needs. We need a more instrumental understanding of ethics. In the end, not only does Kant demand too much of us, he also demands too little.

We need an ends-means ethics which is precisely what the Geneva Conventions provide. War is not a moral activity at all; it is *ethical*. To be moral, an action must be disinterested, it must be independent of the old legal question, *cui bono*: who benefits? Even to save a life of a companion by throwing oneself on a grenade is not a moral duty: it is an ethical gift. A soldier cannot be court-martialled for not offering it (MacIntyre 2002: 28). Most soldiers for that reason live in a distinctive *ethical* community. Ethics is inherently interested. The ethics of war inheres in that most challenging of questions: how do you get the enemy to surrender or to admit defeat, or even to swallow the shame of defeat? Kant's injunction to do nothing in war that puts peace out of reach is not a moral injunction at all: it is a conditional, ethical response.

Of course, all this is problematic for moral philosophers and pacifists who would like to outlaw war altogether. And it is true that the rules of war make it possible for us. The only effective counter to war would be to make it so violent that it became its own deterrent. W.B. Gallie calls this the sub-rational option as opposed to the 'super-rational' as when Christian love meets oppression by non-violent means (Gallie 1978: 119) He draws our attention to a passage in Tolstoy's novel *War and Peace* where we find Prince Andrei on the evening before the battle of Borodino overhearing a snippet of a conversation between two German staff officers in Russian service, one of whom happens to be Clausewitz. Both are talking about extending the war. Andrei is already sickened by the butchery which he has witnessed at first hand and is appalled that the rules of war preach chivalry and flags of truce, but do nothing to stop homes from being plundered, or children killed, or foes treated in the most outrageous fashion. 'To hell with all this magnanimity business in warfare', he thinks. 'It boils down to this. We should have done with humbug and let war be war and not a game' (Gallie 1978: 117).

And this is particularly regrettable because since 9/11 we have been encouraged to see our enemies in terms that make it possible to ill-treat them. The Bush administration was roundly condemned both at home and abroad for sanctioning torture, the abuse of prisoners in detainment centres such as Abu Ghraib and Guantanamo Bay, and the practice of extraordinary rendition (the interrogation and torture of suspected terrorist by third parties at the instigation of the United States). For a typical Western stereotyping, see Sam Harris' book *The End of Faith: Religious Terror and the Future of Reason*. There is, we are told, a Western way of war practised by civilised democracies and there is also a Muslim way of war, 'standing eye-deep in the red barbarity of the Fourteenth Century – a kill-the-children-first approach to war' (Harris 2004: 20) But we ignore the fundamental difference between their violence and ours at our peril. Once you externalise violence onto the 'other', every tool and tactic becomes justified, including torture. Once you externalise your own actions as good, and theirs as evil, you find it easier to humiliate them which may render it, in turn, more difficult for them to come to terms with defeat.

Kant's key insight, that we should respect our enemies, still holds. For he saw that the moment you externalise violence and project it onto the 'other', you may well fail to acknowledge the impulses within yourself that permit you to carry out indefensible acts. In the end – watching at a distance – you end up dismissing Guantanamo Bay or Abu Ghraib as possibly regrettable but inevitable. Like Junger, we may even comfort ourselves with the thought that 'things like that belong to the style of the times'. 'Stuff happens', as the US Defense Secretary said notoriously of the outbreak of the looting in Baghdad within days of the Americans arriving in the city.

UAVs and managing war

In August 2009, a British journalist spent a day at Creech Air Force Base in the Nevada desert, where he visited a mobile ground control station for Predator drones. 'Is this it?' was his first thought, after being shown into the back of a caravan parked beside a two-lane highway about 45 miles outside Las Vegas. The caravan was a US Air Force mobile ground control station and the rather unimpressive-looking machine at the back of it was the flight deck for a remote-controlled Predator aircraft operating 7,000 miles away in Afghanistan.

It is hard to describe how surreal for the journalist it was to watch two young pilots operating such a lethal device on a different continent from the battlefield. The advantages from a logistical standpoint were overwhelming: these twenty-first century pilots got to live essentially the same lives as suburban sales executives. They kept regular hours. They commuted back and forth from home. Their workplace was clean, safe and air-conditioned. But where was the soldiers' honour in killing an adversary 7,000 miles away? What happened to looking your enemy in the eye? How could you understand the consequences of your actions? Surely, the journalist concluded, killing should not be like sending an email – otherwise where would it all lead?

His questions were informed by a new feature of counterinsurgency operations – the use of military robots, especially Unmanned Aerial Vehicles (UAVs) which present a new challenge – in extending the scope of our responsibilities *post bellum* are we in danger of narrowing the scope of our individual moral concerns?

We are engineering robots for many reasons. One of the most important is to reduce human risk. It is precisely because we are weak, vulnerable beings, that the body is exposed to harm, that we are always seeking to put ourselves out of harm's way. Robots may indeed enhance our ability to fight war, but they also offer a chance to reduce suffering, both physical and mental. Among the ethical properties this may be the most important of all. In rebooting war for our own age we aspire to go beyond spreading risks, we aspire to eliminate them altogether. Risk avoidance has now become an absolute military priority. Henry Yuen, an expert in anti-submarine warfare, wrote an internal paper for the Defense Department shortly after the end of the Gulf War. 'One of the foremost objectives in the development of new weaponry', he wrote, 'should be the reduction or total elimination of human risk. Put simply, weapons or equipment in harm's way should, to the extent possible, be unmanned' (Toffler and Toffler 1993: 141).

We use technology as a substitute for risk. We use for instance Pacbots – a ground system that can be used for scouting hostile areas, or which can disable basic IEDs; the advantage of such a system, according to one military officer, is 'when a robot dies, you don't have to write a letter to its mother'. Fanciful or not, as Ralph Peters, a retired Army Officer, has put it 'there's a uniquely American pursuit of the Grail that technology will solve all human problems, that we can have bloodless wars' (Singer 2009: 291). In the years to come the military will be using robots more and more to reduce the risk of combat. Take the case of Pacbots: the service these provide is grounded in risk aversion. John Dyer, the President of I-robot, the company that makes them, plays up the life-saving effects: 'Pacbot allows personnel to safely neutralise roadside bombs, car bombs and other IEDs, and perform other life-threatening missions, helping to save soldiers' lives.' The trade-off seems so obvious and simple: why should a 20-year-old soldier have to look around a corner when a replaceable machine can do the same job? The same is true, of course, for disposing of potentially dangerous ordnance.

But if war is becoming bloodless for one side, at least, as Peters claims, it is quite the opposite for the insurgent, or indeed the troops on the ground. And there is the rub. *For there are moral consequences of using robots in this way.* The armed forces are using them in dangerous operations from which they might otherwise shy away if the risks were greater. Employing robots lowers the threshold for war. Indeed, one commander thinks that these unmanned systems may significantly change how commanders approach war. The conviction that technology can or must substitute the risk to human life has a pernicious tendency to distort the consideration of risks and rewards. A lower threshold for war may encourage us to engage in more operations than might be wise. Technologies, unfortunately, are not ethically or socially neutral. They have a huge impact on the societies that build and maintain them, changing attitudes and even normative assumptions. Technology first changes the environment and then changes our way of thinking and our values, hence the popular adage to the person whose only tool is a hammer, all problems look like nails.

The point is that we build the technology that we need. Michael Ignatieff, writing of the first risk-averse war in Kosovo (1999) in which not a single allied pilot or soldier lost his life, wrote at the time that the West had begun to challenge 'the basic equality of the moral risk, kill or be killed' (Ignatieff 2000: 29). Is killing insurgents from thousands of miles away, as we can do with today's drones, a moral response? 'I hope that many more computer chips will lay down their lives for their country.' This remark is attributed to an American general on the loss of a UAV somewhere in Bosnia. It has become quite well known. It has almost entered folklore as a sign of the times – an anticipation of the shape of things to come. But it has profound implications for the ethics of war. For computer chips do not lay down their lives for their country; soldiers do. UAVs remove the 'sacred' from sacrifice. It is sacrifice – the willingness to run risks and – if necessary – pay the supreme price with one's life that is the chief legitimating factor of war; ultimately, it is what makes it different from common murder. Sacrifice offers a window into a soldier's interior life as well as our own (for we are both human). As the etymology of the word reveals, sacrifice is derived from sacred. All militaries regard the sacrifice of men (and now often women) to be sacred for that reason.

This presents another problem. The warrior ethos – correct behaviour concerns two related moral demands – accepted and acceptable behaviour. Accepted behaviour is behaviour that is legally sanctioned. Acceptable behaviour is behaviour that may be legitimate (in the eyes of others) but which may not necessarily be within the law. The drone pilot still operates within an environment of accepted behaviour; he has rules of engagements (though they are not always standardised), and he has to obey legal conventions. There is a chain of command, and the lawyers are part of it. Acceptable behaviour is different; soldiers often reach a point where they conclude that their own behaviour merits hostility on the part of the enemy; they deserve what they get, translated into the biblical metaphor, one reaps what one sows.

Are UAV pilots likely to be disengaged from the enemy? All technology gets us to see the world differently. This is the warning that we find in John Ellis' splendid book, *The Social History of the Machine Gun*, which shows how it opened up the last phase of imperial expansion in Africa. The gun was the product, clearly, of a rational society because only a rational society could invent it. It was a weapon that was used to get the natives to see reason: to see how foolish it was to resist. It followed that if they continued resisting, they were clearly being unreasonable. The machine gun gave us what no other technology had given the people before; the right to occupy the moral high ground. Except of course when we turned the machine guns against each other in 1914, we found ourselves in a moral No Man's Land. We saw the machine gun in a completely new light precisely because our enemies shared the same moral world with ourselves; both were high-tech.

We must choose our tools carefully, not because they are inhumane (all weapons are), but because the more we come to rely on them, the more they come to shape our view of the world, and it is clear that as we are becoming increasingly reliant on robotics it may be reshaping our inter-subjective experience with the enemy which constitutes what we used to call a community of fate. We are human, wrote Richard Rorty, to the extent that humanity is not a given; it is real only insofar as our humanity is recognised by others in us.

To sustain any ethical discourse on a battlefield requires us to also recognise the humanity in the enemy and this is as old a challenge as war itself. Thucydides describes the exchange between a Spartan prisoner of war and an Athenian ally. The ally asks the captive whether his fellow Spartans who died rather than surrendered had been men of honour. The Spartan replies that a weapon would be worth a great deal if it could distinguish a gallant man from a coward. But of course it cannot (Lendon 2005: 47). A weapon is merely a weapon. It is dumb, not smart. Even today a drone pilot operating a UAV over the skies of Afghanistan does not know when he launches it whether he is killing men who are brave or cowards. He may see more than anyone has ever seen before, but the vision does not help that much; he still cannot see the man within.

The ethics of the suicide bomber

In Plato's *Republic* sons are expected to accompany their fathers into battle to learn their trade young. Today in the West Bank you will find summer camps in which children as young as eight are trained in military drills; they are encouraged to write poems about the suicide bombers and to learn how to take their life – and the lives of others. At al Najah University a student exhibition in 2001 included a recreated scene of the Sbarro pizzeria in Jerusalem after a particularly destructive suicide bombing, with fake blood and body parts hanging from the ceiling as though suspended in mid-air.

The ethics of war for state actors revolves around killing. For non-state actors there is another dimension – it revolves around dying. 'And we must tremble so long as we have not learned to heal the sinister ease of dying.' The words are Victor Hugo's writing after the high death rate in the Paris Commune in 1871. Sacrifice becomes problematic when dying becomes too easy. Sacrifice becomes problematic when it appears to betray a contempt for life which is at the centre not of heroism, but of fanaticism.

One of the chief objections to suicide bombing is that it reduces life to Hobbes' state of nature – the war of all against all, 'every man the enemy of every man'. What is distinctive about the state of nature is the absence of any instrumental dimension. The young (usually young men but sometimes women) are corrupted by the violence to which they resort. It is in this sense that the one-dimensional existential view of war is so deeply corrupting. Referring to the lone individual who takes his own life, Camus also used the same phrase as Hugo – 'a terrible strength'. Yeats used a different phrase about the Easter Rising in Ireland in 1916 – another foolhardy revolt by young men. He called it a 'terrible beauty'. Camus' 'terrible strength' is now, alas, a feature of politics in the Middle East. And because it is 'political' – because it's intended to influence others, particularly, impressionable, young men – it is used to dominate others and allow the bombers (and especially their controllers) to dominate the moral high ground in the region where a willingness to die for one's beliefs is so often taken as a sign of moral conviction.

This terrible strength used to be nourished by secular ideologies; it is now fuelled by religion. 'God has come back into history through the door of terror', wrote Paul Virilio in 1983, the year that witnessed the appearance of the first suicide bomber in the Hezbollah campaign in the Lebanon in 1983. The suicide bomber is an existentialist *tout court*. He kills, of course, as well as dies. He dies in order to kill. The mark of warrior cultures throughout history and the reason why people dislike them is that one can only hazard one's life for glory if one is prepared to take the life of another. This is what makes the warrior such an ambiguous figure in the Western world. But the true warrior is a better man for the experience; whether he survives or not he still masters it. And that is why the world is often a better place because of him.

So, is the suicide bomber an ethical figure? Few ethicists would accept the claim they make for themselves, and the main reason for that is that they have too much rage. Radical Islam sanctifies rage. The violence of the suicide bomber is unmediated which is why suicide is not an act of war, but what Hobbes calls 'warre' – the war of all against all, prior to the state. Like Hobbes' creature in the state of nature he is a lonely, atomised figure finding solace only in the company of like-minded persons. He tends to be driven by impotent rage, easy prey for those who can give their empty lives a sense of significance or meaning. War is the great educator; Hegel claimed it educates for freedom. It is rite of passage; a developer of character; a way by which a warrior may come to know himself, and 'become' what he is as a result of insight into his own nature. In the foot soldiers of jihad or the faith we have killing machines, human bombs, men who find the pain and labour and shame of the world too hard to master.

But the objection goes much further and gets to the very heart of the ethics of war. In a famous essay on suicide the English writer G.K. Chesterton wrote that 'the man who kills a man kills a man. The man who kills himself, kills all men; as far as he is concerned he wipes out the world'. There is much truth in Chesterton's remark. Indeed, we can echo him by asserting that his acts threaten to 'wipe out the world' because they end that dialogue which war constitutes and which makes peace possible. This is an ultimate negation of Kant's injunction that we should do nothing in war that would put permanent peace forever out of reach.

Recommended readings

Amato, J. (1990) *Victims and Values: A History and Theory of Suffering*. New York: Praeger.
Coker, C. (2009) *Ethics and War in the Twenty-first Century*. London: Routledge.
Johnson, J. (1999) *Morality in Contemporary Warfare*. New Haven: Yale University Press.
Jonas, Hans (1999) *Mortality and Morality: A Search for the Good after Auschwitz*. Evanston: Northwestern University Press.
Walzer, Michael (2004) *Arguing about War*. New Haven: Yale University Press.

References

Bourke, Joanna (1999) *An Intimate History of Killing*. London: Granta.
Cicero (1991) ed. M Griffiths. *On Duties*. Cambridge: Cambridge University Press.
Ellis, J. (2004) *The Social History of the Machine Gun*. London: Pimlico.
Gallie, W.B. (1978) *Philosophers of War*. Cambridge: Cambridge University Press.
Gay, P. (1993) *The Bourgeois Experience: from Victoria to Freud, Volume 3: The Cultivation of Hatred*. New York: Norton.
Harris, S. (2004) *The End of Faith: Religion, Terror and the Future of Reason*. New York: Norton.
Ignatieff, Michael (2000) *Virtual War*. London: Chatto & Windus.
James, Alan (2007) *Peacekeeping in International Politics*. Oxford: Oxford University Press.
Jonas, H. (1999) *Mortality and Morality: A Search for the Good after Auschwitz*. Evanston: Northwestern University Press.
Kant, Immanuel (1983) *Perpetual Peace and Other Essays* (trans. Ted Humphry). Cambridge: Hackett Publishing.
Kassimeris, G. (2004) 'The Dynamics of Defeat: Prisoner Taking and Prisoner Killing in the Age of Total War', *War in History*, 11 (1): 34–78.
Kassimeris, G. (2006) *The Barbarisation of Warfare*. London: Hurst.
Lendon, J.E. (2005) *Soldiers and Ghosts: A History of Battle in Classical Antiquity*. New Haven: Yale University Press.
MacIntyre, A. (2002) *After Virtue: A Study of Moral Theory*. London: Duckworth.
Toffler, A. and Toffler, H. (1993) *War and Anti-War: Survival at the Dawn of the Twenty-first Century*. Boston: Little & Brown.
Virilio, P. (1983) *Pure War*. London: Semiotext(e).

11

COUNTERINSURGENCY

The state of a controversial art

David Kilcullen

In 2003, as resistance to occupation intensified in Iraq, Counterinsurgency re-entered main-stream consciousness for the first time in a generation. In 2005, as the Afghan war escalated, Counterinsurgency also began to dominate the discourse of European, American and allied governments, either openly or under cover of terms like 'the comprehensive approach'. After decades in the dark, the controversial art of counterinsurgency was suddenly thrust again into the spotlight, provoking a vigorous and rancorous debate.

By 2007, after a remarkable period of rapid adaptation and organizational change in the US military, a re-introduced Counterinsurgency doctrine was making a major difference on the ground in Iraq. The publication of the Army and Marine Corps field manual, FM 3–24 *Counterinsurgency*, in December 2006, and General David Petraeus' successful application of methods from that manual during the surge in Iraq in 2007–8, led some commentators to see Counter-insurgency (or COIN) as the solution, or at least as the new dominant paradigm in Western thinking on intervention in complex conflicts.

In this chapter, as I have done elsewhere, I will argue the exact opposite: namely, that not only is classical COIN not the new dominant paradigm for Western intervention, but that it *should not be* – and that a debate that focuses too narrowly on the efficacy or applicability of a set of Cold War concepts from the late 1950s is both destructive and distracting.

Key issues in the debate: effectiveness, appropriateness, ethics, policy

The key issues in the counterinsurgency debate are easy to enumerate: does counterinsurgency actually work? Does it take too long, and cost too much, to be sustainable for Western demo-cratic governments? Should Western militaries do more to develop counterinsurgency capabil-ity? Do processes of competitive adaptation and organizational learning drive success in counterinsurgency? Does improving counterinsurgency capability undermine effectiveness in 'conventional' state-on-state warfare, and if so, does this matter? Should civilian organizations (especially diplomatic services and aid agencies) be forced to build their own counterinsurgency capability, whether they want it or not? In the absence of civilian capabilities, should military forces assume the mission of development, stabilization, reconstruction and governance assist-ance, or does this do more harm than good? Does development assistance in counterinsurgency have a stabilizing, neutral or destabilizing effect? Does the counterinsurgent's focus on governance and development assistance hinder and compromise the work of NGOs and humanitarian assistance organizations trying to work in the same space, and does that matter? Is counterinsurgency just a kinder, gentler method of pursuing neo-imperialist goals that are fundamentally harmful to local populations? Is counterinsurgency therefore unethical, even if conducted with respect for human rights? Is counterinsurgency doomed to failure because the enemy will always be more savage than we can be, and because proven methods of suppressing rebellion – involving mass destruction and violence – are unavailable to modern Western democracies? Does the creation of counterinsurgency capabilities make it more likely that governments will choose to intervene in one of the messiest and most problematic forms of conflict? Do we thereby risk locking ourselves into precisely the kinds of conflicts we should avoid? Alternatively, much as Western dominance in conventional warfare has pushed adversaries into other forms of conflict, is mastering counterinsurgency the key to avoiding having to do it?

We might marshal this diverse collection of issues into four debates, over *Effectiveness*, *Appropriateness*, *Ethics* and *Policy*. And yet the answer to these questions, like the answer to almost any important question when applied to complex adaptive systems in real-world environments, is 'it depends'. Of course, it primarily depends on what we mean by 'Counterinsurgency', and the word can mean several very different things, as the following brief intellectual history shows.

A brief intellectual history of counter-insurrection

Generic, 'small c' counterinsurgency – the broadly-defined activity of countering insurrection, suppressing internal rebellion in order to control societies – is an ancient human institution, a traditional (perhaps even a defining) activity of government. It has existed at least as long as the state itself.

In fact, counterinsurgency seems to have been central to the development of the ancient state, and hence of the state as we know it today. Paul Johnston, for example, traces the evolution of counterinsurgency in Egypt under the Ptolemies, following their victory over the Seleucids at the battle of Raphia in 218 BC, a victory that destabilized Egyptian society for more than a century. This instability forced Ptolemaic armies to engage in continual operations against a series of insurgencies, and fundamentally affected the development of the state in Egypt (Johnstono 2009). In a similar vein, Barry Strauss' study of the Third Servile War (73–71 BC) shows that the Roman Republic's suppression of Spartacus' slave rebellion, while aiming to preserve the status quo, in fact contributed – through the boost it gave to the political careers of generals like Marcus Licinius Crassus and Gnaeus Pompey – to that Republic's transformation, through civil war, into the Empire. Both these studies, like others, indicate a link between counterinsurgency and state formation in ancient history (Strauss 2009).

Countering insurrection in the ancient world, of course, bore little resemblance to mid twentieth-century COIN theory. Indeed, the bitter comment of the British guerrilla leader Galgacus ('to robbery, slaughter and plunder, they give the lying name of Empire; they make a devastation and call it Peace' (Tacitus Book 30)), reported in Tacitus, could serve as a universal verdict on the generally ferocious methods of ancient counterinsurgency. As I have remarked elsewhere, in this the Romans seem to have been merely the most systematic and well-developed exemplars of a widespread tendency in the ancient world, but they of course also engaged in political coalition-building, civil governance and economic development programmes, so that highly lethal military operations were only one component of a much more comprehensive approach to counter-insurrection (Kilcullen 2011: 321).

The link between countering insurrection and patterns of state formation is by no means restricted to antiquity however, as Philip Bobbitt showed in *The Shield of Achilles*, his comprehensive survey of the interaction of law, economics and strategy in the formation and evolution of the modern state. Bobbitt showed that the very nature of the state has been shaped by the demands of war, and by the need to create and maintain legitimacy through domestic order. While much of Bobbitt's argument relates to the organization of the state for external or interstate war, many of his examples also demonstrate the effects of internal counter-insurrection on state evolution right up until the end of the twentieth century (Bobbitt 2002). More recently, Ganesh Sitaraman has made the link between counterinsurgency and constitutional (or state) formation explicit for modern conflicts (Sitaraman 2008: 1622). Likewise, the historian Roy McCullough makes a persuasive argument for the role of counterinsurgency (especially in the Languedoc region) as a major shaping element in the evolution of the French state under Louis XIV (McCullough 2007).

Indeed, political theorists including Max Weber, Emile Durkheim and, of course, Karl Marx explicitly define the state, at least in part, via its internal security and counterinsurgency role. Consider, for example, Weber's famous dictum that a state can be defined as such only 'if and insofar as its administrative staff successfully upholds a claim on the monopoly of the legitimate use of violence in the enforcement of its order' (Weber 1946). While this observation is often shorthanded to 'a monopoly on the legitimate use of force', the full quotation makes it clear that Weber is referring here to the use of force under certain specific circumstances, namely coercion by the state to suppress internal disorder. He is also pointing to a process whereby the state legitimizes that suppression through success in maintaining order against opposition – in other words, through countering insurrection.

Generic, 'small-c' counterinsurgency, then, or counter-insurrection, seems to be an enduring human social institution that has been part of the role of virtually every government in history and perhaps even partly defines what we mean by the word 'state'.

The methods states have used to suppress insurgencies have been as enormously varied as states themselves, and have also varied according to the nature of a given insurrection, and the nature of the population group within which that insurrection exists. It is therefore difficult to identify a common approach to counter-insurrection throughout the roughly 385 examples of this form of conflict that have occurred in the last two centuries, or in the hundreds of other examples from earlier periods in history. Ethnic or multi-racial empires, colonial powers, occupation authorities, totalitarian or authoritarian regimes, democracies, or indeed private corporations acting in the role of a state (such as the British East India Company in pre-1857 India, or the Honorable East India Company in the Netherlands East Indies) seem to have adopted widely varying techniques. That said, these techniques appear to have been determined in large part by the state's attitude to the population within the territory it controlled, an attitude that in turn arose largely from the nature of these states or state-like entities themselves. Hence, the nature of the state (in particular, the relationship between the state and its subject population) seems to be one of the few reliable predictors of the types of counterinsurgency techniques it is likely to adopt.

'COIN' or 'big-c' counterinsurgency

Thus 'small-c' or generic counterinsurgency is a longstanding and diverse phenomenon that does not seem to be exclusively associated with any specific content, doctrine or set of core techniques – it simply mirrors the state's relationship with the population, and may involve a very wide variety of methods. 'Big-C' Counterinsurgency, however, is an entirely different matter.

Both the term 'Counterinsurgency' (hereafter, 'COIN') and the doctrine to which it refers have an extremely specific content, a definite origin, and embody a set of ideas that can be very precisely located in time and space: in the late 1950s, in the government-research 'think-tank' community, and on the eastern seaboard of the United States. Indeed it is almost impossible to fully understand the implications of COIN as we know it without grasping the very particular intellectual climate from which it emerged.

A RAND Corporation study, Austin Long's *On 'Other War': Lessons from Five Decades of RAND Counterinsurgency Research* (2006) acknowledges that

> the RAND corporation's ... research is limited in that almost all of it is based on cases that occurred in the context of the Cold War. Some might question the continued relevance of studies centered on conflicts that took place in such a radically different geopolitical context.
>
> *(Long 2006: ix)*

This is significant because RAND (along with ARPA, the forerunner of today's DARPA, the Defense Advanced Research Projects Agency) can be said to have invented COIN as we know it, sometime between 1956 and 1962, in response to the problems of Cold War low-intensity conflict, under conditions of superpower nuclear confrontation, against agrarian communist insurgencies in the former territories of European empires in Asia and Africa. Veteran RAND analyst Stephen Hosmer remembers first hearing the term 'Counterinsurgency' in the mid 1950s, when RAND was first beginning research into the topic, giving some indications that RAND may even have coined the term itself.[1]

The RAND Corporation, originally a project of the Douglas Aircraft Corporation to support the United States Army Air Forces during the Second World War, had by 1946 become a government-sponsored operations research institute focusing on aerospace policy and technology, and in particular on nuclear strategy. RAND theorists like Albert and Roberta Wohlstetter, Herman Kahn, Bernard Brodie, William Kaufmann and Thomas C. Schelling were highly influential in the formulation of US nuclear strategy for the Cold War, through important studies on post-nuclear strategy, nuclear deterrence and game theory (Long 2006: 5). RAND's influence within the priesthood of nuclear strategists who specialized in almost hyper-rational analysis of virtually unthinkable post-apocalyptic scenarios was such that the historian Fred Kaplan described these nuclear researchers as 'Wizards of Armageddon' (Kaplan 1991).

By the mid 1950s, however, communist-inspired nationalist insurgencies had emerged across much of Asia and Africa, in the wake of decolonization by the Dutch, British, French, Belgian, Italian and American empires (in the latter case, the Huk rebellion against the newly-independent former US protectorate of the Philippines). RAND was turning its attention to the much messier problems of ground warfare through Project SIERRA, a series of war games for the US Air Force, led by Edward Paxson of RAND's mathematics department. SIERRA focused in part on the problems of limited war against communist guerrillas in the decolonizing world. According to a recent RAND history of the Vietnam era:

> Starting in 1954 and lasting for several years, these war games focused on Southeast Asia, South Asia, and the Middle East, and on the tactical role that the Air Force might play in such a war in conjunction with the Army and Navy. Among various scenarios, Paxson's SIERRA simulated guerrilla warfare fighting, such as the struggles then being waged by the Viet Minh against the French in Vietnam and by Chinese insurgents against the British in Malaya. Other scenarios included Thailand and Burma.
>
> *(Elliot 2010: 9)*

One key outcome of Project SIERRA was a handbook of Viet Minh insurgent strategy and tactics, written by RAND researcher George Tanham between 1954 and 1957, initially as a classified study, later published by Praeger as the very first work on communist insurgency by an American author (Elliot 2010: 10). Another outcome was a sharp critique of the then-prevailing US nuclear strategy of Massive Retaliation, which the COIN analysts saw as inflexible and lacking in credibility in limited wars outside Europe and the United States (Elliot 2010: 9). This critique paralleled that of General Maxwell D. Taylor in his 1960 book *The Uncertain Trumpet*, which called instead for a strategy of 'flexible response' (Long 2006: 6). Upon President John F. Kennedy's election in November 1960, his administration adopted Taylor's strategy of flexible response, 'but expanded it to cover insurgencies as well as limited wars such as those envisioned by [RAND in Project] Sierra' (Long 2006: 6).

Indeed, John F. Kennedy presided over the first great outpouring of research, debate, policy, public commentary and field practice for what was now, for the first time, being called 'Counterinsurgency'. President Kennedy's inauguration on 20 January 1961 can thus be considered the beginning of what we might call the 'Classical' COIN era.

Classical COIN

In January 1961, the month of Kennedy's inauguration, the National Liberation Front announced its campaign to overthrow the government of South Vietnam, and Soviet Premier Nikita Krushchev gave a speech pledging support for 'wars of national liberation'.

> [Krushchev] classified conflicts into world wars, local wars, and wars of national liberation … National liberation wars began 'as uprisings of colonial peoples against their oppressors, [then] developed into guerilla wars.' The Soviet Union would support wholeheartedly and without reservation wars of national liberation, such as the conflicts in Algeria, Cuba, and Vietnam.
>
> *(Welch Larson 1997: 110)*

Although Krushchev's speech was given on 6 January before a closed Kremlin meeting of party theoreticians and propagandists, the West did not become aware of the speech until it was published on 18 January, two days before President Kennedy's inauguration (Welch Larson 1997: 110). Kennedy's reaction was immediate: the very same day, even before the formal inauguration of his new administration, he directed the development of a counterinsurgency capability within the US government, to include the US Agency for International Development, the Central Intelligence Agency, the State Department and the US Information Agency. President Kennedy also ordered the creation of a counterinsurgency school within the US Army Special Forces. In his speech at the opening ceremony of this school (which today bears his name), the president said:

> We need to be prepared to fight a different war. This is another type of war, new in its intensity, ancient in its origin, war by guerrilla, insurgents, subversives, assassins; war by ambush instead of combat, by infiltration instead of aggression, seeking victory by eroding and exhausting the enemy instead of engaging him. It requires, in those situations where we encounter it, a whole new strategy, a wholly different force, and therefore, a new and wholly different kind of military training.[2]

RAND's response to President Kennedy's call to arms was to ramp up its study of counterinsurgency, prompted in part by patriotism – a genuine wish to contribute to a pressing national security challenge – and in part, according to its own history, by 'its desire not to be left out of the policy loop on an issue that was gaining importance in America's national security considerations' at a time when new conflicts were emerging in which the Air Force, until now RAND's major funder, would play only a supporting role (Elliot 2010: 13).

The 1962 RAND symposium

As part of RAND's expanded counterinsurgency programme, on 16 April 1962, Stephen Hosmer convened a critically important week-long symposium in Washington, DC, attended by civilian researchers and military experts, the results of which were published by RAND in 1963 as *Counterinsurgency: A Symposium, April 16–20, 1962* (Hosmer and Crane 1963). This symposium was a seminal moment in the intellectual history of classical COIN.

The aim was to 'distill lessons and insights from past insurgent conflicts that might help to inform and shape the U.S. involvement in Vietnam and to foster the effective prosecution of other future counterinsurgency campaigns' – in other words, to study contemporary wars of national liberation and draw, by analogy, lessons for current and future counterinsurgency (Hosmer and Crane 1963: iii). This approach depended on reasoning by extrapolation from case studies, bringing together 'best practice' field methods with theoretical insights from RAND's existing stable of scientists and nuclear strategists. The case study method, invented by and beloved of Harvard Business School and the Operations Research community, achieved a neat intellectual fit with the worldview of President Kennedy's new Secretary of Defense, Robert S. MacNamara, himself a former Harvard professor, Air Force operations research analyst, statistician, and president of the Ford Motor Company.

In key ways, then, classical COIN represents an outgrowth of the New Frontier mentality of the early Kennedy administration: an effort by the Washington think-tank community to support Kennedy's vision, and his attempt to counter Soviet support for national liberation movements, by distilling the essence of colonial warfare and updating it for Cold War conditions. The immediate purpose was to develop a scientific, rational, measurable, management-science approach to the Vietnam War. This is not to criticize COIN, but to acknowledge its origins: since COIN theory relies on reasoning by analogy from case studies, we are entitled to ask whether those case studies are representative of the broader phenomenon of guerrilla warfare, and whether the environment in which COIN emerged resembles today's conflict environment sufficiently closely to justify an extrapolation from classical COIN to today's wars in Iraq, Afghanistan and elsewhere.

Some of the most influential theorists and practitioners of classical COIN attended the 1962 symposium: David Galula, Frank Kitson and Edward G. Lansdale among them, along with Charles Bohannan, Wendell Fertig and Napoleon Valeriano. Retired Lieutenant Colonel David Galula of the French Colonial Infantry,[3] in particular, was an active participant in the workshop, and this led him to further work with RAND, including a detailed account of French pacification operations in the Kabylia region of Algeria. This, originally a classified study, remained unpublished for over 40 years before eventually being released by RAND in 2006 as *Pacification in Algeria, 1956–1958* (Galula 2006). The better known of Galula's works (indeed, his only known full-length study until 2006) was his systematic COIN primer *Counterinsurgency Warfare: Theory and Practice*, published by Praeger in 1964, and an intellectual cornerstone of COIN's neo–classical revival after 2003.

And here, perhaps, is the first hint of something problematic about classical COIN as theory. Galula's longer and more detailed study, *Pacification in Algeria* is Algeria-specific and focused at the lower tactical level (Galula had been a captain, commanding a company in two rural districts of one region, at a specific period in the development of the Algerian War). True, Galula had served in Greece (as an observer), and in Hong Kong (as a military attaché) during the Chinese Civil War. But his only first-hand experience of COIN (an experience which, by definition, heavily informed the case-based COIN theory), indeed his only command experience in any campaign, was as a junior officer in Algeria.

French counter-guerrilla tactics in Algeria were not a popular subject in the United States in the early 1960s: President de Gaulle had announced that Algeria would vote on independence only two weeks before President Kennedy's inauguration, a process leading inevitably to French withdrawal in defeat from the colony; General Salan[4] launched a coup against the withdrawal three months later. US popular sympathy was generally on the side of the insurgents, with many Americans seeing them as nationalists rather than communists in orientation, glossing over the extensive atrocities against civilians that followed the French withdrawal. Ann Marlowe, in her biographical monograph on Galula, observes that this sentiment extended to President Kennedy himself:

> Then, too, in the United States, sentiment was often on the side of the Algerian rebels. Anti-colonialism was the order of the day. President Kennedy was fashionably anti-colonialist, and while still a senator, spoke in favor of Algerian independence. His July 2, 1957, speech, the longest of his Senate career, was titled, 'Imperialism—The Enemy of Freedom.' Kennedy argued that the Algerians deserved freedom on its merits, but he also noted that it would be hard to deny it to them in the long run.
>
> *(Marlowe 2010: 8–9)*

Galula, as a research associate at Harvard in 1962–3, therefore appears to have set out to write a more concise, generic and theoretical work, incorporating the same insights as *Pacification in Algeria*, but with minimal explicit reference to Algeria.[5] The book that resulted – *Counterinsurgency Warfare* – is thus not really a general theory of COIN, but rather, to some extent, a theory of COIN tactics in Algeria, with Algeria taken out. *Counterinsurgency Warfare* is essentially an argument (albeit a persuasive one) based on generalization from a single case – and even within this case the method achieved only a 50 per cent success rate: Galula used the same approach in both districts where he operated, but it only worked in one of them. More worryingly, the single-example basis for the theory only became readily apparent some four decades later, when Galula's two major works could finally be compared for the first time.

Sample size and homogeneity in classical COIN

A similar problem with sample size afflicts classical COIN more broadly, given that the case studies used to formulate the theory seem to have been drawn from a very small subset of examples of insurgency and counterinsurgency, and from a very specific historical period (that of communist wars of national liberation in the immediate post-1945 period). Taking the participants in the 1962 symposium as a group, given that they were asked to share insights from their experiences, it is instructive to examine those experiences as reported in the biographical notes in the symposium report, as these provide an insight into the case studies upon which the theory is built.

Of the symposium's 12 formal participants, five were American, four were British and there were one each Australian, French and Filipino. Eleven were Army officers; all were men (indeed, except for Sybille O. Greene, the rapporteur, all attendees were male including the RAND researchers). Eleven of the 12 were white. At least eight had fought in the Second

Table 11.1 Case study base for the RAND COIN Symposium 1962

Conflict: Features:	Huk Rebellion	French Algeria	Malaya	Kenya	South Vietnam	French Indochina
Region	Southeast Asia	North Africa	Southeast Asia	East Africa	Southeast Asia	Southeast Asia
Year began	1946	1954	1948	1952	1954	1946
Year ended	1954	1962	1960	1960	Ongoing in 1962	1954
Winner	Government	Insurgent	Government	Government	Insurgent	Insurgent
Government type	US-dominated former colony	Colonial power (France)	Colonial power (UK)	Colonial power (UK)	US-dominated former colony	Colonial power (UK)
Insurgent type	Communist rural	Communist rural/ urban	Communist rural	Nationalist/tribal rural	Communist rural	Communist rural
Economy type	Subsistence/cash-crop	Subsistence/cash-crop	Subsistence/cash-crop	Subsistence/cash-crop	Subsistence/cash-crop	Subsistence/cash-crop
Population	Tenant farmer	Tenant farmer	Peasant	Tenant farmer	Peasant	Peasant
Main terrain	Farm/village and plantation	Farm/village and plantation	Farm/village and plantation	Farm/village and plantation	Farm/village and plantation	Farm/village and plantation
Second terrain	Jungle	Mountain	Jungle	Jungle	Jungle	Jungle
Insurgent religion	Animist/Christian	Muslim	Buddhist/Confucian	Animist/Christian	Buddhist/Confucian	Buddhist/Confucian

Source: RAND Corporation, *Counterinsurgency: A Symposium, 16–20 April, 1962*, biographical notes pp. xix–xxiii.

World War, and at least six had a background in Special Operations or Unconventional Warfare (that is, in the terminology of the time, in leading guerrilla forces in occupied territory). There were no specialists in logistics, transportation, policing or civilian government, no naval, marine[6] or aviation officers, no diplomats and no former or current insurgents or host-nation civilian populations. Most participants had served at the tactical level in command of army combat units, a fact reflected in the rank structure of the group: one captain, eight colonels or lieutenant colonels, two brigadier generals and a civilian.

Their collective experience included the Huk rebellion in the Philippines, the Algerian War, the Malayan Emergency, the Greek and Chinese Civil Wars, and campaigns in Oman, Kenya, Vietnam, French Indochina, Korea and Thailand. This experience appears more diverse than it was, however, since between them Galula and Lansdale brought experience (as observers only) in five of these campaigns. The vast weight of practical experience of the group was in two theatres only: Malaya and Indochina. Indeed, comparing the campaigns in which seminar participants had fought, remarkable commonalities emerge.

Key commonalities include:

- *timeline* (all conflicts began within nine years after the Second World War);
- *duration* (all lasted eight years except Malaya, which lasted 12, and Vietnam, which was ongoing in 1962);
- *region* (all occurred in Southeast Asia and North or East Africa);
- *government* type (all governments were either European colonial powers or US-dominated former colonies);
- *insurgent* type (all but one insurgency was communist, all had nationalist elements, all were predominantly rural);
- *economic* type (all conflicts occurred in subsistence agriculture or cash-crop economies);
- *population* type (all populations were tenant farmers or peasants and primarily Buddhist/ Confucian or animist/Christian); and
- *terrain* (principal fighting in all campaigns occurred in farm, village or plantation environments with significant secondary fighting in jungle areas or mountains).

Interestingly, there is less commonality of outcome across these six similar cases: the results are an even split between insurgent victory and government victory. Thus while it is possible to say that there is a high degree of homogeneity among the case studies used to formulate classical COIN theory, it is much harder to say that the application of COIN theory (based on best practices by military participants on the government side in these cases) has a strong correlation with government victory. Methods varied, and only in Malaya can the government as a whole be said to have been consciously and systematically applying a version of classical COIN. In other words, while the environments were similar, the methods differed, as did the outcomes, and because the studies rely on personal experience of tactical operations, it is very difficult to draw a clear correlation between method and outcome.

Needless to say, there were dozens of other seminars, studies, symposia and other analyses as part of the initial development of classical COIN theory, and it would be wrong to see the RAND study as the sole point-of-origin of the theory. On the contrary, it was simply representative of many efforts to distil the essence of colonial warfare, drawing from case studies of the revolutionary warfare of the 1950s, and update it for Cold War conditions, that ultimately resulted in the emergence, by the early 1960s, of classical COIN as we know it. Again, this is not to criticize classical COIN but rather to make explicit the theoretical and case study basis from which it emerges, and to point out that the case studies upon which it draws share certain very specific characteristics, so that while the techniques it advocates *may* be effective in environments, or against insurgents, that share these characteristics, its applicability is far more questionable in different circumstances.

Neo-classical COIN

The COIN revival of the early post-9/11 period, as the United States and its allies drifted into an insurgency in Afghanistan, and as resistance to occupation in Iraq gradually also assumed the form of an insurgency, drew heavily on classical COIN theory. Galula, Thompson, Fall and other writers of the classical era were highly influential in the thinking of the group (including myself) that devised the reinvigorated COIN doctrine embodied in the Army/Marine Corps Field Manual, FM 3–24 *Counterinsurgency* in December 2006. The RAND Corporation, likewise, played an important role by re-issuing or re-examining many of its classical-era publications, or publishing for the first time key works like Galula's *Pacification in Algeria* that had remained classified until that time.

In this sense, given the influence of classical COIN over FM 3–24, and its appeal to the authority of historical classics (Galula, Thompson, Mao, Lawrence) the COIN renaissance of 2005–6 can be considered a Neo-Classical Revival, resting on the application and updating of classical precepts for the new campaigns. Clearly, the effort to revisit COIN best practices made eminent sense for a military force that was engaged against two major insurgencies and had not updated its COIN doctrine for more than 20 years. But how applicable is the 1960s version of classical COIN, as a theory, to these modern campaigns? As I have argued elsewhere in detail, and as summarized below, there are significant differences at the strategic, operational and tactical levels.[7]

The strategic environment

Classical COIN theory posits an insurgent challenge to a functioning (albeit often weak) state – the standard situation of a colonial or newly independent state facing a national liberation war, as in the 1960s case studies that form the basis for the theory. The insurgent challenges the status quo; the counterinsurgent seeks to reinforce the state's legitimacy and capacity, to defeat this internal challenge. This clearly applies to some insurgencies today – Southern Thailand, Aceh, Sri Lanka and Colombia are examples. But in other cases, insurgency today is occurring after state failure. It is not directed at taking over a functioning body politic, but rather at dismembering or scavenging its carcass, or contesting an 'ungoverned space'. Chechnya in 1994–9, and East Timor in 1999–2002 are examples of this form of insurgency; Somalia (since 1991 but more especially since 2006) is another. This situation is covered in works on colonial small wars (such as those by C.E. Callwell and the US Marine Corps *Small Wars Manual*; Callwell 1996; US Marine Corps 1987) but was not emphasized in classical COIN, and is an example of circumstances outside the parameters of the case studies on which the theory is built.

Similarly, classical COIN assumes that the insurgent initiates. Thus, Galula asserts flatly that 'whereas in conventional war, either side can initiate the conflict, only one – the insurgent – can initiate a revolutionary war, for counterinsurgency is only an effect of insurgency' (Galula 1964: 3). Classical theorists therefore pay substantial attention to the problem of recognizing insurgency early enough to respond effectively. Thompson observes that 'at the first signs of an incipient insurgency … no one likes to admit that anything is going wrong. This automatically leads to a situation where government countermeasures are too little and too late' (Thompson

1970: 20–1). But several modern campaigns – Iraq and Afghanistan, for example – were initiated by governments or invading forces, and insurgents were reactive. True enough, in Iraq and Afghanistan, inattention after the end of conventional campaigning allowed the insurgents to regroup and launch the first attacks. But though the insurgents thus gained the tactical initiative, the counterinsurgents held the strategic initiative. Such patterns are readily recognizable in historical examples of resistance warfare, but not in classical COIN theory.[8]

Today, in many cases, the counterinsurgent represents the forces of revolutionary change, while the insurgent fights to preserve the status quo of ungoverned spaces, or to repel an occupying force – a political relationship in reverse of that envisaged in classical COIN. Pakistan's campaign against the Pakistani Taliban since 2003 is an example of this. The enemy includes not only al-Qaeda (AQ) linked extremists and Taliban, but also local tribal combatants who fight primarily to preserve their way of life against twenty-first century encroachment on their traditional rights and freedoms.[9] The problem of weaning these fighters away from extremist sponsors, while simultaneously supporting modernization on the frontier, does somewhat resemble pacification operations in classical COIN, of the sort described by Galula in 1963. But it also echoes colonial campaigns in the same region, and includes entirely new elements arising from the effects of globalization.[10]

One of the most strategically significant of these 'globalization effects' is the rise of a worldwide audience, which gives insurgents a near-instantaneous means to publicize their cause. Globalized Internet communication also enables moral, financial and recruiting support, acting as a strategic hinterland or 'virtual sanctuary' that sustains insurgents. Classical COIN theory deals extensively with 'active' and 'passive' sanctuaries, methods to quarantine such sanctuaries, and their effects on insurgent performance (Thompson 1970: *passim*; Galula 1964: 38–41) But it treats sanctuary as primarily a physical space (often straddling an international border) in which insurgents can regroup or through which external support flows.

However, today's Internet-based virtual sanctuary is beyond the reach of counterinsurgent forces or neighbouring governments, and its effects are difficult to quarantine. Insurgents in Iraq were adept at exploiting global media effects, while the 'Global Islamic Media Front' and AQ's *as-Sahab* media production arm have achieved new heights of professionalism in targeting global audiences.[11] Internet-based methods for financial transfers, training and recruitment, clandestine communication, planning and intelligence collection capabilities allow insurgents to exploit virtual sanctuary for more than just propaganda. Classical COIN theory has, of course, little to say about such virtual sanctuary, since the modern electronic environment did not exist in the 1950s cases upon which the theory is built.

The transnational character of modern insurgency is another new feature. Classical-era insurgents copied each other (for example, the Algerian FLN consciously copied the Viet Minh, and EOKA and other insurgent and terrorist movements copied the Jewish *Irgun Zvai Leumi* and *Lehi* in Mandated Palestine) (Hoffman 2006: 45–53). But such emulation typically happened after the event, and direct real-time cooperation between movements was rare. Thus classical COIN typically regards insurgency as something that occurs within one country or district, between an internal non-state actor and a single government (Kilcullen 2005). This is reflected in definitions of insurgency used today in official doctrine.[12] By contrast, today we see real-time cooperation and cross-pollination among movements. AQ and its loose confederation operate across many countries in several continents (Kilcullen 2005; Barno 2006). AQ operatives pass messages from Pakistan and Afghanistan, through Iran to Iraq.[13] Improvised explosive devices (IEDs) that first appear in Palestine or Iraq rapidly proliferate to Chechnya and Afghanistan. Iranian IED technology appears in Iraq (AFPS 2006) or Afghanistan, and Pakistani extremist groups operate in Afghanistan.[14] Insurgents in Iraq mounted operations in response to events in

Lebanon, and conducted attacks in Jordan.[15] Insurgents in Southeast Asia apply methods developed in the Middle East that circulate via the Internet or on CD-ROM.[16] This transnational pattern of cooperation is part of a deliberate AQ strategy, but these materials are also available to other movements and there is evidence that non-AQ groups (including environmentalist extremists) are noting and copying AQ methods.[17]

Classical COIN also tends to assume a bilateral struggle between the insurgent and counterinsurgent: both Galula and FM 3–24 posit two theoretical actors in this type of campaign, the 'insurgent' and the 'counterinsurgent' (Galula 1964). Thompson speaks of the 'insurgent' and the 'government'. But another distinctive characteristic of modern insurgency is its multilateral character. Insurgencies today, including those in Iraq, Afghanistan, the Southern Philippines, Southern Thailand, Chechnya, Pakistan and the Horn of Africa involve multiple diffuse, competing insurgent movements. In contrast to traditional movements these conflicts lack a 'united front' or umbrella organization that directs the insurgency. Rather, dozens of competing groups pursue their own, frequently conflicting agendas. Field experience from Iraq, particularly, suggests that it may be harder, not easier, to defeat such a complex and disorganized swarm of opponents.[18]

Operational art

At the operational level, there are of course many similarities between today's insurgencies and those of the classical era. Insurgent movements remain popular uprisings that grow from, and are conducted through pre-existing social networks (village, tribe, family, urban neighbourhood, political or religious party).[19] Thus the insurgent operational art remains fundamentally a matter of aggregating dispersed tactical actions by small groups and individuals, and orchestrating their effects into a strategically significant campaign sequence. Similarly, the operational art of COIN remains fundamentally concerned with displacing insurgent influence from these social networks, supplanting insurgent support within the population, and manoeuvering to marginalize the enemy and deny them a popular base of support. Thus, while the strategic 'competition for government' may be less relevant today than in the past, at the operational level COIN remains a competition between several sides, each seeking to mobilize the population in its cause.

But today's environment (especially the 'globalization effects' of virtual sanctuary, global audience and cyber-mobilization) ensures that this operational art develops in ways that differ substantially from classical methods. Indeed, modern insurgencies operate more like a self-synchronizing swarm of independent, but cooperating cells, than like a formal organization. In many cases, even the fashionable cybernetic discourse of 'networks', 'vertices' and 'nodes'[20] implies more structure than exists.

Classical COIN theorists considered the aggregated effect of many small incidents – Robert Taber's 'war of the flea' – as a key operational driver[21] even though they recognized the impact of well-publicized single dramatic incidents. By contrast, modern decentralized media capabilities have driven a compression of the operational level of war, so that almost any tactical action by any individual can have immediate strategic impact. This increases the unpredictability and non-linearity of COIN campaigning, rendering statistical trends (Cordesman 2006: 3) less important than public perception. Again, this was accounted for in classical COIN theory, but 'globalization effects' have dramatically increased its influence. In circumstances of pervasive media presence, the demeanour of a single soldier, diplomat or aid official instantaneously communicates more about the success or failure of a campaign than can any public information operation.

Urban insurgent tactics

At the tactical level, one obvious difference between classical COIN and today's campaigns is their urbanized quality. All of the case studies in the 1962 symposium, for example, were primarily rural. Classical insurgencies actually included several campaigns with urban components, such as Algeria, but COIN theory treats the rural component of each campaign as decisive. The reason was straightforward – classical-era insurgencies in 'colonial or independent underdeveloped territories' (Thompson 1970: 21) were indeed primarily rural. But this is often not so today, as is apparent when flying over Afghanistan or Iraq. Incidents in Iraq cluster in urban centres or areas of suburban sprawl around Iraq's major cities.[22] The insurgent, as in classical theory, continues to hide amongst the population. But in urbanized societies (like Iraq) the cover is in the cities.

This urban environment has very significant tactical implications – engagement ranges are short and contacts are fleeting as in traditional insurgencies, but bystanders are now always present and often exploited by the insurgent. Media presence is also greatest in cities, fuelling propaganda-based tactics that target the population to generate shock and provoke sectarian unrest. Traditional COIN tactics like fencing villages, cordon and search, curfew, and food control (accepted as routine in Malaya) have drawn sharp criticism in Iraq and Afghanistan because of the disruption they cause in urban neighbourhoods, combined with the negative propaganda effect of enhanced media coverage (Ricks 2006: 330–5).

Internet, cell phone and television coverage in insurgent areas enables web- and cellphone-based coordination, changing insurgent tactics and countermeasures. Most houses in Iraqi cities have at least one satellite dish, for example,[23] while a recent study found that more than 24 per cent of residents in Mogadishu access the Internet at least once a week (Ledgard 2011). Underground newspapers, pirate radio stations and insurgent posters are still a factor in places like Pakistan's Federally Administered Tribal Areas, which lack the Internet coverage and urbanized population of Iraq or of settled districts in Pakistan.[24] But perception management is vastly more complex when the population has instantaneous access to media broadcasts intended for third nation audiences.[25]

Modern insurgent tactics centre on the urban bomb rather than, as in classical COIN, on the rural ambush. Improvised explosive devices (IEDs), particularly suicide attacks, generate 'good copy' for insurgent propaganda and ensure sponsorship from donors and supporters. IEDs also overcome the lethality 'self-limit' of classical insurgencies, whose rifle-based tactics meant that they had to field a greater number of fighters, and so risk more casualties, in order to generate greater lethality (McCormick *et al.* 2006). The Irish Republican Army developed this approach 20 years ago, but unlike Northern Ireland (where acquisition, storage, transport and caching of IEDs were so difficult that insurgent quartermasters were key players (Dillon 1999)) modern-day theaters like Iraq are awash with military-grade ordnance.

Post-classical COIN

In key respects, then, many of the assumptions that were carried across from specific case studies into the general, classical theory of COIN do not transfer well to today's conflicts, making a straight copy of classical COIN (essentially, the neo-classical approach) problematic. This is, of course, very well understood by practitioners in the field, so that neo-classical COIN is already giving way to a post-classical period, in which techniques and doctrine are based more on empiricism (a data-driven or evidence-based understanding of what is happening on the ground) rather than on appeal to the authority of historical cases, or exegesis from the classical canon of COIN theorists.

This can be seen in two features of the environment since the publication of FM 3–24 in late 2006: the emergence in the field of new techniques not envisaged in doctrine, and the development of new paradigms that explain reality at least as well as classical COIN.

Field innovation: accelerated COIN

As noted earlier, all the case study campaigns in the 1962 RAND symposium lasted eight years, except for Malaya which lasted 12, and Vietnam which eventually took nine years of US direct combat involvement (1965–73). As one of many studies during the same era, this similarity of duration may have contributed to the accepted wisdom that COIN inherently takes a long time (9–12 years is an often-quoted yardstick), and that therefore a long-term, whole-of-government effort, successfully maintaining both the support of the population in theatre, and US domestic public support, is the sine qua non of successful COIN. The neo-classical version of this can be seen in FM 3–24:

> I-134. Insurgencies are protracted by nature. Thus, COIN operations always demand considerable expenditures of time … people do not actively support a government unless they are convinced that the counterinsurgents have the means, ability, stamina, and will to win.…The populace must have confidence in the staying power of both the counterinsurgents and the HN government. Insurgents and local populations often believe that a few casualties or a few years will cause the United States to abandon a COIN effort. Constant reaffirmations of commitment, backed by deeds, can overcome that perception.
>
> *(US Army 2006: 1–24)*

Interestingly, this idea is somewhat foreign to colonial warfare or small wars theory, which recognized that conventional armies are tactically stronger than irregulars, whereas local guerrillas are strategically more resilient than intervening outsiders. Thus, in small wars theory, quick, decisive, often violent action to knock out a nascent rebellion is favoured over protraction, on the theory that this is ultimately cheaper, kinder and more likely to succeed.

In any case, whatever the doctrine, campaigning in Iraq and Afghanistan has been subject to much tighter time constraints than envisaged in classical or neo-classical COIN theory. In January 2007, one month after the publication of FM 3–24, its principal author (General David Petraeus) assumed command in Iraq with nowhere near the length of time that one would expect in a classical COIN paradigm. The 'surge' was slated to last 18 months, giving a total time for the Iraq campaign of only five years (2003–8). Even on the assumption that some units had begun applying COIN as early as 2005, the timeline for the campaign was radically truncated to about three years. What was needed was a dramatically accelerated COIN effect in order to buy time for a political settlement.

The approach that emerged could not easily have been found in FM 3–24. It combined coercive and persuasive elements into a political strategy that sought a peaceful solution to the sectarian conflict that was driving the insurgency – thus, less of a COIN approach, and more civil war termination or heavy peace enforcement. The aim was to marginalize extremists on all sides (including those aligned with the government of Iraq) while co-opting anyone, from any political orientation whatsoever, who proved ready to reconcile, support a peaceful settlement and cease fighting.[26] To do this, the planners recognized that we needed a lengthy period of confidence building to convince people they were safe enough to engage in a political accommodation. We also recognized that, to lift the pall of fear that was preventing all sides from feeling safe enough to negotiate, we would need to kill or capture a substantial number of irrec-oncilable extremists: the plan must have a 'hard', lethal, coercive component directed against terrorists like al-Qaeda in Iraq (AQI), Jaysh al-Mahdi (JAM) and Iranian secret cells, as well as a 'soft', peaceful component of reconciling with anyone willing to put down the gun. The two worked in symbiosis – the more effectively we eliminated the irreconcilables, the more willing others would be to reconcile, and the further we progressed in peace-building the easier it would be to identify and eliminate the irreconcilable minority.

This resulted in what might be called 'accelerated COIN', with population-centric opera-tions across Iraq providing a framework of security, upon which two additional layers rested: highly lethal counter-network targeting (primarily using special operations and air power, sup-ported by an intensive intelligence effort) to destroy the irreconcilable network of terror cells, plus reconciliation and reintegration to make peace with reconcilable elements, bringing them into alignment with the coalition and (ultimately, in theory) the government. Ultimately the decisive aspect of the reconciliation strategy was the Awakening, a tribal revolt against AQI, which spread rapidly across the Sunni part of the country in 2007 and combined reconciliation and peacemaking with direct military action against irreconcilables and public safety in threat-ened communities.

The synergy achieved by this reconciliation/counter-network/security cycle had a flywheel effect, accelerating progress while creating an impetus towards reform and capacity building for civil government. Meanwhile the dramatic drop in Iraqi civilian casualties in mid 2007, and a similar drop in coalition casualties from late summer, restored a certain amount of public confi-dence (both in Iraq and in the United States) and bought enough political space to allow the coalition to eventually withdraw under a negotiated status of forces agreement. All this occurred within three years, dramatically faster than envisaged in COIN theory.

Likewise, in Afghanistan in 2010, General Stanley McChrystal (soon to be followed by General Petraeus) was saddled with what classical COIN theorists would have considered a hopelessly unrealistic timeline, when President Obama announced in December 2009 that US forces would begin a complete withdrawal by July 2011. This had a massively destabilizing effect on the Afghan people, validated Taliban propaganda that the coalition was an unreliable long-term partner, and provoked Afghan elites (most notably, the Afghan president himself) to begin balancing against the international community. Once again, on the most generous possible interpretation, some elements of the force in Afghanistan had begun practising neo-classical COIN in 2006–7, while COIN only became widespread in 2008. Thus the timeline for Afghanistan was again radically truncated to between two and four years, vastly less time than envisaged in COIN theory, and in extremely difficult circumstances due to the loss of confi-dence provoked by the self-imposed timeline.

Again, the approach taken has been 'accelerated COIN', combining extremely intensive counter-network targeting with intensified efforts at reconciliation (of senior Taliban leaders) and reintegration (of lower-level foot-soldiers). This rested on a framework of population and area security operations which looked, on the ground, much like traditional COIN, and on enhanced efforts to create a viable Afghan police and military, supported by an additional, time-limited troop surge.

Again, there have been several attempts to create an 'Awakening-like' uprising against the Taliban. While this has not taken the self-sustaining large-scale form of the Iraqi Awakening, it has resulted in a similar programme, the Village Stability Operations/Afghan Local Policing initiative, which is having similar effects at the local level in some insurgent-affected areas. Thus, once again, in the absence of anything like enough time for traditional COIN, and without the resources (especially troops) traditionally considered necessary for effective COIN, commanders have been forced into a risky attempt to dramatically accelerate COIN effects. The method chosen is, again, to generate a synergy between highly kinetic counter-network targeting of irreconcilables, and a peace-building programme to win over any member of the insurgency who proved willing to reconcile. This approach – not discussed in classical COIN theory and not to be found in FM 3–24 – can therefore be considered to be a field innovation, a form of post-classical COIN. It can be illustrated graphically, as shown in Figure 11.1.

The implications are two-fold. First, in a practical sense, the methods that succeeded in Iraq and that are currently being applied in Afghanistan differ significantly from those of classical COIN, or indeed from FM 3–24 and other neo-classical theories. Second, the intellectual approach to each campaign is profoundly empiricist – identifying techniques and methods that work on the ground, then developing and extending these methods through a series of limited 'field experiments', to form a bottom-up tactically driven campaigning style rather than a doctrinaire approach based on the historical, 1960s theory of insurgency and counterinsurgency.

Beyond COIN: new paradigms

It is dangerous to be prescriptive about these new models, since they are so field-based and pragmatic, and since the outcome of both the Afghan and Iraqi campaigns remains in doubt. But we can discern, in broad outline and with varying degrees of confidence, some emerging paradigms that move beyond COIN.

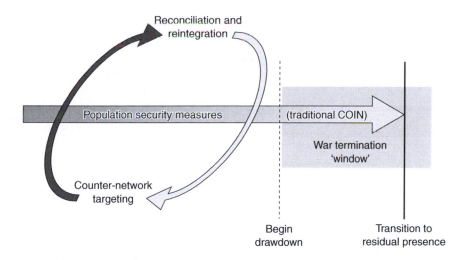

Figure 11.1 Accelerated COIN – Afghanistan and Iraq 2007–11.

A competition to mobilize, not to govern

In today's campaigns, the side may win which best mobilizes and energizes its global, regional and local support base – and prevents its adversaries doing likewise. Most fundamentally, it may be appropriate to move beyond the classical conception of COIN as a competition for legitimate government, seeing it instead as a *competition to mobilize*, interpreted in the broadest sense. Modern guerrillas may not seek to seize control of an existing government, relying instead on their ability to mobilize sympathizers within a global audience and generate local support. Thus the legitimacy of local government may be a secondary factor. Likewise, intervening security forces must mobilize the home population, the host country, the global audience, the populations of allied and neutral countries, and the military and government agencies involved. Success may have less to do with governmental legitimacy than with the ability to energize and mobilize support, and to deny energy and mobility to the enemy's support base.

Beyond 'single-state' COIN

In modern counterinsurgency, the security force 'area of influence' may need to include all neighbouring countries, and its 'area of interest' may need to be global. The classical single-state paradigm for COIN may no longer apply, since insurgents operate across national boundaries and exploit a global 'virtual sanctuary'. Thus, while legal and political considerations will probably prevent military activity outside a single-country 'area of operations', a COIN force must be able to influence the behaviour of neighbouring states. Border security, money transfers, ungoverned areas, ethnic minorities, refugee populations and media in neighbouring states may all play a key operational role for the insurgent – hence the counterinsurgent must be able to influence these. Similarly, the insurgents' propaganda audience, and their source of funds, recruits and support may be global. So the counterinsurgent's parent government must be able to work globally to counter propaganda and disrupt funding and recruiting. This implies a vastly increased role for diplomacy, global intelligence liaison and information operations.

Beyond 'binary COIN'

In modern campaigns, the security force must manage a complex environment, including multiple friendly, enemy and neutral players – rather than defeating a single insurgent adversary. Classical COIN tends to be 'population-centric', focusing on securing the population and gaining its support rather than on destroying the insurgent enemy. But it still fundamentally views the conflict as a binary struggle between one insurgent (or insurgent confederation) and one counterinsurgent (or counterinsurgent coalition). Modern campaigns belie this binary approach, since there are often multiple competing insurgent forces fighting each other as well as the government, and since the 'supported' government's interests may differ in key respects from those of its supposed allies. Hence, as I have argued elsewhere, it may be best to conceive of the environment as a 'conflict ecosystem' with multiple competing entities seeking to maximize their own survivability and influence. The counterinsurgent's task may no longer be to defeat the insurgent, but rather to impose or maximize its own interests in an unstable and chaotic environment.

This approach aligns well with recent thinking in the US military, as embodied in FM 3–07 *Stability Operations*, which conceives of modern campaigns as an attempt to neutralize and deal with sources of instability, and to build community resiliency, in a complex environment, rather than – as in classical COIN – to neutralize and deal with an insurgent enemy, strengthening the government and connecting it more closely to its people. In fact, this approach recognizes that efforts to strengthen or extend the reach of a corrupt, abusive or exploitative government may in fact have seriously destabilizing effects.

Beyond 'unity of effort'

In today's campaigns a common diagnosis of the problem, and common enablers for collaboration, may matter more than unity of effort across multiple agencies. A key principle of classical COIN is unity of effort – in the purest case, unified control of all elements of power, vertically at every level from local to national, and horizontally from district to district. Even 'unity of effort' is a watered-down version of the military's preferred 'unity of command'. But in modern campaigns international aid organizations, global media, non-government organizations and religious leaders are all critical for success, but lie outside the military's control. Many of these entities will not accept direction from the military, yet their actions can deny success unless cooperation is achieved. Since one cannot command what one cannot control, 'unity of effort' (let alone 'unity of command') may be unworkable in this environment. Luckily, international relief organizations have developed methods of collaboration and information sharing, designed to build a common diagnosis of 'complex emergencies', which enable collaboration in precisely this type of situation. A similar approach is beginning to be applied in several contemporary campaigns.

Beyond the '80/20 rule'

General Sir Gerald Templer, the British commander in Malaya, famously asserted that 'the shooting part is only 25% of this business', while Galula described counterinsurgency as '80% political, 20% military' (Galula 1964: 89). This concept certainly remains relevant to modern campaigning, in the sense that non-military elements of national power are more significant (though, in most cases, far less well resourced) than military forces. But it could be misinterpreted as implying that there remains an area – albeit only 20 per cent of the problem – that lies outside political leaders' purview and subject to conventional norms of combat. In modern campaigns, as we have seen, this may not be so. Given the pervasiveness of media presence and the near-instantaneous exploitation of all combat action for propaganda, today's counterinsurgencies may be 100 per cent political. Commanders, even at the lowest tactical level in the most straightforward combat engagement, may need to conceive of what they are doing as a form of 'political warfare' in which perception and political outcomes matter more than battlefield success. COIN specialists are already comfortable with this approach, but broadening it to conventional combat units and 'big army' commanders would be a true paradigm shift.

Beyond 'victory' in counterinsurgency

Classical COIN defines victory as the military defeat of the insurgents, the destruction of their political organization, and their marginalization from the population (Galula 1964: 77). Typically, destruction of the last remnants of an insurgent movement can take decades, but once permanently marginalized they are no longer considered a threat. (For example, the Malayan Emergency ended in 1960. But MCP leader Chin Peng and the last band of MPLA guerrillas surrendered only in 1989.) Yet this paradigm may not apply to today's campaigns, in which cell-based organizations, bomb-based tactics, global communications and vastly improved insurgent lethality make it relatively easy for marginalized insurgent movements to transform themselves into terrorist groups. Pursuing classically-defined victory over insurgents, particularly those linked to AQ, may simply help create a series of virtually-linked, near-invisible 'rump' terrorist movements in former insurgent theatres. Since terrorists do not need a mass base to be operationally effective, this may perpetuate rather than end the broader conflict. Thus, in modern campaigns, victory may need to be re-defined as the disarming and reintegration of insurgent cells into the parent society, combined with popular support for permanent, institutionalized anti-terrorist measures that contain the risk of terrorist cells emerging from the former insurgent movement.

Certainly, in the specific case of Afghanistan and Pakistan, the objective may not be to defeat the insurgency and establish a viable democracy in Afghanistan (something the truncated time-line may not allow), but rather to create a stable enough environment to allow the permanent or near-permanent suppression of AQ and other transnational terrorist organizations in the region. This is not classical or even post-classical COIN: in doctrinal terms, it might be considered stability operations, an effort to create stable enough conditions for a long-term regional counter-terrorism posture.

COIN and its critics

What then of the current COIN debate? As the foregoing history has shown, it is possible to mount a thoroughgoing intellectual critique of classical COIN as a theory. Its case-study basis draws on an extremely limited, and perhaps unrepresentative, sample of conflicts, from a very specific and peculiar set of historical circumstances, and thus may not be applicable in differing circumstances today. Its social-scientific component is based on post-war thinking about development, governance, information and the nature of colonial or post-colonial societies in what was then called the 'Third World' – thinking that is almost certainly out of date due to the effects of globalization, modern mass media, transnational proliferation, virtual sanctuaries, and so on. Thus both classical COIN and its neo-classical revival have some serious intellectual limitations as a basis for contemporary campaigns.

One might argue that this lack of intellectual applicability does not particularly matter in any case, since neither classical nor neo-classical COIN bears much resemblance to the methods that are actually being used today in Afghanistan, or were applied in Iraq. Not only do these methods diverge from classical COIN, they are barely considered in the neo-classical COIN literature such as FM 3–24. Thus, while one could criticize COIN as an inappropriate paradigm for today's wars, this matters less because it is not actually being applied as such.

Interestingly, however, these are not the comments one commonly hears from critics of COIN. Rather, as discussed at the start of this chapter, those criticisms fall into four key areas: effectiveness, appropriateness, ethics and policy. In each debate, some key critics of COIN often seem to be criticizing strawmen of their own creation, to be radically misinformed about the nature of current operations, or to be arguing from a position of institutional self-interest rather than intellectual openness. Some examples follow, but the obvious implication is that this debate misses the point about what is problematic about COIN as a theory, while equally missing the point that this COIN theory is being applied in only an extremely limited way in today's campaigns. A debate that focuses narrowly on the COIN concepts of the late 1950s is therefore both distracting, and potentially very unproductive.

Key critics of COIN in the current debate include Colonel Gian Gentile, a professor at the US Military Academy at West Point, whose argument seems to be that COIN is not appropriate for modern conflicts, has had little to do with any success that was achieved in Iraq, and runs the risk of undermining future US military capability for conventional war against peer adversaries.

Gentile, who served in Baghdad in 2006 during a period when AQI extended its reach and the environment was spiraling out of control, is not an impartial critic (though neither, of course, are the COIN advocates he criticizes) and he has sometimes been regarded unsympathetically, due to the extremely sharp personal animosity that he shows in many of his writings.[27] However, to the extent that a consistent position can be identified, he seems to be offering a critique based on effectiveness (COIN techniques do not work), appropriateness (the US military as currently constituted and trained is incapable of executing COIN techniques, and therefore these are not appropriate for American forces), and policy (the danger that re-orienting the Army, in particular, towards COIN for today's conflicts will undermine its effectiveness in theoretical future conflicts against as-yet-unidentified adversaries).

The academic anthropology community, with some exceptions,[28] has generally been extremely negative towards COIN in its neo-classical form, regarding it as a soft form of imperialism, as a means to the oppression of occupied peoples, as a perversion of social science research on the characteristics, incentives and culture of populations in affected areas, and (perhaps most saliently) as compromising the work of academic anthropologists, who may be mistaken for intelligence or Human Terrain Team operators and thus be put at risk or lose research access to communities.[29] Much of this critique has been dismissed by some commentators as simply anti-American or Left politics, as opposition to the invasion of Iraq by the Bush administration and therefore a desire to see the occupation fail, or (perhaps more accurately) as based on misinformation about the humanitarian benefits of COIN as opposed to counter-terrorism or conventional warfare. One might also argue that the academic community is expressing a perfectly legitimate professional concern about the impact of COIN on research programmes, but that this must be balanced against bigger issues at stake in today's conflicts. Some may also see it as rather disingenuous to express such criticisms as moral or ethical concerns with COIN, when in fact they have more to do with academic or professional self-interest, and when the application of COIN in Iraq and, to some extent, in Afghanistan has coincided with a drop in civilian casualties, so that it arguably has been a moral positive in these campaigns.

Some humanitarian NGOs have mounted a similar critique of the use of development methodologies, humanitarian spending and community stabilization initiatives in today's conflicts, arguing that these programmes – even when undertaken by civilian government aid agencies, but even more so when done by the military – erode the humanitarian space within which NGOs operate, compromise their impartiality, cause them to be identified associated with occupying forces, and put them at risk.[30] These concerns are justified to some extent as a commentary on actual practice in the field today, but are not strictly a critique of COIN theory per se, since similar concerns exist in any stability operation or peacekeeping deployment, as well of course as in conventional war, whether or not COIN is the dominant approach used. Thus this is more properly considered as an issue in NGO–military relations in general, rather than for COIN in particular. One might also argue that NGOs (especially Western-led NGOs focusing on social or gender issues in conflicts like Afghanistan or Sudan) are in fact *not* impartial in any meaningful sense, and that therefore concepts such as humanitarian space have limited applicability in these types of conflict.

A critique by development NGOs, as well as some academics and aid agencies, has argued that high rates of development assistance in COIN campaigns (including programmes like the US Army's Commander's Emergency Response Program, CERP, as well as larger-scale stabilization programming by aid agencies) contribute to instability, corruption and abuse (Wilder 2009). By creating streams of poorly-supervised cash income, monetizing elements of the rural subsistence economy that are not traditionally cash-based, creating incentives for exploitation and corruption, and advantaging aid recipients over neighbouring populations who may then be driven to violence through a sense of relative deprivation, development assistance can indeed destabilize COIN environments. Such assistance can also create inflationary pressure, undermine local markets and producers, and exacerbate local dependency on outside actors. Again, however, although these criticisms are entirely valid, they are not really criticisms of COIN theory as such – similar debates and criticisms attach to the whole construct of Western development assistance generally, whether or not this happens in a COIN environment. And, in fact, the idea that development spending creates stability is actually *not* a generally accepted concept in classical COIN – theorists like Nathan Leites and Charles Wolf were arguing a similarly sceptical position on this issue in the early 1960s (Wolf 1965; Leites and Wolf 1970).

Other critics, including the historian Edward Luttwak, have mounted passionate attacks on COIN, based on the notion that it is somehow 'malpractice' or intellectually dishonest (Luttwak 2007). Luttwak argues that there is, in fact, a universally effective method in countering insurgency, and this is to out-terrorize the insurgent, to so terrify and cow the population through salutary acts of violence that the insurgents can no longer gain support. To support this argument he adduces the Roman Empire and Nazi Germany as examples of successful counterinsurgency using this method. This critique seems to be simply ill-founded in fact: Roman counterinsurgency technique included very significant non-lethal, political, governance and economic development components and applied violence in ways that were in step with contemporary norms in the ancient world, and to apply Nazi approaches on the Eastern Front would be to copy an army that failed dramatically, despite an initially welcoming population, to control the area under its occupation. Luttwak's argument (advanced early in the Surge period in Iraq in 2007, and arguing that since the United States could never be as violent as the insurgents, the Iraq effort was doomed) turned out to be a radical misreading of the situation, which was beginning to turn significantly in the coalition's favour even as Luttwak's article came out, and this criticism of COIN seems to have now been thoroughly discredited by events on the ground.

Ralph Peters, a retired army officer who served as a military intelligence analyst during the Cold War, has mounted a similar personal attack on some advocates of COIN, arguing in essence that COIN is not a 'manly' approach to warfare, that its advocates are soft, gentle, or even defeatist or treacherous in their attitude, and that COIN not only cannot work (the effectiveness critique) but that developing COIN capabilities undermines the military's warlike ethos (appropriateness) in ways that will be extremely dangerous in a future all-out war against an unspecified possible future enemy (policy) (Peters 2006, 2007). Peters has argued that it would have been better to invade Afghanistan, destroy the Taliban in a conventional military campaign, then simply leave – rather than assuming the expense and trouble of post-conflict reconstruction or counterinsurgency. He has argued that it would be cheaper and more effective to simply re-invade if the Taliban or AQ were to re-establish a safe haven, rather than to occupy territory on a permanent basis. This argument makes a great deal of sense, but is perhaps impractical in that it is, in fact, not proven that periodic re-invasion (on the model of colonial punitive expeditions) would in fact be cheaper or more effective than long-term stabilization, and since such a policy would in fact be in breach of international law which imposes certain obligations on an invader to administer conquered territory and protect populations within it. Moreover, given the downside risk that failure to prevent the re-emergence of a safe haven would only be noticed in retrospect following another major international terrorist attack, such a strategy would be quite risky. And, in any case, this was not the strategy adopted – so, like it or not, we are now engaged in a long-term struggle against an insurgency in Afghanistan and must seek an appropriate way out. In this sense, Peters' critique is as useful as that of the proverbial farmer who gives directions that begin 'well, if I were going there, I wouldn't start from here...'. And again, whatever the merits of COIN as a theory, current practice in Iraq and Afghanistan does not in fact bear a particularly close resemblance to that theory, and thus such criticisms, while highly relevant to the Afghan campaign, are less relevant as critiques of COIN.

Some policy critics of counterinsurgency sometimes take another view, suggesting that the acquisition of counterinsurgency capabilities by the military will make it more likely that political leaders will commit the US military to a series of far-flung, unsustainable interventions with little chance of success – in other words, that having the capability for COIN will make COIN more likely. Would that this were so – as Dr Janine Davidson has pointed out, in practice, lack of an effective doctrine for COIN and lack of key capabilities has not typically stopped misguided political leaders from committing to such conflicts, Iraq being only the most recent case in point (Davidson 2010).

Conclusion

In summary, this chapter has examined the state of the controversial art of counterinsurgency from the standpoint of intellectual history. As this history shows, counterinsurgency in its generic format is one of the oldest and most diverse forms of conflict, having existed at least as long as the state. The specific concepts, techniques and tools used to counter insurrection have varied dramatically over time, usually reflecting the nature of the state or government involved, and in particular its relationship with the population groups residing in its territory. This means that, while there is a very large body of historical data on counter-insurrection, there is little commonality between examples and it is difficult to pinpoint a specific set of core concepts or mainstream techniques.

By contrast, 'big-C' Counterinsurgency, the specific set of concepts developed by the US government-sponsored think-tank community, in the late 1950s, does embody a very definite set of ideas about how to counter insurgencies. As we have seen, however, this theory emerged through a process of reasoning by analogy from a very small number of case studies, all of which had very similar features associated with the immediate post-1945 wars of national liberation and the decolonization of European and US empires in Asia and Africa. Thus, to the extent that similar conditions obtain in any particular conflict today, these ideas (which I describe as 'classical COIN') may be quite relevant. Unfortunately, as explained earlier, modern conditions in fact vary quite significantly from the standard assumed conditions that underlie classical COIN, and thus these techniques may not be particularly applicable.

I have criticized what I call 'neo-classical COIN' for attempting to apply classical COIN without due attention to these differences, but in practice this is something of a hollow criticism, since in current campaigns in Afghanistan and Iraq, the methods actually being applied (reconciliation, local irregular forces, high-intensity targeting of irreconcilables and so on) bear little resemblance to either classical COIN theory or to its neo-classical revival.

Thus, it is possible to mount a reasoned critique of COIN as theory – based on limited sample size and extrapolation of general principles from too few case studies – or as practice, since it has so rarely been applied in full in the real world that there are few genuine opportunities to validate the theory. Interestingly, however, this critique is rarely heard in the current debate over COIN, which is generally dominated by ill-informed commentary, or institutional interest, rather than open inquiry. For this reason, as I have argued, COIN (in its classical, 1960s sense or in its neoclassical version) is not only *not* the dominant paradigm for contemporary conflict, it arguably should not be: and a debate that focuses too narrowly on the applicability of a set of Cold War concepts from the late 1950s has the potential to be both distracting and destructive.

Notes

1 Stephen T. Hosmer, RAND Corporation, personal communication to the author by email, Washington, DC, September 2006.

2 Transcribed by the author from a plaque at the US Army John F. Kennedy Special Warfare Center and School, Fort Bragg, North Carolina, during a visit in March 2010.

3 Misidentified in the symposium report (p. xi) as a member of the French Marine Corps, Galula was in fact an officer of the Colonial Infantry, a branch of the French Army whose badge was, somewhat confusingly for some non-French observers, a naval anchor. In point of fact, he had actually retired from the French Army by this time, and was working as a research associate at Harvard University's Center for International Affairs.

4 General Raoul Salan, last French commander in Indochina and a former Commander-in-Chief in Algeria, was one of four organizers of the Algiers putsch of 1961 and went on to found the reactionary terrorist group, Organization de l'Armee Secrete (OAS).

5 The Algerian campaign is in fact mentioned only eight times in the book.

6 As noted earlier, although Galula was misidentified as a Marine officer he was an Army officer of the colonial infantry.

7 The following section draws partly on an updated version of portions of (Kilcullen 2006–7).

8 For examples of this pattern in resistance warfare see (Asprey 1975; Beckett 1988; Laqueur 1977; Orlov 1963).

9 Discussion with Mahsud informant, Northwest Frontier Province, June 2006. The informant noted that each Mahsud family has contributed one fighter to the anti-government insurgency in order 'to protect their traditional ways', while Waziri tribesmen have joined in a less organized but more fanatical manner. These patterns of behaviour are closely consistent with tribal characteristics.

10 For a discussion of these effects in relation to Indonesia, see Kilcullen (2006).

11 See 'Al Qaeda Takes Media Jihad Online' at www.middle-east-online.com/english/?id=14500.

12 See US Joint Publication 1–02 which defines insurgency within a single-state, single-insurgent paradigm, as 'an organized movement aimed at the overthrow of a constituted government through use of subversion and armed conflict'.

13 For example, see the transfer of letters between Ayman al-Zawahiri and Abu Musab al-Zarqawi (noted below), and other correspondence between AQ leadership in Pakistan and Afghanistan, and insurgents in Iraq and Southeast Asia.

14 Interview with Pakistan government official, North-West Frontier Province, Pakistan, June 2006.

15 For example, in July 2006 Shiite militias in Iraq conducted operations in sympathy with Hizballah fighters engaged in conflict with Israel, while in 2005 AQ in Iraq conducted a hotel bombing in Amman, possibly in an attempt to disrupt support for coalition forces in Jordan.

16 See materials captured in the possession of Jema'ah Islamiyah (JI) operative Dr Azahari in November 2005, and the so-called 'Camp Hudaibiya manual' used by JI and ASG insurgents in the Philippines, which drew on AQ source materials produced in South Asia.

17 CIA analyst, unclassified personal communication, July 2006.

18 Personal observation, Taji, January 2006 and discussions with US military intelligence officers, Baghdad and Kuwait, January–February 2006.

19 I am indebted to Dr Gordon McCormick of the Naval Postgraduate School, Monterey and to Colonel Derek Harvey for insights into the 'small world, scale-free' aspects of insurgent social networks and the enduring influence of the pre-war Iraqi oligarchy on the current Iraqi insurgency.

20 See McCormick *et al.* (2006) for comments on this discourse.

21 For a good example of this perspective, see Fall (1965).

22 Cordesman (2006) and interview with Multinational Force Iraq intelligence officer, January 2006.

23 Personal observation, Baghdad, Taji and Basra, February 2006.

24 Interview with Pakistan Government civilian official, Khyber Agency, June 2006.

25 Interview with senior Iraqi government national security official, Green Zone, Baghdad, January 2006.

26 The following account is based primarily on the author's participant observation as a member of the Iraq Joint Strategic Assessment Team, and then as Senior Counterinsurgency Advisor to Multinational Force Iraq, based in Baghdad, during 2007.

27 See smallwarsjournal.com for an extensive selection of commentary by COL Gentile.

28 For example, Thomas Barfield, Montgomery McFate and Carl Philip Salzmann.

29 See, for example, the report of the American Anthropology Association's Commission on the Engage-ment of Anthropology with the US Security and Intelligence Communities, *Final Report on The Army's Human Terrain System Proof of Concept Program*, 14 October 2009, online at www.aaanet.org/cmtes/commissions/CEAUSSIC/upload/CEAUSSIC_HTS_Final_Report.pdf.

30 See, for example, extensive commentary by the Afghanistan NGO Safety Office, available online at www.afgnso.org.

Recommended readings

American Anthropology Association, Commission on the Engagement of Anthropology with the US Security and Intelligence Communities (2009) *Final Report on The Army's Human Terrain System Proof of Concept Program*, 14 October. Available at: www.aaanet.org/cmtes/commissions/CEAUSSIC/upload/CEAUSSIC_HTS_Final_Report.pdf.

Asprey, Robert B. (1975) *War in the Shadows: The Guerrilla in History*, 2 vols. New York: Doubleday.

Barno, David W. (2006) 'Challenges in a Global Insurgency', *Parameters*, (Summer): 15–29.

Beckett, Ian F.W. (1988) *The Roots of Counter-Insurgency: Armies and Guerrilla Warfare 1900–1945*. London: Blandford.

Bobbitt, Philip (2002) *The Shield of Achilles: War, Peace and the Course of History*. New York: Knopf.

Callwell, C.E. (1996) *Small Wars: Their Principles and Practice*, 3rd edn. Lincoln and London: University of Nebraska Press.

Davidson, Janine A. (2010) *Lifting the Fog of Peace: How Americans Learned to Fight Modern War*. Ann Arbor: University of Michigan Press.

Department of the Navy (1987) United States Marine Corps, NAVMC 2890, Reprint of USMC *Small Wars Manual 1940*, Washington.

Elliot, Mai (2010) *RAND in Southeast Asia: A History of the Vietnam War Era*. Santa Monica: RAND.

Fall, Bernard (1965) 'The Theory and Practice of Counterinsurgency', *Naval War College Review*, April.

Galula, David (1964) *Counterinsurgency Warfare: Theory and Practice*. London: Pall Mall.

Galula, David (2006) *Pacification in Algeria, 1956–1958*. Santa Monica: RAND.

Hoffman, Bruce (2006) *Inside Terrorism*, revised edn. New York: Columbia University Press.

Hosmer, Stephen T. and Sibylle O. Crane (1963) *Counterinsurgency: A Symposium, April 16–20, 1962*. Santa Monica: RAND Corporation (republished 2006).

Johnstono, Paul (2009) 'The Evolution of Ptolemaic Counter-insurgent Strategy', paper presented at *And Call it Peace: New Perspectives on Ancient Wars*, Graduate Student Conference, PhD Program in Classics, The Graduate Center of the City University of New York, 25 April 2009. Abstract available at: http://web.gc.cuny.edu/Classics/confs/conf_2009/johstono.htm.

Kilcullen, David (2006) 'Globalisation and the Development of Indonesian Counterinsurgency Tactics', *Small Wars and Insurgencies*, 17 (1): 44–64.

Kilcullen, David (2006–7) 'Counterinsurgency Redux', *Survival*, 48 (4): 111–30.

Kilcullen, David (2011) 'Lawrence's Ladder: Tribal Irregulars and an Actor–Based Theory of Modern War', in Karl Erik Haug and Ole Jorgen Maao (eds), *Conceptualising Modern War: A Critical Inquiry*. London: Hurst and Company.

Laqueur, Walter (1977) *Guerrilla*. London: Weidenfeld & Nicolson.

Larson, Deborah Welch (1997) *Anatomy of Mistrust: U.S.-Soviet Relations during the Cold War*. Ithaca: Cornell University Press.

Leites, Nathan and Charles Wolf (1970) *Rebellion and Authority: An Analytic Essay on Insurgent Conflicts*. Santa Monica: RAND Corporation.

Long, Austin (2006) *On 'Other War': Lessons from Five Decades of RAND Counterinsurgency Research*. Santa Monica: RAND Corporation.

Luttwak, Edward R. (2007) 'Dead End: Counterinsurgency Warfare as Military Malpractice', *Harper's Magazine*, February.

McCullough, Roy L. (2007) *Coercion, Conversion and Counterinsurgency in Louis XIV's France*. Leiden: Brill Academic Publishing.

Marlowe, Ann (2010) *David Galula: His Life and Intellectual Context*. Carlisle, PA: Strategic Studies Institute, US Army War College.

Orlov, Alexander (1963) *Handbook of Intelligence and Guerrilla Warfare*. Ann Arbor: University of Michigan Press.

Peters, Ralph (2006) 'Politically Correct War', *The New York Times*, 18 October.

Peters, Ralph (2007) 'Progress and Peril, New Counterinsurgency Manual Cheats on the History Exam', *Armed Forces Journal International*, 144 (February).

Sitaraman, Ganesh (2008) 'Counterinsurgency and Constitutional Design', *Harvard Law Review*, 121 (6).

Strauss, Barry (2009), *The Spartacus War*, New York: Simon & Schuster.

Thompson, Robert (1970) *Revolutionary War in World Strategy 1945–1969*. New York: Taplinger.

US Army (2006) Field Manual (FM) 3–24 *Counterinsurgency*. Leavenworth: Department of the Army.

Wilder, Andrew (2009) 'A Weapon System Based on Wishful Thinking', *Boston Globe*, 16 September.

Wolf, Charles (1965) *Insurgency and Counterinsurgency: New Myths and Old Realities*. Santa Monica: RAND Corporation.

References

AFPS (2006) 'IED Components Moving Across Iraq-Iran Border, General Says', 17 March.

Asprey, Robert B. (1975) *War in the Shadows: The Guerrilla in History*, 2 vols. New York: Doubleday.

Barno, David W. (2006) 'Challenges in Fighting a Global Insurgency', *Parameters* (Summer): 15–29.

Becket, Ian F.W. (1988) *The Roots of Counter-Insurgency: Armies and Guerrilla Warfare 1900–1945*. London: Blandford.

Bobbitt, Philip (2002) *The Shield of Achilles: War, Peace and the Course of History*. New York: Knopf.

Callwell, C.E. (1996; first published 1896, 3rd edn originally published 1906) *Small Wars: Their Principles and Practice*, 3rd edn. Lincoln and London: University of Nebraska Press.

Cordesman, Anthony (2006) *The Iraq War and Lessons for Counterinsurgency*. Washington, DC: Center for Strategic and International Studies.

Davidson, Janine A. (2010) *Lifting the Fog of Peace: How Americans Learned to Fight Modern War*. Ann Arbor University of Michigan Press.

Department of the Navy, United States Marine Corps (1987) NAVMC 2890, *Reprint of USMC Small Wars Manual 1940*. Washington.

Dillon, Martin (1999) *The Dirty War*. London: Routledge.

Elliot, Mai (2010) *RAND in Southeast Asia: A History of the Vietnam War Era*. Santa Monica: RAND Corporation.

Fall, Bernard (1965) 'The Theory and Practice of Counterinsurgency', *Naval War College Review*, April.

Galula, David (1964) *Counterinsurgency Warfare: Theory and Practice*. London: Pall Mall.

Galula, David (2006) *Pacification in Algeria, 1956–1958*. Santa Monica: RAND Corporation.

Hoffman, Bruce (2006, rev. edn) *Inside Terrorism*. New York: Columbia University Press.

Hosmer, Stephen T. and Sibylle O. Crane (1963, republished 2006) *Counterinsurgency: A Symposium, April 16–20, 1962*. Santa Monica: RAND Corporation.

Johnstono, Paul (2009) 'The Evolution of Ptolemaic Counter-insurgent Strategy', paper presented at *And Call it Peace: New Perspectives on Ancient Wars*, Graduate Student Conference, PhD Program in Classics, The Graduate Center of the City University of New York, 25 April 2009. Abstract available at: http://web.gc.cuny.edu/Classics/confs/conf_2009/johstono.htm.

Kaplan, Fred M. (1991) *The Wizards of Armageddon*, Stanford Nuclear Age Series. Stanford: Stanford University Press.

Kilcullen, David J. (2005) 'Countering Global Insurgency', *Journal of Strategic Studies*, 28: 597–617.

Kilcullen, David J. (2006) 'Globalisation and the Development of Indonesian Counterinsurgency Tactics', *Small Wars and Insurgencies*, 17 (1): 44–64.

Kilcullen, David J. (2006–7) 'Counterinsurgency *Redux*', *Survival*, 48 (4): 111–30.

Kilcullen, David J. (2011) 'Lawrence's Ladder: Tribal Irregulars and an Actor-Based Theory of Modern War', in Karl Erik Haug and Ole Jorgen Maao (eds), *Conceptualising Modern War: A Critical Inquiry*. London: Hurst and Company.

Laqueur, Walter (1977) *Guerrilla*. London: Weidenfeld & Nicolson.

Ledgard, J.M. (2011) 'Digital Africa', in *Intelligent Life* (Spring). Available at: http://moreintelligentlife.com/content/ideas/jm-ledgard/digital-africa?page=full.

Leites, Nathan and Charles Wolf (1970) *Rebellion and Authority: An Analytic Essay on Insurgent Conflicts*. Santa Monica: RAND Corporation.

Long, Austin (2006) *On 'Other War': Lessons from Five Decades of RAND Counterinsurgency Research*. Santa Monica: RAND Corporation.

Luttwak, Edward R. (2007) 'Dead End: Counterinsurgency Warfare as Military Malpractice', *Harper's Magazine*, February.

McCormick Gordon H., Steven B. Horton and Lauren A. Harrison (2006) 'Things Fall Apart: The "End Game" Dynamics of Internal Wars', research paper, October. Available at: www.math.usma.edu/people/horton/EndGame.pdf.

McCullough, Roy L. (2007) *Coercion, Conversion and Counterinsurgency in Louis XIV's France*. Leiden: Brill Academic Publishing.

Marlowe, Ann (2010) *David Galula: His Life and Intellectual Context*. Carlisle, PA: Strategic Studies Institute, US Army War College.

Orlov, Alexander (1963) *Handbook of Intelligence and Guerrilla Warfare*. Ann Arbor: University of Michigan Press.

Peters, Ralph (2006) 'Politically Correct War', *The New York Times*, 18 October.

Peters, Ralph (2007) 'Progress and Peril, New Counterinsurgency Manual Cheats on the History Exam', *Armed Forces Journal International*, 144 (February).

Ricks, Thomas E. (2006) *Fiasco: The American Military Adventure in Iraq*. New York: Penguin.

Sitaraman, Ganesh (2008) 'Counterinsurgency and Constitutional Design', *Harvard Law Review*, 121 (6).

Strauss, Barry (2009) *The Spartacus War*. New York: Simon & Schuster.

Tacitus, Publius Cornelius *De Vita et Moribus Iulii Agricolae*.

Thompson, Robert (1970) *Revolutionary War in World Strategy 1945–1969*. New York: Taplinger.

US Army (2006) Field Manual (FM) 3–24 *Counterinsurgency*. Leavenworth: Department of the Army.

Weber, Max (1946) 'Politics as a Vocation', in H.H. Gerth and C. Wright Mills (eds), *Max Weber: Essays in Sociology*. Oxford: Oxford University Press.

Welch Larson, Deborah (1997) *Anatomy of Mistrust: U.S.-Soviet Relations during the Cold War*. Ithaca: Cornell University Press.

Wilder, Andrew (2009) 'A Weapon System Based on Wishful Thinking', *Boston Globe*, 16 September.

Wolf, Charles (1965) *Insurgency and Counterinsurgency: New Myths and Old Realities*. Santa Monica: RAND Corporation.

Part II

Insurgent movements

12

INSURGENT MOVEMENTS IN AFRICA

William Reno

Since the 1990s, insurgencies in African states such as Sierra Leone, Liberia, Congo, Somalia and Sudan have attracted attention from scholars and policy-makers as evidence of a new generation of warfare. Rather than fighting to replace existing states with more efficient alternatives, insurgents in these wars disrupt political order and hollow out states rather than fighting to replace or reform them. Their leaderships often lack cohesion. Their styles of fighting reflect this fragmented structure, an amalgam of ethnic militias, local gangs, defecting army units and criminal bands. They advertise no core ideology or comprehensive political programmes. In a marked contrast to Africa's Maoist-style anti-colonial and anti-apartheid insurgents of the 1960s to the 1980s that devoted great effort to set up liberated zones and to mobilize and administer populations, these new insurgents neither claim that they represent large segments of the population nor put significant effort into seeking popular support for their objectives. Their actions are geared instead towards protecting and enriching their own members, usually at the expense of the security and material well-being of the people among whom they fight.

Paul Collier explains how the combination of weak state institutions and a dearth of economic opportunities set the stage for insurgents that develop as a kind of criminal enterprise that serves the personal material interests of its members. Insurgent leaders in this context have little option but to appeal to the self-interest of recruits and tolerate uses of violence – looting, for example – that appear to be undisciplined and counterproductive in the Maoist version of insurgency. This kind of insurgent organization overwhelms potential leaders who attend to political organizing instead of prioritizing the quest for income to attract fighters and to buy weapons (Collier 2000). Support from the Diaspora and neighbouring states that use insurgents as proxies to meddle in affairs beyond their borders provides ready sources of income to self-interested insurgents. This external support protects insurgents from consequences of using violence in ways that impoverish people and make them less secure (Collier and Hoeffler 2004). Mary Kaldor explains that this shift in the nature of insurgents follows global economic and political changes producing a 'revolution in the social relations of warfare' (Kaldor 2001: 3). In her analysis, the criminal gangs, paramilitaries, mercenaries and other disparate groups that feature in these wars use violence to control new sources of income linked to changes in the global political economy such as skimming humanitarian aid and illicit trafficking of commodities such as drugs, diamonds and timber.

These analytical approaches provide valuable insights into how and why insurgents in Africa behave as they do and why broad ideological and political programmes and population-centric strategies remain as unrealized possibilities. They show how the weakening of state institutions and the associated ascendancy in relative terms of illicit and criminal economic opportunities drives insurgent behaviour. Given that these trends have been most severe in Africa, insurgencies there operate in a political environment that promotes fragmented organizations, an overriding interest in personal economic gain among fighters, and the exercise of violence in ways that make non-combatants more insecure.

The problem with this formulation is that it does not fit the facts. A survey of insurgencies in Africa uncovers a high degree of simultaneity in organizational behaviour. At the dawn of the twenty-first century, factionalized collections of gangs, militias and renegade army units fought in Congo, Sierra Leone and Liberia while the Sudan People's Liberation Army held and administered substantial 'liberated zones' in southern Sudan under the leadership of a disciplined Leninist-style centralized command. Somalia exhibited a diversity of insurgent organizations, ranging from armed groups that turned to piracy, to local clan-based militias and to religious groups. One insurgent group, the Somali National Movement, has sustained a government administration in areas that it controls from the early 1990s, and has declared an independent Republic of Somaliland. Meanwhile, in 2000, disparate gangs in Nigeria fought in the oil-rich Niger Delta sometimes as armed muscle for local politicians and at other times to attack institutions of state authority as they took advantage of business opportunities as extortionists and looters. Tuareg militias in northern Mali and Niger fought for greater self-determination, while in 1998, a small, disciplined group of al-Qaeda operatives carried out coordinated simultaneous attacks on US embassies in Kenya and Tanzania.

In sum, Africa's contemporary and historic insurgencies demonstrate a wide range of organizational forms and strategies. The next two sections contain the central argument that explains why Africa's insurgencies assume these various forms. The section that follows examines opposite ends of the spectrum of recent and ongoing insurgencies in Africa; the hierarchical bureaucratic Maoist variant and the decentralized amalgamations that resemble diverse collections of armed gangs. The final section considers the future of insurgency in Africa.

The mainsprings of Maoist-style insurgencies

The organization of insurgencies often mirrors the organization of the states that they fight. For example, as the anti-colonial insurgencies of the 1960s fought to create a new kind of politics, they adopted many of the organizational features of the colonial states that were their targets as they set up their 'liberated zones'. These administrations were meant to give substance to insurgent promises to improve and reorient the bureaucracies of the state that they were about to inherit. This was true even when insurgents engaged in asymmetrical battles, attacking state authority through sabotage, while guerrilla forces infiltrated communities in efforts to displace the central authorities and set themselves up as a rival government. The struggle to form a new government required that insurgents focus on non-combatant populations to shape their perceptions and mobilize them in support of the insurgent cause in the model of classic twentieth-century Maoist insurgencies. Mao's admonition that the 'richest source of power to wage war lies in the masses of the people' (quoted in Rejai 1969: 250) appeared in insurgent rhetoric and strategies during Africa's anti-colonial struggles of the 1960s and 1970s. This 'people's war', the mobilization of non-combatant populations, also marked the anti-apartheid insurgencies in Southern Africa to 1990. Anti-government insurgents in Ethiopia in the 1980s fought a self-styled revolutionary regime, taking up the problems of local people and interpreting them in ways that advanced the insurgents' ideological agenda, an emphasis on self-reliance and careful attention to administering 'liberated zones' in preparation for protracted military struggle against the regime (Young 1997: 32–5).

These population-centric strategies and broad ideological frameworks required careful coordination of operations to ensure that disciplined insurgent fighters would use violence in a discriminating fashion geared towards maintaining popular support as much as to engage state forces in battle.[1] This struggle with the state to control territory and to govern people thus played a central role in Maoist insurgent strategies, necessitating constant attention to indoctrinating and controlling fighters, exercising violence carefully, and building and sustaining bureaucracies. Political leadership played a central role in coordinating these strategies and to recognize and navigate around the constraints and opportunities that their situations presented.

Mid-twentieth-century insurgents and the regimes that they fought shared modernist ideals about the nature of state authority. They agreed that states should mobilize and order society to promote economic transformation. Insurgents and state officials alike tried to figure out new ways to boost the capacity of their organizations to accomplish these tasks. Post-Second World War colonial Africa's model farms and villages, extensive rural conservation efforts, and the rapid expansion of infrastructure and services exemplified these aspirations of state power. The elaborate five-year plans of Portuguese colonial officials in the 1960s, for example, included provisions to construct the world's fourth largest dam in Mozambique to generate electricity for huge agricultural projects and to support state-designed industrial development plans (Radmann 1974: 47). The Frente de Libertação de Moçambique (FRELIMO), Mozambique's principal anti-colonial insurgency that was founded in 1962 considered this project as a menacing demonstration of Portuguese power and intent of their colonialist foes to bring more settlers to their colony. Yet upon assuming power in 1975, the successful insurgents incorporated this project in their own five-year plan, modifying the agricultural development portion to reflect what they saw as the positive lessons of the Chinese and Tanzanian agrarian policies to promote rural development and adjusting the industrial component to reflect their emphasis on autonomous development (Gesnekter 1975: 25).

James Scott identified the ultimate incapacity of this high modernist project to break free of the improvisations and illicit acts of the people whose behaviour they were expected to change. He argued that these deviations from rules and procedures took place in realms of social autonomy that exist beyond the capacity of bureaucracies to easily control. Especially in rural areas where even the most capable state bureaucracies could not dominate entrenched local community practices, insurgent forces oriented towards 'people's war' benefited from venues and local personal networks from which they could educate potential recruits, draw followers, and mobilize supporters and their resources to oppose state power. Insurgents took advantage of some of the same personal networks that helped individuals to evade state efforts to tax and regulate economic transactions. The irony was that bureaucrats often had to tolerate this incompleteness of control. Even in the Soviet Union, Scott noted, planners put up with clandestine exchanges between state enterprises and formally proscribed activities such as private garden plots and other improvisations as necessary compromises that were critical to making the rest of the system work (Scott 1998: 309–41).

Other social spaces such as university classrooms – venues to debate and experiment with ideas – also can provide arenas beyond the close scrutiny of bureaucratic state administration. Historically the bulk of the leadership of Africa's Maoist-style insurgencies and their guerrilla armies was drawn from universities. These leaders, highly unrepresentative of the people they later led in battle and tried to administer, took advantage of the limited reach of the state into the classroom and student groups to tap into commercial networks to collect and control the flow of the resources that they needed to recruit fighters and to pursue their political strategies. The greater the social autonomy of these spaces the more leeway for would-be insurgent leaders to improvise and experiment with organizational strategies and political programmes. Insurgent leaders such as Amilcar Cabral, Eduardo Mondlane and Yoweri Museveni wrote about the lessons of their missteps in disciplining fighters and in warding off or co-opting criminal and bandit groups while they were pursuing academic and professional careers (see for example: Handyside 1969; Mondlane 1969; Museveni 1997). Appearing less frequently in their public writings were the harsh adjustments that involved the suppression of critics and the bloody struggles to eliminate rival factions. Ironically, bureaucratic institutions in Africa, seen in development literature as 'strong' alternatives to patronage-based regime strategies, created the social conditions for ideologically-driven insurgents to organize and experiment. The clear division between public and private realms and the inherent limits of purely bureaucratic approaches to the exercise of state authority – the ideal of the modern vision of the state – also provided the context for insurgent leaders to theorize about and then recruit and organize their followers as a counter-state.

State officials historically have been inclined to suppress ethnic militias and criminals and other armed groups in favour of an exclusive state-provided order. But the counterinsurgency strategies of some states have included these groups when officials were confident that these would remain under the guidance of the state and not threaten its control (Cann 1997; Ellis 1999). The limits of this counterinsurgency strategy lay in official concerns that ceding state authority to these armed groups would undermine the capacity of these states to exercise bureaucratic control over their own populations. Those African states with the greatest bureaucratic capacity to conduct surveillance and apply coercion, most notably South Africa, did use proxy militias and gave free reign to special units (Ellis 1998) but state forces in these instances relied primarily on police and regular military forces to prevent insurgents from establishing liberated zones.

Insurgencies that have appeared in the world's most bureaucratic states beyond Africa's shores also illustrate this relationship between the nature of state authority and the organization of insurgencies. Germany's Red Army Faction wrote of the challenges that they faced in the late 1960s: 'The degree to which the political police can monitor these groups, their meetings, their appointments, and the contents of their discussions is already so extensive that one has to stay away if one wants to escape this surveillance' (Red Army Faction n.d.). As in South Africa where the African National Congress and other insurgent groups faced formidable state agencies, creating very small, tight-knit and secretive vanguard organizations offered a way to avoid harsh countermeasures. Urban guerrillas in Latin America encountered similar problems, and considered assaults, raids, the infiltration of demonstrations to provoke police to shoot protestors, and other forms of 'armed propaganda' such as kidnapping, hijackings and bank robberies as alternatives where intensive state control ruled out mass-based insurgencies (Marighella 2002). These insurgents observed, as did counterparts across Portuguese Africa and in the apartheid regimes and in a few other places, that university classrooms and student study groups were among the safest places to discuss ideas with like-minded people and to recruit cadres while minimizing interference from the state.

Insurgents in Africa have mirrored these global patterns of insurgent organizational response to the nature of state authority. Africa's states with the deepest historical experiences with bureaucratic administrations – the Portuguese colonies, the apartheid regimes of Southern Africa, Rwanda and Ethiopia, produced classic Maoist-style insurgents whose leaders originated in universities and who went on to recruit guerrilla armies among rural communities. Their strategies devoted attention to building 'liberated zones' and mounting 'people's wars' to challenge regimes and mobilize the population in a new vision of the future. These mass-based Maoist insurgencies have arisen in contexts where state authorities do not control major elements of everyday life in rural areas. Mid-century bureaucratic colonial states in Africa fit into this category of state–insurgent relations, with insurgents first gaining purchase in peripheral rural areas and later encircling cities. Africa's most urbanized and bureaucratized states, particularly the apartheid regimes of South Africa and Namibia in the 1970s and 1980s, forced insurgents to incorporate the tactics that looked more like the urban guerrilla. But even these insurgents tried to mobilize populations and envisioned carving out their own liberated zones on enemy territory.

More generally, it is not surprising in this light that urban insurgencies throughout the world since industrial societies and dense bureaucratic states started appearing in the late nineteenth century have taken the form of anarchist and ultra-radical cells, and more recently, dispersed networked terrorist cells.[2] Basque separatists, the Baader-Meinhof gang, the Red Army Faction and more recent organizations such as the Greek group, Conspiracy of Cells of Fire that specializes in sending mail bombs to European leaders, and the transnational groups responsible for the 9/11 attacks on New York and Washington adapt the organizational models of the insurgents of the twenty-first century that challenge bureaucratically capable states. But as societies urbanize and rapid economic development in many countries translates into state administrations that are able to conduct intensive surveillance of the movements and transactions of their populations, such capacities are not developing in this direction in a significant portion of Africa, with important consequences for the organization of insurgencies there.

The mainsprings of network–centric insurgencies

The most noteworthy contrast to Maoist guerrillas that fight bureaucratic regimes appears in Africa's most thoroughly non-bureaucratic states. These are the states in which regimes have exercised authority through the manipulation of patronage rather than through building capable bureaucracies. Insurgencies that appear in these states copy this organizational strategy in their own efforts to exercise political authority. In this fight for political power, the insurgents target the patronage networks that are the foundation of regime power. Since these regimes do not put a great deal of effort into actually governing citizens, such as providing them with protection and social services, insurgents face no great need to try to out-govern the regime in a struggle to wrest control of the people as a precondition to rule. This environment, however, presents its own hazards. Insurgent leaders who struggle to infiltrate and control the patronage networks upon which the regime bases its power become highly vulnerable to co-optation. If they successfully resist this danger, they still face the demands of their new clients to tend to the highly parochial demands of ethnic or sectarian interests around which individual state officials often organize the populations that they represent.

These conditions present insurgent ideologues and commanders with serious challenges in coordinating an organizational focus on broad political visions and programmes. These insurgents arise in contexts where regimes have maintained control through allowing key members of patronage networks to field their own armed groups that they are permitted to use for personal agendas, such as exploiting illicit economic opportunities, provided that these armed groups are used to defend regime power when needed. This is partly a regime response to the scarcity of revenues. Unable to build bureaucracies as vehicles of patronage to knit together diverse populations, many rulers of threadbare states opted instead to permit their supporters to exploit other people who enjoyed lesser levels of political favour. While this strategy for asserting authority gives incentives to clients and would-be clients to compete to demonstrate support for a central patron, it is also compatible with mobilizing and arming groups and individuals to pursue their private agendas. For example, a politician's 'political muscle' can prey upon neighbouring communities in the course of claiming to protect one's own. Security forces and even local toughs associated with politicians can set up roadblocks to collect money from travellers while enjoying the protection of (and providing kickbacks to) their superiors. This decentralization and privatization of violence has become a serious problem in places like Kenya and Nigeria where the introduction of competitive elections has intensified the struggle for position within these patronage networks, such that Kenya's own government investigators reported that politicians regularly cultivate ties with armed gangs for mutual interest (Republic of Kenya 2008).[3]

Insurgencies in this kind of environment have to compete with established armed groups for recruits. Would-be insurgent fighters can use this competition to demand that insurgents also cater to their short-term personal interests, such as through tolerating looting, lest these recruits decide to join another group. This initial inability of insurgents to control the flow of resources, even in small areas, denies them the leeway to experiment with political ideas and indoctrinate and discipline recruits. Such insurgents usually prove to be as fragmented and uncoordinated as the various army factions, militias and politicians' personal gangs that are associated with the regimes that they fight. These wars exhibit the character of what Kalyvas calls 'symmetric irregular warfare', much like multi-sided gang warfare (Kalyvas 2006: 67–8).

At first glance, these states with exceedingly weak bureaucracies, particularly in rural areas, should be easy targets for Maoist-style insurgents. A reflection of this incapacity, the American journal *Foreign Policy* lists ten African countries as 'critical' in its 2010 failed states index.[4] This feeble institutional capacity is usually coupled with displays of regime failure in the form of minimal service delivery that generate widespread vocal popular expressions of disgust at misrule. Taken together, this condition may seem to provide fertile ground for insurgent ideologues to promote compelling political narratives of rebellion and renewal and set up 'liberated zones' with fairly little interference. This vision motivates fears in foreign capitals that such 'ungoverned spaces' will become refuges for violent insurgents to promote religious extremism and opposition to the West while exploiting the bureaucratic incapacities of states to plan and launch well-coordinated attacks (Rabasa *et al.* 2007).

The reality is that states with feeble bureaucracies often have regimes that pursue stability and assert their authority through patronage networks, as noted above. These strategies of control are often socially intrusive. Such regimes focus on controlling people through manipulating their access to economic opportunities and incorporating these people into vertical patronage networks that are organized around politically reliable local strongmen that act as intermediaries between officials in the capital and the bulk of the population that remain beyond the reach of state agencies. These intermediaries often come from a wide array of backgrounds, often exercising authority in their own right in some other sphere, such as in local religious institutions or markets. These regimes cultivate this influence in as many social venues as possible, such as in NGOs, student groups, ethnic associations and other networks that are conventionally associated with 'civil society'. Though not part of the formal institutional design of the state, these social venues often play important roles in the political networks of regimes. This control can extend to regime domination of illicit markets through manipulating law enforcement to exempt political favourites from prosecution. Zaire's former president, Joseph Mobutu, summarized how this system of authority worked in his country: 'Everything is for sale, everything is bought in our country. In this traffic, holding any slice of public power constitutes a veritable exchange instrument, convertible into illicit acquisition of money and other goods' (Lemarchand 1979: 248).

This system of authority inhibits cooperation between groups in society. Competition for leadership within these groups often becomes intertwined with struggles over individual and group standing in this wider regime-centric political network, which reinforces tendencies towards factional and even personal conflicts within these groups. The practical effect is that this political activity invades the otherwise autonomous spaces in which people who may hate this kind of regime and the economic hardship and insecurity that it produces could otherwise organize to challenge the regime. This organizational fragmentation means that surprisingly little coercion on the part of state officials is needed to isolate and destroy truly radical challenges and limit the field of manoeuvre for popular critics.[5]

Taken as a whole, this kind of politics has insulated the African continent from durable anti-regime political movements, even though popular activism played a significant role in the advent of political reforms in the early 1990s. The continent is notable in recent decades for the scarcity of radical reformist movements that arise to challenge incumbent regimes. When such regimes are swept from power, it is at the hands of their own agents at the elite levels of these political networks. The focus of competition for political power thus occurs within this framework, even when the capacity of the top echelon in the capital to manage these affairs falters. Thus succession crises and internal competition and not insurgencies are the real challenges facing these regimes. Local intermediaries continue to control access to economic opportunities – in licit and illicit commerce, through the allocations of public offices for private gain, the regulation of 'private' associations such as NGOs, ethnic and religious associations and so forth – and maintain dominant positions in their home communities, even after the political centre collapses. The 'resource wars' that are thought in some quarters to drive conflicts in Africa actually reflect these competitions between different branches of political networks. Instead of the population-centric Maoist 'people's wars', these conflicts are network-centric competitions for control over the resources needed to maintain personal domination over patronage networks. Close scrutiny of these conflicts usually turns up ideologues of the old fashioned type. But these people cannot rise to prominence when they are shut out of access to resources that they need to recruit followers and generate popular support. They cannot find social venues in which to organize followers, even if their messages find resonance in people's political attitudes and opinions.

This form of political control shapes the nature of the recruitment of insurgents. Hatred of political figures that are widely seen as beneficiaries of unwarranted privilege may be widespread. At the same time individuals may feel compelled to join the hated politician's militia to gain access to resources and protection from other predators. This dynamic is familiar to students of mafias. Blok, for example, explained how Mafiosi in Sicily employed criminals and poor peasants to use violence to control the public arena on behalf of local aristocrats. State officials who could not control communities directly sought out these 'violent entrepreneurs' to help them manage opposition in these societies. This exercise of violence produced profits for those involved, particularly those in the upper reaches of this hierarchy. Thus many poor people, rather than taking up arms against a local aristocracy and a state that presented them with few prospects, made their peace with this organization and sought protection, higher status and income through collaboration with this network (Blok 1974). If political activists had enjoyed greater social autonomy to organize followers, perhaps Sicily would have been the site of a Maoist-style rural insurgency. But such an insurgency was very difficult to organize, even though the Italian state was notable for its weak control over this region.

It is very difficult to compel fighters to consistently discriminate in their uses of violence in network-centric warfare. The proliferation of armed groups gives fighters opportunities other than the insurgent organization to pursue their personal interests, often under the protection of incumbent political insiders. Fighters who apply violence arbitrarily against non-combatants, for example, can escape punishment if they shift their support to a political militia or join some other political gang that rewards violent self-interested behaviour. This capacity to shift from one group to another gives individual fighters the capacity to pursue short-term interests and needs, some of which are consistent with the aims of the leaders of surviving branches of the incumbent political network. Population-centric Maoist-style insurgency thus becomes very difficult when insurgents cannot convince populations that they can protect and administer these people, even if the insurgents wanted to set up such 'liberated zones'.

Incumbent political notables who mobilize impoverished young people do not suffer political harm if their fighters attack local non-combatants, since it is the resources associated with the fragmenting political network that are the targets of their struggles. From the perspective of Maoist 'people's war', these conflicts appear to focus on spoiling and disrupting political order. But that perspective reflects the old insurgency warfare focus on the state, whereas these network-centric conflicts in contemporary Africa mirror the pre-conflict regime strategies of authority. It is this domestic political context, particularly regime strategies for asserting political authority, that shapes the organization and behaviour of many insurgent groups in Africa, a development that is examined in more detail immediately below.

The evidence

Nearly all of Africa's Maoist-style insurgencies began under the direction of ideological leaderships that initiated their struggles in university classrooms. Amilcar Cabral, the leader of the Partido Africano da Independência da Guiné e Cabo Verde (PAIGC) offers a prototypical case. One of a handful of indigenes of Portuguese Guinea who was able to gain access to higher education, he discovered opportunities while at a university in Portugal in the 1950s to discuss political ideas with students from other Portuguese colonies. Even though these students were socially removed from the vast bulk of their own societies, the students were in positions to formulate their own political strategies and link them to political debates that were then going on in Europe. Once Cabral and others returned to their homes, the insurgent leaders made tactical alliances with workers in the expanding formal economy who were socially ambitious or were concerned about salaries and job security, and convinced these people that the anti-colonial struggle would solve these problems.

Portuguese authorities used bureaucratic measures to conduct surveillance of the activists and to suppress challenges to their rule. In Portuguese Guinea, the colonial army had 40,000 troops and access to NATO supplies. But the colonial regime's rudimentary bureaucracy and alliances with chiefs and businessman still could not control the entirety of that small country's territory and its population. The PAIGC was able to gain control over commerce in agricultural goods in regions that it operated. This was because the PAIGC could co-opt local notables who had enough local autonomy to be able to switch sides without too much immediate fear of punishment. In this colonial milieu, local youth did not yet owe allegiance to politician militias or the youth wings of patronage-based political parties. Therefore, local notables could still impose direct discipline on how these insurgent recruits used violence in their home communities. Insurgents that could make use of this effective form of social control enjoyed the leeway to experiment and to adjust strategies from the doctrinaire framework that they devised in the rarified atmosphere of the university and cafes. Modifying esoteric political theories was essential to the insurgent capacity to convince people that a broad anti-colonial political narrative could address parochial concerns (Dhada 1998: 572). 'Remember always that the people do not fight for ideas, for things that only exist in the heads of individuals' wrote Cabral. 'The people fight and they accept sacrifices. But they do it in order to gain material advantages, to live in peace, and to improve their lives, to experience progress' (quote from Henriksen 1976: 381).

This and other colonial regimes had few mechanisms through which to easily mobilize grass-roots parochial concerns to counterbalance the insurgents' appeals. The social isolation of the colonial state, which intensified with the bureaucratic reforms of the 1950s and 1960s in Portuguese Guinea left the PAIGC insurgents freedom to coordinate local agendas. This merging of the insurgents' broad political ideology and programme with local traditions of periodic resistance to authority succeeded in directing what James Scott called the 'revolution in the revolution' towards the construction of a new political order (Scott 1979). This process of insurgent indoctrination and control also resembles what David Kilcullen later called the 'accidental guerrilla syndrome' in which insurgents convince local armed groups that external threats are really responsible for their problems and that the insurgents are their defenders (Kilcullen 2009: 34–8). Since the ideological perspectives of student ideologues held little intrinsic appeal among most people, the insurgents also had to build relationships with communities through shared business interests, personal social connections, and through the selective intimidation of those who resisted their domination. These strategies of insurgent control enlisted local notables who pined to regain the authority that they had lost as a result of colonial administrative reforms and others who resented the actions of the state, and extended to people who simply reacted negatively to the impact that outside ideas and social changes had on local values and mores. Cabral was especially adept at this process, having met many local notables in his capacity as an agronomy researcher for the United Nations prior to leading an insurgency. This occupation gave him an opportunity to learn about local problems and to build personal connections.

This social insulation from the regime and state gave the insurgents the capacity to compel fighters to be discriminate in their uses of violence. The capacity to discipline fighters with the help of local authorities made possible the creation of insurgent-run 'liberated zones'. By September 1973, PAIGC leaders concluded that they had liberated enough of the country – about 80 per cent – to make a unilateral declaration of independence and to convince a growing number of governments to recognize them as the rightful rulers of their country.

Anti-colonial insurgency followed a similar trajectory in Mozambique through the 1960s. FRELIMO leader Eduardo Mondlane used his position as a UN research officer on trust territories to meet anti-colonial activists in Mozambique and to develop personal connections to local community leaders and educated nationalists, much as Cabral had used his UN connection.[6] This kind of social autonomy appeared in later insurgencies too. Yoweri Museveni wrote of how his days as a student (1967–70) at the University of Dar es Salaam had shaped his political strategies and gave him access to the recruits to launch an insurgency in Uganda 1981 that succeeded in taking power in 1986 after an extensive experience running liberated zones and mobilizing local populations. 'It is Dar es Salaam's atmosphere of freedom fighters, socialists, nationalists, and anti-imperialism', wrote the young Museveni, 'that attracted me rather than the so-called "academicians" of the University College, Dar es Salaam'.[7] The core of Museveni's National Resistance Army (NRA) included 26 other educated men, among them a law graduate of the University of Dar es Salaam, a fine arts graduate from Makerere University, a student of veterinary medicine, several school teachers, and a number of students who had joined another insurgent group before being absorbed into the NRA (Amaza 1998: 234–41).

Insurgents closer to the present illustrate this link between the capacity to organize population-centric strategies, maintain internal discipline and discriminate uses of violence, and access to socially sheltered environments. The decision of the UN's High Commission for Refugees to provide Rwandan refugees with separate schools – often better than those that Ugandan citizens attended – and scholarships gave some refugees the education that they needed to emigrate to wealthier countries from which they provided support to the Rwandan Patriotic Front (RPF) in the early 1990s. At least as important was the RPF leadership's experience in Museveni's

NRA and from 1986 in the victorious insurgency's new national army. Top RPF leaders served in Uganda in positions such as the political commissar of the Ugandan army's infantry school, as assistant director of counterintelligence, Head of the School of Political Education, and several as high staff members in the Directorate of Military Intelligence (Mushemeza 2007: 113–15). These positions were ideal for giving the insurgent leaders opportunities to recruit and organize followers in an environment where the insurgents could contain other influences on recruits.

All of these population-centric insurgencies faced state regimes that tried to divide insurgent forces through exploiting the ethnic and other social differences of their leaders and their recruits. Strategies include using militias to control communities beyond the limited capacities of regular armies to occupy. These strategies met with some success. Efforts to infiltrate insurgent groups sowed suspicion within them and led to self-destructive searches for enemy collaborators. For the most part, however, these states relied on formal bureaucratic instruments of coercion such as police forces, armies and intelligence agencies to battle the insurgents. With the exception of South Africa where formidable bureaucratic capacity precluded the formation of liberated zones, none of the states that faced insurgents who emphasized population-centric 'people's wars' were able to prevail militarily over their foes.

The argument here is that these state forces could not prevail because the bureaucratic character of their authority permitted the social spaces in which ideologically oriented population-centric insurgents could organize and survive long enough to develop effective strategies. The more bureaucratic the nature of state authority, the more likely it was that ideologues would prevail among organizers and that the insurgencies that they led would pursue a Maoist 'people's war' strategy of mobilization (provided that bureaucratic control was not overwhelming). Regimes that relied upon patronage networks to assert their authority also undermine the social basis for the development of Maoist insurgencies. Thus regimes that are commonly thought of as weak from the perspective of conventional notions of state capacity do a good job of resisting the efforts of reformist and revolutionary groups to overthrow them. They more commonly succumb, however, to the divisions and succession crises that are internal to these regimes.

Liberia's war during the 1990s provides a prototypical portrait of the network-centric warfare in the context of patronage-based regime strategies. Charles Taylor, the leader of the National Patriotic Front of Liberia (NPFL), the main insurgent faction, occupied an important position in the patronage networks of the regime that he sought to replace. He had served from 1981 to 1983 as the Director of General Services, the regime's overseas procurement agency, which gave him access to government purchasing contract procedures. Taylor received this position and the benefits of corruption that were associated with it because of his role as a student leader in the 1970s and his close connections to a popular military commander. Taylor's participation in politics, even as he exploited his office for personal gain, demonstrated to would-be opponents that critics were easily co-opted. The Liberian regime's decision to prosecute Taylor for corruption in 1983 also showed that the regime could punish its clients. Though Taylor was in the United States, the Liberian government invoked an extradition treaty to have Taylor returned to Liberia. But Taylor escaped from a Massachusetts prison in 1985 where he had been detained pending his extradition and fled to Africa.

Taylor's organizational efforts focused on members of the incumbent regime and to others who were connected to the regime's patronage resource networks. These included a former foreign minister and attorney-general, both of whom became close Taylor associates in the 1990s. Taylor also grafted foreign business networks to his insurgent coalition, and a finance minister from the old regime became Taylor's 'economic advisor'. He also received the backing of the president of neighbouring Côte d'Ivoire, whose son-in-law was killed by the previous Liberian regime when it seized power in 1980.

All of these ties marked Taylor and his associates as political insiders. Liberia was not without ideologues who envisioned a population-centric insurgent strategy. Some of these were even attracted to Taylor's NPFL. But such people were dangerous to Taylor as their popularity threatened his position as the leader of the NPFL. Subsequently, many of these people either died under mysterious circumstances or fled from the conflict. Taylor instead based his authority on satisfying the self-interest of NPFL recruits, as his network-centric strategy did not require developing close ties with local communities to mobilize popular support. Even the NPFL's American lobbyists painted a picture of minimal administrative efforts when they visited NPFL-held territory. 'The Taylor forces are not paid—they are all volunteers. Basically they live off the land', they reported (Hyman and Goldfield 1991: 4). Taylor's own agents recorded popular complaints of 'commanders and their subordinates in the habit of harassing and brutalizing peaceful citizens' (NPRAG 1992: 7). Government courts did not function, teachers went unpaid, and insecurity and poverty provoked the flight abroad of over a half a million people from NPFL-held territory, about one-third of the population, and the displacement of another third to areas of Liberia beyond the NPFL's control (Human Rights Watch 1994).

Self-interest, which plays a role in recruitment in all wars, was particularly evident in this conflict. A post-war survey of fighters found that about 35 per cent cited the need to protect their families as their primary reason for joining the NPFL. About 20 per cent said that they joined because they were scared to do otherwise, and about 18 per cent reported that they were abducted. Many reported that they received incentives such as money, food and jobs to join the NPFL (Pugel 2007: 36). These motivations would remain dominant driving forces for fighters in the absence of political commissars and cadres responsible for indoctrinating these recruits. The absence of these figures and the inability and lack of political will of the NPFL's leaders to develop deeper ties with local notables denied the NPFL the tools to discipline recruits to use violence in a more discriminating fashion. But the network-centric goals of this insurgency did not require such extensive and politically risky measures. This was true on all sides of this conflict, and thus the recruits of other factions, including those in government-aligned militias and the state's own armed forces were organized and behaved much like the insurgents that they fought. These political networks had crowded out and destroyed many of the social spaces that ideologues and others otherwise would have used to develop their alternative strategies for fighting.

Liberia's experience reflected trends around the continent. By the 1980s, economic problems associated with patronage-based strategies of rule and institutional decay had hit universities especially hard. During the 1990s, about 20,000 academic staff emigrated from the continent each year, with 10,000 from Nigeria employed in the United States alone at mid-decade (Jumare 1997: 113). World Bank researchers estimated that at the start of the twenty-first century, one-third of Africa's professionals had departed. In an extreme case, every doctor in one graduating class at the University of Zimbabwe left the country (Brown 2002: 20). In countries like Nigeria, armed youths started appearing on university campuses to interfere in student politics. Many observers suspected that such gangs were affiliated with politicians and were deployed to disrupt anti-regime organizing. To the extent that universities were prime sources of leadership for Africa's population-centric insurgencies, these changes closed off the venues that previously favoured ideologues. Even political activists willing to take advantage of electoral reform encountered regime-laid obstacles. In Congo (Zaire), Mobutu agreed to multi-party elections. At the same time he sponsored 'opposition' parties among his clients in an effort to fragment the political terrain and crowd out popular opposition movements. By 1991, over 200 parties were registered, and by 1993, there were 380 parties on the scene (Ngoy-Kangoy 1995: 27–54).

These regime strategies used disorder as a political instrument, much as the insurgents that fought them used disorder in their efforts to seize power (Chabal and Daloz 1999). This crowding out of political space has created what Ernest Wamba-dia-Wamba (himself a former leader of the Kisangani faction of the Rassamblement Congolaise pour la Démocratie as well as the former President of the Council for the Development of Social Science Research in Africa) recognized as a 'crisis of ideology' that left in its place a violent politics that presented enormous obstacles to those who tried to organize population-centric insurgencies around alternative political visions (Wamba dia Wamba 1998).

The future of insurgency in Africa

The central claim of this argument is that the organization and behaviour of insurgencies reflect the strategies that regimes use to exercise political authority. The nature of these strategies has significant consequences for shaping the nature of social spaces, and in particular, the degrees of social autonomy that are available to insurgent leaders. Just as the urbanization in economically developed societies with dense state surveillance and regulation of interactions reduces the opportunities to create rural-based Maoist-style insurgencies, significant parts of the African continent demonstrate their own distinctive category of state–insurgent relations. These regimes that preside over institutionally feeble states in Africa often prove to be remarkably adept at using their political networks – the real sinews of political authority – as a sort of counterinsurgency strategy to undermine organized opposition. This does not protect these regimes from all threats; it simply shifts the focus of those threats to ambitious political actors who challenge regimes from within their own networks. Maintaining the stability of these elite coalitions and managing succession crises stand as their biggest challenges. But even when these political networks collapse into competing armed factions, ideological insurgents still encounter tremendous organizational obstacles.

Consideration of these influential factors helps to shed light on possible future forms of insurgency in Africa. One possibility is that state regimes continue to exercise authority through patronage networks and abjure or downplay serious efforts to create strong bureaucracies. Another possibility is that state regimes in Africa undergo significant reform, boosting their bureaucratic capacities in efforts to increase revenues and seek popular legitimacy on the basis of service provision and economic performance. In fact, both trajectories are possible, and would be associated with different categories of insurgencies.

The first category, fragmented network-centric insurgencies that abjure efforts to administer 'liberated zones' and that employ indiscriminate violence against non-combatants, would be associated with regimes that rely on patronage networks to exercise authority. Electoral politics in some countries from the 1990s appears to have intensified the scramble among politicians in these networks once competitive elections offered the possibility of claiming more status and power. Congo-Brazzaville's elections in the 1990s offered a paradigmatic example of conflict in a patronage-based regime. Politicians turned to armed supporters and helped to field militias in violent campaigns. Groups such as the Cobras, Ninjas and Zoulous dominated the 1992 and 1997 elections.[8] Elections in Nigeria have exhibited a similar propensity to generate violence as politicians compete to control patronage resources (Human Rights Watch 2007). Political leaders in Congo-Brazzaville have done away with truly competitive elections, and thus have restored a measure of stability to their patronage-based political system. Nigeria, however, continues to exhibit the connection between competition in patronage systems and armed struggle to control associated resources. Kenya, noted above, and Côte d'Ivoire show similar connections between elections and violence. Consequently, these states have not seen the appearance of insurgents with autonomous political agendas, even though many citizens express a deep disdain for the status quo and occasionally radical ideas are articulated in popular media and circulate even more widely in music lyrics and rumours.

It is possible that the extremes of violent competition in this kind of political context, particularly after the regimes that once centralized the control of access to patronage resources collapse, could undergo a transformation. Most of Somalia, lacking a centralized state since 1991, and Congo, having largely collapsed by the mid 1990s, now contain young adults who have no personal experience of living in a state. It is doubtful that these young people would be socialized into the world of political competition in the same way that their elders were in the context of presidents who could still more or less regulate the distribution of patronage across their nations. The interstices of highly decentralized competing networks may offer those who reject this politics a new space to organize their own ideologically-driven insurgencies and mobilize followers. These insurgents would need a broadly accessible narrative to cut across parochial divisions. They would also need access to resources that were beyond the reach of incumbent politicians and militia leaders. Though narratives may be available, possibly in the form of millenarian visions, religious extremism or reactions against sinister global forces, resources would be much harder to secure, particularly if insurgents wanted to avoid compromising themselves in agreements with incumbent politicians.

A second broad category of future insurgency might appear where successes in international and domestic efforts to build the capacities of administrative institutions in Africa unintentionally open new social spaces for ideologues to organize armed opposition. If reform is supposed to trim the reach of political networks and end rent-seeking behaviour among officials and regime insiders, the invigorated 'civil society' that arises may include ideologically-driven regime opponents. One can imagine that the anonymity of a commercial sector or religious institutions that are truly autonomous from the dense networks of patronage politics and factional struggle would present more favourable environments for ideologues. Unlike many Northern economies, commerce in Africa is still largely conducted through physical exchanges of currency, which would further insulate insurgent leaders from state surveillance in their collection of resources if these wider political changes were to occur.

It is possible that reformers will take advantage of technological advances to increase state surveillance and hinder the organizational efforts of ideologues. Ethiopia's government, for example, has presided over economic and administrative policies that have resulted in the doubling of the country's economy in the decade from 2000. That government also has promoted electronic transfers of funds, even for very poor people in an effort to collect revenues. Obtaining SIM cards requires the presentation of identity papers, and transmission towers go off-line when political challenges appear. The country's status as a frontline state in the War on Terror has resulted in international aid to upgrade computer databases containing information about the movements of citizens and foreigners, tighten border surveillance capabilities, and more careful screening of international transactions. These measures would force ideological, population-centric insurgents to adopt some of the same measures as urban guerrillas outside of Africa; that is, the insurgents would have to become more secretive and commit highly visible violent acts to announce their presence to the people and demonstrate lapses of government control.

This survey does not exhaust future possibilities. The appearance of violent drugs gangs in Mexico that displaces the state in their core areas of operation signal the development of new kinds of insurgents that combine the control of resource networks with occasional efforts to administer populations, even though these groups do not fight to overthrow the current regime. It is conceivable that the operators of illicit networks in Africa could attain a similar degree of autonomy from the old political establishment that previously protected them. Extensive urban slums, despite their physical proximity to state power, might see armed political groups attain the upper hand vis-à-vis their politician patrons. If this occurred, insurgent violence might take on some of the character of violence in Mexico.

In all of these scenarios, the future of insurgencies in Africa would mirror changes in the strategies of incumbent regimes to assert their authority. Seen more broadly, particular kinds of insurgencies would be associated with particular kinds of regimes. As it is likely that Africa's politics will continue to change, so too will Africa's insurgencies continue their evolution.

Notes

1 This is demonstrated well in Kai Thaler, 'Revolutionary Restraint: Marxism-Leninism and Violence Against Civilians in Mozambique and Angola', Yale University, Program on Order, Conflict and Violence, 2009. Available at: www.yale.edu/macmillan/ocvprogram/papers/ThalerRevolutionaryRestraint.pdf.
2 This idea of the symmetry of state and insurgent forces appears in Kalyvas (2007).
3 On political violence in Nigeria, see Human Rights Watch (2008).
4 'Failed States Index 2010', *Foreign Policy*, June 2010. Available at: www.foreignpolicy.com/articles/2010/06/21/2010_failed_states_index_interactive_map_and_rankings. The ten African states include: Central African Republic, Chad, Côte d'Ivoire, Democratic Republic of Congo, Guinea, Kenya, Nigeria, Somalia, Sudan and Zimbabwe.
5 This idea is developed in Bayart (2009: 180–204).
6 On Mondlane's connections and background see Kitchen (1967).
7 Yoweri Museveni, 'My Three Years in Tanzania', mimeo, n.d. I am grateful to a former NRA fighter who gave me a copy of this in Kampala in June 2001.
8 On the origins of one of these militias, see Ossebi (1998).

Recommended readings

Ali, Taisier and Robert Collins (eds) (1999) *Civil Wars in Africa: Roots and Resolution.* Montreal and Kingston: McGill-Queen's University Press.
Clapham, Christopher (ed.) (1998) *African Guerrillas.* Oxford: James Currey.
Clayton, Anthony (1999) *Frontiersmen & Warfare in Africa Since 1950.* London: University College London.
Spears, Ian (2010) *Civil War in African States.* Boulder: Lynne Rienner.
Williams, Paul (2011, forthcoming) *War and Conflict in Africa.* Cambridge: Polity Press.

References

Amaza, Ondoga ori (1998) *Museveni's Long March: From Guerrilla to Statesman.* Kampala: Fountain Publishers.
Bayart, Jean-François (2009) *The State in Africa: The Politics of the Belly*, 2nd edn. Cambridge: Polity.
Blok, Anton (1974) *The Mafia of a Sicilian Village, 1960–1960.* Oxford: Blackwell.
Brown, Kyle (2002) 'Africa's Loss in the Brain Drain', *West Africa*, 27 May.
Cann, John (1997) *Counterinsurgency in Africa: The Portuguese Way of War, 1961–1974.* Westport: Greenwood Press.
Chabal, Patrick and Jean-Pascal Daloz (1999) *Africa Works: Disorder as Political Instrument.* Oxford: James Currey.
Collier, Paul (2000) 'Rebellion as a Quasi-criminal Activity', *Journal of Conflict Resolution*, 44 (6): 839–53.
Collier, Paul and Anke Hoeffler (2004) 'Greed and Grievance in Civil Wars', *Oxford Economic Papers*, 56: 563–95.
Dhada, Mustafa (1998) 'The Liberation War in Guinea-Bissau Reconsidered', *Journal of Military History*, 62 (July).
Ellis, Stephen (1998) 'The Historical Significance of South Africa's Third Force', *Journal of Southern African Studies*, 24 (2): 261–99.

Ellis, Stephen (1999) 'The New Frontiers of Crime in South Africa', in Jean-François Bayart, Stephen Ellis and Béatrice Hibou (eds), *The Criminalization of the State in Africa*. Oxford: James Currey, pp. 49–68.

Gesnekter, Charles (1975) 'Independent Mozambique and Its Neighbors; Now What?', *Africa Today*, 22 (3).

Handyside, Richard (trans. and ed.) (1969) *Revolution in Guinea: Selected Texts by Amilcar Cabral*. New York: Monthly Review Press.

Henriksen, Thomas (1976) 'People's War in Angola, Mozambique, and Guinea-Bissau', *Journal of Modern African Studies*, 14 (3).

Human Rights Watch (2007) *Criminal Politics: Violence, 'Godfathers' and Corruption in Nigeria*. New York: Human Rights Watch.

Human Rights Watch (2008) *Politics as War: The Human Rights Impact and Causes of Post-Election Violence in Rivers State, Nigeria*. New York: Human Rights Watch.

Human Rights Watch – Africa (1994) 'Testimony of Janet Fleischman', Sub-Committee on Africa, House Foreign Relations Committee, Washington, DC, 18 May.

Hyman, Lester and H.P. Goldfield (1991) 'Notes on Liberian Fact-Finding Visit', Washington, DC: photocopied report.

Jumare, Ibrahim (1997) 'The Displacement of the Nigerian Academic Community', *Journal of Asian and African Studies*, 32 (1).

Kaldor, Mary (2001) *New & Old Wars: Organized Violence in a Global Era*. Stanford: Stanford University Press.

Kalyvas, Stathis (2006) *The Logic of Violence in Civil War*. New York: Cambridge University Press.

Kalyvas, Stathis (2007) 'Civil Wars', in Carles Boix and Susan Stokes (eds), *Oxford Handbook of Comparative Politics*. New York: Oxford University Press, pp. 426–30.

Kilcullen, David (2009) *The Accidental Guerrilla: Fighting Small Wars in the Midst of a Big One*. New York: Oxford University Press.

Kitchen, Helen (1967) 'Conversation with Eduardo Mondlane', *Africa Report*, November, pp. 31–51.

Lemarchand, Rene (1979) 'The Politics of Penury in Rural Zaire: The View from Bundundu', in Guy Gran (ed.), *Zaire: The Political Economy of Underdevelopment*. New York:Praeger.

Marighella, Carlos (2002) *Minimanual of the Urban Guerrilla*. Oakland: Abraham Guillen Press.

Mondlane, Eduardo (1969) *Struggle for Mozambique*. Harmondsworth: Penguin.

Museveni, Yoweri (1997) *Sowing the Mustard Seed*. London: Macmillan.

Mushemeza, E.D. (2007) *The Politics and Empowerment of Banyarwanda Refugees in Uganda 1959–2001*. Kampala: Fountain Publishers.

Ngoy-Kangoy, Kgulu (1995) *La transition démocratique au Zaire*. Kinshasa: Université de Kinshasa.

NPRAG (1992) *Report from the National Security Committee submitted to the Conference Bureau, All-Liberian National Conference*. Gbarnga, photocopy, 25 April.

Ossebi, Henri (1998) 'De la galèrie á la guerre: jeunnes et "Cobras" dans les quartiers Nord de Brazzaville', *Politique Africaine*, 72 (December): 27–33.

Pugel, James (2007) *What the Fighters Say: A Survey of Ex-combatants in Liberia*. New York: United Nations Development Programme.

Rabasa, Angel, Steven Boaz, *et al.* (2007) *Ungoverned Territories: Understanding and Reducing Terrorism Risks*. Santa Monica: RAND.

Radmann, Wolf (1974) 'Zambesi Development Scheme: Cabora Bassa', *Issue: A Journal of Opinion*, 4 (2).

Red Army Faction (n.d.) *The Urban Guerrilla Concept*. Available at: www.germanguerilla.com/red-army-faction/pdf/71_04.pdf.

Rejai, M. (ed.) (1969) *Mao Tse-Tung on Revolution and War*. Garden City: Anchor Books.

Republic of Kenya (2008) *Report of the Commission of Inquiry into Post Election Violence* ['Waki Report']. Nairobi: Nairobi Government Printer.

Scott, James (1979) 'Revolution in the Revolution: Peasants and Commissars', *Theory & Society*, 7 (11): 97–134.

Scott, James (1998) *Seeing Like a State: How Certain Schemes to Improve the Human Condition Have Failed*. New Haven: Yale University Press.

Young, John (1997) *Peasant Revolution in Ethiopia: The Tigray People's Liberation Front, 1975–1991*. New York: Cambridge University Press.

Wamba dia Wamba, Ernest (1998) 'Mobutuism after Mobutu', *CODESRIA Bulletin*, 3 and 4: 73–5.

13

INSURGENCY IN IRAQ 2003–10

Ahmed Hashim[1]

US forces entered Iraq on 19 March 2003 in an invasion dubbed Operation Iraqi Freedom (OIF) in order to overthrow the regime of Iraqi leader, Saddam Hussein, who was viewed as a recalcitrant and irredeemable tyrannical ruler. By the end of the year Iraq was in the throes of a full-scale insurgency by a section of its population, the Sunnis, against the Coalition presence. Irregular warfare was something that the superb conventional US military neither expected nor knew how to deal with. Lacking effective doctrine for countering insurgencies, the United States flailed around and became frustrated; its early failures contributed to fanning the flames of anger and humiliation (see Burton and Nagl 2008: 303–27; Sepp 2007: 217–30). The fighting was so extensive and bitter that between 2003 and 2005 it has produced nearly ten times as many Coalition casualties as the fight to topple the regime and defeat Iraq's army. After 2006 the insurgency evolved into a bitter civil war between Sunnis and Shiites that has only gradually been brought under control in the last two years. The purpose of this chapter is to address the origins/causes, ideologies, goals and evolution of the insurgency after 2003 and assess the factors behind its failures and ultimate decline.

Cradle of civilization

The origins of the Sunni insurgency cannot be understood without reference to the evolution of the Iraqi policy from Ottoman and Persian times to the present. The Ottomans were responsible for the emergence of the Sunni Arabs as the dominant political community in Mesopotamia from the mid-nineteenth century as a 'shield' against the Persian Safavids, a Shiite dynasty. Sunnis in turn took full advantage of the Ottoman educational system, sending their sons through the system to become officers in the Ottoman Army garrisons in the province. The establishment of secular schooling in 1869 was for the Sunni Arabs a way of compensating for their demographic weakness and enhancing their political status.

This situation continued after the First World War when Britain gained control over Mesopotamia. The British formed an interim government in November 1920 predominantly comprised of Sunni Arabs who had curried favour with them. In 1932, Iraq gained its 'independence' although the British still maintained a dominant position within the power structure. The Sunni elite continued to remain entrenched in power despite the emergence of an educated Shiite political class, which did manage to move into key positions such as the premiership. This situation continued after the overthrow of the monarchy in 1958 and the Sunni elite ruled Iraq until 2003.

The onset of insurgency

The insurgency in Iraq can be viewed as a 'communal' insurgency as only one community, the Sunnis, really leads it. It could also be qualified as an 'ethnic' insurgency, as many Sunni insurgents consider themselves as fighting the empowerment of both non-Arab Kurds and Shiite Arabs. It did not emerge from a politically and socioeconomically marginalized ethnic or communal group. Rather, it is a rare phenomenon, an insurgency by a hitherto dominant group seeking to restore its former position of power: a restorationist or 'reactionary' insurgency.

There is a clear set of factors behind the onset of the Sunni insurgency. In a structural sense, the origins of the insurgency in Iraq must be found in the nature of Iraqi state formation and nation-building and the issue of identity politics. Ottoman, British and then Iraqi policies worked in a way to ensure that the Shiites, despite their demographic weight in the country, became a 'minority' in the sense that they were politically marginalized and removed from the centres of political and economic power (Jabar 2003). For the Shiite Arabs Sunni-dominated Iraqi Arab nationalism was a further vehicle for their reduction to the status of a minority within their country (Beinin and Stork 1995: 18–22). The Kurdish population in the north also remained removed from power; it is true that during the early history of modern Iraq they were better represented than the more demographically significant Shiites in the corridors of power. Kurds were recruited into the armed forces and government bureaucracy. They were Sunnis, but they were not Arabs; with the emergence of nationalism among segments of the Kurdish population, there also appeared a desire for autonomy or even independence. This highly skewed and troublesome edifice that had been set up by the Ottomans, reinforced by the British, and consolidated by the Sunni minority came crashing down around the Sunni Arabs in April 2003. It was a massive psychological and physical dislocation to which they have been unable to effectively adjust. It was this massive threat to identity which provided the impetus for the eruption of Sunni insurrection. At its heart, the Sunni insurgency arose out of a loss of Sunni identity.

The Sunnis not only lost their positions in government due to marginal Ba'athist affiliation, but their entire way of life had been upended with the invasion. Additionally, the primacy of the Sunni in governing Iraq was taken away and given to the Shiite majority, further compounding the Sunni loss of prestige. The Bush Administration desired to implement a pluralist democratic society in Iraq, further compounding the loss of Sunni identity

Among the earliest adherents of the insurgency were members of the former regime, Ba'athist security personnel and officials who had the most to lose from the downfall of the regime. Initially, they were very disorganized and merely lashed out wildly at their perceived tormentors. As Shiite-dominated and US-sponsored national governments were formed, Sunni resistance took on a defensive character, as Sunnis began to fear Shiite retribution for years of Sunni rule over Iraq. Yet while indigenous factors – a loss of identity and the need to restore a sense of social balance – were critical in the development and growth of the Sunni insurgency, mistakes by Coalition forces made at the tactical, operational and strategic levels contributed to increasing levels of Sunni resistance to the presence of the United States and its allies in Iraq.

At the tactical level, the lack of cultural understanding of Iraqi society was largely absent from Coalition forces' interaction with the population after the fall of the Ba'ath regime. The insensitive manner in which soldiers conducted house-to-house searches and handled detainees inflamed Iraqi sensitivities. The absence of any coherent post-invasion planning done in the run up to the invasion, including the failure to consider the possibility of an insurgency and the Bush Administration's ill-conceived policy to impose the Coalition Provisional Authority (CPA) (in Iraqi eyes a governing apparatus much akin to the British Mandate of the previous century) also contributed to the rapid growth of the insurgency through the summer and autumn of 2003. Yet, even in the midst of these grave errors, the ignominious actions at Abu Ghraib prison in the autumn and winter of 2003, and its shoddy handling, stand out as a key accelerant to the growth of a nascent Sunni insurgency.

An important factor in initiating Sunni resistance was the early American policy of either ignoring the Sunnis or of perceiving them collectively as the 'enemy' because they had been the mainstay of the deposed regime. The American indifference and hostility towards the Sunnis was deliberate in the early days of the occupation; and it led to their marginalization in accordance with the Bush Administration's strategy of relying on the more 'reliable' Shiite Arabs and Kurds, who together constituted a majority of the population. The first post-Saddam ruling structure, the CPA, under 'proconsul' Paul Bremer, took the highly inflammatory and ideologically-driven step of dissolving the Iraqi army because it was heavily identified with the former regime and thus with the Sunni community. This was not how Iraqi army officers saw it; for the vast majority of them, the defunct Iraqi military was a professional force that had been founded in 1923, long before Saddam, and had been corrupted and misused by the Iraqi dictator. The decision to disband the armed forces was ultimately to ensure that large numbers of officers and enlisted men were to become insurgents beginning in the autumn of 2003.

The rise of Islamist feelings within the Sunni community strengthened the power and voice of the Sunni clerics and preachers who began to take an activist political role in order to articulate Sunni grievances and goals and to present a cohesive Islamist narrative legitimizing resistance to foreign occupation. However, the impetus for the rise of Islamism within what was ostensibly a secular state lies within the political and socio-cultural dynamics of Iraqi society in the 1990s. The political activism of the Sunni clerical establishment started in the 1990s under the former regime when clerics began to rail against the sanctions regime and the 'moral' and ethical collapse of Iraqi society. Those clerics who deigned to attack the regime, whether implicitly or explicitly, were imprisoned or exiled (Hottiger 2004). With the downfall of the regime, Sunni clerics began to take charge of the sociopolitical space because there was a distinct lack of worthy or decisive political leaders to act on behalf of the community or to negotiate with other political forces in the post-Saddam Iraqi political scene.

The clerics adopted a Salafist interpretation of Islam promoted their views among the Sunni population, particularly during Friday sermons (Shihab 2003). With the capture of Saddam in late 2003, the local Salafists believed that this was their opportunity to pick up the torch of resistance ideologically from the dominant Ba'athist and nationalist strands. The invasion and occupation had led to a steady increase in recruits. In 2004 local Salafists were 'on the rise' among the ranks of the resistance. Although still modest, their networks grew, aided by the fact that a handful of senior officers joined the Islamists while many former soldiers also returned to religion.

The majority of early Sunni insurgent groups had a nationalist aspect to their rhetoric. The core groups of the secular Sunni nationalists formed around former Ba'athists and are known by Coalition forces as Former Regime Elements (FRE) or Former Regime Loyalists (FRL), with the capture of Saddam in December 2003, the secular nationalists were largely discredited. As they tried to cast off the ties to Ba'ath secularism, many moved towards the Islamist nationalist camp.

In the spring of 2004 Shia elements under the leadership of the young populist cleric Moqtada al-Sadr joined in the violence against the Coalition forces. Coalition forces were hard-pressed to deal with what was seemingly becoming a national liberation struggle. But there was little, if any, coordination between Sunni and Shia insurgents. The growing mutual alienation between Sunni and Shiites provided a backdrop to the infiltration into Iraq of transnational Islamists who were to declare allegiance to the al-Qaeda movement of Osama bin Laden. These groups subscribed to a rigid and inflexible form of Salafist Islamism. Unlike the more 'moderate' local Salafists these groups did not hesitate to pronounce *takfir* (excommunication, i.e. rendering non-Muslim) against Muslims who do not subscribe to their ideology. This group has been profoundly hostile to the Shias who are referred to as Rafidis or rejectionists (of Islam).

The presence of a plethora of insurgent groups in Iraq has had adverse implications for the articulation of a unified ideology and set of goals. It is not clear what the myriad groups had in common with one another at the beginning of the insurgency beyond a desire to rid the country of the foreign presence, fight the rise of the Shia majority and ensure a return to Sunni hegemony. The wide variety of ideological currents within the insurgency was a reflection of deep divisions and fissures within the Sunni community, divisions which had barely been kept in check during the last decade of Saddam's rule.

Internal structures and organizational dynamics

When addressing Iraqi insurgent internal structures and organizational dynamics, two major structural characteristics stand out. The first one is the fact that the Iraqi insurgent organizations are *hybrids* in that the vast majority of them consist of a mix of *hierarchical and decentralized structures*. No Iraqi insurgent organization or group, not even the hitherto rigidly hierarchical Ba'ath party, is purely hierarchical. If they were they would be susceptible to penetration by hostile forces and to leadership decapitation. Similarly, none is completely decentralized without a leadership structure. Such organizations would not be able to undertake operations effectively or exercise some form of command, control and coordination. They would collapse due to endogenous weaknesses.

The second structural characteristic is the range of *functional specialization*. The largest insurgent organizations, often characterized by a substantial cadre of personnel with special skills, prevalence of bureaucratic skills, sufficient funding, an ability to undertake a wide range of operations ranging from the simple to the complex ambushes and raids. They have a nationwide reach and can be defined as having high functional specialization because they are able to create a wide range of specialized combat and combat support cells.

The Ba'athists and their affiliates are characterized by high functional specialization for a wide variety of reasons. They used to control the state and its various institutions; they re-created some of them in a decentralized manner in order to conduct an insurgency. One of the better-known insurgent groups, Jaysh al-Fatihin or Al-Fatihin Army (AFA), seems to have developed an extensive and highly functionally specialized organizational structure. This may have been due to the fact that it learned from its parent organization, the IAI. The AFA claims to have a wide variety of internal institutions and councils. These include Leadership, General Command, Shura, Sharia, Military and Media councils. Its military council is allegedly in charge of ten combat brigades which operate in various cities in central and northern Iraq (OSC Report, 28 November 2006). al-Qaeda in Iraq (AQI) developed an advanced level of functional specialization which it passed on to the umbrella organization, the MSC and then the Islamic State of Iraq (ISI).

The military wing has combatant battalions, security and reconnaissance units which carefully examine new members, collect intelligence about the enemy, recruit agents in the Iraqi security forces, the contractor companies and the transportation and logistics support for the Coalition. Those groups that cannot afford to have a wide range of specialized cadre and may be forced to 'borrow' such cadre from other groups (Improvised Explosive Device or IED-makers), do not have the ability to undertake a wide range of operations, and may, by choice, be dedicated to 'defending' their local turf against Coalition forces, Iraqi Security Forces, Shi'a militia, and increasingly AQI and its affiliates, rather than fighting in a nationwide insurgency, can be defined as organizations of low functional specialization. The tribal insurgents and very small localized '*kata'ibs*' (brigades) are characterized by low functional specialization. For many this is not a particularly onerous constraint as they do not aspire to do more.

Targeting, operational art and tactics

The Iraqi insurgency has a large range of targets available to them. These include Coalition forces and their associated networks and infrastructure such as supply convoys, and private security companies. They also include the foreign companies and foreign workers who flooded into Iraq in the wake of the invasion to participate in the expected windfall from reconstruction, development and the provision of services to the enormous Coalition military and civilian presence.

In the case of the Sunni insurgents in Iraq terrorism has also increased as the insurgency gathered steam. There are groups whose entire modus operandi has been predicated on the use of terror through the use of 'suicide' or martyrdom operations, large-scale assassinations of individuals or groups associated with or collaborating with the Coalition, and kidnapping and execution of foreigners.

Most of Iraq's suicide bombers are foreigners, with the highest percentage coming from Saudi Arabia and other Gulf states. Since August 2003, as the US-led coalition forces gradually strengthened their defences, suicide car bombs have been increasingly used as weapons by guerrilla forces. There have also been many attacks on non-military and civilian targets, beginning in earnest in August 2003 and steadily increasing since then. Kidnapping, and in some cases beheadings, have also emerged as another insurgent tactic since April 2004. Foreign civilians have borne the brunt of the kidnappings, although US military personnel have also been targeted.

Guerilla tactics

Iraqi insurgents use the traditional guerilla tactics of hit-and-run, raids, ambushes, the use of car bombs and IEDs, and assassinations. Usually, Iraqi insurgents operate in small teams of five to ten men. This facilitates mobility, reduces complexity in command and control and the chances of detection; but it improves the ability to escape capture. However, it also lessens the amount of firepower they can bring to bear against heavily armed Coalition forces. The improved training of the insurgents was reflected in the increase in written tactical manuals and instructions issued by insurgent groups. These are often distributed electronically on the Internet where many other groups can access them.

Not surprisingly, the insurgents' ability to learn was reflected in their developing the skills to launch larger, more complex and well-executed attacks involving as many as 150 men. This happened in and around the large city of Ramadi in Al-Anbar province where complex attacks were led by former Iraqi army commanders. In April 2005 two particularly audacious attacks by large insurgent forces occurred against Abu Ghraib prison south of Baghdad and against a US Marine outpost. In the first attack two separate columns of insurgent forces launched an assault against the prison following an accurate and sustained bombardment of US positions by 80mm and 120mm mortars and two VBIED assaults aimed at breaching the prison walls. In the second case a group of 100 insurgents launched a well-coordinated complex attack on a US Marine base at Husaybah (Galloway 2005; Knickmeyer 2005: A1). The guerillas in Diyala became increasingly well organized and trained, and the province was the third deadliest place for US troops in Iraq in 2006 after Baghdad and Anbar.

This ability to learn and adapt is very evident in the insurgents' deployment of IEDs and in the ways they have countered US attempts to defeat the IED threat. The first-generation IEDs were relatively small and simple, often a 155mm or 152mm artillery shell hidden in a wall or embankment along a road. Insurgents would run wires from the device to a hand-held trigger, which they could activate from a nearby hiding place. As US troops devised countermeasures to detect those IEDs, by spotting the wires or suspicious individuals nearby, insurgents changed their approach and began using remote triggers – garage door openers, cell phones – to detonate the devices from greater distances. They also turned to more powerful explosives, sometimes 'daisy-chaining' multiple artillery rounds to boost destructive force.

By March 2004, the insurgents were using daisy chains, emplacing 155mm rounds in a row. In the spring of 2004 US troops also started getting their first large-scale deliveries of jammers: devices that can be mounted in a vehicle or, in some cases, carried in a backpack, to block the wireless signals insurgents used to set off IEDs. The insurgents adapted faster. By early 2004, they began burying IEDs under roads, so they would blast up through the thin floors that proved to be the Achilles heel of even the armoured Humvees. The triggers changed, too. As more jammers arrived, insurgents switched to hard-wired devices or pressure-plate IEDs, which explode when a vehicle goes over them. By 2007 they were adapting again and using explosively formed projectiles (Eisler 2007: 1).

The Iraqi insurgency has been responsible for one innovation: the efforts of some groups to formulate and implement insurgent chemical warfare. The first indication of interest in the creation of an insurgent chemical warfare capability came in March 2004 when a series of site exploitations and detentions of men intrigued the Iraq Survey Group (ISG) which then began investigating a network of Iraqi insurgents – referred to as the al-Aboud network – who had begun to actively seek a chemical weapons capability in late 2003. ISG created a team of experts to investigate and dismantle the al-Aboud network. By June 2004, ISG was able to identify and neutralize the chemical suppliers and chemists, including former regime members, who supported the al-Aboud network. A series of raids, interrogations and detentions managed to disrupt key activities at al-Aboud-related laboratories and safe-houses. But the leaders of the network eluded capture.

The 'surge' strategy

By the autumn of 2006 many observers in Washington concluded that Iraq's future was bleak. It was increasingly dawning upon the Bush Administration that the United States was headed for a monumental defeat in Iraq. Bush declared that failure in Iraq was not an option; but domestic forces were clamouring for the United States to do something decisive, preferably such as creating a definite timetable for withdrawal. The grim situation forced the Bush administration to consider the few options remaining. The Administration decided, on the advice of retired officers and civilian strategic analysts, on a 'surge' of US troops. President Bush articulated this in January 2007. The purpose of the surge of US troops was to damp down the violence and establish the conditions for the Iraqis to bring about national reconciliation.

However other factors weighed in to help the surge strategy. The homogenization of neighbourhoods by 2007 due to 'ethnic cleansing' meant that there was less opportunity for Sunnis and Shia to kill each other. The decision in August 2007 of Moqtada al-Sadr to stand down his militia which had been heavily engaged in fighting the Sunnis and in provoking US forces was another significant factor in the diminution of the violence. Moqtada and his senior commanders then went after alleged rogue elements within the Mahdi Army (AM) and weeded them out through the simple expedient of gunning them down. The AM's history begins in a most unlikely place. In September 2006, Ramadi was arguably the most dangerous city in Iraq. AQI and local Sunni insurgents were so active that the number of attacks against Coalition and Iraqi forces per capita was three times higher than in any other part of the country. Insurgents enjoyed complete freedom of movement in the city and the Iraqi government's authority extended no further than the government centre in the heart of downtown. US and Iraqi forces in the area operated from large Forward Operating Bases in the area, patrolling periodically and then returning to base. This non-persistent presence failed to secure the population or provide protection for local leadership, allowing insurgents to retain control of the city. The ability of insurgents to operate with impunity allowed them to deploy extensive IED belts making the city even more forbidding for US and Iraqi forces.

Early US efforts in Ramadi focused on establishing political alliances with local political and tribal leaders designed to isolate and defeat the insurgency. In November 2005, US commanders met with local sheiks and convinced them to break with AQI. Since late 2007, scholars have offered a multitude of explanations for the decline of violence and the abatement of AQI. As this debate has played out over time, the positions have largely gelled into two distinct positions – those actions that originated with the US-led Coalition and those actions that originated indigenously.

By looking at the literature from a broader perspective, we can see similar causes that leap out in explaining the demise of AQI and can be roughly classified as belonging in either one of these two positions. It appears that the Sunni revolt against AQI was at its heart a reaction to protect local identity from being subsumed by an outside group. As much as the demonization of Sunni identity by the United States and its Iraqi quislings created the insurgency in 2003–4, the perceived belief by the Sunnis that AQI would destroy their identity caused AQI's demise. The Sunnis attempted to resist this imposition of a new identity on numerous occasions, only to see each attempt quickly suppressed by AQI, and it was not until the Ramadi-based Anbar Salvation Council in late 2006 that the Sunni resistance to AQI actually stood firm.

The widening of sectarian conflict

The most important factor, however, in promoting the diminution of violence was the dramatic change in the Sunni insurgency. Even as Sunni and Shiite were busy killing each other, there were signs of a split within the Sunni insurgency between local insurgents including the tribes – who see themselves as fighting to rid Iraq of foreign occupation and to restore Sunni dominance – on the one side and the Salafi-Jihadist strain – fighting to establish a purist Islamist political system – coalescing around al-Qaeda in Iraq (AQI) and its creation the Islamic State of Iraq (ISI) on the other. Many of the local insurgents, including even some of the most Islamist in orientation, were annoyed with the AQI extremists because of differences in goals, strategies and modus operandi.

The Sunni tribes in particular bore the brunt of AQI's disruptive strategies and tactics in the rural hinterlands; slowly but surely the tribes began to turn against the extremism of AQI which was disrupting their way of life, beliefs and mores, and economic activities. As a result of the growing distaste with AQI in Anbar province by the summer of 2007 several tribal sheiks had created armed 'Awakening Councils' throughout the province of Al-Anbar. These were known in Arabic as the *Sahwa*. These councils pitted their militias against the transnational jihadists – foreign Islamists from other Arab countries – and their Iraqi allies. Initially, the tribal forces made little headway due to the better armaments of the AQI/MSC/ISI fighters. The brutality of the jihadists' response to the challenge posed by the 'contemptible' tribesmen only further strengthened the latter group's determination to eradicate the extremists in their midst. In a practical application of the old cliché that the 'enemy of my enemy is my friend', the tribes turned to their former foe, the US forces, for aid.

There was no core ideological set of principles vis-à-vis the Americans espoused by the tribes that would preclude a pragmatic quid pro quo between the two sides. This is not say that the tribes viewed the American presence in Iraq and specifically in their respective tribal areas in any positive light; but they proved that they were willing to bargain with the occupier, if the latter satisfied both material and ideational interests. The impetus for the emergence of collective bargaining between tribe and occupier was provided by AQI whose actions threatened the entire spectrum of tribal interests and identity. The extremists muscled in on tribal economic interests, extracted 'protection money' from merchants and travelers, they imposed taxes, they shut down barber shops and coffee shops. As AQI's funding needs increased – in order to finance operations and recruit members – the greater the exactions against the tribes.

The Americans had deeper pockets and were willing to part with the money, to involve the tribes in reconstruction projects, and to hire the men of the tribes. AQI imposed strict and doctrinal principles on tribal culture, they trod on tribal norms, honour and dignity by publicly flogging or beheading tribesmen who 'strayed'. And lastly, they committed horrific acts of terror. The Americans may have been boorish, particularly in the early days of the insurgency. They were not interested in imposing doctrinaire ideas upon the tribes. In the final analysis, as several tribal sheiks put it when tribal–AQI relations were frayed and turned to violence: the Americans maybe an enemy, but AQI is the worst enemy (author observations in Iraq November–April 2003, July–September 2005 and October–November 2007; Baram 1997: 1–31; Glain 2000; Pope and Spindle 2002; Kilcullen 2007; Jabar and Dawood 2003).

In autumn 2007 US forces seized letters written by Sahwa or AQI leaders which documented the startling turnaround in AQI fortunes due to the rise of the Awakening movement in the Sunni province. One letter by 'Abu Tariq', details how his force of 600 men had shrunk to less than 20 and proceeded to lament the fact that the organization had been 'mistreated' and duped by the Iraqi insurgent groups and the tribes. Americans may have been naïve in their understanding of tribal dynamics, but AQI and its leadership was even more naïve and ignorant of culture and history of tribal behaviour and of Iraqi needs. They finally recognized that their ideology and tactics had succeeded in turning the populace against the movement and allowed the Americans to recruit them to their side. This helped turn the tide. The successes of the tribal councils in Anbar contributed to the rise of copycat awakening councils in Baghdad itself and other provinces such as Salahedin and Diyala where the inhabitants and local insurgents had finally had enough of the depredations of the extremists. They took the initiative to organize their struggle against the extremists in their midst.

It was not long before the US military began to recognize the benefits of providing support in the shape of arms and money to these groups. The decline of the insurgency is largely attributable to the incorporation of mainly Sunni tribal leaders and their militias in the *Sahwa* ('Awakening') movement (assisted by the increasing rifts between the Sunni insurgency and AQI). This marks the latest in a series of oscillations in Iraqi history between attempts to build a strong centralized state (as under the revolutionary government of Abd al-Karim Qasim from 1958 to 1963 and, most successfully, between the 1973 oil price rise and the Iran–Iraq War) and a reliance on relations of patronage with tribal sheiks (as under the British Mandate, the Hashemite monarchy and the latter years of Saddam Hussein's rule) (Tripp 2000; Dodge 2003; Hechter and Kabiri 2008).

The American military, having at first attempted to impose a direct rule regime in complete disregard of local institutions, now appear to have reinvented the system of tribal patronage.

They have been aided by the ineptitude of AQI, which, having at first successfully allied itself with the Sunni insurgency, proceeded to alienate many of these allies by its indiscriminate violence, by challenging the authority of tribal power structures it perceived as un-Islamic, and by attempting to take control of the insurgency (ICG 2008; Simon 2008). At first referred to by the Americans as 'concerned local citizens', the 'Awakening Councils were rebranded as *abna al-Iraq*' or 'Sons of Iraq'. These concerned citizens were, in fact, largely former Sunni insurgents, although 18–20 per cent of the 100,000 officially registered 'Sons' are Shia (O'Hanlon and Campbell 2008: 12). The United States was paying $360 for each, of which up to 20 per cent went to tribal leaders, allowing some to amass considerable wealth (Simon 2008) and some to restore the powers of patronage. There was a significant reduction in violence and a return to near normalcy in 2008, but the situation in Iraq remained very fragile.

As the former Sunni insurgents celebrated their victories against AQI, touted their alliance with the Americans, and expanded their militia organizations, tension emerged between them and the government of Nuri al-Maliki. Neither side had the highest regard for the other. The Sunnis viewed with distaste the entrenchment of the Shia in the Iraqi body politic. Some were still fanatically dedicated to removing that domination; others were more pragmatically demanding resources for reconstruction in their areas and the absorption of militia personnel into the security services. Having helped the Americans defeat a common enemy in the fanatics of AQI, the Sunni militias were now wondering whether they would be facing their second biggest enemy once again, the Shia, but this time one that dominates the state and is increasingly self-confident. Ironically, members of the Sunni militia, *abna' al-Iraq* (Sons of Iraq) do not want to see the Americans leave, such is their distrust of and hostility towards the government of Prime Minister Nuri al-Maliki which they see as a tool of Shia Iran. The Status of Forces Agreement (SOFA) that the United States has signed with the Iraqi government was actually not welcomed by many within the Sunni community, despite the public statements of Sunni leaders and politicians that this was a good step towards full sovereignty.

The government of Nuri al-Maliki does not feel the need to 'reward' the Sunni militias, whom it sees as former insurgents with blood on their hands. There is also the hidden fear that a massive re-entry of Sunnis into the armed forces could threaten the hard-won Shia dominance of the military; like the Sunnis before them, the now dominant Shiite elite recognize that one of the key structures of power in Iraq remain the security forces. The existence of a large group of armed former Sunni insurgents led by men with political ambitions has worried the Shia-dominated government in Baghdad. This would give these groups considerable clout should they effectively execute an entry into national politics. The deep-seated hostility sets the stage for a possible renewed outbreak of violence.

A number of prominent mainstream Sunni insurgent organizations – not AQI whose remnants continue to bluster and threaten the Awakening Councils (AC) – have suggested that the ACs should reconsider rejoining the ranks of the insurgency in order to revitalize it. There was also great concern in spring 2008 that AQI showed signs of revival. Much of the concern was expressed by the Sons of Iraq leadership. It was not clear if this were true or merely a tactic in order to promote their relevance and importance to the maintenance of security. However, a letter found in a raid on an AQI hideout in March 2008, by an unknown operative named Abu Sufiyan outlined a strategy to destabilize the country by targeting Awakening members, economic infrastructure and Shia. Dozens of Awakening Council members were killed in the early months of 2008. The head of ISI issued a call for the Sunnis to return to the fold of AQI or to face certain death.

Many members of the ACs – particularly those leaders who were prominent within the ranks of the mainstream insurgency – felt betrayed by the US decision to leave them at the mercy of the Shia-dominated government. An umbrella organization of Sunni insurgent groups, The

Front for Change and Jihad has been in the forefront in expressing and highlighting the alleged betrayal and in suggesting that the Sunnis as a community should prepare to fight the government in Baghdad. The government's stubbornness stems in part from the perception, probably accurate, that the balance of power in the country has turned almost irrevocably in favour of the Shia majority; and that they do not need to curry favour with the heavily-armed Sunni groups. This is dangerous and although the Shia are likely to ultimately triumph – particularly in light of the build-up of the military and because of support from neighbouring Iran – a possible renewal of the civil war as the United States slowly but surely reduces its presence is likely to make the 'undeclared' civil war of 2005–06 look tame by comparison.

Note

1 The author would like to thank Grégoire Patte, intern at the International Center for Political Violence and Terrorism Research at the Rajaratnam Center for International Studies, Nanyang Technical University Singapore, who collaborated in the final preparation of the chapter.

Recommended readings

Ahmed, Hashim (2006) *Insurgency and Counterinsurgency in Iraq*. Ithaca: Cornell University Press.

Kagan, Kimberly (2008) *The Surge: A Military History*. New York: Encounter.

Munson, Peter (2009) *Iraq in Transition: The Legacy of Dictatorship and the Prospects for Democracy*. Herndon: Potomac Books.

Ricks, Thomas (2006) *Fiasco: The American Military Adventure in Iraq*. New York: Penguin.

Ricks, Thomas (2009) *The Gamble: General David Petraeus and the American Military Adventure in Iraq 2006–2008*. New York: Penguin.

Robinson, Linda (2008) *Tell Me How this Ends: General David Petraeus and the Search for a Way Out of Iraq*. New York: Public Affairs.

References

Baram, A. (1997) 'Neo-Tribalism in Iraq: Saddam Hussein's Tribal Policies 1991–96', *International Journal of Middle Eastern Studies*, 29(1): 1–31.

Beinin, Joel and Stork, Joe (eds) (1995) *Shi'ism and the Revolution*. Bloomington: Indiana University Press.

Burton, B. and Nagl, J. (2008) 'Learning as We Go: The US Army Adapts to Counterinsurgency in Iraq, July 2004–December 2006', *Small Wars and Insurgencies*, 19 (3): 303–27.

Dodge, Toby (2003) 'The Social Ontology of Late Colonialism: Tribes and the Mandated State in Iraq', in Faleh Jabar and Hosham Dawod (eds), *Tribes and Power: Nationalism and Ethnicity in the Middle East*. London: Saqi, pp. 257–82.

Eisler, P. (2007) 'Insurgents Adapting Faster to U.S. Defenses', *USA Today*, 16 July, p. 1.

Galloway, J. (2005) 'Bolder Insurgent Tactics Unleashed in Iraq', *The State.com*, 24 April. Available at: www.thestate.com/mld/thestate/living/11474953.htm?template=contentModules/prin.

Glain, J. (2000) 'Tribalism in Iraq', *The Wall Street Journal*, 23 May.

Hechter, M. and Kabiri, N. (2008) 'Attaining Social Order in Iraq', in Stathis N. Kalyvas, Ian Shapiro and Tarek Masoud (eds), *Order, Conflict, and Violence*. Cambridge: Cambridge University Press, pp. 43–74.

Hottiger, A. (2004) 'Die befreite Stadt des Sunniten predigers Janabi', *Neue Zurcher Zeitung*, 15 September. Available at: www.nzz.ch/dossiers/2002/irak/2004.09.15-al-article9UVGR.html.

ICG (2008) 'Iraq's Civil War, the Crisis and the Surge', Middle East Report No. 72, February.

Jabar, F. (2003) 'Sheikhs and Ideologues: Deconstruction and Reconstruction of Tribes under Patrimonial Totalitarianism in Iraq, 1968–1998', in Falah Jabar and Hosham Dawood (eds), *Tribes and Power: Nationalism and Ethnicity in the Middle East*. London: Saqi Books.

Kilcullen, D. (2007) 'Anatomy of a Tribal Revolt', *Small Wars Journal*, August. Available at: http://small-warsjournal.com/blog/2007/08/print/anatomy-of-a-tribal-revolt.

Knickmeyer, E. (2005) 'Zarqawi Said to Be Behind Iraq Raid', *Washington Post*, 5 April, p. A1.

O'Hanlon, M. and Campbell, K. (2008) *Hard Power: The New Politics of National Security*. New York: Basic Books.

OSC Report (2006) GMP20061128281001, *Jihadist Websites*, Al-Fatihin Army Hostile to US, Iran, Shiite Militias, Open Source Center, 28 November; GMF20060808281005, Open Source Center, 8 August.

Pope, H. and Spindle, B. (2002) 'Tribes May Play Crucial Role In Political Future of Iraq', *Wall Street Journal*, 16 December. Available at: http://ebird.dtic.mil/Dec2002/e20021216126659.html.

Sepp, K. (2007) 'From "Shock and Awe" to "Hearts and Minds": The Fall and Rise of US Counterinsurgency Capability in Iraq', *Third World Quarterly*, 28 (2): 217–30.

Shihab, S. (2003) 'Resurgence of Salafist Current in Sunni Crucible Reflects Radicalization Against Americans', *Le Monde*, 16 November in FBIS Report, EUP20031118000024, Open Source Center, 16 November.

Simon, S. (2008) 'The Price of the Surge', *Foreign Affairs*, May–June.

Tripp, C. (2000) *A History of Iraq*. Cambridge: Cambridge University Press.

14

HEZBOLLAH AND HAMAS

Islamic insurgents with nationalist causes

Judith Palmer Harik and Margret Johannsen

The cases of Hezbollah and Hamas illustrate a regional trend that features the use of asymmetric warfare by sub-state actors against a conventional army of overwhelming military power. Through rapidly expanding armouries and fighting capacities these Arab actors have recently succeeded in nudging the strategic balance in the Arab–Israeli conflict arena off balance. As a result, mounting tensions between Israel and its neighbours have drawn increased attention from scholars and practitioners who seek formulae for containing or eliminating these insurgencies.

What is known about Hezbollah and Hamas? What are the accepted positions and where are the lacunae in the state of our knowledge about these organizations? After reviewing information about which there is little debate on the origins, structures, ideologies and practices of each organization, we then present the major points of disagreement concerning their intent and the questions that remain unanswered about the two organizations. Finally we outline what we see to be the challenges that lie ahead for Hezbollah and Hamas.

As Hezbollah preceded the development of Hamas and in several ways has served as the model to emulate for the Palestinian group, we begin with the Lebanese organization.

Hezbollah in review

An adequate understanding of Hezbollah's emergence and growth must take as a point of departure Lebanon's experience of the Arab–Israeli conflict, the weakness of the state and the plight of Lebanon's Shiite community from which the sub-state actor emerged.

Transnational intervention in a weak state

Squeezed between warring neighbours Syria and Israel, Lebanon's internal confessional problems left it open to intervention by both actors in the 1960s. The civil war (1975–90) well demonstrates how each fished in Lebanon's troubled waters by training and arming clashing Lebanese militias as surrogate forces. To this day authentic Lebanese sovereignty has not been regained (El-Khazen 2001; Harik 2010).

While Beirut was sinking into chaos Syria and other Arab states were backing leftist-Muslim militias and PLO forces operating against Israel from within Lebanon's southern border. When the PLO was evacuated as a result of the 1982 Israeli invasion of Lebanon the individual yet concurring strategic calculations of Syrian President Hafez al-Assad and ally Ayatollah Ruhollah Khomeini of Iran resulted in a replacement force for the Palestinian fighters. That replacement force was introduced later as Hezbollah (Byman 2005; Hinnebusch and Ehteshami 1997: 207–22).

In control of the Bekaa Valley where Hezbollah was materializing, Syria provided logistics and security for the fledgling movement and Iran handled organizational, training and financial details as well as supplying weapons for the insurgency. These arrangements remain unaltered despite efforts by Lebanese, regional and international actors to interrupt them.

Shiite deprivation and alienation

Concentrated in the South, the Bekaa and Beirut's southern suburb, the Shiites rank lowest on Lebanon's socio-economic scale (UNDP and CDR 1998: ES-2) Members of this deprived group joined leftist parties to express their discontent until communal mobilization occurred in the 1970s (Cobban 1986: 137–59). Led by Imam Musa Sadr, the Movement of the Dispossessed (*al-Harakat al-mahrumin*) eventually spun off a pool of militant young islamists who formed and led Hezbollah. Among them was General Secretary Hassan Nasrallah, a charismatic cleric who over the course of his tenure has won broad admiration for his role in the political setbacks handed Israel by his militants as well as for his personal reliability (Harik 2003: 25–6; 2004: 72–3).

The repeated Israeli attacks that led thousands to seek refuge in South Beirut, a squalid and densely populated area, provided impetus for recruitment into the fighting wing forming in the Bekaa Valley as did Hezbollah's ideological appeal and the salaries and benefits provided by the organization through the good offices of Iran (Kramer 1993: 539–56).

Over the years, with Iran's help, donations from expatriates, regional supporters and self-financing, Hezbollah has cemented its popularity by addressing the substandard living conditions and lack of public facilities in all areas of Shiite concentration (Harik 1994: 81–93). Among the institutions the organization has established are hospitals, clinics, agricultural stations, schools, a micro-credit institution (*al-Qurd al-Hasan* – 'the Benevolent Gift') and more than half dozen charitable associations (Harb forthcoming 2011: 106–36; Harik 2006). Hezbollah's *Jihad al-Binaa* (Reconstruction Campaign) is credited with the construction and highly efficient management of some of these as well as other projects (el-Moubayed 1999: 23–8).

Ideology and organization

Hezbollah's goals and beliefs were first publicly announced in an open letter published in Beirut's *as-Safir* daily newspaper in February 1985. The letter contained a note of reassurance for Lebanese Christians who might fear an Islamic takeover of the state and stated that Hezbollah's enemies were limited to those who furthered US and Israeli aims in Lebanon (Schapiro 1987).

Hezbollah professes the Twelver Shiite ideology and fully espouses Ayotallah Khomeini's vision of Shiite activism as distinct from the passive role played by sect leaders over the centuries (Saad-Ghorayeb 2002: 69–78). It affirms that an individual is to resist injustice by whatever means he or she possesses. According to Hezbollah's Under-Secretary Na'im Qassim 'Resistence is a way of life' (Saad-Ghorayeb 2002: 112; Qassim 2005: 58–69; Kramer 1990a). The Party of God applies the Islamic injunction to protect and serve the *umma* (Community of the Faithful) and to combat the usurpers of Islamic lands as the moral underpinning of its holistic concept of warfare.

Hezbollah is governed by the *majlis ash-Shura* – a consultative council of elected members headed by Secretary General Hassan Nasrallah. Policy decisions are taken by discussion among members until consensus is reached. Hezbollah's military and security branches are directly linked to this council. An Executive Council linked to the organization's administrative and political apparatus oversees foreign, social, educational, financial unionist and parliamentary affairs (Hamzeh 2004: 46, 71–3; Rabil 2008: 5–12). There are reports of an overseas branch governing activities in the United States, Latin America and Africa (Farah 2006; Diaz and Newman 2006).

The three areas of Shiite concentration are administered in top-down fashion and on a street-by-street basis in Beirut's southern suburb where tight security prevails (Harb 2011: 132–34).

From guerrilla organization to Arab army

The 1982 Israeli invasion

Hezbollah's emergence during the Israeli invasion and, according to Israeli and US sources, its implication in a string of terrorist activities during that turbulent period, place it on the US State Department's list of terrorist organizations. However, the 1985 withdrawal of Israeli forces to a so-called 'Security Zone' within Lebanon at the frontier afforded the Party of God a legitimate resistance persona that it capitalized on during its 17-year-long guerrilla campaign to oust the foreign troops and their South Lebanese Army (SLA) allies. The war of attrition drew major Israeli air and land incursions in 1993 and 1996 to drive out Hezbollah but increased Israeli casualties finally forced Israeli withdrawal behind a blue line designated by UN forces in May 2000 (see also Chapter 21 by Sergio Catignani in this volume). In full control of the frontier Hezbollah was now able to increase the range of its rockets and to fortify the area despite the presence of UN peacekeeping troops stationed there.

The 2006 conflict and its political aftermath

The 34-day battle unleashed after Hezbollah's capture and killing of Israeli soldiers on 12 July 2006 resulted in the deaths of 159 Israeli and 1,019 Lebanese and massive displacement on both sides of the frontier (Harel *et al.* 2009). While Lebanon was subjected to intensive Israeli bombardment of infrastructure, dwellings and businesses, Israel's ground offensive was nevertheless thwarted by well-trained Hezbollah cadres and village fighters (Exum 2006: 9–10). During the battle the Israeli state came under a relentless barrage of Katyusha rockets and medium range missiles that for the first time reached as far as Haifa (Makovsky and White 2006, Exum 12–13).

Military analysts noted Hezbollah's new blend of conventional and guerrilla tactics (Biddle 2007: 29–45) and its effective use of weapons (Exum 2006: 3–4; Kulik 2006; Cordesman *et al.* 2007).

In the autumn of 2006 Hezbollah sought to protect its arms by pressuring the anti-Syrian authorities to form a national unity government in which its allies would have a blocking veto. The refusal by these authorities to cooperate led to a paralysis of the government by a massive sit-in spearheaded by Hezbollah that closed down Beirut's commercial sector for close to two years. In 2007 opposition MPs also boycotted parliamentary sessions called to nominate a president whose election might jeopardize the resistance (Harik 2007: 123–5). A compromise candidate was finally endorsed in 2008. In May Hezbollah consolidated its political grasp by scotching a government move to close down its intelligence system and by forcibly disarming opposing militias. These acts together with its possession of increasingly powerful weaponry augmented the survivability of the Hezbollah power structure in Lebanon (Cordesman and Nerguizien 2010).

Outstanding issues

Hezbollah and the Lebanese state: hidden Islamic agenda or pragmatic politics?

Those who suggest Hezbollah has a pragmatic inclination (Hamzeh 1993; Norton 1998, 1999; Harik 2004: 47; Harb and Leenders 2005: 189–91) point to several factors that limit the scope of the movement's future plans for Lebanon. Foremost is the impossibility of any one group's capacity to overturn the well-entrenched, multi-confessional political system without engendering a bloodbath. In part the Lebanese civil war was fought to establish a more equitable representation of the Muslim portion of the population rather than to change the political formula of sectarian power sharing.

Moreover any plans to overturn the prevailing Lebanese political system have also been found to be impractical given Syria's interest in keeping the various communities in Lebanon divided and thus manageable. Pragmatic Hezbollah leaders are therefore thought to be more intent on integrating into the existing political system, enabling them to build power and preserve and expand their resistance agenda; this will enable them to maintain their hegemony in the Shiite community rather than attempt to create an Islamic state.

On the other side of this debate are those who assert that Hezbollah's commitment to an Islamic state for Lebanon is programmatic rather than ideological (Kramer 1990a; Sharara 1996; Badran 2009). Citing organic ties with Iran and the expansion of mosques and seminaries in Lebanon over the years, and underlining leaders' insistence that resistance is Hezbollah's *raison d'être* and that all of Lebanon should join it, Badran makes the case that the latter plans to engulf the Lebanese state rather than to integrate it.

All the way to Jerusalem – ideology or programme?

Hezbollah's larger intent is the subject of considerable debate among analysts and scholars. Those who argue that the organization has fixed goals to destroy Israel refer to the Islamist premises that underpin its actions and Iran's and the discourse of its leaders (Kramer 2006, 1990a; Harel *et al.* 2009: 259–60; Karman 2003: 15–16; Zisser 2002, 11). Others refute this position arguing that the Party of God's limited agenda focuses on the recovery of Lebanese and Syrian occupied territories and on assistance to Hamas' struggle rather than on plans to liberate Jerusalem through its own efforts (Hamzeh 2004: 80, 108–35; Harik 2004: 47–8; Byman 2003; Hajjar 2002: 16; Norton 1999: 3; 1998: 46). Nevertheless, Hezbollah's expanding and more sophisticated weaponry makes a greater role for Hezbollah in the Palestine–Israel conflict arena more plausible than previously thought.

The challenges that lie ahead

Hezbollah faces two major challenges related to its survival as a resistance organization and both concern its capacity to retain the allegiance of domestic and foreign supporters in the face of US and Israeli efforts to erode its support.

Shiite and national solidarity vis-à-vis Israel's strategy of 'cumulative deterrence'

'Cumulative deterrence' attempts to elicit the compliance of a recalcitrant actor by repeated applications of force assuming that resistance will eventually become too costly to continue (Almog 2004–5). This strategy has guided Israel's destruction of Lebanese infrastructure as a means of coercing Beirut to rein in Hezbollah. Yet while it has caused grumbling about Hezbollah's independent resistance agenda among officials the strategy has failed to elicit any effective government action against the Party of God.

This strategy was also applied to the Shiite community in 2006 in a drive to erode its continued support for the Party of God. Many Shiite villages as well as Shiite streets and homes in divided villages were targeted by Israeli aircraft and destroyed at that time. Most notable was the Israeli Air Force's levelling of 200 high-rise residential buildings in the southern suburb.

Hezbollah was able to overcome the negative fallout of this strategy by the anger generated among Shiites and others at the extent of Israeli damage and pride in the Party of God's resistance. The large amounts of cash distributed by Hezbollah to those who had suffered loss or damage to property immediately after the ceasefire also went a long way towards mollifying discontent. Property owners and renters in Beirut have since received new dwellings at Hezbollah's expense as part of its *al-Waad* (The Promise) project. Despite these measures it is nevertheless uncertain how much the 'resistance community' can continue to take from the Israeli air force without abandoning Tel Aviv's real target.

Relationship with regional allies and institutional autonomy

The durability of Hezbollah's relationship with Iran and Syria under changing geopolitical conditions might be problematic for the Party of God in the future. For example a land for peace deal worked out between Israel, Lebanon and Syria could cause the redundancy of Hezbollah's fighting wing. Abandoning Hezbollah might also be a part of a future Iranian deal struck with the United States. The challenge for the organization's resistance agenda is therefore to work towards autonomy while at the same time maintaining positive relations with its allies. This brings up the question of whether what seems to have developed into a partnership with its allies rather than surrogacy will continue in another war with Israel that might feature an escalation of asymmetric warfare.

Hamas: an overview

Hamas' emergence and growth originate from the Israeli–Palestinian conflict, in particular the Palestinian resistance to the Israeli occupation of the West Bank and Gaza Strip since the War of 1967, and the internal rivalry between Hamas and Fatah for leadership in the occupied territories.

The making of a national-religious resistance movement

Hamas[1] was established in response to the outbreak of the first Intifada in December 1987 (Aronson 1990; Legrain 1990; Alimi 2006). It emerged out of the Society of the Muslim Brothers founded in Egypt in 1928 (El-Awaisi 1991). In 1945, the Brotherhood created a Palestinian offspring, which spread quickly until in 1948 its branches were severed by the results of the first Israeli–Arab war. Until the War of 1967, when both territories fell under Israeli occupation, the Palestinian Brotherhood was more or less marginalized, whereas the Palestinian secular nationalists flourished in exile. Under Israeli occupation, the Brotherhood re-emerged in the mid 1970s. They initially focused on institution-building as well as social, educational and welfare activities, turning the Gaza Strip with its large refugee population into its stronghold. By the late 1970s, they had established themselves as a notable civil society actor and competed successfully for representation in professional, student and trade union organizations – more so in the Gaza Strip, less so in the West Bank. In the first half of the 1980s, the Gaza branch under the guidance of its spiritual leader Sheikh Ahmad Yassin established a military arm and began collecting weapons and organizing weapon training. Early in 1988, the Palestinian Muslim Brothers joined the Intifada under the name of Hamas. Through its charitable programmes Hamas could establish a reputation for efficiency and integrity.

Pinned against political compromise

In the course of the uprising, Hamas developed into a formidable political rival to the secular nationalists (Schiff and Ya'ari 1991). In 1991, Hamas formally established as its military organization the Izz ad-Din al-Qassam Brigades. The Brigades were to support the goals of Hamas, which after the signing of the Oslo Accords in 1993 was determined to sabotage any progress towards Israeli–Palestinian agreement and conciliation through negotiations, doubting that they would achieve the Palestinians' legitimate rights (Ghanem 2008: 473f.) and at the same time viewing the vision of compromise as an ideological and political threat (Kurz 2009: 76). Hamas carried out numerous attacks against both Israeli soldiers and civilians. In the mid 1990s, the attacks took the most violent form of suicide bombings (Ahmed 2005). These bombings served various purposes, including retaliation against Israeli assassinations of Hamas leaders, battling for popular support, undermining the legitimacy of the Palestinian Authority, derailing the peace process and increasing Palestinian leverage over Israel (Bloom 2005: 19–44; Gunning 2007a: 213). Ten years later, these so-called martyr operations had practically been replaced by rocket and mortar-grenade fire emanating from the Gaza Strip (Israel Intelligence Heritage & Commemoration Center 2009). These attacks are far less deadly than the suicide bombings, but Israel nevertheless sees them as a strategic threat, especially as the range of the rockets has increased over the years (Johannsen 2009a: 181). The value of the rockets was captured by Mahmoud az-Zahar, co-founder of Hamas and a member of the Hamas leadership in the Gaza Strip, when in 2007 he stated that

> Rockets against Sderot will cause mass migration, greatly disrupt daily lives and government administration and can make a much huger impact on the government. We are using the methods that convince the Israelis that their occupation is costing them too much.
>
> *(Israel Ministry of Foreign Affairs 2007)*

Ideology and religion

Unlike the PLO, Hamas rejects eventual partition of the land as a basis for resolving the conflict with Israel. Its charter of 1988 gives expression to this refusal in religious terms stating that 'the land of Palestine is an Islamic Waqf consecrated for future Moslem generations until Judgement Day. It, or any part of it, should not be squandered: it, or any part of it, should not be given up'.[2] According to the document, Hamas' goal is to liberate all of Palestine, extending from the River Jordan to the Mediterranean Sea, from Zionist occupation. However, while clothing this goal in religious term, Hamas has always '"Palestinianized" the universal claim of Islam and given the movement a national-religious-political profile' (Klein 1997: 112f.), while limiting its military operations to Israel, the West Bank and the Gaza Strip.

Structure and decision-making

Hamas is composed of three wings which engage in social welfare, political leadership and military activities. In principle, the political leadership oversees all activities of the movement. Strategic control of the military wing's behaviour by the political leadership is of high significance, as the focal points of the two can differ considerably. Gunning identifies the military wing's concerns as focusing on operational efficiency and secrecy, whereas the political wing is predominantly aiming at popularity, legitimacy and visibility (Gunning 2004: 236). Hamas' political body consists of the political bureau with its office residing in Damascus, a national council and regional councils, which are chaired by local leaders in the West Bank and the Gaza Strip. The national council and the political bureau include members of both Hamas' internal and external leadership. A consultative council considered to be the movement's overarching political and decision-making body supervises Hamas' activities through a number of committees. It includes representatives from the Gaza Strip and the West Bank, from abroad and from Israeli prisons.

In order to avoid detection, the Qassam Brigades are highly decentralized, providing individual cells with a high level of autonomy. This has enabled them to develop individual links with the external leadership and occasionally bypass both the Brigades' own hierarchy and the internal leadership in the occupied territories (Gunning 2007b: 134). The external leadership exercises control over much of the military wing's funding. It is generally considered to be more hawkish than the internal leadership as the latter has to cope with the situation on the ground and hence tends to be more pragmatic (International Crisis Group 2007: 24).

External support

Until the freeze on the transfer of money to Hamas through the global banking system in 2006, Hamas could rely on the generosity of the Muslim Brotherhood organizations in more than 80 countries. It received funding from Palestinians living abroad as well as private donors in the wealthy Arab oil states such as Saudi Arabia, Bahrain and Kuwait, as well as those in the West (Zuhur 2008: 56f.). The 1979 Iranian revolution was a source of inspiration to Hamas. Still, Sunni Hamas' suspicion of Iranian ambitions to export a Shiite revolution precluded any close relationship until the drying up of its sources of capital in 2006 caused Hamas to turn to Iran for alternative funding (Schanzer 2008: 139). Iran supports the Gaza government financially and facilitates equipping Hamas with weapons that are employed against Israeli targets, including rockets with a longer range than the home-made Qassams (Ben-David 2009: 7).

However, Hamas has not become an Iranian surrogate, with Syria's political and logistical support remaining crucial to balancing Iran's influence. This support ranges from harbouring Hamas' political bureau to approving weapons delivery to the Gaza Strip to tolerating Hezbollah's providing military training to Hamas fighters (Congressional Research Service 2006). The security cooperation between Iran, Syria, Hamas and Hezbollah serves the perceived interests of all four members of the so-called 'axis of resistance', with Iran and Syria viewing Hamas as instrumental in antagonizing Israel, and Hezbollah occasionally strengthened its resistance credentials by emphasizing its solidarity with the embattled sister movement (International Crisis Group 2010: 8).

From rebel movement to ruling party

Within less than two decades, Hamas has developed from a rebel movement to the ruling party of an embattled would-be state. Following the establishment of the Palestinian Authority (PA) in 1994, Hamas boycotted the ensuing presidential and parliamentary elections, viewing them as part of 'Oslo' (Declaration of Principles 1993) and hence illegitimate. Acting as extra-parliamentary opposition, it was not held responsible for the failure of the peace process and was spared the charges of corruption and mismanagement that the Fatah-dominated PA had to face. It nevertheless participated in the political structures of the semi-autonomous territories through its elected representatives in student bodies, trade unions and professional associations. Four years into the second Intifada, Hamas started out to attain a new role in Palestinian politics by translating the popularity accrued from armed struggle and welfare work into political power. In the municipal elections of 2004/2005 Hamas fared well even in a number of alleged Fatah strongholds (Litvak 2005). In the national elections of 2006, the Hamas list 'Change and Reform' successfully campaigned on an agenda with emphasis on good governance and managed to win a comfortable majority of seats in the Palestinian Legislative Council (PLC).

Governing a quasi-state under quarantine

In its new role as governing party, Hamas fared less well. Driven into bankruptcy through a financial boycott orchestrated by Israel and the Western donor states (Johannsen 2010: 181) and fearing to be ousted from power by Fatah-led militias equipped by the United States, Hamas seized control of the security apparatus in Gaza and has since June 2007 ruled as the Gaza Strip's de facto government, albeit under an Israeli imposed blockade. Hamas survived the devastations of the 22-day war of December 2008/January 2009, has since consolidated its control over Gaza's territory, political institutions and society, and has moved towards a defensive, rather than offensive, posture vis-à-vis Israel (ICG 2010: 14). The political opposition has been more or less silenced and governance has become increasingly authoritarian. By taxing the tunnel trade, Hamas has additional sources of revenue, which, however, due to the blockade it cannot use to rebuild the economy and infrastructure. Finally, power consolidation in the tiny territory with a population of 1.5 million has been achieved at the expense of Hamas' profile as a resistance movement and has practically nullified the ambitious reform goals of its election campaign.

Outstanding issues

As long as Hamas was primarily perceived as a resistance movement, the better part of the discussion concerned its long-term goals in the Israeli–Palestinian conflict. Since Hamas has assumed control of the Gaza Strip, however, its domestic agenda has also sparked some debate.

Erasing Israel from the map of the Middle East?

Controversy over the goals of Hamas' charter takes a prominent place in the academic and political debate on Hamas. In light of Hamas' principled refusal to recognize Israel (Goerzig 2010: 16), some see Hamas' charter as evidence that the destruction of Israel has remained a long-term goal of the movement to this very day (Committee for Accuracy in Middle East Reporting in America 2009). Others dismiss the text as more or less obsolete, merely reflecting Hamas' involvement in the beginnings of the first Intifada (Hroub 2006). In the aftermath of the terror attacks of 9/11, Hamas commissioned a draft for a new charter in order to counter efforts to identify all Islamic movements and organizations with al-Qaeda. After Hamas' electoral victory in 2006, however, the project was put on hold so as not to nourish speculation that Hamas was bowing to outside pressure (Tamimi 2007: 147–50).

Long-term ceasefire: ploy or strategic decision?

According to Hamas, the way to achieve a Palestinian state in the West Bank, including East Jerusalem and the Gaza Strip, is by a long-term truce (*hudna*), offered time and again by Hamas leaders (Amayreh 2004; The Palestinian Information Center 2008; Haaretz 2008). In the light of Hamas' ambiguous behaviour on the ground, phases of frequent attacks alternating with phases of restraint, the offer can be read as a mere tactical move. In fact, as long as Hamas has not departed from its vision of a liberated Islamic state in all of Palestine and refuses to commit to a final status settlement, the offer actually reinforces Israel's fears that the time of a truce will be used for military entrenchment and build-up not only in the Gaza Strip but also in the West Bank (Al-Hashimi 2009: 59). Others argue that the past ceasefires declared by Hamas served a number of purposes, namely to trigger a political process, to test Israeli intentions, to demonstrate political leadership as well as standing on equal ground with internal political rivals. As such they testify to the movement's ability to respond to changes in political opportunity structures (McAdam 1996: 27) and develop a greater interest in shaping Palestinian society than in liberating all of Palestine (Gunning 2007a: 235).

Resistance and governance: complement or contradiction?

The participation of Hamas in local and national elections has met with a mixed response. On the one hand, it was seen as evidence that the organization was prepared to face up to the electorate, accept the challenge of democratic accountability and integrate into the political system (Baumgarten 2006). This process, it was argued, would exert a moderating influence on the organization, encouraging it to sharpen its profile as a conservative party with a societal agenda based on a religious outlook which in turn implied encouraging electoral participation (Gunning 2007a: 170f.). Others warned that democratic elections were fundamentally incompatible with the participation of an organization in arms. They doubted that integrating into the political system provided enough of an incentive for Hamas to discard its violent traits rooted in the armed resistance. In this view, admitting Hamas to the elections under these circumstances merely encouraged the movement to emulate the Lebanese Hezbollah and tap both sources of power: one emanating from the ballot box, the other one from the gun barrel.

Islamizing the Gaza Strip: long-term goal or default option?

In the election campaign of 2006, Hamas ran on a platform of good government, with only a few references to Islam (Hroub 2006), two of them of a very general character, the other two policy oriented but none in any way indicative that Hamas, if it were to govern, intended to forcefully Islamize the Palestinian society and institutions. After having assumed power in the Gaza Strip in June 2007, however, Hamas set out to Islamize society systematically, by introducing codes of conduct in the public sphere, controlling the courts, the media and the education system, and sustaining this process by introducing Islamic legislation (White 2009; McCarthy 2009).

It could be argued that by underplaying its religious planks (Malley 2006), Hamas had intentionally misled those of its voters who merely wanted to show their dissatisfaction with the Palestinian Authority. One could also make the case that for want of material resources to take care of the needs of the residents, Hamas saw streamlining society as a means of securing its power. Finally, Hamas could try to appease its own radicalized base and jihadi Islamist rivals, who had initially denounced Hamas for running in the parliamentary elections and later criticized it for not implementing the *sharia* on the ground (Amayreh 2007: 7; International Crisis Group 2008: 26; Cohen and Levitt 2010: 15).

The challenges that lie ahead

Hamas faces two major challenges related to its dual character as a resistance movement and a de facto government. Both of them concern its capacity to retain the allegiance of domestic and foreign supporters in the face of efforts by rivals and enemies to undermine its popularity and eventually marginalize it as a factor in Palestinian politics.

Resistance and good governance

While it may be tempting for Hamas to pose as a government in Gaza, its enduring capability to escape accountability for the well-being of the population under its rule is questionable. Moreover, its entrenchment in Gaza collides with its professed commitment to Palestinian unity, which a majority of the population wants to be restored (Schanzer 2008: 191f.; Palestinian Center for Policy and Survey Research 2010). If real progress in the renewed negotiations between the PA and Israel occurs, Hamas' uncompromising stance will be more difficult to uphold. Short of overcoming the split, the challenge for the organization's agenda is therefore to demonstrate to its rival Fatah that it can undermine progress towards accommodation with Israel and at the same time signal to Israel that it is able and willing to contain violence emanating from the Gaza Strip if it sees it in its interest to do so (Johannsen 2009b: 229f.).

Despite efforts by Hamas to calibrate its resistance operations so as to reconcile both aims, it is uncertain how much its popular support base is willing to sacrifice for not abandoning its rulers. Renewed efforts to crack down on Hamas' network of social and charitable organizations (Zuhur 2008: 52) or build up competing charities (Levitt 2006) could aggravate this problem for Hamas. Faced with the risk of losing ground in Gaza, Hamas may seek to facilitate a normalization of life by going along with arrangements for opening and regulating the border crossings (Agreement on Movement and Access 2005). As this would include prevention of weapons smuggling, the organization would have to put up with a weakening of its military capabilities. The challenge Hamas faces under these circumstances is to take along the military wing in order to prevent fragmentation of the movement. At the same time, past excuses for bad governance can no longer be credibly upheld. Here the challenge for Hamas lies in proving its ability to enforce law and order with the welfare of the residents in mind. If it fails it may decide to return to its roots and escalate the struggle for the liberation of all of Palestine.

Easing of regional tensions

Syria's and Iran's support for Hamas is connected to the latter's capability to involve Israel in military conflict without risking direct confrontation with the Jewish state. An easing of regional tensions will therefore decrease Hamas' value for its state sponsors. Advances towards a settlement of the Israeli–Syrian conflict over the Golan might dry up Syria's support for Hamas' military posture. In the same vein, a solution to the crisis related to Iran's nuclear programme could weaken Iran's motivation to support Hamas financially. Without material and logistical support from its two external sponsors, Hamas will find it increasingly difficult to continue its policy of pinpricks vis-à-vis Israel and at the same time legitimize its rule in the Gaza Strip vis-à-vis its residents. The challenge for Hamas' agenda as de facto government is therefore to seek cooperation with its rival Fatah in stabilizing the volatile situation in the Gaza area. However, such a turnaround could very well put the organization's cohesion to a test that it may not pass.

Conclusions

In spite of several similarities, the Lebanese and Palestinian insurgencies differ considerably in a number of aspects, most notably in their origins, military strength and political clout.

Hezbollah, an insurgency by design, has monopolized violence in Lebanon for more than 30 years and is now in a position to call the political and security shots in that country. It appears to retain the solidarity of a majority of Shiites based in no small part on the uninterrupted delivery of public and social services and on strong allegiance to its leadership.

Moreover reports of advanced weaponry and more effective Katyusha rockets flowing to Hezbollah indicate continued firm support from its transnational allies. In fact, while Shiite/Sunni tensions remain high in the region, Israel poses a threat to the implementation of the Islamic Republic's nuclear programme; as long as issues of occupied Arab land remain unresolved there is little question of serious disruptions in the Iranian–Syrian–Hezbollah alliance. The Party of God seems to have covered all bases to insure the durability and dynamism of its brand of asymmetrical warfare.

Compared to Hezbollah, *Hamas*' ability to safeguard its status is doubtful. Yet since its inception at the early stages of the first Intifada more than 20 years ago, it has developed into a serious stakeholder in Palestinian society and politics. Part of the territory slashed for future Palestinian sovereignty has fallen under its control and its military capabilities enable it to manipulate the PA's dealings with the occupying power. However, the durability of its reign in the Gaza Strip is by no means certain while in the West Bank its political representatives have been sidelined and its activists persecuted.

As long as the US–Iranian tension persists and the conflict over territory involving Israel, Syria and Lebanon remains unresolved, Hamas can expect continued support from its allies. However, Hamas' fortunes stand and fall with the future of the Israeli–Palestinian conflict. Resolving this seemingly intractable conflict and securing the consent of the Palestinians at large to the agreed solution would call into question Hamas' rejectionist *raison d'être*. In what way Hamas would adapt to the new reality is a function of the balance of power between military commanders, absolutists and pragmatists.

Notes

1 Hamas is the acronym of al-Harakat al-Muqawwama al-Islamiyya, meaning Islamic Resistance Movement.
2 The Covenant of the Islamic Resistance Movement, Yale Law School, The Avalon Project, http://avalon.law.yale.edu/20th_century/hamas.asp.

Recommended readings

Hamas

Goerzig, Carolin (2010) *Mediating Identity Conflicts. Potential and Challenges of Engaging with Hamas*, Berghof Occasional Paper No. 30, Berlin.
Gunning, Jeroen (2007) *Hamas in Politics. Democracy, Religion, Violence*. London: Hurst Publishers.
International Crisis Group (2009) *Gaza's Unfinished Business*, Middle East Report N°85, 23 April, Gaza City/Ramallah/Jerusalem/Washington/Brussels.
McGeough, Paul (2009) *Kill Khalid. The Failed Mossad Assassination of Khalid Mishal and the Rise of Hamas*. New York: The New Press.
Tamimi, Azzam (2007) *Hamas. A History from Within*. Northhampton, MA: Olive Branch Press.

Hezbollah

Biddle, Stephen and Friedman, Jeffrey (2006) *The 2006 Lebanon Campaign and the Future of Warfare*. Carlisle, PA: Strategic Studies Institute, US Army War College.

Byman, Daniel (2005) *Deadly Connections: State Sponsors of Terrorism*. London: Cambridge University Press.

El-Khazen, Farid (2001) 'Lebanon – Independent No More', *Middle East Quarterly*, 8 (1): 43–50.

Harik, Judith Palmer (2004) *Hezbollah: The Changing Face of Terrorism*. London: I.B. Tauris.

Harik, Judith Palmer (2010) 'Force of Arms and Hezbollah's Staying Power', in: Abdulaziz Sager and Klejda Mulaj (eds), *Violent Non-State Actors in World Politics*. New York and London: Columbia University Press and Hurst, pp. 137–55.

Qassim, Na'im Hizbullah (2005) *The Story from Within*. London: Saqi Books.

Rabil, Robert (2008) 'Hezbollah: Lebanon's Power Broker', *Journal of International Security Affairs*, 15 (autumn): 5–12.

Saad-Ghorayeb, Amal (2002) *Hezbollah: Politics and Religion*. London: Pluto.

References

Hamas

Al-Hashimi, K. (2009) 'Understanding Hamas's Radicalisation', in Michael Emerson, Kristina Kausch and Emerson Youngs (eds), *Islamist Radicalisation. The Challenge for Euro-Mediterranean Relations*. Brussels and Madrid: Centre for European Policy Studies, pp. 52–68.

Alimi, E. (2006) *Israeli Politics and the First Palestinian Intifada*. London: Routledge.

Amayreh, K. (2004) 'Running out of Time', *Al Ahram Weekly*, 675, 29 January–4 February.

Amayreh, K. (2007) *Hamas and al-Qaida. The Prospects for Radicalization in the Occupied Palestinian Territories*. Beirut, London and Washington, DC: Conflicts Forum, October.

Aronson, G. (1990) *Israel, Palestinians, and the Intifada: Creating Facts on the West Bank*. London: Kegan Paul International.

Baumgarten, H. (2006) *Hamas. Der politische Islam in Palästina*. Kreuzlingen/München: Diederichs.

Ben-David, A. (2009) 'Iran is Rearming Hamas in Gaza', *Jane's Defence Weekly*, 28 (January).

Bloom, M. (2005) *Dying to Kill. The Global Phenomenon of Suicide Terror*. New York: Columbia University Press.

Cobban, Helena. (1986) 'The Growth of Shi'i Protest in Lebanon and its Implications for the Future' in Nikki R. Keddi and Juan R. Cole (eds) *Shi'sm and Social Protest*. New Haven, Conneticut: Yale University Press, pp. 137–59.

Cohen, Y. and Levitt, M. with Wasser, B. (2010) *Deterred But Determined. Salafi-Jihadi Groups in the Palestinian Arena*. Washington, DC: The Washington Institute for Near East Policy, Policy Focus #99, January. Available at: www.washingtoninstitute.org/pubPDFs/PolicyFocus 99.pdf.

Committee for Accuracy in Middle East Reporting in America (2009) *Backgrounder: The Facts about Hamas*, 3 February. Available at: www.camera.org/index.asp?x_context=7&x_issue=20&x_article=1618.

Congressional Research Service (CRS) (2006) *Lebanon: The Israel-Hamas-Hezbollah Conflict*, CRS Report for Congress, 15 September. Available at: www.fas.org/sgp/crs/mideast/RL33566.pdf.

Declaration of Principles (1993) 'The Oslo Declaration of Principles'. Available at: www.mideastweb.org/meoslodop.htm.

El-Awaisi, A. (1991) 'The Conceptual Approach of the Egyptian Muslim Brothers Towards the Palestine Question', *Journal of Islamic Studies*, 2 (2): 225–44.

Ghanem, A. (2008) 'Palestinian Politics after Arafat. The Predicament of the Palestinian "National Movement"', *Journal of Developing Societies*, 24 (4): 465–87.

Goerzig, C. (2010) *Mediating Identity Conflicts: Potential and Challenges of Engaging with Hamas*, Berghof Occasional Paper No. 30. Berlin: Berghof Conflict Research.

Gunning, J. (2004) 'Peace with Hamas? The Transforming Potential of Political Participation', *International Affairs*, 80 (2): 233–55.

Gunning, J. (2007a) *Hamas in Politics. Democracy, Religion, Violence*. London: Hurst Publishers.

Gunning, J. (2007b) 'Hamas: Socialization and the Logic of Compromise', in Marianne Heiberg, Brendan O'Leary and John Tirman (eds), *Terror, Insurgency, and the State*. Philadelphia: University of Pennsylvania Press, pp. 123–54.

Haaretz (2008) 'Meshal Offers 10-year Truce for Palestinian State on '67 Borders', *Haaretz*, 21 April. Available at: www.haaretz.com/hasen/spages/976662.html.

Hroub, K. (2006) 'A "New Hamas" through its New Documents', *Journal of Palestine Studies*, 35 (4). Available at: www.palestine-studies.org/journals.aspx?id=7087&jid=1&href=fulltext.

International Crisis Group (2007) *After Mecca: Engaging Hamas*, Crisis Group Middle East Report No. 62, 28 February.

International Crisis Group (2008) *Ruling Palestine I: Gaza Under Hamas*, Crisis Group Middle East Report No. 73, 19 March.

International Crisis Group (2010) *Drums of War: Israel and the 'Axis of Resistance'*, Middle East Report No. 97, 2 August.

Israel Intelligence Heritage & Commemoration Center (2009) *Summary of Rocket Fire and Mortar Shelling in 2008*. Available at: www.terrorism-info.org.il/malam_multimedia/English/eng_n/pdf/ipc_e007.pdf.

Israel Ministry of Foreign Affairs (2007) www.mfa.gov.il/MFA/Terrorism-+Obstacle+to+Peace/Hamas+war+against+Israel/Missile+fire+from+Gaza+on+Israeli+civilian+targets+Aug+2007.htm#hamasstatements.

Johannsen, Margret (2009a) 'From Resistance to State-Building: Dealing with the Ambiguities of the Hamas Experiment in Gaza', *S+F. Sicherheit und Frieden/Security and Peace*, 27 (3): 180–5.

Johannsen, Margret (2009b) 'Der Gaza-Krieg 2008/2009 – Was lehrt uns die Wiederkehr des ewig Gleichen?', in Österreichisches Studienzentrum für Frieden und Konfliktlösung (ed.), *Söldner, Schurken, Seepiraten. Von der Privatisierung der Sicherheit und dem Chaos der 'neuen' Kriege*. Wien/Münster: Lit, pp. 221–35.

Johannsen, Margret (2010) 'External Security Governance and Intractable Conflict: Constraints of the EU's Support to Police Reform in the Palestinian Territories', in Hans-Georg Ehrhart and Martin Kahl (eds) *Security Governance in und für Europa – Konzepte, Akteure, Missionen*. Baden-Baden: Nomos, pp. 169–90.

Klein, M. (1997) 'Competing Brothers. The Web of Hamas-PLO Relations', in Bruce Maddy-Weitzman and Efraim Inbar (eds), *Religious Radicalism in the Middle East*. London: Frank Cass, pp. 111–32.

Kurz, Anat N. (2009) *The Palestinian Uprisings: War with Israel, War at Home*, Institute for National Security Studies, Memorandum No. 98, April. Available at: www.inss.org.il/upload/%28FILE%291239086658.pdf.

Legrain, J. (1990) 'The Islamic Movement and the Intifada', in Jamal R. Nassar and Roger Heacock (eds), *Intifada. Palestine at the Crossroads*. New York: Praeger Publishers, pp. 175–90.

Levitt, M. (2006) *Hamas. Politics, Charity, and Terrorism in the Service of Jihad*. New Haven/London: Yale University Press.

McAdam, D. (1996) 'Conceptual Origins, Current Problems, Future Directions', in D. McAdam, J.D. McCarthy and M.Y. Zald (eds), *Comparative Perspectives on Social Movements. Political Opportunities, Mobilizing Structures, and Cultural Framings*. Cambridge: Cambridge University Press, pp. 23–40.

McCarthy, R. (2009) 'Hamas Patrols Beaches in Gaza to Enforce Conservative Dress Code', *Guardian* (Internet Edition), 18 October. Available at: www.guardian.co.uk/world/2009/oct/18/hamas-gaza-islamist-dress-code.

Malley, R. (2006) 'Hamas: The Perils of Power', in *The New York Review of Books*, 9 March. Available at: www.crisisgroup.org/en/regions/middle-east-north-africa/israel-palestine/hamas-the-perils-of-power.aspx.

Palestinian Center for Policy and Survey Research (2010) *PSR Poll No. (36), 10–13 June*. Available at: www.pcpsr.org/survey/polls/2010/p36epressrelease.html.

The Palestinian Information Center (2008) 'Haniyeh to Reiterate that the Truce must be Mutual and Comprehensive', 23 April. Available at: www.palestine-info.info/ar/default.aspx?xyz=U6Qq7k%2bcOd87MDI46m9rUxJEpMO%2bi1s7ywuWtgFXMRCLwX/tIXaRy/aQnqZ7bZDKM9kRMfzcDUrG44hI186aQE9OZCmomn%2bYtCYslbloD6ggsMGykZ2llZte8dUmv657nXvC3hc1fyc=.

Schanzer, J. (2008) *Hamas Vs. Fatah. The Struggle for Palestine*. New York: Palgrave Macmillan.

Schiff, Z. and Ya'ari, E. (1991) *Intifada. The Palestinian Uprising Israel's Third Front*. New York and London: Simon & Schuster.

Tamimi, A. (2007) *Hamas. A History from Within*. Northhampton, MA: Olive Branch Press.

White, B. (2009) 'Hamas Turns its Attention to Virtue', *Guardian* (Internet Edition), 10 August. Available at: www.guardian.co.uk/commentisfree/2009/aug/10/hamas-gaza-islam.

Zuhur, S. (2008) *Hamas and Israel: Conflicting Strategies of Group-Based Politics*, Strategic Studies Institute. United States Army War College, December. Available at: www.strategicstudiesinstitute.army.mil/pubs/download.cfm?q=894.

Hezbollah

Almog, Doran (2004–5) '"Cumulative Deterrence": The War on Terrorism', *Parameters*, 34 (4): 4–19.

Badran, Tony (2009) 'Hezbollah's Agenda in Lebanon', *Current Trends in Islamic Ideology*, 8, 16 May.

Biddle, Stephen (2007) 'Strategy in War', *PS: Political Science and Politics*, 40 (3): 461–6.

Biddle, Stephen and Friedman, Jeffrey (2008) *The 2006 Lebanon Campaign and the Future of Warfare*. Carlisle, PA: Strategic Studies Institute, US Army War College.

Byman, Daniel (2003) 'Should Hezbollah be Next?', *Foreign Affairs*, 82 (6): 54–66.

Byman, Daniel (2005) *Deadly Connections: State Sponsors of Terrorism*. London: Cambridge University Press.

Cordesman, Anthony H. and Nerguizien, Aram (2010) *The Arab-Israeli Military Balance in 2010: Conventional Realities and Asymmetric Challenges*. Washington, DC: Center for Strategic and International Studies.

Cordesman, Anthony H., Sullivan, George and Sullivan, William D. (2007) *Lessons of the 2006 Israel-Hezbollah War*. Washington, DC: Center for Strategic and International Studies.

El-Khazen, Farid (2001) 'Lebanon – Independent No More', *Middle East Quarterly*, 8 (1): 43–50.

El-Moubayed, Lamia (1999) *Strengthening Institutional Capacity for Rural Community Development: Two Case Studies from Lebanon*. Beirut: Economic and Social Commission for Southwest Asia.

Exum, Andrew MacDonald (2006) 'Hezbollah at War: A Military Assessment', Policy Focus 63, Washington, DC: The Washington Institute for Near East Affairs.

Farah, Douglas (2006) 'Hezbollah's External Support Network in West Africa and Latin America', International Assessment and Strategic Center, 4 August.

Hajjar, Sami G. (2002) *Hizballah: Terrorism, National Liberation, or Menace?* Carlisle, PA: US Army War College.

Hamzeh, A. Nizar (1993) 'Lebanon's Hizbullah: From Islamic Revolution to Parliamentary Accomodation', *Third World Quarterly*, 14 (2): 321–37.

Hamzeh, A. Nizar (2004) *In the Path of Hizbullah*. Syracuse: Syracuse University Press.

Harb, Mona (forthcoming 2011) *Le Hezbollah a Beyrouth: de la Banlieu a la Ville*. Paris: Karthal-IFPO.

Harb, Mona and Leenders, K. (2005) 'Know Thy Enemy: Hezbullah, "Terrorism" and the Politics of Perception', *Third World Quarterly*, 25 (1): 175–97.

Harel, Amos, Issacharoff, Avi, Cummings, Ora and Tlamin, Moshe (2009) *34 Days: Israel, Hezbollah and the War in Lebanon*. New York: Palgrave Macmillan.

Harik, Judith Palmer (2004) *Hezbollah: The Changing Face of Terrorism*. London: I.B. Tauris.

Harik, Judith Palmer (2006) 'Iran and Hezbollah's Social Services', in Houchang Chehabi (ed.), *Lebanon and Iran: The Long Relationship*. Oxford: Oxford Centre for Lebanese Studies, pp. 61–83.

Harik, Judith Palmer (2007) 'Hezbollah and Today's Battle for Beirut', *Fletcher Forum of World Affairs*, 31 (2): 11–132.

Harik, Judith Palmer (2010) 'Force of Arms and Hezbollah's Staying Power', in Abdulaziz Sager and Klejda Mulaj (eds), *Violent Non-State Actors in World Politics*. New York and London: Columbia University Press and Hurst, pp. 137–55.

Hinnebusch, Raymond and Ehteshami, Anoush (1997) *Syria and Iran: Middle Powers in a Penetrated Region*. London: Routledge.

Karman, Ely (2003) 'Fight on all Fronts: Hizbollah, the War of Terror and the War in Iraq', Memorandum 45. Washington, DC: The Washington Institute for Near East Policy Research.

Kramer, Martin (1990a) 'Redeeming Jerusalem: The Pan-Islamic Promise of Hezbollah', in D. Manashri (ed.), *The Iranian Revolution and the Muslim World*. Boulder: Westview Press, pp. 105–30.

Kramer, Martin (1990b) 'The Moral Logic of Hizbullah', in Walter Reich (ed.), *Origins of Terrorism: Psychologies, Ideologies, Theologies, States of Mind*. Cambridge: Cambridge University Press, pp. 131–57.

Kramer, Martin (2006) 'The Israeli-Islamist Conflict', Occasional Paper, *Middle East Program*.

Kulik, Amir (2006) 'Hisbullah vs the IDF: The Operational Dimension', *Strategic Assessment* 9, 3 Tel Aviv: Jafee Center for Strategic Studies, November.

Makovsky, David and White, Jeffrey (2006) 'Lessons and Implications of the Israel-Hezbollah War: A Preliminary Assessment', *Policy Focus 60*, The Washington Institute for Near East Affairs (October).

Newman, Barbara and Diaz, Tom (2006) *Lightning out of Lebanon: Hezbollah Terrorists on American Soil*. Novato: Presidio Press.

Norton, Richard Augustus (1998) 'Hizbullah from Radicalism to Pragmatism?', *Middle East Policy*, 5: 147–58.

Norton, Richard Augustus (1999) *Hezbullah of Lebanon: Extremist Ideals vs Mundane Politics*. New York: Council on Foreign Relations.

Qassim, Na'im (2005) *Hizbullah: The Story from Within*. London: Saqi Books.

Rabil, Robert (2008) 'Hezbollah: Lebanon's Power Broker', *Journal of International Security Affairs*, 15 (autumn): 5–12.

Saad-Ghorayeb, Amal (2002) *Hezbollah: Politics and Religion*. London: Pluto.

Schapiro, Simon (1987) 'The Origins of Hezbollagh', *The Jerusalem Quarterly*, 46 (spring).

Sharara, Waddah (1996) *dawlat Hizb'allah lubnan mujtawa'm islamiyya* [*Hezbollah's Lebanese State: An Islamic Society*]. Beirut: Dar al-Nahar.

Zisser, Eyal (2002) 'The Return of Hizbullah', *Middle East Quarterly*, (autumn): 3–11.

15

INSURGENCY IN SOUTHEAST ASIA

Lawrence E. Cline

Southeast Asia has faced some of the most complicated insurgency environments of any region in the world. In several countries, there are multiple insurgencies, at times having little or no common ideological basis. The region also has had some of the longest lasting and seemingly intractable insurgent environments. All these issues are overlaid by broader internal security failures within the countries, complicating adequate responses focused directly on the insurgent movements. The three countries that continue to have the most significant insurgencies – Thailand, Burma and the Philippines – are the focus of this chapter.

Thailand

Throughout much of the 1960s and beyond, Thailand has faced an immensely complicated insurgent situation. By the beginning of the 1980s there were three principal insurgent movements: 'poorly organized' Muslim separatists; remnants of the Malay Communist Party that had conducted the insurgency in Malaya and Malaysia; and the Communist Party of Thailand (CPT) (Randolph and Thompson 1981: 16). Most of the members of the latter two groups were ethnically Chinese, and during that period both maintained relatively large numbers of members (Prizzia 1985: 22). The CPT, however, faced a significant amount of factionalization after Hanoi and Beijing split, with various CPT leaders leaning to one side or the other. After the end of the Cold War, both Communist groups appear to have precipitously faded into insignificance.

Muslim separatists have, however, proven to be more problematic. Splits between the central government in Bangkok and the southern provinces have existed since the incorporation of the Sultanate of Pattani in 1902. The local populace did not respond well to their new status, and unrest quickly developed (Pojar 2005: 8–22). Ethnically and religiously, over 80 per cent of the roughly two million people in the three southern provinces are Malay and Muslim, with most southerners speaking Yawi, a Malay dialect (Pauker 2005/2006: 78). Historically, the majority of the ethnic Malay population continued to identify more with their kinsmen still in Malaya and Malaysia than with the concept of being Thai. Their status as Muslims almost certainly further exacerbated their alienation from the Thai Buddhist majority, but religion likely should be viewed more as a marker for larger ethnic differences than as being the key element of the unrest (Harish 2006: 48–69).

Unrest has been bubbling in southern Thailand for many years, with multiple forms of resistance from banditry – very active for years – to separate educational systems, political movements, and ultimately small-scale insurgency. The Thai governance of the south exacerbated the unrest. The consensus among analysts is that the south became the 'dumping ground for incompetent or corrupt officials' (Randolph and Thompson 1981: 15). At the same time, many demographic, social and economic conditions in the southern provinces lagged significantly behind those of Thailand as a whole.

Lesser or greater levels of unrest in southern Thailand, including occasional uprisings, continued for decades (International Crisis Group, 18 May 2005, pp. 2–6). Major groups have included the National Patani Liberation Front (BNPP), formed in 1959; the National Revolutionary Front (BRN), formed in the early 1960s; and the Patani United Liberation Organization (PULO), formed in 1968. Most of these groups numbered in the low hundreds. The PULO in particular has had strong foreign contacts, with much of its leadership based in Mecca. The group has received considerable financial support from Arab countries, particularly from Syria and Libya, and has had training camps in Syria (International Crisis Group 2005: 8).

As unrest continued, other ephemeral groups emerged, conducting some operations but quickly fading. Even the major three groups began fracturing by the 1980s. As the groups split apart, factions adopted new names, but most of these small groups had limited impact. The PULO likely retained the largest number of fighters, albeit very reduced in numbers. Perhaps the key point, however, is that the hard core insurgents were not eliminated, leaving a cadre for future activities.

After the splits in the insurgent groups, several new or reorganized groups emerged as the principal players in the insurgency. Most of these new groups consisted of both younger and more militant members. Both PULO and a splinter group calling itself New PULO have continued their activities. A splinter group of the BRN, the BRN-Coordinate (BRN-C), launched its own operations. A youth group, the Permuda – with reported links to the BRN-C – has provided many of the insurgents. Another group, the Gerakan Mujahideen Islam Pattani (GMIP) has emerged, with its ideology based much more on Islamic terms. In the last few years, the various militant groups have formed a coalition known as Bersatu (Unity), also known as the United Front for the Independence of Pattani. Just how well this umbrella group has actually coordinated activities is however subject to considerable question.

Although sporadic violence continued for many years, a major upsurge in unrest began in Thailand's southern provinces in 2001. According to Thai Ministry of Interior statistics, insurgent attacks numbered 50 in 2001, 75 in 2002, 119 in 2003 and over 1,000 in 2004 (International Crisis Group, 16). In January 2004, insurgents raided an army depot in Narathiwat, stealing about 300 weapons and killing four soldiers. Simultaneously, arson attacks hit 18 government schools. Shortly after, a wave of operations was conducted against local police stations. Since then, a series of attacks have been conducted against police, Buddhist monks, teachers and government officials. Over 1,500 people have been killed in the region since January 2004. Most attacks have occurred in the three southern provinces, but a few bombings have been conducted outside the region.

Several patterns have marked the insurgency. Attacks generally have been well coordinated and, in many ways, the insurgents have maintained the initiative. Targets have included government offices, police stations and homes of government and police officials. Government-sponsored schools and school teachers have been a particular focus for insurgent attacks. Many of the attacks have come in waves. For instance, in June 2006, about 70 small bombs were detonated over a three-day period in a widely dispersed area; likewise, in early August, about 130 targets were hit in only a few days. Attacks dropped in 2007–8, but began intensifying again in 2009 (International Crisis Group 2009: 2).

According to Thai government analysis of captured insurgent documents, the insurgent groups are pursuing a seven-step strategy. The first step is propaganda and agitation; second is infiltration of mass organizations; third is establishment of a united front, with the intention of having 30,000 supporters, 3,000 armed militants and 300 'commandos'. Succeeding steps are recruitment and organization, indoctrination and training, preparation and 'revolution' (Thailand Interior Ministry, cited in Lumbaca 2005: 26–7). It should be noted that these steps are very similar to virtually all insurgent movements.

One interesting development in the most recent unrest is that the ethnic-religious component of the Thai Muslim unrest may have developed a more religious underpinning. After an insurgent attack in 2004, a manual titled *Berjihad di Pattani* was found on the bodies of several insurgent casualties. This document, using Islamic terminology, calls for the liberation of the south as an independent kingdom from 'colonialists' (Liow 2006: 100–3). Government of the new polity would come from the traditional Malay rulers. The document also directs that 'hypocritical' Muslims should be attacked along with Thai security forces. Significantly, it does not mention global sufferings of the Muslim community (the *umma*) or the creation of a regional caliphate; instead, it focuses solely on local issues, albeit in more intensified religious terms.

This ideological emphasis on religious issues has been reflected in operational patterns in some insurgent operations. The combination of Sufi-style Islam and folk religious beliefs was apparent in the preparations for attacks in April 2004:

> [The leader] claimed to have supernatural powers that would help them fight. He taught ... recruits from his village how to perform *zikir* (recitation of the name of Allah) and special prayers over and over – as many as 70,000 times a day for 40 days – in order to become invisible at will and be impervious to bullets and knives. He gave recruits in Songkhla sacred water to make them invisible. Some members travelled ... to Malaysia, to visit Ayoh, the Kelantanese they referred to as 'the master', to receive special blessings, for which some paid 450 baht.
>
> *(International Crisis Group 2005: 22)*

Probably as a result of the increasing religious content of the insurgency, Buddhists living in the south increasingly have become targets of the insurgents. There have been a number of public beheadings of Buddhists, particularly monks, and at least 34,500 persons, mostly Buddhist, had fled the area by mid 2005 (Montlake, 2005, online). Overall, however, it appears that in fact more Muslims have been killed by the insurgents for 'collaboration' than have Buddhists.

The actual number of insurgents remains somewhat uncertain. One assessment suggested that there are an estimated 1,000 insurgents, who control some 247 villages (Abuza, 2007, online). A more official estimate from a Thai police official suggests that the numbers are closer to 3,000 insurgents active in some 500 towns (Shinworakomoi, 2006, online). One feature of the most recent incarnation of the insurgency has been the significant role that the *ponohs* (Islamic schools) have played in the movement; many of these schools have been centres for recruitment and leadership of the various insurgent groups.

At least one senior Thai officer has argued that support for the insurgency follows a typical pattern: 10 per cent of the local population supports the use of violence to achieve the separatist goal; 10 per cent oppose the use of violence; and 80 per cent are ready 'to support the side that is able to protect their lives and property, so they can live and work peacefully' (Not-for-attribution briefing by a senior Thai Special Forces officer, 2005). General Kitti Rattanachaya, a government security adviser expressed similar realistic sentiments: 'People will always be [siding] with those who have power. If we are stronger, they will be with us. If [the insurgents] are stronger, people will be with them' (Thammasathien, BBC, 8 January 2004).

Although the high-water mark for insurgent operations seems to have been in the mid 2000s, with operations waning since then, the insurgency appears far from over. The various insurgent groups continue to be rather disorganized and unlikely to threaten the existence of the larger Thai state, but at the same time the Thai security forces appear unable to completely end the insurgency. Greater political, social and economic efforts in the south would help remove at least some of the underlying local grievances, and the Thai military appears well aware of this crucial component. Given the larger ongoing political problems within Thailand, it remains unlikely that the Thai government will be capable of focusing enough attention to the south to stop the insurgency environment from continuing to exist.

Philippines

The Philippines has faced two very different strands of insurgent movements. The first, and seemingly viewed by the Philippines government for many years as being by far the most significant, has been the New People's Army (NPA). The NPA, the armed wing of the Communist Party of the Philippines, began operations in 1969. The NPA, together with some 13 smaller armed Communist groups, is part of the New Democratic Front. Several key leaders, including Jose Maria Sison, the chairman of the CPP's Central Committee and the NPA's founder, live in exile in the Netherlands. There have been repeated splits within the leadership, with the Philippines government claiming the latest split – reportedly based on whether to continue a Maoist armed strategy or to shift to a political strategy – began in January 2010. Earlier splits, to include a number of mass executions of those suspected of being collaborators, reportedly occurred in 1982–8 and again in the 1990s.

The NPA now probably has about 9,000 to 10,000 members, down significantly from its peak strength of about 25,000 in the 1980s. Although it has conducted some urban operations, it generally has focused its main efforts in rural areas of Luzon, Visayas, and parts of northern and eastern Mindanao. The group conducted some major operations from its inception and represented a significant threat to stability for a considerable period. Some 40,000 have been killed in the fighting since 1969. In the last few years, although fighting has continued (with about 200 soldiers and guerrillas killed in 2008), the level has decreased significantly. Despite frequent abortive ceasefire talks and frequent governmental claims of 'victory' against the NPA, there seem to be few prospects of completely eliminating the group's activities. Unless the NPA self-destructs, continued operations are likely to remain at least on low levels, with occasional upsurges of violence.

The second strand of insurgency in the Philippines has been the various groups under the rubric of the Moros, i.e. Filipino Muslims. The Moro insurgency has involved a varying mix of ethnically and religiously based organization and ideology. The relative appeal of the ethnic and religious components of the insurgency appears to have shifted over time. Although the religious bases of the insurgency have been significant throughout the conflict, the saliency of religious factors as distinct from ethnicity seems to have increased in recent years.

Given that Muslim Filipinos are a distinct minority of the overall Filipino population, comprising only about 4 to 5 per cent of the population, they have only limited chances for a nationwide movement. Muslims are, however, concentrated in the southern Philippines, providing a potential critical mass for concerted political activity. Filipino Muslims have had a number of legitimate grievances. Government land reform policies frequently have provided land to Christians at the expense of Muslims, whose land tenure system has been informal. Filipino Muslims generally have a lower per capita income than that of Christians, and the majority of the more lucrative jobs in the Mindanao economy typically have gone to Christians (Che Man 1990). Historically Christians have viewed the Muslim community as 'uncivilized' and as needing outside assistance in becoming 'true' Filipinos. Although Muslims in the Philippines have had a distinct identity for several hundred years, a sense of 'nationhood' became more prominent after the Second World War. The first significant post-war Islamic secessionist group was the Muslim Independence Movement (MIM), launched in 1968. Although the MIM never was of particular significance, it did serve as a training ground for leaders and members of larger movements.

The most significant figure to emerge from the MIM was Nur Misuari. A teacher of political science at the University of the Philippines, in 1969 he and other secularly educated Muslims founded the Moro National Liberation Front (MNLF), with Misuari as Chairman. Beyond the overall Moro independence movement, the environment has been greatly complicated by localized political feuds. In many cases, severe political violence has had less to do with any particular liberation or insurgent movements, but instead has been local. Politicians have used armed gangs – such as the Barracuda and Blackshirts by an Islamic congressman, and the Rats by a Christian provincial governor – to settle political conflicts (Mercado 1984: 157). One aspect of this local political violence has been to further poison the environment between Muslims and Christians. According to *The Economist* (20 February 2010), there have been few if any improvements in this situation, with one politician's militia in the province of Maguindanao massacring 58 civilians in November 2009.

On 24 October 1972, a group of several hundred guerrillas, based on a loose temporary alliance, attacked a Philippine constabulary station and seized the campus of the Mindanao State University. This attack reportedly caught the MNLF leadership by surprise (Mercado 1984: 161). The guerrillas were driven out of the city in about 24 hours, but unrest spread rapidly throughout the area. This attack was followed by a massive deployment of Philippine army troops to the Moro areas, and marked the beginning of the armed campaign.

After the resulting martial law declaration, the various Philippine Islamist groups sought and received support from other Islamic countries. They received particular support from Libya, and the MNLF moved its political headquarters to Tripoli, Libya. Leaders both of the MNLF's political and military wings tended to be young and college educated, although some traditional elites also belonged to the MNLF, primarily in the political wing.

The NPA, although originating in Luzon, also was very active in Mindanao. The MNLF as an organization kept a considerable distance between itself and the NPA. Misuari in fact was quoted as stating that he would be willing to join forces with the Philippine military against the NPA if the Communists posed a significant threat (Chapman 1988: 238). At the same time, however, there were some tactical alliances between the NPA and some Moro commanders.

Early operations of the Moro guerrillas were marked by their seizing towns or rural areas and attempting to hold the areas against government counter-attacks. Needless to say, such a strategy – given the military's preponderance of heavy weaponry and equipment – resulted in a heavy toll of guerrilla casualties. After a series of such disasters, the insurgents adopted more 'conventional' unconventional tactics of hit-and-run operations and ambushes. These tactics proved much more successful, and the Philippine security forces began ceding large areas of Mindanao to de facto insurgent control.

The first phase of the insurgency from 1972 to 1975 was very bloody, with estimates of about 60,000 soldiers, insurgents and civilians killed. This phase was ended by the Tripoli Agreement of 1976 in which a ceasefire was declared and the establishment of an Autonomous Regional Government in 13 provinces of Mindanao and Sulu. Although the first phase of the insurgency was under putative MNLF leadership, its actual control must be viewed with some scepticism.

The group's political wing was located in Libya, with the geographical separation between the politicians and the fighters continuing to present difficulties. Moreover, many of the guerrillas appeared to have only tenuous loyalty to the MNLF as an organization, with some clearly more interested in fighting for relatively local issues (McKenna 1998: 183–5).

The MNLF and succeeding insurgent groups have suffered from a steady stream of surrenders and defections to the government, frequently 'in bulk', as when in 1978 the MNLF Vice-Chairman and all his followers surrendered to the government. In many cases, the defections seemed more a result of economic than ideological reasons, with important defectors receiving large cash payments, special export licenses, or even government positions. In many cases, though, although putatively returning to the government fold, defectors remained relatively independent of any realistic government control and became local power brokers.

The MNLF has been marked by continual splits and dissent, particularly after the collapse of the 1976 Tripoli Agreement. Three major factions emerged: the Misuari 'mainstream' MNLF and the MNLF Reformist Group led by Dimas Pundato. The third major faction was led by Hashim Salamat (a former vice-chairman of the MNLF), who in 1977 left with a group of his followers to form the Moro Islamic Liberation Front (MILF), formally established in March 1984.

The MILF's publicly expressed ideology has been much more religiously based than that of the MNLF. Although also calling for Moro independence, the group called for the imposition of Sharia law in the proposed state. Clerics have been much more prominent among the leadership of the MILF than in the MNLF; the MILF also has had a significant presence of traditional aristocrats. The MILF also has demonstrated stronger links with foreign groups, training a number of members of other regional groups in its camps (Abuza 2005: 453–70).

Strength estimates of the MILF have varied widely. The Philippine government has used figures of 8,000; Western estimates normally are in the 40,000 range; the MILF itself claims 120,000 troops. Beyond the normal propaganda games played with such estimates, much of the disparity can be ascribed to the MILF's system of troop mobilization. MILF military forces are organized into six divisions, but most soldiers are only part-time. Each brigade within the individual division has one full-time battalion with about 600 soldiers, with another battalion on active service for a month on a rotational basis. According to MILF sources, the training of their forces is very professional, with soldiers receiving three months of full-time training and officers one year of training (Tiglao 1996: 28).

The MNLF has largely disappeared as a cohesive organized group. In 1986, the Philippines government and leaders of the MNLF reached an agreement in which the government ceded considerable autonomy to the provinces in which the MNLF was strongest, and the MNLF agreed to enter the 'normal' Filipino political process. This process was eased by many MNLF leaders and members being given various economic incentives and appointments to potentially lucrative political positions. The MILF, however, has continued its opposition despite on-again, off-again peace talks. Nevertheless, fighting between the government and the MILF has dropped significantly, with only sporadic fighting. The MILF reportedly controls about 10 per cent of Mindanao. Even in 'government-controlled' areas, the MILF is said to have an influential shadow government.

Another splinter group of the MNLF is the Abu Sayyaf Group, which probably has received more foreign attention than any of the other organizations. Although a significant group in terms of its terrorist activities, it has exhibited limited popular support and some of its cells may have degenerated more into warlord or criminal groups than a political movement. Its primary significance may lie more in its continued role as an additional security stressor in the southern Philippines and the possibility that its members could serve as the possible nucleus for yet newer insurgent movements.

Burma

Some ethnic opposition movements have been struggling against the Burmese regimes for 60 years. Although the level of armed operations against the government has decreased significantly from its peak, these ethnic movements remain a significant factor in the internal stability of Myanmar. Beyond the ethnic conflicts – and for a considerable period, more significant – the Communist Party of Burma (CPB) launched a major insurgency in 1948 that lasted until 1989. Since 1988, with the seizure of power by military officers as the State Law and Order Restoration Council (SLORC), renamed in 1997 as the State Peace and Development Council (SPDC), the levels of ethnic insurgent activities have increased.

As of 2006, there were at least 41 armed ethnic groups in Burma (Smith 1999: 308). Although some efforts have been made to unify these ethnic movements – and to forge alliances with various pro-democracy activists – these efforts generally have had little impact. Over a third of these groups were splinters of other organizations, and most have only a handful of armed troops. Only the Karen National Union, the Karen National Progressive Party, Shan State Army-South, Chin National Front and National Socialist Council of Nagaland maintain armed forces of several hundred troops or more (Smith 1999: 296). Of these 41 groups, roughly two-thirds have reached some form of ceasefire with the government. There are some ten groups still formally in armed opposition to the government. The three major non-ceasefire armed groups are the Shan State Army-South (SSA-S), the Karen National Liberation Army (KNLA) operating as part of the KNU, and the Karenni Army. In many ways, the KNU remains the most important of the ethnic opposition groups in terms of its overall political impact, both within Myanmar and within the region.

According to a Western source with extensive experience in working with Burmese ethnic groups, all ethnic resistance organizations suffer from the following in varying degrees:

- no stable forms of revenue/tax basis;
- no retirement system, a fact that keeps elders in power past their prime;
- deference to elders, no matter how poorly they lead;
- leaders do not rely on staffs the way we do in developing courses of action – leaders tend to do all the work themselves;
- they also are often quintuple-hatted, being members of various coalitions or consortia. This keeps them in endless meetings;
- disempowerment by Western NGOs who generally bypass ethnic governments in order to empower the people at lowest levels;
- no professionalization of ethnic governments;
- little appreciation of what strategy is;
- tendency to focus on near-term survival;
- no unifying strategy;
- no apparent leader development within ethnic governments;
- no stable or coherent Western support other than through niche interest groups and faith-based donors;
- vulnerable leadership in exile (discussions and email follow-up with source requesting anonymity).

The most consistent observation of reporters and analysts who have visited ethnic groups within Burma and Burmese refugees in the region is that of war weariness. This is hardly surprising. Most ethnic opposition groups are now in their third or fourth generation of resistance. Insurgencies typically have a 'shelf life', and 60 years represents an extraordinarily long time.

Maintaining motivation among fighters and supporters likely is becoming increasingly difficult for the movements' leaders.

The insurgent groups essentially are operating on the strategic defensive. In almost all cases, their remaining strategic goals seem to centre around protecting what civilians they can. Sanctuaries generally have shrunk in size and few if any fixed bases remain within Myanmar. The various ethnic groups remain very subject to splits and unilateral ceasefires among their members.

The Burmese government, however, is far from having achieved any sort of outright victory. Despite the reduction of areas controlled by the non-ceasefire groups, they still retain areas in which the army has difficulty operating. Borders remain porous even if neighbouring governments are more prone to cooperate with the Burmese regime. Regional refugee camps remain a good source of recruits and support for the insurgent groups. The army's extreme brutality also continues to drive many to support the insurgents.

The regime's political strategy of ceasefire negotiations with the various groups and their breakaway factions does not represent an unalloyed success for the government. Although certainly reducing the level of violence directed against the government, few of the ceasefire groups have actively supported the SPDC. Most remain as quasi-independent power centres with very mixed allegiances. If pushed too hard by the military government, they easily can slip back into active opposition. Longer term, several of these groups could convert into full-scale warlord armies (which already seems to be occurring with at least two groups).

Two other factors will play a role in future developments within Myanmar. The first are the internal dynamics within the military regime. Internal dynamics within the junta remain opaque, but there have been some clear differences among its members in the past. Although even the purported moderates are almost certainly not ever going to make significant concessions to either the ethnic groups or pro-democracy groups, they may be more prone to reach further negotiated agreements.

The second factor involves the SPDC's proposed plans for some form of elections in 2010, which already are having an impact on the various opposition groups. The regime reportedly has ordered all ethnic groups, whether or not in a formal ceasefire, to form approved political parties to contest the elections. The apparent goal is to remove the military leadership of the opposition groups and to have them replaced by purely political figures. Given the history of factional struggles within the various ethnic insurgent groups, such efforts may well bear fruit for the current regime. As mentioned, there is considerable weariness after 60 years of struggle, and a significant number of ethnic group members may view some form – however limited – of political representation to be preferable to seemingly endless conflict and suffering.

Overall, the most probable situation in the near term is continued strategic stasis. As long as the military retains control of what it views as the core areas of Myanmar, it probably will continue its current strategies and tactics. The junta generally can meet its major interests, including reasonable economic enrichment, by simply maintaining its current policies. At the same time, the existing insurgent groups are unlikely to regain the initiative and must focus simply on maintaining their existence and some ability to protect at least part of their population. The ethnic resistance – factionalized, with continued ceasefires that come and go as the situation changes – and the Burmese army's brutal counterinsurgency campaign are almost certain to continue to be a running sore for the region.

Patterns among the countries

Several similarities exist among all three countries. The first is the very complex security environment in the areas of active insurgency. Each has been marked by a long history of banditry, varying levels of warlordism, and overall lack of effective governmental control. Also, each country's government has faced significant levels of corruption creating public distrust among significant segments of the population. In the cases both of Burma and the Philippines, the insurgencies have been active for decades. Although the formal insurgency has not lasted as long in Thailand, lower levels of unrest have existed for as long. Finally, each faces multiple insurgent groups, with various goals and distinct identities. Again, Thailand has somewhat a lesser problem with this issue in terms of significantly different ideologies, but must face a number of separate groups in the south. The splits among the insurgent groups in all three countries means that each group is individually weaker than if a unified movement were in place, but the divisions also make it much more difficult for the governments to devise a straightforward unitary political and military strategy, much less a single negotiating strategy.

The Philippines presents the clearest picture of one other aspect of insurgencies. Even as governments succeed in negotiations with some of the more moderate elements of insurgent movements, 'true believers' may split to continue the struggle. Although the new groups will be smaller, they probably will be more radical and less willing to compromise their objectives. As such, they may be even more dangerous to the population than the more broadly-based groups. Even if such radicalized groups are controlled, a significant number of insurgents may prove to be incapable of returning to a 'normal' life and to continue as members of criminal or warlord groups. This of course particularly is the case where governments are unwilling or incapable of conducting legitimate reconciliation programmes, which would seem to apply to a greater or lesser extent to all three countries. While some progress may be made through negotiations and more effective counterinsurgency operations, there is little reason to be sanguine about the restoration of governmental control in the affected areas or the end of armed unrest.

Recommended readings and references

Abuza, Zachary (2005) 'The Moro Islamic Liberation Front at 20: State of the Revolution', *Studies in Conflict and Terrorism*, 28.

Amnesty International (June 1999) *Myanmar: The Kayin (Karen) State: Militarization and Human Rights*.

Askew, Marc (2008) 'Thailand's Intractable Southern War: Policy, Insurgency and Discourse', *Contemporary Southeast Asia*, 30 (2).

Ba Saw Khin (1998, revised 2005) *Fifty Years of Struggle: A Review of the Fight for the Karen People's Autonomy*. Available at: www.kwekalu.net.

Black, Michael (13 December 2006) 'On Myanmar-China Border, Tensions Escalate Between SPDC, Narco-Militias'.

Bosson, Andrew (May 2007) *Forced Migration/Internal Displacement In Burma With An Emphasis On Government-Controlled Areas*, Internal Displacement Monitoring Centre (Norwegian Refugee Council).

Chapman, William (1988) *Inside the Philippine Revolution: The New Peoples Army and its Struggle for Power*. London: I.B. Tauris 1988.

Che Man, W.K. (1990) *Muslim Separatism: The Moros of Southern Philippines and the Malays of Southern Thailand*. Singapore: Oxford University Press.

Croissant, Aurel. (2007) 'Muslim Insurgency, Political Violence, and Democracy in Thailand', *Terrorism and Political Violence*, 19.

Free Burma Rangers (April 2008) *A Campaign of Brutality: Report and Analysis of Burma Army Offensive and Ongoing Attacks Against the People of Northern Karen State, Eastern Burma*. Chiang Mai, Thailand.

Gowing, Peter G. (1980) *Muslim Filipinos: Heritage and Horizon*. Quezon City: New Day Publishers.

Gowing, Peter G. and McAmis, Robert D. (eds) (1974) *The Muslim Filipinos*. Manila: Solidaridad.

Harish, S.P. (2006) 'Ethnic or Religious Cleavage? Investigating the Nature of the Conflict in Southern Thailand', *Contemporary Southeast Asia*, 28 (1).

Human Rights Watch (June 2005) *They Came and Destroyed Our Village Again: The Plight of Internally Displaced Persons in Karen State*, 17/4(C).

Human Rights Watch (October 2007) *Sold to Be Soldiers: The Recruitment and Use of Child Soldiers in Burma*, 19/15(C).

Internal Displacement Monitoring Center (Norwegian Refugee Council) (14 February 2008) *Myanmar (Burma): No End in Sight for Internal Displacement Crisis*.

International Crisis Group (7 May 2003) ICG Asia Report Number 52, *Myanmar Backgrounder: Ethnic Minority Politics*.

International Crisis Group (16 February 2009) Asia Briefing Number 88, *The Philippines: Running in Place in Mindanao*.

International Crisis Group (8 December 2009) ICG Asia Report Number 181, *Southern Thailand: Moving Towards Political Solutions?*

Islam, Syed Serajul Islam (2007) 'State Terrorism in Arakan', in Andrew T.H. Tan (ed.), *A Handbook of Terrorism and Insurgency in Southeast Asia*, UK: Cheltenham.

Karen Human Rights Group, www.khrg.org/background_on_burma.html.

Karen National Union Website, www.karen.org/knu.

Karenni National Organization Website, www.kachinland.org.

Liow, Joseph Chinyong (2006) *Muslim Resistance in Southern Thailand and Southern Philippines: Religion, Ideology, and Politics*. Honolulu: East-West Center.

Lumbaca, Jeremiah C. (2005) *Islamic Insurgency and Transnational Terrorism in Thailand: Analysis and Recommended Solution Strategy*. Monterey: Naval Postgraduate School.

McKenna, Thomas M. (1998) *Muslim Rulers and Rebels: Everyday Politics and Armed Separatism in the Southern Philippines*. Berkeley: University of California Press.

Malik, Mohan (18 January 2005) 'Regime Shake-Up in Rangoon: A Setback for Beijing?', *China Brief* 5/2, The Jamestown Foundation.

Marks, Thomas A. (1996) *Maoist Insurgency Since Vietnam*. London: Frank Cass.

Mercado, Eliseo R. (1984) 'Culture, Economics, and Revolt in Mindanao: The Origins of the MNLF and the Politics of Moro Separatism', in Lim Joo-Jock and Vani S. (eds), *Armed Separatism in Southeast Asia*. Singapore: Institute of Southeast Asian Studies.

Moro Islamic Liberation Front Website, at www.luwaran.com.

Pauker, Benjamin (winter 2005/2006) 'Thailand: A Fire This Time', *World Policy Journal*.

Phan, Poe Shan K. and Hull, Stephen (n.d.) 'Supporting IDP Resistance Strategies', *Forced Migration Review*.

Pojar, Daniel J. (March 2005) Unpublished thesis, 'Lessons Not Learned: The Rekindling of Thailand's Pattani Problem', Monterey, CA: Naval Postgraduate School.

Prizzia, Ross. (1985) *Thailand in Transition: The Role of Oppositional Forces*. Honolulu: University of Hawaii Press.

Randolph, R. Sean and Thompson, W. Scott (1981) *Thai Insurgency: Contemporary Developments*, The Washington Papers Vol IX, No. 81. Washington, DC: Georgetown University Press.

Smith, Martin (1999) *Burma: Insurgency and the Politics of Ethnicity*. London: Zed Books.

Smith, Martin (2007) 'Ethnic Conflicts in Burma: From Separatism to Federalism', in Andrew T.H. Tan (ed.), *A Handbook of Terrorism and Insurgency in Southeast Asia*. Cheltenham, UK.

The South Asia Human Rights Documentation Centre (SAHRDC), www.hrdc.net/sahrdc/resources/burmese_refugee.htm.

South, Ashley (2007) 'Karen Nationalist Communities: The "Problem" of Diversity', *Contemporary Southeast Asia*, 29 (1).

Tiglao, Rigoberto (28 March 1996) 'The Fire Next Time', *Far Eastern Economic Review*, 159.

United Nations (16 November 2007) *Report of the Secretary-General on Children and Armed Conflict in Myanmar*.

16

INSURGENCIES IN INDIA

Namrata Goswami

India has been plagued by multiple insurgencies for many decades. Prominent amongst them are the ethnic insurgencies in the northeast of India, the Sikh insurgency in the Punjab, and the Maoist or the left-wing insurgency in states like Andhra Pradesh, Bihar, Chhattisgarh and Jharkhand, Orissa. While it is argued by existing literature (Verghese 1996) that there are several causes for armed insurgencies in India such as a demand for a separate independent state; greater political representation within the Union of India; assertion of cultural identity; and the lack of governance, this chapter isolates four significant factors that have sustained multiple insurgencies in India across time and space. These are: exclusive homeland narratives; political mobilization; the use of violence; and external connections.

Five cases studies of insurgencies will be used to illustrate these ideas: the Dima Halam Daogah (DHD) and the United Liberation Front of Asom (ULFA) in Assam; the National Socialist Council of Nagalim led by Thuingaleng Muivah and Isak Chisi Swu-NSCN (IM) based in Manipur and Nagaland; the United National Liberation Front (UNLF) based in Manipur; the Sikh insurgency in the Punjab in the 1970s, 1980s and 1990s and the Maoist insurgency (see Figure 16.1)

A brief overview

With an international border stretching up to 4,500 kms, the northeastern region of India has been plagued by multiple insurgencies since India's independence. The oldest insurgency is the Naga insurgency which can be traced back to 1918 with the formation of the Naga Club. In 1946, the Naga National Council (NNC) was formed and it declared Naga independence on 14 August 1947, a day before India declared its own independence. The Naga movement turned violent in the 1950s and is still active today. Manipur has also been grossly affected by armed violence with the formation of the UNLF on 24 November 1964. Another significant Manipuri separatist armed group known as the Revolutionary People's Front (RPF) and its armed wing, the People's Liberation Army (PLA) have been engaged in armed struggle since 1976. Other insurgent groups in Manipur include the Peoples' Revolutionary Party of *Kangleipak* (PREPAK) established in the 1970s and the Kanglei Yawol Kanna Lup (KYKL) formed in 1994. Neighbouring Assam has also been plagued by insurgent violence since 1979 with the formation of the ULFA. The hill districts of Assam, North Cachar Hills and Karbi Anglong are

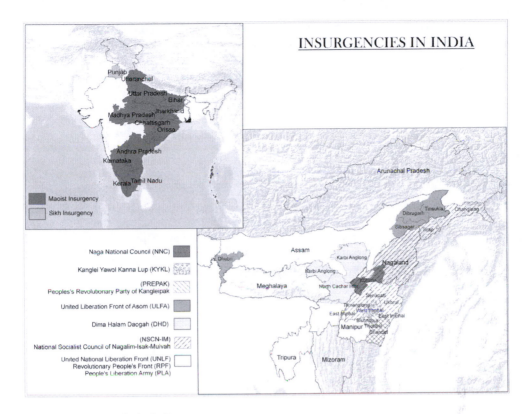

Figure 16.1 Insurgencies in India.

dominated by the DHD and the United Peoples' Democratic Solidarity (UPDS) since the 1990s. Significantly, most of the northeast insurgent groups have thrived primarily due to strong external connections. Countries like China in the 1960s and the 1970s as well as Pakistan and later on Bangladesh have supported many of these armed groups by providing arms, training and, most importantly, base areas for underground camps (Bhaumik 2007: 1–16). Matters rather changed however when Banglasdesh closed these camps when Sheikh Hasina came to power in 2008.

The Sikh insurgency had a turbulent beginning as the Indian state oscillated in its response between limited and excessive use of force. Due to the lack of a 'trust and nurture' doctrine in Indian counterinsurgency strategy (Goswami 2009: 66–86), Punjabis started fearing that the *Panth* (greater Sikh community) was in danger within India (Latimer 2004: 14–16). This resulted in a plethora of insurgent groups, namely the Khalistan Liberation Force, the All India Sikh Student's Federation (AISSF), the Khalistan Commando Force and the Babbar Khalsa (Gill 1997: 48). Insurgent violence peaked during 1983–91 killing nearly 21,000 people.[1]

A Maoist insurgency started in 1967 in a place called Naxalbari in West Bengal as a peasant uprising against unjust landlords, though some semblance of it had already started taking roots in the state of Hyderabad as early as 1948 (Bajpai 2002: 18–22). While the movement was contained by the Indian state in the 1970s, it re-appeared in the 1980s and started spreading across many states in India. According to the 2010 Government of India statistics, 20 out of 28 states in India were affected in some way or other by Naxalite activities. The reasons for this spread of the Maoist insurgency lay in the inability of the legitimate political authority in India to provide avenues for structural upliftment of the deprived sections of society in the affected states. The tribal population in these states views the Maoist insurgency as a viable alternative out of desperate social and economic conditions.[2] Violence is also seen as an instrument for political assertion and attention (Coser 1956: 6–10).

Four significant factors for sustenance of insurgencies in India

As noted, four significant factors have given rise to multiple insurgencies in India: exclusive homeland narratives; political mobilization; the use of violence; and external connections. These will now be discussed in turn.

Exclusive homeland narratives: though the depth of insurgent movements across India varies, there are certain similarities weaving them together. When one probes deeper into the antecedent causes of the conflicts, assertions of minority ethnic identity and aspirations of political empowerment are at the core of the conflicts, be it in Assam, Manipur, Nagaland, Chhattisgarh, Jharkhand or the Punjab. The northeast insurgencies have another added feature: the colonial residue of being treated as 'excluded or partially excluded' areas based on the Inner Line Regulation of 1873.[3] Due to the lack of a pre-colonial and colonial integrative policy with the rest of India, the hill tribes resist the post-colonial Indian state's entry into their territories. Consequently, in order to safeguard their political space, most of the ethnic communities demand a separate ethnic homeland. Interestingly, these factors are evident in the ethnic movements pertaining to the NSCN (IM), UNLF, ULFA and the DHD. For instance, the NSCN (IM) in its negotiations with the Union government, ongoing since 1997, demands an exclusive ethnic homeland for Nagas, Greater Nagalim (Nagaland) comprising of Naga inhabited areas in Arunachal Pradesh, Assam, Manipur, Nagaland and across the border in Myanmar. The flip side of this exclusive ethnic homeland demand is that the territories included in the Greater Nagalim map are inhabited by ethnic 'others' and as a result the claim is perceived as a serious security threat given the risk of serious inter-communal and inter-ethnic violence.

A case in point is the response of the Meitei community in Manipur. The Meiteis are deeply apprehensive that the current Naga peace process could end up in the balkanization of Manipur. Geographically, the hills which are included in Greater Nagalim constitute 70 per cent of Manipur's territory and any further slicing of territory would leave Manipur at a disadvantage. Meiteis also claim that their culture is a synthesis of Naga and Meitei cultures and they are embittered by the identity and historical exclusivity discourse of the Nagas. Under pressure from the NSCN (IM), in a joint statement issued on 14 June 2001 in Bangkok, the Indian government extended the Naga ceasefire 'without territorial limits' to Manipur.[4] This led to violent protests in Manipur. Many civil society organizations were united in a mass movement against the decision to extend the Naga ceasefire to the Naga-dominated hill districts of Manipur.[5] The end result was the state assembly building being burned down with 13 protesters killed on 18 June 2001.

The ULFA and the DHD in Assam also base their armed movements on the demand for exclusive homelands for the Assamese and the Dimasa ethnic communities, respectively. The ULFA seeks to revert Assam's status to the Ahom ruled Assam, as conceived of in the 1826 treaty of Yandaboo between the British and the Burmese, which ushered in British rule in Assam (Baruah 1994: 863–97). ULFA's Vice Chairman, Pradip Gogoi, has stated that his organization's political objectives are the creation of a 'sovereign, socialist Assam' in which 'All indigenous people must stay, all others must leave'. The stated demand of the DHD is a unified Dimaraji state comprised of Dimasa inhabited areas of N C Hills district, Karbi Anglong district,

Cachar district, parts of Nagaon district in Assam, and Dimapur and Dimasa inhabited areas in Dhansiripar in Nagaland. The UNLF in Manipur draws its credence from the historical argument that Manipur was forcefully inducted into India in 1949. The DHD is based on a leftist ideology vis-à-vis the economic and social alienation of the people of Manipur. The armed group asserts that the backwardness of Meitei society can be better addressed with the establishment of a Meitei state to the exclusion of all ethnic 'others' (Goswami 2007: 287–313).

Interestingly, the demands of the NSCN (IM) for a unified Nagalim (Greater Nagaland), the DHD for a Dimasa state, the ULFA for Independent Assam and the UNLF for Independent Manipur consist of overlapping claims to the same territorial space. Indeed, the emergence of multifarious insurgent groups with claims over the same territory has further complicated the situation in these remote areas of India.

The Punjab insurgency was also propelled by deep-seated fears of the Sikh community that a Hindu dominated country like India would have little space for their religion, language and culture (Bajpai 2002: 55–6). As a result, the major political party in Punjab, the Akali Dal, argued that Punjab had to either become sovereign or granted a high degree of political autonomy to safeguard the Sikh community. When the Union government appeared to be lacklustre in meeting these demands, the movement took on an insurgent turn with the political goal of establishing an exclusive Sikh state called Khalistan, based on the Anandpur Sahib resolution of 1973.

Drawing inspiration from the Maoist ideology of heartland 'revolutionary warfare', the Maoist insurgency aspired to establish a 'red corridor' in India, stretching from the border of Nepal in central India in the north to Karnataka in the south by violent struggle. The Maoists claim that this Maoist state will be anti-imperialist, anti-bourgeois and pro-proletariat. Apparently, the political goal of the Maoist insurgency differs from that of the northeast and the Punjab insurgencies with its focus on regime change in India. However, in reality, the dynamics of allegiance of the Maoist cadres to the armed insurgency is similar to that of the other insurgencies. The most committed cadres of the Maoist insurgency are the tribals of Andhra Pradesh, Chhattisgarh, Jharkhand and Orissa whose support is based on the political goal of establishing an exclusive homeland in which their rights are paramount.[6] Hence, the red corridor that the Maoists want to establish is coterminous with that of the tribal population inhabiting these areas. Significantly, the goal of regime change that the Maoists are fighting for is also similar to that of the other insurgencies in India. The northeast armed groups and the Sikh insurgency also seek regime change with the ultimate political goal of undoing the so-called illiberal and non-representative character of the present local state regimes and replacing them with a democratic ethnic leadership. The only difference is that the Maoist insurgency wants to achieve this at a pan-India level whereas the other insurgencies have been largely limited to a local and regional level.

Political mobilization: politics forms the core of insurgent groups' mobilization strategy (Grey 1999: 283–5). Most insurgent groups garner popular support for their violent activities by citing a political cause, significantly important to the target population. According to Mao Zedong, the promise of mobilizing for revolution will exist in any country where the formal administrative structures fail to meet their basic obligations of providing the minimum standard of life to their citizens (Griffith 1962: 5–6). Political mobilization is the first critical phase in any insurgency to acquire critical mass. Historical evidence also suggests that there is very little hope of destroying an insurgency once it survives the first phase and succeeds in acquiring a level of social support (Griffith 1962: 27–43). It must also be noted that insurgent groups construct a 'social imaginary' (Schmidt and Schroder 2001: 4) based on real or perceived political alienation and cultural subjugation by dominant 'others' thereby vindicating the need for violent assertion of legitimate concerns of the insurgent groups' social base. Insurgent leaders also behave like socially powerful individuals by openly projecting their armed cadres, weapons and financial prowess. This visible showcasing attracts unemployed youths in areas where the state is unable to provide decent alternative livelihoods.

The NSCN (IM) cites political reasons for the use of force. It argues that its political objective is Naga territorial unification and sovereignty based on the group's historical narrative of Naga independent status before the British occupied Naga territories in the nineteenth century (Goswami 2007: 134–54). During the 6th Naga Peoples' Consultative Meeting for Discussion on Extension of Cease-Fire at Camp Hebron on 27 July 2007 and attended by nearly 5,000 people from across the Naga areas, Thuingaleng Muivah, the General Secretary of the NSCN (IM) asserted the importance of the political objectives.[7] He also committed to improve the overall economic and social standing of Nagas knowing full well that such arguments strike an emotional cord amongst Naga society as development in these areas is dismal. The ULFA, the DHD and the UNLF also utilize the perceived sense of social alienation and political neglect cutting across societal spaces in the northeast. Historical narratives are constructed based on a nostalgic interpretation of past events and earlier ethnic communities are projected as leading an idyllic independent political life. It is also argued that if such an ethnic based state is established, all the present ills of under-development and dominance by India's northern heartland will end. This was also the case with the Punjab. Sikh society was mobilized by insurgent actors who projected the idea of an independent Khalistan which would guarantee the preservation of the Sikh language, religion and politics.

The Maoist insurgency is perhaps the most well organized to carry out political mobilization.[8] The People's Liberation Guerrilla Army (PLGA) of the Communist Party of India (Maoist) or the CPI (M) is the chief instrument of the insurgency. It is through the PLGA that most of the political mobilization and training has been conducted.[9] Central to the factor of political mobilization are the violent means used for the political objective of regime change. Most crucially, the fact that young recruits are turned into forces capable of unleashing social violence must be kept in focus. The interaction between insurgent groups, the armed forces of the state and civilian population is central to understanding not only political mobilization patterns but also the all important variable of dynamics of allegiance. What is at stake here is the loyalty of the non-combatant population. Civilian support is crucial for the advancement of a conflict. Resources like crucial food supply, manpower and information come from the people. Building support through the correct political mobilization strategy wrapped around core issues linked to the population is therefore critical (Weinstein 2007: 7–22).

Another important political factor for insurgent mobilization is the disproportionate government response to insurgent violence. As mentioned earlier, during the Punjab insurgency, the years 1983–91 witnessed a brutal suppression of the insurgency leading to widespread alienation of the local people. The Akali Dal government under Prakash Singh Badal was dismissed by the Indira Gandhi government on the mere suspicion that it was supporting pro-Khalistan groups and a state of emergency was imposed on Punjab. Military operations were intensified with little regard for human rights (Final Report on Punjab Disappearances, 2003). This strengthened the hands of militants like Jarnail Singh Bhindranwale who, taking advantage of the widespread hardships of the local people, further radicalized them under the pretext that Sikh religion was under threat (Marwah 1996: 59; Joshi 1984: 126–34). The Akali Dal party also joined this militant nexus. Operation Wood Rose, an army operation aimed at wiping out Bhindranwale's supporters in the aftermath of his death in 1984 ended up further alienating the population due to its use of indiscriminate force and critical lack of knowledge of the terrain and its people. According to K.P.S. Gill, Operations Blue Star and Wood Rose 'in combination, gave new lease of life to a movement that could have been easily contained in 1984 itself' (Gill 1997: 95–7).

The Sikh insurgency intensified after Operation Blue Star of June 1984 was seen by local Sikh communities as an assault on their religion. Worse still, it was undertaken on 5 June, the day that marked the death anniversary of the founder of Amritsar's Golden Temple, Guru Arjan Dev. An estimated 10,000 pilgrims were present in the temple site that day. In a large-scale operation involving six tanks, heavy artillery, four infantry fighting vehicles and three armoured personnel carriers, 4,712 civilians including Bhindhranwale were killed (Latimer 2004: 22). Several old manuscripts of the Sikhs, as well as the temple itself, suffered severe damage. The entire Sikh community was outraged, not so much by Bhindhranwale's death, but by the attack on their holy site. This discontentment culminated in the assassination of the Indian Prime Minister, Indira Gandhi, in October 1984 by her two Sikh bodyguards.

The use of violence: the tactic and strategy of guerrilla warfare is followed by the insurgent actors in India providing them with the genesis of a protracted conflict aimed at wearing down the will of the stronger party. Violence is utilized by insurgent actors for three significant reasons:

1   assertion of power in a given territory;
2   as a bargaining chip; and
3   as a coercive means to get support from the local population.

Most of the insurgent groups in the northeast utilize violence to establish their hold on a given territory. For instance, show of force is essential in the Naga inhabited areas as there are multiple insurgent actors at a given time inhabiting the same territorial space. According to Phunthing Shimrang, self-styled Brigadier in the Naga Army and Chairman, NSCN (IM) Cease-fire Monitoring Cell, the use of violence by the NSCN (IM) is critical to signal to their rival armed faction, the NSCN (K) who is the dominant actor in a given territory.[10] Consequently, the use of violence should be viewed as a consequence of power-battles with factional fights mainly aimed at dominating the authoritative allocation of resources and territory. Given the fact that insurgent groups are heavily dependent on the extortion networks run in common areas, the violence is mostly about who dominates what, where and how. The Sikh and Maoist insurgencies follow a similar pattern. With regard to the latter, it is critical for the Maoist insurgency to dominate states like Jharkhand whose illegal coal mines add the highest percentage of money to Maoist budgets.[11]

Violence is utilized as a bargaining chip to get concessions from the stronger actor (read the Indian state). This also gets insurgent actors visibility, space for dissent and a place at the negotiating table with the Union government, as is the case with northeastern insurgent actors like the NSCN (IM), the DHD and the ULFA. Violence is also utilized as a viable tool to get support from the insurgent groups' target population through 'fear and intimidation'. ULFA is known for its terror tactics of killing non-Assamese Hindi-speaking people, especially migrant workers from Bihar. Most societies affected by insurgent violence in India support insurgent actors out of a need to 'self-preserve' because if they do otherwise, they fear some kind of physical harm, given that they inhabit remote inaccessible terrain still not penetrated by the state (Goswami 2009: 66–86). Usually, insurgency affected societies suffer from high stress levels and genuinely fear destructive social forces prevalent among them.

External support: insurgencies garner support from external sources especially with regard to the hardware of violence and in updating their strategies. External support is contingent on the geography of the area where the insurgent groups are active. Support from neighbouring countries could be political, moral, military, economic, territorial or cultural based on ethnic ties (Bajpai 2002: 98–104).

The northeastern states share a 4,500 km highly porous border with China in the north, Myanmar in the East, Bangladesh in the southwest and Bhutan in the northwest whereas it precariously clings to the rest of India by a 22 km narrow strip of land known in Bengal as the 'Chicken's Neck'. Both the ULFA and the NSCN (IM) have had training camps in Myanmar and Bangladesh. Significantly, the unified National Socialist Council of Nagaland (NSCN) was formed in Myanmar on 31 January 1980. In 1986, ULFA established linkages with the unified NSCN. Both insurgent groups had strong connections with the Kachin Independence Organization (KIO) of Myanmar (Tucker 2000: 82–5). (See also Chapter 15 by Lawrence E. Cline) Southern Bhutan also offered a safe haven for insurgent bases in the 1980s and 1990s. Things however changed when in December 2003, the Royal Bhutan Army (RBA) and the Royal Body Guards (RBG) comprising 6,000 military personnel forcefully expelled 3,000 insurgent cadres of the ULFA and KIO from Bhutan and destroyed nearly 30 training camps. Many top ULFA functionaries were also arrested. The ULFA then shifted to Myanmar and Bangladesh. The ULFA camps in Bangladesh remained a bone of contention between India and Bangladesh for a long time. Most of the top ULFA leaders, like its chairman, Arabinda Rajkhowa, and commander-in-chief, Paresh Barua, remained in Bangladesh. It is only recently that there has been some gainful cooperation between India and Bangladesh in this regard and top ULFA leaders like Rajkhowa were arrested by Indian security personnel in the Bangladesh-Meghalaya border area in December 2009.

The NSCN (IM) receives the help of the Karen National Union (KNU) fighting the Myanmar junta since 1947. The group has also ventured into the Chinese black market in Yunnan province. Small arms are shipped by the NSCN (IM) through the Chittagong port in Bangladesh. Anthony Shimray is the NSCN (IM)'s procurement officer in Philippines enjoying close connections with the Southeast Asian small arms network (Egreteau 2006: 78).

China also began to support revolutionary movements across the world after the Communist takeover in 1949. Thereafter, it provided strong political, economic and logistical support to various insurgent groups in northeast India in order to counter so-called Western imperialism and Soviet revisionism in Asia. In return, most of these insurgent groups supported the 'One China policy' with regard to Taiwan. The Nagas were greatly inspired by the Chinese ideas of 'People's War' and 'protracted struggle'. In 1966, Muivah, then member of the NNC, led a 130-strong Naga guerrilla force in a three-month trek to Yunnan province in China mostly helped by the Kachins. He later moved to Beijing to get political training, followed by Isak Chisi Swu and Moure Angami in 1968. China's help to the Mizos is also well documented, subsequently followed by support to the UNLF. However, Deng Xiaoping's 'good neighbour policy' stopped Chinese aid to these insurgent groups except for the flow of illegal Chinese arms through the black market in Yunnan.

The Sikh insurgency was backed by Pakistan with regard to supply of arms, money and training. Without this external help, the insurgency would have most likely failed to sustain itself for nearly three decades in the face of India's counterinsurgency operations (Wallace 2007: 425–79). The Maoist insurgency depends on internal sources within India like illegal small arms factories in Bihar and looting for the hardware of violence. However, there have been growing linkages regarding strategy and ideology following the formation of the Coordination Committee of the Maoist Parties and Organizations in South Asia (CCOMPOSA) in 2001. This body includes ten Maoist groups from Bangladesh, India, Nepal and Sri Lanka. In a joint statement issued on 1 July 2001, subsequently followed by a declaration in August 2002, the CCOMPOSA identifies resistance to US imperialism, globalization, the 'centralized' Indian state and its internal repression of minority people through the Naxalite People's War, and India's expansionist designs backed by US imperialism in South Asia as its goals.[12]

Conclusion

This chapter has outlined a framework for further research to analyse insurgencies in India. It is equally important to do substantive work on conflict resolution mechanisms. Conflict resolution by definition indicates a comprehensive framework, going much beyond conflict management, which addresses the deep sources and root causes of any particular conflict. The Mizo peace process (1968–86) in India indicates that the conflict was transformed from violent assertion to peaceful resolution as the root causes of the conflict were addressed; attitudes of the conflicting actors changed over time; and issues became reframed. Another critical issue in a democracy like India is popular support for insurgencies. Consequently, while 'use of force' is a necessary counterinsurgency response, it must be proportionate and should not end up further alienating the insurgency affected population by doing more harm than was intended. Use of force in a democracy must visibly demonstrate accountability and restraint by a responsive state. Consequently, security forces must realize that counterinsurgency in a democracy is not merely a military operation; it is a political act as well. Further research should particularly be undertaken on important concepts like 'non-combatant immunity' and 'proportionality' and their relationship to insurgencies and counterinsurgencies.

Notes

1 Atal Vihari Vajpayee, 'Indian Prime Minister Vajpayee's Address to US Congress', Washington, DC, 14 September 2000, at www.usindiafriendship.net/statements/vision/vision.htm (accessed 2 September 2007). Also see K.P.S. Gill, 'End Game in Punjab, 1988–93', *Faultlines*, at www.satp.orgtp/publication/faultlines/volume/articles3_htm (accessed 5 January 2007).

2 See Independent Citizens Initiative, *War in the Heart of India An Enquiry into the Ground Situation in Dantewada District*, Chhattisgarh, 20 July 2006. Also *Naxal Monitor*, A Quarterly Newsletter of the Asian Centre for Human Rights, Vol. 11, April–June 2006.

3 The Inner Line Regulation of 1873 prohibited any British Indian subjects from entering Naga inhabited areas without having prior permission. The policy continues to be upheld after India became independent in 1947 and is still in force today.

4 For full text of the agreement see South Asia Terrorism Portal, 'Countries; India; States; Nagaland; Papers; Extension of the cease-fire with the NSCN-IM', www.satp.org (accessed 21 June 2006).

5 The ULFA has said that the NSCN (IM)'s claim of eight Assam districts as part of Nagalim has 'neither credibility nor any historical basis'. Arabinda Rajkhowa, the ULFA chairman, has called upon the NSCN (IM) to remove the eight Assam districts from its Nagalim map. See Ajai Sahni 'Survey of Conflicts and Resolution in India's Northeast', at www.satp.org/satporgtp/publication/faultlines/volume12/Article3.htm (accessed 10 August 2006).

6 Field interviews conducted by author in Orissa with the tribal community in Kandamal, Nayagarh and Malkangiri, October 2008.

7 The 6th Naga Peoples' Consultative Meeting was held on 27 July 2007 at Camp Hebron near Dimapur, Nagaland, which I attended as an observer. The meeting comprised nearly 5,000 Naga peoples' representatives from Naga areas in Arunachal Pradesh, Assam, Manipur and Nagaland. Civil society organizations like the Naga Hoho (Apex Council) representatives, Presidents of Tribal Hohos, Naga Mothers' Association, Naga Students' Federation, Human Rights Organizations, Village Headmen Association, Senior Citizens' Forums, members of the intelligentsia and media were also in attendance.

8 'Party Constitution Central Committee (P)CPI (Maoist)', at www.satp.org/satpgtp/countries/india/maoist/documents/papers/partyconstitution.htm (accessed 1 March 2008).

9 Ibid. Also see 'CPI (ML) People's War: Functioning of Military Commissions and Commands Coordination of Main, Secondary and Base Forces', at http://satp.org/satporgtp/countries/india/maoist/documents/papers/Functioning.htm (accessed on 1 March 2008).

10 Insurgent leaders interviewed with regard to insurgent strategy included self-styled Brigadier of the rebel Naga army and Chairman, NSCN (IM) Ceasefire Monitoring Cell, Punthing Shimrang, at Diphupar, Dimapur, Nagaland, 26 July 2007 and self-styled Commander-in-Chief of the Dimasa Army, Pranob Nunisa, Dima Halam Daogah, Haflong, Assam, 19 July 2007.

11 Jason Miklian and Scot Carney, 'Fire in the Hole', *Foreign Policy*, September–October 2010, at www. foreignpolicy.com/articles/2010/08/16/fire_in_the_hole (accessed 17 February 2011).

12 See 'Declaration of CCOMPOSA', at http://cpnm.org/new/ccomposa/cco/cco_dclr.htm (accessed on 9 April 2007). For joint statement, see www.satp.org/satporgtp/southasia/documents/papers/ CCOMPOSA.htm (accessed 9 April 2007).

Recommended readings

Baruah, Sanjib (2005) *Durable Disorder Understanding the Politics of Northeast India*. Oxford: Oxford University Press.

Gill, K.P.S. (1997) *The Knights of Falsehood*. New Delhi: Har Anand.

Goswami, Namrata (2007) 'The Naga Narrative of Conflict: Envisioning a Resolution Roadmap', *Strategic Analysis*, 31 (2): 287–313.

Goswami, Namrata (2008) 'Unraveling Insurgent Groups' Strategy: The Case of the National Socialist Council of *Nagalim* in India', *Strategic Analysis*, 32 (3): 413–38.

Hassan, M. Sajjad (2006) *Reconstruction from Breakdown in Northeastern India Building State Capacity*. Tokyo: United Nations University.

Kohli, Atul (1997) 'Can Democracies Accommodate Ethnic Nationalism? Rise and Decline of Self Determination Movements in India', *Journal of Asian Studies*, 56 (2): 325–44.

Marwah, Ved (1996) *Uncivil Wars: Pathology of Terrorism in India*. New Delhi: Centre for Policy Research.

Verghese, B.G. (1996) *India's Northeast Resurgent: Ethnicity, Insurgency, Governance, Development*. New Delhi: Konarak.

References

Bajpai, Kanti P. (2002) *Roots of Terrorism*. New Delhi: Penguin.

Baruah, Sanjib (1994) 'The State and Separatist Militancy in Assam: Winning a Battle and Losing the War?', *Asian Survey*, 34 (10): 863–97.

Bhaumik, S. (1996) *Insurgent Crossfire: Northeast India*. New Delhi: Lancer.

Bhaumik, S. (2007) *Insurgencies in India's Northeast: Conflict, Co-option & Change*. East-West Center Washington Working Paper No. 10. Washington, DC: East-West Center.

Coser, Lewis A. (1956) *The Functions of Social Conflict*. New York: Free Press.

Egreteau, Renaud (2006) *Instability at the Gate: India's Troubled Northeast and its External Connections*. New Delhi, Centre de Sciences Humaines.

Final Report on Punjab Disappearances (2003) *Reduced to Ashes The Insurgency and Human Rights in Punjab*. Kathmandu: South Asian Forum for Human Rights.

Gill, K.P.S. (1997) *Punjab: The Knights of Falsehood*. New Delhi: Har Anand.

Gill, K.P.S., 'End Game in Punjab, 1988–93', *Faultlines*, at www.satp.orgtp/publication/faultlines/volume/ articles3_htm (accessed 5 January 2007).

Goswami, Namrata (2007a) 'The Naga Narrative of Conflict: Envisioning a Resolution Roadmap', *Strategic Analysis*, 31 (2): 287–313.

Goswami, Namrata (2007b) 'Twilight over Guerrilla Zone Retracing the Naga Peace Process', in Jaydeep Saikia (ed.), *Frontier in Flames North East India in Turmoil*. New Delhi: Penguin, pp. 134–54.

Goswami, Namrata (2009) 'India's Counter-Insurgency Experience: The "Trust and Nurture" Strategy', *Small Wars & Insurgencies*, 20 (1): 66–86.

Grey, Colin (1999) *Modern Strategy*. Oxford: Oxford University Press.

Griffith, Samuel B. (1962) *On Guerrilla Warfare*. New York: Praeger.

Jafa, Vijendra Singh, 'Counter-insurgency Warfare, The Use and Abuse of Military Force', at www.satp. org/satporgtp/publication/faultlines/volume3/Fault3-JafaF.htm (accessed 6 February 2008).

Joshi, Chand (1984) *Bhindranwale Myth and Reality*. New Delhi: Vikas.

Latimer, William S. (2004) *What Can the United States Learn from India to Counter-Terrorism?* Monterey, CA: Naval Post Graduate School.

Marwah, Ved (1996) *Uncivil Wars: Pathology of Terrorism in India*. New Delhi: Centre for Policy Research.

Schmidt, Bettina E. and Ingo W. Schroder (eds) (2001) *Anthropology of Violence and Conflict*. London: Routledge.

Tucker, Shelly (2000) *Among Insurgents, Walking Through Burma*. Delhi: Penguin.

Verghese, B.G. (1996) *India's Northeast Resurgent: Ethnicity, Insurgency, Governance and Development*. Delhi: Konark Pub.

Wallace, Paul (2007) 'Countering Terrorist Movements in India: Kashmir and Khalistan', in Robert J. Art and Louise Richardson (eds), *Democracy and Counterterrorism Lessons from the Past*. Washington, DC: United States Institute of Peace, pp. 425–82.

Weinstein, Jeremy M. (2007) *Inside Rebellion: The Politics of Insurgent Violence*. Cambridge: Cambridge University Press.

17

INSURGENCY IN AFGHANISTAN

Antonio Giustozzi

The state of knowledge

Origins

Although much has been written on the post-2001 insurgency in Afghanistan, little of it is systematic in its analysis or has been carefully researched on the ground. The history of the Taliban and how they emerged as a powerful insurgent movement is however quite clear. The best analytical discussion of the Taliban before 9/11 and their transformation into a regime is in Dorronsoro (2005). The Taliban's origins are important to understand their modus operandi after 2001, because the nature of the movement has changed but not wholly transformed. The clerical nature of the pre-2001 Taliban is very clear, for example, and the core of the Taliban as an insurgent movement remains clerical in essence. Before 2001, the Taliban had little experience in handling a guerrilla war. Most of its members had been active in the 1980s jihad against the Soviet Army and the pro-Soviet government, but mainly in junior roles, leading small fronts of fighters and usually not the best organized ones. By 2001, the year when their regime was overthrown by American intervention, the Taliban had expanded their original alliance of southern clerical networks into a nationwide 'network of networks', a development which would later help them organize an insurgency on a much larger scale. Similarly the history of the relationship between the Taliban and al-Qaeda until 2001 may be relevant to understand post-2001 developments (Lia 2008; Al-Masri 2005; Brown 2010).

The collapse of the Taliban regime has not been studied in detail, but it seems to have occurred faster than anticipated by the Taliban and their Arab allies. The solidity of the network and of a range of external alliances with militias and former warlords in the face of American onslaught had clearly been overestimated. After the collapse followed a time of demoralization and loss of direction, which lasted some months. By the summer of 2002 there were already signs of the leadership trying to re-organize, although initially with little success. Helped by friendly Pakistani networks, which contributed help and volunteers to start military operations across the Pakistani border, the Taliban managed to gradually re-establish a sense of faith in the movement among a portion of their old supporters, and started actively recruiting a new generation in the madrassas and refugee camps of Pakistan. Although largely under-reported, the insurgency steadily grew from a very low base throughout 2002–5. The year 2006 is usually seen as the turning point, when the pace of violence and of the spread of the insurgency acceler-ated dramatically (Giustozzi 2008). From 2006 onwards the insurgency has arguably been growing without interruption. At the time of writing (August 2010) a debate was still going on, whether 2010 represented yet another year of further expansion for the insurgency or whether the American 'surge', started in 2009, had succeeded in containing the insurgency. In any case, the indicators of violence all point to a steady growth of the insurgency year after year without interruptions.

The dimensions of the insurgency

The overall map of the insurgency, its spread and its composition are quite well known. The dominant force within the insurgency is the Army of the Islamic Emirate of Afghanistan, popularly known as the Taliban. It accounts for about 80 per cent of the total force of the political insurgents. The second group in terms of strength is Hizb-I Islami, which accounts for about 10 per cent, but has also links to many former members who operate as part of the Taliban, particularly away from eastern Afghanistan where the organizational structure of the party is strongest. The rest of the insurgency is largely marginal: a couple of small Salafi groups in eastern Afghanistan, with a strength of no more than a few hundred each; some independent commanders here and there, mostly in western Afghanistan, and a number of non-Afghan organizations operating inside Afghan territory. These include mostly Pakistani groups, of which the most active is Lashkar-e Taiba, and Central Asian groups, of which the main one is the Islamic Movement of Uzbekistan (IMU). The contribution of these groups to the 'jihad' in Afghanistan is significant mainly at the local level; eastern Afghanistan for most Pakistani groups and northern Afghanistan for the IMU. Their contribution appears valuable mostly in terms of their indirect support: training seems to be provided to Taliban by both the IMU and the Pakistani groups. Some complex attacks are carried out with the infusion of groups of spe-cialists from Pakistan, which contribute skills in sniping, explosive and team weapons (Gius-tozzi 2008; Giustozzi and Reuter 2010).

The size of the insurgency is more or less clear too, although there are different ways of counting. The number of full-time fighters in mid 2010 was around 30,000, of which up to 4,000 may have been foreigners; there are also tens of thousands of part-time fighters, facilita-tors, political cadres, of which almost none are foreigners. There are also tens of thousands of men active in illegal armed groups, which are not directly connected to the insurgency, although sometimes may entertain relations with them. Mostly the latter groups avoid fight-ing the security forces and the foreign troops, but sometimes clash with the police. The mass of part-timers, facilitators and political cadres are the least discussed component of the insur-gency, because they either operate in the shadows or are local in character. Part-timers might sometimes be seen by the Taliban as integral part of the movement, but other times they might be seen as external allies mobilized by communities in defence of their own interests. The degree of involvement of each community can vary greatly, from full Talibanization, where pro-Taliban clerics take over control of the community, to a superficial alliance of community elders who have little to share with the Taliban's ideology and worldview. There is some evidence that many community elders might have allowed the Taliban into their ter-ritory initially as a way of signalling their displeasure to the central government, which has been neglecting local elders since its inception in 2001. The Taliban, however, have demon-strated themselves as quite adept at manipulating local elders for their own purposes and once they establish themselves in a region it has proven difficult to get rid of them (Giustozzi 2008, 2009a, 2009b).

The size of the post–2001 insurgency compared to the 1980s can be a useful benchmark of the overall picture in Afghanistan. Around the peak of that insurgency, there were around 75–90,000 full-time insurgents, with a total of 250,000 active and another 500,000 in non–state armed groups which were not particularly interested in fighting the Soviet Army, but which contributed to the general climate of insecurity. In other words, the size of the insurgency now might be around a third of the size it had reached in the 1980s. The Taliban suffer from some disadvantages compared to the mujahidin of the 1980s: the level of international support is far from having reached the same level (it amounted to US$ billions per year in the 1980s and is in the low hundreds of millions now) and the refugee population in Pakistan, a privileged recruitment ground for insurgents then and now, is much smaller than it was in the 1980s. The quality of the weaponry in the Taliban's hands is also modest; the Kalashnikovs are not as effective now as they were in the 1980s, because bullet-proof vests have become the standard in NATO armies; anti-tank missiles and Manpads were available in relatively large quantities in the 1980s and are hardly available at all now; plastic mines (hard to detect) were also available in very large numbers then and are not available now. Given these constraints and the greater availability of financial resources to NATO (compared to the Soviet Union) as well as the greater commitment of troops to Afghanistan from 2009 onwards, the Taliban could be said to have done remarkably well as an insurgent movement (Giustozzi 2000, 2008).

The structure and organization

Where controversy begins is in the discussion of the internal structure of the insurgency. While Hizb-I Islami is clearly separate from the Taliban as an organization, the relationship of different Taliban networks to each other and to the leadership of the Islamic Emirate is still very much a matter of debate. Undoubtedly, two of the three main regional councils of the insurgents affiliated with the Islamic Emirate have a large degree of autonomy: the MiranShah Shura and the Peshawar Shura. The former is dominated by the Haqqanis, to the extent of being often referred to as the 'Haqqani network', while the latter has a strong Islamist presence (as opposed to the 'fundamentalism' of the Taliban) (Giustozzi 2009, 2010b; JTSM 2009a, 2009b).

It is also obvious that the insurgents have been trying to develop a system of shadow government. Although on the whole still primitive, there is a consensus that some aspects of it are helping the insurgents to gain a degree of legitimacy; in particular the judiciary sponsored by the Taliban seems to be very popular, not least because the Taliban quickly and ruthlessly implement any sentence or determination. The system of governors put in place by the Taliban has not had much of an impact, except in playing a role in dispute resolution (Giustozzi 2010b; Dressler and Forsberg 2009).

Much information about the leadership of the Taliban is available in the public domain, although the constant changes in the line-up make it difficult to monitor accurately the exact composition at any given time. In general the Taliban are not a very secretive movement; they tend to be quite keen to circulate information and in recent times they have even been encouraged by the leadership to open up to journalists. Much communication occurs openly and is regularly intercepted by the International Security Alliance Force (ISAF); in the aggregate this information potentially provides a lot of information about the way the Taliban operate, although probably ISAF's capacity to process it might not be sufficient. Several Taliban leaders and hundreds of mid and low-rank commanders have lost their lives due to this relative transparency of the Taliban.

Not as much is known about the other components of the insurgency, except to some extent Hizb-I Islami. The further from the northeast, the weaker the the organizational presence of the party. Strong in Kunar, Laghman, Kapisa and Nangarhar, it is only able to mobilize pockets in the southeast and does not exist at all in the south, where Hizb–I Islami activists operate under Taliban control. In the 1980s and 1990s, Hizb–I Islami fielded a comparatively centralized and disciplined system of command and control from the centre; this does not seem to exist any longer and Hizb–I Islami appears to operate in the field in a way similar to that of the Taliban, centred on networks and the charisma of individual commanders. Most of the old Hizb–I Islami networks around Afghanistan have not been remobilized into the insurgency; notably not even in Nangarhar, where the party is still popular among the youth. In part these non–mobilized networks even cooperate with the government or with international organizations: quite a few former Hizb–I Islami members are today ministers, governors, chiefs of police, etc. This has led to allegations that some of these individuals have been cooperating with the insurgency. Hizb–I Islami has been expanding since 2002, but despite its ambitions is not getting any closer to be able to compete for the hegemony of the insurgency with the Taliban; its organizational weakness means that much of its insurgent potential does not benefit the party but the Taliban; some estimates suggest that a good quarter of the insurgents or more in some southern provinces have a background in Hizb–I Islami (Giustozzi 2008; Ruttig 2009).

The inner organization of the Taliban, as already mentioned, is one of the topics most debated in the literature. The so-called Haqqani network is often seen as a separate organization, but some authors contest this. The Haqqani network seems to have its own sources of funding, but the level of cooperation with other Taliban networks is very high. Although the Haqqanis are often believed to have been the main sponsors of suicide terrorism in Afghanistan after the death of Mullah Dadullah, as far as the actual implementation of attacks is concerned the different networks seem to cooperate without problems. There are sometimes some significant ideological differences among Taliban networks and other components of the insurgency: as already mentioned, Hizb–I Islami's Islamism differs from the fundamentalism of the Taliban with regards to women's rights, elections (both of which the Taliban reject and Hizb accepts) and the role of the clergy (which Hizb–I Islami tends to minimize). Within the Taliban, some members have an Islamist background as well, particularly in the Peshawar Shura. Other sources of friction within the Taliban concern tribal rivalries (thinking tribally is very deeply rooted particularly in the south) and personal jealousies (Giustozzi 2008, 2009a; Ruttig 2009; JTSM 2009b).

Certainly the Taliban operate as a decentralized movement; the field commanders are given some general directives, a set of rules of behaviour, a certain amount of supplies, and a lot of leeway on how to operate tactically. The tendency of the Taliban to form tactical alliances with bandits, communities and other illegal armed groups has produced even more confusion with regard to their operations, leading many observers to believe that there is little role for a central leadership apart from offering incentives to fight, mostly economic ones. However, others have pointed out that the deployment of cadres far away from their provinces, the ability of the insurgency to expand gradually following the development of supply lines and the ability to concentrate force on a number of occasions all point to a strategic vision which must be embodied in a leadership with a degree of overall authority. The role of foreign advisers among the Taliban is also contentious; all that can be said is that the relative sophistication of the Taliban's strategy seems uncharacteristic of a movement which had little experience of actual guerrilla warfare until 2002 (Giustozzi 2008, 2009a, 2010b; Ruttig 2009).

The exact organization of the leadership is not fully clear yet. There is a Leadership Council, which leads the Islamic Emirate and was originally based in Quetta although it seems to have moved now, there are abut ten commissions dependent on it, and then there are four regional military councils (Shuras): Quetta, MiranShah, Peshawar and Gerdi Jangal. The four councils are in charge of managing military operations; provincial commissions deal with the political side of operations at the provincial level. What is not clear is the exact attribution of responsibilities and powers; the situation gets even more confused by the fact that there is some overlap between the individuals staffing the various commissions and councils. The extent to which the commissions and the councils carry authority as opposed to the individual leaders is not fully clear; documents are issued by the councils and by the commissions but Taliban rank-and-file tend to refer to individual leaders as sources of authority (Giustozzi 2008, 2010b; Roggio 2010a).

The recruitment

The recruitment base of the insurgents is rather well known, both in geographic and social terms. The Islamic Emirate mainly draws support in the south and in isolated pockets in the northeast, southeast and east and among clerics and religious students everywhere in the country. Hizb-I Islami largely recruits in the east, mostly among students and among families previously linked to the party when it was a much larger and powerful organization in the 1980s and 1990s. Mostly in the south, the Taliban have established strong connections with a number of local communities, which have mobilized to fight on their side. Over half of Afghanistan was in 2010 affected by the politicized insurgency, while illegal armed groups were reactivating themselves almost everywhere, contributing to the chaos (Giustozzi 2008 and 2009a).

As the insurgency spreads, the picture gets more complicated in terms of base of recruitment and constituencies. As of 2010, about 90 per cent of the Taliban's full-time fighters were Pashtuns; since 2006 the percentage of Pashtuns among the full-time fighters seems to have declined by just a few percentage points, from 95 per cent. However, these percentages do not do justice to the spread of the Taliban to northern Afghanistan. In some areas, by 2009 significant recruitment of non-Pashtuns such as Uzbeks, Tajiks, Turkmen and Aimaqs was going on throughout the north and northeast of Afghanistan. The recruitment of Tajiks was also confirmed in areas like Logar and Ghazni, where Tajiks live mixed with Pashtuns. The potential for further expansion of the insurgency is inevitably a matter of controversy. Until 2009, few observers believed that the Taliban could really recruit to any significant extent among non-Pashtuns; scepticism remains despite their first signs of success in this regard. The Taliban are known to have been recruiting Tajiks, Uzbeks and others in Pakistani madrassas since the 1990s; the expanding capabilities and logistics of the movement from 2006 onwards have enabled them to deploy some of these old cadres in northern and northeastern Afghanistan to sound out local potential for recruitment and identify suitable pockets where to focus efforts. Once again, it appears that the cadre structure is really what matters within the Taliban: the should and skeleton of the insurgency. Everything else rotates around it (Giustozzi and Reuter 2010; Giustozzi 2010c).

External support

Although the external support received by the insurgents is still a matter of debate at the diplomatic level, almost all analysts agree that a very substantial level of support has been provided since 2002 and increasingly so by the Pakistani authorities; recently leaked documents have only confirmed what nearly everybody was already arguing. Evidence of support coming from the Iranian Revolutionary Guards has also been mounting during 2009 and 2010. Otherwise, there is an agreement that the insurgents have been receiving support from jihadist networks in the Muslim world and particularly in the Gulf and that they raise a growing amount of tax inside Afghanistan and among Afghan communities in Pakistan and in the United Arab Emirates (Waldman 2010b; Giustozzi 2008; Gohel 2010).

Equipment

The equipment of the insurgents is not very sophisticated by any standard. Standard weapons are Kalashnikovs of various models, Soviet machine guns (mostly PKM and some DSchK), rocket launchers (RPG) and increasingly precision rifles (Dragunov); mortars and recoilless guns are also sometimes used. Improvised Explosive Devices (IEDs) have been used on an increasingly large scale since 2006 but their technology has not changed much. The insurgents prefer to adapt tactically than to invest in advanced technology. Over the last two years anti-aircraft machine guns have become increasingly common (ZSU-1 and -2); the use of Manpads is sometimes reported but rarely confirmed. It seems to occur occasionally, with equipment left over from previous wars or purchased on the black market in small quantities (Giustozzi 2008).

Aims

The political aims of the Taliban are only understood up to a certain point. There is no question that they aim to get foreign troops out of the country, that they consider to be fighting a jihad and that they oppose most of the changes that have occurred in Afghanistan after 2001. The official line of the insurgents is that they struggle to re-establish the legitimate government of Afghanistan that is the Islamic Emirate led by Mullah Omar. This line seems to be accepted by their allies too, not only the IMU and the Pakistani jihadists, but also Hizb-I Islami, although it is not clear how deeply heartfelt this position is. It is known that Hizb-I Islami uses the same 'judicial system' of the Taliban at least in a number of locations. The Taliban are ambiguous with regard to any claim to return to the pre-Enduring Freedom status quo, perhaps because they realize how this would make any alliance with other groups, whether tactical or strategic, more difficult. In the Taliban propaganda the point that they are re-fighting a jihad like in the 1980s against the Soviets is stressed continuously; appeals to other 'mujahidin' who fought in the 1980s jihad are constantly repeated.

The Taliban seem to see the large pool of active and inactive non-state armed groups in the country, mostly staffed by former mujahidin, as a key potential reservoir of new recruits. Starting from 2006, they have enjoyed some success in attracting former mujahidin who had not been previously involved with the Taliban. Although those who joined up with the Taliban only represent a small percentage of the non-state armed groups in the country, they have had an impact in specific areas. They mostly come from Hizb-I Islami (both the Hekmatyar and the Khalis wings of the party), Jamiat-i Islami and Ittehad-i Islami (Giustozzi, 2009a, 2010b; Giustozzi and Reuter 2010; Ruttig 2009; Tellis 2010).

The relationship with Hizb-I Islami is also of some importance in order to establish the credibility of the Taliban's claim that they are open and even keen to ally with other Islamic groups. The alliance with Hizb-I Islami was threatened by a major clash in Baghlan province in 2010, where the local front of Hizb-I Islami was virtually annihilated by the Taliban. Opinion remains divided with regard to the long-term consequences of this clash; other smaller clashes have occurred in Kapisa, Logar and other places, usually as a result of local rivalries.

The relationship with al-Qaeda is probably not one of the most important aspects of the Taliban insurgency, but attracts a disproportionate amount of media and policy interest, not least because the relationship with al-Qaeda was the cause of American intervention in the first place. If al-Qaeda had been reduced to a negligible presence on the ground, the intervention would lose its original justification. We know from the memoirs of former jihadists that the pre-9/11 relationship between Taliban and al-Qaeda was not smooth; Mullah Omar might have been upset by Bin Laden's behaviour and the disgrace it brought to the Taliban, although he seems to have kept cooperating with al-Qaeda after 9/11, probably because of the funding al-Qaeda could offer to help remobilizing the Taliban. The role of al-Qaeda in running the insurgency in Afghanistan seems to have declined gradually; US intelligence sources indicate that perhaps just 100 al-Qaeda operatives were left in Afghanistan by 2010 (Brown 2010; Al-Masri 2005; Lia 2008; Roggio 2010b). Opinion was still divided in 2010 over the Taliban's relationship with al-Qaeda, although a growing number of analysts believe that al-Qaeda was by 2010 a marginal force in Afghanistan. Denouncing al-Qaeda is one of the preconditions that Western negotiators are likely to place in the event of a peace deal being discussed.

An accurate mapping of the Taliban, of their internal currents and of any internal differences can only be done through extensive fieldwork, which is difficult and expensive under the current circumstances. The most pressing question at the time of writing concerned the inclination (or disinclination) of the Taliban towards negotiations with the Afghan government and their vulnerability to buy-off offers from ISAF and the Afghan government. As for the first question, the signals sent by the Taliban until the summer of 2010 were mixed, sometimes indicating a readiness to negotiate, but also showing inflexibility about preconditions and terms to be offered. Analysts remained therefore much divided over whether the Taliban were likely to make a deal or not (Giustozzi 2010b; Masadykov et al. 2010; Waldman 2010a).

Strengths and weaknesses

The secret of the Taliban's success is still a matter of debate. One explanation is simply that democracies are not very good at fighting wars away from home, where arguing that a defensive war is going on is hard sell back on the home front. As far as the Taliban themselves are concerned, one factor that might explain their resilience has been their decentralized structure, which limits their ability to develop sophisticated strategies, but at the same time allows for a very high degree of resilience. Great damage can be taken by the Taliban without long-term harm being inflicted. The availability of a sanctuary in Pakistan (and according to some views increasingly in Iran too) is certainly a factor of strength for the Taliban, although as argued above the same factor was present in even greater strength in the 1980s.

There is plenty of evidence that the Taliban have been facilitated since 2002 by the Pakistani security agencies, particularly the Frontier Corps and the ISI, but the actual extent of Pakistani support is unclear. The degree of dependence of the Taliban on Pakistan is another issue that has been discussed with increasing frequency from 2009 onwards. Iranian supplies, although still much smaller than Pakistan's, seemed by 2009 to have reached the stage where they could affect relations between the Taliban and Pakistan, emboldening the former (Waldman 2010b; Giustozzi 2008).

The Taliban also enjoy a reliable recruitment ground in the madrassas of Afghanistan and particularly Pakistan, which not only produce a steady output of recruits but also guarantee their 'high quality' in terms of commitment and indoctrination. Perhaps this is the greatest strength of the Taliban, because a homogenous core of cadres and fighters is important to maintain the functionality of the movement in a situation where 'bureaucratic' command and control is very difficult. Oversight of operations on the ground cannot take place effectively through occasional radio or mobile phone calls, because of ISAF listening all the time. Messengers and couriers are employed and a sophisticated 'mail system' has been developed, but inevitably this is not a technology that can allow micromanagement on the ground. Decentralization can only allow an insurgent movement to aim for strategic targets and the leadership to retain a degree of control if there is a pool of committed cadres large enough to be present in all areas affected by the insurgency. It could indeed be argued that the production of cadres by the Taliban has been the main factor enabling them to expand; their presence allows the Taliban to exploit local griev- ances and social discontent in an ever growing number of corners of the country (Giustozzi 2008, 2010b).

The nature of the insurgency is still largely a matter of debate. Sometimes the Taliban are described as a nationalist reaction to foreign presence, other times as an umbrella organization offering a multitude of disgruntled communities the possibility of mobilizing for collective action, other times still as a Ghilzai tribal revolt against the dominance of Durrani tribes in gov- ernment (Johnson and Mason 2007; Ruttig 2010; JTSM 2009a; Giustozzi 2008).

Recent writings on the Taliban are increasingly exposing the nature of their organization as a clerical movement, which pragmatically allies with local causes in order to gather strength against the government and the foreign forces. It is from the clergy that the 'cadres' of the movement are taken. Certainly xenophobia (more than nationalism) plays a role in the recruit- ment of rank-and-file fighters, who are often illiterate village or urban boys (Giustozzi 2008, 2009a, 2010b).

The impact of counterinsurgency on the Taliban was the object of bitter debates from 2006 onwards. Several counterinsurgency approaches and strategies have been applied during this lapse of time, which makes assessing their impact difficult. One relatively consistent effort in counterinsurgency since late 2007 has been the deliberate targeting of Taliban commanders; this is a relatively uncontroversial approach, but the degree of its success is disputed. There is no question that every year hundreds of Taliban commanders have been killed since at least 2008, accounting for a large percentage of the field leadership. The Taliban clearly have been able to replace the losses, but the average age and experience of the new commanders has been steadily declining, until it stabilized at around 20, a very low level. The matter of dispute is whether this decline in the average age of commanders represents a sign of crisis of the insurgents, or not. Population-centric counterinsurgency, adopted with great fanfare in 2009, did not outlive its original promoter, Gen. McChrystal. In practice it proved difficult to implement against an adaptive and tactically flexible movement like the Taliban; experiments carried out in Helmand in 2010 did not produce conclusive results, despite the massive (and unsustainable) commitment of troops. In many areas, the Taliban had enough of an underground structure to continue operating even when facing a strong military presence of ISAF and Afghan government forces (Dorronsoro 2010; Keane 2010).

As for the issue of the vulnerability of the Taliban to reconciliation from the bottom, that is the co-optation of individual commanders onto the government side, during 2009 and 2010 there was much optimism in ISAF in this regard. Contacts in the field seemed to be yielding positive answers in many cases, but after a year and a half of intensified engagement, there has still been little to show. Most observers are sceptical about the prospects of luring significant numbers of Taliban cadres away from the insurgency; many of those who recon- ciled in 2002–9 went back to fighting for a variety of reasons, and other regretted having reconciled in the first place. Some factors appeared particularly important in preventing reconciliation efforts from taking off: threats from the Taliban who in many areas maintained an underground structure of cadres and hit teams; the danger of mistreatment and worse from the government security forces, often driven by personal hostility to the Taliban; the desire for high status and recognition, as well as financial packages capable of offsetting the loss of face involved in reconciling and the possible necessity to relocate (Waldman 2010a; Masa- dykov *et al.* 2010; Giustozzi 2010b).

Recommended readings

Dorronsoro, G. (2005) *Revolution Unending*. London: Hurst.

Dressler, J. and Forsberg, C. (2009) *The Quetta Shura Taliban in Southern Afghanistan: Organization, Operations, and Shadow Governance*. Washington, DC: Institute for the Study of War.

Giustozzi, A. (2008) *Koran, Kalashnikov and Laptop: The Rise of the Neo-Taliban Insurgency in Afghanistan*. London: C. Hurst & Co.; New York: Columbia University Press.

Giustozzi, A. (ed.) (2009) *Decoding the New Taliban: Insights from the Afghan Field*. London: C. Hurst & Co; New York: Columbia University Press.

Ruttig, Thomas (2009) 'The Other Side: Dimensions of the Afghan Insurgency: Causes, Actors and Approaches to "Talks"', Kabul: Afghan Analysts Network.

Ruttig, Thomas (2010) *How Tribal Are the Taleban?* Kabul: Afghan Analyst Network.

References

al-Masri, Abu al-Walid (2005) 'The Story of the Afghan Arabs: From the Entry to Afghanistan to the Final Exodus with the Taliban', *Asharq al-Awsat*, 29 June and 1, 6 and 10 July.

Brown, Vahid (2010) 'The Facade of Allegiance: Bin Ladin's Dubious Pledge to Mullah Omar', *CTC Sentinel*, 3 (1).

Dorronsoro, G. (2010) 'Afghanistan: Searching for Political Agreement', Washington, DC: Carnegie.

Dressler, J. and Forsberg, C. (2009) *The Quetta Shura Taliban in Southern Afghanistan: Organization, Operations, and Shadow Governance*. Washington, DC: Institute for the Study of War.

Giustozzi, A. (2000) *War, Politics and Society in Afghanistan, 1978–1992*. London: Hurst.

Giustozzi, A. (2008) *Koran, Kalashnikov and Laptop: The Rise of the Neo-Taliban Insurgency in Afghanistan*. London: C. Hurst & Co.; New York: Columbia University Press.

Giustozzi, A. (2009a) 'One or Many? The Issue of the Taliban's Unity and Disunity', Brief N. 48, Bradford: Pakistan Security Research Unit (PSRU).

Giustozzi, A. (ed.) (2009b) *Decoding the New Taliban: Insights from the Afghan Field*. London: C. Hurst & Co; New York: Columbia University Press.

Giustozzi A. (2010a) 'Afghanistan', in Barry Rubin (ed.), *Guide to Islamist Movements*. Armonk: ME Sharpe.

Giustozzi, A. (2010b) *Negotiating with the Taliban: Issues and Prospects*. New York: The Century Foundation.

Giustozzi, A. (2010c) *The Taliban beyond the Pashtuns*, the Afghanistan papers no. 5. Waterloo (Ontario): CIGI.

Giustozzi, A. and Reuter, C. (2010) 'The Northern Front: The Afghan Insurgency Spreading beyond the Pashtuns', Briefing Paper, Kabul: Afghan Analyst Network.

Gohel, Sajjan M. (2010) 'Iran's Ambiguous Role in Afghanistan', *CTC Sentinel*, 3 (3).

JTSM Jane's Terrorism and Security Monitor (2009a) 'Taliban Chain of Command', November.

JTSM Jane's Terrorism and Security Monitor (2009b) 'Unravelling Haqqani's Net', 30 June.

Johnson, Thomas H. and Mason, M. Chris (2007) 'Understanding the Taliban and Insurgency in Afghanistan', *Orbis* (winter).

Keane, Jack (2010) 'Why the Surge Worked in Iraq and its Implications for Afghanistan', The Henry Jackson Society, 11 June. Available at: www.henryjacksonsociety.org/stories.asp?id=1613.

Lia, B. (2008) *Architect of Global Jihad: The Life of Al Qaeda Strategist Abu Mus'ab Al-Suri*. London: Hurst.

Masadykov, T. *et al.* (2010) 'Negotiating with the Taliban: Toward a Solution for the Afghan Conflict', Working Paper 66.2. London: Crisis States Research Centre (LSE).

Roggio, Bill (2010a) 'The Afghan Taliban's Top Leaders', *The Long War Journal*, 23 (February).

Roggio, Bill (2010b) 'Analysis: Al Qaeda Maintains an Extensive Network in Afghanistan', 29 July.

Ruttig, Thomas (2009) 'The Other Side: Dimensions of the Afghan Insurgency: Causes, Actors and Approaches to "Talks"', Kabul: Afghan Analysts Network.

Ruttig, Thomas (2010) *How Tribal Are the Taleban?* Kabul: Afghan Analyst Network.

Tellis, Ashley J. (2010) 'Beradar, Pakistan, and the Afghan Taliban: What Gives?, Washington, DC: Carnegie.

Waldman, M. (2010a) *Golden Surrender*. Kabul: Afghan Analysts Network.

Waldman, M. (2010b) *The Sun in the Sky: The Relationship between Pakistan's ISI and Afghan Insurgents*. London: Crisis States Research Centre (LSE).

18

INSURGENT MOVEMENTS IN PAKISTAN

Shehzad H. Qazi

Introduction

In its brief history of 64 years, Pakistan has already faced four prominent insurgent conflicts: Bengali nationalist-separatist rebellion in East Pakistan (1971), low-intensity Baloch nationalist insurgency (1948–present) with heightened conflict between 1974 and 1977, Muhajir nationalist insurgency in Karachi (1990–9), and now the Pakistani Taliban insurgency in the Federally Administered Tribal Areas of Pakistan (FATA) and Khyber Pakhtunkhwa (KP) (2001–present). In addition, Pakistan faces some militant separatism in Sindh and Gilgit-Baltistan. Out of these four, the most successful movement was that of the Bengali nationalists who were able to secure a separate homeland for themselves at the end of the civil war.

The outbreak of multiple insurgencies in Pakistan is not anomalous. This characteristic it shares with other states in its neighbourhood in South and Central Asia. Moreover, it also shares this phenomenon with other developing or under-developed countries of the world where state institutions are weak and armed conflict persists.

In this chapter I explore the current Pakistani Taliban insurgency and keep the focus geographically circumscribed to the tribal areas and KP. Moreover, I limit the attention to insurgent groups that are directly engaged in challenging or resisting the Pakistani state and its armed forces in this region, i.e. the Pakistani Taliban, Punjabi Taliban and al-Qaeda. It should be noted that I use the term Pakistani Taliban and Taliban interchangeably to refer to the same conglomeration of militant outfits.

The chapter begins with a brief history of the conflict, tracing the rise of the Pakistani Taliban to the participation of the Pashtun tribesmen in the fight against invading US and international forces in Afghanistan and the radicalization that subsequently took place as al-Qaeda re-settled within the tribal areas. The dynamics of the conflict are then discussed, followed by a survey of the actors involved in the insurgency, with special attention paid to strategic and tactical collaboration that takes place amongst them.

Next, the structure and organization of the Pakistani Taliban, especially Tehrik-e-Taliban Pakistan (TTP), is explained, with special emphasis on its decentralized nature. I then explain the insurgents' military strategy and discuss observed trends in the tactics used by them. Here I highlight the influence al-Qaeda and Kashmiri groups have had. The chapter then analyses militant recruitment. The use of selective incentives, coercion and the ability to exploit grievances

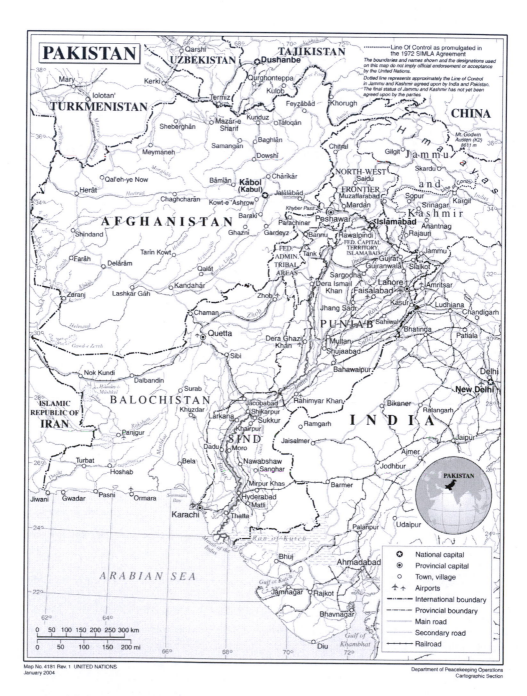

Figure 18.1 Pakistan.

against the state are three essential factors of the Taliban's recruitment strategy. Finally, I make some observations about the nature of the Taliban's governance, pointing out that social repression, political authoritarianism and economic predation are three major characteristics of Taliban rule. The provision of quick and swift justice, however, remains one area of service that has at times made the insurgents popular.

Insurgency in FATA

Origins

Several authors (Hussain 2008; Gul 2010b; Hussain 2010; Rana *et al.* 2010) have now narrated the rise of the Pakistani rebels and in this chapter the history is summarized only to provide a background for the subsequent analysis of the insurgency. Whereas the Tehrik-e-Taliban Pakistan (Student Movement of Pakistan) was officially established in 2007, its members had been involved in militancy against the US–NATO Forces and the Pakistan Army since 2002. Many leading figures of the Pakistani Taliban have also been active inside Afghanistan during the Soviet-Afghan War, the 1990s Taliban movement, and the anti-US–NATO resistance militias of 2001. The origins of the Pakistani rebels can be traced from this period.

Following the US invasion and bombing of Afghanistan in 2001 the senior leadership of the Afghan Taliban and al-Qaeda escaped into Pakistan's tribal areas to seek refuge. Along with them came hundreds of Afghan fighters and al-Qaeda's Arab, Chechen, Uzbek, East Asian and Sudanese insurgents. According to Zahid Hussain 'bin Laden's men distributed millions of dollars among tribal elders in return for shelter'. Most of the two groups' leadership and cadre escaped to South Waziristan where they were offered protection by the Ahmedzai Wazir tribe, who after two decades of engagement had become sympathetic towards both the Afghan Taliban and al-Qaeda (Hussain 2008; Rana *et al.* 2010).

By this time thousands of Pakistani Pashtun tribesmen had also gone to Afghanistan to fight the invading US and NATO forces. Nek Mohammad of the Ahmedzai Wazir tribe and Abdullah Mehsud of the Saleemikhel Mehsud tribe were two notable fighters who would later also resist the Pakistan Army. Nek Mohammad was a veteran of the Soviet-Afghan War who like Abdullah Mehsud had also fought alongside the 1990s Afghan Taliban movement. Another Pashtun cleric, Sufi Mohammad, leader of the Tehrik-e-Nifaz-e-Shariat-e-Mohammadi (Movement for Enforcement of *Shariah* Law) took close to 10,000 young boys from Swat with him to Afghanistan to fight the invading forces in 2001. At least 3,000 of them were killed and the remaining captured inside Afghanistan or sent back to Pakistan (Hussain 2008; Abbas 2009).

The rise of the Pakistan's Pashtun tribal militants can be seen most discernibly from these two developments. To resist the US-led invasion and protect their co-ethnics and fellow tribal members Pakistani Pashtun tribesmen began participating in militant activities inside Afghanistan. In addition to the individual radicalization of these tribesmen, a culture of militancy was cultivated – merely revived in some ways – inside FATA by the Afghan Taliban and al-Qaeda fighters who were forced to flee there because of the US-led invasion. To organize an insurgency in Afghanistan Mullah Omar and Mullah Dadullah got in touch with tribal leaders in FATA in 2002 to recruit Pakistani tribesmen and *madrassah* students to fight in Afghanistan. According to Behuria (2007), the Afghan Taliban were interested in creating a Taliban chapter inside FATA to sustain the movement (Giustozzi 2007). Furthermore, al-Qaeda gave large sums of money to locals to lease their compounds for training camps and command and control centres within FATA. al-Qaeda also began recruiting local Pashtun tribesmen and paid each rebel around $250 a month (Hussain 2008). Whereas these two factors helped militarize and radicalize the locals, it was the 2002 invasion of the Pakistani Army to root out al-Qaeda that catalysed widespread militancy and helped create full-scale rebellion in FATA.

Under pressure from the US government, the Pakistan Army entered Tirah Valley in Khyber Agency and Shawal Valley in North Waziristan and South Waziristan in 2002 (initially with the permission of tribal elders) intending to capture or eliminate al-Qaeda operatives who were mainly foreigners. Pro-bin Laden sentiment was quite high in the tribal areas and the US invasion had caused intense anger amongst Pashtun tribesmen. Military action in South Waziristan thus turned the tribal elders hostile to the Army. They refused to hand over foreign fighters and the subsequent fight between the Pakistan Army and foreign al-Qaeda insurgents turned into a combat between the Pakistan Army and rebel tribesmen. The Army's decision to impose collective punishment by demolishing the houses of defiant tribesmen and seizing their property increased anger. Many Waziri tribesmen had been active as guerrilla fighters in the Soviet-Afghan War and by this time many of these tribesmen had become members of Islamist organizations (Hussain 2008). Nek Mohammad was one such fighter, and soon after the invasion he mobilized armed resistance against the Pakistan Army. Heavy resistance also came from the Zali Khel clan of the Ahmedzai Wazir tribe and later, as mentioned, by the Mehsud of South Waziristan. Civilian casualties increased anger within the larger public, creating support for the rebel movement (Hussain 2008; Kilcullen 2009).

The insurgency, which was initially limited to North and South Waziristan, then spread over the next few years to all of FATA. The Pakistan Army suffered casualties and desertions arising from the troops' lack of training, low morale and ideological opposition to the war. Pakistan, at the time both unable and unwilling to execute a counterinsurgency in the tribal regions and lacking domestic support for the war, did not hold ground that was cleared and signed several ceasefire agreements with the militants between 2004 and 2009. This allowed militants to regroup and increase their control in the region (Hussain 2010; Abbas in Gartenstein-Ross and May 2010). Moreover, between 2002 and 2006 several local rebels groups had been formed in the seven agencies of FATA and Swat District. These rebels gathered in a secret meeting and on 13 December 2007 announced the formation of the umbrella group Tehrik-e-Taliban Pakistan which would coordinate their activities against US and NATO forces in Afghanistan and the Pakistan Army in FATA and Khyber Pakhtunkhwa (Abbas 2009). By mid 2007 Swat District had also been taken over by the rebels and by early 2009 the insurgency had spread to Dir and Buner districts, which are merely 60 miles from Islamabad.

Dimensions of the conflict

The conflict in FATA is neither simply a tribal revolt nor a violent movement of criminals, thugs and the mafia. It is also not just a militant Islamist movement. The conflict features multiple actors and agendas and subsequently has multiple and often overlapping dimensions.

First, the war has a significant tribal component. This conflict has featured strife between various tribes and the Pakistani state, inter/intra-tribal conflicts, and fighting between state-backed tribal militias and the rebels. For example, the Waziri and Mehsud tribes were both fighting the Pakistan Army since 2002. Nevertheless, in 2007 a rift happened between Baitullah Mehsud and Mullah Nazir, after which he and Hafiz Gul Bahadar split and formed the Muqami Tehrik-e-Taliban (Local Taliban Movement) in Waziristan. Their goal was 'to defend the Wazir tribes interests in North and South Waziristan' (Abbas 2009). Moreover, the Pakistani government has sponsored tribal militias and groups, such as that of Qari Zainuddin Mehsud and Haji Turkistan Bhittani, to fight the TTP (Nawaz 2009).

This pattern of conflict is by no means a new development. Ahmed's (1983) work illuminates reasons and patterns of intra-tribal conflict, especially between the Wazir and Mehsud tribes. Moreover, Johnson and Mason (2008) have also pointed out, this region has seen several examples of charismatic religious leaders waging insurgencies against invading powers. Thus, they argue, the current insurgency is a mere contemporary manifestation of a historically recurrent pattern.

Second, the insurgency in FATA has a strong link to transnational Islamist militancy. Leaders and factions of the Afghan Taliban, such as Gulbuddin Hekmatyar and Hizb-I-Islami, Jalaluddin and Sirajuddin Haqqani and their Haqqani Network, and the Islamic Movement of Uzbekistan (IMU) operate out of FATA (2009c; Abbas 2009). Moreover, the Pakistani Taliban are allies of al-Qaeda and its fighters participate in the insurgency against the Pakistan Army. While the relationship between the locals of FATA and al-Qaeda dates back to the days of the Soviet-Afghan War (Rana *et al.* 2010) its presence in the tribal areas is also part of a global strategy to seek sanctuary in conflict zones, align with groups with long-standing grievances against their governments, and exploit those fissures to gain control (Kilcullen 2009).

Third, FATA features an extensive black economy and the insurgency, especially in Khyber and Bajaur, is heavily enmeshed with crime and criminal syndicates. Drug trafficking, gunrunning and illegal arms and ammunitions trade, foreign currency counterfeiting, car theft and 'custom-free' smuggling of goods are major illicit trades in the region. Smugglers and criminal gangs predominate the region and often attack NATO supply cargoes and steal the fuel, clothing and foodstuffs, selling them later on the black market (Gul 2010b). The Taliban have also been smuggling timber, weapons and narcotics (Rana *et al.* 2010). Many locals have also benefited by sheltering illegal foreign fighters and providing them with food at very high costs. Others have leased their houses and compounds to al-Qaeda to use them as training centres (Hussain 2008).

Fourth, the conflict in Kurram features an overlapping sectarian and inter-tribal dynamic, where the Shia Turi tribe is fighting the Sunni Banghash tribe. The Punjabi Taliban have intervened and attacked the Turi tribe and have long blocked off the tribe's access to basic commodities. Similarly, Orakzai features Sunni–Shia violence as well, while Khyber features conflict between Deobandi Lashkar-e-Islami and Barelvi Ansarul Islam militias (Nawaz 2009).

Fifth, there is an element of class warfare to the militancy as well. The conflict has featured the rise to power of poor men belonging to lesser or minor lineages against the traditional control of powerful tribal elders. Profiles of many rebel leaders confirm this. For example, Baitullah Mehsud was a former bus conductor, Hakimullah Mehsud was a village *madrassa* drop out, Maulvi Omar sold perfumes on a vending cart, Mangal Bagh was a truck driver and small-time criminal involved in car-jacking, and Mullah Fazalullah operated ski lifts in Swat. The Soviet-Afghan War spurred this social movement that was reinforced by the US invasion of Afghanistan. Changes in political opportunities and access to resources (economic and military) allowed tribesmen to contest traditional tribal leadership. In FATA, the militants have assassinated over 600 elders to gain control of the political leadership (Nawaz 2009).

Finally, a Maoist/Communist aspect also appeared in the insurgency. Members of the Mazdoor Kissan Party (Peasants and Workers Party) have used violence to air grievances over unequal distribution of land (Nawaz 2009).

Insurgent actors

The tribal areas of Pakistan have become a global militant metropolis. The insurgents operating from and within FATA can be classified into four major groups. These include the Afghan

Taliban, the various groups of the Pakistani Taliban, foreign fighters (primarily al-Qaeda) and the Punjabi Taliban. Given the parameters of this chapter, I focus on the latter three.

The Pakistani Taliban are a collection of roughly 40 al-Qaeda aligned militant groups based inside FATA. The largest of these groups is the umbrella organization, Tehrik-e-Taliban (TTP), currently led by Hakimullah Mehsud. The TTP has provided training and operational guidance for several international terrorists, including Faisal Shahzad, the 'Times Square bomber', and Humam al-Balawi, who bombed a CIA outpost in Afghanistan in 2009 (Hussain 2010). Furthermore, the Pakistan Taliban can be divided into two groups: one that sees the war against Pakistan and its army as a primary pursuit, and participation in the war in Afghanistan as being secondary. The second group emphasizes fighting NATO and ISAF in Afghanistan and argues against fighting with the Pakistan Army. The second group is also closer to the Afghan Taliban, who have repeatedly urged the Pakistani Taliban to focus on the war against the United States inside Afghanistan and not the Pakistan Army. The Pakistan Taliban are a fractured movement and suffer from indiscipline, disagreement and rebel infighting (Abbas 2009). Moreover, like the Afghan Taliban, the Pakistani Taliban are very localized and make decisions based on domestic interests.

A host of foreign fighters belonging to al-Qaeda or allied groups also operate out of Pakistan's tribal areas. Leading members of al-Qaeda, including Ayman Al-Zawahiri and the interim leader Saef Al-Nidal reside in FATA (Mir 2011b). Other notable al-Qaeda leaders such as Abu Faraj al-Libi, Abu Lait el Libi, Abu Jihad al Masri, etc., have all either been killed or arrested in FATA (Gul 2010b; Rana *et al.* 2010). A large number of Arab, Chechen, Sudanese and some Uighur al-Qaeda militants also live and fight in this region. Moreover, the al-Qaeda-aligned Islamic Movement of Uzbekistan (IMU) is another prominent foreign militant organization in the area. IMU operates alongside the Pakistani Taliban and al-Qaeda fighters (Abbas 2009).

Finally, various militant outfits that fought in Kashmir have located to the tribal areas since 2002 when the Musharraf regime curtailed Pakistani sponsorship of the insurgency. For many of the leaders and fighters this is a mere return, as their initial training and battlefield experience took place during the Soviet-Afghan War in either Afghanistan or Pakistan's tribal areas (Rana *et al.* 2010). These groups, which include Lashkar-e-Taiba (LeT), Harkatul-Jihad al Islami (HuJI), Jaish-e-Mohammad (JeM), Lashkar-e-Jhangvi al-Almi (LeJ), Sipah-e-Sahaba Pakistan (SSP) and Harkatul Mujahideen al-Alimi (HuM), amongst others, began referring to themselves collectively as the Punjabi Taliban. With relationships dating to the 1980s, these groups remain operationally aligned to al-Qaeda (Mullick 2010). For example, Ilyas Kashmiri, late

Table 18.1 Estimated strength of insurgents in FATA, Khyber Pakhtunkhwa and other areas of Pakistan (Qazi 2011)

	2002	2004	2006	2010
Pakistani Taliban (all factions)		<40,000	40,000	20,000–25,000
North Waziristan				10,000–15,000
Punjabi Taliban				2,000
Foreign Fighters				
(Arab, Uzbek, Tajik, Chechen, Uighur and Sudanese fighters)	<3,000			9,000–14,000
Total		<40,000	40,000	31,000–41,000
Total Pakistani Taliban				22,000–27,000

leader of HuJI and the 313 Brigade, worked with al-Qaeda and was purportedly its chief for global operations (Shahzad 2009). The Punjabi Taliban mostly carry out operations within Pakistan-proper.

Organization and structure

The organization of militant groups inside FATA can be best understood as a complex web of networks. This web includes the Afghan Taliban – itself composed of at least five major groups – al-Qaeda, IMU, Punjabi Taliban, Pakistani Taliban and various criminal syndicates. Whereas these organizations have their own structures, collaboration for purposes of strategic planning, propaganda and operations is a common feature. The structure of al-Qaeda and the various Kashmiri militant groups has been explained elsewhere (Mullick 2010) and here I focus on briefly explaining the complex structure and organization of the Pakistani Taliban.

As mentioned, the Pakistani Taliban is a conglomeration of roughly 40 militant outfits. Within the Pakistani Taliban, the largest alliance or umbrella group consisting of militants fighting Pakistan is the TTP. The TTP has created a hierarchical organizational structure, but lacks centralized control. It has a *shura* (parliament) that meets to plan tactics and discuss strategies and an *Amir* (president) who recommends and decides the overall strategy of the organization (Abbas 2009). The Taliban structure also features departments and officials with specialized tasks such as propaganda and training for bomb-making and suicide missions (Wolfe 2010). Given its decentralized nature, however, tactical decision-making is mostly undertaken by the participating militant groups and field commanders and is influenced by their own domestic political needs and considerations (Qazi 2011).

The TTP's current leader is Hakimullah Mehsud. Every tribal agency has a TTP commander and deputy commanders who are responsible for coordinating the resistance on behalf of the group. For example, Wali-ur-Rahman is the Agency Commander in South Waziristan, while Wali Mohammad is the local commander for the city of Wana in South Waziristan. At times, of course, there have been disagreements and commanders have split from the umbrella group, such as Hafiz Gul Bahadur and Maulvi Nazir. Major towns of FATA and Khyber Pakhtunkhwa such as Wana, Damadola, Bara area and Darra Adamkhel also feature TTP commanders. Furthermore, the agencies also feature Taliban groups that are anti-TTP, such as those of Hafiz Gul Bahadur and Maulvi Nazir, and Mangal Bagh's Lashkar-e-Islami.

Military strategy and tactics

The strategy and tactics of the Pakistani Taliban mirror those of the Afghan rebels of the 1980s and the present-day neo-Taliban. As explained by Sial (Rana *et al.* 2010) the Taliban in FATA are using the classic 'war of the flea' model of guerrilla warfare to fight the Pakistan Army. Taliban fighters normally launch attacks on the Army in small bands of 15–20 fighters and quickly disperse within the populace (Gul 2010b).The strategy of the Taliban includes targeting the security forces, tribal elders, civilian administration, political parties and then civilians. Between January 2008 and June 2009 alone 254 security force personnel, 57 tribal elders and seven political party members were targeted. Militants seek out their support base within the people of FATA and also use them as human shields. They have regularly used improvised explosive devices (IEDs) and landmine explosions to target security forces (Rana *et al.* 2010).

Furthermore, with the aid of the Kashmiri militant groups and al-Qaeda, the TTP has also launched several urban guerrilla attacks inside Pakistan. The main targets have been the government's military and police security agencies. The most recent example was the attack launched at PNS Mehran, Pakistan's largest naval base, in Karachi (Mir 2011a). Guerrillas were able to engage Pakistani naval commandos in an overnight battle and wreak havoc at the base. Previously in 2009 the TTP had also attacked the General Headquarters (GHQ) of the Pakistan Army. The siege lasted for around 24 hours.

Similar to the neo-Taliban in Afghanistan, suicide bombings have also become a very regular feature of the Taliban's assault on Pakistan. According to the Pakistan Body Count (2011), 294 suicide bombings have taken place in Pakistan between November 2000 and April 2011 in which between 3,116 and 4,570 people have died. The targets of suicide attacks have been offices of security agencies, leaders and politicians, markets and hotels and restaurants frequented by foreigners.

As Gul (2010b) explains, suicide bombings are a new phenomenon in Pakistan and were introduced by al-Qaeda. Suicide attacks in Pakistan are a prominent example of al-Qaeda's strong influence on the strategic and tactical thinking of the Pakistani Taliban as well as the Afghan Taliban. The larger strategy of the Pakistani Taliban and al-Qaeda appears to be to cut domestic support for military action in FATA and raise the costs of occupation and fighting so that they can consolidate their control in the region.

Recruitment

While the Punjabi Taliban recruit most of their fighters through extended networks of seminaries and presence in different Pakistani cities and villages (Mullick 2010), the Taliban recruits fighters from settled populations instead of madaris and from areas where it operates in FATA and KP. As I have detailed elsewhere (Qazi 2011), three main tactics are used by the Taliban to recruit fighters: access to selective incentives, coercion and exploiting grievances.

FATA is a tremendously underdeveloped part of Pakistan where poverty and unemployment are widespread and further exacerbated by the conflict (2009c; Rana *et al.* 2010). In such a situation, many recruits have joined due to the monetary compensation offered by the Taliban. In 2009 a foot soldier received approximately $180 a month (2009c). Moreover, similar to the Afghan case, joining the Pakistani Taliban provides access to social networks and this brings recruits a sense of validation, power and prestige. According to Imtiaz Gul, militants 'prey on young unemployed men who have no prospects and no hope for education and work'. The Taliban scout these men and then approach them, inviting them for informal conversations. By offering them company, says Gul, they give the individual a sense of belonging to a peer group. The interaction is then used to convince the people to join the movement. Several have joined the Taliban because it brings political backing and clout (Gul 2010a).

The Taliban have also abducted young boys to join their movement (2010b). According to Hussain (2010), in Swat alone anywhere from 1,200 to 1,500 children may have been taken by the Swat Taliban up until 2009. There are others who are coerced into joining through their associations with madaris which are frequented by the Taliban or affiliated with them (Hussain 2009). In Tank district militants forced school-age children to sign up for suicide bombing missions in early 2007 and also kidnapped 30 children for this purpose (Abbas 2009, 2010a). In Swat the Taliban asked locals to send a member of the household to join the militants as a means of showing political allegiance (Meo 2009).

Finally, genuine grievances against the Pakistani Army and state have also motivated tribesmen to join the Taliban. As several analysts have written, including Schofield in this volume (Chapter 26), the Pakistani Army has lacked a population-centric counterinsurgency strategy (Shah 2008). In 2009 alone at least 1,150 civilians were killed because of military operations (2009a). The Pakistan Army, untrained in counterinsurgency operations, has relied on a heavy firepower and airpower-based approach (Kilcullen 2009), for example, during Operation Rah-e-Rast (Straight Path) in Swat (Khan 2009b). Moreover, collective punishment of tribes, economic blockades, mass and arbitrary arrests and detentions, extrajudicial executions and deliberate destruction of property have all occurred during the counterinsurgency campaigns, pushing the locals into the waiting arms of the Taliban (2010a, 2009b).

Aerial strikes from Pakistani helicopter gunships and CIA-operated Unmanned Ariel Vehicles (UAVs) have produced collateral damage, resulting in the deaths of innocent women and children (Abbas 2009; Nawaz 2009). According to the New American Foundation, between 2004 and 2010 158 UAV strikes have occurred, causing anywhere from 311 to 530 civilian casualties (2010d, 2010c). Over 700 civilians died in these strikes in 2009 alone (2010c). Apart from Taj (2010), most analysts agree that the backlash aided militant recruitment. Baitullah Mehsud highlighted this idea once, saying, 'I spent three months trying to recruit and got only 10–15 persons. One U.S. attack and I got 150 volunteers!' (Nawaz 2009). Many young men have joined the Taliban to avenge the deaths of their family members who were killed because of indiscriminate bombings by the Army (Latif 2009).

The Pakistani Taliban have also been able to recruit hundreds of young Pashtuns living in refugee camps after being displaced by intense clashes between them and the Pakistani military. Taliban militants reportedly regularly visit these camps and speak to small groups of youth to convince them to participate. Many have joined over frustration at the government because of the lack of basic human facilities in these camps, where people suffered from pneumonia and diarrhoea (Latif 2009).

It is also worth mentioning here that a flow of al-Qaeda recruits have either attempted to or successfully made their way to the tribal areas from Western countries. These have included Pakistanis arrested in the failed Barcelona terrorist plot in January 2009, the five young men from Washington, DC who were arrested in 2009, Najibullah Zazi and Faisal Shahzad. These men were not recruited directly by al-Qaeda, but themselves made the effort to seek out contacts with militant Islamists and ultimately travelled to Pakistani to obtain requisite training and instructions to carry out attacks. In all cases, the men have sought to join al-Qaeda and its affiliates because of their opposition to their home country's military engagement in Afghanistan, Pakistan and/or Iraq. They have received training and operational guidance from the Pakistani Taliban and al-Qaeda (Hussain 2010).

Governance

The Pakistani Taliban have instituted a system of governance that is politically authoritarian, socially repressive and economically predatory, and their control is largely premised on the use or threat of violence. Ironically, the one oft-quoted redeeming value is that the militants have been able to provide some judicial services when the Pakistani state has failed to.

The rule of the Pakistani Taliban is analogous to that of the 1990s Taliban in Afghanistan. They adhere to a literalist interpretation of Islam and enforce a very strict version of the *Shariah* law. The Taliban have banned listening to music, CDs and radio (apart from their FM stations) and viewing television and DVDs. The sale of these goods is also prohibited. Moreover, girls' schools have been shut down, men are forced to grow beards and barbers are forbidden from shaving them, and women cannot move in public without covering their faces and without a male companion. Those who violate these rules have been disciplined through public floggings and sometimes executions. In Swat, for example, militants roaming the streets and using loudspeakers warned locals to abide by Islamic law or face dire consequences (Khan 2009a).

Like the current Afghan Taliban, the Pakistani Taliban have attacked NGO offices and workers. They oppose their presence, accusing them of spreading obscenities. For example, they have opposed polio vaccination drives (Gul 2010b).

Furthermore, they have instituted a reign of terror in the region. Upon gaining control of a region, the Taliban tell locals to stop negotiations with the government, cease organizing anti-Taliban *jirgas* and militias, and aid the Taliban in implanting *Shariah*. Violators are threatened with death, and in this manner the Taliban have killed hundreds of tribal leaders to eliminate opposition to their rule. Hundreds of men and one woman have also been accused or suspected of being spies, and publicly executed (Gul 2010b; Rana *et al.* 2010).

The Taliban have, however, been adept at providing judicial services and in places created law and order. They have established Islamic courts and centres for dispute resolution and provision of justice. Locals do come to these courts to settle family and social disputes. In places disputes between the Taliban and the locals over taxation have been referred to these courts (Khan 2009a; Rana *et al.* 2010).

Finally, the Taliban have undertaken predatory economic practices. From 2006 they began raising taxes in North Waziristan and also forcefully collected donations for 'Islam and jihad' the annual mandatory *zakat* (alms). The Swat Taliban levied *jiziya* (protection tax) on minority communities, while in other places the Taliban levied fines on people disobeying their laws. For example, fining people for listening to music after it was banned or men for not having beards. The Taliban have also taxed property and businesses, collected tolls, and extorted money from truck drivers. While in Swat the Taliban controlled emerald mines and timber forests, in FATA they have taken over mills of business people and private lands and orchards (Abbas 2009; Rana *et al.* 2010; Roul 2009).

Conclusion

This case study has aimed to survey seven major facets of the insurgency in Pakistan. While acknowledging that the current insurgency is inexorably linked to the social, political, ideological and economic changes that were brought about by the Soviet-Afghan War and when the tribal areas and populace became heavily involved in the insurgency (Rana *et al.* 2010), I trace the rise of the Pakistani Taliban to more recent political upheavals. It was the tribesmen's participation in the latest Afghan war and their rekindling of relations with al-Qaeda that catalysed the birth of the Pakistani Taliban. As mentioned, the impact of al-Qaeda and Taliban on the Pakistani militants is very influential. Al-Qaeda is active in assisting the Taliban strategically and operationally, especially in carrying out terrorist attacks in Pakistan-proper, while the Afghan Taliban remain an inspiration in terms of governance and strategy for guerrilla warfare inside FATA.

Furthermore, the chapter has explored the various dynamics of the insurgency. It must be stressed that the conflict features a variety of factors, including tribal warfare, transnational militancy, crime, sectarian violence, class war, and some elements of Maoism. Similarly, a plethora of actors are involved in the fighting. Moreover, the Pakistani Taliban is far from monolithic. The movement is decentralized, features tens of leaders and at times suffers from infighting and fissures.

Lastly, in investigating recruitment tactics one finds that the Taliban have taken advantage of FATA's underdevelopment and impoverishment and have used selective incentives to recruit young men, i.e. offering them financial incentives for joining and allowing them to access social networks that bring them clout and power. Moreover, coercion – abduction or forceful conscription – remains a regularly utilized tool. Genuine grievances against the abusive behaviour of the Pakistan Army have also motivated tribesmen to join the insurgency, whether to seek revenge or protection.

It is important to note that whereas the insurgency in Pakistan's tribal areas has been under-way for close to a decade, before 2010 literature on the conflict was sparse. Only over the past year have four new books appeared on the topic: Gul (2010b), Hussain (2010), (Rana *et al.* 2010) and Shahzad (2011). Still, however, three of these are journalistic accounts. Like the Afghan insurgency, much of the knowledge of the insurgency in Pakistan comes from NGO and think-tank reports and other journalistic contributions. Academic literature on the topic is thin and existing literature leaves much to be desired. An extensive study of the Pakistani Taliban and the various aspects of the insurgency, one that draws on existing literature on insur-gencies and insurgent movements, such as the work published in this volume, is yet to be produced.

Recommended readings

(2009) *Pakistan: Countering Militancy in FATA*. Islamabad/Brussels: International Crisis Group.

(2010) *'As if Hell Fell on Me': The Human Rights Crisis in Northwest Pakistan*. London: Amnesty Interna-tional.

Abbas, H. (2009) *Pakistan's Troubled Frontier*. Washington, DC: Jamestown Foundation.

Giustozzi, A. (2007) *Koran, Klashnikov, and Laptop: The Neo-Taliban Insurgency in Afghanistan*. New York: Columbia University Press.

Gul, I. (2010) *The Most Dangerous Place*. New York: Viking.

Hussain, Z. (2008) *Frontline Pakistan: The Struggle with Militant Islam*. New York: Columbia University Press.

Hussain, Z. (2010) *The Scorpion's Tail: The Relentless Rise of Islamic Militants in Pakistan-and How it Threatens America*. New York: Free Press.

Johnson, T.H. and Mason, M.C. (2008) 'No Sign Until the Burst of Fire: Understanding the Pakistan-Afghanistan Frontier', *International Security*, 32 (36).

Kilcullen, D. (2009) *The Accidental Guerrilla: Fighting Small Wars in the Midst of a Big One*. Oxford: Oxford University Press.

Mullick, H.A.H. (2010) *Al Qa'eda and Pakistan: Current Role and Future Considerations*. Washington, DC: Institute for Social Policy and Understanding.

Nawaz, S. (2009) *Crossed Swords: Pakistan, its Army, and the Wars Within*. Karachi: Oxford University Press.

Nawaz, S. et al. (2009) *FATA – A Most Dangerous Place*. Washington, DC: Center on Strategic and Inter-national Studies.

Qazi, S.H. (2011) 'Rebels of the Frontier: Origins, Organization and Recruitment of the Pakistani Taliban', *Small Wars & Insurgencies*, 22.

Rana, M.A., Sial, S. and Basir, A. (2010) *Dynamics of the Taliban Insurgency in FATA*. Islamabad: Pak Insti-tute of Peace Studies.

Shah, A. (2008) 'Pakistan After Musharraf: Praetorianism and Terrorism', *Journal of Democracy*, 19 (9).

Shahzad, S.S. (2011) *Inside al-Qaeda and the Taliban*. London: Pluto Press.

References

(2009a) *2009 Human Rights Report: Pakistan*. Washington, DC: US Department of State.

(2009b) 'Pakistan: Avoid Civilian Casualties,' *Human Rights Watch*. Available at: www.hrw.org/en/news/2009/05/11/pakistan-avoid-civilian-casualties.

(2009c) *Pakistan: Countering Militancy in FATA*. Islamabad/Brussels: Interntaional Crisis Group.

(2010a) *'As if Hell Fell on Me': The Human Rights Crisis in Northwest Pakistan*. London: Amnesty Interna-tional.

(2010b) 'The Making of a Suicide Bomber', *Dawn*. Available at: www.dawn.com/wps/wcm/connect/dawn-content-library/dawn/news/pakistan/03-Behind-the-scenes-of-a-Pakistani-suicide-bombing-ss-03.

(2010c) 'Over 700 Killed in 44 Drone Strikes in 2009', *Dawn*. Available at: www.dawn.com/wps/wcm/connect/dawn-content-library/dawn/news/pakistan/18-over-700-killed-in-44-drone-strikes-in-2009-am-01.

(2010d) *The Year of the Drone*. Available at: http://counterterrorism.newamerica.net/drones – 2010chart.

(2011) 'Pakistan Body Count'. *Suicide Bombing*.

Abbas, H. (2009) *Pakistan's Troubled Frontier*. Washington, DC: Jamestown Foundation.

Ahmed, A.S. (1983) *Religion and Politics in Muslim Society: Order and Conflict in Pakistan*. Cambridge: Cambridge University Press.

Behuria, A.K. (2007) 'Fighting the Taliban: Pakistan at War With Itself', *Australian Journal of International Affairs*, 61 (14): 529–43.

Gartenstein-Ross, D. and May, C.D. (eds) (2010) *The Afghanistan-Pakistan Theater*. Washington, DC: FDD Press.

Giustozzi, A. (2007) *Koran, Klashnikov, and Laptop: The Neo-Taliban Insurgency in Afghanistan*. New York: Columbia University Press.

Gul, I. (2010a) *The Most Dangerous Place: Pakistan's Lawless Frontier*. London: Penguin Books.

Gul, I. (2010b) *The Most Dangerous Place*. New York: Viking.

Hussain, Z. (2008) *Frontline Pakistan: The Struggle with Militant Islam*. New York: Columbia University Press.

Hussain, Z. (2010) *The Scorpion's Tail: The Relentless Rise of Islamic Militants in Pakistan-and How it Threatens America*. New York: Free Press.

Johnson, T.H. and Mason, M.C. (2008) 'No Sign Until the Burst of Fire: Understanding the Pakistan-Afghanistan Frontier', *International Security*, 32 (36): 41–77.

Khan, A.R. (2009a) 'The Rise of "Talqaeda"', *Current*, 4.

Khan, M.A. (2009b) 'Pakistani Government Offensive in Swat Heading for the Taliban of Waziristan', *Terrorism Monitor*. Available at: www.jamestown.org/single/?no_cache=1&tx_ttnews%5Btt_news%5D=35149&tx_ttnews%5BbackPid%5D=7&cHash=625b4c7d36.

Kilcullen, D. (2009) *The Accidental Guerrilla: Fighting Small Wars in the Midst of a Big One*. Oxford: Oxford University Press.

Latif, A. (2009) 'Taliban Finds Fertile Recruiting Ground in Pakistan's Tribal Refugee Camps', *U.S News & World Report*. Available at: www.usnews.com/articles/news/world/2009/02/09/taliban-finds-fertile-recruiting-ground-in-pakistans-tribal-refugee-camps.html.

Meo, N. (2009) 'Taliban Recruits Teenage Suicide Bombers for Revenge Attacks', *Telegraph*. Available at: www.telegraph.co.uk/news/worldnews/asia/pakistan/5413052/Taliban-recruits-teenage-suicide-bombers-for-revenge-attacks.html.

Mir, A. (2011a) 'al-Qaeda's Saif-Ilyas Duo Behind Navy Attack', *The News*. Available at: www.thenews.com.pk/TodaysPrintDetail.aspx?ID=48981&Cat=2&dt=5/25/2011.

Mir, A. (2011b) 'New al-Qaeda Chief in North Waziristan', *The News*. Available at: www.thenews.com.pk/TodaysPrintDetail.aspx?ID=47811&Cat=2&dt=5/19/2011.

Mullick, H.A.H. (2010) *Al Qa'eda and Pakistan: Current Role and Future Cosiderations*. Washington, DC: Institute for Social Policy and Understanding.

Nawaz, S. *et al.* (2009) *FATA – A Most Dangerous Place*. Washington, DC: Center on Strategic and International Studies.

Qazi, S.H. (2011) 'Rebels of the Frontier: Origins, Organization and Recruitment of the Pakistani Taliban', *Small Wars & Insurgencies*, 22 (4): 574–602.

Rana, M.A., Sial, S. and Basir, A. (2010) *Dynamics of the Taliban Insurgency in FATA*. Islamabad: Pak Institute of Peace Studies.

Roul, A. (2009) 'Gems, Timber and Jiziya: Pakistan's Taliban Harness Resources to Fund Jihad', *Terrorism Monitor*, 7. Available at: www.jamestown.org/programs/gta/single/?tx_ttnews%5Btt_news%5D=34928&cHash=39d6075765.

Shah, A. (2008) 'Pakistan After Musharraf: Praetorianism and Terrorism', *Journal of Democracy*, 19 (9): 16–25.

Shahzad, S.S. (2009) 'Al-Qaeda's Guerrilla Chief Lays Out Strategy', *Asia Times Online*. Available at: www.atimes.com/atimes/South_Asia/KJ15Df03.html.

Shahzad, S.S. (2011) *Inside al-Qaeda and the Taliban*. London: Pluto Press.

Taj, F. (2010) 'The Year of the Drone Misinformation', *Small Wars & Insurgencies*, 21 (6): 529–36.

Wolfe, B. (2010) 'The Pakistani Taliban's Suicide Bomber Trainer: A Profile of Qari Hussain Mehsud', *Current Threats*. Available at: www.criticalthreats.org/pakistan/pakistani-talibans-suicide-bomber-trainer-profile-qari-hussain-mehsud-may-25-2010.

19

POST-COLD WAR INSURGENCY AND COUNTERINSURGENCY IN LATIN AMERICA

David E. Spencer

Post-Cold War counterinsurgency (COIN) in Latin America has gone through a subtle, yet significant transformation. To understand this transformation, a short discussion of COIN in the region during the Cold War era is necessary.

In general, counterinsurgency went through three stages. An initial phase occurred during the 1960s when the United States provided relatively unconditional military aid to countries pursuing counterinsurgency campaigns against Cuban inspired *focos*. The emphasis was largely military and tactical. This was followed by a stage of general US disengagement as a consequence of the over-throw of democratic regimes by Latin American militaries and subsequent brutal campaigns in the 1970s against urban guerrilla movements. The continuing focus on the military and tactical aspects of counterinsurgency, combined with the perception of the insurgents as agents of foreign powers, led to strategies focused on the physical elimination of the enemy combat force as the strategic condition for victory. Because insurgents did not wear uniforms, civilian supporters of the insurgents were considered fair game, and many were killed, tortured and or imprisoned as a result. Both the US government and Latin American militaries suffered considerable loss of legitimacy due to this approach.

This actually opened up political space for insurgents in some countries, particularly in Central America. After the revolutionary triumph in Nicaragua in 1979, and the emergence of much stronger insurgencies following variants of Mao's prolonged war, the United States re-engaged. While much of the focus continued to be on the military aspects of the campaign, there was recognition that local conditions, such as political exclusion, were creating fertile ground for the recruitment of people to insurgent causes. This time the United States provided significant political and economic assistance in addition to military aid conditioned on significant political reform to include democratization and respect for human rights. All of the insurgencies after Nicaragua failed to take power. However by the end of the Cold War, every country in Latin America, with the exception of Cuba, had adopted democratic government.

Despite this, insurgency refused to disappear. The end of the Cold War terminated outside intervention and support for insurgency, and democratization supposedly ended political motives for insurgency, but there were still a number of groups that continued to hold out, despite the changes: in Guatemala, Chile, Colombia and Peru. The former two were impossible to sustain as their existence responded to Cold War dynamics that no longer existed. Mostly the groups prolonged their existence to get better terms for themselves in the process of negotiations, demobilization and reconciliation. Colombia and Peru were different, marking the boundary between the transition from insurgencies of the Cold War to those of the post-Cold War era. Never part of the main-stream, and thus not supported by Cuba, Fuerzas Armadas Revolucionarias de Colombia (FARC), to a lesser degree Ejército de Liberación Nacional (ELN) in Colombia, and Sendero Luminoso (Shining Path) in Peru had to find alternative means to sustain their organizations. Between 1982 and 1995 they all turned to drugs trafficking as a major source of finances, and this breathed life into the movements. It allowed them to acquire weapons, recruit people and suborn government offi-cials on unprecedented scales. One of the myths is that these insurgencies transformed into drug traffickers and lost their ideology. This is simply not true. The strategic goal of these insurgencies remained to take power through Marxist revolution, but drug trafficking did transform them. Money and the acquisition of money became elevated in importance to the detriment of political mobilization of the mass base. The money made the groups less dependent on the people for their sustenance, and viewed more as potential business rivals, so population control rather than popu-lation mobilization became pre-eminent. Also, since most of the activity of the illegal economies in the region, with some exceptions, took place in remote, depopulated or underpopulated areas of the country, the control of these empty or 'ungoverned' spaces became of strategic importance to the insurgent movements. These ungoverned spaces could be turned into true base areas from which strategic power could be generated. This meant that the strength of an insurgency in the post-Cold War era was often a function of government weakness and lack of will or capacity to control ungoverned spaces, rather than the ability of the insurgency to mobilize people against the government. In Latin America, political control has been traditionally maintained by controlling major centres of the population and the legal economy. Other areas could be ignored or controlled with economy of force. It was Che Guevara's foco theory of the 1960s that first tried to take advant-age of this fact by creating insurgent movements in the remote countryside where the government was not present. The idea was that the insurgent movement would become strong enough before the government could realize what was happening and concentrate enough force to destroy it. In practice this never worked because the ungoverned regions could never generate enough recruits and resources for the movement to consolidate before the government, particularly with US assist-ance, could react. In the post-Cold War era, the resources generated by the illegal economies made Guevara's idea possible. Counterinsurgency then became a function of recovering empty space, filling the vacuums left by traditional methods of political and economic control that were no longer relevant in the post-Cold War world. However, post-Cold War governments were slow to realize this or develop sufficient capability to perform this task. As of this writing, many have still not. There were several reasons for this.

First, although virtually all were now democracies, institutions were weak. Providing effective services outside of major urban centres like health, education, justice or infrastructure like electric-ity, water and paved roads has been difficult for some countries due to a variety of factors. Another very important issue was that in general the new democratic governments mistrusted the military and deliberately kept them weak to prevent them from launching coups as in the past. In many countries militaries were constitutionally prohibited from carrying out internal defence missions. The internal defence mission was given to the police, but police forces were not sufficiently strengthened under the misguided notion that the resolution of the political tensions through democratization meant that there would be a decreased need for security overall. In some coun-tries the result was immediate. In others it took several years. Crime in general and violent crime specifically jumped to unprecedented levels. Over the years the combination of weak police forces and huge profits from illegal markets would result in the rise of gangs and mafia organizations with insurgent-like characteristics. They armed themselves with military weapons: automatic rifles, machine guns and grenades. The more advanced groups acquired grenade launchers, light mortars, rocket launchers, and even improvised mines. Using increasingly sophisticated irregular warfare tactics they dominated terrain, co-opted or expelled government representatives, dominated and mobilized populations, established varying degrees of a counter-state, and otherwise subverted the sovereignty of the state in the areas they came to dominate. For criminal insurgent-like groups these areas were, in many cases, urban space rather than rural areas, mostly among the unplanned slums and poor areas that ring most Latin American cities. Long neglected by security forces, they became perfect breeding grounds for the violent gangs and mafias. The groups were not insurgents in the sense that their strategic purpose was to overthrow the state, but they did seek to weaken the state so they could grow and do business. They are included here because the most successful solutions to date have, even if the governments have not used the term, employed classic counter-insurgency approaches. Remarkably, both the post-Cold War counterinsurgencies and post-Cold War anti-criminal campaigns have followed similar paths, making the same mistakes and subsequently adopting similar solutions to both the political and the criminal problems. While there are other cases, this chapter will look at four cases: Peru's current campaign against the new generation of Sendero Luminoso, Colombia's struggle against FARC, the struggle against the drug trafficking gangs of Rio de Janeiro, and Mexico's ongoing struggle against the narcotrafficking mafias.

In all cases initial approaches were a combination of denial and mis-analysis. In Colombia, despite public availability of FARC strategic documents stating that their final goal was to take power, politicians and academics wasted a lot of time and effort debating over what their strategic goal really was, denying that in the post-Cold War world a Communist insurgency could seriously think about taking power. All signs that they were systematically following their publicly available strategic plan were completely ignored, except by the military. This was because the military, and to a slightly lesser degree the police, were assigned the mission to fight them. The military had a role because the fighting was fairly intense, and constantly increasing, beyond the ability of the police to confront them. However, Colombia's government spent less of its budget on the military, which was at war, than several neighbouring Latin American governments did on their armies, which were at peace. The political establishment generally tried to avoid the war, except to criticize the security forces when they failed. As far as they were concerned, the military was only temporarily involved, dealing with a public order mission. What few wanted to recognize was that this temporary mission had been ongoing for over 30 years and showed no signs of abating. Effectiveness was measured by how many guerrillas were killed or captured compared to how many military and police were killed. During the mid 1990s the numbers of killed/captured insurgents were increasing, causing some to claim that the military was winning the war, when in fact FARC was making significant organizational advances inevitably increasing the intensity of the fighting. Counter-guerrilla operations largely consisted of forays against FARC-dominated areas. These settled into a pattern of temporarily driving FARC forces out of the zone, skirmishes with FARC security rings, the capture of abandoned equipment, and subsequent withdrawal of the military from the area of operations. As a result, the bulk of FARC forces would wait out the foray in well-established alternative camps and then return to occupy their normal camps once the military had withdrawn. The guerrillas in turn would make forays against towns, attacking the police station, robbing the banks and destroying the local government centre. They would occupy the town and harangue the people until rescuing army units would drive them out. These attacks occurred very frequently and some towns were hit multiple times over the years. Although major military encounters were rare, the intensity and frequency of these encounters was systematically increasing. The military were rudely shaken in mid 1996 when FARC launched a nationwide offensive of 22 separate attacks, including overrunning an isolated company outpost at Las Delicias, Caquetá. It took an additional 18 months of a string of defeats culminating in the decimation of an understrength elite battalion at El Billar for the military to get serious about making significant changes in its approach to the war.

In Peru, the original Sendero Luminoso was largely defeated by 1994. The Peruvian police and military were able to capture most of the leadership, including Abimael Guzman, as they had foolishly concentrated in Peru's capital city, Lima. In the countryside, Sendero units reeled in confusion. A combination of local militias known as 'Rondas Campesinas' and army or navy commandos hunted down and killed or captured what remained. Fighting was intense and vicious with no quarter asked or given. Sendero divided into two factions; one that remained loyal to Guzman and the other that blamed Guzman for the disaster. It is not surprising that the two groups survived in the drug trafficking zones, particularly the Upper Huallaga Valley and in the Apurimac and Ene River Valley, known by the acronym VRAE. By 2001 the counterinsurgency had been scaled back significantly, and the fight against Sendero had become essentially a counter-terrorism mission with intelligence and special forces going after individual Sendero leaders. Local security and development was de-emphasized if not discontinued in many areas. The main focus became counter-drug operations under the control of the police. It should be no surprise then that when Sendero began to make a comeback in 2006–7, there was a great deal of denial among both the government and the press that it was in fact Sendero and not drug traffickers. In fact, the terms 'Sendero', 'guerrillas' or 'insurgency' were not mentioned in many accounts when a string of attacks and ambushes were carried out starting in 2007. Sendero was not the same organization it had been. It had evolved, attempting to correct the mistakes that had caused its downfall in the early 1990s. Where it had tried to control population through terror, it now tried to win them over through social action. It openly allied itself with drug traffickers, and particularly the coca-growing population. However, like FARC, it maintained its Marxist ideology. The government focused on the drug trafficking aspect of the organization and denied the importance of the political. This denial caused it to dismiss the socio-political aspects of the movement and reduce combat against it to law enforcement. As a consequence, the organization grew and expanded its activities. The government got a wake-up call when Sendero Luminoso carried out a series of ambushes and attacks, inflicting between 2007 and 2009 some of the most significant losses on the Peruvian military that it had ever suffered at the hands of insurgents, including the death of 12 soldiers in a single ambush and the shooting down of a helicopter gunship (*Caretas*, 16 October 2008 and *Caretas*, 10 September 2009).

In Mexico, there had long been accommodation with drug trafficking organizations going back to the 1960s and 1970s. This accommodation varied from government to government, but over time many national, state and local officials from a variety of parties and at varying times either were suborned, made deals or ignored the drug traffickers for a variety of reasons. The problem was not considered a Mexican problem but rather a US problem. This did not mean that the Mexican police and military did not fight drugs, they did, and there were notable successes against drug kingpins and against some illegal drug crops. However, there were too many failures, and examples of impunity. Furthermore, the demand for drugs grew, both in the United States as well as in Mexico. Also, increasing effectiveness against guerrillas and drug traffickers in Colombia created opportunities for the Mexican organizations, which they gladly took up. On balance the drug trafficking organizations became more important, richer, stronger and more violent. This growth was reflected in increasing war between the cartels as rivalries came to a head. It was the savage violence between the cartels that prompted the government of Calderón to declare war on the drug trafficking organizations in 2006. However, as the war heated up, the government realized that its capability to combat the narcotraffickers was completely undermined by the long history of corruption and accommodation, particularly at the state and local level. Those that were not corrupted were in serious danger, and many police lost their lives or were too afraid to operate effectively. Furthermore, not only were state and local police forces compromised, but local society as well. Drug traffickers spent money and provided jobs. There was a degree of popular support in some areas that was difficult to eradicate. Finally, the drug traffickers were well armed and organized. They had acquired large and very sophisticated arsenals. This included fleets of armoured all-terrain vehicles, assault rifles, machine guns, rocket launchers, grenade launchers, mortars and copious amounts of ammunition. They had recruited former military and policemen that had provided training and tactical advice to the cartels. To many both inside and outside Mexico, the government had bitten off more than they could chew (Aguilar and Castañeda 2009).

In Rio de Janeiro, Brazil, landless poor people occupied the slopes of the many karsts that are scattered throughout the city as well as other less valuable or unoccupied land and built slums called *favelas*. One of the unique characteristics of these slums is that unlike many other Latin American cities, where they are concentrated on the outskirts of the cities, the favelas are scattered throughout the city occupying space next to very wealthy neighbourhoods. Furthermore, they dominate key transportation arteries. The successive governments adopted different approaches to the favela problem. In sum, law enforcement generally did not seek to establish law and order within the favelas, but rather to prevent crime from spilling from the favelas into the wealthier parts of the city. This allowed gangs to flourish and establish local dominance. Second, a succession of governors did try to improve conditions within the favelas through social programmes. However, the social programmes and security forces were never linked together, and in fact they often worked at cross purposes. Humanitarian organizations often viewed the police as the enemy. The outcome of this was that the social programmes actually strengthened the power of the gangs since NGOs and social workers could not enter the favelas without the acquiescence of the gangs. Rio society developed a taste for drugs, and the gangs became the ideal vehicle through which to satisfy that demand. This in turn brought an infusion of money into the favelas, which created violent rivalries between the gangs. Over time the weaponry and organization of these gangs became increasingly sophisticated, not only to combat each other for the domination of markets, but also to resist the police. Inter-gang violence and crime began to spill over into the wealthy neighbourhoods, scaring tourists, interrupting traffic and generally making life difficult for the citizens. Murders across the city spiralled out of control. The police made an increasing number of incursions into the favelas to arrest the perpetrators of the crimes. Resistance to those incursions became increasingly violent and sophisticated. The gangs acquired automatic rifles and grenades. This forced the police to wear body armour and then to acquire armoured vehicles as resistance became increasingly heavy. Videos show the vehicles being struck by Molotov cocktails and hundreds of rounds of ammunition in the space of a few minutes. The gangs escalated, acquiring increasing numbers of both general purpose and heavy machine guns as well as constructing concrete roadblocks and fighting positions to prevent police penetration of the neighbourhoods. Despite large numbers of kills and captures, the violence was only getting worse. In 2008, of a city of 11 million there were approximately 5,000 murders committed and almost 1,200 people killed by the police in shootouts. In 2009, shortly after it was announced that Rio de Janeiro had been selected for the 2016 Olympics, the gangs shot down a police helicopter, killing two of the crew.

In all of the countries, the initial denial or mis-diagnosis led to significant failures which then led to a re-evaluation of the situation whether at the national or sub-national level. Subsequently new strategies and approaches were adopted which led to increasing levels of success. All of these approaches, whether against true insurgents or insurgent-like criminal organizations, involved efforts with strategic direction at the highest political level, strengthened security or military elements, and coordinated non-military components aimed at increasing governance, social services and economic openings.

In Colombia, the first step was to change the concept of the conflict. Where the military had regarded their mission as a temporary ad hoc public order or security mission, the slogan became 'we are at war', meaning that the conflict became the permanent central focus of the armed forces.

Training, education, acquisition and promotion were determined by the requirements of the conflict. The enemy strategy became the central focus of a series of general officer meetings and planning focused on how to counter that strategy. This was made somewhat difficult by the Pastrana government's policy of peace negotiations with the FARC, for which the government ceded temporary sovereignty over five rural municipalities to the guerrillas for the purpose of talks. This area was known as the demilitarized zone (DMZ). When it became apparent that peace talks in the DMZ did not mean a cessation of FARC offensive actions outside the zone, the Pastrana government gave the military the green light to proceed. The first step was to blunt FARC offensive action by creating a Rapid Deployment Force known by the acronym FUDRA. This force could be deployed anywhere in the country within 24 hours. Several bloody battles occurred between 1999 and 2002 in which every major FARC offensive was neutralized. The second step was to identify and attack all of the intermediate regional base areas from which FARC offensives were being launched in each of the then five division areas. These offensives took place between 2000 and 2001. Critical locations were recovered all over the country and new units were created, such as the High Mountain Battalions to occupy and control these former intermediate base areas.

Around the end of this phase, President Alvaro Uribe was elected, and this changed the government approach to the war. For the first time, the main objective of the government as a whole, and not just the security forces, was to establish security and governance. The government wrote a national strategy known as the Democratic Security Policy. The major objective of the strategy was to establish security for every Colombian no matter where they lived or what political party they favoured. This facilitated the implementation of the military's third phase, which consisted of establishing local area control. When FARC had been on the offensive, a large amount of territory had been abandoned. Small military outposts and police stations had been abandoned either because they had been overrun or because they were too vulnerable to FARC offensive action. Every abandoned municipality was recovered and local forces known as 'peasant soldiers' and later 'village soldiers' were implemented. Colombia had had a bad experience with civil defence and local militia forces. All of these forces were collectively called 'paramilitaries'. Many had degenerated into death squads or had made common cause with drug traffickers. Like the guerrillas, the paramilitaries had also gotten involved in illegal economies for financing. The Colombian solution to create necessary local defence forces was to recruit local men into the regular army, and have them serve under regular officers in their home villages. This way local forces operated under national control. To prevent these forces from being overrun by the guerrillas, each platoon was supported by a regular army platoon as well as the local police station, and mobile police forces known as *carabineros*. The combination of these forces plus regular forces within a few minutes call, guaranteed that no element was left in isolation. In general the combination of regional offensive and local security completely shut down the guerrillas' ability to launch attacks against towns and military posts. In addition, it had a significant impact on both organized and common crime. All crime indicators dropped significantly due to increased security.

This in turn allowed government to function the way it was designed. Mayors and judges returned to their towns. Increased security meant that licit economic activity could return, and despite the significant costs of the security plan, economic growth took off, more than offsetting the increased military and security spending.

To insure that local government was re-establishing governance the way that it should, President Uribe established the Community Councils. Most weekends he travelled with much of the national cabinet to different areas of the country and met with the local government, military and police commanders and the populace. The meetings would last most of the day and people would talk about governance and security problems. The president would make assignments and hold local and national officials accountable for the assignments and promises that were made. These councils boosted confidence in the government because for the first time, for many people, the national government actually cared about local conditions.

An important outcome of the establishment of security and governance was the demobilization of the paramilitaries. The atrocities of the paramilitaries had delegitimized the government as individual government representatives had tolerated or even encouraged the formation and existence of these groups. Acknowledging that they no longer had a reason to exist, the paramilitaries agreed to demobilize. While controversial and imperfect, 32,000 paramilitaries turned in weapons in exchange for reduced punishment and rehabilitation. Although marred by controversy this programme increased government legitimacy and let them focus on the guerrillas.

FARC was still essentially intact. The government had mainly filled vacuums in the portion of the country where it already had significant presence and infrastructure. FARC's power however was generated from ungoverned space. They had established significant base areas from which they projected strategic power against the rest of the country. In order to strategically defeat the insurgency, the government had to eliminate these base areas. In 2003 the military launched Operation Libertad I, the first phase of the national plan known as Plan Patriota. FARC's strategy contemplated a siege of Bogota from base areas centred in the eastern *cordillera* surrounding the capital. It was vital to eliminate this base area to remove this threat. Around 10,000 army troops spread out into the areas dominated by FARC. For the first six months they pushed patrols deep into guerrilla territory seeking to systematically cut off logistics and communications routes. FARC, misreading the operation's intent, moved to more remote ground, thinking that after a few weeks the soldiers would leave. However, they did not. Furthermore the army took measures to win over the civilian population. Cut off and surrounded, the guerrillas soon began to suffer desertions. This allowed the development of intelligence which was used by army special forces to carry out strikes and ambushes. In the last three months of the operation most of the operational level FARC commanders were killed. A captured FARC after action analysis revealed that every guerrilla front in the area of operations lost between 50 per cent and 90 per cent of their forces to the point where FARC high command ordered these fronts out of the area to prevent their annihilation.

The next phase of the plan, Operation JM, was implemented in 2004. The Colombian military created Joint Task Force Omega composed of 18,000 mostly army, but also important air force and navy riverine components. The main role of the United States was to provide logistics, communications, intelligence and maintenance support to sustain this force in the field. This force was launched deep into the Colombian jungle against the main FARC base area in Caquetá and Meta departments. FARC's plan to resist this advance consisted of attrition operations, particularly with mines and indirect fire, while attempting to manoeuvre and draw a military unit into a kill zone where they could inflict an important tactical and psychological defeat. While the army did suffer combat casualties the main enemy was disease, particularly leishmaniasis. The advance was heavily harassed by copious amounts of mortar bombs either rigged as mines or fired from tubes. The mortar tubes and bombs were made in jungle factories. This diminished considerably when the army captured the shops where the mortars were made. No large battles took place, but the guerrillas suffered steady attrition from combat, disease and desertion. Furthermore, huge amounts of guerrilla infrastructure and logistics were captured and destroyed. Finally, the operation fragmented guerrilla forces that were only able to communicate with each other remotely. This set up the organization for penetration and deception. Another significant benefit of government domination of formerly ungoverned space was a great reduction in drug cultivation and trafficking.

Like other areas, once security was established the efforts at consolidating governance began. However, because these areas were remote, and dependent in most cases on illegal economies, a special effort needed to be made to bring governance to these zones. It was decided to create a special coordinating body known as the Centre for the Coordination of Integrated Action (CCAI). The director of this organization had a direct line to the president. The CCAI was not a new agency, but rather a committee to coordinate and prioritize the efforts of existing government ministries. Their job was to work together with each other and the local communities to identify the needs and programmes to be implemented. Supported by the United States the initial efforts were modest but increased in importance, coverage and size over time.

By 2008, FARC forces had been reduced to relatively isolated pockets in a number of very geographically difficult zones around the country. This allowed the government to carry out a number of attacks on medium- and high-level leadership targets. In March 2008, the military, in Operation Fenix, attacked and killed Raul Reyes, a member of the ruling FARC seven-man Secretariat. Another member of the Secretariat, Ivan Rios, was killed by his own bodyguard when military pressure on his unit caused him to become paranoid and threaten those closest to him. Finally, Manuel Marulanda, long time leader of FARC, died of old age in the jungle. In June 2008 the military was able to launch Operation Jaque and rescue 15 political hostages from under the noses of the FARC, including three Americans that had been kidnapped in 2003. In September 2010, the Colombian military launched Operation Sodoma, in which they killed FARC military strategist, Jorge Briceño, aka 'Mono Jojoy'.

However, FARC did not collapse. The three members of the Secretariat killed in 2008 were replaced and a new leader, Alfonso Cano, was appointed who reaffirmed FARC's commitment to the strategic plan. FARC began to operate in increasingly irregular and dispersed forms through the use of expendable militias and massive use of remotely detonated mines and explosives. In addition, remnants of the paramilitaries that either decided not to demobilize, remobilized or formed new groups occupied space not consolidated by the government, in some cases replacing guerrilla forces. However, unlike the previous paramilitaries they are almost wholly dedicated to illicit economies and are not tied to the government or military. Today they are called criminal bands or BACRIM. So while insurgents and irregular threats are on the defensive in Colombia, they have not been defeated. This is due primarily to two factors: enormous profits and continuing ungoverned space where they can function. Second, FARC has found sanctuary and support in neighbouring countries. Raul Reyes was killed just across the border in Ecuador, and evidence was found of complicity between FARC and individuals of the Ecuadorean government. Not only were Ecuadoreans involved, but also individuals and organizations from the radical left from nearly every country in the hemisphere as well as Spain and others. Venezuela and the Chávez government played a particularly important role to the degree that the Colombian government officially complained to the Organization of American States (OAS) in August 2010 and presented a long list of evidence of Venezuelan complicity. So while it is clear that the Colombian government, particularly under President Uribe, made great strides towards achieving a counterinsurgency victory, the final consolidation of that victory due to drug trafficking and international collusion may take many more years of effort.

Efforts in the other countries are much less advanced than in Colombia. In Peru, the government came to the conclusion that in the VRAE it had to defeat both drug trafficking and the guerrillas. In order to do this it had to attack the reasons that people participated in these activities, which were largely social and economic. They developed Plan VRAE, an inter-agency effort to reduce poverty, by increasing access to health care, education and legal economic opportunities combined with a significant security effort. The policy strengthened police counter-narcotics activities and military counter-terrorist operations (Government of Peru 2009). While news from the VRAE is scarce, levels of violence fell in 2010 and important guerrilla leaders were killed or captured. However, Sendero expanded its efforts in Lima making it unclear whether the advances have been due to Plan VRAE or whether the organization had adapted.

In Mexico, the president launched a war against narcotrafficking in December 2006. This plan has multiple lines of operation. First, Mexican police and justice were deemed insufficient to combat the drug trafficking organizations. In particular local and state police forces were ill trained and riddled with corruption. A national level process to reform and retrain police forces and overhaul the justice system was initiated. Meanwhile, federal police forces were duplicated and committed to the effort. Because this process was going to be long and difficult, the military was ordered into the gap. The military had a cleaner image and was considered less corrupt than the police. Troops were deployed, largely to the northern border states where the violence was the worst. The military is supposed to hand the mission back to the police gradually as the police and justice reforms are completed. Other lines of operation included the development of a dedicated intelligence organization, reducing funding through the control of money laundering, developing a national information campaign and reducing weapons trafficking, particularly from the United States. While it is clear that many weapons in the hands of the traffickers were originally manufactured in the United States, a majority of these are military weapons not available on the civilian market. An examination of the numbers suggests that no more than 17 per cent of the weapons come from the civilian market of the United States (La Jeunesse and Lott 2009). However, what is likely is that a great deal of military grade ammunition does cross the border as it is openly available on the US market. Between 2006 and 2010, 45,000 troops and 5,000 federal police were deployed to 18 states. Meanwhile over 28,000 people were killed. While the military have scored some notable successes, as of this writing, they were still in a steep learning curve. Also, untrained for irregular war, human rights complaints jumped from 182 in 2006 to 1,230 in 2008. Furthermore, levels of violence were only reduced by 5 per cent. Interviews with military sources indicate that the drug traffickers have developed the capability of carrying out sophisticated ambushes and even manoeuvre warfare attempting to isolate and overrun platoon size military units by drawing them into kill zones, setting up blocking forces to prevent reinforcements and then annihilating the unit through the combination of support weapons and manoeuvre (Mexican officers 2009–10).

In 2010 President Calderón announced a social component to the strategy consisting of increasing health care, education and promoting small and medium business. This was due to the realization that many young people were joining the cartels for as little as 45 dollars a week because there were no alternative opportunities. Also, cartel leaders were winning the loyalty of locals by providing services that the government had failed to provide. The steady supply of recruits and view that the cartels could get things done where the government could not undermined the ability of the government to fight them. This programme is too new to have generated results but the unmistakable parallels to the classic counterinsurgency approach are not lost on the informed observer.

Similar approaches have been adopted in Rio de Janeiro. In late 2008 the military police fought a particularly fierce battle to kill, capture or expel drug traffickers from *favela* Santa Marta. This culminated in December. However, instead of leaving the *favela* as in the past, the police stayed. They established a permanent base inside the *favela* and created a new 'community police' unit. The community police operated much like US provincial reconstruction teams (PRTs) in Iraq or Afghanistan. They worked with local community leaders to provide security but also identified local needs and brought in development projects. This included improved housing, day care, vocational training and education. Crime dropped dramatically, prosperity and governance went up. Since then, the programme has been gradually extended to other favelas in Rio. Regular and special units first went in and battled with the drug traffickers, occupying the neighbourhood. Once recovered, a community police unit was established. The units were given the official name of Permanent Police Units (UPPs). While as of this writing there were eight units, the plan is to have 60,000 new police in UPPs by 2016. Where the UPP units have been located, crime has dropped by as much as 85 per cent according to official statistics.

In conclusion, the application of counterinsurgency principles in Latin America has been found to be useful against a whole range of irregular threats, not just classic political insurgency, although it is too early to tell what the final results will be in places like Peru, Mexico and Rio de Janeiro. Like insurgency, the violent criminal organizations and gangs subvert governance, use irregular tactics, dominate terrain and have roots in social and economic grievances. The strategic whole-of-government approach to counterinsurgency, which seeks to repress violent behaviour challenging the sovereignty of the state, but simultaneously deal with the source of social grievances from gaps resulting from obsolete and dysfunctional societal organization and economy, effectively strengthens democratic governance.

References

Aguilar, R. and Castañeda, J. (2009) *El Narco: La Guerra Fallida*. Mexico: Punto de Lectura.

Arias, E. (2006) *Drugs and Democracy in Rio de Janeiro: Trafficking, Social Networks and Public Security*. Chapel Hill: University of North Carolina Press.

Army of Peru (2010) *En Honor a la Verdad: Version del Ejercito sobre su participacion en la defensa del sistema democratico contra las organizaciones terroristas*. Lima: Ejercito del Peru.

Barcellos, C. (2003) *Abusado, O Dono do Morro Dona Marta*. Rio de Janeiro: Editora Record.

Caretas (2008) 'Guerra Desatada', 16 October, p. 46.

Caretas (2009) 'Punto de Quiebre', 10 September, p. 23.

Felbab-Brown, V. (2010) *Shooting Up: Counterinsurgency and the War on Drugs*. Washington, DC: The Brookings Institute.

Government of Peru (2009) *Plan Vrae*.

Interviews with Mexican military officers during 2009 and 2010 who prefer to remain anonymous.

La Jeunesse, W. and Lott, M. (2009) 'The Myth of 90 Percent: Only a Small Fraction of Guns in Mexico Come From U.S.', *Fox News*, 2 April. Available at: www.foxnews.com/politics/2009/04/02/myth-percent-small-fraction-guns-mexico-come.

Molloy, M. and Bowden, C. (2010) *El Sicario: The Autobiography of a Mexican Assassin*. New York: Nation Books.

Moroni, J. and Spencer, D. (1995) *Strategy and Tactics of the Salvadoran FMLN Guerrillas: Last Battle of the Cold War, Blueprint for Future Conflicts*. Westport: Praeger.

Spencer, D. (1996) *From Vietnam to El Salvador: The Saga of the FMLN Sappers and Other Guerrilla Special Forces in Latin America*. Westport: Praeger.

Spencer, D. (2009) 'Paraguayan People's Army: Challenging a Populist Regime', *Security and Defense Studies Review*, 9 (1 & 2): 105–14.

Spencer, D. (2011) *Colombia's Road to Recovery: Security and Governance 1982–2010*. Washington, DC: Center for Hemispheric Defense Studies.

Part III

Counterinsurgency cases

20

TRENDS IN AMERICAN COUNTERINSURGENCY

Thomas R. Mockaitis

Professional officers, politicians and the general public have long agreed that the US military's primary mission (its only mission, some would argue) is to fight and win the nation's wars. By 'war' they mean a conventional conflict between regular armed forces along clearly delineated lines of battle. Unconventional conflict, fraught with ambiguity and rife with problems for regular forces, was at best an inconvenience and at worst a major distraction from their proper mission. When unconventional operations cannot be avoided, they should be gotten over quickly or, better yet, left to Special Forces, whose mission list includes all those activities the regulars wish to avoid.

Counterinsurgency in particular became the dirtiest word in the American military lexicon. This aversion to counterinsurgency stemmed from the experience of Vietnam. 'Are Americans and their cultural values adaptable to the concept and techniques of unconventional warfare?' a 1962 article asked in its title. The author concluded that while US forces could engage in such activities, doing so ran counter to popular perceptions of national values (Williams 1962: 86–9). In other words, there was something profoundly un-American about unconventional conflict. While the United States did develop effective counterinsurgency tactics and employed them in Vietnam, the war proved so deleterious to the morale and effectiveness of US armed forces that they wished to avoid any future large-scale counterinsurgency campaign. Not until a year into the Iraq War would the military as whole again become interested in this important form of warfare.

The disdain for counterinsurgency coupled with popular perceptions that this type of conflict was not a core task of the US military led to the misperception that prior to Vietnam the Army and Marines had confined themselves to conventional warfare. As this chapter will demonstrate, nothing could be further from the truth. From the early days of the Republic to the present, US forces have fought in a wide range of unconventional conflicts. They engaged in intermittent irregular warfare against Native American tribes as the country expanded westward. While nineteenth-century Indian wars, clearances, and round ups were not full-fledged counterinsurgency campaigns, they had many of the same characteristics. During the entire span of the twentieth century as well, US forces conducted a series of counterinsurgency campaigns. Study of these campaigns reveals that although the military never liked unconventional operations, it always managed to conduct them effectively albeit after a costly period of trial and error.

The Philippines

The US military's first full-fledged counterinsurgency campaign took place at the turn of the twentieth century in territory it had acquired following the Spanish-American War. The United States occupied the Philippines as the Spanish withdrew. Emilio Aguinaldo, who had led a revolution against Spain in 1897, aided the Americans during the war with the expectation that his country would receive independence. When the United States decided to remain in control of the islands for the foreseeable future, Aguinaldo realized he had traded one colonial master for another and mounted an insurgency against the new occupiers.

The conflict began with an offensive by Aguinaldo's Army of Liberation in the spring of 1899. With their superior firepower and organization US forces easily defeated the insurgents in open battle and cleared the Luzon plain of them. They also nearly captured the rebel leader, who fled to a mountainous region in the northeast of the island. Realizing his mistake in using conventional tactics, Aguinaldo shifted to guerrilla warfare. He reorganized his forces into semi-autonomous bands of 30–50 fighters, which carried out hit-and-run operations against American units up to company strength. Aguinaldo created what is today being called a 'shadow government' or a 'parallel state' in the communities he controlled. The insurgents collected taxes, dispensed justice, requisitioned supplies and recruited members. At the height of the insurgency, Aguinaldo may have had as many as 80,000 fighters operating in familiar terrain among people whose language and culture they understood, thus enjoying a significant advantage in garnering intelligence on US forces (Williams 1962: 86–9).

American troops responded to the insurgency as conventional soldiers often do. Unable to find and destroy the enemy, they took out their frustration on the general population, punishing entire communities suspected of supporting the insurgents, even if that support had been coerced. Soldiers destroyed property, murdered civilians and summarily executed prisoners. A century before the Abu Ghraib scandal they also tortured suspects for information. To deprive the guerrillas of support from sympathetic (or intimidated) civilians, the Army rounded up ordinary people, most of whom had no connection to the insurgency, and detained them in concentration camps, where thousands died of disease. Such brutality declined as the conflict progressed, though it never entirely stopped, but contrary to popular belief, these harsh tactics did not defeat the insurgents (Gates 2007). The United States had too few troops (24,000 at the height of the emergency) to terrorize a population of seven million into submission (Boot 2002: 127). Only an effective counterinsurgency strategy could accomplish that goal.

After its initial failures, the Army developed such a strategy and the tactics to implement it. US forces employed what later would be called a 'hearts-and-minds' approach, identifying and addressing the causes of unrest. Washington promised the Philippines eventual independence and offered some degree of local autonomy immediately. The administration of William McKinley created the Philippine Commission to oversee civil administration of the islands and appointed William Howard Taft to direct it. The military and civil efforts combined in what today are known as 'clear-and-hold' operations. The soldiers handed control of pacified areas over to the Commission, which appointed and paid Filipinos to run their own affairs.

The Army also adapted its approach to combating the guerrillas. Rather than focus on killing and capturing them, they concentrated on breaking the link between the insurgents and their supporters. However, instead of re-concentrating people into squalid concentration camps, they deployed troops both to prevent subversion and to protect the population from insurgent retaliation. The army created four military districts, subdivided into smaller units in which commanders were deployed for extended periods, so that they got to know the area and its people well (Linn 1989: 163–70). This approach prefigured the French 'oil stain' strategy in Morocco and the British 'framework deployment' in Malay. General Orders No. 100, which had first been issued by President Abraham Lincoln to govern occupied Confederate territory during the Civil War, provided the legal framework for the counterinsurgency campaign.

Although they would be considered harsh by today's standards, most contemporary legal experts considered the Orders humane (Linn 2002: 63–4). The Orders promoted unity of effort by vesting both civil and military power in a governor general who had the power to impose severe penalties on insurgents and those who supported them, including capital punishment. The Orders also insisted that civilians and captured insurgents be treated humanely. 'Military oppression is not Martial Law', they asserted. 'It is the abuse of the power which that law confers.... It is incumbent upon those who administer it to be strictly guided by the principles of justice, honor, and humanity (*General Order No. 100*).'

In addition to avoiding counterproductive measures, military commanders also took positive steps to win popular support. American soldiers built schools and roads, improved sanitation, and inoculated Filipinos against smallpox. Military commanders appointed mayors and local councillors, empowering them in turn to hire labourers for public works projects. This ability to dole out patronage gave the mayors leverage and credibility with local populations (Deady 2005: 59). This hearts-and-minds effort facilitated military operations by reducing support for the insurgents and inducing people to provide intelligence on their whereabouts.

The US Army also employed Filipino scouts, who spoke the local language and knew the terrain. In March 1901, one of these indigenous units finally helped secure the capture of Aguinaldo, who on 1 April swore an oath recognizing American authority over the Philippines. He then issued a proclamation calling on his followers to lay down their arms. A generous amnesty induced many insurgents to surrender. In July 1902, Congress passed the Philippine Organic Act, which called for the establishment of a local legislature and extended the US Bill of Rights to the islands. The insurrection ended that month, and President Theodore Roosevelt pardoned those who had taken part it.

The Philippine insurrection required the United States to mount its first full-scale counter-insurgency campaign. While US forces did develop an effective strategy, victory occurred under very favourable circumstances. The insurgency occurred primarily within a single ethnic group and was confined to two islands of the vast archipelago. Naval supremacy enabled the United States to prevent supplies reaching the guerrillas. Because they fought on islands, the insurgents lacked a safe haven across a friendly border. Although its conduct improved as the conflict progressed, the Army never completely abandoned the brutal methods it had employed early in the campaign. However, these qualifiers notwithstanding, the US Army and civil administration devised a sound counterinsurgency strategy and implemented it effectively. Unfortunately, the army did not preserve the lessons of the Philippine insurrection in formal doctrine, and so the lessons of the campaign were largely forgotten.

The Caribbean

Following the First World War, US forces once again found themselves confronting internal unrest, this time much closer to home and handled by the Marine Corps rather than the Army. Between 1898 and 1940, the era of 'gunboat diplomacy', the Leathernecks intervened in Cuba, Panama, Haiti, the Dominican Republic, Mexico and Nicaragua. Intervention stemmed from a strategic desire to forestall European colonial expansion in the region, the perceived need to safeguard American economic interests, and a desire to protect the Panama Canal. In each of these cases, the United States had to do much more than project force ashore. The Marines were called upon to restore order and promote stability, which often required application of sound counterinsurgency principles.

Of all these small wars, the intervention in Nicaragua came closest to being a full-blown counterinsurgency campaign. In 1927, the United States intervened to resolve a civil war that had destabilized the country in an area of vital American interest. US representative Henry L. Stimson succeeded in reconciling the various factions, with the exception of one rebel leader. Augusto Sandino switched to guerrilla operations after suffering defeats in conventional battles with government forces and their American backers. Sandino made excellent use of the mountainous country between Nicaragua's Pacific and Atlantic regions, which also divided the country ethnically. The Spanish and *mestizo* peoples lived on the Pacific side; European settlers occupied the few towns on the Atlantic coast, where Muskito Indians made up the majority, who also dwelt in the interior along with the indigenous Sunu people. Most American-based economic activity (mining and fruit production) occurred in the Atlantic region. Sandino operated in a remote area along the Honduran border, which gave him access to both regions and safe haven in Honduras.

The US campaign against Sandino was led by Marine Captain Merritt 'Red Mike' Edson. After considering the situation, Edson decided that controlling the Rio Coco, which runs 400 miles from the Honduran border to the Caribbean Sea, would restrict Sandino's ability to operate. He could use the river as an avenue to invade Sandino's territory and blockade it to restrict the insurgents' movement between eastern and western Nicaragua. Controlling the river required befriending the native population living along it and hiring them as river guides, boatmen and interpreters. Edson also hoped to exploit the animosity of the Indians towards the Spanish-speaking Nicaraguans.

Edson devised a three-phased strategy to defeat the insurgents. He would first lead his forces on a reconnaissance mission up the Rio Coco. The Marines would then garrison the lower reaches of the river near the Atlantic. Finally, Edson would launch an offensive from the east deep into Sandino territory coordinated with a corresponding attack out of Managua from the west. The first phase of the plan went well as Marines reconnoitered the river from the Atlantic to the central mountains. Garrisoning the lower reaches of the Coco proved more problematic. The Indians posed the same difficult questions that have often been asked of American intervention forces ever since. How long will you stay, and what will happen to us when you leave? Uncertainty over the Untied States' long-term commitment made recruiting locals difficult. Their reluctance to support such an uncertain ally proved well founded. In 1934, President Herbert Hoover withdrew the Marines and left the counterinsurgency campaign to the Nicaraguan National Guard supported by US advisors. The Guard abducted and murdered Sandino during peace talks in 1936 and his rebellion collapsed.

Despite limited success due to conditions beyond his control Edson understood modern counterinsurgency. 'It was my belief', Edson concluded, 'that, if we were to succeed in our mission of eradicating the bandit element in Nicaragua, we should make every effort to gain the friendliness and cooperation of the peaceful citizenry' (Edson 1936). He lived among the people to learn their language and customs and to protect them from insurgent reprisals. Given time and enough troops his strategy might have worked.

While the Philippine conflict made little impression on US Army doctrine, the Marine Corps produced an entire volume on irregular warfare. Published in 1940, the *Small Wars manual* contained over 400 pages of theoretical and practical guidance on combating insurgency. In language similar to General Petraeus' pronouncements on Afghanistan, it warned that 'the application of purely military measures may not, by itself, restore peace and order because the fundamental causes of the condition of unrest may be economic, political, or social' (*Small Wars*

Manual 1940). Force had to be combined with efforts to address these underlying causes (*Small Wars Manual* 1940: I-9, 16). Unfortunately, the Marines forgot most of this wisdom when they shifted to conventional operations during the Second World War.

Cold War counterinsurgency

Following the Second World War the United States planned on reducing its armed forces as it had after the Civil War and the First World War. The advent of the Cold War and the outbreak of the Korean Conflict in 1950 made this reduction impossible. Defending Western Europe from a Soviet attack would be the primary mission of US forces deployed overseas and protecting South Korea (and with it Japan) a close second. At the same time, the United States and its allies faced the problem of communist 'wars of national liberation' supported by Moscow and/or Beijing. The nuclear stalemate, which made the cost of a confrontation between the US and the USSR unacceptably high, encouraged both sides to pursue their agenda through proxy wars, localized internal conflicts in which they supported one side in the hopes of either gaining an ally or forcing the other superpower to mount a costly intervention. The Soviets used the Vietnam War in this way, and the Americans returned the favour when the Soviets invaded Afghanistan.

The first such conflict occurred in Greece (1946–9), where communist insurgents challenged an American and British-backed government. Fiscal constraints forced the British to withdraw support in March 1947. With communist governments controlling Yugoslavia, Albania, Hungary, Romania and Bulgaria, Greece looked to be the last bastion of democracy in southeast Europe. Determined that the country should not fall, President Harry Truman provided $723.6 million in aid plus 800 military and 700 civilian advisors (McClintock 1992: 12). The Americans pursued a conventional approach, insisting that the Greek infantry move in to fix the enemy so that artillery could destroy them (Birtle 2006: 47–8).

This conventional approach, which under different circumstances would have cost the government popular support, succeeded largely because of insurgent mistakes and fortuitous circumstances. Believing that conditions favoured moving to the phase of mobile war in Mao's model, the communists reorganized their forces from small bands of 50 to 100 into formal 'brigades' and 'divisions' (Birtle 2006: 52). These larger formations could be more easily targeted by the regular Greek forces supported by the Americans. The following year the Soviet Union broke off relations with the communist leader Josef Broz Tito, who responded by closing the Yugoslav border to the Kremlin-backed Greek insurgents, depriving them of the safe havens and supply bases. Thus with minimal attention to winning hearts and minds, the Greeks achieved a conventional military victory over an unconventional foe.

HUK revolt

Like so many national liberation movements, the Hukbalahap (Filipino acronym for 'People's Liberation Army') developed out of the political chaos at the end of the Second World War. The 'Huk', as they were generally known in the West, were the military wing of the Communist Party of the Philippines. During the war they had allied with other guerrilla groups to fight the Japanese. When the United States granted the islands independence in 1946, the Huk launched an insurgency against the new government. The United States assisted its ally with military equipment and advisors via the Joint US Military Assistance Group (JUSMAG).

The Huk based its rural insurgency on poor peasants, primarily in central Luzon, promising them land in return for support. Despite their distrust of the government, only about 10 per cent of the population supported the insurgents, 10 per cent opposed them and 80 per cent remained neutral, preoccupied with the day-to-day struggle to survive (Tierney 2007: 55). At the height of the insurgency, the Huk had around 12,000 fighters supported by approximately 150,000 civilians out of a total population of two million in the affected area (Bohannan 1962: 21). They faced an American trained and equipped Filipino force of 25,000 (Bohannan 1962: 21). Under the circumstances victory might well go to the side that succeeded in winning over the 80 per cent of undecided peasants.

Initially, the Philippine government made the usual mistakes of a state threatened by insurgency. It refused to engage in land reform or take any significant measures to address the causes of unrest that fuelled the insurgency. It sought a purely military solution to the conflict, and the military for its part engaged in conventional operations learned from the Americans. These operations consisted of large sweeps supported by the air force. Over-reliance on firepower, requisitioning of supplies, and ill-treatment of civilians undermined government legitimacy and did little to hamper the elusive guerrillas.

The situation changed with the appointment of two outstanding individuals. In 1948, Colonel Edward Lansdale took charge of JUSMAG, and in 1950, Ramon Magsaysay became Philippine Defense Minister. The two men understood counterinsurgency and thoroughly revised the government strategy. With Lansdale's support Magsaysay launched the 'All-out Friendship or All-out Force' programme. This strategy combined an extensive hearts-and-minds campaign with aggressive counter-guerrilla operations. To begin with, the government engaged in genuine reform enabling poor peasants to acquire their own land. By providing medical assistance, digging wells, building schools and engaging in other development projects, they won over the peasant population, who were concerned more with their quality of life than with political ideology. Magsaysay also energized the military aspect of the campaign, replacing large-scale sweeps with small-unit counter-guerrilla patrols. The new approach produced dramatic results in a relatively brief time. By 1954 the Huk had been reduced to an active strength of around 200 (Bohannan 1962: 25–8).

During the 1960s, the US Army considered defeat of the Huk a textbook case of effective counterinsurgency. Although it employed the right principles in an effective strategy, the campaign also benefited from the favourable circumstances in which the government conducted it. The insurgents operated primarily on a single island, isolated from outside support and with no safe haven across a friendly border. Once the government began to engage in real reform, the Huk could not win a bidding war for the hearts and minds of the local people. Finally, defeat of the Huk did not end the communist threat to the Philippines, which flared up in later decades. Nonetheless, it was an impressive victory.

Vietnam

No conflict in American history has been so traumatic to the US military as Vietnam. The war lasted more than a decade, took 58,000 lives, and left the Pentagon with what many called a 'broken' army. Diehards still insist the United States never really lost the war in Vietnam but on the American home front. A conversation between an American and a North Vietnamese colonel following the war captures the frustration of the US military and makes an important point about insurgency. 'You never defeated us on the battlefield', the American observed. 'That may be so', the Vietnamese replied. 'It is also irrelevant' (Taw and Leicht 1992: 12).

Vietnam was the most complex conflict the American military had faced to date. The United States inherited the war from the French following their withdrawal and division of the country into North and South in 1954. Concerned that the communist North would overrun the South, the United States gave the Saigon government $85 million a year in aid and sent in advisors to assist its military (Herring 1986: 59). Emphasis on heavy armoured divisions and conventional-war training at the expense of counterinsurgency left the Army of the Republic of Vietnam (ARVN) ill prepared for the war it would have to fight (Krepinevich 1986: 23–4). That war was a hybrid affair in which ARVN and US forces faced both a conventional threat along the demilitarized zone separating North and South Vietnam and in the central highlands and an insurgency in the Mekong Delta and the heavily populated coastal zone (Dunn 1985: 77).

The military mistakes in Vietnam have been thoroughly analyzed and can be briefly summarized here. As the conflict escalated, the United States poured in more and more troops. However, the mission suffered from a very poor tooth-to-tail ratio. Of the 543,000 men and women deployed at the peak of the conflict, only 80,000 were combat troops (Krepinevich 1986: 197). These troops used conventional means that made a bad situation worse, especially excessive use of force. The commander of Military Assistance Command Vietnam, General William Westmoreland, maintained that the answer to insurgency was 'firepower', while Secretary of Defense Robert McNamara insisted the measure of effectiveness in the conflict should be 'body count' (Krepinevich 1986: 194–7). Westmoreland also concentrated disproportionately on search-and-destroy operations in the central highlands and neglected control of the delta and the coastal plain, where 90 per cent of the population lived (Boot 2002: 301).

These failures notwithstanding, US forces did develop some effective counterinsurgency programmes. These programmes fell into the operational category known as 'pacification', what today would be called 'clear and hold'. Based on is experience in Latin America during the interwar period, the Marine Corps developed the Combined Action Platoons (CAPs) initiative. Each CAP consisted of a Marine Rifle section (12–15 men) and a South Vietnamese Popular Forces (militia) platoon (30 men) stationed in a village. The CAP lived among the locals, built trust, engaged in patrolling, and gathered intelligence on the Viet Cong (Boot 2002: 304–8). Another successful counterinsurgency operation targeted the insurgent organization. Run by the Central Intelligence Agency (CIA), the Phoenix programme concentrated on taking out the Viet Cong political leadership. By the end of the war, the programme had killed 26,000 insurgents and persuaded 22,000 others to work with the South Vietnamese government. The CIA considered those it turned far more important that those it killed, as they provided intelligence on their erstwhile comrades (Boot 2002: 310). Finally, the creation in 1967 of an office of Civil Operations and Rural Development brought disparate programmes under a single roof.

However, these effective measures were a classic example of too little too late. They could not redeem a flawed strategy or compensate for the over-reliance on firepower. The 1968 Tet Offensive, which revealed that the enemy was far from defeated, and the end to college draft deferments the same year eroded popular support in the United States for continuing the struggle. Anti-war protests rocked college campuses and disrupted the 1968 Democratic Convention. Despite campaigning on a promise to end the war, the new President Richard Nixon prosecuted it with renewed vigour, switching to Vietnamization only in 1973. Two years after the American withdrawal, Saigon fell to North Vietnamese troops.

From Vietnam to 9/11

Counterinsurgency was one of the casualties of the Vietnam War. After the debacle in Southeast Asia, the Pentagon wanted nothing to do with it. A sea change in strategic thinking reflected this attitude. The Nixon doctrine eschewed direct participation in favour of 'foreign aid for internal defense'. The new approach promised to provide 'military and economic assistance when required' but insisted that the host nation must 'assume the responsibility of providing the manpower for its defense' (Nixon 2010). Military doctrine adopted the same posture, subsuming counterinsurgency into broad task categories such as 'Low-Intensity Conflict' (LIC) and 'Operations Other than War' (OOTW) catch-all terms for tasks it wished to avoid. The 1986 Goldwater-Nichols Defense Reorganization Act created Special Operations Command, an entity to which the military could gladly hand responsibility for counterinsurgency. As a result of these changes, counterinsurgency became a specialized task which few conventional soldiers learned. This approach worked well enough until 9/11; afterwards it had disastrous results.

In the three decades between the advent of the Nixon Doctrine and the beginning of the Global War on Terrorism the United States participated in only one protracted counterinsurgency campaign. The Salvadoran Civil War (1980–92) developed out of widespread poverty and a gross inequity that left 15 families with 90 per cent of the country's assets. When the army moved to block land reform in 1979, a series of resistance groups combined to form the Farabundo Marti National Liberation Front (FMLN), a Marxist organization committed to political reform and social change. From 1980 to 1983, the FMLN fought so successfully against the Salvadoran armed forces filled with reluctant conscripts that US advisors warned that without a massive infusion of US aid, the insurgents might very well win the war (Stanley 2006: 102). The US government responded with an infusion of cash and arms. It also sent a small number of advisors, most of them Special Forces, to advise the Salvadoran military. Although willing to accept tactical training from the Americans, Salvadorans officers resisted pressure to cease human rights violations, which were costing the government popular support. They understood that the Reagan administration cared more about fighting communism than it did about promoting human rights or fostering political reform (Schwarz 1991: 9, 44).

By the end of the 1980s, however, circumstances conspired to make possible a negotiated settlement of the conflict facilitated by the United States. The administration of George H.W. Bush was more willing than its predecessor to pressure the Salvadoran government into reform, especially after the fall of the Berlin Wall in 1989. The Marxist Sandinistas' electoral loss in Nicaragua also made fighting communism less of an imperative. That same year the FMLN launched an offensive against the capital San Salvador, occupying some of its wealthy neighbourhoods and disproving optimistic claims by the army that they were winning the war. The two sides had achieved a strategic stalemate, a situation that allowed the United States to work towards a negotiated settlement by making aid conditional upon an improved human rights record by the Salvadoran military and by nudging the government towards the bargaining table. By 1992, the United Nations (UN) had facilitated a peace accord that reduced the power of the Salvadoran army, incorporated FMLN fighters into a new civilian police force, and provided land grants to veterans from both sides (Mockaitis 2011).

While El Salvador was the United States' last major counterinsurgency effort before 9/11, US forces did deploy on missions with a striking similarity to counterinsurgency. In December 1992, the Marines intervened in Somalia to protect humanitarian aid shipments. They handed responsibility to a UN mission with a hefty US Army contingent the following spring. American forces found themselves in the midst of an escalating conflict that culminated in the infamous 3 October 1993 'Blackhawk Down' incident. The United States had to choose between a protracted counterinsurgency campaign and withdrawal. It chose withdrawal.

Bosnia confronted the United States with a similar dilemma, although one it could not as easily escape. After witnessing three years of genocide and brutal civil war, the United States finally intervened with its NATO allies to end the conflict with an air campaign in the autumn of 1995. Following the Dayton Peace Accords signed that December, it contributed 20,000 troops to the International Stabilization Force sent into Bosnia. However, the Clinton administration kept that contingent on a short leash, leading to charges that avoiding casualties was more important than any other goal. A similar mentality characterized the mission to Kosovo four years later. The

United States willingly led an air campaign against Yugoslavia to end genocide against the Kosavars, but it kept US troops in the Kosovo Force safely behind barbed wire or in heavily armed convoys. Clearly the ghosts of Vietnam had yet to be exercised.

Iraq

Ironically, President George W. Bush, who had campaigned on a pledge to avoid nation-building committed the United States to the two biggest nation-building missions in its history. However, the administration never envisioned either the Afghanistan or Iraq operation as a protracted counterinsurgency campaign. Once the US forces reached Kabul and Baghdad, they were to hand each country over to a pro-Western government and withdraw as soon as possible. This narrow approach devoid of any real contingency planning not only contributed to the outbreak of insurgencies in both countries, but guaranteed that those insurgencies would be more difficult to counter than they might have been had the United States prepared for them.

Although the regime of Saddam Hussein had not been involved even indirectly in 9/11, the Bush administration used the climate of fear created by the terrorist attacks to argue for an invasion of Iraq. Following the overthrow of the Taliban regime in Afghanistan but before the Taliban and al-Qaeda were decisively defeated, the Pentagon began to prepare for the invasion of Iraq. However, rather than use the existing invasion plan devised by former Central Command Commander General Anthony Zinni, Rumsfeld demanded a new plan that would require far fewer troops. Recognizing that the real challenge would come not from defeating the Iraqi Army, but from the need to occupy and control a country of 26 million just over twice the size of Idaho, OPLAN 1003–98 called for an invasion force of 400,000 troops (Gordon and Trainor 2006: 29–30). In 1999, Zinni's staff conducted a table-top seminar exercise to test the assumptions of the plan, during which they identified all of the problems the United States eventually encountered in Iraq (*Desert Crossing Seminar* 1999). Despite the predictions of the exercises, Rumsfeld ignored it. Consequently, the United States entered Iraq with more than enough troops to defeat Saddam's hollow military but not nearly enough to stabilize Iraq.

Mistakes made during the first year of the war have been thoroughly documented and exhaustively analyzed and can be briefly summarized here (Ricks 2006). A shortage of troops and lack of counterinsurgency training left the Army and Marines ill-prepared for a complex insurgency involving several resistance groups and foreign terrorists. Widespread looting wrecked an already fragile infrastructure and alienated ordinary Iraqis, who remarked bitterly that they had been better off under Saddam Hussein. In the face of escalating violence, soldiers defaulted to conventional tactics, relying on firepower to compensate for numbers. The decision to disband the Iraqi Army without pay and ban former Ba'ath Party members of a certain rank from holding office in the new Iraqi government further alienated people (Mockaitis 2008).

By 2006, many analysts considered Iraq a lost cause and advised withdrawal of American troops sooner rather than later. That autumn the bipartisan Iraq Study Group issued its report, warning that the situation was 'grave and deteriorating' (Baker and Hamilton 2006: 6). In an effort to reverse this trend, the White House adopted a surge strategy, sending in more than 20,000 additional troops to combat the insurgents. While putting additional boots on the ground certainly helped, success may have depended more upon the 'Anbar Awakening', the decision of concerned local citizens' committees to work with the US-led coalition to get rid of foreign mujahideen led by al-Qaeda in Iraq. This grassroots approach began to produce significant results. At the same time, the United States concentrated on training Iraqi military and police to take over security. By 2010, the situation in Iraq had improved to the point where the United States could reduce its troop strength from over 120,000 to 55,000.

Afghanistan

Although the United States has finally adopted an effective counterinsurgency strategy, the situation in Afghanistan is far more precarious than that in Iraq. The United States overthrew the Taliban in December 2001 by providing logistics and air support to the Northern Alliance leavened by CIA and Special Forces teams. No sooner did US troops reach Kabul, however, than Rumsfeld pushed to start withdrawing them. A State Department Advisor to the Bush administration argued for a continued US deployment of 25–30,000 US troops combined with an equal number of NATO personnel to maintain security in the post-conflict phase, but his proposal received no support (Haass 2010). The White House did not wish to become embroiled in a protracted nation-building mission. The International Stabilization Force (ISAF) that did deploy is a polyglot mission of 47 nations with differing mandates and rules of engagement and little unity of effort, never mind command. Numerous international, non-governmental, intergovernmental and private volunteer organizations descended on Afghanistan to engage in humanitarian aid, development and capacity building. Unfortunately, much of their effort has been characterized by 'incompetence, incoherence, and conflicting strategies' (Rashid 2008: 21). Finally, the US military focused on killing and capturing terrorists rather than employing a comprehensive counterinsurgency strategy.

As a result of this lacklustre approach, the United States missed a window of opportunity from late 2001 through 2004 in which it might have finished off the Taliban and built a stable Afghanistan. Instead, the insurgents and their al-Qaeda allies regrouped in the Federally Administered Tribal Area of Pakistan. (See Chapter 17 and 18 in this volume.) They gained sufficient strength to go on the offensive in Afghanistan and become a major security threat to Pakistan. Funded by opium cultivation and trafficking, which they taxed, the Taliban expanded their control (Peters 2009: 6–22). While the Taliban do use intimidation, much of their success comes from exercising effective 'shadow governance' in the areas they occupy. For example, Taliban courts have a greater reputation for fairness than the official Afghan courts (Kilcullen 2009: 276).

To recoup the deteriorating situation, the United States adopted a new strategy in December 2009. 'Clear and hold' replaced 'kill or capture' as the central strategic concept. President Barak Obama 'surged' an additional 30,000 troops to augment the 32,000 already deployed, promising to begin withdrawing them by the summer of 2011 (Obama 2010). The United States and its NATO allies ramped up training Afghan security forces, emphasizing counterinsurgency. Whether this new strategy achieves the desired result or proves to be too little too late remains to be seen.

The future of US counterinsurgency

Since 2001, the US military has undergone a dramatic change in its attitude towards and approach to counterinsurgency. The Army and Marine Corps accept it as a core task, no matter how much they may dislike it, and have adapted doctrine and created educational and training institutions to prepare for counterinsurgency operations. In 2006, they produced the first major overhaul of counterinsurgency doctrine since the Vietnam era. *FM 3–24: Counterinsurgency* examines the origin and development of insurgencies and contains a wealth of theoretical and practical information on how to combat them. Based upon the experience of past campaigns and the lessons of Iraq and Afghanistan, the manual sets military operations within the context of a comprehensive campaign employing all elements of national power (*FM 3–24* 2006).

In 2009 the Military Affairs Bureau of the State Department produced a strategic document explaining how to integrate those elements into a unified strategy. *U.S. Government Counterinsurgency*

Guide identifies security, economic development and information operations as crucial to success in counterinsurgency. These elements, the *Guide* maintains, need to be integrated by a political strategy combining them in a unified effort (*U.S. Counterinsurgency Guidelines* 2009: 17). However, because its counterinsurgency campaigns support threatened allied governments, the United States cannot easily get those governments to engage in the kind of reform necessary to defeat a counterinsurgency campaign. It faces the added difficulty of maintaining public support for protracted, often expensive, wars in which the survival of the country is not at stake. The overwhelming public support for the invasion of Afghanistan following 9/11 has declined as the conflict has surpassed Vietnam as the United States' longest war.

The future of US counterinsurgency will depend in large measure on how the military processes and preserves the experience of Afghanistan and Iraq long after those conflicts end. It might, as it did during the Second World War and the Cold War and following Vietnam, reject counterinsurgency as a core task. Since the Pentagon realizes that such a policy proved disastrous on both occasions, however, it seems unlikely that the US military will once again forget its own experience. The continuing challenge will be to develop and maintain a military capable of conducting both conventional and unconventional operations. The reorganization of the division-based army into brigades that can be combined in various ways for specific missions has produced flexibility absent from the pre-9/11 military. Nonetheless, as US armed forces emerge from the two present wars, the tension between preparing for conventional versus unconventional conflicts will remain. No matter how the Pentagon deals with this tension, one thing is certain: insurgencies will occur for the foreseeable future and the United States will undoubtedly get involved in some of them.

Recommended readings

Birtle, Andrew J. (2006) *U.S. Army Counter Insurgency and Contingency Operations Doctrine, 1942–1976*. Washington, DC.

Boot, Max (2002) *The Savage Wars of Peace: Small Wars and the Rise of American Power*. New York: Basic Books.

Gordon, Michael R. and General (ret.) Bernard Trainor (2006) *Cobra II: The Inside Story of the Invasion and Occupation of Iraq*. New York: Vintage Books.

Herring, George (1986) *America's Longest War: the United States and Vietnam, 1950–1975*. New York: Knopf.

Kilcullen, David (2009) *The Accidental Guerrilla: Fighting Small Wars in the Midst of a Big One*. New York: Oxford.

Krepinevich, Andrew F. (1986) *The Army and Vietnam*. Baltimore: Johns Hopkins.

Linn, Brian McAllister (1989) *The US Army and COIN in the Philippine War, 1899–1902*. Chapel Hill: University of North Carolina Press.

Mockaitis, Thomas R. (2008) *Iraq and the Challenge of Counterinsurgency*. Westport: Praeger.

Mockaitis, Thomas R. (2011) *Resolving Insurgencies*. Carlisle Barracks, PA: Strategic Studies Institute, US Army War College.

Rashid, Ahmed (2008) *Descent into Chaos: The United States and the Failure of Nation Building in Pakistan, Afghanistan, and Central Asia*. New York: Penguin.

Schwarz, Benjamin C. (1991) *American Counterinsurgency Doctrine and El Salvador: The Frustrations of Reform and the Illusions of Nations Building*. Santa Monica: RAND.

References

Baker III, James A. and Lee H. Hamilton (2006) *Report of the Iraq Study Group*. Washington, DC: USIP.

Birtle, Andrew J. (2006) *U.S. Army COIN and Contingency Operations Doctrine, 1942–1976*. Washington, DC.

Bohannan, Charles T.R. (1962) 'Anti-guerrilla Operations', *Annals of the American Academy of Political and Social Science*, 341 (May): 19–29.

Boot, Max (2002) *The Savage Wars of Peace: Small Wars and the Rise of American Power*. New York: Basic Books.

Deady, Timothy K. (2005) 'Lessons from a Succesful Counterinsurgency: the Philippines, 1898–1902', *Parameters* (spring): 53–68.

Desert Crossing Seminar After Action Report (28–30 June 1999) Declassified 2 July 2004. Available at: www. gwu.edu/~nsarchiv/NSAEBB/NSAEBB207/Desert%20Crossing%20After%20Action%20 Report_1999–06–28.pdf (accessed 22 December 2010).

Dunn, Peter M. (1985) 'The American Army, 1965–1973' in Ian Beckett and John Pimlott (eds), *Armed Forces and Modern Counterinsurgency*. New York: St. Martins, pp. 77–111.

Edson, Merritt (1936) 'The Coco Patrol', *Marine Corps Gazette* (August).

FM 3–24: Counterinsurgency. Washington, DC: Headquarters Department of the Army.

Gates, John M. (1982) 'The Pacification of the Philippines', in Joe E. Dixon (ed.), *The American Military in the Far East: Proceedings of the 9th Military History Symposium, USAF Academy*. Washington, DC: GPO.

Gordon, Michael R., and General (ret.) Bernard Trainor (2006) *Cobra II: The Inside Story of the Invasion and Occupation of Iraq*. New York: Vintage Books.

Haass, Richard N. (2010) 'We're Not Winning. It's Not Worth it', *Newsweek*, 18 July.

Herring, George (1986) *America's Longest War: the United States and Vietnam, 1950–1975*. New York: Knopf.

Kilcullen, David (2009) *The Accidental Guerrilla: Fighting Small Wars in the Midst of a Big One*. New York: Oxford.

Krepinevich, Andrew F. (1986) *The Army and Vietnam*. Baltimore: Johns Hopkins.

Laws of War: General Orders No. 100. Instructions for the Government of Armies of the United States in the Field. Prepared by Francis Lieber and promulgated by Abraham Lincoln, 24 April 1863. Available at The Avalon Project at Yale Law School: www.yale.edu/lawweb/avalon/lieber.htm#sec1 (accessed 11 May 2007).

Linn, Brian McAllister (1989) *The US Army and COIN in the Philippine War, 1899–1902*. Chapel Hill: University of North Carolina Press.

Linn, Brian McAllister (2002) *The Philippine War 1899–1902*. Lawrence: University Press of Kansas.

McClintock, Michael (1992) *Instruments of Statecraft: U.S. Guerrilla Warfare, COIN, and Counter-Terrorism, 1940–1990*. New York: Pantheon Books.

Mockaitis, Thomas R. (2008) *Iraq and the Challenge of Counterinsurgency*. Westport: Praeger.

Mockaitis, Thomas R. (2011) *Resolving Insurgencies*. Carlisle Barracks, PA: Strategic Studies Institute, US Army War College.

Morrison Taw, Jennifer and Robert C. Leicht (1992) *The New World Order and Army Doctrine: The Doctrinal Renaissance of Operations Short of War?* Santa Monica: RAND.

Nixon, President Richard. Speech on Vietnamization. 3 November 1969. Available at: http://vietnam. vassar.edu/doc14.html (accessed 20 December 2010).

Obama, President Barak. Speech Delivered at West Point. 1 December 2010. Available at: http://abcnews. go.com/Politics/full-transcript-president-obamas-speech-afghanistan-delivered-west/ story?id=9220661 (accessed 28 December 2010).

Peters, Gretchen S. (2009) 'The Taliban and the Opium Trade', in Antonio Giustozzi (ed.), *Decoding the Taliban: Insights from the Afghan Field*. London: Hurst, pp. 7–22.

Rashid, Ahmed (2008) *Descent into Chaos: The United States and the Failure of Nation Building in Pakistan, Afghanistan, and Central Asia*. New York: Penguin.

Ricks, Thomas (2006) *Fiasco: The American Military Adventure in Iraq*. Harmondsworth: Penguin Press.

Schwarz, Benjamin C. (1991) *American Counterinsurgency Doctrine and El Salvador: The Frustrations of Reform and the Illusions of Nations Building*. Santa Monica: RAND.

Small Wars Manual United States Marine Corps (1940) Washington, DC: GPO.

Stanley, William Dean (2006) 'El Salvador: State Building Before and After Democratization, 1980–1995', *Third World Quarterly*, 27 (1): 101–14.

Tierney, John J. Jr. (2007) 'Can a Popular Insurgency be Defeated?', *Military History* (March).

U.S. Counterinsurgency Guidelines (2009) Washington, DC: Department of State.

Williams, Jr., Robin M. (1962) 'Are Americans and Their Cultural Values Adaptable to the Concept and Techniques of Unconventional Warfare?', *Annals of the American Academy of Political and Social Science*, 341 (May): 82–92.

21

ISRAELI COUNTERINSURGENCY

The never-ending 'whack-a-mole'

Sergio Catignani

This chapter examines Israel's counter-terrorism and counterinsurgency strategy and campaigns particularly vis-à-vis Palestinian groups on the West Bank and Gaza Strip. It will also briefly look at the Israeli Defence Forces' (IDF) conduct in Lebanon during its occupation of the country between 1982 and 2000; thereafter it will focus on Israel's counterinsurgency campaigns during the two Intifadas (1987–91 and 2000–6), periods in which its counterinsurgency and population control measures were seriously put to the test.

There are considerable complexities and challenges when a state adopts such a series of kinetic campaigns. This is because, rather than achieving a quick 'battlefield decision', 'victory' or even diplomatic resolution, the Israeli state has usually succeeded in postponing further rounds of hostilities by temporarily suppressing the level of insurgent violence or shifting the problem to another geographical area until such hostilities reappear, often in a more virulent manner.

Israeli counterinsurgency 'strategy'

Although Israel has dealt with low-intensity threats to its national security since (and before) its establishment in 1948, its defence establishment has customarily focused on deterring full-scale conventional warfare. This was largely due to the perception that Israeli's enemies had the potential to wipe the state off the map should the state suffer a major defeat in conventional war. Accordingly, Israel's force posture and doctrine regarding low-intensity threats such as terrorism and insurgency have not been clearly formulated. As David Rodman has contended, the 'concept of "massive retaliation" captures best Israel's deterrent posture in the area of unconventional warfare. To deter low-intensity conflict, Jerusalem has consistently promised to retaliate disproportionately against terrorist [and guerrilla] organizations' (Rodman 2001: 77).

Such retaliation was often carried out beyond Israel's borders into countries that harboured terrorist/insurgent groups, chiefly against Palestinian *fedayeen* paramilitary units originating from Egypt (until the 1956 Suez War), against Palestinian terrorist groups in Jordan (until the 1970 Black September events), in Lebanon (from the 1970s onwards given the influx of Palestinian terrorists/insurgents from Lebanon following Black September) as well as Syria. Retaliatory operations have also been conducted through targeted killings across the world – most notably following the 1972 Munich Olympics massacre of Israeli athletes by the Palestinian Black September terrorist group. Retaliatory strikes frequently involved not only seizing or killing terrorists, but carrying out punitive reprisal operations inflicting collateral damage and casualties on states or local communities harbouring such groups. Such retaliatory operations could often escalate into full-scale war – as in the case against Egypt during the 1956 Suez War, against the Palestinian Liberation Organization (PLO) in Lebanon in 1982, against Hezbollah again in Lebanon in 2006 or into major military offensives – as in the case of Operation Litani against the PLO in 1978 and of Operations Accountability and Grapes of Wrath against Hezbollah carried out respectively in 1993 and in 1996 in Lebanon.

In any case, by 1967 Israeli counter-terrorist strategy had become firmly entrenched. It was by and large designated as a strategy of retaliation and pre-emption based on deterrence (Catignani 2009a: 68). Israeli counter-terrorist and counterinsurgent strategy has not really changed substantially in the years since. The IDF's emphasis on its qualitative edge, sought increasingly by developing its technological capabilities and the need to achieve a quick battlefield decision, have customarily dictated military operations and these have been pretty much been adapted in order to deal with asymmetric threats (Adamsky 2010: 93–129). Such constancy has been due to the fact that its operational doctrine has remained in part static over the years. Only at the tactical levels have Israeli security forces demonstrated significant innovation, often as a result of improvisation.

Such a lack of innovation at the operational and strategic levels have in part been a product of the nature of Israel's unique civil–military relations whereby politicians, lacking adequate intelligence and policy-making institutions as well as the political will to adopt long-term strategic goals, have often left it to the military to second-guess Israel's security strategies (Ben-Eliezer 1998; Peri 2006). This has proven problematic, though, because

> the military echelon has its own aspirations and needs. Internal forces are generated which are activist, vigorous, and targeted toward action and operational success. To the military, it seems as if political considerations are foreign to their *raison d'être* ... [T]o the military, creating and maintaining a record of operational success stands above any other consideration.
>
> *(Drory 2005: 4)*

The military, thus, has usually been engrossed with immediate tactical challenges rather than on Israel's future strategic options. During a period in which operational missions increased (as during the peak of Israel's counterinsurgency and counter-terrorist campaigns against Palestinian and Lebanese organizations during the Intifadas and Israel's occupation of Lebanon between 1982 and 2000) military commanders' views have also increased in influence and their recommendations are often willingly approved by higher leadership echelons within the IDF. As Brig.-Gen. Dov Tamari has argued, the military leadership echelons were 'molded to a tactical environment, not an operational one, and this is the reason behind the lack of innovation in military thought' (Tamari 2009: 707). The military has often pushed tactical operations which in hindsight have proved detrimental to Israel's strategic interests. And yet, such short-sighted military activism has repeatedly been used by Israel's political elites as a panacea for their inability to provide longer-term strategic thinking.

Overall, Israeli counterinsurgency/counter-terrorist activities have historically comprised the following three major elements:

1   Offensive operations, which are instigated by the IDF against terrorist/insurgent targets in order to prevent terrorist organizations from planning and organizing the initial stages of future terrorist/insurgent attacks.

2   Defensive operations, which are intended at pre-empting and disrupting attacks while ter-
      rorists/insurgents are on their way to target Israeli civilian and/or military targets.
3   Reprisal operations, which are intended to punish the planners and operatives of terrorist/
      insurgent attacks, as well as the supporters of terrorist organizations.

The combination of these three types of operations have been aimed at preventing attacks and
re-establishing deterrence if enemy attacks have actually been made on Israeli targets. Israel put
into place defensive measures at a fairly early period in the country's history against terrorist
attacks and in order to interdict insurgent infiltrations. Israel built fortified outposts along its
borders, placed minefields all along easily accessible passageways and strengthened these outposts
and minefields with armoured vehicle patrols, all in order to impede the Arab terrorist's and
insurgent's infiltration into Israel. 'Over the years the IDF's "perimeter defence system" continually expanded to incorporate such assets as ultra-sophisticated electronic equipment, maritime and airborne reconnaissance, border fences and patrol roads' (Catignani 2009a: 68). Such a
defence system was, moreover, extended during the 1982 Lebanon War into southern Lebanon
itself following the IDF's re-deployment in 1985 to 45 kilometres from its northern border.[1]

   The principal task for fighting terrorism throughout Israel's existence has been consigned to
the three main branches of Israeli intelligence: the Sherut haBitachon haKlali, the General Security Service, also known by its Hebrew acronyms, Shin Bet and Shabak), the Mossad (the Israeli
Intelligence Agency) and AMAN (the Israeli Defence Forces Intelligence Directorate). By
relying on a far-reaching intelligence-gathering network centred on both technologically
advanced electronic as well as human means, the Israeli intelligence services try to monitor and
infiltrate terrorist organizations in order to impede their operations at the earliest stage possible.
Over the last two decades this has often entailed the use of arrests or even 'targeted killings' by
Special Forces units, and if deemed too dangerous to conduct ground operations (usually led by
Special Forces units) then helicopter gunships, and more recently unmanned aerial vehicles
(UAVs), have been used to eliminate such operatives. Aerial strikes have also been employed in
order to 'decapitate' the political-military leadership echelons.

Israeli security policies in occupied land

Fighting terrorism and insurgency has been a constant concern for Israel, but it has proven even
more challenging when trying to 'pacify' populations under its control in south Lebanon
between 1982 and 2000 and in the Territories since 1967. Having taken control of the Sinai,
Golan Heights and the Territories of the Gaza Strip and West Bank with the lightning victory
achieved during the 1967 Six-Day War, Israel confronted the problem of having to control and
manage a large local Palestinian population. Moshe Dayan, the Israeli Minister of Defence from
1967 to 1974, was responsible for devising and applying Israel's security policy in the Territories
during the first seven years after the war. Dayan made sure that the IDF maintained a light foot-
print, that is, an 'invisible occupation' in the Territories in order to reduce the chances of friction between the Palestinian population and local IDF forces. This in turn helped to avoid the
local Palestinian population from radicalizing and providing support to the PLO and other Palestinian organizations clamouring for nationhood and self-determination. Such a policy lasted as
long as Dayan was minister of defence.

   By the mid 1970s, Israeli policy in the Territories became blatantly expansionist – with the
rise to power in 1977 of the right-wing Likud party Israeli settlements mushroomed – and
security measures became more widespread and stifling. By expanding settlements in the Territories Israel forcibly took control of local water resources, expanded road networks linking

communities and increased checkpoint and border controls as well as the number of permits required by Palestinians to move, work and basically live in the Territories.[2] So effective were Israeli security measures in the Territories that no significant armed Palestinian faction was able to operate from there. Palestinian factions consequently operated from neighbouring countries. Following the PLO's resettlement into south Lebanon in 1970, Israel's main security concerns increasingly derived from its northern neighbour.

Interlude: the Lebanon (mis)adventure

The PLO and other Palestinian factions from the early 1970s took control of southern Lebanon and began building significant terrorist and paramilitary capabilities, which were increasingly employed to attack northern Israel (through rocket and mortar barrages and terrorist infiltrations) and Israeli/Jewish targets abroad (through spectacular terrorist attacks). Israel progressively carried out incursions and bombardments in south Lebanon in order to try and deter further Palestinian attacks, which nevertheless still continued. Both the invasion of Lebanon in 1982 and the IDF's subsequent re-deployment and establishment of the south Lebanon 'security zone' were carried out in order to stop Palestinian guerrilla/terrorist infiltrations and their highly disruptive Katyusha rocket and mortar attacks into northern Israel. Whilst Israel's invasion managed to bring the PLO into temporary disarray by getting its leadership exiled to Tunis in 1985, Israel's security patrols and operations, conducted with the assistance of the predominantly Christian Maronite South Lebanese Army (SLA), as well as the establishment of the southern security zone comprised of company-sized fortified outposts and security checkpoints led to the alienation of the initially welcoming local Shi'ite population.

By late 1982, in fact, the Islamist Shi'ite Hezbollah ('Party of God') was established and began to conduct suicide terrorist attacks against IDF units and command centres and suicidal assaults on IDF/SLA outposts. (See Chapter 14 in this volume.) These attacks, aided by Iranian and Syrian training and funding, became increasingly coordinated, sophisticated and most of all lethal.[3] During the mid-to-late 1990s, Hezbollah's growing ability to inflict casualties on IDF units increasingly led the IDF to conserve its regular units by reducing their patrols and operations. It also brought about growing domestic opposition to the continued presence of Israel in south Lebanon. So, whilst Israel's 1982 invasion into Lebanon set out to reduce threats originating from its northern neighbour, the IDF/SLA deployment galvanized Shi'ite opposition to the Israeli occupation to the point where rocket attacks and terrorist/guerrilla infiltrations against Israel paradoxically increased the threat originating from south Lebanon.

Frustration with Hezbollah's increasingly effective terrorist/guerrilla campaign led Israel, consequently, to carry out two large-scale artillery and air bombardment campaigns against south Lebanon and Beirut in Operation Accountability (1993) and Operation Grapes of Wrath (1996). 'In these two operations the principle of transferring the war to the enemy's territory was substituted by the concept of transferring fire to the enemy's territory instead' (Catignani 2009a: 71). This change was due to two main issues. First, Israeli domestic and international public opinion could not stomach another large-scale ground offensive into Lebanon. Second, this feeling was underpinned by the Israeli military and political leadership echelon's growing casualty aversion, common amongst post-military Western societies (Ben-Eliezer 2004). The use of airpower in counterinsurgent warfare increasingly became Israel's preferred method for fighting Hezbollah units in Lebanon (Gordon 1998). In any case, Israel's bombing campaigns did not really have the desired effect of deterring further Hezbollah guerrilla/terrorist activities. Paradoxically, Israel's operations helped Hezbollah establish a modus vivendi with the IDF/SLA, whereby Hezbollah would not attack Israeli civilian targets in north Israel as long as the

IDF's and SLA's security operations in south Lebanon did not cause a priori civilian casualties or collateral damage. Thereafter most skirmishes remained within the confines of the security zone. Despite attempts on the part of several Israeli prime ministers to reach, during the 1990s, a peace agreement with Syria and, by extension, Lebanon, Israel was not able to come to an agreement with either country.

This finally led Prime Minister Ehud Barak to order the unilateral withdrawal of Israel from south Lebanon in accordance with United Nations (UN) Security Resolution 425. This occurred speedily and without any major incident in May 2000. Without an agreement in hand and still at odds with Hezbollah, which continued to claim that the Shebaa Farms were part of Lebanese occupied territory within the Golan Heights,[4] the Lebanese quagmire would in any case drag Israel into war again in the summer of 2006. Notwithstanding its poor operational performance,[5] after the cessation of hostilities in mid-August 2006 and with the subsequent reinforcement of the peace-keeping UN Interim Force in Lebanon contingent in southern Lebanon, an uneasy quiet has persisted. But such 'quiet' could easily deteriorate into another war, given Hezbollah's continued militancy and re-armament efforts sustained with the help of Iran and Syria (Eshel 2010; Opall-Rome 2009).

The Intifada

Israel's ability to suppress Palestinian self-determination in the Territories together with the PLO's disarray caused by Israel's invasion of Lebanon in 1982 intensified resentment towards the Israeli occupation on the part of the Palestinian indigenous population. This ultimately manifested itself in a spontaneous uprising against Israeli occupation on December 1987 and came to be known as the Intifada. Such an uprising was widespread and unremitting. During the first two years of the Intifada there were 60,243 disturbances (about 110 a day); 2,701 Molotov cocktails were launched; 140 explosive charges were set off; and there were 715 instances of intentional fires (Cohen-Almagor 1991: 21). Whilst political frustration was a significant factor in encouraging local Palestinians to demonstrate, relative economic deprivation was a key cause for the outburst and initial phases of the first Intifada. An initial IDF study of the Intifada found that most of the detained demonstrators did not have former records as political activists and that many took part in demonstrations for the very first time in their lives. The study also found that 'the most basic principles of politics did not mean anything to most of those detained. They were not familiar with the Palestinian Covenant, and some even did not know about its existence' (Cohen-Almagor 1991: 20).

However, within the first six months of the start of the Intifada the PLO was able to co-opt most of the popular resistance committees and coordinate further unrest in the Territories. As in the past, the Israeli security services' reach often went far beyond the Middle East region. With the increasing participation of the PLO in the uprising, the Israeli security forces did not limit their operational activities within the Territories. PLO activists were, for example, killed in Cyprus. In Tunis, PLO Chairman Yasser Arafat's deputy, Khalil al-Wazir (aka Abu Jihad) was also assassinated in order to deter further PLO interference in the Territories.

In order to deter local populations from providing logistical, intelligence and any other form of assistance to the various terrorist organizations involved in fighting against it, Israel increasingly made use of several emergency security measures, which had already been set up by the British Mandatory Government in Palestine with the 1945 Defence (Emergency) Regulations. This has allowed it to employ a variety of punitive measures against terrorists, terrorist suspects and by extension anyone actively (or even passively) supporting terrorist organizations. These measures comprised, amongst others, the incarceration of terrorists, the administrative detention of suspects, who cannot be put on trial in Israeli civilian courts for various reasons, the expulsion of key local political leaders/agitators, and the demolition or sealing up of homes of terrorists either apprehended or killed during their failed terrorist attack. In the last case, for example, between 9 December 1987 and the end of 1993, the Israeli security services completely or partially demolished 493 homes (87 per cent of which were demolished between 1988 and 1990) as well as completely or partially sealed 443 homes (62 per cent of which were sealed between 1988 and 1990) as a punitive measure (B'Tselem n.d.a).

Untrained in civilian pacification measures, during the initial stages of the Intifada, the IDF resorted to a 'policy of beatings' and utilized non-lethal and semi-lethal weapons, such as plastic bullets, rubber-coated bullets and tear gas. Rules of engagement (ROE) allowed for the use of firearms, but their use was sanctioned only in life-threatening situations. However, such ROE were not firmly enforced after some initial court-martials against ROE violators proved demoralizing for IDF units on the ground. These units often struggled to demarcate clearly between life-threatening and non-life-threatening scenarios and routinely defaulted to the use of live fire in order to protect themselves. Consequently, Palestinian deaths and casualties were not insubstantial. B'Tselem, the Israeli Information Centre for Human Rights in the Occupied Territories, revealed the following statistics regarding the first Intifada (9 December 1987 to 13 September 1993): 1,070 Palestinians were killed in the Territories by Israeli security services (39 per cent of whom were minors under the age of 17), whilst 118 Israelis were killed in the Territories by Palestinians (40 per cent of whom were civilians) (B'Tselem n.d.b). Furthermore, the lack of clear guidance from upper military echelons, together with the thorny nature of having to control an unarmed civilian population through the threat or actual use of violence, proved particularly demoralizing and led to the rise in the phenomenon of conscientious objection within the IDF lower ranks.[6]

The effectiveness of these reprisal measures was dubious even though they were justified by Israeli security officials as a means for reinstating some form of deterrence vis-à-vis terrorist organizations and their supporters. Their employment was really more the reflection of Israeli frustration with terrorism and, particularly during the Intifada, with the local population's insubordination expressed through demonstrations, strikes and low-scale violence. Even large-scale and sweeping curfews on Palestinian villages and towns as well as the closure of the Territories in the aftermath of severe attacks within Israel have demonstrated to be of unsatisfactory operational efficiency. Very often such punitive measures have been carried out in order to placate Israeli public opinion. However, such measures have in turn galvanized Palestinians' determination to fight the Israeli occupation in the Territories, particularly within Palestinian Islamist factions such as Palestinian Islamic Jihad and, most notably, Hamas (Islamic Resistance Movement).

An offshoot of the local Islamic Brotherhood, Hamas was established in 1987 and initially operated like its precursor as a charitable Islamic organization. (See Chapter 14 in this volume.) This enabled it to recruit and increase its membership through the provision of legitimate educational, welfare and health activities. At the same time Hamas – with its decision to participate in early 1988 in the Intifada's violent activities – was also able to indoctrinate with extremist Jihadist doctrine and to train in suicide terrorist and guerrilla warfare tactics new members within the military wing of the organization (Behrendt 2007). By the early 1990s Hamas was already vying for political primacy in the Territories and played a major role in trying to derail the Israeli–Palestinian peace process outlined in the 1993 Oslo Peace Accord through the use of spectacular suicide terror attacks, which intensified once the Al-Aqsa Intifada broke out. As Hatina has aptly put it, 'if the first intifada (1987–92) witnessed the canonization of civic resistance, the second intifada (al-Aqsa) witnessed the sanctification of suicide acts' (Hatina 2006: 40).

When the Oslo peace process' permanent status negotiations between Prime Minister Ehud Barak and President Yasser Arafat failed in July 2000 at Camp David,[7] Arafat sought to gain further concessions by encouraging violent demonstrations in the Territories. After Ariel Sharon's provocative visit to the Temple Mount on 28 September 2000,[8] violent demonstrations broke out, which gradually escalated to the point that the Voice of Palestinian radio could declare the following day that a new Intifada had begun.

The Al-Aqsa Intifada

The Al-Aqsa Intifada, in the first year of its occurrence, progressed over four overlapping stages. During the first four to five weeks of the conflict – that is, until mid-November 2000 – the conflict exhibited the connotation of a popular uprising similar to that of the first Intifada. Following lessons learned from its experiences from previous armed clashes with the Palestinian security forces during the September 1996 Hasmonean tunnel and the May 2000 Naqba riots, the IDF adopted effective ROE that significantly limited the numbers of own casualties suffered during the initial three months of the Al-Aqsa Intifada. The IDF's tactics, which included the employment of 'sophisticated gear and personal mobile shelters, reduced casualties to a minimum' (Eshel 2001: 36).

Nevertheless, the IDF did not possess a sufficient amount of non-lethal anti–riot weapons and was required to rely on 'less-than-lethal' weapons, such as tear gas, stun grenades and rubber-coated plastic bullets. As in the case of the first Intifada, these could often cause a significant number of casualties and occasional fatalities if fired outside the maximum stand-off combat ranges (100–150 m) (Eshel 2001: 37). With significant Palestinian civilian casualties and a real lack of popular enthusiasm for a prolonged uprising, Palestinian Security Services forces, set up under the Oslo peace process to fight terrorism, began to shoot at IDF units from within groups of stone-throwing civilians (usually youths). Guerrilla and terrorist ambushes began also to be employed by the various Palestinian factions, most notably Hamas, Palestinian Islamic Jihad, Fatah Tanzim and Force 17, which began operating together under the umbrella terrorist organization, the Al-Aqsa Martyrs' Brigade. Attacks were normally aimed at settler and IDF traffic on roads adjacent to Palestinian towns. They ranged from sniper shootings to subsequently more intricate techniques such the use of Lebanese-style roadside improvised explosive devices (IEDs) and mortar barrages. By early 2001 Palestinian terrorist groups essentially adopted a mixture of guerrilla warfare tactics in the Territories and increasingly lethal suicide terrorist attacks against Israeli civilian targets which peaked in early 2002.

As the second Intifada progressed, both the escalation and militarization of Palestinian violence made it easier for the IDF to adopt and employ its full arsenal and military-style incursions. Given that Palestinian insurgents were able to attack IDF units with insidious IEDs and with large calibre assault rifles, the IDF decided to employ not only armoured personnel carriers, but also introduce *Merkava* (Chariot) main battle tanks in early 2001 into urban operations involving close-quarter combat. Up until then previous chiefs of staffs had vetoed their use in such scenarios due the detrimental effect they could have on Israel's international image. However, then outgoing IDF Armoured Corps commander Brig.-Gen. Udi Shani shrugged off such concerns by contending that, 'The bottom line is that the tank is performing excellently and is very effective.... We don't exactly think it is a wise and an ethical way to operate tanks against the masses. But that's the way it is' (Rodan 2001: 16). His successor, Brig.-Gen. Avigdor Klein, justified the use of main battle tanks as a way for the IDF is able to better protect its forces 'and use less manpower to accomplish necessary missions' (Opall-Rome 2003). Such measures became common practice once Ariel Sharon came to power in early 2001.

Israel's government under Ehud Barak had officially pursued a defensive 'policy of containment' during the first year of the Intifada, in order to maintain some resemblance of continued diplomatic relations and negotiations with the Palestinian Authority. However, the increasing spiral of violence brought about tit-for-tat Palestinian attacks and Israeli reprisal operations. These contributed, along with Barak's inability to reach a peace agreement with Yasser Arafat, to the electoral victory of Ariel Sharon's Likud party in February 2001. Sharon and Likud were decidedly more intent in crushing the Palestinian insurgent/terrorist campaign given that they did not see any serious peace partner for peace negotiations. In December 2001, the Israeli government defined the Palestinian Authority as a 'terror-supporting entity'. Such a definition had clear policy implications given that many politicians as well as military leaders saw terrorism as an existential threat that had to be extirpated by any means and which necessitated Israeli refusal to concede to Palestinian terrorist organizations' demands.[9]

Under Sharon's leadership Israel adopted a proactive, if not offensive, posture vis-à-vis Palestinian terrorism following the Passover *seder* night massacre which resulted in 30 deaths and over 140 civilian casualties at the Park Hotel in Netanya. The IDF was unleashed with Operation 'Defensive Shield' and around 30,000 IDF personnel organized in various joint forces, comprised of mainly infantry and armour supported by field intelligence, combat engineer and Special Forces units, 'swarmed' the Territories.

IDF infantry units advanced whilst surrounded by an aerial and intelligence 'bubble', which proceeded ahead of them, targeted the enemy and opened up the terrain. The operational doctrine of using a 'bubble' entailed three facets:

1   the land dimension comprised of observation posts and snipers concealed in the terrain employed in order to gather information and neutralize targets;
2   the aerial dimension comprised of mini-UAVs and other aircraft also employed in order to gather real-time surveillance on ground movement and, together with attack helicopters, to neutralize targets;
3   the intelligence dimension comprised of both human and electronic intelligence sensors both employed to provide intelligence on both friendly and non-friendly activity. Improved real-time intelligence capabilities led to the reduction of the sensor-to-shooter cycle (Fischman 2004).

These joint task forces carried out multiple operations into many of the main Palestinian towns known for supporting terrorist activities such as Jenin, Tul Karem, Nablus, Ramallah, Gaza City, Khan Yunis and Rafah, in order to destroy bomb and weapons factories, kill terrorists, kill or detain suspected terrorists, seize weapons and explosives as well as re-establish control of the territories that had been under the PA's control.

In addition in the months following October 2000, Cobra helicopter units equipped with little more than personal protective equipment, night-vision goggles and radio communications operated almost constantly in support of Israeli ground and air units. The helicopter's almost total lack of armour was not an issue in operations that benefited from total air superiority over operationally familiar ground (Opall-Rome 2002: 21). Fixed-winged aircraft, other more protected attack helicopters and especially UAVs were increasingly used in order to attack insurgents operating in densely populated urban areas with growing precision. UAVs were particularly employed in order to provide live imagery of targets to commanders coordinating and approving attack helicopter strikes that could entail the risk of collateral damage (Fulghum and Wall 2002: 26). Such precision was enhanced during the Al-Aqsa Intifada by a system developed by the Israeli defence industry that partitions 'the urban battlefield into precise increments and gives each building in a city … an individual four-digit designation so that both land and air forces know exactly which target they are trying to hit' (Fulghum and Wall 2002: 25). Employment of precision-guided munitions and other targeting assets did not mean, though, that collateral damage or civilian casualties were always deliberately avoided. Indeed, on several occasions, the IDF rashly employed disproportionate force.[10]

The IDF's coordinated attacks were also subsequently facilitated even more through its 'Digital Ground Forces' programme called *Tsayad* ('Hunter'), which has endeavoured to provide broadband communications capabilities to all ground units. A new secure cellular communications network dubbed *Vered Harim* ('Mountain Rose') was deployed in July 2004 in order to facilitate personal and secure communications between commanders from company level upwards and brigade or division headquarters (Ben-David 2004b: 20). This communications network was used in subsequent urban operations particularly during IDF incursions into the Gaza Strip.

Following Defensive Shield's five-week offensive, the IDF subsequently launched the 13-month Operation 'Determined Path' in which it deployed units around major towns in order to continue the interception of suspected terrorists and the seizure of weapons and explosives on an ongoing basis. Curfews, closures and house demolitions increased in number, partially in reaction to continued successful Palestinian terror attacks in Israel. Israel's security establishment understood that they had a rather detrimental effect on Israel's international public image given that such measures often had negative humanitarian consequences, but as former coordinator of government activities in the territories, Maj.-Gen. Amos Gilad, has argued,

> It is very difficult to solve this contradiction between terror, on the one side, and humanitarian assistance, on the other. For example, to ease the daily life of Palestinians we must open the roads between cities, but the moment we do that, we are hit with terrorist attacks.
>
> *(Gilad 2002: 13)*

Shrugging off the negative political consequences of various security policies has been a common practice within the Israeli security establishment and has been justified by quite a few military commanders who have stated often that Israel's security imperative vis-à-vis terrorist threats trump other more 'ephemeral' considerations, such as international public opinion or negative strategic repercussions. During quieter periods, when the IDF has been able to normalize Israeli security by reducing the threat of terror to a tolerable level, internal investigations or committees have time and again reached different conclusions. For example, punitive house demolitions carried out by the Israeli security services during the Al-Aqsa Intifada resulted in the demolition of ten homes in 2001, 252 in 2002, 225 in 2003 and 177 in 2004 (B'Tselem n.d.a). Despite declarations by the Israeli commanders that house demolitions had a deterrent effect on terrorist activities during the first four years of the conflict, a military committee headed by Maj.-Gen. Udi Shani concluded in early 2005 that 'the damage to Israel caused by the demolitions was greater than the benefits because the deterrence, limited if at all, paled in comparison to the hatred and hostility toward Israel that the demolitions provoked among the Palestinians'. This conclusion led the IDF to officially renounce the use of house demolitions as a standard operational procedure for deterring further terrorist attacks (Harel 2005).

In any case, the rise in successful Palestinian suicide terrorist attacks in Israel during the first three years of the Intifada together with the continuing inability to reach a peace settlement under the US-sponsored 2002 Road Map for Peace produced a situation where it was becoming too costly for Israel to remain indefinitely enmeshed in the Territories. The financial and human costs associated with the fight against terror in the Territories were taking their toll on the IDF. Training, for example, beyond company level became almost non-existent and conscientious objection became even more widespread. Regular army conscripts, who in the past underwent 17-week rotations of training and operational activities during their three-year mandatory service, were continually deployed in operational missions. During the Al-Aqsa Intifada, 'regular units receive[d] only two periods of four weeks of training each year'. Battalions were the largest unit that underwent full exercise, whilst full brigade exercises were virtually unheard of (Ben-David 2004a). The IDF's force preparedness had deteriorated significantly and proved to be one of the reasons for the IDF's poor operational performance during the 2006 Lebanon War.

This state of affairs led Prime Minister Sharon to decide to unilaterally withdraw from parts of the Territories as well as approve in 2003 the construction of a security fence that would enable Israel to keep suicide bombers and other attacks out of Israel. Prime Minister Ariel Sharon approved the creation of the 650 km security fence, known in Israel as the 'separation fence', in order to impede the infiltration of further terrorists through Israel's porous 'Green Line' borders. By late 2005, almost 80 per cent of the fence had been constructed. Along this buffer zone troops together with UAVs and aerostat surveillance carried out surveillance and interdiction activities, which were coordinated by sophisticated C4I centres. Despite international condemnation and the non-binding ruling by the July 2004 International Court of Justice declaring the fence illegal, the fence actually led to a dramatic reduction in the number of successful suicide terror attacks in Israel (Kaplan *et al.* 2005).

Yet, a resolution to the conflict was still far out of sight by 2005. Palestinian groups, Hamas in particular, were able to adapt their tactics into an 'over/under' conflict in which rather than resorting to suicide bombings, mortar and *Kassam* rockets were instead used to target Israeli targets within the Green Line and with IEDs within the Territories. The IDF conducted several large-scale incursions into the Gaza Strip with Operations 'Rainbow' and 'Days of Penitence' in 2004 in order to dismantle Hamas' terrorist weapons and bomb-making workshops. These periodic incursions occurred after Israel's unilateral disengagement from the Gaza Strip and from several towns in the West Bank in August 2005, mainly Operations 'Summer Rains' and 'Autumn Clouds' in 2006 and 'Hot Winter' in 2008. All of these incursions set out for the most part to take apart Hamas rocket-making capabilities and stop the relentless mortar and rocket launches against Israel following the IDF's deployment from the Gaza Strip. They reached their pinnacle with the reprisal operation carried out in January 2009 known as Operation 'Cast Lead' which set out to debilitate Hamas' military capabilities and destroy it as a viable terrorist organization.[11] The operation was prompted by Israeli irritation with Hamas' declaration that it had defeated the IDF by forcing its redeployment from Gaza as a result of unilateral disengagement in 2005 together with several abductions of IDF personnel patrolling the border with Gaza. In addition Hamas' victory in the Palestinian Authority's parliamentary elections in January 2006 and the organization's continuous rocket attacks on Israel were the major factors that led Israel to launch Operation Cast Lead. Although the IDF achieved significant tactical successes – obtained mainly through a more lethal and improved joint manoeuvring performance that was enhanced by the IDF's increasingly effective network-centric and intelligence capabilities – it was not able to dismantle Hamas' political and military infrastructure, which even after having received a significant blow is today restocking its arsenal and regrouping itself particularly with the help of Hezbollah.

Conclusion

As seen in this chapter, the state of Israel has been constantly involved in counter-terrorist and counterinsurgent operations since its establishment in 1948. Whilst Israel has never developed a fully fledged counterinsurgent strategy, its continual engagement with terrorist and insurgent threats helped it to develop a de facto policy of 'massive retaliation' in order to quickly re-establish deterrence vis-à-vis terrorist/insurgent organizations. The IDF's tactical inventiveness and assertiveness enabled it to wear down temporarily through attrition Palestinian and Arab organizations' capabilities. IDF campaigns, following the escalation of violence, led occasionally to brief interludes of relative calm or to the forced removal of an organization from a particular geographical area.

Yet, as Noemi Gal-Or has persuasively argued, 'the Palestinian struggle ... changes sectors, wears different forms, and passes from intensity on the military level to intensity on the political-diplomatic one, but Israel has continued to respond with "operationalist" solutions' (Gal-Or 1990: 223). Such '"operationalist" solutions' have usually tended to postpone a further round of hostilities, but they have not been able to undermine the motivations that often help Palestinian and other Arab organizations to re-animate and continue their terrorist and insurgent fight against Israeli occupations. Without further political and diplomatic efforts that could re-ignite Israeli–Palestinian and even Israeli–Arab peace negotiations, it will only be a matter of time before another major operation or even war breaks out; whether this will be in the guise of sub-conventional or unconventional warfare remains to be seen. Clearly, a military can (poorly) manage, but not resolve an insurgency through military means alone. This is a lesson that Israel (and other states) continues to struggle to apply when appraising its strategy vis-à-vis the Palestinian problem and the greater Middle East. Consequently, Israel finds itself repeatedly whacking an insurgent in one area only to find it reappear in some other place or form.

Notes

1 On the rationale behind Israel's decision to invade Lebanon, on the IDF campaign and the resulting quagmire Israel experienced, see Schiff and Ya'ari (1984).
2 For a detailed overview of Israeli security policies in the Territories between 1967 and 2000, see Gazit (2003).
3 On Hezbollah's combat tactics, see Blanford (1999).
4 The United Nations has agreed with Israel that the area is not covered by UN Security Council Resolution 425, which called for the return of Israeli-occupied Lebanese territories.
5 On the issue of the Lebanon Summer War, see Harel and Issacharoff (2008); Bar-Joseph (2009); Kober (2008).
6 On conscientious objection during the first Intifada, see Linn (1996).
7 On the failed Oslo process final status negotiations, see Bregman (2005).
8 Such a visit had, in fact, been approved beforehand by the chief of the Palestinian Security Services and Israel's Minister of Internal Security.
9 The IDF Chief of Staff declared in July 2002 that, 'I believe as a military man, that this confrontation obligates us to win in a fashion that will be burned into the consciousness of the Palestinian side, that terror and violence have no chance of bringing any achievements whatsoever' (Ya'alon 2002: 11).
10 The most notorious case was when the Israel Air Force F-16 dropped a one-tonne bomb in a densely populated neighbourhood of Gaza City in the middle of the night of 22 July 2002 in order to assassinate then leader of Hamas' military wing, Salah Shehade. In the attack 15 people died, including Shehade, his wife and nine of his children. Fifty other civilians required medical attention following the attack as well.
11 For a detailed analysis of Operation Cast Lead, see Catignani (2009b).

Recommended readings

Catignani, Sergio (2009) *Israeli Counter-Insurgency and the Intifadas: Dilemmas of a Conventional Army*. London: Routledge.

Cohen, Stuart A. (2008) *Israel and Its Army: From Cohesion to Confusion*. London: Routledge.

Gazit, Shlomo (2003) *Israel and Hizbollah: An Interstate and Asymmetric War in Perspective*. London: Frank Cass.

Jones, Clive A. and Sergio Catignani (2009) *Israel and Hizbollah: An Interstate and Asymmetric War in Perspective*. London: Routledge.

Kober, Avi (2009) *Israel's Wars of Attrition*. London: Routledge.

References

Adamsky, Dima (2010) *The Culture of Military Innovation: The Impact of Cultural Factors on the Revolution in Military Affairs in the USSR, the US and Israel*. Stanford: Stanford University Press.

Bar-Joseph, Uri (2009) 'The Hubris of Initial Victory: The IDF and the Second Lebanon War', in Clive Jones and Sergio Catignani (eds), *Israel and Hizbollah: An Asymmetric Conflict in Historical and Comparative Perspective*. London: Routledge, pp. 147–62.

Behrendt, Sven (2007) *The Secret Israeli-Palestinian Negotiations in Oslo: Their Success and Why the Process Ultimately Failed*. London: Routledge.

Ben-David, Alon (2004a) 'All Quiet on the Eastern Front, so Israel will Revise IDF Organization and Doctrine', *Jane's International Defense* (March): 37.

Ben-David, Alon (2004b) 'Israel Deploys Cellular Comms Network', *Jane's Defence Weekly*, 41 (21).

Ben-Eliezer, Uri (2004) 'Post-Modern Armies and the Question of Peace and War: The Israeli Defense Forces in the "New Times"', *International Journal of Middle East Studies*, 36 (1): 49–70.

Ben-Eliezer, Uri (1998) *The Making of Israeli Militarism*. Bloomington: Indiana University Press.

Blanford, Nicholas (1999) 'Hizbullah Attacks Force Israel to Take a Hard Look at Lebanon', *Jane's Intelligence Review*, 11 (4): 32–7.

Bregman, Ahron (2005) *Elusive Peace: How the Holy Land Defeated America*. London: Penguin.

B'Tselem (n.d.a) *House Demolitions as Punishment*. Available at: www.btselem.org/english/Punitive_Demolitions/Statistics_Since_1987.asp (accessed 5 May 2010).

B'Tselem (n.d.b) *Statistics: Fatalities in the First Intifada*. Available at: www.btselem.org/English/statistics/First_Intifada_Tables.asp (accessed 5 May 2010).

Catignani, Sergio (2009a) 'Israeli Counter-insurgency Strategy and the Quest for Security in the Israeli–Lebanese Conflict Arena', in Clive Jones and Sergio Catignani (eds), *Israel and Hizbollah: An Asymmetric Conflict in Historical and Comparative Perspective*. London: Routledge.

Catignani, Sergio (2009b) 'Variation on a Theme: Israel's Operation Cast Lead and the Gaza Strip Missile Conundrum', *RUSI Journal*, 154 (4): 66–73.

Cohen-Almagor, Raphael (1991) 'The Intifada: Causes, Consequences and Future Trends', *Small Wars and Insurgencies*, 2 (1): 12–40.

Drory, Ze'ev (2005) *Israel's Reprisal Policy 1953–1956: The Dynamics of Military Retaliation*, London: Frank Cass.

Eshel, David (2010) 'Hamas, Hezbollah could Push Israel to War', *Aviation Week*, 1 April. Available at: www.aviationweek.com (accessed 10 June 2010).

Eshel, David (2001) 'The Al-Aqsa Intifada: Tactics and Strategies', *Jane's Intelligence Review*, 13 (5).

Fischman, Alex (2004) 'The IDF Proudly Presents: "The Bubble"', *Yedioth Ahronoth (Saturday Supplement)*, 15 October, pp. 6–7 [In Hebrew].

Fulghum, David A. and Robert Wall (2002) 'UAVs Validated in West Bank Fight', *Aviation Week and Space Technology*, 156 (19).

Gal-Or, Noemi (1990) 'The Israeli Defense Forces and Unconventional Warfare: The Palestinian Factor and Israeli National Security Doctrine', *Terrorism and Political Violence*, 2 (2): 212–26.

Gazit, Shlomo (2003) *Trapped Fools: Thirty Years of Israeli Policy in the Territories*. London: Frank Cass.

Gilad, Maj. Gen. Amos (2002) 'Inside the Maelstrom', *The Review*, 27 (12).

Gordon, Shmuel (1998) *The Vulture and the Snake. Counter-guerrilla Air Warfare: The War in Southern Lebanon*. Ramat Gan: Begin–Sadat Center for Strategic Studies.

Harel, Amos (2005) 'IDF Panel Recommends Ending Punitive House Demolitions for Terrorists' Families', *Ha'aretz*, 17 February.

Harel, Amos and Avi Issacharoff (2008) *34 Days: Israel, Hezbollah, and the War in Lebanon*. New York: Palgrave Macmillan.

Hatina, Meir (2006) 'The "Ulama" and the Cult of Death in Palestine', *Israel Affairs*, 12 (1).

Kaplan, Edward H., Alex Mintz and Shaul Mishal (2005) 'What Happened to Suicide Bombings in Israel? Insights from a Terror Stock Model', *Studies in Conflict and Terrorism*, 28 (3): 225–35.

Kober, Avi (2008) 'The Israel Defense Forces and the Second Lebanon War: Why the Poor Performance?', *Journal of Strategic Studies*, 31 (1): 3–40.

Linn, Ruth (1996) 'When the Individual Soldier Says "No" to War: A Look at Selective Refusal During the Intifada', *Journal of Peace Research*, 33 (4): 421–31.

Opall-Rome, Barbara (2002) 'Older Cobras Key for Israel Now', *DefenseNews*, 27 May–2 June.

Opall-Rome, Barbara (2003) 'Tanks Fill Wider Role in Israel's Anti-terror War', *DefenseNews*, 17 March.

Opall-Rome, Barbara (2009) 'Iran, Lebanon Loom Large in Israeli War Plans', *Defense News*, 14 December. Available at: www.defensenews.com (accessed 10 June 2010).

Peri, Yoram (2006) *Generals in the Cabinet Room: How the Military Shapes Israeli Policy*. Washington, DC.

Rodan, Steve (2001) 'IDF Debates Main Battle Tank Role in Intifada', *Jane's Defence Weekly*, 36 (8).

Rodman, David (2001) 'Israel's National Security Doctrine: An Introductory Overview', *Middle East Review of International Affairs*, 5 (3).

Schiff, Ze'ev and Ehud Ya'ari (1984) *Israel's Lebanon War*. New York: Simon & Schuster.

Tamari, Dov (2009) 'Who Really Dictates what an Existential Threat is? The Israeli Experience', *Journal of Strategic Studies*, 32 (5): 687–713.

Ya'alon, Major General Moshe (2002) 'On the Offensive', *The Review*, 27 (9).

22

FROM BELFAST TO LASHKAR GAR VIA BASRA

British counterinsurgency today

Warren Chin

The Good Friday Agreement in 1998 brought to an end a religious sectarian conflict which had raged in Northern Ireland for nearly three decades and resulted in over 3,500 deaths. During that time the British government developed a sophisticated strategy that aimed to prevent a Protestant insurrection whilst at the same time convincing the Irish Republican Army (IRA), that 'the ballot box and not the Armalite' was the only viable solution to resolving this internal conflict. A vital component of this strategy was the deployment of a garrison force of between 11,000 and 14,000 soldiers whose job it was to support the civilian government, restore order and contain the threat posed by terrorism. Fundamental to the success of this campaign was the recognition that, in spite of a massive numerical superiority enjoyed by the security services (25,000 soldiers and police versus 300 active terrorists) there was no military solution in Northern Ireland. This campaign reinforced Galula's maxim that counterinsurgency is 80 per cent political and 20 per cent military (Galula 1964: 63). In essence, this conflict demonstrates that in this kind of war force works best when used in support of a wider political and economic strategy which attacks the root causes of the conflict.

Much of what was seen as 'best practice' in this internal war supposedly grew out of a set of values and traditions which could be equated to a British way in small wars which was based on the British military's experience of past colonial campaigns (Strachan 2006). According to Pimlott, the recognition by the British military that force had such a limited role to play in counterinsurgency stemmed from the paucity of resources available to the British. This imbalance between resources and commitments was most pronounced in the inter-war period when the British Empire was at its maximum size at a time when the political consciousness of those colonised was starting to challenge the legitimacy of empire (Gwynn 1936). Lacking sufficient force to impose its will resulted in the British understanding that success depended on dealing with the political roots of a conflict rather than prosecuting a campaign to annihilate the threat. In practice this meant using force discriminately and proportionately so that reconciliation became possible (Pimlott 1988: 17–20). In a similar vein, Strachan emphasised the importance of the civil–military relationship which emerged in the era of colonial warfare as an additional force multiplier. As such the military became accustomed to working closely with the political authorities. Equally important, the British military also played a key role in establishing governance in newly conquered territories. An important question that Strachan addresses is how this experience was captured and survived within the memory of an institution which had little in the way of formal written doctrine. Within the context of the era of decolonisation he believes this experience was captured in the first instance by soldiers who served in campaigns in the inter-war period on the North West Frontier and Palestine. This experience was then brought to bear in Malaya. Again little in the way of formal doctrine emerged from this conflict and so lessons learned were disseminated as officers left Malaya for other theatres of war. A second important repository of information came from books written by the likes of Sir Robert Thompson and Sir Julian Paget. In the case of Northern Ireland, Frank Kitson's *Low Intensity Operations* provided a contemporary overview of how to make colonial counterinsurgency operate within the social, political and economic setting of Northern Ireland (Strachan, 2007).

Although it took many years to apply these lessons properly, both the government and the security services learned from earlier failures and by the late 1970s both possessed a range of capabilities and skills which made them quite formidable in this largely urban conflict. In the case of the army a key part of its ability to learn and adapt was helped by the creation of the Northern Ireland Training and Assistance Team (NITAT) in 1972 which drew upon the latest operational experience to provide comprehensive pre-deployment training to all units going to Northern Ireland. Another component of the army's increased effectiveness was the conceptual and doctrinal application of tactics, techniques and procedures taken from earlier campaigns and their fusion with new ideas developed to deal with the specific challenges of fighting the IRA. Most important was the focus placed on intelligence. To this end the army created a new intelligence unit called 14 Intelligence which became heavily involved in the surveillance and infiltration of the IRA. They also invested heavily in the creation of an extensive system of passive and active surveillance across the province as a whole based upon cameras, telephone bugs, the use of other electronic sensors and powerful computers which were connected to all units down to the level of the company. Equally important was the use of ordinary soldiers on the street providing information based on their observation of changes in day-to-day life in their sector and information provided by the local Catholic community. To obtain this information it was important for the military to treat the Catholic population with a modicum of respect and to compete with the IRA for the hearts and minds of the people. Of even greater importance was the role of the police and in particular Special Branch in penetrating the organisation of the IRA and providing valuable intelligence which allowed a more discriminate campaign to be carried out (Chin 2007: 119–47).

These contemporary lessons were captured in the 1977 edition of the British army counterinsurgency (COIN) doctrine, the main tenets of which were represented by the six principles of British counterinsurgency. These principles were as follows:

1   recognition of the political nature of the problem;
2   civilian supremacy of the campaign and application of a coordinated government and security plan which ties civil, police and military agencies together;
3   the development of an effective intelligence and surveillance network;
4   split the insurgents from the people via propaganda, winning hearts and minds and imposition of physical security;
5   destroy the isolated insurgent;
6   conduct political reform to prevent a recurrence of conflict.

Although this did not represent an explicit theory of COIN it served to provide a framework within which to develop a strategy for defeating an insurgency and it is claimed provided the basis for much of the success the British enjoyed in the 'brush fire' wars it fought in the period of decolonisation and Northern Ireland (Mockaitis 1995).

However, the insurgencies in Iraq and Afghanistan have called into question the validity of this framework (Metz 2007: 1–29). Interestingly, British army doctrine writers warned in the 2001 edition of British COIN doctrine that relying on the recent experience of Northern Ireland was potentially dangerous because it could constrain military thinking on the subject in the post–Cold War world (AFM Vol. 1 Part 10, B–2–1, 2001). Having said that the 2001 COIN manual continued to rely on an insurgent type which was driven by a secular or nationalist ideology, usually a variation of Marxism, Leninism and/or Maoism, which was not helpful in understanding the causes and prosecution of insurgency in the post–Cold War era (Metz 1995: 35). However, this intellectual inertia was understandable given that the immediate problem facing the British military in the 1990s was the crisis in Bosnia and the challenges this posed to its existing peacekeeping doctrine. This conflict absorbed much of the intellectual energy of the army and resulted in the production of not one but two new peacekeeping doctrines between 1994 and 1997.

In addition, many of the tactics, techniques and procedures used by the British in past counterinsurgency campaigns were used to good effect in this peacekeeping mission, which probably served to reinforce the impression that existing counterinsurgency doctrine remained 'fit for purpose'. It is also important to remember that in the immediate aftermath of the Cold War the future of insurgency looked bleak. As Metz explained, by the end of the twentieth century Maoist insurgency was on the verge of extinction because most states possessed the means and the knowledge to contain and defeat this phenomenon (Metz 2004: 12). This over-optimism was also reinforced by the end of the Cold War which resulted in state sponsorship of insurgent groups ending (Mackinlay 2002: 17–23).

In general, most experts recognised that insurgency would persist, but from the perspective of the British, this remained a phenomenon very much on the periphery of their own vital interests. In truth, even the cataclysmic event of 9/11 did not result in an immediate and profound revision of British counterinsurgency doctrine. Thus, in the view of the military, the main challenge posed by the war on terror was not doctrinal (House of Commons Defence Committee, HC 93, 2003, Q51). The focus instead was to ensure we were better able to conduct what could be described as global counter-terrorist campaign (MOD, Cm 556, 2002). Unfortunately, as the war against terror progressed, it became increasingly clear that al-Qaeda was pursuing a more complex and multi-faceted strategy which included terrorism but also incorporated a global guerrilla war (Cassidy 2005: 336). In fact, according to one former CIA analyst, al-Qaeda was and always had been primarily a guerrilla as opposed to a terrorist group. Its aim was to build an army capable of fighting 'jihad' (Scheuer 2005: 63–7). The failure of the Americans to realise this was cited as one reason why operations in both Iraq and Afghanistan mutated from rapid decisive operations to bloody and protracted wars (Benjamin and Simon 2005: 159). But such debates tended to support the view that British COIN doctrine remained relevant, even in a post-modern world dominated by non-state actors such as al-Qaeda.

However, as Mackinlay explains, this event could be interpreted as a manifestation of a new kind of insurgency which served to challenge the logic of British COIN. In his view migrant communities have become increasingly radicalised by Western military intervention in 'Islamdom' caused by access to satellite television, the Internet and the DVDs produced by insurgents as a way of promoting their cause (Mackinlay 2009: 167–73). But the British response to events like 7/7 was to see this as a problem for domestic counter-terrorism rather than requiring a new COIN doctrine (JDCC 2006).

But even in the specific cases of Afghanistan and Iraq, the British were slow to realise that the nature of these conflicts posed a serious challenge to the logic of its COIN doctrine. In the case of Iraq, the British were quicker off the mark than their American counterparts to realise that the country was descending into a state of insurgency. However, initially at least, this was seen very much as an American problem caused largely by an American strategic and organisational culture which resulted in a brutal and indiscriminate response to the Sunni insurgency (Aylwin-Foster 2005: 3). This merely reinforced the validity of the British approach. Thus, in 2004, the Chief of the General Staff, Sir Mike Jackson, distanced the British military from their American ally stating: 'we must be able to fight with the Americans. That does not mean we must be able to fight as the Americans'. In his view, the British approach to post-conflict situations was doctrinally different from that of the United States (Defence Committee, HC 65, 2005, Q361). He like many others in the UK believed that the British army played an important role in creating a permissive environment in Multi National Division South East (MND SE) in 2004. According to one observer the key to success was the ability of the British to draw on its experience in past counterinsurgency campaigns and apply tactics, techniques and procedures which ranged from 'a willingness to abandon the dehumanising effect conferred by wearing a helmet to simply removing one's sunglasses when communicating with people' (HCDC, HC 65, 2005, para 81).

Unfortunately, such a view failed to take into account the very different environments facing the British and American forces. In the case of the British they controlled an area containing a population of six million people, but the majority of these were Shia Muslims who had every reason to celebrate regime change when it came in 2003. Although the British received a mixed response from the population nearly all the people were prepared to wait and see what the occupation brought in terms of change. However, the British failure to seize this window of opportunity resulted in increased instability and from 2004 until the end of 2008 the British became embroiled in a cycle of violence which stemmed from an array of motivations reflecting the complexities of local politics, culture, religion, corruption and crime that existed within Iraq. In the first instance, the military response to this challenge was to externalise the very obvious problems that confronted them in Iraq and blame Whitehall's departmental system of government which militated against an effective reconstruction and development plan. The most important articulation of this position was published in early 2006. Called *The Comprehensive Approach* it argued that we needed to do more to link and coordinate the military, economic and political levers of power within the theatre of operations (JDCC 2006). This became an issue because, in Iraq, the perceived absence of this coordination played a key role in causing the British to fail in terms of delivering security and reconstruction, which played a critical role in allowing an insurgency to erupt in MND SE (Synott 2008: 19). Although not technically COIN, the Comprehensive Approach provided a framework which reinforced rather than contradicted past experience in COIN campaigns in terms of the institutional set-up required for success. Most important it shaped our approach to campaigns in both Iraq and Afghanistan. The most obvious manifestation of this can be seen in the creation of the Stabilisation Unit, an interdepartmental organisation whose primary function is to provide assistance in post-conflict situations. In addition, the British also adopted an American idea: provincial reconstruction teams (PRTs) which brought together the military and civilian agencies at the local level in each theatre of operations. First established in Afghanistan they were quickly applied to Iraq and one was set up in Basra in 2006.

In the case of Afghanistan, the British perceived this to be essentially a peacekeeping mission and little happened between 2001 and 2006 to challenge this view. The catalyst for change was the decision to deploy 16 Air Assault Brigade to Helmand in summer 2006. Although the deployment of the brigade looked like a haphazard exercise in planning, the sad truth is that the government went to great lengths to ensure that the Comprehensive Approach was at the centre of its efforts to re-establish governance in this province. In December 2005 all the key departments of state met over a two-week period to create a joined up comprehensive plan (Ferguson 2008: 25–46). Equally important, although there was no expectation of large-scale resistance, the military drew heavily on the classic counterinsurgency campaign in Malaya to shape and inform their operations in Afghanistan. One of the most important outcomes of this exercise was the view that the focus of operations in Helmand was reconstruction not war (Tootal 2009: 30–1). Yet, in spite of these good intentions, both the Comprehensive Approach and the icon of Malaya were stillborn as British military operations came to be dominated by what became known as the platoon blockhouse strategy; in essence a series of defensive battles to hold key towns and villages from the Taliban. Although less dramatic, it was also clear that the British faced a similar fate in Iraq. By September 2005, they were not just fighting the militias but had also become locked in a violent battle with elements of the Iraqi security forces in Basra.

Although both conflicts were fundamentally different they also shared common traits which presented important challenges to existing COIN doctrine. Realising that the problem was not due entirely to the structural weaknesses of the Whitehall machine, the military began to reflect on its own practices and to question whether their doctrine was appropriate for the new conditions in which counterinsurgency operated. The first doctrine publication to specifically address this issue was *Countering Irregular Threats* (CIA). Published in 2007 it attempted to create a new taxonomy for insurgency which captured the rise of a range of groups that presented an armed threat to the authority of the state. Irregular activity was defined as behaviour that attempted to achieve political change through the illegal use, or threat, of violence 'conducted by ideologically or criminally motivated non-regular forces, groups or individuals, as a challenge to authority' (JDCC 2007: para 102).

Most important given the array of different insurgent types, the CIA questioned the relevance of British experience of counterinsurgency and questioned the extent to which principles derived from past campaigns could be applied to these more complex, internationalised and multi-faceted insurgencies (JDCC 2007: para 104).

The CIA acted as a catalyst for change and helped shape and inform the debate about the future of British COIN. A second milestone in this process of reflection was the production of the American COIN manual FM3–24, in December 2006. This huge tome set a new standard in doctrine writing and provided the start point for the British who responded by producing two new doctrine publications, a new counterinsurgency manual for the army (AFM 10, Vol. 1, 2009) and a joint manual for all three services called Stabilisation (JDP 340, 2009). Both publications drew heavily on the experience of operations in Iraq and Afghanistan. These two doctrines were justified on the grounds that the Army COIN manual was designed to assist planning at the tactical level and JDP 340 focused on the campaign plan or operational level within the theatre of operations.

Both doctrines acknowledged the perceived change in terms of the motivation and behaviour of the insurgent and the contemporary operating environment and accepted this required a new approach. With regard to the insurgent it was recognised that insurgency was mutating and becoming more hybrid in nature, meaning that past distinctions between high and low intensity combat were becoming increasingly blurred. As a result, one of the cherished assumptions of British counterinsurgency – that it falls generally into the low-intensity bracket – was no longer valid. Now insurgents employed 'a mix of conventional weapons, irregular tactics, terrorism, and criminal behaviour in the same "battlespace" to achieve their political objectives' (AFM 10, 2009, 1–1). It is also recognised that the number of armed groups had increased significantly and, as in the case of CIA, a broader categorisation of what constituted an insurgent was required. Again experience in Iraq and Afghanistan provided ample evidence to support this position. In the case of Iraq it is estimated that the British faced over 300 different militias in

Basra during the latter stages of the occupation (Munson 2009: 103). Similarly in Afghanistan it is estimated that the British faced at least six armed groups who were connected to the Taliban insurgency and countless numbers of warlords and militias (Foreign Affairs Committee, HC 302, 2009, ev 78). Most important were the connections between these groups, the drug trade and al-Qaeda. Giustozzi notes that the Taliban's support for global jihad and the exploitation of the Internet is evidence that this is now a very different movement from the one which governed Afghanistan until 2001 (Giustozzi 2007: 13–14) and this raises important questions about how doctrine tackles transnational insurgents.

Even more important however is the environmental context of counterinsurgency today. British success in COIN in the past was due to the fact that these campaigns were largely conducted in colonies controlled by the British and as such there was usually a functioning administration and local security force through which to prosecute the campaign. In addition, the legitimacy of these operations often went unquestioned because it was deemed to be an internal affair within the empire or homeland. In contrast, British counterinsurgency today is generally conducted in support of a sovereign government and consequently British operations must take into account the wishes of the host government. Although the British have experience of this practice from their campaign in Dhofar in the 1970s, this was the exception rather than the rule and British experience in Afghanistan and Iraq demonstrate how frustrating they found having to liaise with a host government.

In the case of Iraq this problem became acute in terms of the effect it had on the ability of the British to stabilise Basra. In a strange twist of fate, the principal insurgent group, the Sadrists, were represented in the provincial and national government and opposed any attempt to reduce the power of their militias in the area. This political fix presented an unprecedented problem for the British when in 2006 they planned a large-scale sweep of Basra to clear all the militias, but were forced to scale this down to a more modest reconstruction and development project because of pressure exerted by the Sadrists on the Malaki government. As a result, Operation Sinbad failed to remove the militias and made the British withdrawal from Basra in 2007 look like an act of desperation; there were even rumours in the press that the British had been forced to negotiate terms with the militias to ensure this action was not contested. In truth, the withdrawal happened because the British realised that most of the violence in Basra was directed at them and if they left they hoped the violence would decline dramatically, which it did. Similar problems occurred again in 2008 when the Malaki government decided to launch an offensive against opposition groups in Basra. Operation 'Charge of the Knights' proved to be a surprise to both the Americans and the British, but it was the British who were perceived to be the biggest losers in this campaign as the media inferred that the Iraqi government and the Americans had lost confidence in the British (Cockburn 2008), something which the British military have been eager to contest. Very similar problems have been experienced in Afghanistan. Indeed as soon as the British deployed into Helmand province in 2006, they were forced to deviate from the plan by the provincial governor and president Hamid Karzai who saw the threat of the Taliban as a challenge to the authority of the government and demanded the British send forces to protect the towns in the north of Helmand. Some have argued that if the military had not bowed to this pressure that the Taliban would have left Helmand and headed to Kandahar, which was their main objective, but once the British moved into the area they fixed the attention of the insurgents and the result was a summer of heavy fighting (Chin 2010). However, as Brigade Commander Ed Butler explained, how could the British deny the request of a sovereign government in whose country they were in? (Ferguson 2008: 153).

The political domain of counterinsurgency today is made more complicated because most campaigns are conducted largely through coalitions frequently led by the United States. As a result the British have had to fuse their plans with those of their allies as well as the host government. Again recent operational experience demonstrates that this adjustment to being the junior partner has created problems for the British. This was most apparent in post-war Iraq as the insurgency got underway. A good illustration of this was the way in which British plans were undermined by the American decision to disband Iraq's security services and implement a policy of de-Ba'athifcation, both of which had a huge impact on the security situation. It is not entirely clear if the British government was even consulted on these decisions before they were announced but many within the British military opposed them. The British were also frustrated in their efforts to advise their American counterparts on how to deal with the insurgency that was growing in the American controlled areas of Iraq, but again were unable to influence their ally until the arrival of a new US commander and ambassador in summer 2004, but this was over a year after the Sunni insurgency began. Many of the same problems were present in the US–UK relationship in the Afghan campaign. At its most basic level there was a fundamental tension between what the British thought they needed to do, which focused on nation-building, and the US military's emphasis on carrying on with counter-terrorist operations. Inevitably, the Americans did their best to limit the role and size of the International Security Force (ISAF) set up by the British so that it did not come into conflict with their operations. This tension persisted even when the British pushed into Helmand in 2006 and British efforts to win hearts and minds were undermined by US attacks against the same population which frequently caused civilian casualties; a good example of this occurred in area around Now Zad. The British and Americans also came into conflict over the role of counter-narcotics in the context of the wider counterinsurgency campaign. The British military feared eradication would alienate the population and so tried to ignore it, but the Americans remained adamant that eradication was the immediate and long-term solution to stabilising Afghanistan.

The third environmental factor which has complicated the application of British counterinsurgency is the way in which such campaigns have increasingly come to be conducted within failed and failing states. British defence policy views failed states as one of the principal security concerns facing the UK because it could be exploited by transnational terrorist groups like al-Qaeda (MOD, Cm 6041, 2003, para 2.8). Dealing with this phenomenon is the central focus of JDP 340 which envisages COIN as a component part of a wider strategy which seeks to support states weakened by conflict and help in the restoration of governance and security within its borders. Equally important is the assistance given to create political institutions which provide a legitimate and non-violent way to resolve the distribution of political power and ensure sustainable and economic development. The role of the military within this process is primarily to provide security for the population and support the indigenous government. Most important and reminiscent of the doctrinal debate which surrounded peacekeeping in the 1990s, was the realisation that armed forces had an important role to play in nation-building, especially in those states where conflict continued to rage. In such life-threatening situations, charities and civilian development agencies are unable to operate which means the military have to carry this burden. These new tasks include the provision of economic assistance, facilitating disarmament, demobilisation and reintegration of former insurgents and militia fighters, training new security forces and assisting in the creation of an effective judicial system (DCDC 2010).

However, in spite of these potentially dramatic changes, the British military's new doctrine represents an evolutionary rather than revolutionary change. A good illustration of this can be seen if you compare the six principles of counterinsurgency with those articulated in the new doctrines:

Principles of counterinsurgency in Army Field Manual:
1 primacy of political purpose
2 unity of effort
3 understand the human terrain
4 secure the population
5 neutralise the insurgent
6 gain and maintain popular support
7 iperate in accordance with the law
8 integrate intelligence
9 prepare for the long term
10 learn and adapt. (AFM Countering Insurgency: 1–1)

The principles of stabilisation are very similar:
1 primacy of political purpose
2 understand the context
3 focus on the population
4 foster host nation governance, authority and indigenous capacity
5 unity of effort
6 neutralise and isolate irregular actors
7 gain consent and maintain credibility
8 prepare for the long term
9 anticipate, learn and adapt. (DCDC 2010: viii)

The British army's latest edition of COIN and JDP 340 both accept that the world has changed, but both remain insistent that classical COIN theorists like Galula, Thompson and Kitson continue to provide useful insights and in particular the emphasis placed on securing and controlling the population, (DCDC 2010: 1–3 and AFM 10 2009: 4–3).

Frank Hoffman notes that the US military's COIN manual FM 3–24 contains within it a paradox. One the one hand it claims that you cannot fight insurgents today in the same way you fought the Viet Cong, but the manual also states that most insurgencies follow a similar course of development and consequently the past remains an important source of learning (Hoffman 2007: 72). A similar criticism could be made of the latest iteration of British counterinsurgency doctrine. But it is nevertheless an important evolution which attempts to address some of the weaknesses highlighted in FM 3–24. Both British doctrines demonstrate an awareness of the importance of consent and legitimacy in counterinsurgency, which are important factors to take on board when in the midst of what is frequently a military occupation of a country. They also attempt to move beyond the Maoist model of insurgency by identifying a range of different insurgent groups which in the case of AFM 10 reflects a taxonomy which recognises the importance of identity and religion as significant sources of motivation within insurgency today. In theory this should allow a more flexible approach than is normally associated with classical counterinsurgency doctrine. In addition, both doctrines recognise the importance of the propaganda war and a lot of time is invested in developing the theme of 'Influence' as a way of countering the insurgent's exploitation of the information domain. However, the doctrines offer little insight into what the British can do to improve the legitimacy of the host government in the eyes of its own people and other governments; especially when that government is riddled with corruption and is unwilling or unable to reform itself. Similarly it does not provide a convincing solution to the problem of how to generate sufficient force to secure the population. The idea of relying on security sector reform often creates its own problems. This was clearly demonstrated in Iraq in 2006 when the US strategy of relying on poorly trained and unreliable Iraqi security services as a substitute for American soldiers very nearly caused the United States to lose the conflict. Most important, the situation was only saved by the United States reinforcing Iraq with 30,000 additional troops, which were used to generate the time needed so that the training and mentoring of Iraq's security forces could be improved (Ricks 2009: 3–21). Obviously, the British military lacks this capacity and consequently this has weakened its ability to conduct COIN. This deficiency has been exacerbated because the British also lack the financial muscle to conduct an effective reconstruction and development programme to support a COIN operation in a failed and failing state. Consequently, in spite of the doctrinal agility displayed by the British military so far, the future of British COIN looks uncertain.

Recommended readings

Bishop, P. (2007) *3 PARA*. London: Harper.

Bishop, P. (2009) *Ground Truth*. London: Harper.

Bulloch, G. (1996) 'The Application of Military Doctrine to Counter Insurgency (COIN) Operations: A British Perspective', *Small Wars and Insurgencies*, 7 (2): 165–77.

Chin, W. (2008) 'Why Did it all Go Wrong? Reassessing British Counterinsurgency in Iraq', *Strategic Studies Quarterly*, 2 (4): 119–35.

Dewar, Michael (1997) *The British Army in Northern Ireland*. London: Arms and Armour Press.

Dixon, Paul (1997) 'Counterinsurgency in Northern Ireland', in Paul Rich and Richard Stubbs (eds), *The Counterinsurgent State: Guerrilla Warfare and State Building in the Twentieth Century*. Basingstoke: Macmillan; New York: St. Martin's Press, pp. 175–211.

Faligot, Roger (1983) *Britain's Military Strategy in Ireland: The Kitson Experiment*. London: Zed Press.

Farrell, Theo and Stuart Gordon (2009) 'COIN Machine: The British Military in Afghanistan', *Orbis*, 53 (4): 18–25.

Greenall, G. (2004) 'Winning the Peace', *British Army Review* 134 (summer): 21–3.

Grey, S. (2009) *Operation Snakebite*. London: Viking.

Hamil, Desmond (1985) *Pig In The Middle*. London: Methuen.

Kitson, Frank (1971) *Low Intensity Operations: Subversion, Insurgency, Peacekeeping*. London: Faber.

McInnes, Colin (1997) 'The British Army in Northern Ireland 1969–1972: From Policing to Counter-Terror', *Journal of Strategic Studies*, 20 (2): 1–24.

Miller, S.N. (2009) 'A Comprehensive Failure in British Civil Military Strategy in Helmand Province', *British Army Review* 146 (spring): 36–7.

Mockaitis, T. (1995) *British Counter Insurgency in the Post Imperial Era*. Manchester: Manchester University Press.

Nagl, J. (2005) *Learning to Eat Soup With Knife: Counter Insurgency Lessons from Malaya and Vietnam*. Chicago: Chicago University Press.

Newsinger, J. (1995) 'From Counter-Insurgency to Internal Security: Northern Ireland 1969–1992', *Small Wars and Insurgencies*, 6 (1): 88–111.

Rangwala, G. (2009) 'Counter-insurgency amid Fragmentation: The British in Southern Iraq', *Journal of Strategic Studies*, 32 (3): 495–513.

Steele, J. (2008) *Defeat: Why America and Britain Lost Iraq*. Berkeley: Counterpoint.

Taylor, Peter (2001) *Brits: The War Against the IRA*. London: Bloomsbury.

Ucko, D. (2010) 'Lessons from Basra: The Future of British COIN', *Survival*, 52 (4): 131–58.

References

Aylwin-Foster, Brigadier Nigel (2005) 'Changing the Army for Counter Insurgency Operations', *Military Review* (November–December): 2–15.

Benjamin, D. and S. Simon (2005) *The Next Attack: The Globalization of Jihad*. London: Hodder & Stoughton.

Cassidy, R. (2005) 'Feeding Bread to the Luddites: The Radical Fundamentalist Islamic Revolution in Guerrilla Warfare', *Small Wars and Insurgencies*, 16 (3): 334–59.

Chin, W. (2007) 'British Military Operations in Northern Ireland 1972–94', in *The British Approach to Low Intensity Operation's: Network Centric Operations, Case Study Part 2*. Washington DC: US Department of Defence.

Chin, W. (2010) 'Colonial Warfare in a Post Colonial State British Military Operations in Helmand Province Afghanistan', *Defence Studies Journal*, 10 (1–2): 215–47.

Cockburn, Patrick (2008) 'A Gross Failure that Ignored History and Ended with a Humiliating Retreat', *The Independent*, 17 March.

Defence Committee 6th Report (2005) *Iraq: An Initial Assessment of Post Conflict Operations* HC 65-I, 2004–2005. London: HMSO.

Development, Concepts and Doctrine Centre (2010) *A Guide to Joint Doctrine Publication 3–40 Security and Stabilisation: The Military Contribution*. Shrivenham: MOD.

Ferguson, J. (2008) *A Million Bullets*. London: Bantam Press.

Foreign Affairs Committee (2009) *Global Security: Afghanistan and Pakistan 8th Report HC 302*. London: HMSO.

Galula, D. (1964) *Counterinsurgency Warfare Theory and Practice*. London: Praeger.

Giustozzi, A. (2007) *Koran Kalishnikov and Laptop: The Neo-Taliban Insurgency in Afghanistan*. London: Hurst & Company.

Gwynn, Sir Charles (1936) *Imperial Policing*. London: Macmillan.

Hoffman, F. (2007) 'Neo Classical Counter Insurgency', *Parameters* (summer): 71–87.

Joint Doctrine and Concepts Centre (2006) *The Comprehensive Approach, Joint Discussion Note 4/05* (January).

Joint Doctrine and Concepts Centre (2006) *Countering Terrorism; The UK Approach to the Military Contribution*. London: MOD.

Joint Doctrine and Concepts Centre (2007) *Countering Irregular Activity within a Comprehensive Approach*. JDN 2/07 (March).

Mackinlay, J. (2002) *Globalisation and Insurgency*. London: IISS.

Mackinlay, J. (2009) *The Insurgent Archipelago: From Mao to Bin Laden*. London: Hurst.

Metz, S. (1995) 'A Flame Kept Burning Counterinsurgency Support After the Cold War', *Parameters* (autumn): 27–41.

Metz, S. (2004) *Insurgency and Counterinsurgency in the 21st Century: Reconceptualising Threat and Response*. Carlisle, PA: US Army War College, Strategic Studies Institute.

Metz, S. (2007) *Rethinking Insurgency*. Strategic Studies Institute, June.

Mockaitis, T. (1995) *British Counter Insurgency in the Post Imperial Era*. Manchester: Manchester University Press.

MOD (1977) *Land Operations, Vol III Counter Revolutionary Operations*. London.

MOD (2001) *The Army Field Manual, Vol. 1, Part 10, Counter Insurgency Operations*, July.

MOD (2002) *The Strategic Defence Review: A New Chapter*. London.

MOD (2003) *Defence White Paper 2003: Delivering Security in a Changing World*, Cm 6041. London: HMSO.

MOD (2009) *Army Field Manual Part 10, Countering Insurgency*. London: MOD.

Munson, P. (2009) *Iraq in Transition*. Washington, DC: Potomac Books.

Pimlott, J. (1988) 'The British Experience', in I. Beckett (ed.), *The Roots of Counter Insurgency Armies and Guerrilla Warfare 1900–1945*. London: Blandford Press, pp. 17–39.

Ricks, T.E. (2009) *The Gamble: General David Petraeus and the American Military Adventure in Iraq, 2006–2008*. London: Penguin Press.

Scheuer, M. (2005) *Imperial Hubris: Why the West in Losing the War on Terror*. Potomac Books.

Strachan, H. (ed.) (2006) *Big and Small Wars: The British Army and the Lessons of War in the Twentieth Century*. London: Routledge.

Strachan, H. (2007) 'British Counter Insurgency from Malaya to Iraq', *RUSI Journal* (December): 8–11.

Synott, Sir Hilary (2008) *Bad Days in Basra*. London: I.B. Tauris.

Tootal, Col. S. (2009) *Danger Close*. London: John Murray.

23

COUNTERINSURGENCY IN A NON-DEMOCRATIC STATE

The Russian example

Yuri M. Zhukov

The influence of regime type on the outbreak, conduct and resolution of low-intensity conflict has been the subject of considerable debate. Democracies and non-democracies face different levels of conflict risk and confront different types of challenges from non-state opponents. They employ different instruments and strategies in fighting their enemies and may have different track records of victory and defeat. Democratic sceptics argue that these differences favour closed regimes, which face fewer constraints on the use of coercion and have a higher tolerance for sustaining the human and material costs of war (Mack 1975; Chalk 1995; Inbar 2003; Merom 2003; Li 2005; Luttwak 2007; Peters 2007). Democratic optimists maintain that democracies are less likely to provoke violent opposition in the first place and, by emphasizing legitimacy over intimidation, are better able to secure the peace (Dernado 1985; Elbadawi and Sambanis 2000; Regan and Henderson 2002; Elkins 2005; Sambanis and Zinn 2005; Abrahms 2007).

Both sides have drawn on evidence from a limited number of well-documented West European and American cases. The optimistic argument is derived largely from the best practices of the British in Malaya, and the less spectacular performance of the French in Algeria and the United States in Vietnam (Galula 1963; Thompson 1966; Kitson 1971; Aylwin-Foster 2005; Nagl 2005; Kilcullen 2009). The sceptical argument cites the British and US experiences in Kenya and the Philippines as examples in which harsher methods – like mass relocation and pseudo-gangs – helped achieve mission goals (Cline 2005; Peters 2007; but also see Elkins 2005).

The bulk of modern counterinsurgency expertise, however, resides in countries with less democratic political systems. Since the Bolshevik Revolution of 1917, Russia has confronted two dozen insurgent movements and large-scale insurrections.[1] Its responses to these challenges present a counterinsurgency model diametrically opposed to the 'hearts and minds' approach espoused by the British school and the most recent US Army Field Manual on Counterinsurgency.[2] Despite serious setbacks in Afghanistan and the first Chechen War, Russia has one of the most successful track records of any modern counterinsurgent.

The Russian experience challenges our understanding of regime type and counterinsurgency. It highlights the need to distinguish between different types of non-democracies and the threats they face, different types of coercion and when each is used, different definitions of success and the role of repression in attaining them. Yet apart from several notable studies of the Soviet-Afghan War (Grau 1997; Grau and Gress 2002; Lyakhovskiy 1995; Varennikov 2002;

Gareev 1999) and the ongoing conflict in the North Caucasus (Toft 2003; Kramer 2005; Lyall 2009, 2010b), the authoritarian model of counterinsurgency has largely eluded systematic empirical investigation.

This chapter reviews our current knowledge of regime type and counterinsurgency, with an emphasis on three areas of inquiry: the emergence, conduct and outcome of low-intensity conflict in countries with different political systems. Throughout, the Russian example is presented as an illustration of how such conflicts have been brought about, fought and resolved in a non-democratic state. The chapter concludes with summary remarks and a few thoughts on future research.

Regime type and insurgency onset

A substantial body of research argues that democracies are relatively peaceful actors at home and internationally, while autocratic and transitional regimes are more conflict-prone (Krain and Myers 1997: 109–18; Benson and Kugler 1998; Gurr 2000; Henderson and Singer 2000: 275–99; Hegre *et al.* 2001: 33–48; Mansfield and Snyder 2005; Davenport 2007a). Many theories have been proposed to support this claim: democracies are richer and more capable of providing security and controlling territory (e.g. Fearon and Laitin 2003); dissidents in democracies have more non-violent channels for expressing dissent (e.g. Elbadawi and Sambanis 2000; Regan and Henderson 2002: 121–2); the pluralism of democratic politics necessitates non-violent debate, negotiation and conflict resolution (e.g. Madison 1787; Rummel 1995: 4); electorally vulnerable leaders tend to initiate only those wars in which they expect a high probability of success (e.g. Bueno De Mesquita and Siverson 1995: 841–55; Reiter and Stam 1998: 378; Fearon 1994: 577–8, 585–6). Although the causal mechanism behind democratic pacifism remains a subject of debate, the theory's central empirical claim is consistent with the historical record. Fewer than 30 per cent of the governments involved in major counterinsurgency campaigns since 1808 – and 26.6 per cent since the First World War – have been institutionally mature democracies.[3]

States with different political systems are also expected to face different types of opponents. Autocracies are considered more likely to view domestic dissent as threatening to the regime, thereby escalating anti-government activity into the realm of violence (Davenport 1995). Democracies encounter relatively few domestic threats and are more likely to fight insurgents outside their own borders (Lyall 2010b: 179–80). Historically, 53 per cent of democratic counterinsurgent campaigns took place during foreign wars of occupation, compared to 31 per cent for non-democracies.[4] This difference stems in part from the superior material resources of democratic states.[5] However, even powerful non-democracies have often had their hands full with domestic opponents, avoiding overseas adventures while more pressing and proximate challenges persist.

The Russian example

The Russian experience supports the view that 'most violence is in the middle' of the spectrum of political regimes, with institutionally weak transitional governments at greater risk of conflict than consolidated autocracies (Hegre *et al.* 2001; Regan and Henderson 2002).

Russia has never been a liberal democracy. Of the 93 years since the Bolshevik Revolution, the country spent six as a fledgling semi-autocracy (1917–22), almost seven decades as a totalitarian dictatorship (1923–88), and the remainder meandering between semi-autocratic and semi-democratic forms of government (1989–present).[6] During those 93 years, Moscow encountered 24 significant insurgencies and rebellions, shown in Figure 23.1.[7] These conflicts erupted in three waves: the first in multiple regions of European and Asian Russia during and immediately following the Civil War, the second in the USSR's western borderlands after the Second World War II, and the third in the North Caucasus following the disintegration of the Soviet Union. The first wave consisted mostly of peasant uprisings, large-scale mutinies and two ethno-nationalist insurrections in the wake of the Bolsheviks' victory over Wrangel's White Army in the Civil War. The second wave primarily involved nationalist insurgencies in territories newly acquired by the USSR. The third wave started with the first Chechen War in late 1994 and later expanded to other southern Russian regions.

Seventeen of the 24 conflicts originated during times of regime transition (pre-1923 and post-1989), and five of the remaining seven emerged in regions only recently introduced to Soviet rule (West Ukraine, West Belarus and the three Baltic states). All three waves of insurgencies occurred at times of economic devastation, weak central authority and varying degrees of military demobilization. Periods of strong central authority – such as the 1930s and much of the Cold War era – were almost entirely devoid of new insurgent movements. Periods of transition were violent without exception.

The Russian case further reinforces the image of autocratic counterinsurgency as a mostly domestic affair. Only two of the conflicts shown in Figure 23.1 were fought on foreign soil: the Soviet occupation of Afghanistan and Russian peace operations in Tajikistan. Moscow embarked on the Afghan campaign at a time of relatively low domestic threat; over two decades had passed since the last incidents of insurgent violence in Western Ukraine. In the second case, Russia's

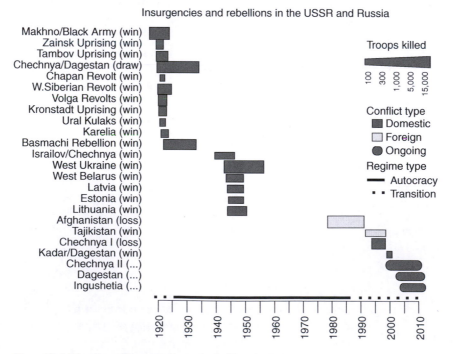

Figure 23.1 Timeline of insurgencies and rebellions in Russia.

Note

Outcomes, shown in parentheses, are coded from the perspective of the incumbent. For coding rules see note 17.

formal military role was initially limited to border security, humanitarian aid and the defence of critical infrastructure. Firefights with Tajik opposition groups and smugglers – while not uncommon – were more mission creep than mission.

Regime type and the conduct of counterinsurgency

Given that different regimes face threats of different frequency and origin, are there systematic differences in how they confront these security challenges? It has become widely accepted that autocracies are more brutal counterinsurgents than democracies (Merom 2003; Abrahms 2007). Pressure from various domestic groups is expected to exert normative constraints on the strategic and tactical choices of democratic governments.[8] Under these constraints, democracies are less likely to engage in actions that risk unnecessary civilian deaths or otherwise violate international treaties and norms, particularly those concerning basic human rights (Neumayer 2005). Although intentional noncompliance may incur the risk of international sanctions and intervention, autocratic regimes have no comparable sources of domestic restraint on the use of coercion.

Empirical support for a negative relationship between democracy and brutality, however, has been mixed. Some studies have found highly authoritarian regimes more likely to resort to mass killing than highly democratic ones, but the substantive and statistical significance of this difference is comparatively weak (Poe and Tate 1994; Valentino *et al.* 2004: 402). Indeed, coercion is more widespread in mixed and transitional regimes than at either of the two extremes (Fein 1995; Regan and Henderson 2002).[9]

One distinction that has received less attention in the literature is that between two varieties of brutality: indiscriminate force, as in the case of civilian deaths resulting from kinetic operations, and collective punishment, as in the case of mass repression, where coercion is administered to group, rather than individual, targets.[10]

While it is plausible that democratic regimes are more constrained in entertaining overtly repressive policies, their ability to prevent indiscriminate killing is largely a function of capabilities – the local balance of power, the quality of intelligence and the accuracy of weapons systems (Kalyvas 2006; Kocher *et al.* 2008). High collateral damage from mass firepower can be a sign of weakness as much as callousness.

By the same logic, unconstrained decision-making is not sufficient for collective punishment to be employed. Unlike an artillery strike, which could be planned and executed on the initiative of a Soviet battalion commander, repression typically requires political authorization, extensive material resources and joint execution by a multitude of centrally and locally based units and administrative offices. Its effective use requires not simply a non-democratic state, but a strong state.

The Russian example

The Russian case illustrates how capabilities and regime type interact in the use of coercion. Collective punishment – typically in the form of mass repression – was most common under autocratic governments with strong local capabilities, and indiscriminate killing – typically a result of mass firepower – was more common when Russia was a transitional regime with weak local capabilities.

Artillery, the main mechanism of indiscriminant violence, has long played a dominant role in Soviet and Russian ground combat power. Its primacy in counterinsurgency was driven in part by a desire to substitute firepower for infantry, avoid close combat and save soldiers' lives

(Grau 1997). During the Tambov Uprising of 1920–1, Mikhail Tukhachevsky employed high-intensity artillery barrages to completely flatten the villages of Koptevo, Khitrovo and Verkhne-spasskoye, and clear forested areas with chemical weapons.[11] Such indiscriminant use of firepower emerged from the difficulty of executing alternative combined arms tactics in rugged areas where civilian support was overwhelmingly on the side of the insurgents. Raids and ambushes claimed heavy casualties among the infantry, driving military leaders to rely increasingly on indirect fire (Sennikov 2004).

Russia's reliance on indiscriminate firepower where local superiority is elusive has endured in more recent cases. In Herat, a city overrun by urban guerillas since before the Soviet occupation of Afghanistan, three-quarters of the urban centre was shelled into rubble (Elkhamri *et al.* 2005: 21–2; Gareev 1999; Grau 1996: 51–2). In the most recent Chechen War, mass firepower was similarly used in lieu of manpower (Oliker 2001: xii). Still shaken by the disastrous 1994 Battle for Grozny, Russian forces sought to avoid urban combat as much as possible. They employed conventional and thermobaric explosives to destroy large sections of the city and clear guerilla positions in bunkers and heavily fortified emplacements (Grau and Smith 2000; Maksakov 2000).

If indiscriminate force was often used where Soviet and Russian forces were weak, collective punishment was used where they were strong. Reflecting on the lessons of the Tambov Uprising, Tukhachevsky wrote, 'The struggle must be waged not primarily with the rebel bands, but with the entire local population' (cited in Kantor 2005: 257). Rather than separating civilians from insurgents by catching the 'fish swimming in the sea', Tukhachevsky's approach was to drain the sea in which the fish swim. He instituted a pilot program of this sort in the Tambov province, where concentration camps were established for families and associates of known insurgents. Yet the scale of these early efforts did not approach the levels of the 1930s and 1940s, after Stalin's regime had solidified and the Great Purge ushered in a new era of mass government repression.

Forcible resettlement was one of the most extreme forms of repression used in Russian counterinsurgency. In a practice inherited from Czarist times, the Peoples Commissariat for Internal Affairs (NKVD) and its successor agencies gave thousands of civilians only hours to collect their belongings, boarded them onto freight cars, and relocated them for a decade or more to Central Asia, the Far East or another remote part of the country.[12] The intent was to deny insurgents their flows of provisions, intelligence and new recruits by applying punishment collectively, to combatants as well as their potential supporters (Vladimirtsev and Kokurin 2008: 6). A secondary objective was to deter the remaining local population from supporting insurgents in the future. The scope of these operations ranged from relatively selective – targeting the immediate family and close associates of known insurgents, as in the cases of Ukraine and the Baltic States after 1944 – to expansive – targeting all persons belonging to an ethnic group or class, as in the cases of Chechens and Kulaks.

Polyan (2001) identified 79 major resettlement operations in Russia between 1920 and 1952, 70 per cent of which took place in the decade 1935–45.[13] Most were cases of one-sided government coercion, but a sizable share (19 of 79) consisted of responses to ongoing or recent insurgent activities. Resettlement efforts during armed conflicts relocated almost twice as many people as operations undertaken in peacetime: 124,632 versus 64,228 persons per operation, on average.

These activities required tremendous organizational capacity to execute. Following a five-month planning period, it took 119,000 NKVD personnel three days in February 1944 to load 387,229 Chechens and 91,250 Ingush onto the trains. In April 1949, 76,000 interior ministry troops took three days to arrest and relocate 29,687 families (89,874 individuals) from Lithuania,

Latvia and Estonia (Polyan 2001: 122, 139). The terrifying efficiency of the Soviet secret police made such operations difficult to replicate. Only at the height of Soviet power was it possible to accomplish the logistical feat of rapidly deploying multiple divisions across extended lines of communication, maintain the secrecy and deception required to prevent mass flight or acts of sabotage, identify and locate tens of thousands of targets, and closely monitor them upon arrival to destination. The operational challenge of physically rounding up entire villages, districts and even republics was enormous. It is not surprising that massive resettlement has only been used where the government already enjoyed some combination of local military superiority, territorial control and low levels of armed resistance. Where this has not been the case – in Afghanistan, in the latest Chechen Wars, in the early 1920s, even in Western Ukraine and the Baltics immediately following the German retreat – this form of repression was not an option.

Even in the assertive, semi-autocratic Russia of the Putin era, collective punishment has proven surprisingly difficult to implement. Democratization is one plausible explanation for the trend away from repressive counterinsurgency in Russia, but an incomplete one. During the first Chechen War, when a pervasive media presence publicized the most egregious uses of force to the electoral benefit of Yeltsin's political opponents, many of the hallmarks of repressive counterinsurgency, like resettlements and sweeps, were not seriously considered. In contrast, the Afghan and second Chechen conflicts were both conducted in controlled media environments. Even so, the state's repressive impulses were largely unfulfilled or ineffective.[14]

This is not to say that Russia's most recent wars were not brutal. But indiscriminate firepower and deliberate repression are not the same thing – one compensates for local asymmetries favouring the insurgent, the other is an exploitation of much greater asymmetries that favour the incumbent. The Russian case suggests that a reliance on collective punishment is a function not simply of regime type, but of an interaction between regime type and capabilities.

Regime type and counterinsurgency success

Given differences in the threats they face and how they fight, are democracies and non-democracies differentially likely to achieve success? Theoretical arguments fall into three camps: 'democracy hurts', 'democracy helps' and 'democracy does not matter'. The first, sceptical view maintains that democracies are cost-sensitive and reluctant to escalate the use of force. Because they are unable to get their hands dirty and commit sufficient resources to avoid defeat, democratic regimes experience a disadvantage in low-intensity conflict (Merom 2003: 19, 21–4, 46–7; Inbar 2003: ix; Mack 1975: 184; Li 2005: 283; Reiter and Stam 2002: 164–92, 347, 349, 363; Chalk 1995: 35; Peters 2007; Luttwak 2007). This view has not gone unchallenged. As several scholars have pointed out, the costliest campaigns, like the foreign internal defence missions favoured by democracies, are generally more difficult from the outset (Edelstein 2008: 5; Lyall 2010b: 178). Indiscriminate violence and repression, moreover, do not always ensure victory: repression can inflame, suppress or have no effect on future insurgent violence (Lichbach 1987; Moore 1998; Davenport 2007b).

In explaining how democracy can be an asset in counterinsurgency, democratic optimists have turned many of the sceptics' arguments on their head. Because democracies are risk-averse, optimists expect them to become involved in only those conflicts where victory is relatively easily attainable (Bueno De Mesquita and Siverson 1995: 841–55; Reiter and Stam 1998: 378; Fearon 1994: 577–8, 585–6). Because they face constraints on the use of excessive force, democracies are expected to avoid escalating a conflict by inflaming and provoking dissidents (Dernado 1985: 188, 209; Sambanis and Zinn 2005; Abrahms 2007: 242–6).

The third position is that – after adjusting for other potential sources of variation – regime type has no discernible impact on success. Lyall (2010a: 183) and Getmansky (2010) argue that the success–regime type relationship is spurious, and that earlier findings were compromised by no-variance research designs and failure to account for differential selection into conflict by regime type.

Empirically, social scientists and policy analysts have had a surprisingly difficult time finding common ground. Quantitative analyses have largely failed to find a strong and consistent relationship between regime type and counterinsurgency success (Zhukov 2008; Lyall 2010a; Getmansky 2010), although some research on counter-terrorism has supported the more optimistic view (Abrahms 2007). In general, social scientists have been wary of treating victory and defeat as subjects of direct study. Most academic research has focused instead on more easily quantifiable measures of conflict cessation, like basic numerical thresholds of war-related casualties (say, 1,000 or 100 battle deaths per year), and conflict duration. To policy analysts, such metrics are neither satisfying nor informative as measures of success.[15] Recently, social scientists have begun to consider the impact of democracy on ordinal and categorical measures of victory, like 'win-lose-draw' (Lyall and Wilson 2009: 71; Lyall 2010a) or 'strong' and 'lenient' definitions of success (Zhukov 2008: 7; Getmansky 2010: 13, 44). These measures combine criteria for pacification and insurgent military defeat with changes in the political status quo, potentially conveying more policy-relevant information.

If future empirical studies of counterinsurgency are to inform strategic design and policy-makers' evaluation of past performance, the continued conceptual refinement of victory and defeat warrants priority attention. Few studies, for instance, have embraced the intersubjectivity of the 'success' concept, or potential divergences in its meaning across different types of regime.[16] The current US government is unlikely to deem an outcome successful if it were achieved largely through a massive programme of forcible resettlement; if we lose sight of our basic norms and principles, one might say, we have lost the war. The same could not be said of Stalin's Soviet Union, or even Andrew Jackson's United States.

The Russian example

By the Lyall and Wilson (2009) definition of success, Russia has 'won' almost every counterinsurgency campaign it has fought (Figure 23.1).[17] With the outcomes of three conflicts still uncertain and one case coded as a draw, Russia's overall success rate is 18 in 21, or 85.7 per cent.[18] Afghanistan and the first Chechen War are the only cases of outright defeat since 1917. By contrast, the cross-national historical average for the same time period is 35.1 per cent, including 29.7 per cent for democracies, 32.8 per cent for transitional regimes and 42.8 for autocracies.[19]

The cost of Russia's participation in these conflicts has been considerable: excluding the ongoing cases, mean duration was 4.01 years, with a median of 3.38 years and an average of 3,583 security service personnel killed per conflict.[20] Casualty rates were slightly greater in conflicts initiated under transitional regimes – 3,902 on average, compared with 2,786 under the Soviet Union – contrary to claims that autocracies are highly cost-acceptant.[21]

Given the conventional wisdom that autocracies are willing to fight longer wars (Reiter and Stam 2002), Russia's campaigns may seem surprisingly short. Indeed, their duration has been less than half the historical average from the same time period (8.27 years).[22] Half of the 18 successful Russian cases were terminated in less than 2.5 years, and 90 per cent in less than 6.2, compared to 4.5 and 20.4 years for successful counterinsurgencies worldwide. On this metric, Russia has been far closer to her democratic rivals (50 per cent of cases won under two years and 90 per cent under 5.42) than to her non–democratic peers (4.08 and 14.83 years for autocracies, 4.25 and 11.5 years for transitional regimes). Russia's victories have been unusually swift and decisive.[23]

One may ask whether – outlier or not – Russia's track record is one to hold in high esteem. After all, Russian counterinsurgency has traditionally been the domain of coercion, much of it crude and indiscriminate. It is not immediately clear whether Russia's successes have been achieved due to this systematic brutality, or in spite of it. On this point, the main insight from the Russian example might be, 'repression works, but not in moderation'.

Of the 79 major episodes of forcible resettlement since 1917, 11 either failed to suppress an insurgency or could not prevent its recurrence. The risk of inflammation was particularly high in cases where these operations were implemented in response to insurgent activity. Five of the 19 wartime resettlements (26.3 per cent) were followed by new or continued conflict within the next decade, compared to six out of 60 peacetime resettlements (10 per cent).[24]

Under what conditions, then, has mass repression succeeded in suppressing insurgency? There has been little regional variation – both suppressive and inflammatory resettlement operations were conducted in the North Caucasus, the Baltic states and the western borderlands of Ukraine and Belarus. The target groups have also been similar: active members of 'counter-revolutionary' movements and their families, pre-Soviet intellectual and military elites, 'criminals', wealthy landowners and peasants (Vladimirtsev and Kokurin 2008: 36).

The clearest distinction between 'successful' and 'failed' resettlement operations appears to have been their scale.[25] The average number of people relocated in operations that failed to suppress violence was 43,131, compared to 86,838 for the successful cases. Among the 19 wartime operations, this difference was 73,600 to 142,857. This contrast is even starker within the separate regions. In the Baltic states, the total number of people relocated in failed versus successful cases was 45,000 to 143,000. These figures were 345,000 to 864,600 in the North Caucasus, and 62,000 to 2,457,000 in the borderlands of Ukraine and Belarus.[26]

In sum, the larger the scale of mass repression, the more likely it was to suppress fighting. Half-measures, if tens of thousands of deportees can be seen as such, were more likely to make things worse.[27] Repression is a resource-intensive activity. Even localized, small-scale actions like cordon-and-search can place heavy burdens on manpower, intelligence and logistics. While it is possible to employ repression effectively in counterinsurgency, the Soviet Union's 'anti-hearts and minds' model is unlikely to offer a workable blueprint. The Soviets, it appears, were successful not simply because they repressed, but because – on most occasions – they had the capabilities to repress efficiently and on so large a scale that remaining insurgents were separated – literally, by thousands of miles – from major sources of popular support. Repression, as the Russian case suggests, is highly risky. The only way to reduce this risk is to go 'all in', which – fortunately for civilians – is not an option most governments are capable of implementing.

Conclusion

The Russian experience yields several lessons for governments attempting to cope with domestic and expeditionary counterinsurgency. First, not all non-democracies are alike. Transitional, semi-autocratic regimes are at far greater risk of experiencing insurgent violence than consolidated dictatorships. They are also less efficient in the employment of coercive instruments of power. Second, coercion comes in different forms. Repression, of the sort employed during the massive resettlement operations of the 1930s and 1940s, requires not simply a lack of normative constraints on the use of force, but also the capacity to mobilize significant manpower, intelligence and operational resources. Indiscriminate mass firepower, on the other hand, is more likely to be used where these requirements cannot be met. Third, a lack of restraints on coercion does not by itself ensure success. Repression is most likely to suppress insurgent violence if it is used on a massive scale. Small and even medium-scale repression is likely to be inflammatory or simply ineffective.

The Russian case also highlights a number of puzzles yet to be resolved. It remains unclear, for instance, why Russia has been an outlier in so many areas. It faced an average of one insurgency every four years, yet managed to defeat 85.7 per cent of these opponents. Historically, it was expert in rapidly crushing insurrections, yet recently it has struggled to contain several protracted conflicts. Why has Russia been unable to replicate the 'magic formula' of its Soviet past? Regime characteristics are likely insufficient as explanations for these peculiarities.

Many of the political factors that make the Russian case so intriguing also make empirical investigation difficult. The overclassification of primary sources on Soviet counterinsurgency has kept in-depth study of the subject off limits to all but a small circle of analysts within Russia's intelligence services and interior ministry. Despite an extensive declassification of Soviet-era documents in the early 1990s and a 30-year secrecy limit imposed by the 1993 Law on State Secrets, much of the data remains in closed archives.[28]

Despite these challenges, there is a growing volume of superb archival sources yet to be exploited by Western research.[29] Relatively little of the material has been translated into English, but those willing to parse it will find a wealth of historical data on the location and timing of insurgent attacks and government operations, detailed rosters of combatant and civilian casualties, and thousands of official memoranda, strategy papers and directives. These data can enable empirically rich micro-level study of civil conflict, repression and dissent.

There is an old, cynical Soviet joke: 'Is there opposition in the USSR? If there *were* any, there would no longer *be* any.'[30] While not particularly funny, the punchline is faithful to the empirical pattern illustrated in this review. Rigorous investigation of why there has been so much violent opposition in Russia, and how so much of it came to be violently suppressed, can enrich our understanding of the emergence, conduct and outcome of low-intensity conflict.

Notes

1 These include Nestor Makhno and the Black Army (1918–21), the Zainsk Uprising (1920), the Tambov Uprising (1920–1), the post-Civil War insurgency in Chechnya and Dagestan (1920–32), the Chapan Revolt (1921), the West Siberian Revolt (1921–2), Volga Revolts (1921), the Kronstadt Uprising (1921), insurrections by Ural Kulaks (1921), an uprising in Karelia (1921–2), the Basmachi Rebellion (1922–31), Khassan Israilov's insurgency in the Chechen-Ingush ASSR (1940–4), post-Second World War nationalist insurgencies in Western Ukraine (1944–54), Western Belarus (1944–7), Latvia (1944–7), Estonia (1944–8) and Lithuania (1944–8), the occupation of Afghanistan (1979–89), the civil war in Tajikistan (1992–7), the First Chechen War (1994–6), the Islamist insurrection in the Kadar Gorge of Dagestan (1999), the Second Chechen War (1999–2009), and low-intensity violence in Dagestan (2002–present) and Ingushetia (2004–present).
2 'Hearts and minds' is defined as a strategic emphasis on the protection of civilians, economic assistance and government legitimacy. See paragraphs 1–3, 1–108 and 1–113 in FM 3–24.
3 Ninety-one of the 307 cases of insurgency included in Lyall and Wilson's (2009) dataset involve a democratic incumbent, defined as a country with a Polity2 score greater than 6, where –10 represents full autocracy and 10 represents full democracy.
4 Conditional probabilities of occupation by incumbent regime calculated from Lyall and Wilson's (2009) dataset.
5 Expeditionary operations entail heavy costs and logistical burdens, requiring high readiness, sustainable force generation, protection of extended and vulnerable lines of communication, and a capability to sustain operations in austere environments where host-nation support may be deficient or unavailable. Few countries beyond the great powers of North America and Western Europe have been able to field such capabilities. See Gongora (2004), Fry (2005), Deverell (2002).

6 Russia had a Polity2 score of –1 in 1917–22, –7.7 on average in 1923–88, and 3.6 on average in 1989–2009.

7 These cases were selected on the following criteria: they involved the use of political violence by non-state actors against the central government, involved mostly irregular warfare, and resulted in at least 100 government fatalities. This definition excludes conventional warfare against non-state adversaries like the White Army during the Russian Civil War, as well incidents of one-sided government repression, such as the forcible resettlement of ethnic Koreans to Central Asia in 1937.

8 Non-governmental organizations, political parties and policy activists facilitate the adoption of norms through agenda-setting, electoral challenges and the reform of institutional procedures (Finnemore and Sikkink 1998; Keck and Sikkink 1998).

9 In this view, decisions to coerce are driven primarily by the perceived level of threat emanating from insurgents. Where the threat to regime survival is high and the government's capacity to monitor and regulate the threat is low, coercion is expected to be more likely (Davenport 1995: 708; Regan and Henderson 2002). Transitional regimes are expected to be most repressive because their reins of power are highly contested, security services are weak and fractured, and adherence to non-coercive norms is not institutionalized.

10 Definition of mass repression from Polyan (2001: 12). Examples of repression include 'scorched earth' policies of crop, livestock and infrastructure destruction, forcible resettlement and deportation, detention in concentration camps, systematic use of cordon-and-search and comparably invasive activities. For alternative definitions, which appeal to intent and tactics rather than the scope of the repressed targets, see Davenport *et al.* (2008: 9), Davenport (1995: 685; 2007b: 2), Besley and Persson (2009: 1) and Regan and Henderson (2002: 3).

11 In the words of Tukhachevsky's Chief of Staff, Nikolay Kakurin, the latter approach was used 'to ensure that the cloud of asphyxiating gases is completely dispersed across the entire forest, killing everything that hides within' (Sennikov 2004).

12 The typical sentence was 5–8 years in a hard labour camp, followed by 20 years of residence in a remote resettlement location, where family members would already be waiting. All the family's private property would be confiscated upon arrest (Polyan 2001: 99).

13 These include only large-scale resettlement efforts (over 1,000 relocated per operation).

14 An example of this difficulty is the recent use of cordon-and-search, colloquially called zachistka (mop-up) in Russian. A defining feature of NKVD's post-Second World War campaign against Ukrainian nationalists (Zhukov 2007: 447–8), cordon-and-search operations have far fewer moving pieces than mass resettlement, but still call for significant resources and depend on surprise (to prevent early detection), extensive planning (to avoid rushing into position), robust intelligence (to identify and locate targets), overwhelming numbers (to maximize coverage of escape routes), territorial control (at least of roads leading to the village) and significant combined arms capabilities (to synchronize arrival and provide artillery support). Unlike the post-Second World War cases, which were carried out only after the NKVD and SMERSH ('Death to Spies') had assembled extensive rosters of suspected insurgents and their whereabouts, the Chechen mop-ups were – at least initially – implemented hastily and with inadequate intelligence preparation. In the absence of preliminary data on insurgents' identities and whereabouts, interrogations often became sole sources of evidence, resulting in indiscriminate arrests, disappearances and forced confessions (Souleimanov 2007: 173–5).

15 Violence levels may drop as a result of the establishment of incumbent or insurgent territorial control (Kalyvas 2006), stalemate, third-party intervention or a host of other factors, irrespective of whom the resulting status quo may favour.

16 I thank Jeff Friedman for this insight.

17 As defined by Lyall and Wilson (2009: 71–2):

> a win occurs when the insurgency is militarily defeated and its organization destroyed, or the war ends without any political concessions granted to insurgent forces.... A draw occurs when an incumbent is forced to concede to some, but not all, insurgent demands, and neither side obtains its maximal aims.... [A] loss [is] a situation in which the incumbent unilaterally concedes to all, or nearly all, insurgent demands.

18 Afghanistan and the first Chechen War are coded 'loss'. The 1920–32 counterinsurgency in Chechnya and Dagestan – which succeeded in temporarily stemming the violence, but did not prevent its recurrence less than a decade later – is coded 'draw'. All other completed cases are coded 'win'. The

Lyall–Wilson dataset includes nine of the 24 Russian and Soviet cases, although it does not include casualty statistics and uses different names for some conflicts. Among the duplicates, outcome codings given here agree with those provided by Lyall and Wilson.

19 Success rates calculated with Lyall and Wilson (2009) data. The success rate for Russia and the Soviet Union is six in eight completed cases, or 75 per cent, in the Lyall–Wilson dataset.

20 The Ukrainian Insurgent Army (UPA) of 1944–56 and the Chechnya-Dagestan insurgency of 1920–32 share the position of longest case. The bloodiest cases were Afghanistan in 1979–89, which claimed 15,051 military casualties, closely followed by campaigns against Nestor Makhno's Black Army in 1921–2 (14,935 troops killed) and the UPA (14,128).

21 Casualty figures for the conflicts in Figure 23.1 are taken from multiple sources, primarily Krivosheyev (2001) and the 'Isroricheskaya Pamyat' [Historical Memory]' Foundation's casualties database (http://lists.historyfoundation.ru).

22 Of 188 post-1917 counterinsurgencies worldwide, duration has been 8.27 years on average, with 9.27 years for democracies, 8.74 for autocracies and 7.82 for transitional regimes. The respective median durations have been five years overall, 4.88 for democracies, eight for autocracies and 4.46 for transitional regimes. Data from Lyall and Wilson (2009).

23 The causal arrow, of course, may conceivably point in either direction – protracted counterinsurgencies are more difficult to win, but difficult counterinsurgencies are also likely to become protracted.

24 Cross-tabulations calculated with data from Polyan (2001).

25 A 'successful' resettlement operation is understood as one followed by pacification and no resumption of insurgent violence within the following decade (suppressive). A 'failed' operation is one followed by either an increase in insurgent violence (inflammatory), no change (ineffective), or a recurrence of violence within the following decade.

26 Descriptive statistics calculated with data from Polyan (2001).

27 This pattern is consistent with recent research by Friedman (2010: 20), who finds that small-scale repression can have disastrous consequences. It undermines both the perceived legitimacy of the government and the government's credibility in carrying out threats.

28 This state of affairs can be explained by a lack of mechanisms to ensure archival compliance with new declassification requirements, as well as by official reluctance to publish tactics and procedures while Russia continues to be embroiled in armed conflict with several insurgent groups in the Caucasus.

29 Primary source literature on Soviet-era counterinsurgency has been of three sorts: collections of insurgent documents published by pro-insurgent émigré groups (e.g. Mirchuk 1953), collections of declassified material from non-Russian post-Soviet archives (e.g. Bilas 1994; Anusauskas 1999; Serhiychuk 1998; Strods 1996; Adamushko 2004; Andreev and Shumov 2005), and collections from the much larger but more secretive Russian archives (e.g. Litvinov and Sedunov 2005). Because selection of documents for these volumes is to varying degrees partisan, researchers are advised to pursue data collection strategies that draw, with due caution, from all three categories of sources.

30 In Russian: *Yest' li v SSSR oppozitsionery? Yesli by oni byli, ikh by uzhe ne bylo!*

Recommended readings

Burds, J. (1997) 'AGENTURA: Soviet Informants' Networks in Galicia, 1944–1948', *Eastern European Politics and Societies* (January).

Burds, J. (2007) 'The Soviet War against "Fifth Columnists": The Case of Chechnya, 1942–1944', *Journal of Contemporary History*, 42 (2).

Grau, L. (1996) *The Bear Went Over the Mountain: Soviet Combat Tactics in Afghanistan*. Washington, DC: NDU Press.

Grau, L. (1997) 'Artillery and Counterinsurgency: The Soviet Experience in Afghanistan', *Field Artillery Journal*, May–June.

Grau, L. and M. Gress (eds) (2002) *The Soviet-Afghan War: How a Superpower Fought and Lost*. Lawrence: University Press of Kansas.

Grau, L. and T. Smith (2000) 'A Crushing Victory: Fuel-Air Explosives and Grozny 2000', *Marine Corps Gazette*, August.

Kramer, M. (2005) 'Guerilla Warfare, Counterinsurgency, and Terrorism in the North Caucasus: The Military Dimension of the Russian-Chechen Conflict', *Europe-Asia Studies*, 57 (2): 209–90.

Lyall, J. (2009) 'Does Indiscriminate Violence Incite Insurgent Attacks? Evidence from Chechnya', *Journal of Conflict Resolution*, 53 (3): 331–62.

Lyall, J. (2010a) 'Do Democracies Make Inferior Counterinsurgents? Reassessing Democracy's Impact on War Outcomes and Duration', *International Organization*, 64 (winter): 167–92.

Lyall, J. (2010b) 'Are Coethnics More Effective Counterinsurgents? Evidence from the Second Chechen War', *American Political Science Review*, 104: 1–20.

Lyall, J. and I. Wilson (2009) 'Rage Against the Machines: Explaining Outcomes in Counterinsurgency Wars', *International Organization*, 63 (winter): 67–106.

Oliker, O. (2001) *Russia's Chechen Wars 1994–2000: Lessons from Urban Combat*. Santa Monica: RAND.

Robinson, P. (2010) 'Soviet Hearts-and-Minds Operations in Afghanistan', *The Historian*, 72 (1): 1–22.

Souleimanov, E. (2007) *An Endless War: The Russian-Chechen Conflict in Perspective*. Frankfurt: Peter Lang.

Statiev, A. (2005) 'Motivations and Goals of the Soviet Deportations in the Western Borderlands', *The Journal of Strategic Studies*, 28 (6): 977–1003.

Statiev, A. (2009) 'Soviet Ethnic Deportations: Intent versus Outcome', *Journal of Genocide Research*, 11 (2–3): 243–64.

Statiev, A. (2010) *The Soviet Counterinsurgency in the Western Borderlands*. Cambridge: Cambridge University Press.

Toft, M. (2003) *The Geography of Ethnic Violence: Identity, Interests, and the Indivisibility of Territory*. Princeton: Princeton University Press.

Zhukov, Y. (2007) 'Examining the Authoritarian Model of Counter-Insurgency: The Soviet Campaign Against the Ukrainian Insurgent Army', *Small Wars and Insurgencies*, 18 (3): 439–66.

References

Abrahms, M. (2007) 'Why Democracies Make Superior Counterterrorists', *Security Studies*, 16 (2): 2233–53.

Adamushko, V.I. *et al.* (eds) (2004) *Osvobozhdennaya Belarus. Dokumenty i materialy* [Liberated Belarus. Documents and Materials]. Minsk: NARB.

Andreev A. and S. Shumov (eds) (2005) *Banderovshchina*. Moscow: EKSMO.

Anusauskas, A. (ed.) (1999) *The Anti-Soviet Resistance in the Baltic States*. Vilnius.

Aylwin-Foster, N. (2005) 'Changing the Army for Counterinsurgency Operations', *Military Review*, 85 (6): 2–15.

Benson, M. and J. Kugler (1998) 'Power Parity, Democracy, and the Severity of Internal Violence', *Journal of Conflict Resolution*, 42 (2): 196–209.

Besley, T. and T. Persson (2009) 'Repression or Civil War?', *American Economic Review*, 99 (2): 292–7.

Bilas I.G. (1994) *Repressivno-karal'na sistema v Ukrayini: 1917–1953* [The Repressive-Punitive System in Ukraine: 1917–1953]. Kyiv: Lybid', Viys'ko Ukrayiny.

Bueno de Mesquita, B. and M. Siverson (1995) 'War and the Survival of Political Leaders: A Comparative Study of Regime Types and Political Accountability', *American Political Science Review*, 89 (4).

Chalk, P. (1995) 'The Liberal Democratic Response to Terrorism', *Terrorism and Political Violence*, 7 (4): 10–44.

Cline, L.E. (2005) *Pseudo Operations and Counterinsurgency: Lessons from Other Countries*. Monograph, US Army War College, Strategic Studies Institute, June.

Davenport, C. (1995) 'Multi-Dimensional Threat Perception and State Repression: An Inquiry into Why States Apply Negative Sanctions', *American Journal of Political Science*, 39 (3): 683–713.

Davenport, C. (2007a) *State Repression and the Domestic Democratic Peace*. Cambridge: Cambridge University Press.

Davenport, C. (2007b) 'State Repression and Political Order', *Annual Review of Political Science*, 10: 1–23.

Davenport, C., D. Armstrong and M. Lichbach (2008) 'From Mountains to Movements: Dissent, Repression and Escalation to Civil War'. Unpublished Manuscript.

Dernado, J. (1985) *Power in Numbers: The Political Strategy of Protest and Rebellion*. Princeton: Princeton University Press.

Deverell, J. (2002) 'Coalition Warfare and Expeditionary Operations', *RUSI Journal*, 147 (1): 18–21.

Edelstein, D. (2008) *Occupational Hazards: Success and Failure in Military Occupation*. Ithaca and London: Cornell University Press.

Elbadawi, Ibrahim and Nicholas Sambanis (2000) 'Why Are There So Many Civil Wars in Africa? Understanding and Preventing Violent Conflict', *Journal of African Economies*, 9 (3): 244–69.

Elkhamri, M., L. Grau, L. King-Irani, A. Mitchell and L. Tasa-Bennett (2005) 'Urban Population Control in a Counterinsurgency'. Foreign Military Studies Office, Ft. Leavenworth.

Elkins, C. (2005) 'The Wrong Lesson', *The Atlantic Monthly*, 296, July/August.

Fearon, J. (1994) 'Signaling versus the Balance of Power and Interests: An Empirical Test of a Crisis Bargaining Model', *Journal of Conflict Resolution*, 38 (June, Special Issue): 236–69.

Fearon, J. (2004) 'Domestic Political Audiences and the Escalation of International Disputes', *American Political Science Review*, 88 (3).

Fearon, J. and D. Laitin (2003) 'Ethnicity, Insurgency, and Civil War', *American Political Science Review*, 97 (1): 75–90.

Fein, H. (1995) 'More Murder in the Middle: Life-Integrity Violations and Democracy in the World, 1987', *Human Rights Quarterly*, 17 (1): 170–91.

Finnemore, M. and K. Sikkink (1998) 'International Norm Dynamics and Political Change', *International Organization*, 52 (autumn): 887–917.

Friedman, J. (2010) 'The Optimal Counterinsurgent: A Theory of Hearts, Minds, and Intimidation'. Unpublished Manuscript.

Fry, R. (2005) 'Expeditionary Operations in the Modern Era', *RUSI Journal*, 150 (6): 60–3.

Galula, David (1963) *Pacification in Algeria, 1956–1958*. MG-478-1. Santa Monica: RAND.

Gareev, M. (1999) *Afganskaya strada (s sovetskimi voiskami i bez nikh)* [Afghan Campaign (with Soviet Forces and without them)], 2nd edn. Moscow: Insan.

Getmansky, A. (2010) 'Who Wins Counterinsurgency Wars? The Role of Regime in Counterinsurgency Outcomes'. Unpublished Manuscript, 16 August.

Gongora, T. (2004) 'Expeditionary Operations: Definitions and Requirements', *Military Technology*, 28 (6): 106–14.

Grau, L. (1996) *The Bear Went Over the Mountain: Soviet Combat Tactics in Afghanistan*. Washington, DC: NDU Press.

Grau, L. (1997) 'Artillery and Counterinsurgency: The Soviet Experience in Afghanistan', *Field Artillery Journal*, May–June.

Grau, L. and M. Gress (eds) (2002) *The Soviet-Afghan War: How a Superpower Fought and Lost*. Lawrence: University Press of Kansas.

Grau, L. and T. Smith (2000) 'A Crushing Victory: Fuel-Air Explosives and Grozny 2000', *Marine Corps Gazette*, August.

Gurr, T. (2000) *People Versus States: Minorities at Risk in the New Century*. Washington, DC: United States Institute of Peace.

Hegre, H., T. Ellingsen, S. Gates and S.P. Gleditsch (2001) 'Toward a Democratic Civil Peace? Democracy, Political Change, and Civil War, 1816–1992', *American Political Science Review*, 95 (1): 33–48.

Henderson, E. and D. Singer (2000) 'Civil War in the Post-Colonial World, 1946–92', *Journal of Peace Research*, 37 (3): 275–99.

Inbar, E. (ed.) (2003) *Democracies and Small Wars*. London: Frank Cass.

Kalyvas, S. (2006) *The Logic of Violence in Civil War*. New York: Cambridge University Press.

Kantor, Yu. (2005) *Voina i mir Mikhaila Tukhachevskogo* [War and Peace of Mikhail Tukhachevskiy]. Moscow: Ogonyok.

Keck, M. and K. Sikkink (1998) *Activists beyond Borders: Advocacy Networks in International Politics*. Ithaca: Cornell University Press.

Kilcullen, D. (2009) *The Accidental Guerilla: Fighting Small Wars in the Midst of a Big One*. New York: Oxford University Press.

Kitson, F. (1971) *Low Intensity Operations: Subversion, Insurgency, Peace-keeping*. Harrisburg: Stackpole Books

Kocher, M., T. Pepinsky and S. Kalyvas (2008) 'Into the Arms of the Rebels? Aerial Bombardment, Indiscriminate Violence, and Territorial Control in the Vietnam War', paper prepared for presentation at the 49th Annual Convention of the International Studies Association, San Franciso, 26–29 March.

Krain, M. and M. Myers (1997) 'Democracy and Civil War: A Note on the Democratic Peace Proposition', *International Interactions*, 23 (1): 109–18.

Kramer, M. (2005) 'Guerilla Warfare, Counterinsurgency, and Terrorism in the North Caucasus: The Military Dimension of the Russian-Chechen Conflict', *Europe-Asia Studies*, 57 (2): 209–90.

Krivosheyev, G. (ed.) (2001) *Rossiya i SSSR v voynakh XX veka. Poteri vooruzhennykh sil. Statisticheskoye issledovaniye* [Russia and the USSR in the Wars of the 20th Century. Military Casualties. Statistical Study]. Moscow: Olma-Press.

Li, Q. (2005) 'Does Democracy Promote or Reduce Transnational Terrorist Incidents?', *Journal of Conflict Resolution*, 48 (2): 278–97.

Lichbach, M. (1987) 'Deterrence or Escalation? The Puzzle of Aggregate Studies of Repression and Dissent', *Journal of Conflict Resolution*, 31 (2): 266–97.

Litvinov, M. and A. Sedunov (2005) *Shpiony i diversanty: bor'ba s pribaltiyskim shpionazhem i natsionalisticheskimi bandformirovaniyami na Severo-Zapade Rossii* [Spies and Saboteurs: The Struggle against Baltic Espionage and Nationalist Bands in Northwest Russia]. Pskov: Pskovskaya Oblastnaya Tipografia.

Luttwak, E. (2007) 'Dead End: Counterinsurgency Warfare as Military Malpractice', *Harper's*, 314 (1881): 33–42.

Lyakhovskiy, A. (1995) *Tragediya i doblest' Afgana* [Tragedy and Valor of the Afghanistan War]. Moscow: GPI Iskona.

Lyall, J. (2009) 'Does Indiscriminate Violence Incite Insurgent Attacks? Evidence from Chechnya', *Journal of Conflict Resolution*, 53 (3): 331–62.

Lyall, J. (2010a) 'Do Democracies Make Inferior Counterinsurgents? Reassessing Democracy's Impact on War Outcomes and Duration', *International Organization*, 64 (winter): 167–92.

Lyall, J. (2010b) 'Are Coethnics More Effective Counterinsurgents? Evidence from the Second Chechen War', *American Political Science Review*, 104: 1–20.

Lyall, J. and I. Wilson (2009) 'Rage Against the Machines: Explaining Outcomes in Counterinsurgency Wars', *International Organization*, 63 (winter): 67–106.

Mack, A. (1975) 'Why Big Nations Lose Small Wars: The Politics of Asymmetric Conflict', *World Politics*, 27 (2): 175–200.

Madison, J. (1787) 'The Utility of the Union as a Safeguard Against Domestic Faction and Insurrection [Federalist No. 10]', *Daily Advertiser*, 22 November.

Maksakov, Ilya (2000) 'Operatsii na Severnom Kavkaze ispolnyayetsya god' [The Operation in the North Caucasus becomes One Year Old], *Nezavisimaya Gazeta*, 2 August.

Mansfield, E. and J. Snyder (2005) *Electing to Fight: Why Emerging Democracies go to War*. Cambridge, MA: Harvard.

Merom, Gil (2003) *How Democracies Lose Small Wars*. New York: Cambridge University Press.

Mirchuk, P. (1953) *Ukrainskaya Povstancheskaya Armiya. 1942–1952. Dokumenty i materially* [Ukrainian Insurgent Army. 1942–1952. Documents and Materials]. Munich: Khvil'yovyi.

Moore, W. (1998) 'Repression and Dissent: Substitution, Context, and Timing', *American Journal of Political Science*, 42 (3): 851–73.

Nagl, J. (2005) *Learning to Eat Soup with a Knife: Counterinsurgency Lessons from Malaya and Vietnam*. Chicago: University of Chicago Press.

Neumayer, Eric (2005) 'Do International Human Rights Treaties Improve Respect for Human Rights?', *Journal of Conflict Resolution*, 49 (6): 925–53.

Oliker, O. (2001) *Russia's Chechen Wars 1994–2000: Lessons from Urban Combat*. Santa Monica: RAND.

Peters, R. (2007) 'Progress and Peril', *Armed Forces Journal*, February.

Poe, S. and C. Tate (1994) 'Repression of Human Rights to Personal Integrity in the 1980s: A Global Analysis', *American Political Science Review*, 88 (4).

Polyan, P. (2001) *Ne po svoyey volye ... Istoriya i geografiya prinuditel'nykh migratsiy v SSSR* [Not of Their Own Will ... The History and Geography of Forced Migrations in the USSR]. Moscow: Memorial.

Regan, Patrick M. and Errol A. Henderson (2002) 'Democracy, Threats and Political Repression in Developing Countries: Are Democracies Internally Less Violent?', *Third World Quarterly*, 23 (1): 119–36.

Reiter, D. and A. Stam (1998) 'Democracy, War Initiation and Victory', *American Political Science Review*, 92 (2): 377–89.

Reiter, D. and A. Stam (2002) *Democracies at War*. Princeton: Princeton University Press.

Rummel, R. (1995) 'Democracy, Power, Genocide, and Mass Murder', *Journal of Conflict Resolution*, 39 (1): 3–26.

Sambanis, N. and A. Zinn (2005) 'From Protest to Violence: An Analysis of Conflict Escalation with an Application to Self-determination Movements'. Manuscript, Yale University.

Sennikov, B. (2004) *Tambovskoye vosstanie 1918–1921 gg. i raskrestyanivaniye Rossii 1929–1933 gg.* [Tambov Uprising of 1918–1921 and the Elimination of Peasantry in Russia 1929–1933]. Moscow: Posev.

Serhiychuk, V. (1998) *Desyat' buremnykh lit. Zahidnoukrayins'ki zemli u 1944–1953 rr. Novi dokumenty i materially* [Ten Turbulent Years. West Ukrainian Lands in 1944–1953. New Documents and Materials]. Kyiv: Dnipro.

Souleimanov, E. (2007) *An Endless War: The Russian-Chechen Conflict in Perspective*. Frankfurt: Peter Lang.

Strods, H. (1996) *Latvijas nacionalo partizanu kars. 1944.-1956* [The Latvian National Partisan War, 1944–1956]. Riga: Preses Nams.

Thompson, R. (1966) *Defeating Communist Insurgency: Experiences from Malaya and Vietnam*. London: Chatto & Windus.

Toft, M. (2003) *The Geography of Ethnic Violence: Identity, Interests, and the Indivisibility of Territory*. Princeton: Princeton University Press.

United States Department of the Army (2006) *Counterinsurgency. Field Manual 3–24*. Washington, DC: Headquarters, Department of the Army.

Valentino, B., P. Huth and D. Balch-Lindsay (2004) '"Draining the Sea": Mass Killing and Guerilla Warfare', *International Organization*, 58 (spring): 375–407.

Varennikov, V. (2002) *Nepovtorimoye* [Unrepeatable]. Moscow: Sovetskiy pisatel'.

Vladimirtsev, N. and A. Kokurin (2008) *NKVD-MVD SSSR v bor'be s banditizmom i vooruzhennym natsionalisticheskim podpol'yem na Zapadnoy Ukraine, v Zapadnoy Belorussii i Pribaltike 1939–1956* [NKVD-MVD in the Struggle against Banditry and Armed Nationalist Guerillas in Western Ukraine, Western Belarus and the Baltics]. Moscow: MVD.

Zhukov, Y. (2007) 'Examining the Authoritarian Model of Counter-Insurgency: The Soviet Campaign Against the Ukrainian Insurgent Army', *Small Wars and Insurgencies*, 18 (3): 439–66.

Zhukov, Y. (2008) 'Evaluating Success in Counterinsurgency, 1804–2000: Does Regime Type Matter?', paper presented at 21st International School on Disarmament and Research on Conflicts (ISODARCO) Winter Course, Andalo, Italy.

24

COUNTERINSURGENCY IN INDIA

David P. Fidler and Sumit Ganguly

The country with the most continuous and diverse involvement in waging counterinsurgency (COIN) campaigns is India. From the first years after its independence until today, India has been engaged almost continuously against insurgencies fuelled by tribal, ethnic, religious, ideological and external political forces. Certainly, no other democracy since the Second World War has had as much involvement with COIN as India. Yet, India's experiences with COIN have been largely ignored by the United States and other countries (Gill and Lamm 2009) and treated with political neglect and military ambivalence within India (Goswami 2009). The reasons for this lack of external and internal interest in India's COIN experiences are complex, but understanding India's efforts at waging COIN is important for grasping the political and military difficulties democracies face in confronting insurgencies at home and abroad. This chapter describes India's COIN campaigns and identifies themes that emerge from looking across the many and diverse COIN efforts India has mounted. It then proceeds to analyse the key features of the Indian experience of COIN ranging from overarching strategic principles to tactical military adaptations. We also explore persistent problems and future challenges facing India's relationship with COIN theory, doctrine and practice.

India's counterinsurgency campaigns

Overview of the campaigns

Starting in the mid 1950s, India has waged COIN in multiple northeastern provinces (Assam, Manipur, Mizoram, Nagaland and Tripura), Punjab, Sri Lanka, Jammu and Kashmir (Kashmir), and multiple Indian states (e.g. Chhattisgarh, Orissa, Jharkhand, West Bengal and Maharashtra) against the Naxalites. These campaigns are outlined in Table 24.1. Although the beginning and end dates of these COIN campaigns are only approximate because of the difficulty of assigning definitive time periods, the dates reveal that Indian federal and state governments have been engaged in fighting insurgencies in every decade since India's independence in 1947. The violence perpetrated has not been identical in scope and intensity or in the danger posed to the integrity of the Union of India, which has been provoked into using a range of different labels to describe these threats including terrorism, low-intensity conflict and insurgency.

Table 24.1 Summary of India's counterinsurgency campaigns

COIN campaign (approximate dates)	Brief description
Assam (1988–2003)	Members of disaffected tribal communities resorted to violence in pursuit of an independent state after negotiations for more autonomy within Assam failed. Agreements in 1993 and 2003 ended the violence, except for continued armed struggle by one militant group.
Kashmir (1988–2002)	Frustration among Muslims in Kashmir with Indian rule turned violent after fraudulent state elections in 1987. Pakistan began to support the insurgency, eventually turning the conflict into a proxy war between Pakistan and India. By the elections of 2002, India had stabilized Kashmir and effectively defeated the insurgency.
Manipur (1978–present)	Despite granting statehood to Manipur in 1972, militant groups, with training provided in China, sought independence. Efforts to end the violence, including elections and ceasefire offers, have not, to date, succeeded.
Mizoram (1966–86)	Led by the charismatic Laldenga, the Mizo peoples launched an insurgency in the mid 1960s. Twenty years later, the insurgency ended with an agreement that had Laldenga becoming Chief Minister of the new Indian state of Mizoram.
Nagaland (1955–97)	India's first and longest COIN campaign came in response to the Naga insurgency's drive for an independent Nagaland. Through trial and error, the Indian government and military wore down the insurgency until the 1997 ceasefire agreement, which is still in force.
Naxalites (1967–73; 2000–present)	Naxalites are adherents of Maoist ideology who use violence to achieve a socialist revolution. The first Naxalite insurgency started in the late 1960s but lasted only a few years. The second Naxalite insurgency arose in the past decade, becoming a threat to India's national security that is not yet contained.
Punjab (1978–93)	The Punjab insurgency involved Sikh nationalists wanting an independent Khalistan. Indian efforts to defeat the Sikh insurgency in the mid 1980s worsened the violence. Improved COIN tactics led to the defeat of Sikh militancy by the early 1990s.
Sri Lanka (1987–90)	India intervened in the civil war in Sri Lanka in order to bring the government and the Tamil Tigers into negotiations for a peaceful settlement. The peacekeeping mission morphed into COIN when the Tamil Tigers refused to negotiate. India withdrew after the Sri Lankan government ordered Indian forces to leave the country.
Tripura (1978–present)	Frustrated by the failure to achieve autonomy through political means, Tripuran militants resorted to violence to secure Tripura's freedom from Indian rule. A peace agreement in 1988 did not end the violence because new secessionist groups formed that have continued fighting until the present day.

Sources: Chadha 2005; Fair 2009; Marwah 2009; Mehta 2009; Patankar 2009; Shekatkar 2009.

Internal counterinsurgency campaigns

As Table 24.1 reveals, all India's COIN campaigns have been within its territory except the one in Sri Lanka. The overwhelmingly internal nature of India's COIN experiences provides one potential reason why US and other Western experts have overlooked India in analysing COIN. With the exception of the wars against Native Americans in the nineteenth century, the United States has engaged in COIN exclusively in foreign countries, with the campaigns in the Philippines, Vietnam, Iraq and Afghanistan being the most prominent examples. These internal and external COIN contexts help explain differences between Indian and US doctrines developed to guide COIN operations (Indian Army 2006; US Army and Marine Corps 2007; Fidler 2009).

The insurgencies India has confronted within its territory have aimed at secession and/or the creation of independent states. In each case, India has prevented this outcome and has, in this respect, been successful in preventing the breakup of India. In this sense, the Indian democratic polity has been the graveyard of insurgencies. Although India has not 'lost' an internal COIN campaign, opinions vary markedly as to whether India's COIN campaigns have been political and military successes. For critics, India's defeat or containment of insurgencies has come at an unnecessarily high price in terms of lives lost, economic resources expended, political legitimacy damaged, human rights violated, and democratic principles compromised. Criticism of India's COIN campaigns reveals that the internal context of these efforts creates higher expectations and standards for success within a democracy than might be the case for countries engaging in COIN in foreign nations (e.g. the gradually decreased expectations of what the United States hopes to accomplish through COIN in Afghanistan).

Reinventing the wheel in counterinsurgency

The frequent resort to COIN by the government and military within Indian territory might suggest that India has absorbed lessons from past campaigns and developed sophisticated and integrated capabilities for waging this peculiar type of warfare. However, one of the most striking conclusions that emerges from analyses of India's COIN experiences is that Indian civilian and military personnel have been unprepared each time an insurgency has erupted, forcing the federal and state governments and the Indian Army to scramble to implement an effective COIN campaign. Such ad hoc reactions have led to serious mistakes, which strengthened the insurgencies and increased the costs of defeating the militants.

This painful and costly phenomenon of repeatedly 'reinventing the wheel' reveals that neither the Indian military nor federal and state civilian authorities have embraced the need to prepare and sustain their capabilities for COIN. Goswami has noted for instance that the India Army has continued, despite repeated and intensive use of COIN operations over decades, to treat counterinsurgency as 'secondary to its primary duty of defending India from external threats. Consequently, little serious thought has been given to doctrinal innovations within the Army with regard to insurgent contingencies' (Goswami 2009: 66). Civilian institutions have proven no more adept at becoming COIN competent despite the strategic imperative that resolving insurgencies is, ultimately, a political not a military task. The return and spread of Naxalite violence, for example, has been associated with failures of federal and state authorities in terms of governance, economic development and fielding adequate police forces (Chadha 2005; Oetken 2009).

The 'reinventing the wheel' pattern in India's responses to insurgencies also reveals that India has not discovered any 'silver bullet' for the dangerous and difficult tasks of COIN. The evolution of the Indian Army's doctrine for such operations largely reflects the tenets other countries have developed for COIN. Even when India has turned the tables on insurgents, the Indian experience offers no shortcuts or undiscovered techniques that reduce significantly the burden governments and militaries bear in fighting insurgencies. This reality reinforces the warnings of COIN experts that engaging in COIN effectively is an expensive, long-term and risky business. India's resilience over decades in combating insurgencies demonstrates the government's ironclad determination not to permit secession from the Union. India's experience highlights moreover that, with internal insurgencies seeking to break apart the state, there is no 'exit strategy'.

External counterinsurgency contexts

The general consensus on India's COIN campaign in Sri Lanka is that India failed to achieve its political and military objectives (Mehta 2009; Rajagopalan 2008). What began as a peacekeeping mission to separate the military forces of Sri Lanka and the Liberation Tigers of Tamil Eelam (Tamil Tigers) became a peace enforcement/COIN operation when the Indian Peacekeeping Force began operations against the Tamil Tigers to bring them back to political negotiations. Political and military preparations for such a shift were inadequate, producing serious problems for India strategically and tactically that Indian civilian officials and military officers could not overcome despite efforts to adapt to the dramatically changed mission.

In addition to this has been India's ongoing effort to support the government of Afghanistan in its struggle against the Taliban-led insurgency (Government of India 2005). To date, India's involvement in Afghanistan has been civilian-only in the form of development-related projects, such as building roads and hospitals. India has deployed no military forces in Afghanistan for any purpose, including training Afghan security forces. Thus, India's efforts in Afghanistan do not, at present, constitute a comprehensive civilian-military COIN campaign. However, India's activities support and contribute to the COIN strategy implemented by the Afghan government and it allies, led by the United States. These activities – and the problems India encounters in Afghanistan – constitute a new aspect of India's experiences with COIN.

India's involvement in external COIN endeavours in Sri Lanka and Afghanistan share similar features but differ in critical respects. India's intervention in Sri Lanka and its willingness to support nation-building in Afghanistan connect to Indian policy-makers' perceptions of direct threats to India's strategic interests and national security. New Delhi viewed the worsening conflict between the Sri Lankan government and Tamil Tigers as a threat because of Sri Lanka's geostrategic importance in the Indian Ocean and the conflict's potential to inflame Tamil passions in the Indian state of Tamil Nadu. Similarly, in Afghanistan, India's core interests were perceived as being best served by achieving a secure, prosperous and pro-India Afghan government, economy and society. Creating this Afghanistan would improve India's security, strengthen its influence in South Asia, improve access to economic and natural resource opportunities in Central Asia and also mitigate the impact of the rivalry with Pakistan on India's ambitions as a great power.

The largest difference between the Indian COIN involvement in Sri Lanka and Afghanistan is the deployment of Indian military forces in the former but not, as yet, in the latter. Unlike in Sri Lanka, India's participation in the Afghan COIN effort has been dependent for security on the Afghan government and its foreign allies. In the context of worsening security in Afghanistan, concerns about the dangers to India's development assistance have increased, leaving India in a dilemma between accepting the deteriorating status quo or escalating Indian participation by involving the Indian military in training Afghan security forces and/or providing better security for Indian development projects. Pakistan would consider such escalation a provocation to its interests in Afghanistan, and, with the United States and Afghanistan increasingly reliant on Pakistani cooperation, India appears to be in a weak position to increase its COIN role in Afghanistan. In other contexts, Pakistan has made India's COIN endeavours more difficult by supporting insurgent groups within India (e.g. Pakistani assistance to Kashmiri insurgents). Pakistan's ability to frustrate India's support for COIN in Afghanistan adds a new twist to the problems Pakistan has in the past created for Indian COIN efforts.

Features of India's experiences with counterinsurgency

Over the decades India has engaged in COIN; strategic principles, effective practices and persistent problems have emerged that characterize the Indian COIN experience. Boiling down India's efforts across such diverse COIN operations shortchanges factors that make each insurgency and COIN response unique. However, given the published case studies of India's COIN campaigns and specific operations (Chadha 2005; Rajagopalan 2008; Ganguly and Fidler 2009) this chapter focuses on characteristics repeatedly identified as important in the Indian government's and military's participation in COIN.

Strategic principles

The Indian approach to COIN reflects a commitment to strategic principles rooted in the idea that COIN is ultimately a political and not a military endeavour. As mentioned above, India has refused to countenance secession from the Union sought by internal insurgency movements. India's behaviour over decades demonstrates that it will bear the costs of defeating an insurgency that remains uncompromising in its demands for secession. This commitment is, of course, connected with India's interest in not setting any precedent that would weaken its territorial integrity, power and influence, especially as a multi-ethnic, religiously pluralistic country located in the dangerous South Asian neighbourhood. The commitment also acts as a deterrent because any group seeking secession knows that it will have to overcome the full force of the Indian state – a daunting task that promises an unequal war of attrition the Indian state believes it will win over time, every time. The tendency of insurgent groups within India to fragment, become divided, and turn to crime and thuggery for survival, reveals the unlikelihood of an insurgent group prevailing through uncompromising zeal for its cause.

The second principle is civilian control of the military, a bedrock tenet of the Indian constitutional order that takes on additional significance in COIN operations within India. The criticism that the Indian Army has played too big a role in responding to insurgencies does not reflect a weakening of this principle but rather highlights inadequate capabilities of civilian authorities, such as state and local police, for security and governance in the face of insurgent violence. The emergence of insurgency in India has often occurred in conjunction with persistent, overlapping and cascading governmental failures at local, state and national levels – a problem exacerbated by India's struggles as a large developing country with enormous governmental, economic and social challenges.

Third, India has emphasized the importance of fighting insurgencies in ways that uphold and respect the rule of law. Civilian control of the military serves this principle, but upholding and advancing the rule of law in the complex civil-military operations required in COIN are difficult challenges. Criticisms about violations of the rule of law, especially concerning the protection of individual rights, have dogged every COIN campaign within Indian territory, which calls into question the commitment and capabilities of Indian COIN operations to respect the rule of law. Nevertheless, the rule of law remains a central strategic principle in Indian COIN because it undergirds the value of the Indian political system being defended against militant violence.

A fourth overarching principle enshrined by Nehru in the early years of India's struggle with insurgencies is that COIN campaigns are about bringing disaffected citizens back into constitutionally ordained political processes. The measure of the success of a COIN effort is not the number of militants killed or captured or the amount of territory cleared of insurgent influence. The overriding objective is political reconciliation and reconstitution, which requires addressing political and economic grievances of disaffected populations and reintegrating insurgents and their supporters back into society and democratic processes. Thus, Indian COIN efforts have repeatedly involved the Indian government applying pressure through military, paramilitary and other security forces while simultaneously offering compromises and actions to produce political reconciliation with and reintegration of insurgents and their sympathizers.

Doctrine and effective counterinsurgency practices

Over time, the Indian government and military developed doctrine and effective practices to employ in COIN. Although many of these practices had to be re-learned in successive COIN operations, India accumulated field-tested 'best practices' for COIN campaigns. For a good deal of the time India has been fighting insurgencies, this body of knowledge was passed along rather informally as the cumulative wisdom of civilian and military practitioners. However, the process of communicating these practices through education and training was haphazard and ineffective. Commenting on the historical development of COIN doctrine in the Indian Army, Banerjee (2009: 191) has argued that 'training and doctrinal literature in the Indian Army lacks quality and is not standardized. What is available does not fully reflect the wealth of knowledge, skills, and experiences that the Indian Army possesses'. The first military-generated formal doctrine for COIN operations only appeared in December 2006 (Indian Army 2006). An equivalent doctrinal document for civilian authorities has not, to date, been developed, even though 'there is a pressing need to craft a comprehensive doctrine at the national level that involves all relevant actors, and not just the Indian Army' (Banerjee 2009: 206).

As a general matter, Indian military doctrine contains many similarities with the US COIN doctrine which was also finalized in 2006 in response to the insurgencies in Iraq and Afghanistan (Fidler 2009: 215–17). Interestingly, India and the United States developed their doctrines independently and without cross-fertilization of experiences. The commonalities shared by the two COIN doctrines point to a more universal set of COIN practices that address the challenges COIN operations face. These practices counsel, among other things, that counterinsurgents should:

- use all elements of national power in defeating insurgencies;
- focus on the population as the 'centre of gravity';
- understand the society, culture and languages of the populations affected by the insurgency;
- integrate and coordinate civilian and military efforts;
- accept that military forces have multiple roles in COIN, including provision of military assistance to civilian authorities;
- attempt to cut off external support for insurgencies;
- minimize the use of force and carefully craft and enforce rules of engagement to reduce loss of life in the civilian population;

- engage in extensive intelligence gathering and comprehensive information operations;
- respect human rights and the rule of law in conducting COIN operations;
- assess the effectiveness of COIN actions through metrics and indicators;
- emphasize training for COIN, especially the importance of civil–military coordination, small unit activities, and leadership and initiative by junior officers and civilian personnel; and
- support economic and political development as priorities in COIN operations.

Indian experiences with COIN reveal the Indian Army and government applying these best practices through various policies, techniques and mechanisms, many of which revealed adaptation and innovation in the face of insurgent challenges. For example, the Indian Army has developed new tactical approaches, capabilities and training for COIN operations. In terms of military tactics, the Indian Army adopted and refined the use of the 'counterinsurgency grid' to protect the population, put pressure on the insurgents, maximize the utility of small unit patrols, create space for political and economic development projects, and collect more effective intelligence. Apart from one early episode in the Nagaland insurgency and the selective use of helicopter gunships in Sri Lanka, India has not used air power against insurgents in order to minimize the use of force against militants and reduce civilian casualties from military operations.

In terms of capabilities, the Indian Army has tried many approaches to bolster its COIN capabilities. These approaches include creating special military units specifically trained in COIN (e.g. the Rashtriya Rifles) or drawn from the regions affected by insurgency violence (e.g. the Assam Rifles). The Indian military has experimented with strengthening its COIN performance by (1) using former militants in identifying and apprehending insurgents and collecting intelligence, and (2) forming village defence committees to improve security against insurgent violence and intimidation. India has developed different kinds of security forces with capabilities relevant to COIN operations, including the National Security Guards and Central Reserve Police Force. India's COIN experiences have also taught it the importance of strong police forces at the state and local levels as critical capabilities for effective COIN campaigns. As Marwah (2009: 104) argued in reflecting on the COIN campaign in the Punjab, '[t]he police are the most appropriate security force in COIN operations, and COIN campaigns should make every effort to strengthen police capabilities'.

The Indian Army has also attempted to improve COIN training for its forces by establishing training centres in Vairangte, Mizoram and Khrew, Kashmir. These facilities are designed to heighten the awareness and skills of troops concerning the challenges of COIN operations, including identifying improvised explosive devices, conducting search operations, respecting human rights, coordinating with civilian authorities, supporting and participating in development projects, and developing an understanding of the cultures, mores, politics and languages of the region of deployment.

In terms of political practices, India has adopted many practices to resolve grievances of disaffected populations. In the northeast, it created new states within the Union (e.g. Nagaland, Mizoram) to provide the peoples of these areas with more of a direct stake in the Indian constitutional order. India has made extensive efforts to encourage insurgents to renounce violence and return to the established political processes, perhaps most famously exemplified by a former insurgent leader Laldenga becoming the chief minister of the newly created Indian state of Mizoram. The Indian central government has also made efforts to improve governance and security capabilities in state and local governments, especially with respect to building up governmental administrative capacities and strengthening police forces in insurgency-affected regions.

In addition, Indian political strategies during COIN have emphasized the importance of holding state and federal elections under the shadow of insurgent intimidation and violence. Elections have frequently played critical roles in efforts to defeat insurgencies within India, as happened with the 1992 restoration of an elected government in Punjab (Marwah 2009). These elections have not always gone well for various reasons, including fears of militant attacks and retaliation against people who vote. For example, elections in 1996 in Kashmir produced only 40 per cent voter turnout because of militant threats (Ganguly 2009). The Indian government has, however, usually sought to maintain democratic governance as part of the political strategy of defeating insurgencies.

India has also attempted to address problems of economic and social development in regions afflicted by insurgency violence. COIN campaigns have included various economic development projects (e.g. infrastructure building) and social programmes (e.g. education and health services) funded by central government revenues. For example, Ladwig (2009: 49) noted how, in northeastern areas affected by insurgencies, '[r]oads and bridges were built in inaccessible areas, schools and hospitals were opened, and many villages received electricity and piped water for the first time'. Such efforts not only address immediate needs of the population but also demonstrate the benefits of the population remaining within the Indian political and economic system. Often, because of the security situation, the Indian Army has played an important role in such projects and programmes until civilian authorities could shoulder more of the stabilization and reconstruction burdens.

Persistent problems in India's counterinsurgency experience

Just as India has developed strategic principles, doctrine and effective practices for engaging in COIN campaigns, it has suffered persistent problems that have undermined the effectiveness of its COIN efforts. One of the largest persistent problems has already been highlighted – the phenomenon of the Indian government and military having to re-learn the lessons of COIN in addressing each new insurgent threat. This tendency has produced a costly COIN dynamic observable in most Indian COIN operations that makes the tasks of the government and military unnecessarily harder.

Insurgencies have arisen through breakdowns of governance and security in various regions, producing the need for the induction of the Indian Army to provide security. Unprepared for COIN operations and hampered by the lack of adequate civilian capabilities (e.g. police forces), the military response starts too heavy-handed, which further alienates the disaffected population and fuels the narrative of the insurgent group. Foreign powers interested in harming India become involved in assisting the growing insurgency by providing arms, training and sanctuary. Civilian–military coordination proves poor in the early stages of a COIN operation, meaning that all elements of Indian national power are not being applied as effectively as possible. Through painful and time-consuming trial and error, the civilian authorities and military personnel re-calibrate and coordinate their offensive, defensive and stability operations to put the insurgency under increasing political and security pressure. Very often the insurgency fragments under such escalating pressure, increasing the prospects for the COIN campaign to bring insurgents back into the political process. Remaining elements of the insurgency become more extreme and turn to terrorism and organized crime to survive, which alienates the population from what's left of the insurgency.

Within this common dynamic other persistent problems with India's COIN campaigns appear. One such problem is structural. Under the Indian Constitution, law and order governance functions are responsibilities of state and local governments. The central government's power to intervene arises only in emergency contexts, which usually has meant that an insurgency has established a foothold because of state and local government incompetence, corruption and/ or lack of adequate capabilities. The powers available to the central government, such as emergency rule and induction of the Army, have consistently proved blunt instruments that take time to be refined for effective COIN operations to unfold. The 'reinventing the wheel' problem illustrates that India has not yet found a more efficient way to bring central government resources and capabilities to bear more swiftly and effectively when insurgency threats overwhelm state and local authorities. This dynamic and this structural problem are again apparent with the difficulties India is having with the resurgence of Naxalite violence.

India has struggled with cutting off external support to insurgencies it is battling within its territory. In the COIN campaigns in the northeast, the rugged terrain in border areas (such as those with Burma) have contributed to the difficulty of working with foreign governments in stopping militants from using geography as an ally in hiding, training and launching operations. In other cases, foreign countries, namely China and Pakistan, have supported insurgents in India as part of their geostrategic competition for power and influence with India. Pakistan has been the biggest thorn in India's side in this respect, especially in the northeast (until the independence of Bangladesh eliminated East Pakistan as a source of insurgency succour) and Kashmir. More transnationally, India's early blunders in handling the Sikh insurgency produced Sikh diaspora support for the insurgency that complicated India's efforts to bring this threat under control.

Another persistent problem seen across India's COIN campaigns are concerns over the excessive application of force by military and other security forces. Despite the long-acknowledged importance of minimizing the use of force in COIN, the Indian state's responses to insurgencies have repeatedly involved large-scale, intensive uses of military force, which have backfired each time. Prominent examples include the disastrous Operation Blue Star in 1984 to flush Sikh militants from the Golden Temple in Amritsar (Marwah 2009), the resort to conventional warfare tactics against the Tamil Tigers in Sri Lanka (Banerjee 2009) and the initial 'mailed fist' approach used against the insurgency in Kashmir in the late 1980s and early 1990s (Ganguly 2009). Much of this problem connects to the Indian Army's continued ambivalence about preparing for and participating in COIN operations as opposed to focusing on training for conventional warfare. The Indian Army is, for example, reluctant to address the worsening Naxalite insurgency (Gokhale 2010a).

India's COIN experience is also marred by rule of law problems. As noted above, India strives to conduct COIN operations within the rule of law, but critics have, in every COIN campaign, accused the Indian government and military of engaging in widespread violations of human rights. These accusations include allegations of excessive and indiscriminate use of force, abusive behaviour towards civilian populations, extrajudicial killings of suspected militants and torture of detained persons by security forces. In the eyes of critics, India compounds these human rights problems by providing military forces with effective immunity from acts committed in 'disturbed areas' under the controversial Armed Forces (Special Powers) Act (AFSPA). According to Human Rights Watch (2008: 5):

> The AFSPA gives the armed forces wide powers to shoot to kill, arrest on flimsy pretext, conduct warrantless searches, and demolish structures in the name of 'aiding civil power.' Equipped with these special powers, soldiers have raped, tortured, 'disappeared,' and killed Indian citizens for five decades without fear of being held accountable.

Despite these criticisms, the Indian Army remains committed to defending the protections the AFSPA provides its troops. In June 2010, an Indian Army general in Kashmir stated that the AFSPA is critical to the military's COIN operations (NDTV.com 2010). In July 2010, the

Indian Army Chief of Staff argued that 98 per cent of investigated accusations of Indian Army abuse under the AFPSA have been found to be false (1,473 of 1,511 cases (NDTV.com 2010)) and that the AFPSA remains important to Indian Army operations within India (Gokhale 2010b).

Another persistent problem seen in India's COIN campaigns has been an inability to finish off threats from recalcitrant militants and address grievances of disaffected populations. As Shekatkar (2009: 25) observes in connection with the Nagaland saga, after the 1997 ceasefire agreement,

> negotiations between the Indian government and the remaining insurgent factions have failed to achieve a breakthrough, while allowing the factions to continue to remain armed and to participate in criminal activities that erode the potential for good governance and economic development in Nagaland and the Northeast.

The failure of local, state, and central governments on governance, economic and social development in many Indian states helps fuel the violent return of the Naxalties. Serious disturbances in 2010 in Kashmir reveal that India has still not adequately addressed what ails this restive province, and, although these disturbances have not sparked a new insurgency, such a development might happen if India's responses to the crisis do not significantly improve its authority in Kashmir.

Conclusion

Looking into the future, India faces immediate challenges and longer-term tasks in terms of insurgency threats and its COIN acumen and capabilities. In terms of immediate challenges, India confronts the growing Naxalite threat, the discontent boiling over again in Kashmir, the mounting drag on governance and development caused by 'rump insurgencies' in the northeast, and the increasing vulnerability of its nation-building support to COIN efforts in Afghanistan. In each case, India has hard COIN-related choices that it needs to make. In the longer term, India has to grapple with how it better prepares civilian and military policies and capabilities to address more effectively insurgency threats within its borders. These tasks include improved planning between central and state government authorities to prevent population grievances from morphing into insurgency violence, preparations by civilian authorities and agencies for insurgency contingencies, and less ambivalent attitudes in the Indian military about its role in battling insurgency threats.

India's history with COIN has not garnered the attention one might expect from a country with such extensive experience in this difficult political-military task. With India emerging as a new great power, it will come under more scrutiny across all policy areas, including how it tries to prevent discontent from becoming militant (e.g. Kashmir), responds to internal insurgency threats (e.g. Naxalites) and participates in COIN campaigns outside its borders (e.g. Afghanistan). The next phase of India's relationship with COIN theory, doctrine and practice will not unfold in the obscurity that has characterized this relationship in the past.

Recommended readings

Chadha, V. (2005) *Low Intensity Conflicts in India: An Analysis*. New Delhi: Sage Publications.
Ganguly, S. and Fidler, D.P. (2009) *India and Counterinsurgency: Lessons Learned*. London: Routledge.
Indian Army (2006) *Doctrine for Sub-Conventional Operations*. Simla: Army Headquarters Training Command.
Rajagopalan, R. (2008) *Fighting Like a Guerilla: The Indian Army and Counterinsurgency*. New Delhi: Routledge.

References

Banerjee, D. (2009) 'The Indian Army's Counterinsurgency Doctrine', in S. Ganguly and D.P. Fidler (eds), *India and Counterinsurgency: Lessons Learned*. London: Routledge, pp. 189–206.

Chadha, V. (2005) *Low Intensity Conflicts in India: An Analysis*. New Delhi: Sage Publications.

Fair, C.C. (2009) 'Lessons from India's Experience in the Punjab, 1978–93', in S. Ganguly and D.P. Fidler (eds), *India and Counterinsurgency: Lessons Learned*. London: Routledge, pp. 107–26.

Fidler, D.P. (2009) 'The Indian Doctrine for Sub-Conventional Operations: Reflections from a U.S. Counterinsurgency Perspective', in S. Ganguly and D.P. Fidler (eds), *India and Counterinsurgency: Lessons Learned*. London: Routledge, pp. 207–24.

Ganguly, S. (2009) 'Slow Learning: Lessons from India's Counterinsurgency Operations in Kashmir', in S. Ganguly and D.P. Fidler (eds), *India and Counterinsurgency: Lessons Learned*. London: Routledge, pp. 79–88.

Ganguly, S. and Fidler, D.P. (2009) *India and Counterinsurgency: Lessons Learned*. London: Routledge.

Gill, J.H. and Lamm, D.W. (2009) 'The Indian Peacekeeping Force Experience and U.S. Stability Operations in the Twenty-First Century', in S. Ganguly and D.P. Fidler (eds), *India and Counterinsurgency: Lessons Learned*. London: Routledge, pp. 173–85.

Gokhale, N. (2010a) 'Will the Cabinet Send in the Army to Tackle Naxals?', NDTV.com, 10 June. Available at: www.ndtv.com/news/india/will-the-cabinet-send-in-the-army-to-tackle-naxals-30800.php (accessed 19 August 2010).

Gokhale, N. (2010b) 'Special Powers for Special Needs: Army Chief to NDTV', 11 July. Available at: www.ndtv.com/article/india/special-powers-for-special-needs-army-chief-to-ndtv-36856 (accessed 19 August 2010).

Goswami, N. (2009) 'India's Counter-Insurgency Experience: The "Trust and Nurture" Strategy', *Small Wars & Insurgencies*, 20 (1): 66–86.

Government of India (2005) *Rebuilding Afghanistan: India at Work*. New Delhi: Ministry of External Affairs.

Human Rights Watch (2008) *Getting Away with Murder: 50 Years of the Armed Forces (Special Powers) Act*. New York: Human Rights Watch.

Indian Army (2006) *Doctrine for Sub-Conventional Operations*. Simla: Army Headquarters Training Command.

Ladwig, W.C. (2009) 'Insights from the Northeast: Counterinsurgency in Nagaland and Mizoram', in S. Ganguly and D.P. Fidler (eds), *India and Counterinsurgency: Lessons Learned*. London: Routledge, pp. 45–62.

Marwah, V. (2009) 'India's Counterinsurgency Campaign in Punjab', in S. Ganguly and D.P. Fidler (eds), *India and Counterinsurgency: Lessons Learned*. London: Routledge, pp. 89–106.

Mehta, A.K. (2009) 'India's Counterinsurgency Campaign in Sri Lanka', in S. Ganguly and D.P. Fidler (eds), *India and Counterinsurgency: Lessons Learned*. London: Routledge, pp. 155–72.

NDTV.com. (2010) 'Army Defends Armed Forces Special Powers Act', 10 June. Available at: www.ndtv.com/news/india/army-defends-special-powers-act-31642.php (accessed 19 August 2010).

Oetken, J.L. (2009) 'Counterinsurgency Against Naxalites in India', in S. Ganguly and D.P. Fidler (eds), *India and Counterinsurgency: Lessons Learned*. London: Routledge, pp. 127–51.

Patankar, V.G. (2009) 'Insurgency, Proxy War, and Terrorism in Kashmir', in S. Ganguly and D.P. Fidler (eds), *India and Counterinsurgency: Lessons Learned*. London: Routledge, pp. 65–78.

Rajagopalan, R. (2008) *Fighting Like a Guerilla: The Indian Army and Counterinsurgency*. New Delhi: Routledge.

Shekatkar, D.B. (2009) 'India's Counterinsurgency Campaign in Nagaland', in S. Ganguly and D.P. Fidler (eds), *India and Counterinsurgency: Lessons Learned*. London: Routledge, pp. 9–27.

US Army and Marine Corps (2007) *Counterinsurgency Field Manual (FM 3–24)*. Chicago: University of Chicago Press.

25

COUNTERINSURGENCY IN SRI LANKA

A successful model?

David Lewis

In 2009, after 30 years of conflict, the government of Sri Lanka declared victory over the Liberation Tigers of Tamil Eelam (LTTE), one of the most innovative and resilient insurgent organisations in modern history. They had maintained an armed separatist movement for nearly 30 years, and from the late 1990s onwards had run a de facto separatist state of 'Tamil Eelam' in the northeast of the island. Government attempts to defeat the LTTE through counterinsurgency campaigns in the 1980s and 1990s had failed, but a two-year military offensive in 2007–9 completely routed the group, and called the government to regain control over the whole of the island.

This remarkable outcome led some to examine the 'Sri Lankan model' of counterinsurgency as a possible export to deal with other ongoing insurgencies in South Asia and elsewhere. On closer inspection, however, the example of Sri Lanka raises significant problems and challenges. In military terms, government tactics were often very effective, but may not always be replicable in other situations, where insurgent groups have not developed a nascent state apparatus, or where they still have a deep hinterland or third-party support. More significantly, the campaign was accompanied by reliable allegations of widespread and serious war crimes during the fighting, resulting in international censure of the government, and continuing grievances and resentment among many of the minority Tamil community. In addition, the counterinsurgency had a very negative impact on the country's domestic political system, undermining political pluralism and civil liberties, and contributing to the emergence of an increasingly authoritarian regime. Nevertheless, it is a case study that offers potentially significant lessons for counterinsurgency in the twenty-first century, not least in its open challenge to the more population-centric doctrines developed by Western COIN experts.

Insurgency and counterinsurgency in Sri Lanka: historical overview

The roots of Sri Lanka's conflicts are highly contested, but date back at least to the late British colonial period, when competition between the majority Sinhalese and minority Tamil groups became more acute in the run-up to independence in 1948. Resentment among Sinhalese at apparent over-representation of Tamils in the civil service and in the professions led to legislation (such as the 1956 Sinhala-only act, which promoted the Sinhalese language) that limited minority rights. Tamil opposition to such moves was initially expressed through peaceful demonstrations, strikes and political campaigns, but in the early 1970s Tamil youth began to develop more militant tactics. In 1976 Velupillai Prabhakaran, a young radical from the north of Sri Lanka, founded the Liberation Tigers of Tamil Eelam (LTTE). At the time, it was just one among many radical, Tamil nationalist groups, but it slowly emerged as the most powerful advocate of Tamil secessionism, both through clever political manoeuvring and by ruthlessly eliminating its rivals.

Figure 25.1 Sri Lanka (© United Nations).

Full-scale war first broke out in 1983, following an LTTE attack on an army convoy in Jaffna and subsequent mass anti-Tamil riots in Colombo. These events initiated what was subsequently termed Eelam War I (1983–7), a brutal conflict which only ended with the intervention of the Indian Peacekeeping Force (IPKF) in 1987. The intervention, however, was a disaster: instead of acting as a peacekeeping force, the IPKF became embroiled in a counterinsurgency campaign against the LTTE, which refused to disarm. (See also Chapter 24 in this volume.) The failure of the IPKF to disarm the LTTE led to Indian withdrawal from Sri Lanka in 1990, and continues to have an impact on official thinking in Delhi about involvement in military interventions overseas. The LTTE, on the other hand, emerged from the IPKF period significantly strengthened, both psychologically, having taken on the Indian army and effectively won, and materially, having gained significant military resources during the conflict with the IPKF.

During the IPKF period, government forces had been fighting a second insurgency, led by a leftist group in the south of the country, the Janathā Vimukthi Peramuna (JVP), which combined Maoism and virulent Sinhalese nationalism in an unlikely ideological cocktail. The JVP had led a militant uprising in 1971, and then a more serious campaign in 1987–90, in which many officials and military officers were assassinated. This latter insurgency was crushed brutally by the government, involving mass abuses of human rights, severe restrictions on civil liberties and the widespread use of extrajudicial methods. Many of the lessons of this apparently successful counterinsurgency campaign appear to have inspired elements of the campaign against the Tigers after 2006.

Fighting broke out again between the LTTE and government forces in July 1990, after the failure of peace talks, and following a series of massacres and expulsions committed by the LTTE, particularly targeting Muslim residents in the north and east of the island. During Eelam War II (1990–5) massacres and atrocities were committed by both sides. The LTTE had by now developed the capability to engage in significant military confrontations with the much larger Sri Lankan army, such as the battle of Elephant Pass in 1991, when 5,000 LTTE fighters laid siege for a month to a Sri Lankan army base. Government offensives in 1992 might have defeated the LTTE, but they were again forestalled by Indian diplomatic intervention. Gradually, the LTTE began to take control of territory in the north and was developing parallel state structures in those areas it controlled.

A short-lived ceasefire in 1995, brokered under new president Chandrika Kumaratunga, was broken by the LTTE in April, and led to Kumaratunga's so-called 'war for peace' (Eelam War III), a major military offensive against the LTTE, which led to the government retaking control of Jaffna after heavy fighting for the first time in a decade. However, subsequent military campaigns were repulsed by the LTTE, which also carried out a series of devastating terrorist attacks in civilian areas in the south, using suicide bombers, the so-called 'Black Tigers'. These had first been used in 1987, but in the mid 1990s they became a central tactic in the LTTE's military campaign. The most audacious LTTE attack came in 2001, when a commando raid on the country's only international airport destroyed 12 planes. The airport attack left the government demoralised, and helped open the way to peace talks brokered by Norway.

The failure of the counterinsurgency against the LTTE in the 1980s and 1990s was partially the result of poor military strategy, an often corrupt and poorly managed procurement system, and inadequate training. However, successive governments also felt significant international pressure during military campaigns. In both 1987 and 1992 Indian diplomatic and military intervention forced the Sri Lankan government to halt potentially successful offensives against the LTTE. Support for the LTTE in Tamil Nadu in India was an important factor in the politics of the military campaign, and it was augmented by a large Tamil diaspora in Western Europe, Canada and Australia, who ran an extensive fundraising campaign for the LTTE and put often vocal pressure on Western politicians. These experiences informed the post-2006 campaign, when there was a strong rejection of international pressure on the government to limit its military offensive.

The new regime

The peace process (2002–6) failed for multiple reasons, including problems with the design of the process itself (ICG 2006), but its failure was accelerated by a change of president in late 2005, when Mahinda Rajapakse was elected with support from the extreme nationalist JVP, and also as a result of an LTTE-imposed boycott of the election by Tamils. The new president's scepticism about the peace process was well known, and his new team, which included his two brothers, Gotobaya (as Minister of Defence) and Basil (as political adviser), began planning a possible military response to the LTTE, although there is no evidence that they had a genuine plan for an extensive military campaign before they came to office.

In 2005 few observers believed that the situation could be resolved only by military means: previous government offensives had demonstrated serious problems in the Sri Lankan military, including corruption, lack of discipline and high levels of desertion. By contrast, the LTTE were highly disciplined, with almost legendary skills in commando operations, and a growing capacity to carry out conventional military warfare on land and sea. By 2003 the LTTE had developed a de facto state, Tamil Eelam, which had exclusive control of 15,000 sq km of territory in the north and east of Sri Lanka; in the north, the government only controlled Jaffna, which was cut off from the south of the island, and had to be resupplied by air and sea. This proto-state had its own state services, including police, welfare and other bodies, and a full range of military capabilities, including both traditional military capacity, heavy weaponry and some sea-going capability, and non-traditional units, including suicide squads. Often these capabilities were mixed, with small boats designed for use in suicide missions against larger Sri Lankan naval vessels, for example. A small air force became apparent in during Eelam War IV, but consisted only of a small number of Cessna light aircraft.

Arguably, the peace process, far from strengthening the LTTE as many of its opponents argued, had made the LTTE complacent, forcing it to focus on state-building and political and administrative tasks at the expense of the military. Above all, the peace process probably played a role in undermining the LTTE's unity. In 2003 the group suffered an extremely damaging split, with the defection of a key commander from Eastern Province, Vinayagamoorthy Muralitharan, generally known by his *nom de guerre* of Col. Karuna. The reasons for the split were disputed, but probably combined personal and political issues, accentuated by a traditional, regional divide between eastern and northern Tamils. However, the defection of Karuna seriously weakened LTTE control of Eastern Province (where there was also a large Muslim population, many of them opposed to the LTTE). Not surprisingly, it was in the east that the first successes of the government emerged.

Renewal of conflict: Eastern Province

Although there were increasing skirmishes between the two sides in 2005–6, the beginning of Eelam War IV is usually dated to July–August 2006, when the government launched what it termed a 'humanitarian operation' to take control of sluice gates at Mavil Aru, which had been closed by the LTTE, cutting off water supplies to farmers. This event gave the government a useful justification for a major assault on key strategic LTTE positions on the east coast, most importantly retaking control of Sampur, from which the LTTE had been able to use artillery against the strategically vital port at Trincomalee. The resumption of control over Sampur involved retaking territory from the LTTE for the first time since the 1990s. Although neither side abrogated the ceasefire and peace talks were held in October 2006, in reality the battle for control of Eastern Province had begun.

The government had significant advantages in the east: the demographics were in its favour, with a large Muslim population, which was equally suspicious of both Karuna and LTTE Tamil militias, interspersed among Tamils along the heavily populated coastal strip. The defection of Karuna made it relatively easy to take control of Batticaloa, his main political base, and gradually during late 2006 government forces, primarily the paramilitary police charged with counter-terrorist actions, the Special Task Force (STF), asserted control of major roads and towns along the coast. An important battle was for control of Vakarai, a strategic point that linked the LTTE in the east with their northern territories, which was retaken by government troops in January 2007.

LTTE bases in the east remained in the interior, in remote areas away from the major cities of Trincomalee and Batticaloa. The military and STF, together with Karuna militias, combined a variety of methods to cut them off from supply routes and to hunt them down inside the region. First, they used both pressure and physical attacks to eliminate many LTTE sympathisers or supporters who acted as conduits with the major cities. These attacks on individuals and groups involved in the supply route for the interior were often carried out by Karuna militia, acting outside the law, and with impunity. Karuna bases began to appear in government-controlled areas, often located close to the military or next to STF bases. These proxy forces were initially useful to the military in the east, since they often knew LTTE sympathisers personally or at least had the local language and cultural skills to find out the key actors in the LTTE support network. However, the human rights abuses committed by Karuna also attracted increased international attention and pressure on the government, and reduced any genuine support among ethnic Tamils.

Attacks on LTTE sympathisers also began to undermine LTTE extortion networks, cutting off important local sources of funding for the LTTE, and instead channelling funding to pro-government militias. A similar pattern could be observed in recruitment, with many young Tamils (including children) being recruited by the Karuna group, denying the LTTE an important source of military personnel. However, outside Sri Lanka there was also increased pressure on LTTE funding, with Western governments generally combining some criticism of the government for its renewed military campaign with an effort to cut down on LTTE fundraising in their countries, much of which seemed to increasingly represent extortion rackets.

In early 2007 the STF launched attacks on LTTE bases in Thopigalla and Kanchikudich-charu, and cleared the LTTE presence in Ampara district. Once the LTTE was restricted to the interior in the east, they appear to have made the decision to effectively withdraw their remaining forces, and concentrate on the northern front. Any other decision would have left them over-extended in the east with unreliable supply lines, serving no useful strategic purpose; since much of the fighting was carried out by the STF and Karuna group, the LTTE presence in the east was not diverting significant military resources from other fronts.

The northern front

The heartland of the LTTE was in the Vanni, a broad swathe of the Northern Province south of the Jaffna peninsula, much of it covered in dense forest. The 'Vanni operation' targeting LTTE positions in the north had begun rather tentatively in March 2007, while fighting still continued in the east. During 2007 a frequently murky war of attrition gradually gathered momentum on the northern front, with increased activity by Long-Range Reconnaissance Patrols (LRRPs) across the front, followed by conventional attacks on LTTE positions on the A9 road to Jaffna, and in the northwest regions up to Mannar. For several months fairly conventional modes of attack and counter-attack continued around a series of small villages in the Vavunia area. At first it appeared that the LTTE could hold these positions indefinitely: during 2007 the government made no significant gains in the north, and the LTTE made several powerful counter-attacks against government positions. However, the loss of the Eastern Province – which was an important source of recruitment for the LTTE – and the increasing intercepts of shipping and funding streams, weakened the depth of the LTTE's fighting capability, and during 2008 government forces began to make significant gains, and force the LTTE further into the interior.

Feeling increasingly confident, the government finally abrogated the largely fictional 2002 ceasefire in January 2008, and the Sri Lankan Monitoring Mission (a group of Scandinavian observers monitoring the ceasefire) closed on 16 January, leaving the government in full control of information emerging from the battlefield. The fighting caused significant casualties on both sides, with considerable resistance from the LTTE at certain points, where they decided to make a stand, but gradually the significant superiority of the army in numbers and materiel pushed the LTTE back from their forward positions in the Vanni. The army significantly increased its recruitment following early successes in the east, and also managed to cut a previously high level of desertion.

The government strategy was designed to retake coastal areas in the northwest, cutting the LTTE off from another key supply route from India, and linking up government forces in Jaffna and the south. Gradually, government forces moved up the coast to take control of the A32 road, which linked up north and south under government control. From those positions, they began to take control of the even more strategic A9 route, which would link Jaffna with the south under government control for the first time in two decades. Movement was slow and often incremental, facing LTTE positions heavily defended using mined earthworks. As the campaign progressed, the LTTE was in the difficult position of effectively being a guerrilla army defending static positions, but with almost no air support and limited heavy weaponry to defend itself. Although an LTTE air capability did demonstrate its existence in early 2007 with bombing runs by light aircraft over Colombo, in reality these excursions demonstrated no significant military effect, although they were important for boosting morale and undermining the government's narrative of ongoing success.

In January 2009 the incremental progress of the army up the coastline and around Kilinochchi suddenly showed significant progress. The army gained control of the key strategic junction on the A9 road at Paranthan, and retook the highly symbolic Elephant Pass, which guards the entry to the Jaffna peninsula, and had been much fought over in previous wars. The 53rd and 55th Divisions now threatened LTTE positions from the Jaffna peninsula. The LTTE faced probing attacks on four fronts, with the 58th and 57th divisions driving north and northeast towards the heavily defended town of Kilinochchi. The LTTE finally abandoned the defence of Kilinochchi in mid-January to avoid being encircled, and retreated to the interior. Meanwhile the 59th division was moving up the east coast towards Mullaitivu, pushing the LTTE further back into a small territory in the Vanni.

Between January and April 2009 government forces gradually closed the ring around remaining LTTE cadres, declaring a succession of ever smaller No-Fire Zones (NFZs) in which they claimed civilians would be safe from military attack. In reality, it appears that there was much less regard for civilian casualties than claimed by the military, and independent groups have argued that 'the security forces intentionally and repeatedly shelled civilians, hospitals and humanitarian operations' (ICG 2010: 5). UN agencies estimated that nearly

7,000 civilians were killed from January to April 2009, but other reports suggest the figure may have been as high as 30–40,000, including thousands killed in the last days of fighting in the final NFZ (ICG 2010: 5).

The final defeat of the LTTE came in the space of several days of intense fighting around this small NFZ in the northeast of the island. At this point the government was engaged in an intense diplomatic struggle to avoid international pressure for a ceasefire, which would have forced them to negotiate the surrender of the LTTE leadership or allow in some international presence to manage the final stages of the conflict. These initiatives reinvigorated fears among the leadership that international intervention would prevent their victory at the last moment. As a result, while strongly resisting a range of diplomatic initiatives to achieve a ceasefire, the military accelerated their push to defeat the LTTE completely. The exact details of the final days in May 2009 have been much disputed and have become the subject of a variety of investigations, but the military took control of the NFZ, killing most of the LTTE military leadership in the process, and taking about 280,000 civilians into internment camps; about 10,000 people, whom they claimed were LTTE military cadres, were placed in secure detention. This complete control of the LTTE movement, including civilians, effectively prevented any possibility of low-intensity conflict developing after the main military campaign was ended.

The end of the military part of the campaign initiated a new stage dominated by resettlement of internally displaced persons (IDPs), controversial government 'filtration' mechanisms of former LTTE activists, and redevelopment of the north and east. At the same time, President Rajapakse consolidated his hold on power, winning presidential elections in January 2010, in which he competed against Gen. Sarath Fonseka, the victorious army commander who had fallen out with the political leadership and resigned after the end of the military campaign. Fonseka was later arrested, and court-martialled on charges that were clearly provoked by the political rift between him and the political leadership. The arrest of Fonseka was only the most significant moment in a gradual trend towards a more authoritarian political system, dominated by the Rajapakse team, and with increasing pressure on any political opponents.

Key military factors

Recruitment and tactics

There are several reasons suggested for the improvement in military performance in 2006–9 compared with previous military campaigns. One simple explanation is a huge growth in recruitment to the armed forces during this period. During 2007 alone the army recruited 34,000 new personnel, bringing its strength in February 2008 up to 150,000, and the strength of the entire armed forces up to 200,000 (The Island 2008). There were frequent recruitment drives backed by increasing nationalist propaganda, which were also assisted by early successes in the war in the Eastern Province. Recruitment was also probably boosted by the difficult economic situation, partly caused by the resumption of conflict, which had badly affected the tourist industry and foreign investment. Increased recruitment allowed the army to open up more fronts, and to form new Task Forces and Divisions. By the last stages of the war, there were seven Divisions and eight Task Forces engaged in the campaign. In addition, four Special Forces regiments were active along and behind the front lines. By contrast, at the end of the war, there were probably only 10–11,000 LTTE fighters remaining, and even allowing for heavy losses, they were always significantly outnumbered and outgunned by government forces.

The military had enjoyed numerical superiority on the ground in the 1990s, but had nevertheless been defeated. Military tactics in 2006–9 were all informed by past failures, notably the temptation to seek rapid gains in territory, which tended to leave forward units on over-extended supply chains, which were often easy for the LTTE to attack. Instead of seeking territory, government forces engaged in a war of attrition, seeking to achieve as high a rate of killing of LTTE cadres as possible, aware of the difficulties faced by the LTTE in recruitment, with reports emerging of forced recruitment of children and men over fighting age. Significantly improved training also appears to have contributed to improved performance in the 2006–9 conflict. Many more infantry underwent special commando training, which made them better prepared for flexible, small-team tactics led by younger commanders, moving away from the inflexible, top-down attitudes that had characterised previous campaigns. In addition, there was a rapid increase in the number of special forces organised in Long-Range Reconnaissance Patrols, which carried out attacks on LTTE positions behind formally accepted lines of control, forcing the LTTE to shift resources to protect their rear and flank (DeSilva-Ranasinghe 2010: 4). Using these tactics and infantry troops trained in commando techniques, combined with Special Forces and LRRPs, the military was able to often act as an effective guerrilla force against LTTE forces, which were forced to adopt inflexible stances, defending static positions behind mined earthworks.

LTTE static positions were easy targets for repeated attacks by government multi-barrel rocket launchers (MBRL) and other artillery, to which the LTTE had little response. Moreover, with an almost complete monopoly of air power, government forces always had the advantage in these confrontations. The air force had procured Kfir jets under a previous administration, but procurement of aviation equipment and training was stepped up, and Pakistan provided significant technical support. By December 2008 the air force had carried out some 400 air strikes, and aerial surveillance also played an important role in the military campaign, including, for the first time, the use of Unmanned Aerial Vehicles (UAVs). Air strikes in the later part of the campaign were primarily carried out against LTTE positions, but earlier in the offensive there were multiple strikes designed to decapitate the LTTE leadership. An air strike near Kilinochchi in November 2007 killed LTTE peace negotiator and head of its political wing S.P. Thamilselvan. The LTTE had little response to government air power. Although the LTTE had some level of anti-aircraft defence, its capability appears to have been quickly depleted. Anti-aircraft weapons were regularly sought in arms operations overseas but intercepted by law enforcement agencies.

Once the LTTE had abandoned its key defensive lines, many observers expected the LTTE to revert to its classic role as an insurgency using traditional guerrilla tactics. However, the LTTE was no longer the agile, flexible force of the 1990s, but the armed forces of a nascent state, cast in the difficult role of having to defend territory and defensive lines. It did attempt a series of terrorist attacks in the south, but some appear to have been foiled by police action, and others were less effective than in previous campaigns. In addition, as the LTTE retreated, it forced thousands of civilians to accompany it. This was probably a strategic error by the LTTE, which expended considerable energy on maintaining resources for maybe 250,000 civilians. It expected these civilians to serve as an effective 'human shield' to prevent complete military defeat, but this turned out not to be effective, largely owing to the government's frequent disregard for civilian casualties in the final assault.

In contrast to contemporary US thinking, there was no stress on civilian protection in the Sri Lankan counterinsurgency. In the east, Tamil civilians were at the mercy of pro-government Tamil militias, while in the north, the civilian population was forced to move with the LTTE, ensuring that the military did not have to deal with a civilian population. When forward military units entered settlements, they were almost always already abandoned. In many confrontations, however, civilians were clearly present in areas under attack by the government, and in many cases there were high numbers of civilian deaths. It appears that government forces did not take sufficient care to discriminate between combatants and non-combatants in these offensives; reliable reports document repeated violations of the laws of war with regard to civilians (ICG 2010). The LTTE, of course, deliberately used civilians in this way and also blurred the lines between civilian and non-civilian, with much of the population forced to work in support of the military campaign in various capacities.

Supply routes

A key factor in the defeat of the LTTE was the ability of the military to cut off supplies to the interior, both from the sea and from corrupt relationships with state and commercial agents in the south. One of the main complaints of the military during the 2002–5 ceasefire was that they were not permitted to intercept arms transfers by sea, allowing the LTTE to rearm with impunity. During 2007 an important front opened up at sea, with several interceptions by the Sri Lankan navy of LTTE arms shipments. The LTTE was reputed to control several commercial shipping networks, some of which were involved in arms smuggling.

In previous campaigns, the LTTE had always maintained a route to India, both for smuggling in weapons and for key individuals to travel back and forth. These routes partly followed traditional smuggling routes to India, and relied on support structures in Tamil Nadu. During this campaign, it appears that the Sri Lankan navy was increasingly successful in cutting off this supply route, and was probably aided by increased pressure from the Indian side on pro-LTTE Tamils. Effectively, this deprived the LTTE of their 'hinterland', which ensured that when they were forced back into Mullaitivu, there was no possibility to escape and reignite a low-level insurgency later.

Political factors

While the military campaign demonstrated significant innovations in strategy, tactics and above all equipment and recruitment, President Rajapakse and his allies demonstrated an approach to the political aspects of the counterinsurgency entirely at odds with emerging COIN doctrine elsewhere. From the very beginning, Rajapakse was uncomfortable about the peace process with the LTTE, and after late 2006, with the peace talks over, he moved to a more uncompromising position, which ruled out negotiations with 'terrorists'. At the same time, he came under strong pressure from the opposition and the international community to develop a political strategy that would include commitments to autonomy for the Tamils, which could win over the 'hearts and minds' of the Tamil people. Rajapakse responded with a series of essentially fictive institutions and roundtables to discuss the issue, but none had any political weight behind them, and they were all ignored. India pushed for implementation of the so-called thirteenth amendment to the constitution, which allowed for effective autonomy for a northeastern province, but Rajapakse demonstrated opposition to any such autonomy by demerging the northern and eastern provinces.

While failing to develop a political solution that would appeal to the broad mass of Tamils, Rajapakse did develop the co-optation of pro-government Tamils such as Karuna and long-term allies such as Douglas Devananda. Such pro-government Tamils were always at risk of assassination by the LTTE, but they were frequently used to dismiss accusations against the government of Sinhala chauvinism. However, the government was more responsive to right-wing nationalist forces, such as militant Buddhist groups, and parties such as the Jathika Hela Urumaya (JHU), who rejected any concessions to Tamils, and supported extreme nationalist positions in favour of the Sinhalese majority. Politically, the president benefited from the weakness of the mainstream opposition party, which was unable to mount any effective campaign against the government during the war.

It was in the sphere of communications that the government's real ruthlessness emerged. Before the war, Sri Lanka had a lively and often critical press, including Tamil nationalist media outlets. After 2006, attacks and pressure on independent media intensified, with frequent attacks on journalists, including several murders. Media employees were targeted in the so-called 'white van' disappearances, in which individuals were abducted by unknown persons, often in Colombo. The government asserted almost complete control over television coverage of the war, and slowly critical voices were also limited in print media. The Ministry of Defence set up a comprehensive media operation, with a strong presence on the Internet, and complete control over access to the conflict zones. For the most part, there was only very limited access to the battlefield in the north for any foreign journalists, and some more critical journalists found it difficult to get visas to enter the country. NGOs and human rights organisations also found it difficult to conduct research. Although this media operation did not prevent critical reporting of the war in the international media, it did provide an alternative narrative that stressed Sri Lanka's role in the 'war on terror', and prevented critics from gaining detailed accounts of the conduct of the war while it continued.

The international environment

The military activities of 2007 in Eastern Province gave the government increasing confidence that they could engage in a military confrontation with the LTTE and win. However, they remained particularly concerned about the potential for the international community, and India in particular, to attempt to stop any offensive before the LTTE was defeated. This fear of external intervention was largely the result of a particular nationalist reading of history, in which Indian intervention in 1987 and again in 1992 had prevented a defeat of the LTTE; whether correct or not, it was a powerful factor in fuelling often virulent reactions to any international criticism. These attitudes were compounded by a complex post-colonial situation which affected Sri Lankan attitudes to the UK in particular, and the West in general.

The government pursued this strategy in several key ways. First, they increased pressure on domestic NGOs, with particular links to the international community, and on the activities of international NGOs and humanitarian organisations. This made many international organisations more cautious about criticising military actions. Second, they took an aggressive stance towards any criticism of the government by international interlocutors, labelling critics as 'terrorist sympathisers' or 'lackeys' of the LTTE. Third, they strongly resisted any type of international intervention, including proposals for a UN human rights mission. Above all, they benefited from a changing diplomatic landscape, in which China and other allies were able to counteract Western pressure and provide Sri Lanka with financial and diplomatic support. In a key event in May 2009, liberal states failed to gain sufficient votes to censure Sri Lanka's human rights record at the UN Human Rights Council in Geneva, with China, India, Brazil and other major powers blocking a critical resolution (Lewis 2010).

Conclusion: a successful counterinsurgency?

After several years of discussion among COIN experts in the West about downplaying military aspects of strategy and promoting political and civilian protection issues, the Sri Lankan case appears to be a sharp response to such views. The view promoted by Rajapakse that 'Terrorism has to be wiped out militarily and cannot be tackled politically' (Shashkumar

2009: 13) is sharply at odds with emerging thinking in the US military and elsewhere. The apparent conclusion from Sri Lanka that highly repressive methods can be effective in counterinsurgency campaigns, contradicting other COIN doctrines, has been noted with some concern by US observers (Kaplan 2010; Lewis 2010; ICG 2010). However, the apparent success of the Rajapakse strategy may be rather specific to Sri Lanka, and not easily replicable elsewhere.

Certainly the military improved their training, procurement and organisation markedly since the 1990s, and recruitment increased rapidly. Improved air power proved a significant advantage, as did new tactics at sea that helped to block off shipping lanes. However, the government also owes much to changes in the capability and positioning of the LTTE. By 2005 the LTTE was no longer primarily an insurgent fighting force, but a conventional force with non-traditional tactics, including the use of suicide bombers. It occupied territory, patrolled front lines, was based in static positions and headquarters, and had substantial reliance on traditional supply routes by land and sea. However, it did not have sufficient strength in depth, either in manpower or in equipment, to fight a drawn out conventional war, and it was peculiarly vulnerable to a well-planned concerted military campaign that would attack the weaknesses of its conventional positioning. It had no strategic hinterland to withdraw to, and was therefore unable to resume a low-level insurgency, at least initially. The military planned its strategy around these vulnerabilities, using the LRRP as an effective guerrilla force to attack behind front lines, and air power and artillery to dismantle defensive positions. While very effective, the campaign may not offer significant strategic lessons for tackling other insurgencies, which do not suffer from similar liabilities.

The ability to cut off the LTTE from funding and supplies was extremely important and relied not only on physical interceptions but on an understanding of a huge network of corrupt supply routes that were an important part of Sri Lanka's political economy. Some of this took the form of extra-legal killings of suppliers or businessmen; in other cases, legal avenues were used. Often other Tamil militias were used to replace LTTE extortion rackets, usually by simply taking over the same mechanisms. At the same time, the government pushed for international interception of LTTE arms smuggling and financial dealings with some success. All these methods were effective in severely limiting supplies to the LTTE, but also did little to actually dismantle these informal networks of organised crime and politics, which continue to be important in the Sri Lankan context. Nevertheless, the Sri Lankan case points towards the importance of an understanding of the complex nexus between legal business, organised crime and insurgency.

In the political sphere, there was almost no concession made to the Tamil nationalist parties; instead Rajapakse concentrated exclusively on buttressing his own power at the expense of opposition parties, using patronage politics to encourage defections from the opposition, and to win the support of minority parties. This provided him with a streamlined political system, in which the views of the opposition could be ignored during the course of the war, but left Sri Lanka at the end of the war with a significantly weakened democratic system, in which almost all political power was concentrated in the hands of the presidency. Judicial and parliamentary checks on the executive became almost non-existent, and high-level corruption and abuses of rights became commonplace, while patronage became the main means of control. The strong reliance on Sinhala nationalism to increase support for the war was also likely to make post-conflict reconciliation more difficult, as was the political leadership's refusal to seek a political solution acceptable to the Tamil minority. Meanwhile, accusations of war crimes continued to undermine Sri Lanka's reputation abroad and limited potential international assistance to deal with the post-conflict environment.

While militarily highly successful, Sri Lanka's counterinsurgency campaign contained some worrying trends, which had broader consequences than the short-term military campaign. Widespread abuse of human rights during the campaign changed the nature of the state itself, confirming the view that counterinsurgency campaigns often have a major impact not only on the battlefield, but also on domestic political institutions. In addition, Sri Lanka's place in the world changed as a result of the war, with much closer relations emerging with countries like Iran and China at the expense of the United States and EU states. While Sri Lanka's counterinsurgency tried to focus solely on the military goal of defeating the LTTE, the way it was conducted had and will continue to have very significant political consequences.

Recommended readings

Bandarage, Asoka (2008) *The Separatist Conflict in Sri Lanka: Terrorism, Ethnicity, Political Economy*. London: Routledge.

Goodhand, J. (2010) 'Stabilising a Victor's Peace? Humanitarian Action and Reconstruction in Eastern Sri Lanka', *Disasters*, 34 (October): 342–67.

Goodhand, J., B. Korf and J. Spencer (eds) (2010) *Conflict and Peacebuilding in Sri Lanka: Caught in the Peace Trap?* London: Routledge.

International Crisis Group (ICG) (2010) *War Crimes in Sri Lanka*, Brussels, 17 May.

Lewis, D. (2010) 'The Failure of a Liberal Peace: Sri Lanka's Counterinsurgency in Global Perspective', *Conflict, Security and Development*, 10 (5): 647–71.

References

DeSilva-Ranasinghe, S. (2010), 'Strategic Analysis of Sri Lankan Military's Counter-Insurgency Operations', Future Directions International, 12 February. Available at: www.futuredirections.org.au/admin/uploaded_pdf/1266992558-FDIStrategicAnalysisPaper-12February2010.pdf (accessed 1 October 2010).

International Crisis Group (ICG) (2006) 'Sri Lanka: The Failure of the Peace Process', Colombo/Brussels. Available at: www.crisisgroup.org.

International Crisis Group (ICG) (2010) 'War Crimes in Sri Lanka', Brussels, 17 May. Available at: www.crisisgroup.org.

Kaplan, R. (2010) 'To Catch a Tiger', *Atlantic Monthly*, 14 November. Available at: www.theatlantic.com/magazine/archive/2009/07/to-catch-a-tiger/7581 (accessed 30 September 2010).

Lewis, D. (2010) 'The Failure of a Liberal Peace: Sri Lanka's Counterinsurgency in Global Perspective', *Conflict, Security and Development*, 10 (5): 647–71.

The Island (2008) 'Sri Lanka Army now 150,000 Strong; Recruits More; Readies for Big Battles on the Vanni Front', *The Island*, 11 February. Available at: www.lankanewspapers.com/news/2008/2/24596.html (accessed 1 October 2010).

Shashkumar, V.K. (2009) 'Lessons from the War in Sri Lanka', *Indian Defence Review*, 24 (3).

26

COUNTERINSURGENCY IN PAKISTAN

Julian Schofield

This chapter examines the evolution of counterinsurgency in Pakistan and Pakistani counterinsurgency doctrine. Generally speaking Pakistan practices a more population-centric approach to counterinsurgency (hereafter CI) in its core territories of the Punjab and Karachi and by contrast resorts to pacification operations in its dealings with peripheral regions such as East Pakistan, Balochistan, Sindh and Khyber Pakhtunkwa (hereafter KP, formerly the NWFP – Northwest Frontier Province) (Gazdar 2006: 1952). (See map of Pakistan on page 228.)

In terms of the implementation of CI in peripheral areas, Pakistan has under-emphasized the components of population security, economic development and political strategy because these are costs usually beyond the reach of Pakistan's treasury (Lalwani 2009: 5). It has relied instead on pacification, with an emphasis on the intimidatory use of firepower, and exploitation of regional ethnic tensions to deter centrifugal resistance. While operations in the Sindh and Balochistan have achieved pacification, the application of military force in East Pakistan in 1971, Karachi in 1992–7, and since 2002 in KP achieved either an unsustainable stalemate, or have an uncertain future. Popular explanations for Pakistan's failure in regard to pacification centre on its lack of civilian oversight of the military, the lack of political will in a fragmented democracy, and a perceived lack of skill and interest in counterinsurgency by the Pakistan Army (Jones and Fair 2010: 83; Mullick 2009: 1–9). Moreover, Pakistan's military is reluctant to engage target populations that constitute its Punjabi, Pashtun or Muhajir soldiery. Pakistan consists of a military and political system centred around the Punjab (with a population of 90 million). The remaining 36 million Sindhis, 27 million Pashtun, 13 million Mohajirs, eight million Kashmiris and six million Baloch, play either a semi-peripheral or peripheral role in the state apparatus, and are therefore occasionally exposed to less liberal applications of CI. Pakistan also lacks the finances for long-term socio-economic development outside its core territory of the Punjab, and is reluctant to intervene against non-separatist regional populations where existing ethnic tensions permit divide-and-conquer rule.

Counterinsurgency

Pakistani scholar Eqbal Ahmed (2006: 37–64, 38–42; 1999, pers. comm., 22 April) distinguished four kinds of CI applicable to Pakistan:

1   the Conventional-Establishment approach uses military force to hunt the insurgents and
    the police to re-establish order (Karachi);
2   the Punitive-Militarist approach, where pacification is achieved through terror rather than
    a political solution (East Pakistan, Baluchistan, Khyber-Pakhtunkwa);
3   the Technological-Attritive approach which is a genocidal application of force; and
4   the Liberal-Reformist (approximated by counter-terror operations in the Punjab 1994–7)
    approach involves the use of military and police forces within a broader socio-economic
    and political strategy, and is the preferred strategy NATO and the United States would like
    to see Pakistan adopt.

Pakistan's typical practice is a combination of Conventional Establishment if CI is conducted in
a friendly population, and Punitive-Militarist approach if conducted against a peripheral population. Pakistan's prospects for adopting a Liberal-Reformist approach are hampered by a lack of
resources for development, low interest in improving local representation in governance, and
political costs in accessing local resources (such as the Sui natural gas fields in Balochistan)
(Lalwani 2010: 1; Jones and Fair 2010: xv, 129).

Pakistan does not formally have a CI doctrine, though it is widely believed to be in the
process of finalizing one (Iqbal, Major Ali 2010, pers. comm., 24 August). Pakistan has traditionally employed the Westminster terminology of air-to-civil power (Cohen 1975: 208), and
of Low Intensity Warfare (LIW) (Lalwani 2009: 10; Iqbal 2009: 203; Jones and Fair 2010: 8).
The first and politically significant application of an aid-to-civil power operation was the March
1953 deployment of the Pakistan Army in Lahore to quell the anti-Ahmadiya riots. Many of
Pakistan's former military leaders received CI training at Fort Bragg during the heyday of
Vietnam, such as General (later President) Zia ul-Haq, but there is a general reluctance to distract attention from the pressing Indian conventional threat preoccupying most of Pakistan's
military (Housepian 1980: 141; Jones and Fair 2010: 37). Consequently CI training in the Pakistan Army is reduced to historical studies of major Western experiences, such as wars in Malaya
and Vietnam (Rashid 2009: 8). In 2008 the Pakistan Chief of the Army Staffs (COAS) resisted
a US offer to train two brigades of the Interior Ministry's Frontier Corps (FC). The Pakistan
army is therefore poorly structured, equipped and trained for CI (Markey 2008: 12; Rashid
2009: 8; Lalwani 2009: 4). Pakistan's junior and mid-range officers also have little interaction
with other armies (Markey 2008: 43) and consequently have little knowledge of population-
centric approaches to CI (Jones and Fair 2010: xiii) and recommended force ratios (Lalwani
2009: 12). What CI terminology it does use appears mainly to be an appeasing form of public
diplomacy for the benefit of the United States, and its close ally China (with which it is conducting joint counter-terror operations against Uygur insurgent groups hiding out in Pakistan)
(Jones and Fair 2010: xiv; Fair and Jones 2009–10: 162).

Pakistan's military, when it does act in the CI role, does so with less restraint when operating
against the periphery, and more reluctantly in the Punjab or KP because of the sympathetic ethnic
composition of the army. The army is constrained by the over-representation of Punjabis (60 per
cent, mostly from Pindi, Jhelum and Attock) and Pashtuns (Yusufzai, Utman Kel and Kataka from
Kohat and Mardan) in the Inter Services Intelligence Agency (at 30–40 per cent) (Kukreja 2003: 51;
Jones 2002: 139; Elliot 1968: 70, 73, 77–85; Korbel 2002: 73), the officer corps (22–25 per cent)
and soldiery (22 per cent) (Nawaz 2008: 571; Roberts 2009: 33; Johnson and Mason 2008: 65;
Tellis 2008: 39), and Mojahirs in the senior positions of the army and bureaucracy (Frotscher
2008: 107). The 1971 attempt to restore order in East Pakistan resulted in large-scale defections of
East Bengalis from the ranks of the army, navy and air force, and there are concerns that operations
against the Pashtun could again fissure the army (Gazdar 2006: 1952; Masood 2010: 6–8).

The Conventional–Establishment approach: pacification of East Pakistan (1971)

Pakistan's crackdown and subsequent occupation of East Pakistan from March 26 to December 1971 was achieved through a combination of a Conventional–Establishment approach, in which the Pakistan military occupied key urban centres, and a Punitive–Militarist approach, in which paramilitaries terrorized separatist-minded Awami League activists and Hindus (Zaheer 1994: 164). As with other peripheries of Pakistan, a divide-and-rule method of governance was applied, in which the Pakistan armed forces, consisting primarily of Punjabis and Pashtun, was aided by immigrant Bihari Muslims engaged in an quasi-ethnic conflict with the local Bengali population (Cohen 1975: 208). Against a largely hostile population of 60 million Bengalis and approximately 100,000 Indian-trained Mukti Bahini insurgents, by October Pakistan deployed 34,000 soldiers, Special Services Group commandos (SSG) and Rangers, 11,000 Civil Armed Forces (CAF), 16,500 mostly non-Bengali police and another 20–35,000 paramilitaries of the Industrial Security Force (ISF – 3,000 strong), Vulnerable Points Force (VPF – 3,000 strong), Razakar Mujahids (consisting primarily of Bihari and non-Bengali militia), Razakar Ansaris (lathi-armed Bengalis), Shanti Committees and religiously-motivated al-Badr and al-Shams militia organized by Pakistan's Jamaat-i-Islami political–religious organization (Ziring 1992: 69; Garg 1984: 125, 130–1; Niazi 1998: 52, 76–9, 82; Clodfelter 2002: 669; Sisson and Rose 1990: 162–5; Zaheer 1994: 170, 180–1; Mullick 2009: 20).

The initial crackdown was called Operation Searchlight and consisted of seizing and killing key leaders of the Awami League (such as Mujibur Rahman), though most escaped, and overcoming approximately 50,000 combined Bengali army, police and Awami activists (Zaheer 1994: 167, 169; Garg 1984: 117; Sisson and Rose 1990: 165; Mascarenhas 1971: 114–15). Within eight weeks the Pakistan Army had asserted control over East Pakistan, with the final tally of losses by December 1971 between 200–300,000 Bengalis and Biharis killed in ethnic conflict, 9.8 million refugees fleeing to India and 2,950 Pakistani Army deaths (Siddiqui 1972: 152; Niazi 1998: 65; Laporte Jr. 1972: 105; Frotscher 2008: 43; Clodfelter 2002: 669).[1] The pacification operation relied on firepower, such as the use of artillery at Dacca University (Laporte 1972: 102; Ali, Rao Farman 1999, pers. comm., 26 April).[2] The Pakistan Army had already had experience of this type in its operations in Baluchistan and KP (Payne 1973: 53; Khan, Tkka 1999, pers. comm., 25 April). The lack of clearly defined army rules of engagement prompted different standards of treatment of locals, and there were undoubtedly abuses of the local population, rapes, reprisals against villages, lethal enforcement of curfews and collateral damage, some of which resulted in prosecutions by the Pakistan Army against its senior officers (Zaheer 1994: 175, 323; Niazi 1998: 50, 282–3; Mascarenhas 1971: 115; *Torture in Bangladesh 1971–2004* 2004, p. 8; The Secretariat of the International Commission of Jurists 1972, p. 36).

However, most of the actual killing was conducted by the Islamist Al-Badr militias, with their better knowledge of East Pakistan, and their assigned task of targeting the Awami League, its many sympathisers, and East Pakistan's Hindu population (Garg 1984, p. 165; Zaheer 1994, p. 172; Mascarenhas 1971, p. 117; Ziring 1992, pp. 71–2; *Torture in Bangladesh 1971–2004* 2004: 7–8; The Secretariat of the International Commission of Jurists 1972: 23–5, 36; Rushbrook 1972: 74–5; Ali, Rao Farman 1999, pers. comm., 26 April). The Pakistan Army had little difficulty overcoming organized resistance, but in the following months it was confined to urban areas, cantonments and border outposts linked by air and water resupply due to the threat of rural interdiction by insurgents. Rural sweep operations temporary restored access between

May and October of 1970, but the emerging conventional threat from India caused the Pakistan Army to relinquish control of the countryside by October (Zaheer 1994: 167–9, 171, 175, 177, 182; Niazi 1998: 51–2, 82; Garg 1984: 133; Johnson 2005: 152–3).

The Punitive-Militarist approach: the five uprisings of Balochistan

Pakistan's pacification technique of punitive raiding and direct application of force against Baloch insurgents mimics the Khan of Kalat's nineteenth-century tax collection raids against the Baloch town of Dera Bugti (Lalwani 2010; Matheson 1967: 62). When the Khan of Kalat (Balochistan) refused to merge with Pakistan and declared independence, the Pakistan Army invaded on 14 August 1947, and remained to suppress a subsequent tribal uprising in 1948 (Bansal 2008: 184; Khan 2009: 1072). Similar revolts followed in 1958: a Baloch reaction to its merger into a larger Punjabi-dominated West Pakistan necessitated the Pakistan government's dispatch of the Pishin Scouts to the town of Dera Bugti to preempt any mass tribal uprising. In 1962 the Pakistan Army was deployed to suppress a low level insurgency of left-wing separatist militants, which was to last until 1969 (Khan 2009: 1072, 1076; Matheson 1967: 186–7). From 1973 to 1977, a major uprising of 55,000 Baloch tribals in Khuzdar and Kohlu was suppressed by 80,000 Pakistani troops using aircraft, napalm and borrowed Iranian helicopters, resulting in 5,000 insurgent and 3,300 military deaths (Bansal 2008: 184; Khan 2007: 126; Khan 2009: 1077; Lalwani 2009: 28; Gazdar 2006: 1952). The operation was successful and deterred, in combination with political engagement, any further uprising for two decades (Lalwani 2010; Khan 2009: 1077; Sahadevan 2002: 132). The underlying cause of the insurgency was Pakistan's exploitation of resources without Baloch consent or benefit (such as natural gas), and their political marginalization (Bansal 2008: 183, 185–6; Weinbaum 1977; Mullick 2009: 22–3).

The Punitive-Militarist approach was successful because of an absence of significant numbers of Baloch in the military, the non-Baloch composition of the Baloch Regiment, the FC (primarily Pashtun), and that only 25 per cent of the Baloch provincial police were Baloch (Sahadevan 2002: 132; Bansal 2008: 185–6). An inter-tribal divide-and-conquer form of governance by Islamabad has not worked among the well-coordinated Baloch tribes. Pakistan has encouraged, therefore, ethnic inundation by Afghan Pashtun refugees, who have been granted the right to vote, and has supported immigration by Punjabis and Sindhis along the strategic Mekran Coast (though this has resulted in ethnic riots, such as in 1991) (Bansal 2008: 188–9; ICG 2007: 8, 1087).

Since 2003 renewed insurgency among the Dera Bugti and Marri tribesmen of Kohlu led the army to begin pacification operations in December 2005 (Bansal 2008: 182). To that end Pakistan has deployed army artillery elements, 750 Defense Security Guards (DSG) and 10,000 FC and Frontier Constabulary. Pakistan primarily conducts vital point security of gas fields and other infrastructure, combined with mass detentions (12,000 plus 600 missing), raids and assassinations, such as that of Baloch insurgent leaders Nawab Akbar Khan Bugti in August 2006 by gunship, and Nawabzada Ballach Marri in November 2007 (Bansal 2008: 183, 196; Khan 2009: 1082; ICG 2007: 3–5; Khan 2007: 126). When the resistance is substantial, Pakistan routinely blockades Dera Bugti and conducts punitive artillery strikes, as the army did in 2002 (Khan 2009: 1082; Bansal 2008: 184, 190, 192, 196).

The Punitive-Militarist approach: anti-Dacoit operations in the Sindh (1983–9, 1992)

As part of operations by the military government of Zia ul-Haq to suppress Sindhi separatism in the form of the Movement to Restore Democracy (MRD), 40,000 soldiers of the Pakistan army were deployed between 1983 to 1989 to combat bandit attacks on police stations, trains and local administration. Through the use of helicopters, special courts, thousands were detained, villages were raised and order restored, with the loss of several hundred lives (Frotscher 2008: 108; Ahmar 1996: 1048; Gazdar 2006: 1952; Khan 2002: 213, 225, 228; Newberg 1987: 319). The military also made use of private landowner armies, while the ISI helped sponsor the creation of the Islamic Jamhoori Ittehad (IJI) to counterbalance the influence of the main Sindhi nationalist parties (Khan 2002: 226–7, 229). Again in 1992, as a preliminary to operations in Karachi (Operation Clean-up), the Pakistan army conducted anti-Dacoit sweeps through rural Sindh (Operation Sindh) (Frotscher 2008: 136; Mullick 2009: 21).

The Liberal-Reformist approach: Karachi and the MQM (1992–7)

In response to the Sindhi-Mohjir ethnic conflict in Karachi that instigated the formation of the pro-Mohajir Muhajir Qaumi Movement (MQM) and the effective paralysing of Pakistan's wealthiest city by use of terror and attacks on police stations, Nawaz Sharif dispatched the army in 1991 (Frotscher 2008: 127, 174, 185, 187, 217). The army was initially reluctant to become involved because of the significant Mohajir population, who were well represented in the national bureaucracy (Ahmar 1996: 1046, 1048; Frotscher 2008: 37, 225). Operation Clean-up, begun in May 1992, involved two infantry brigades, 20,000 Rangers, SSG, and the ISI-sponsored Haqiqi faction to suppress the MQM's urban guerrilla war (for a force to population ratio of 3.2 to 1,000) (Frotscher 2008: 218–19; Lalwani 2009: 28; Mullick 2009: 21–2).

The hub of MQM activity, Karachi University, was secured, and the city isolated by cordon and search operations that involved the shutting down of basic utilities for extended periods in hostile neighbourhoods (Ahmar 1996: 1041; Frotscher 2008: 115). The primary goal was capturing the MQM leadership cadre, though this was not achieved and the army's activity stoked up greater levels of popular support for the MQM (Ahmar 1996: 1053, 1047). The army employed Punjabi, Sindhi and Jamiat-i-Islami-sponsored student groups, criminal gangs (such as the Salam group), detention of relatives, extrajudicial killings and raids (Frotscher 2008: 115–16, 220–1, 223).

The Terrorist Affected Areas Act of 1992 and the removal of the regulation banning forced confessions permitted torture, but the army could not overcome the MQM's solid community base of support, and so it withdrew on 30 November 1994 (Frotscher 2008: 223–4; Ahmar 1996: 1035; Haq 1995: 1001).

A second Operation Clean-up, along the lines of a Liberal-Reformist approach, was conducted primarily by the Rangers and police in July 1995, and relied more heavily on intelligence and informants rather than neighbourhood sieges, but was supplemented by state-sanctioned extrajudicial killings. It consisted of 35,000 personnel versus 1,500 MQM militants and 4,000 supporters (Waseem 1996: 628; Frotscher 2008: 226–7, 230). The MQM leadership was more effectively dealt with so that by 1997 relative peace was achieved (though assassinations by both sides continued) (Frotscher 2008: 228–31, 235, 240; Abbas 2009: 17).This operated in parallel with political success by the MQM in municipal and national political representation (Frotscher 2008: 222–3).

The Liberal-Reformist approach: counter-terrorism in the Punjab (1994–7)

Pakistan's counter-terrorism operations in the Punjab are the penultimate example of Pakistan's Liberal-Reformist approach to CI (ICG 2009: 7). In the Punjab success was achieved through an orthodox population security approach involving community policing, intelligence and legal and extrajudicial methods, and made politically possible by strong public support for the operation (Lalwani 2010: 2). Under Prime Minister Benazir Bhutto, the PPP (People's Party of Pakistan) government cracked down on militants in the Punjab between 1994 and 1995 (ICG 2009: 18). Prime Minister Nawaz Sharif's PML (Pakistan Muslim League) did the same in February–May 1997 and January 1999 against the SSP (Sipah-e-Sahaba Pakistan) and the LJ (Lashkar-e-Jhangvi), arresting 1,500 militants and sympathisers and pushing them into Afghanistan (ICG 2009: 4; Abbas 2009: 17; Nasr 2000: 185). The ISI was subsequently tasked with conducting the extra-legal disappearances of a large number of Pakistani militants between 2004 and 2007 (ICG 2009: 19; Tellis 2008: 4). When the Pakistan state faced a direct challenge from militants at the Lal Masjid Red Mosque in Islamabad in July 2007, the Pakistan SSG (Special Service Group) was dispatched to neutralize its occupants (ICG 2009: 11).

The Punitive–Military approach: the tribal Pashtun problem

Pakistan's policy in the KP at Partition was too under-funded to mimic the British practice of tribal subsidies, and its military was too preoccupied with India to permanently pacify the Pashtuns, so it granted more local autonomy than had the British (Schofield 2003: 250). Pakistan relied for its governance on the 1902 Frontier Crimes Regulation, which permitted punitive and collective punishment (ICG 2009: ii, 2, 4–5, 18). Pakistan's general governance strategy in the Federally Administered Tribal Areas (FATA), Provincially Administered Tribal Areas (PATA) is divide-and-conquer, in which tribes are counter-balanced by the political agent, and favourite leaders are temporarily supported (a practice that might be termed 'crown the warlord') while more hostile leaders are assassinated. This approach was exemplified by the backing of Pashtun militant leaders Hafiz Gul Bahadur, Maulvi Nazir Ahmed, Jalaludin Haqqani and the Uthmanzai (N. Waziristan) and Bhittani Ahmedzai (S. Waziristan) militias, or the neutralization of Abdul Gaffar Khan, the Faqir of Ipi, Fazl Akbar and Abdus Samad Khan Achakzai (ICG 2009: 7, 18; Rehman 2009; Franco 2009: 278–9, 286; Jones and Fair 2010: 57–8).

Recent divide-and-conquer approaches have largely failed due to the coalescence of 30 clans under the Tehreek-e-Taliban Pakistan (TTP). In cases of failure Pakistan relies on punitive raids, bombardment and economic blockades to maintain law and order, while generally neglecting development and political strategies due to their high cost (Lalwani 2009: 11–12, 39; ICG 2009: ii; Tellis 2008: 25–6; ICG 2009: 21; Rashid 2009: 9). Kilcullen characterizes Pakistani operations in the KP as largely static and dependent on firepower instead of patrolling, reliant on insurgent killing rather than population security, and focused on the marginalizing of local forces (Kilcullen 2009: 10–13; Lalwani 2009: 9; Jones and Fair 2010: 31, 80). Fair and Seth have also identified a preoccupation among the Pakistani military with conventional warfare training that results in low mobility in mountainous terrain and a reluctance to hold territory after it has been cleared of insurgents; this results in the creation of a large flow of internally displaced persons (IDPs) as well as poor local cooperation and follow-on political-economic development planning (Jones and Fair 2010: 81–2).

Operating in KP and the FATA since 2010 are 150,000 personnel of the Army's 11th Corps, including the primarily Pashtun-manned FC, Frontier Constabulary and provincial police (Lalwani 2009: 33; ICG 2009: 17–18). In an auxilliary role under the control of the political agents are the organized tribal Levies and the self-armed tribal Khassadars (ICG 2009: 17). The Federal Ministry of States and Frontier Regions (SAFRON) is ultimately responsible for coordinating the political agents and their responsibility in turn for allowances to cooperative Maliks (traditional political leaders), and is often at odds with the locally elected officials. Estimated government killed-in-action has ranged from 1,000 to 3,000 between 2004 and 2010 (Jagadish 2009: 41; Markey 2008: 7).

Peace deals have usually been the equilibrium outcome in the absence of Pakistani domestic support for CI in the KP and the tribal areas. The underlying principle is that selected tribes can be neutralized to counter-balance others, or even simply to remain anti-separatist within their autonomous areas, regardless of the resulting violence (Markey 2008: 30). Pakistan has learned, in its management of Pashtun uprisings since 1951 and especially between 1960 and 1963 in Bajaur and Dir, that local lashkars, or armed gangs, can remain loyal even against Afghan instigation and infiltration (Dupree 1973: 538–42).[3] This policy has failed because it provided time for insurgents to re-group for further resumption of hostilities (Fair 2009; ICG 2009: 1; Lalwani 2010: 3). Support for military action grew in Pakistan following the collapse of the Swat peace in July 2009 and the October attack on the army's General Headquarters in Rawalpindi (Kilcullen 2009: 2–3; Jones and Fair 2010: 31, 80; ICG 2009: 7).

From 2001 until 2008 Pakistan practised an alternating combination of Conventional-Establishment CI in the KP and PATA, and Militarist-Punitive CI in the FATA and tribal areas. Pakistani support for the US operations at Tora Bora in the autumn of 2001 until 2004 consisted of porous blocking operations along the tribal frontier and limited raids against al-Qaeda (Operation Kazha Punga in S. Waziristan) (Franco 2009: 275–7, 280; Jones and Fair 2010: 41–3, 46–7). Operation Al Mizan (2004) in S. Waziristan was intended to clear the FATA of foreign Chechen and Uzbek militants, but resulted in the introduction of the army (as part of Operation Kalosha II) after an ambush of the FC. Tactically the army had poor cordon-and-search techniques which alienated the local population through a scorched earth policy and airstrikes; it also strategically instigated the consolidation of the insurgents against pro-government Maliks, as well as failed to destroy foreign militant cells. It did mark the first use of US-trained Pakistani CI special forces (Lalwani 2009: 7; Jones and Fair 2010: xiv, 3, 47–50, 53–5). Operation Azam Warsak (June 2006) in Mohmand Agency, a sweep against foreign militants, was executed successfully because of local support (Franco 2009: 275–7, 280; ICG 2009: 6). Operation Zalzala (2008) in South Waziristan was provoked by an insurgent uprising against the FC, and targeted foreign militants, their militant Mehsud hosts and the source of suicide bombings, and was, at least temporarily, successful (Jones and Fair 2010: 34, 57–60). The operation made heavy use of firepower and the creation of outposts for rapid reoccupation by the army. It made innovative use of combat engineering support, armour and jamming of militant communications, but produced significant destruction through collateral damage and collective punishment of villages, resulting in 200,000 IDPs, and failed to stem the return of militants (Jones and Fair 2010: 59–62).

From 2008 onwards Pakistan shifted to a hybrid Conventional-Establishment and Liberal-Reformist CI technique in Bajaur Agency, where the government had a modicum of urban support. Operation Sher Dil (2008–9) in Bajaur made more effective use of mobile and dispersed forces, targeted SSG raids, local follow-on aid, basing for population security, local political and community contact and intelligence, and favourable kill ratios. However, it continued its heavy reliance on air and artillery bombardment producing collateral damage, weak patrolling, concentration in large bases, failure to isolate the battlefield against an influx of militants (though successful at blocking escape), failure to weaken local tribal support for militants, absence of a successful clear-hold-build approach, and produced 500,000 IDPs (Lalwani 2010: 7; Rashid 2009: 8; Jones and Fair 2010: 64–5, 75; Khan 2009; ICG 2009: 5–6; Mullick 2009: 55).

Operation Rah-e-Rast (2007 and 2009) in Swat consisted of two phases, both targeting the Tehreek-e-Nafaz-e-Shariat-e-Mohammadi (TNSM). When the FC failed in its intervention against resurgent activity in October 2007 (Operation Mountain Viper), the army was deployed in November and successfully applied its standard practice of battlefield isolation followed by cordon-and-search. But this local level strategy was coupled with weak applications of civil–military coordination, population security, media support, social development through quick impact projects, community consultation, intelligence, and worsened by a paralysed regional and national political strategy (Iqbal 2009: 5, 15–29, 42–7, 54–81, 84, 87, 89, 91–103, 121, 207, 209, 217; Jones and Fair 2010: 66–8). Normalcy was restored for a period in 2008, facilitating elections, but the overall lack of political strategy led to a resurgence of militant activity in 2009 and the second phase of Operation Rah-e-Rast (Iqbal 2009: 124, 137–48, 167–70). The army augmented its usual practice of cordon-and-search with significant use of artillery, fixed and rotary-wing firepower, coupled with more successful application of dispersed night patrols, SSG raids in Fighting in Built Up Areas (FIBUA) conditions, base locations for population security, air strikes against leadership targets, and the setting-up of local lashkars, resulting in favourable kill ratios for the army, but also producing one million IDPs (Perlez and Shah 2009). While there persists an absence of a national strategy, in Swat the army has managed to maintain continuous operations in lieu of a ceasefire (Iqbal 2009: 200, 223).

Operation Rah-e-Nijat (2009–10) in S. Waziristan was intended as a follow-on to Operation Zalzala after a resumption of terror attacks in the Punjab, and reverted to a Punitive-Militarist mode of CI. The army did engage friendly clans and militias (such as Mullah Nazir and Hafiz Gul Bahadur) in an operation that opened with air strikes (October 2009) against militant concentrations, and successfully overran the primary urban centres of the TTP by December. In conjunction with the United States, drone attacks killed both Beitullah (August 2009) and Hakimullah (January 2010) Mehsud, the leaders of the TTP. The army made heavy use of firepower, deliberate movement to counter Improvised Explosive Devices (IEDs), Unmanned Aerial Vehicles (UAVs), scorched earth tactics, with a low emphasis on winning of hearts and minds, resulting in 100,000 IDPs. Attempts to stem the TTP terror were of limited initial effectiveness as an unprecedented 12,632 died from terror attacks in Pakistan in 2009 (a greater number than suffered by Afghanistan) (Jones and Fair 2010: 8–9).

Pakistan has nevertheless evolved its tactics, however imperfectly, since beginning operations in 2001, and it appears that the Liberal-Reformist approach, as exemplified in operations in Bajaur is likely to be applied more widely in KP and the PATA. But in the absence of a large scale foreign-funded development programme, the Pakistan Army is likely to continue its reliance on the Punitive-Militarist approach to CI in the tribal belt.

Achievements of counterinsurgency

Assessments vary on the final tally of Pakistan's success with its hybrid pacification (Conventional-Establishment and Militarist-Punitive) and CI (Liberal-Reformist) approaches to insurgency. One estimate suggests that Pakistan succeeded in all instances except East Pakistan, but in that case, without Indian military intervention, Pakistani military domination was sustainable (Mullick 2009: 24). If the Pakistan military could have dispensed with the need to prepare for a conventional war against India in 1971, its available military assets would very likely have been sufficient to restore order to East Pakistan, though not legitimacy. For that matter, if Pakistan's sizable military could be diverted from its deployment areas along the Indian frontier, Pakistan could at a minimum triple its assigned forces in KP and the FATA.

Alternately, Pakistan had achieved resounding success in its use of Reformist-Liberal CT in the Punjab, and managed to pacify the Baloch and Sindhis, but achieved no more than a political stalemate in Karachi in the 1990s and among the Pashtun. Insurgencies do poorly in the Punjab, which is the more or less satisfied core of the Pakistan state. What terror does occur in the Punjab is either imported or very far outside the mainstream interests of the population.

Public cooperation with the state in the Punjab is easily obtained. The Baloch and Sindhi under-representation in the army (which is no longer the case among the Sindhis), permitted a far more aggressive punitive response in those peripheries. Operations against the Pashtun areas are far more problematic, given the over-representation of the Pashtun in the army coupled with their political under-representation. The Pashtun are divided by their suspicion of Punjabi domination of Pakistan, coupled with their seemingly compatible views of militant Islam. The result is not a measured response, but overwhelmingly disruptive uses of force followed by political-economic paralysis.

Increasing democratization and socio-economic development of the peripheries, and the shifting recruitment base of the Pakistan Army may make pacification approaches to resolving regional grievances less politically palatable for Islamabad. The result seems to have played out in the FATA, where successful cordon-and-search operations are followed by extended military occupations without economic development or popular mobilization. It is this paucity of funds that seems to drive Pakistan's practice of Militarist-Punitive CI, rather than simply an historical inheritance from British practice.

Notes

1 For alternate estimates, see Garg (1984: 146); Payne (1973: 29, 101); and *Torture in Bangladesh 1971–2004* (2004: 7).
2 Rao Farman Ali asked me what I would have done had I been in his shoes and students were shooting at my artillery train.
3 The peace deals have included: March 2004 Shakai, February 2005 Sararogha (with Beitullah Mehsud), September 2006 North Waziristan, July 2007 Mohmand, 2007 Malakand, and February 2009 Bajaur.

Recommended readings

Ahmed, Eqbal (2006) 'Counterinsurgency', in Carollee Bengelsdorf, Margaret Cerullo and Yogesh Chandrani (eds) *The Selected Writings of Eqbal Ahmad*. New York: Columbia University Press, pp. 37–64.
Franco, Claudio (2009) 'The Tehrik-e-Taliban Pakistan', in Antonio Giustozzi (ed.), *Decoding the New Taliban*. New York: Columbia University Press, pp. 269–91.
Gazdar, Haris (May 20 2006) 'Counter-insurgencies in Pakistan', *Economic and Political Weekly*, 1952–3.
Lalwani, Sameer (2010) *Pakistan's COIN Flip*. Washington, DC: New America Foundation.
Tellis, Ashley (2008) *Pakistan and the War on Terror*. Washington, DC: Carnegie Endowment.

References

Abbas, Hassan (2009) *Police & Law Enforcement Reform in Pakistan*. Michigan: ISPU. http://www.jamestown. org/programs/gta/single/?tx_ttnews%5Btt_news%5D=1056&tx_ttnews%5BbackPid%5D=182&no_cache=1.
Ahmad, Eqbal (2006) 'Counterinsurgency', in Carollee Bengelsdorf, Margaret Cerullo and Yogesh Chandrani (eds), *The Selected Writings of Eqbal Ahmad*. New York: Columbia University Press, pp. 37–64.
Ahmar, Moonis (1996) 'Ethnicity and State Power in Pakistan: The Karachi Crisis', *Asian Survey*, 36 (10): 1031–48.
Bansal, Alok (2008) 'Factors Leading to Insurgency in Balochistan', *Small Wars & Insurgencies*, 19 (2): 182–200.
Clodfelter, Michael (2002) *Warfare and Armed Conflicts*. London: McFarland.
Cohen, Stephen (1975) 'Security Issues in South Asia', *Asian Survey*, 15 (3): 202–14.
Dupree, Louis (1973) *Afghanistan*. Princeton: Princeton University Press.
Elliott, J.G. (1968) *The Frontier 1839–1947*. London: Cassell.
Fair, C. Christine and Jones, Seth (2009–10) 'Pakistan's War Within', *Survival*, 51 (6): 161–88.

Fair, Christine C. (2009) 'Pakistan's Own War on Terror: What the Pakistani Public Thinks', *Journal of International Affairs*, 63 (1): 39–56.

Franco, Claudio (2009) 'The Tehrik-e-Taliban Pakistan', in Antonio Giustozzi (ed.), *Decoding the New Taliban*. New York: Columbia University Press, pp. 269–91.

Frotscher, Ann (2008) *Claiming Pakistan: The MQM and the Fight for Belonging*. Baden-Baden: Nomos.

Garg, S.K. (1984) *Spotlight: Freedom Fighters of Bangladesh*. New Delhi: Allied.

Gazdar, Haris (2006) 'Counter-insurgencies in Pakistan', *Economic and Political Weekly*, pp. 1952–3.

Haq, Farhat (1995) 'Rise of the MQM in Pakistan: Politics of Ethnic Mobilization', *Asian Survey*, 35 (11): 990–1004.

Housepian, Nubar (1980) 'Pakistan in Crisis: an Interview with Eqbal Ahmad', *Race & Class*, 22: 129–46.

ICG (2007) *Pakistan: The Forgotten Conflict in Balochistan*. Asia Briefing 69.

ICG (2009) *Pakistan: The Militant Jihadi Challenge*. Brussels: No. 164.

ICG (2009) *Pakistan: Countering Militancy in Fata*. Asia Report 178.

Jagadish, Vikra (2009) 'Reconsidering American Strategy in South Asia: Destroying Terrorist Sanctuaries in Pakistan's Tribal Areas', *Small Wars and Insurgencies*, 20 (1): 36–65.

Johnson, Robert (2005) *A Region in Turmoil: South Asian Conflicts Since 1947*. London: Reaktion Books.

Johnson, Thomas and Mason, M. Chris (2008) 'No Sign until the Burst of Fire', *International Security*, 32 (4): 41–77.

Jones, Owen (2002) *Pakistan*. New Haven: Yale University Press.

Jones, Seth and Fair, C. Christine (2010) *Counterinsurgency in Pakistan*. Santa Monica: RAND.

Khan, Adeel (2002) 'Pakistan's Sindhi Ethnic Nationalism', *Asian Survey*, 42 (2): 213–29.

Khan, Adeel (2007) 'Pakistan in 2006', *Asian Survey*, 47 (1): 125–32.

Khan, Adeel (2009) 'Renewed Ethnonationalist Insurgency in Balochistan, Pakistan', *Asian Survey*, 49 (6): 1071–91.

Khan, Mukhtar A. (2009) 'A Profile of Militant Groups in Bajaur Tribal Agency', *Terrorism Monitor*, 7 (6). http://www.jamestown.org/single/?no_cache=1&tx_ttnews%5Btt_news%5D=34729

Kilcullen, David (2009) *Terrain, Tribes and Terrorists: Pakistan, 2006–2008*. Washington DC: Brookings, Counterinsurgency and Pakistan Paper Series No. 3.

Korbel, Josef (2002) *Danger in Kashmir*. Oxford: Oxford University Press.

Kukreja, Veena (2003) *Contemporary Pakistan*. New Delhi: Sage.

Lalwani, Sameer (2009) *Pakistani Capabilities for a Counterinsurgency Campaign: A Net Assessment*. Washington, DC: New America Foundation.

Lalwani, Sameer (2010) *Pakistan's COIN Flip*. Washington, DC: New America Foundation.

Laporte, Jr., Robert (1972) 'Pakistan in 1971: The Disintegration of Nation', *Asian Survey*, 12 (2): 97–108.

Major Ali Iqbal (2009) 'Swat Operation', *Counter Insurgency Leader's Workshop*, Ft. Leavensworth, Kansas.

Markey, Daniel (2008) *Securing Pakistan's Tribal Belt*, CSR No. 36. New York: Council on Foreign Relations.

Mascarenhas, Anthony (1971) *The Rape of Bangladesh*. Delhi: Vikas Publications.

Masood, Talat (2010) 'Pakistan's Military Examines its Options in North Waziristan', *Terrorism Monitor*, 8 (5): 6–8.

Matheson, Sylvia (1967) *The Tigers of Baluchistan*. London: Arthur Barker.

Mullick, Haider (2009) *Pakistan's Security Paradox: Countering and Fomenting Insurgencies*. Hurlburt Field, Florida: Joint Special Operations University.

Nasr, Vali R. (2000) 'International Politics, Domestic Imperatives, and Identity Mobilization', *Comparative Politics*, 32 (2): 171–90.

Nawaz, Shuja (2008) *Crossed Swords*. Karachi: Oxford University Press.

Newberg, Paula (1987) 'Pakistan's Troubled Landscape', *World Policy Journal*, 4 (2): 313–31.

Niazi, A.A.K. (1998) *The Betrayal of East Pakistan*. Karachi: Oxford University Press.

Payne, Robert (1973) *Massacre*. New York: Macmilan.

Perlez, Jane and Shah, Pir Zubair (2009) 'Pakistan Says It Has Seized Taliban Spokesman', *New York Times* 11 September.

Rashid, Ahmed (2009) 'Pakistan's Continued Failure to Adopt a Counter-Insurgency Strategy', *CTC Sentinel*, 2 (3): 7–9.

Rehman, I.A. (2009) 'Pakistan's neo-Taliban', *Dawn*, 30 April.

Roberts, Adam (2009) 'Doctrine and Reality in Afghanistan', *Survival*, 51 (1): 29–60.

Sahadevan, P. (2002) 'Ethnic Conflicts and Militarism in South Asia', *International Studies*, 39 103–38.

Schofield, Victoria (2003) *Afghan Frontier*. New York: Tauris Parke.

The Secretariat of the International Commission of Jurists (1972) *The Events in East Pakistan, 1971; A Legal Study*. Geneva: International Commission of Jurists.

Siddiqui, Kalim (1972) *Conflict, Crisis and War in Pakistan*. London: Macmillan.

Sisson, Richard and Rose, Leo (1990) *War and Secession*. Berkeley: University of California Press.

Tellis, Ashley (2008) *Pakistan and the War on Terror*. Washington, DC: Carnegie Endowment.

Torture in Bangladesh 1971–2004 (2004) London: Redress.

Waseem, Mohammad (1996) 'Ethnic Conflict in Pakistan: The Case of the MQM', *The Pakistan Development Review*, 35 (4): 617–29.

Weinbaum, M.G. (1977) 'The March 1977 Elections in Pakistan: Where Everyone Lost', *Asian Survey*, 17 (7): 599–618.

Zaheer, Hasan (1994) *The Separation of East Pakistan*. Karachi: Oxford University Press.

Ziring, Lawrence (1992) *Bangladesh*. Karachi: Oxford University Press.

27

CHINA'S SOCIETY-CENTRIC COUNTERTERRORISM APPROACH IN XINJIANG

Martin I. Wayne[1]

China quietly confronted a predominantly indigenous insurgency in the country's far northwest for over two decades by increasing the security forces' capability to respond to incidents with less brutal methods and simultaneously investing political and financial capital in hardening society to insurgency's call. Although far from perfect, China's tactics evolved to meet the insurgency's new challenges and China nevertheless remained focused on the long-term project of transforming society's vision of the future, one tied to the Chinese state's promise of security, rights and opportunity. Under separatist and Islamist banners, and with inspiration and a few direct links to the global jihad, riots, ambushes, bombings and assassinations in trickle and deluge threatened the government's grip on the massive region of northwest China known as Xinjiang, the 'new frontier'. Possibly hundreds of China's Uyghurs, Xinjiang's once predominant ethnic minority, trained at a camp in Tora Bora, Afghanistan, and probably elsewhere in the region specifically intending to return home and wage a new jihad, a new fight against the Chinese government. China, for its part, prevented the nascent insurgency from gaining momentum by acting early and forcefully, constantly refining its approach down the spectrum of violence and increasingly relying on social methods, thereby limiting the insurgency from escalating into what could have become the country's Chechnya, Gaza, Afghanistan or Iraq (e.g. Chinese Communist Party, author unknown, 2005; Gladney 2002).

After greatly reducing the prevalence of insurgency in mainstream society, Chinese authorities now face problems on both ends of the spectrum of violence: society's increased demand for civil rights, a demand that if met would increase the state's longevity, and terrorist plots, a direct challenge to the state's power that Chinese authorities apparently remain intent on confronting with tactical suppression and strategic integration – with Chinese characteristics. It is unclear if Chinese authorities, seemingly more comfortable fighting terrorists than wrestling with public demands for redress of grievances, have come to grips with the nature of the current political landscape, but judging by the continued calls for investment and education perhaps Chinese leaders sense that the next move is theirs as they press forward transforming society in Xinjiang.

The evolving insurgency in Xinjiang

The gruesome separatist attacks that rocked cities and villages across Xinjiang in the past two years, and the increased plotting and propaganda activity – including by al-Qaeda associated militants outside China – though a poignant reminder of the continued contest, to date have failed to set the region alight. In the days surrounding the opening ceremonies for the 2008 summer Olympics in Beijing, an event some commentators trumpeted as celebrating China's emergence as a pre-eminent global power, two men in Kashgar slept in a parked truck overnight, poised for morning, according to international press reporting. In the early hours of 4 August the pair found their mark: a military police formation out for their morning jog. The pair struck the formation with deadly simplicity, mowing their truck into the paramilitary crowd then reportedly wielded knives and lobbed a few home-made grenades among them, which killed at least 16 and injured as many (e.g. Wong 2009: A5, A8).

The Olympics opened on 8 August without incident far to the east of Beijing, an event to which we will soon return; however events in Xinjiang continued to simmer. Insurgents in the following days reportedly attacked other police and government facilities and a local trade centre, as well as security volunteers manning rural checkpoints. These attacks are visible symptoms of the lingering idea of insurgency within society, yet to understand the strength of the idea within society writ large we must also investigate the claimed or planned and disrupted plots, to the extent possible with the information available from international media reporting, Chinese official statements and insurgent media.

As the 2008 Olympics approached, the al-Qaeda allied Turkestan Islamic Party (listed by the United Nations as the East Turkestan Islamic Movement – ETIM, and also known as the East Turkestan Islamic Party – ETIP; the name 'East Turkistan' referencing the Xinjiang region) publicly asserted its intent to attack (Turkestan Islamic Party 2008; Xinhua 2008; Haq 2009) China's major cities to disrupt the Olympics and warned fellow Muslims to avoid the Olympics to not get injured in the planned attack. According to press reporting of China's ambassador to Pakistan and United Arab Emirates court proceedings, the group also targeted Chinese interests abroad from Pakistan and the Middle East (Islamabad Jinnah 2008: P10; Hassan 2010).

The Turkestan Islamic Party had been nearly silent in the years since international forces entered Afghanistan in late 2001, capturing or killing an unknown number of the group's members alongside Taliban, al-Qaeda and other allied fighters (Tenet 2007: 221), 22 of whom were imprisoned at Guantanamo Bay, Cuba, according to the US Congressional Research Service (Kan 2006). Five remained at Guantanamo Bay the time of writing. The Turkestan Islamic Party since before 9/11 received sanctuary and training for possibly hundreds of fighters in Afghan and other camps and perhaps received modest financing and material support from its al-Qaeda and Taliban allies, according to a published interview with the group's emir (Haq 2009).

Despite the cross-border and international nexus, Xinjiang's insurgency remained fundamentally indigenous: local people focusing on a local fight even as they travelled abroad in search of shelter from security service pressure and paramilitary training, and as in many similar fights, elements of Xinjiang's insurgency reportedly received external support from like-minded militants. While directly benefiting from the cauldron of global jihad, the Turkestan Islamic Party apparently quietly had maintained its focus on returning home to become the vanguard of jihad in Xinjiang. The group's silence persisted after the Turkestan Islamic Party's founding emir and an unknown number of followers died in military activity in Pakistan in late 2003.

By early 2007 the group appears to have reconstituted at least enough strength to attempt terrorist activity inside China. According to Chinese authorities, the People's Armed Police (PAP) in January of 2007 raided a mining facility being used by terrorists with unspecified international ties near the country's borders with Afghanistan and Pakistan and the PAP killed 17 group members (e.g. Wayne 2007a, 2007b). Police in January 2008 raided a safe-house in Urumqi that reportedly housed 17 individuals, at least some of whom police suspected of having ties to the Turkestan Islamic Party's leaders abroad and, at the group's inspiration or direction, plotting an unspecified attack against the Olympics (Eturbonews.com 2008).

By April of 2008 China claims that its security forces had disrupted a Turkestan Islamic Party plot to attack Chinese cities with poisons and explosives. The Turkestan Islamic Party, for its part, in May 2008 publicly claimed to have bombed buses in Shanghai and Kunming and threatened further attacks to disrupt Beijing's hosting of the Olympics in August. It is unclear if the Turkestan Islamic Party in fact conducted the bus bombings; however, the group's threatened attacks targeting China's major cities did not materialize, probably indicating that the Chinese security forces had indeed gained the upper hand.

To step back for a moment, perhaps a few words on insurgency are in order. Insurgencies most tangibly are composed of people generally acting in groups to resist an idea – usually a political regime embodied by a government. Armed struggle is the element that most visibly distinguishes an insurgency from political movements, and in some cases insurgencies have matured to the point where there is a single or a few predominant groups leading the contest for power and influence against the standing regime. In Xinjiang, it is nearly impossible to reliably track across the past two decades the progress of probably many local groups as they formed, pursued elements of armed struggle (i.e. plotting, preparation, attack), and then dissolved or returned underground under security force pressure. This epistemological problem is largely due, I believe, to the difficulty of collecting data on the formation and dissolution of groups contesting the Chinese government's hold on power, a problem exacerbated by the country's historically tight media controls, paucity of reporters, and possibly social-systemic or cultural norms of altering and embellishing accounts to influence and not simply inform the audience.

At least seven additional potentially violent groups are identified by Chinese, American or scholarly sources as conducting activities in Xinjiang spanning the insurgent's tactical spectrum, and it seems highly likely that a new group or groups – to-date unnamed in international media coverage and unpublicized past Chinese Internet and media controls – participated in the violence of the past two years. Specifically, there is insufficient information to identify the affiliations – if any – for example, of the two individuals police killed and 15 detained in a January 2008 raid against an Urumqi safe-house suspected of plotting a possibly separate attack against the Olympics; the Uyghur woman detained in March 2008 aboard an airplane flight accused of attempting to blow up the airliner (eturbonews.com 2008), or the groups that conducted attacks in August 2008 across Xinjiang (AFP 2008).

The contemporary insurgency in Xinjiang probably began in Baren, near China's border with Pakistan and Afghanistan, in 1990, with protesters challenging the Chinese state's claims to legitimate rule and placing authorities on notice, some protesters fielding religious messages to further support their separatist calls. Although unrest in Xinjiang predated the People's Republic of China, the dream of insurgency awoke in the 1990s as a new wave of terrorism rose internationally in the Afghan war's wake. Insurgency infected society and began severing the state from the people. According to a Western diplomat then serving in the region, a band of insurgents crossed into Xinjiang once the Soviet threat was neutralized in Afghanistan, only to be repulsed with relative ease using military and diplomatic tools.

Violence in Xinjiang itself persisted at a low level throughout the 1990s, including occasional rioting, attacks against military and government facilities, bombings of buses and public spaces, and a few reported assassinations or attempts (e.g. United States Department of State 2004; Millward 2004; Dillon 2004). Portending a more enduring threat, some young local men, along with their closest friends, fled China and what they perceived to be suffocating security force pressure and ultimately pursued a path of violence to, in their view, defend themselves from an invading, predatory Chinese state. If China's claims about the Turkestan Islamic Party's activities in the past two years are correct, then it appears that young men from a new generation continued to pursue this path of seeking shelter and training abroad for armed resistance at home.

Taking the trends of insurgency as an organic whole, Xinjiang's dynamic and evolving insurgency outlived successive leaders and a generational shift in operatives, and even the transformation of the insurgency's organizational milieu: the Turkestan Islamic Party has apparently persisted since at least the late 1990s, yet other smaller groups have formed and dissolved.

Nevertheless, some readers clamour for numbers, in a belief that they might be explanatory. Body and incident counts are a flawed indicator of an insurgency's strength despite the seeming ease and attractiveness to quantifying the armed struggle because not only is the data usually flawed (skewed by honest collection constraints, bias, or intentional manipulation to influence perceptions), there is potentially a significant time lag between actors joining the cause and taking deadly action. China in 2002 asserted that over 200 attacks occurred in recent years that killed at least 160 people and wounded 440 (Information Office of the State Council 2002; *People's Daily* 2002). Add to this the August 2008 attacks – in which possibly three dozen security forces and local officials were killed or wounded, and the August 2010 reported vehicle-borne improvised explosive devices in Aksu that killed seven and injured 14 (BBC 2010). It is unclear if Chinese officials would include the two killed and others wounded in the January 2008 Urumqi safe-house raid or the officially reported 197 killed and over 1,000 wounded in the July 2009 ethnic rioting (Anna 2010: A20; Cha 2009a: A8; Cha 2009b: A9). If the 2009 riots are seen as demands for the government to fulfil its responsibilities to provide justice and security for Uyghurs and Han alike, then – no matter how heartbreaking and tragic the spiralling violence – this event marks a new phase and must be excluded from violence intended to challenge the state's authority.

Beyond any measurable 'hard facts' of body counts, let alone economic development or political progress, society's deep perceptions of power and security – future even more than present, and informed by the past – are the constant and immeasurable centre of gravity. To overcome a myopic focus on terrorist attacks isolated from the full political context in which these individuals act and the meaning they hope to create, we must also examine the other side of the political struggle in Xinjiang.

Ethnic rioting tore through southern Urumqi, the regional capital, after police intervened in a protest against the brutal and organized killings of two Uyghur factory workers by their Han counterparts far to the east in Guangdong province. A video posted online (Cha 2009a: A8; Cha 2009b: A9), showing the slow evil of the murderous beatings and seeming government inaction, spurred the outrage, and probably tens of thousands of people eventually took to Urumqi's streets demanding justice. In successive waves of violence, Uyghur mobs attacked Han and then Han mobs attacked Uyghurs. In the end, the ethnic violence killed 197 people and wounded at least 1,000 more. A prominent US-based political dissident claimed, and Chinese officials strongly denied as 'fabricated', that 10,000 people had disappeared into police custody with little trace (Branigan 2009; Cara 2010). The carnage was a heartbreaking human tragedy of a protest – that demanded equal justice and protections for Uyghurs as for other Chinese people – gone horribly awry.

Al-Qaeda senior leader Abu Yahya al-Libi publicly responded to ethnic rioting with a video message posted to al-Qaeda's al-Fajr web forum in October 2009 titled 'East Turkestan: The Forgotten Wound', the first al-Qaeda senior leadership media statement devoted entirely to China. Al-Libi made a clear case for defensive jihad – the theologically less controversial defence of attacked and oppressed Muslims – and called for a media campaign to educate Muslims abroad about the situation in Xinjiang, and for those Muslims to support their 'brothers' in Xinjiang with every means.

It is a duty for Muslims today to stand by their oppressed and wounded brothers in East Turkestan, stand for brotherhood and faith, and support and aid them with everything they can. Let the first steps in doing so be a wide, concentrated, and continuous media campaign in order to let the Islamic nation know the truth about what is going on over there, and expose the pagan Chinese imperialists who pretend to be gentle and forgiving in front of Islamic people in order to protect their interests.

(Abu Yahya al-Libi 2009)

Al-Libi used what he assesses as the Chinese oppression in Xinjiang as a further indictment of the illegitimacy of 'apostate governments' that are friendly with China and already in al-Qaeda's sights, probably an opaque reference to countries already at odds with al-Qaeda like Pakistan, Afghanistan, Saudi Arabia and Turkey. Continuing, Al-Libi then addressed the people of Xinjiang and advised them to carry weapons and rely on God's aid in the face of the Chinese 'invaders'.

Apostate governments appease it while it draws its claws and fangs in order to secretly tear up that remote section of our nation and inflict on its people all kinds of torture and punishment. Let our brothers in Turkestan know that there is no way for salvation, or any method to remove oppression and injustice, except for an honest return to their religion, holding on to it as much as possible, serious preparation for the cause of God the Exalted, carrying weapons in the face of the harsh invaders, patience, sacrifice, depending on God the Exalted.

(Abu Yahya al-Libi 2009)

Al-Libi with the October 2009 video statement began the media campaign; the consequences of China's new taint for 'apostate' governments or Muslims' widespread willingness to take up arms within China as al-Libi urged has yet to materialize. Interestingly, however, al-Libi appears to have a solid sense of Xinjiang's reduced insurgent proclivities and varying levels of religiosity.

Countering insurgency in Xinjiang

Chinese leaders – enabled by their core constituents' seemingly infinite support for securing Xinjiang – endeavoured to fundamentally reshape society in Xinjiang with grassroots institutions and police work. Chinese authorities looked to economic development to solve unrest in the long term, however the increased material wealth and reduction of absolute poverty in Xinjiang has yet to draw its desired impact. The conventional wisdom holds that China simply, repeatedly crushed opposition to its rule with force alone. Chinese security forces have in fact responded brutally to repeated challenges to the state's rule, yet the counterinsurgency's effectiveness across the past two decades increased as Chinese authorities reduced security force brutality – an ongoing project, the success of which is due in large part to the creation and professionalization of services and units trained specifically to suppress angry mobs or interface with peaceful families. International watchdog organizations such as the United Nations and Human Rights Watch assert that torture and summary executions persisted in Xinjiang, if greatly diminished in frequency (Khan 2005; Human Rights Watch 2005 and 2006). Simply stated, these symptoms of an un-free political system are present to varying degrees throughout the country and should not be falsely attributed causal import. Society in Xinjiang today at times loudly demands that the government provide civil rights and justice, at times quietly looks to a future tied to a changing Chinese state.

Insurgency – a form of warfare and politics – fundamentally is a contest for enemy and core constituent political will. Countering an insurgency without the will to act is impossible, no matter how rich the country, capable the forces, or necessary the fight. Conversely, effective counterinsurgency is possible only with the core's political will – a set of deep beliefs and preferences held by society. Here we must make a distinction from public opinion, which is both ephemeral and subject to the fast machinations of politicians, opinion leaders and events. Political will then is a shared enduring emotion within society, a subterranean reservoir that sustains a polity across tumultuous events. Insurgency is the struggle for this centre of gravity, and a state can not long persist in the fight nor likely persist at the helm if it loses the core through perceived inaction or incompetence.

China's counterinsurgency in Xinjiang is enabled and driven by seemingly infinite political will derived from socio-structural and historical factors. Three key factors within the core's society together build this critical resource: the Chinese Communist Party's (CCP) primacy, the state's pursuit of security, and the people's demand for stability.

The CCP must counter insurgency in Xinjiang to maintain its jealously guarded primacy in China's social structure, achieved through its own historic insurgent struggle against a brittle and corrupt regime. The CCP today sits atop a one-party state with the self-fulfilling need of maintaining power. At every level of government, from the grassroots up to the top leadership, the CCP has a concurrent and slightly more equal officer working in tandem with the corresponding state official. Communism itself in China has changed dramatically with the once lustrous ideals now tarnished and faded in eastern China's large cities, yet the appeal of privilege and power endures. The Mao era's economic communism has nearly vanished in China, replaced by a rough and rugged crony-capitalism. Political communism morphed into a new authoritarianism.

Political communism's veneer of ideology wore thin, revealing a fundamentally authoritarian system: power for power's sake. Maintaining its grip on the state's power is the sole motivating force, and the sole ideology, left within the CCP. Countering Xinjiang's insurgency bolsters the CCP claims of serving the national interest, providing viable, if not effective, leadership.

The state must rebuff Xinjiang's insurgency because China perceives that threats in the inner periphery are multiple, linked, unitary: unrest in one area invites challenge in the next; if one area of China secedes the country will disintegrate. With details different in each case, China believes that Tibet and Taiwan (and perhaps other areas) have repeatedly come close to splitting from the mainland. Security is the fundamental job of any state; beyond preventing 'renegade provinces' from splitting, the state must provide internal stability. The question of stability is particularly important in China today because the people demand it; the Chinese people's perceptions of domestic stability and steady progress towards a more healthy political life legitimize the state.

Insurgency in Xinjiang threatens the state by demonstrating the state's inability to manage both unrest in the periphery and provide stability for the core demands. Because when states are perceived as weak, challengers rise and because of China's unique socio-structural and political-historic factors, in this view if China is to survive the state must strongly confront insurgency in Xinjiang: failing this, not only would the periphery rupture but the core would rebel.

At times silently or alternately in blogs, quasi-official editorials and mobs in Xinjiang, the Chinese people demand that the state and the Party counter Xinjiang's insurgency. While knowledge of Xinjiang's troubles is limited even among the most educated in China's east, and knowledge of Uyghurs' social condition seems untouched even among many Han in Xinjiang, the Chinese people demand that their state hold the territory which it claimed decades ago. For the state to back-pedal on this would be to relinquish claims of legitimately representing the will of the Chinese people, and to relinquish its claim to the entirety of China. After decades of socio-political tumult, most prominently the self-inflicted wounds of the Great Leap Forward and the Cultural Revolution, Chinese today are tired of unrest and crave security, security provided by a bold-fisted state if need be.

Chinese society demands that the Party and the state provide a stability which can bring progress at a measured pace, a pace which seems glacial to outside observers; the Chinese people repeatedly have suffered the disastrous self-inflicted effects of revolutionary movements. Not needing the details, the core society cries for movement – however incremental – towards the dream of a better, unified and freer future, and this is the primary reason the core society demands effective counterinsurgency in Xinjiang. Fear of an ethnic 'other' is a powerful contributing factor.

The CCP imperative to retain its preeminent position in society and atop the state, the state's daily attempt to avoid disintegration, and the people's thirst for stability combine into unified purpose: Xinjiang's insurgency cannot be tolerated. China writ large has not only a large reservoir of political will for confronting the insurgency, but the reservoir is refilling and expanding. The greater the challenge Xinjiang poses, the greater the core's will and the state's imperative to counter the threat.

The July 2009 ethnic rioting vividly demonstrates this process of political demand and will: Uyghur mobs – enraged by the state's perceived failure to provide justice for an anti-Uyghur hate crime far to the east – turned against Urumqi's Han residents. In response, Han mobs first demanded the police and state provide security and, when this sense of security was unmet, Han mobs took to the streets. Police ultimately restored order and apparently a perception of state-provided security balanced with fear in both populations. Xinjiang's then top communist Wang Lequan first publicly weathered the political storm to show that the Party refused to be bossed around by anyone's demands – Uyghur or Han – and then quietly moved on to other responsibilities outside the region. Urumqi's Party Secretary Li Zhi lost his post in April 2010 after seemingly implausible rumours of needle attacks, again roiling not only the local but the core Han population's sense of security (Ramzy 2010).

State and CCP officials at all levels in 2009–10 announced what they asserted as new aggressive measures to increase economic development in Xinjiang, intended to alleviate the root causes of unrest, as the flood of police and paramilitary presence gradually ebbed into normalcy. Top suspects still at large were publicly encouraged to turn themselves in to authorities as criminal investigations continued in the background, and at least 200 of the 1,500 suspects arrested ultimately stood trial, according to Chinese press and international media reports, for charges that included organizing crowds to cause bodily harm, vandalizing public property, arson, robbery and murder (BBC 2009). Nevertheless, local Public Security Bureau and PAP units in July 2009 reportedly were ill prepared for the ethnic rioting's speed, scope and scale, possibly indicating that security forces had grown overly confident in their ability to pre-empt or contain threats (e.g. Cha 2009; Cara 2010).

China's response to the July 2009 ethnic rioting coupled with the 2007–10 counterterrorism activity also demonstrates how China's use of force to counter political violence in Xinjiang dramatically changed since 1990 and shifted overwhelmingly down the spectrum of violence in favour of a bottom-up approach. Probably a mix of human informants – either tipsters or infiltrators, China's legendary full-court press to monitor all electronic communications in the country (Beiser 2010) – and alert officials enabled the police and security services to act against these reported camps, plots and cells before they could strike. When bombers eluded the dragnet in August 2008, the military crackdown prominent Western-based dissidents publicly predicted failed to materialize. In defence of Western-based dissidents, most have resided in the West for at least a decade and their impressions of China's security activity in Xinjiang formed when brutal force was a faster default.

At first China employed brutal force as the primary tool to manage incidents because force was the single effective tool in the state's kit, yet over time the state added to its repertoire less deadly and more nuanced security tactics as well as more effective social tools. The military's role transformed from leading the charge against unrest to supporting – at first visibly and then fading behind the curtains – paramilitary and security forces. Increasingly capable forces at each level – national, regional and local – allowed China to push responsibility down the spectrum of violence to forces increasingly capable of adjusting their preparations to local conditions and responses to an incident's specific demands.

Military and security forces can kill or capture insurgents, hypothetically removing troublesome elites from the battle-space or these same tools can coerce society into recalculating, rethinking, re-perceiving the situation's balance of risks and rewards. Counterterrorism almost by its nature draws security forces at first into a capture/kill mind-trap: if only you could catch the bomb-maker/remove the operational commander the group would seemingly crumble. While some terrorist groups might implode without key members, most will not. China's campaign began as an effort against troublesome elites and, if one were to consider the continued demonization of prominent political dissidents as orchestrating or instigating unrest and terrorism from abroad, then perhaps at least some elements of China's security apparatus remain locked in this mental-trap (e.g. Ramzy 2010). This same scapegoating could also be seen as an instrumental attempt to isolate China from international pressure on what it considers its internal affairs, at the same time casting blame abroad for fundamentally internal problems. The problem then becomes that some officials might begin to believe their own rhetoric and misdiagnose the fundamental problems with which they must ultimately deal.

China's counterterrorism campaign in Xinjiang began as an effort to remove troublesome elites yet the country's approach quickly evolved into targeting society's support for insurgency. Even as Chinese police disrupt successive terrorist plots and networks, and capture or kill leaders and operatives, regional officials announce increased economic development and orchestrate counter-messaging campaigns, which gain varying degrees of traction in society. China dampens and suppresses society's support for insurgency through pressure.

Military and paramilitary forces are augmented, Uyghur residents assert, by the massive influx of ethnic Han from China's east that now probably constitute nearly 50 per cent of Xinjiang's population. Perhaps partially by design and part by default, across two decades, the force-mix in Xinjiang shifted from military to paramilitary and local security forces as the state professionalized and created new instruments of power, new instruments down the spectrum of violence and more capable of legitimately, or at least tolerably, interfacing with local society – in part due to increased local membership, and local knowledge, in these services.

As insurgency is violent politics, we must move past the myopic focus on the violence and see the political struggle as well. China found itself under increasing threat from the ideas of insurgency that had infiltrated the Party-state's points of connection in society. These reportedly included local Party, government, educational and religious institutions. Local institutions are often the sole point of actual interface between society and government, and brief interactions even of single individuals can carry ripples of perception of the state's nature and future nonlinearly and far out through society. In many insurgencies the state's position is also undercut by the combination of systemic corruption or simple incompetence hobbling effective interaction with society, a function needed to ultimately provide society that vision for a viable and convincing future path with the state and without actioned doubt.

China – under Wang Lequan's leadership – re-examined and reconstructed grassroots Party, government and security institutions, and pressed outwards. Focused on the insurgency's true ideational core, China strategically turned the social institutions of family, friendship, work-group and neighbourhood into counterinsurgency tools. A generation of educated Uyghurs has entered governance along with highly educated and less paramountly ideological Han, and these officials and institutions began the long slog of professionalizing an expansive and far-reaching bureaucracy at all levels. The Party-state enticed and coerced social and work units to manage responsibility for members, police themselves in concert with the authorities: families for their sons and fathers; work-groups like schools or factories for their workers. By understanding society's structure, the Party-state established and maintained pressure on the nascent insurgency and thus far has kept Xinjiang's society from being set alight.

Long-term stability will depend on the degree to which China is able to craft, sell and deliver a positive vision of the future for Xinjiang's society – a daily and local struggle waged not only, or even principally, by security forces but by educational, religious and cultural, economic, and governance policies. Together these elements reshape society's perceptions of state and insurgent power and shape society's hopes for the future, one intertwined with the state.

A functioning educational system provides the structure and much of the informational content society uses to filter their contemporary civic world. In Xinjiang, schooling presents a pathway up and out of villages and towns, and for some out of the region. Uyghur language curriculum is available in some schools, yet Uyghur families increasingly select Han language (*Hanyu*, also known as Mandarin) schooling and even extra-curricular English for their children to pursue college and business. Like Uyghurs entering the security forces, Uyghurs teach in Xinjiang's elementary and high schools, presenting the state's curriculum at times in the Uyghur language.[2] The Party-state jealously guards two subjects in particular because of their political import, their ability to shape and reshape society's perceptions and people's understanding of their lives within the broader context of human experience and meaning: history and international affairs.

History, when taught in a state school, directly combats the insurgency's narrative of where society has been and where it is going. International affairs, when unfiltered by the state, are potentially contagious. Every society is in many ways a historically unique entity unto itself, its own structures, dynamics, tolerances and dreams; nevertheless, tactics and local society's understanding of the fortunes of similar struggles abroad at key moments can seep and flood in. For example, while Uyghur society generally thus far has rejected the models of Chechnya, Gaza or Iraq for Xinjiang, Urumqi's July 2009 ethnic unrest echoed the protests rocking Tehran earlier in 2009, thousands taking to the street in protest, demanding the government deliver justice promised and denied.

The Party-state's religious and cultural policy in Xinjiang aimed to remove what the state considered political content and political challenge, and not necessarily aimed at blocking the average Uyghur's pursuit of spiritual enlightenment. China trained imams, banned unauthorized gatherings, and the regime leveraged informants and spies to enforce its rules. Uyghur officials and social leaders are pressured to not publicly worship. Perhaps unique to China's heavy-hand, people over 18 are allowed to study and worship openly, relatively freely, in sanctioned gatherings that the government could monitor, should it so choose. If cast in a more positive light, China's actions countered support for one vision of political Islam, the one that yearns for a caliphate, by removing radical voices and empowering moderate ones.

Economic development – the government's go-to answer for all of Xinjiang's problems – probably was never, nor is it now, a crucial element in countering the insurgency. The government has doubled-down on this public strategy, perhaps believing it in earnest, and is pursuing 'leapfrog development' in Xinjiang, designed to rapidly advance the region's standards of living and alleviate any economic-disparity causes for unrest (Xinhua 2010). Historically, the

Party-state's economic policies built animus: tangibly showing the state's power to build roads, skyscrapers and pipelines through the deserts, yet having little perceived benefit for Uyghur residents, making society's vulnerability more salient.

Governance policies, the final element in China's project to reshape society, enabled higher numbers and, most importantly, more educated Uyghur cadres to enter local and regional leadership posts. China has continued its project to bring more capable, less corrupt, socially knowledgeable cadres into leadership posts who can interface with society, represent society's needs and the state's demands. People across China, including society in Xinjiang, dream of a future where local tyrants are no longer unchecked. The task remains for the Chinese state on a daily basis to ensure the path to this dream runs through the state.

Xinjiang's society today seems to anticipate a change in the nature of the Chinese state itself. Why support an insurgency that could unleash violent chaos, harsh Islamist dictates or increased state repression? Tyrannical government today can be suffered, at times challenged, to provide increased justice and minimal – if not equal – rights: just look at the freedoms of eastern China; witness the coloured revolutions of Central Asia.

China's society-centric approach has to date suppressed Xinjiang's nascent insurgency by acting early and comprehensively. Needlessly brutal measures wasted state energy and alienated potential allies, yet the counterinsurgents gained traction when China focused on responsibly interacting with Xinjiang's society. The idea of insurgency, the dream of evicting the Han in favour of a new caliphate, has not disappeared. Insurgency episodically reappears when it perceives the state weakening, when it sees an opportunity or vulnerability.

The counterinsurgency too continues to evolve. Rather than focusing myopically on killing and capturing what inevitably turns into an ever expanding pool of terrorists, instead defining the struggle as a battle for the hopes and soul of society, and building and then refining security, governance and social tools, China increased the campaign's effectiveness. China focused on the political nature of the threat. As governments internationally confront al-Qaeda – less an organization than a cause, a movement unified by the dream of avenging Islam's dignity through bloodshed (e.g. Hoffman 2006) – they would do well to take a new critical look at China's war on terrorism.

Notes

1 Disclaimer: the ideas and opinions in the chapter are the author's alone and in no way represent the US government.
2 In an action reminiscent of the French headscarf controversy or more dated debates in Turkey, since 2000 Uyghur language education has been curtailed at the university level, being currently allowed only for courses in which the language is deemed directly necessary (such as Xinjiang's history). Restrictions on beards and clothing also follow this pattern of forced acculturation as well.

Recommended readings

Lattimore, Owen (1975, 1995) *The Desert Road to Turkestan*. New York: Kodansha International.
Lilley, James and Jeffrey Lilley (2004) *China Hands: Nine Decades of Adventure, Espionage, and Diplomacy in Asia*. New York: Public Affairs.
Millward, James A. (2007) *Eurasian Crossroads: A History of Xinjiang*. New York: Columbia University Press.
Starr, S. Frederick (ed.) (2004) *Xinjiang: China's Muslim Borderland*. Armonk: M.E. Sharp.
Wayne, Martin I. (2008) *China's War on Terrorism: Counter-insurgency, Politics and Internal Security*. New York: Routledge.
Zhao, Suisheng (2004) *A Nation-State by Construction: Dynamics of Modern Chinese Nationalism*. Stanford: Stanford University Press.

References

Anna, Cara (2010) 'China Installs Security Cameras in Xinjiang as Anniversary of Riots Nears', *Washington Post*, 3 July, p. A20.

AFP (2008) 'Months Later, Xinjiang "Terror" Raid Remains a Mystery', 7 April, afp.google.com.

BBC (2009) 'Trials Due Over Xinjiang Riots', 24 August. Available at: news.bbc.co.uk/2/hi/8217427.stm.

BBC (2010) 'Blast Kills Seven in China's Xinjiang', 19 August. Available at: www.bbc.co.uk/news/world-asia-pacific-11021645.

Beiser, Vince (November 2010) 'Over, Under, and Through', *Wired*.

Branigan, Tania and Associated Press (2009) 'China Denise 10,000 Have Disappeared', 30 July. Available at: guardian.co.uk.

Cha, Ariana Eunjung (2009) 'Death Toll Debated in China's Rioting', *Washington Post*, 11 July, p. A8.

Cha, Ariana Eunjng (2009) 'China Unrest Tied to Labor Program', *Washington Post*, 15 July, p. A9.

Chinese Communist Party, author unknown (2005) *Zhongguo Gongchandang Yu Xinjiang Minzu Wenti* (The Chinese Communist Party's Xinjiang Ethnic-Minority Problem).

Dillon, Michael (2004) *Xinjiang—China's Muslim Far Northwest*. London: Routledge Curzon.

Eturbonews.com (2008) 'Airline Crew Thwarted Hijack Bid', 9 March. Available at: www.eturbonews.com/1634/airline-crew-thwarted-china-hijack-bid.

Gladney, Dru (2002) 'Xinjiang: China's West Bank?', *Current History*, 106 (656).

Hassan, Hassan (2010) 'Revealed: The Plot to Blow Up Dragon Mart', 8 July. Available at: www.thenational.ae.

Haq, Abdul (3/26/2009) 'Turkistan Islamic Party Magazine', Interview with Turkistan Islamic Party Amir Abdul Haq, 26 March.

Hoffman, Bruce (2006) *Inside Terrorism*. New York: Columbia University Press.

Human Rights Watch (2006) *Human Rights Watch World Report 2006*. 18 January. Available at: www.hrw.org.

Human Rights Watch (2005) 'Essential Background Overview of Human Rights Issues in China', 31 December. Available at: www.hrw.org.

Islamabad Jinnah (2008) 'Separation Movement in Xinjiang and Chinese Ambassador's Warning', *Islamabad Jinnah*, 28 April, P10.

Kahn, Joseph (2005) 'Torture is "Widespread" in China, U.N. Investigator Says', *The New York Times*, 3 December.

Kan, Shirley A. (2006) 'U.S.-China Counterterrorism Cooperation: Issues for U.S. Policy', Congressional Research Service, The Library of Congress, 27 June.

Millward, James (2004) 'Violent Separatism in Xinjiang: A Critical Assessment', East-West Center, Washington, DC.

People's Daily (2002) 'FM Spokesman: ETIM a Wholly Terrorist Organization', 13 September.

People's Republic of China (2002) 'East Turkistan Terrorist Forces Cannot Get Away with Impunity', Information Office of State Council, 21 January.

People's Republic of China (2003) 'China's National Defense in 2002'. Available at: news.xinhuanet.com.

People's Republic of China, Information Office of the State Council (2004) 'China's National Defense in 2004', 27 December. Available at: www.fas.org.

People's Republic of China, Information Office of the State Council (2006) 'China's National Defense in 2006', 31 December. Available through Xinhua.

Ramzy, Austin (2010) 'A Year after Xinjiang Riots, Tensions Remain High', 7 May. Available at: www.Time.com.

Tenet, George (2007) *At the Center of the Storm*. New York: HarperCollins.

Turkestan Islamic Party (2008) 'Turkistan Islamic Party In Action', 26 June. Video posted on www.Youtube.com.

United States Department of State (2004) *Patterns of Global Terrorism 2003*.

Wayne, Martin I. (2007a) 'Al Qaeda's China Problem', *PacNet* 8A, CSIS, 23 February.

Wayne, Martin I. (2007b) 'Five Lessons from China's War on Terrorism', *Joint Force Quarterly* (October): 42.

Wong, Edward (2009) 'Doubt Arises in Account of an Attack in China: Tourists' Claims Challenge Official Details', *New York Times*, 29 September, pp. A5, A8.

Xinhua (2003) 'Role of Xinjiang Production, Construction Corps Important: White Paper', 26 May.

Xinhua (2008) 'China Identifies 8 Alleged "Eastern Turkistan" Terrorists', 21 October.

Xinhua (2010) 'Efforts to Boost "Leapfrog Development" in Xinjiang', 5 July. Available at: www.chinad-aily.com.cn/china/2010–07/05/content_10058467.htm.

Yahya al-Libi, Abu (2009) 'East Turkestan: The Forgotten Wound', al-Sahab Media Center, al-Fajr, thesis. haveford.edu, 10 July.

28

SOUTH AFRICAN COUNTERINSURGENCY

A historiographical overview

Abel Esterhuyse

The most outstanding feature of the historiography of the South African counterinsurgency campaign between 1966 and 1989 is that very little indeed has been written about South African counterinsurgency. Most publications about the South African military at the time focus either on the nature of the military or on the war in Namibia and Angola in general. At the same time, writers have been very careful to write about the role of the South African military in the counterrevolutionary campaign against the African National Congress (ANC) and other revolutionary movements within South Africa (SA) at the time. It is possible to argue that this is a reflection of changing political sentiments within South Africa. However, a whole range of factors, as would be clear from this discussion, are influencing this reality.

In the analysis of the South African counterinsurgency campaign, it is important to take note of what has been written by those 'on the other side of the hill'. Very little has been written by the revolutionary forces that opposed the South African security forces at the time. What has been written 'on the other side of the hill' predominantly captures the experiences of the Russians and Cubans in support of the revolutionary armed forces and does not necessarily focus on the insurgency approaches, doctrine and techniques of the revolutionaries. The counterinsurgency of the South African Defence Force between 1966 and 1989 was directed predominantly against South West Africa People's Organisation (SWAPO) and its People's Liberation Army of Namibia (PLAN) in the case of Namibia and, in the case of South Africa, the ANC with its armed wing Umkhonto we Sizwe (or MK) and the Pan Africanist Congress (PAC) with its armed wing the Azanian People's Liberation Army (APLA). Very little material is available from these forces about the military struggle against the apartheid forces.

The words 'terrorists' and 'revolutionaries' are often in the eyes of the beholder and the fact that the ANC and SWAPO are governing South Africa and Namibia respectively after democratisation makes the use of these terms even more controversial. This chapter focuses on the South African counterinsurgency effort between 1966 and 1990 exclusively, and the terminology is used as it was used by the South African military at the time. In some cases, reference is made to publications from the revolutionary side of the conflict. These publications are mentioned only if they contribute to an understanding of the South African counterinsurgency effort.

What influences the writing and debate?

Objectivity is an almost unattainable goal for social scientists in general and historians and political scientists in particular. Searching for the truth in a counterinsurgency campaign in which both the insurgents and the counterinsurgents were operating in a cloud of ideology and where they deliberately tried to undermine the truth in an effort to manage perceptions about the so-called threat and support for the war effort represent a real challenge. Applying Leopold von Ranke's idea of 'bloss zeigen, wie es eigentlich gewesen' (simply show how it actually was) is simply impossible in the case of the South African counterinsurgency effort in South West Africa/Namibia and South Africa (Van Jaarsveld 1982: 74). Consequently, a comprehensive understanding of the South African counterinsurgency approach requires a broad effort to gain insight into the ideological, political, strategic, operational and tactical dimensions of the war.

Writing about South African counterinsurgency, just like the unfolding of the counterinsurgency campaign between 1966 and 1994, is influenced, shaped and sometimes even dominated by three very particular considerations. The first factor is of a political nature and rooted in the harsh, often ideological, realities of the unfolding political landscape of the time. From an international and global perspective, the Cold War played itself out in southern Africa and had a defining influence on the ideological, political and military involvement of China, the former Soviet Union and Cuba in support of a variety of revolutionary organisations on the one hand, and the subtle indirect support of the West, particularly Britain and the United States, and the crumbling white-dominated states in southern Africa in general and South Africa in particular, on the other. At a continental level, it was a time of de-colonisation in Africa, and most of the wars in Southern Africa were seen, at least by the revolutionary movements, as wars of 'national liberation'. At a national level, the apartheid ideology and subsequent policies reached its apex in South Africa in the 1960s and 1970s.

In the same way that there is more to war than warfare, it is important to understand that, within the ideological context of the Cold War and de-colonisation, there was more to apartheid in South Africa than segregation and racism. Writing about South African counterinsurgency is, thus, often shaped by questions about a particular author's position and nuanced understanding of the Cold War, de-colonisation and apartheid ideologies in Africa in general and southern Africa in particular. The influence of this factor is vividly demonstrated through Chester Crocker's view that, in Angola, the United States finally managed to 'win the Cold War in the Third World' (Crocker 1992: 17). This view was countered by Shubin and Tokarev with questions such as 'Who rules Namibia (currently): SWAPO or the Democratic Turnhalle Alliance (DTA)? Who becomes the President of Angola: Dos Santos or Savimbi? And who became the first President of democratic South Africa: Mandela or Buthelezi?' (Shubin and Tokarev 2001: 607)

A second factor that shaped South African counterinsurgency, and therefore also writing about the counterinsurgency, is of a strategic nature and concerns the South African strategic choices at the time. More specifically, the South African military made a (not necessarily deliberate) strategic choice to focus its military *Schwerpunkt* in Namibia and to leave the domestic South African situation largely for the police to deal with. This strategic reality was underpinned by a number of considerations. Most important was the nature of the perceived ANC-driven threat to apartheid South Africa. The ANC's strategic approach was based on urban mass action by millions of South Africans through the trade unions, the United Democratic Front (UDF), the Mass Democratic Movement (MDM) and the thousands of individual actions and mass actions, as well as armed propaganda (O'Brien 2003: 63). And, as Anthea Jeffrey in her recently published book, *People's War: New Light on the Struggle for South Africa* (2009; also see O'Brien 2003), clearly demonstrates, the National Party government never really considered the ANC and its armed wing, Umkhonto we Sizwe, much of a military threat, or something that could not be dealt with by the South African Police. The military were therefore free to focus most of their effort on the counterinsurgency campaign in Namibia.

Of course, the war in SWA/Namibia and Angola served a number of (political) purposes for the apartheid government – besides the strategic necessity of fighting the war itself. It kept the military – the most powerful tool of the apartheid state – out of domestic politics and controversy. There was a (proud) so-called 'a-political' tradition in the South African Defence Force (SADF), meaning that politics was never discussed and that there was (supposed to be) no individual involvement in politics.[1] The truth is that no military can be un-political (in the sense of being non-political) and, as an organisation, the SADF was a key political player in SA at the time. The SADF, for example, was the key actor in the State Security Council that was seen by many as a sort of politburo of the apartheid state. One of the most controversial deeds of the De Klerk administration in the early 1990s was the 'back to barracks' message that was sent out by firing a number of SADF generals suspected of dirty tricks (Carlin 1992: 13). In the end, the military permeated every dimension of South African society. The militarisation of the South African society was indeed one of the 'success stories' of the apartheid government. The military became a power instrument admired by friend and feared by foe. In the domestic security environment, the SADF was always deployed 'in support' of the police. At the same time, though, the military was indirectly the senior partner through the mobilisation of the society at large.

In addition, the war in SWA/Namibia and Angola provided the National Party government with tangible proof that it was making progress in the war against both the so-called *swart* and *rooi gevaar* (black and red danger). The extent to which these threats were creations of the National Party government itself is still an issue of intense debate. However, even the most extreme of autocratic governments need to keep their core constituency happy. The war in SWA/Namibia and Angola was a 'clean' war for white South African constituents. In typical heroic Afrikaner tradition, mothers could watch their sons go off to fight what they considered a 'just war' (SANDF Military Archives).[2] The pre-emptive and follow-up cross-border operations in SWA/Namibia provided easy and tangible proof of the threat by highlighting dead PLAN guerrillas and captured Soviet equipment. Indeed, these tangible proofs of the threat were needed to mobilise the population or to keep them mobilised for the protracted nature of the counterinsurgency effort. Both the sense of threat and that of progress were essential elements of the SADF's internal and external warfighting efforts.

It was strategically important for the National Party political and strategic decision-makers to maintain a buffer between itself and the *swart* and *rooi gevaar*. One of the successes of the South African government's foreign policy was the extent to which it succeeded in keeping the Frontline States (FLS) from joining the fight in SWA/Namibia and Angola. This argument is rooted in the question about why the other FLS did not join the fight against the SADF forces in SWA/Namibia and Angola. To a considerable degree, the National Party government had economic leverage over these countries; some were struggling with their own internal challenges, while others, like Zimbabwe, were suffering from battle fatigue. From a South African perspective, the use of this economic leverage by the National Party government, however, was only part of the story (Potgieter 2007; Sanders 2006). For the South African government, it was strategically necessary to keep the fight against the SWAPO/Cuban/Russian forces in Angola from physically linking up with the internal fight by the ANC/PAC and others (Shubin 2008).[3] The presence of the ANC and other SA freedom fighters in Angola provided ample proof to the South African government that there was a definite possibility that the fight in northern SWA/Namibia and Angola would shift to Namibia if the SADF withdrew from SWA/Namibia and Angola. From this perspective, the war in SWA/Namibia and Angola was buying time for the National Party government in its effort to find solutions for a long list of items on the domestic political agenda.

Another key factor in the strategic focus of the South African government and its military on SWA/Namibia and Angola was the need to be strategically effective. There was a fair chance that the military could play a key role in solving the problem in SWA/Namibia and Angola. It may be argued that the SADF was indeed strategically effective in the end in creating the battlefield stalemate in Angola and the impression in the minds of the belligerent forces (SWAPO/Angola/Cuba/Russia) that they needed to talk about a political solution because there was not going to be a battlefield solution. This argument makes the debate about who won the so-called Battle of Cuito Cuanavale almost irrelevant since South Africa succeed in doing what it set itself out to do – to get the Cuban/Russian forces out of Angola as a prerequisite for Namibian independence.

Because of the South African strategic prioritisation of the Namibian counterinsurgency, that particular campaign shaped the counterinsurgency doctrine that was eventually also employed domestically against the ANC and other so-called liberation movements. True understanding of South African counterinsurgency (and this is also reflected in the writings about that strategy and doctrine) necessitates a strong focus on South African military involvement in Namibia.

A third factor that influences the writing and the professional and scholarly debate about South African counterinsurgency is the South African conventional military support for *União Nacional para a Independência Total de Angola* (UNITA) in the Angolan Civil War. South Africa, together with Zaire, CIA advisers and the forces of the Front for the National Liberation of Angola (FNLA), intervened in the Angolan Civil War for the first time in 1975. This intervention, known in South Africa as Operation Savannah, ended when South Africa withdrew its forces in 1976. Yet, by the mid 1980s, the South African military was sucked into the mud pool of the Angolan Civil War for the second time. South African operational and US equipment support for UNITA against the Cuban and Soviet-supported *Movimento Popular de Libertação de Angola* (MPLA) forces in Angola resulted in the fiercest conventional battles on the African continent since the Second World War.

Many of the authors, defence analysts and scholars writing about the South African military involvement in SWA/Namibia and Angola failed to distinguish between the South African counterinsurgency war against SWAPO within SWA/Namibia that sometimes led to pre-emptive operations into Angola on the one hand, and the South African conventional military support to UNITA against the combined MPLA, Cuban and Soviet forces in southeast Angola, on the other. This oversight often directs the analysis of the counterinsurgency campaign and doctrine. It leads to an overemphasis on the military dimensions of the counterinsurgency doctrine to the detriment of the often-successful non-military dimensions of the counterinsurgency campaign in Namibia (De Visser 2010). The oversight also meant that the debate about who won the so-called Battle of Cuito Cuanavale that shaped the outcome of the Angolan Civil War became a metaphor for the success (or failure) of the South African counterinsurgency in SWA/Namibia (Labuschagne 2009). The support of the South African ANC government for the view of the so-called destruction of the apartheid forces at Cuito Cuanavale reiterates this particular view (Sithole n.d.).

Who is writing, why are they writing and what are they writing about?

Widely divergent reasons underpin the motivation of individuals from different backgrounds who write about the South African counterinsurgency effort in SWA/Namibia and South

Africa. And since they are writing for different reasons, the quality of research and writing differs substantially. Often those who write are not interested in quality research but are only concerned about sharing their own experiences of the war, or trying to justify their role in the conflict. Others are still living with the legacy of the ideological indoctrination of the time of the war and are interested in highlighting the 'true' nature of the threat and the righteous nature of their actions.

Consequently, serious researchers are often confronted with at least two widely divergent views about a particular issue in the war: those who viewed Soviet and Cuban influence in southern Africa as the real threat versus those who see the total onslaught ideology of the apartheid state as a myth. In the case of the latter, the Soviet-Cuban presence in Angola and support for the liberation movements is portrayed as a reaction to South African destabilisation in the region. Any reading about the war, therefore, necessitates an in-depth search and understanding of the motivations of the different authors. This is true of the writings of both the insurgent and the counterinsurgent-oriented authors. This particular issue highlights the need for a comprehensive history of South African counterinsurgency by scholars who are preferably not linked to any of the belligerent groupings of the South African wars from the 1960s to the 1980s. More than 20 years after South Africa had withdrawn from Namibia and 15 years after the 1994 democratisation in South Africa such studies have yet to be done.

It is possible to distinguish between at least three groups of individuals who write about South African counterinsurgency in SWA/Namibia and South Africa. As is the case with most wars, the first easily identifiable group of authors are those who were in policy-making and strategic decision-making positions at the time. In most cases, they are writing to justify not only the war but also their own decisions and actions in the war. In terms of an understanding of the South African counterinsurgency campaign, the most important publications in this regard are the books by generals Magnus Malan (2006) and Jannie Geldenhuys (1993, 2009). Both served at different times during the 1970s and 1980s as Chief of the South African Army and later as Chief of the South African Defence Force. Malan ended his career as Minister of Defence (1980–91) in the cabinet of P.W. Botha. Malan never served in any operational command and, though being respected for the institutional changes he instituted as chief of the SADF, is generally seen as a political general. One source describes him as 'a classroom general rather than a battlefield general' and someone who then 'turned into a propagandising politician' (Liebenberg *et al.* 2010: 144). Elsewhere, Malan is described as a 'uniformed technocrat turned securocrat' (Baines 2009: 314). Geldenhuys, by contrast, is generally seen as 'a soldier's general' (Liebenberg *et al.* 2010: 144). In a transforming society like South Africa, many of the primary documents that should have been in the archives have been destroyed.[4] The books by these senior military decision-makers, therefore, make an important contribution as primary sources and a holistic understanding of the counterinsurgency campaign from a South African perspective.

There is no doubt that both Malan and Geldenhuys firmly believed in the idea of the total onslaught and the *swart* and *rooi gevaar* ideologies that featured so prominently as a means of mobilisation in South Africa at the time. Indeed, Malan, first as Chief of the Army and Defence Force and later as Defence Minister, was one of the main military architects of the apartheid state. Though his book is extremely lifeless reading, it is critical in understanding the South African counterinsurgency mindset and the ideological and political thinking about the South African counterinsurgency approach. It also provides valuable insights into the institutional and technological changes of the South African military in fighting the counterinsurgency war, particularly in Namibia. It could be argued that his work falls within the heroic military historiographical tradition with his efforts to glorify the South African military endeavours during the 1970s and 1980s.

The book by Geldenhuys by contrast has a somewhat sociological approach on account of the author's efforts to speak on behalf of everyone who was part of the South African military at the time. Geldenhuys writes with honesty about his own experiences that would speak to the lieutenants and corporals who, in his view, were responsible for fighting the war. The sociological approach is clearly visible in his description of the 2007 edition of his book as a story about life and a story about people – great people who are small and small people who are great, friend and foe who have paved the way and walked the path (Geldenhuys 2007: I). Geldenhuys succeeds in providing a more insightful look of life as a general in the South African military at the time. As a general who was primarily responsible for the design and implementation of the South African counterinsurgency effort in Namibia, Geldenhuys' book ought to be read by those who are interested in the story of the South African military.

Hilton Hamann (2001), in his book *Days of the Generals*, provides an interesting overview of the minds of the South African generals, their differences, their views of South African politicians in general and politicians like Pik Botha, Roelf Meyer and F.W. de Klerk in particular, and their general dislike of the South African police. The book is based, primarily, on interviews with the most influential South African generals. As a journalist who, as a conscript, served in the South African military and often accompanied the South African forces on operations, Hamann's book is rooted in the idea that 'South Africa's new-found democracy and constitution – a constitution held up as a model – would never have been possible without the SADF' (Hamann 2001: xi).

Ending counterinsurgencies is almost as challenging as fighting them. Chester Crocker (1992) in *High Noon in South Africa: Making Peace in a Rough Neighborhood* outlines the role that the United States played in the ending of the wars in both Angola and Namibia. When read in conjunction with Vladimir Shubin's (2008) book *The Hot 'Cold War': The USSR in Southern Africa* and the book by Jannie Geldenhuys (2009) it will help the reader to develop a nuanced understanding of the intricacies involved in ending these types of conflict. Shubin was deeply involved in the support from the former Soviet Union to liberation movements in Southern Africa. His book, written from a Soviet academic perspective, offers interesting insights about the wars in southern Africa in general and Angola/Namibia in particular.

A second very interesting genre in the counterinsurgency literature is the growing number of histories 'from below' that have been published in the last couple of years. These are publications from individuals who participated in the war at a technical, tactical and, in some cases, operational level. In many cases, the authors have served as conscripts in the South African Defence Force and they are now writing about their own experiences in the war and as members of the South African military at the time. As such, the publications do not necessarily contribute to the scholarly debate about the insurgency campaign or the South African counterinsurgency doctrine. Neither are these books necessarily well researched or well written. However, they do provide some interesting sociological insights into the life of a soldier involved in counterinsurgency in general and life in the apartheid military forces in particular. Examples of this category are numerous: Paul Els (2000), Piet Nortjé (2008), Clive Holt (2008), Steven Webb (2008), David Williams (2008), Jan Breytenbach (1990, 2002) and others.

In a number of these works, the reader is confronted with honesty about the realities of counterinsurgency warfighting and a deep respect for the efforts of the insurgents (Baines n.d.). Many of the authors were motivated to write about the dismal experiences they went through in order to deal with the post-traumatic stress syndrome with which many are still struggling. Publications like *Journey without Boundaries: The Operational Life and Experiences of a SA Special Forces Small Team Operator* (Diedericks 2007; also see O'Brien 1998, 2001) and *First in Last Out: The South African Artillery in Action 1975–1988* (Wilsworth 2010) place the emphasis on a particular component of the South African military.

Two recently published books in this genre are, in my view, comparable with the well-known publication *Chickenhawk*, Robert Mason's (1984) account of his experiences as a UH-1 Iroquois helicopter pilot in Vietnam. *Buffalo Battalion, South Africa's 32 Battalion: A Tale of Sacrifice* (Bothma 2008) is a book by an Afrikaans-speaking white South African conscript who served as a platoon commander in the well-known South African 32 'foreign legion' Battalion. It is a translation of a book that was originally published in Afrikaans as *Die Buffel Struikel: 'n Storie van 32 Bataljon en sy Mense* (Bothma 2006). The book, obviously, was also not written with a military or academic audience in mind. The author describes it as a book for those people who never participated or understood South African participation in the border war in far-off Namibia, such as parents, spouses and children of those who had to fight the war. It is above all a book written to show how 'politicians can squander people in a war' (Bothma 2008: 5).

The book places 32 Battalion, one of the most controversial and renowned South African military units, under the spotlight. The author highlights the fact that the book has been written not just about the war but from a deep-rooted respect for the enemy – the SWAPO guerrillas. The aim of the book is to provide an appreciation for 32 Battalion, 'who we were, how we came together, what we learned from each other, and what happened in the bush; our fears and expectations, our tears and happiness, our camaraderie and loyalty' (Bothma 2008: 5). Readers will gain insight into the struggle of individuals, generals and colonels, captains and corporals, to make sense of a war and a history that has not always turned out to be positive for these participants. The most important contribution of the book is the insights the reader develops for the unconventional nature of unconventional war. Yet, one develops some comprehension for the uneasiness of conventional bureaucratic militaries towards an environment and a problem that requires unorthodox thinking and solutions. This is the kind of challenge with which conventional bureaucratic militaries often have to deal, but for which they are often ill prepared. 32 Battalion was indeed created in an unorthodox way by unorthodox soldiers to deal with an unorthodox environment. This is a way of thinking and doing that needs to be studied in greater depth by all bureaucratic armed forces of the world, especially by large militaries that have developed a tradition of fighting small wars badly.

19 with a Bullet (Korff 2009) is a book by a white English-speaking conscript, who served in the hard-fighting parachute battalion during the border war. Through the experiences of the author, the reader develops a grasp for the training and preparation of specialist forces deeply involved in the warfighting dimension of the counterinsurgency campaign. From a counterinsurgency perspective, the description and use of the so-called Fireforce concept and the cross-border pre-emptive operations make some very interesting reading. The books by both Bothma and Korff are of Hollywood quality. They may not necessarily make a huge contribution to an understanding of counterinsurgency but they provide an in-depth conception of the forces and people involved in such a war, their experiences and, ultimately, the effect of the war on their lives.

The Fireforce concept was closely tied to the use of airpower during the counterinsurgency campaign in Namibia. Dick Lord (2009) in his book *From Fledgling to Eagle: The South African Air Force During the Border War* provides an interesting exposition of his experiences in the airpower domain from the first 'incident' at Ongulumbashe on 26 August 1966 to the end of the counterinsurgency campaign in Namibia with the so-called 'April Fool's Day War' in 1989. Lord's book is an important contribution to the debate about the proper use (if any) of airpower in a counterinsurgency campaign. Lord was a key role-player in the South African Air Force during the border war. He received his flight training in the Royal Navy, flying Sea Venoms and Sea Vixens from the aircraft carriers Centaur, Victorious, Hermes and Ark Royal, and Hunters from the naval air stations at Lossiemouth (Scotland) and Brawdy (Wales). He also did a two-year exchange tour with the US Navy, flying A4 Skyhawks and F4 Phantoms out of San

Diego, California (Lord 2010). The value of Lord's contribution is the international perspectives that came to the fore in the discussion of airpower.

A final category of individuals writing about South African counterinsurgency comprises journalists, defence analysts and scholars who write from a more scholarly and analytical perspective and who are primarily responsible for the debate about the South African counterinsurgency. They write from different paradigms, and approach the South African military involvement in South and southern African during the 1970s and 1980s from different perspectives. In an article, and with reference to the scholarly writings about the so-called Battle of Cuito Cuanavale, Leopold Scholtz (2011) differentiates between what he calls 'non-researchers' and 'serious researchers'. There is little doubt that serious researchers are those scholars who attempt to see through the cloud of propaganda that was raised during the war and who rely predominantly on research from a South African military perspective, the South African military archives and interviews with South Africans who have actually been involved in the war on the side of the counterinsurgents to provide clarity.

Some of the earlier works that were published in this regard were by journalists and defence analysts who had served in the SADF or who were very well connected with the apartheid military. Elsewhere, they are described as 'partially embedded' (Liebenberg *et al.* 2010: 136). The best known in this regard are journalist and author Willem Steenkamp (1983, 1989) and defence analyst Helmoed-Römer Heitman (1985, 1990a, 1990b; Heitman and Hannon 1991). Non-South Africans who fall into this category are probably Francis Toase (1987), Paul Moorcraft (1990) and Fred Bridgland (1990). These authors often provide an insider's view on account of their connections with the apartheid military establishment. They had access to the operational area, the opportunity to interview commanders and eye-witnesses, and often accompanied the South African military on operations. They also had close links with the news media in South Africa and elsewhere and access to the military archives in Pretoria. Some may not have been as closely connected, but were also writing from an insider South African perspective.

In *The Military in the Making of Modern South Africa*, Annette Seegers (1996) provides a thorough analysis of the role of the military in the developments in South Africa. The book does not necessarily address counterinsurgency and also covers a much wider timeframe than the counterinsurgency campaigns of the 1960s, 1970s and 1980s. The book, although somewhat unsystematic, is relatively well researched and provides an in-depth analysis of the South African military from the creation of the Union in 1910 to democratisation in 1994. It should be read in conjunction with Chris Alden's (1996) book *Apartheid's Last Stand: The Rise and Fall of the South African Security State*. Alden presents a detailed analysis of the operationalisation of apartheid through André Beaufre's ideas of a total strategy and total onslaught and John J. McCuen's ideas on a counterrevolutionary strategy. Of particular importance is Alden's analysis of the so-called National Security Management System that formed an integral part, if not the most important pillar, of the domestic counterrevolutionary campaign of the South African government.

More recently, academics from across the ideological and political spectrum in South Africa have shown renewed interest in the border war, though not necessarily the South African counterinsurgency approach. Recently published articles in journals such as *Scientia Militaria*, *South African Journal of Military Studies* and the *Journal of Contemporary History* confirm this trend (editions 2006 [31 (3)] and 2009 [34 (1)] in particular). The articles in these journals are generally well researched and cover a wide variety of perspectives on South African counterinsurgency. The article by Leopold Scholtz (2006) in *Scientia Militaria* titled 'The Namibian Border War: An Appraisal of the South African Strategy', for example, is a good overview of the counterinsurgency campaign in Namibia. In addition, graduate students are also increasingly examining the

South African counterinsurgency effort or dimensions thereof in their studies (Van der Merwe 1985; Veldthuizen 1994; Labuschagne 2009; De Visser 2010). One such study by a senior SADF operational commander on the so-called Cassinga Raid led to a heated debate amongst former SADF commanders about the nature of the raid and their roles in the operation (Alexander 2003; Baines 2007).

Conclusion

Within South Africa, all official interest in counterinsurgency came to an end with democratisation and the 1994 rise to power of the African National Congress. The idea that South Africa may face a low-intensity threat in future did not feature in the ideological framework of the ANC in the period after it came to power. Ten years after the 1994 political transition the ANC government has found itself faced with the appearance of international terrorism and an increase in transnational organised crime; in addition it has also been hampered by escalating service delivery problems and a return of domestic civil unrest. The government and security services in particular have thus realised that such an effective counterinsurgency and counter-terrorist capacity is an indispensable part of contemporary Third World security governance – and after 9/11 even in the developed First World. The South African military, unfortunately, lost most of its counterinsurgency institutional knowledge, specialised skills and doctrine during the 1990s. No deliberate effort was made within the South African security sector to learn from both the insurgents and the counterinsurgents through an institutional process that could have culminated in a very refined insurgency/counterinsurgency doctrine (depending on who the South Africans may have to fight) (Gossman 2008; Baker and Jordaan 2010). As a result, there is at present renewed interest from the security sector in both insurgency and counterinsurgency.

One of the most outstanding features of South African counterinsurgency is the absolute lack of comprehensive studies in the vein of Jakkie Cilliers' (1982, 1984) study about the Rhodesian counterinsurgency campaign. Due to political changes in the country and driven by a need for political correctness in the scholarly community, no official studies were conducted in the aftermath of the insurgency and counterinsurgency campaigns of the 1960s to the late 1980s. Those interested in South African insurgency or counterinsurgency search in vain for a book containing a comprehensive treatment of the topic. It is really only possible at present to develop an understanding of South African counterinsurgency by reading a host of articles and books that are dealing with the topic as part of a broader discussion of either the South African military at the time or of the war in general. Thus, South African counterinsurgency is, in essence, a target-rich environment for scholars interested in serious primary research on insurgency/counterinsurgency.

Notes

1 The irony was that some of the most senior SADF members did enter politics, albeit after resignation from the military. The most obvious example in this regard is Gen. M.A. de Malan who resigned as chief of the SADF in order to take up the position of Minister of Defence. In this way, the SADF was catapulted into the heart of apartheid governmental decision-making, i.e. militarising the political discourse about the military and politicising the military organisationally.

2 In one of the after-action reports on Operation Protea in 1981, two sections were set aside for a discussion of 'oorwinning 'n tradisie' (winning a tradition) and the 'profiel van 'n wenner' (profile of a winner). This discussion draws on the South African participation in the First and Second World Wars to underline the justness and success in Operation Protea as 'die voortsetting van   trotse militêre tradi-

sie eie aan die lewensuitkyk van die Suid-Afrikaanse soldaat' (the continuation of a proud military tradition unique to the worldview of the South African soldier).

3 There is no doubt that the threat of communism was real and that South Africa was part of a broader Soviet strategy to expand its control over the mineral riches of southern Africa and its influence in Africa. That explains to some extent the policy of constructive engagement by the United States and the positive stance of some European governments towards apartheid South Africa – France and the UK in particular. The book by Vladimir Shubin provides an interesting exposition of the involvement of the former Soviet Union in southern Africa.

4 In a discussion on the South African military archives during the 2008 XXXIII International Congress of the Society of Military History in Cape Town it came to the fore that certain documents have been removed from the military archives in the period just before the 1948 takeover in 1948 and the transition to democracy in 1994.

Recommended readings

Alden, C. (1996) *Apartheid's Last Stand: The Rise and Fall of the South African Security State*. London: Macmillan Press.

Baker, D. and Jordaan, E. (eds) (2010) *South Africa and Contemporary Counterinsurgency: Roots, Practices, Prospects*. Claremont: UCT.

Bridgland, F. (1990) *The War for Africa: Twelve Months that Transformed a Continent*. Gibraltar: Ashanti Publishers.

Crocker, C. (1992) *High Noon in South Africa: Making Peace in a Rough Neighborhood*. Parklands: Jonathan Ball.

Gossmann, A. (2008) 'Lost in Transition: The South African Military and Counterinsurgency', *Small Wars & Insurgencies*, 19 (4): 541–72.

Jeffrey, A. (2009) *People's War: New Light on the Struggle for South Africa*. Johannesburg: Jonathan Ball.

Moorcraft, P.L. (1990) *African Nemesis: War and Revolution in Southern Africa, 1945–2010*. London: Brassey's.

O'Brien, K.A. (2003) 'A Blunted Spear: The Failure of the African National Congress/South African Communist Party Revolutionary War Strategy 1961–1990', *Small Wars and Insurgencies*, 14 (2): 63.

Seegers, A. (1996) *The Military in the Making of Modern South Africa*. London: Tauris.

References

Alden, C. (1996) *Apartheid's Last Stand: The Rise and Fall of the South African Security State*. London: Macmillan Press.

Alexander, E.G.M. (2003) *The Cassinga Raid*. Pretoria: University of South Africa. Unpublished MA thesis.

Baines, G. (n.d.) *Breaking Rank: Secrets, Silences and Stories of South Africa's Border War*. Available at: www.inter-disciplinary.net/ptb/wvw/wvw4/baines%20paper.pdf (accessed 20 February 2011).

Baines, G. (2007) *The Battle for Cassinga: Conflicting Narratives and Contested Meanings*. In Basler Afrika Bibliographien Seminar. 11 December 2007. Basel, Switzerland. (Unpublished). Available at: http://eprints.ru.ac.za/946/1/baines_Cassinga.pdf (accessed 1 March 2011).

Baines, G. (2009) 'The Life of a Uniformed Technocrat turned Securocrat', *Historia*, 54 (1): 314–27.

Baker, D. and Jordaan, E. (eds) (2010) *South Africa and Contemporary Counterinsurgency: Roots, Practices, Prospects*. Claremont: UCT.

Bothma, L.J. (2006) *Die Buffel Struikel: 'n Storie van 32 Bataljon en sy Mense*. Bloemfontein: Handisa.

Bothma, L.J. (2008) *Buffalo Battalion, South Africa's 32 Battalion: A Tale of Sacrifice*. Bloemfontein: Handisa.

Breytenbach, J. (1990) *They Live by the Sword*. Alberton: Lemur.

Breytenbach, J. (2002) *The Buffalo Soldiers: The Story of South Africa's 32-Battalion 1975–1993*. Alberton: Galago.

Bridgland, F. (1990) *The War for Africa: Twelve Months that Transformed a Continent*. Gibraltar: Ashanti Publishers.

Carlin, J. (1992) 'De Klerk Sacks Generals Suspected of "Dirty Tricks"', *The Independent*, 20 September.

Cilliers, C.K. (1982) *A Critique of Selected Aspects of the Rhodesian Security Forces' Counter-insurgency Strategy, 1972–1980*. Pretoria: University of South Africa. Unpublished MA thesis.

Cilliers, C.K. (1984) *Counter-Insurgency in Rhodesia*. London: Croom Helm.

Crocker, C. (1992) *High Noon in South Africa: Making Peace in a Rough Neighborhood*. Parklands: Jonathan Ball.

De Visser, L. (2010) *Winning the Hearts and Minds: Legitimacy in the Namibian Border War*. Utrecht: Utrecht University. Unpublished MA thesis.

Diedericks, A. (2007) *Journey without Boundaries: The Operational Life and Experiences of a SA Special Forces Small Team Operator*. Durban: Just Done Productions.

Els, P. (2000) *We Fear Naught but God: The Story of the South African Special Forces 'The Recces'*. Johannesburg: Covos Day.

Geldenhuys, J. (1993) *Die wat wen – 'n Generaal se Storie uit 'n Era van Oorlog en Vrede*. Pretoria: J.L. van Schaik.

Geldenhuys, J. (2007) *Dié wat gewen het: Feite en Fabels van die Bosoorlog*. Pretoria: Litera.

Geldenhuys, J. (2009) *At the Front: A General's Account of South Africa's Border War*. Jeppestown: Jonathan Ball.

Gossmann, A. (2008) 'Lost in Transition: The South African Military and Counterinsurgency', *Small Wars & Insurgencies*, 19 (4): 541–72.

Hamann, H. (2001) *Days of the Generals: The Untold Story of South Africa's Apartheid-Era Military Generals*. Cape Town: Zebra Press.

Heitman, H. (1985) *South African War Machine*. United Kingdom: Galago Publishing.

Heitman, H. (1990a) *South African Armed Forces*. Johannesburg: Buffalo Publications.

Heitman, H. (1990b) *War in Angola: The Final South African Phase*. Gibraltar: Ashanti Publishers.

Heitman, H. and Hannon, P. (1991) *Modern African Wars 3: South-West Africa*. Osprey Military Men-At-Arms Series No. 242. London: Osprey Publishing.

Holt, C. (2008) *At Thy Call We Did Not Falter*. Cape Town: Zebra Press.

Jeffrey, A. (2009) *People's War: New Light on the Struggle for South Africa*. Johannesburg: Jonathan Ball.

Journal of Contemporary History. Available at: http://humanities.ufs.ac.za/templates/journals.aspx?journal=13&DCode=147.

Korff, G. (2009) *19 with a Bullet – A South African Paratrooper in Angola*. Johannesburg: 30° South Publishers.

Labuschagne, B. (2009) *South Africa's Intervention in Angola: Before Cuito Cuanavale and Thereafter*. Stellenbosch: Stellenbosch University. Unpublished MA thesis.

Liebenberg, I., Du Plessis, T. and Van der Westhuizen, G. (2010) 'Through the Mirage: Tracing Moments of a War "up there"', *Scientia Militaria – Journal of South African Military Studies*, 2: 131–49.

Lord, D. (2009) *From Fledgling to Eagle: The South African Air Force during the Border War*. Johannesburg: 30° South Publishers.

Lord, D. (2010) *From Tailhooker to Mudmover: An Aviation Career in the Royal Naval Fleet Air Arm, United States Navy, and South African Air Force*. Johannesburg: 30° South Publishers.

Malan, M. (2006) *My Life with the South African Defence Force*. Pretoria: Protea Boekhuis. First published in Afrikaans as Malan, M. (2006) *My Lewe saam met die SA Weermag*. Pretoria: Protea Boekhuis.

Mason, R. (1984) *Chickenhawk*. Kent: Corgi.

Moorcraft, P.L. (1990) *African Nemesis: War and Revolution in Southern Africa, 1945–2010*. London: Brassey's.

Nortjé, P. (2008) *32 Battalion: The Inside Story of South Africa's Elite Fighting Unit*. Cape Town: Zebra Press.

O'Brien, K.A. (1998) 'The Use of Assassination as a Tool of State Policy: South Africa's Counter-revolutionary Strategy 1979–1992' (Parts I and II), *Terrorism and Political Violence*, 10 (3) (1998): 86–105 and 13 (2) (2001): 107–42.

O'Brien, K.A. (2003) 'A Blunted Spear: The Failure of the African National Congress/South African Communist Party Revolutionary War Strategy 1961–1990', *Small Wars and Insurgencies*, 14 (2): 7–70.

Potgieter, D.W. (2007) *Total Onslaught: Apartheid's Dirty Tricks Exposed*. Cape Town: Zebra.

Sanders, J. (2006) *Apartheid's Friends: The Rise and the Fall of South Africa's Secret Service*. London: John Murray.

SANDF Military Archives (Directorate Documentation Services), Archive Group Diverse 2, Box 78, Directorate Military Intelligence, Informasiesamevatting: Operasie Protea en die plaaslike bevolking in Suid-Angola, pp. 28–33.

Scholtz, L. (2006) 'The Namibian Border War: An Appraisal of the South African Strategy', *Scientia Militaria, South African Journal of Military Studies*, 34 (1): 19–48.

Scholtz, L. (2011) 'The Standard of Research on the Battle of Cuito Cuanavale, 1987–1988', *Scientia Militaria, South African Journal of Military Studies*, 39 (1): 115–37.

Scientia Militaria, South African Journal of Military Studies. Available at: www0.sun.ac.za/scientiamilitaria.

Seegers, A. (1996) *The Military in the Making of Modern South Africa*. London: Tauris.

Shubin, V. (2008) *The Hot 'Cold War': The USSR in Southern Africa*. London: Pluto Press.

Shubin, V. and Tokarev, A. (2001) 'War in Angola: A Soviet Dimension', *Review of the African Polical Economy*, 90: 607–18.

Sithole, J. (n.d.) *Cuba's Internationalism in Africa, 1962–1991*. Pietermaritzburg: The Freedom Park Trust.

Steenkamp, W. (1983) *Borderstrike! South Africa into Angola*. Durban: Butterworth.

Steenkamp, W. (1989) *South Africa's Border War, 1966–89*. Gibraltar: Ashanti.

Toase, F. (1987) 'The South African Army: The Campaign in South West Africa/Namibia since 1966', in I.F.W. Beckett and John Pimlott (eds), *Armed Forces and Modern Counterinsurgency*. London: Croom Helm, pp. 77–111.

Van der Merwe, J.C.K. (1985) *'n Ondersoek na aspekte van die ontstaan en verloop van die insurgensie in Ovamboland tot 1983*. Pretoria: University of South Africa. Unpublished MA thesis.

Van Jaarsveld, F.A. (1982) *Moderne Geskiedskrywing*. Durban: Butterworth.

Velthuizen, A. (1994) *Applying Military Force for Political Ends: The Case of South Africa in Southwestern Africa, 1987–1988*. Pretoria: University of South Africa. Unpublished MA thesis.

Webb, S. (2008) *Ops Medic: A National Serviceman's Border War*. Alberton: Galago.

Williams, D. (2008) *On the Border, 1965–1990: The White South African Military Experience*. Cape Town: Tafelberg.

Wilsworth, C. (2010) *First in Last Out: The South African Artillery in Action 1975–1988*. Johannesburg: 30° South Publishers.

29

INSURGENCY AND COUNTERINSURGENCY

Some conclusions

Isabelle Duyvesteyn and Paul B. Rich

What is the state of the art in the field of insurgency and counterinsurgency studies? This is the central question we posed the authors at the outset of this volume. Answering this question unavoidably leads to arguments and examples that are time and also place specific. By bringing together established scholars and some up-and-coming young thinkers, we have sought to provide the reader with an insight into what is available at present and where the challenges lie. The study has been an effort to take stock of current points of view. We asked the contributors to focus on three questions:

1 What is the state of knowledge and the accepted positions?
2 What are the topics that are currently subject of debate?
3 What are the challenges and pressing questions for future research?

The approach we have adopted in this volume is in some ways artificial. We have asked the authors to discuss insurgency and counterinsurgency separately, whereas in practice they feed off each other and are intertwined in an enduring interactive relationship. Moreover, Part II of the volume mostly focused on states rather than organizations or actors, though some authors also took a more regional approach. This of course does not fully engage with the complex and transnational nature of many insurgencies past and present. However the volume as a whole has been able to provide a general picture of the field of insurgency and counterinsurgency studies at the beginning of the twenty-first century and it is through these three general questions that we seek in this concluding chapter to provide an overall assessment of the field of study at the present time before looking forward, in the final section, to where the field might be going in the years ahead.

The state of knowledge

A number of chapters, especially that of Ian Beckett, have pointed to insurgency's long historical roots. Beckett argues that we should see insurgency as deriving from an elevation of traditional hit-and-run tactics to a strategy in its own right by adding political, social and environmental factors at the start of the twentieth century. As discussed in the introduction, this is one of several ways of conceptualizing insurgency. Increasingly prominent, especially in the American literature, seems to be a conceptualization of insurgency as a tactic of war, e.g. the chapter by Ucko. Geraint Hughes also concludes that the prominent instruments employed to deal with insurgency – he discusses in particular the role of intelligence, targeted killing, the use of special forces and air strikes – all amount to tactical rather than strategic effect. Steven Metz, on the contrary, presents an argument in the volume to see counterinsurgency primarily as strategy.

Despite these diverging insights, the study of the past remains important. Contexts have changed and questions abound about applicability of counterinsurgency ideas to current day exigencies, the past remains about the only source we have available for inspiration. As Chin notes, 'you cannot fight insurgents today in the same way you fought the Viet Cong, but [at the same time] … most insurgencies follow a similar course of development and consequently the past remains and important source of learning'.

A common thread in almost all chapters is the centrality of the political challenge in insurgencies. Insurgencies can arise out of a lack of effective governance, security and lack of political access. An important differentiation can be made between internal and external insurgency; in the case of India, the indivisibility of the stakes, secession from the Union, could not be negotiated, leading, according to Fidler and Ganguly, to a certain extent to a deterrent effect for other militant groups. The price to pay to achieve the goal of independence became extremely high. It led most groups to fall apart and revert to crime in order to assure survival. The political challenge was recognized by the state and translated into more autonomy, the creation of new provinces and federated states, improvements in governance and security structures, elections, social and economic development.

Insurgency is also a social phenomenon and therefore a product of the society from which it derives. William Reno argues in his chapter that African insurgencies even mirror the governments against which their main actions were directed. He distinguishes two ideal types of insurgency: a hierarchical Maoist variant and a network type of insurgency. Their individual logic they largely derive from the context in which they are formed and carried out. In a hierarchical Maoist variant, conducted in many post-colonial states, the insurgents aim at building up a shadow government in preparation for an eventual takeover of power. In the network variant, displayed in a patronage predatory state, the access to resources and economic opportunity is used as a means of population control. Challengers in the Maoist variant need to have developed some measure of social autonomy for an ideologically infused struggle. While in the network-centric insurgency, the challengers almost exclusively come from the ruling circles themselves.

An important feature of many of the insurgencies dealt with in this volume concerns the prevalence of a shadow government, not only in the cases of India, Hezbollah and Hamas, but also Iraq and Afghanistan. This could be interpreted as a sign of the strategic nature of insurgency, rather than the tactical. This organizational feature makes it stand out from other expressions of political violence, such as terrorism (see also Duyvesteyn and Fumerton 2009). The latter, because of its secretive nature, does not invest in building up structures capable of taking over political power and responsibility. In the cases of the Taliban in Afghanistan and Pakistan, the insurgencies in the Punjab, Assam, Nagaland and Manipur in India but also in the cases of Hamas and Hezbollah, the chapters conclude that these organizational structures help in attaining some measure of legitimacy for the insurgents. The existence of a shadow government or state-like structures could place these insurgents in the category of Maoist rather than the post-Maoist variant, as discussed in the introduction.

When insurgency is seen as a social phenomenon, it changes with its environment. Developments in information technology have provided a new dimension to current insurgencies, as they have changed society in which they gestate. David Betz notes that 'as the organizing principles of human society have changed with technological development, above all in the range, forms and velocity of communications, so too has changed the pattern of warfare generally and the character of insurgency specifically'.

It has also been confirmed in the cases under consideration in this volume that the role of neighbouring states as facilitators and safe havens can act as a catalyst for insurgencies (Record 2007; Staniland 2005–6). The role of Pakistan is of paramount importance to understand the Taliban insurgency in Afghanistan and the many insurgencies in India. Iran is crucial to Hezbollah and Hamas. In fact, Antonio Giustozzi in his contribution notes that the raising of the backbone of the insurgent cadres in Pakistan has enabled the Taliban to continue and expand its struggle over the past few years within Afghanistan. Cutting off supply lines from abroad formed the key to success in defeating the Tamil Tigers, according to David Lewis. Namrata Goswami argues along similar lines for the cases of insurgency within India's borders.

As with insurgency, counterinsurgencies also possess long historical roots. Despite the reluctance among Western militaries to deal with counterinsurgency, academic interest in the subject, while steady over the course of the twentieth century, has risen steeply over the last few years. As the introduction pointed out, much modern counterinsurgency can be traced back to debates over the management of 'small wars' in nineteenth-century European empires. Beckett in his chapter also notes that one of the problems with historical approaches to counterinsurgency is the widespread temptation to generalize from a very limited number of cases. Kilcullen also reinforces this in his chapter when he points to the evolution of counterinsurgency in the United States in the early 1960s on the basis of a very narrow range of colonial counterinsurgencies. Both authors in fact go as far as questioning whether the comparison of the Malaya and Vietnam cases has not been exhausted. The use of the 'lessons' of Malaya, which are quite prominent among others in the latest American Counterinsurgency Manual FM 3–24, might in fact stretch their utility. There is a dominant stream in the literature about the role of 'hearts and minds'. Almost elevated to law in the American doctrine, the support of the population is seen as a sine qua non for successful insurgency and counterinsurgency. It forms the central battleground and the essence of the strategy employed in Afghanistan in the past few years. Giustozzi, however, sceptically writes that the implementation of the hearts and minds strategy turned out to be difficult to realize against an opponent excelling in adaptation and fluidity.

Furthermore, Alice Hills contends in this volume 'support [of the population] may be achieved by coercion, rather than conviction'. Elsewhere, Paul Dixon and Huw Bennett have shown that the Malaya case has been successful because of – and not despite of – the use of coercion and force, rather than the acclaimed hearts and minds idea (Dixon 2009; Bennett 2009). These ideas go against the prevalent recipe about how to conduct a successful counterinsurgency today. They might also go against the fundaments of ethics, as Christopher Coker notes, to not undertake any action in war that makes subsequent peace impossible. Nevertheless, this forms an important and pressing research challenge; there is a mismatch between historical fact and counterinsurgency ideology.

The apparent consensus on the hearts and minds idea, however, runs skin deep. The case of Israeli counterinsurgency, discussed by Sergio Catignani, is also illustrative of the coercive approach. He concludes that the Israeli heavy-handed campaigns usually have the effect of temporarily halting the violence for it to reappear later in a different locale with higher intensity. The violent methods have also had the function to placate the domestic Israeli audience, showing that something is being done. Yuri Zhukov argues in the Russian case that it 'has one of the most successful track records of any modern counterinsurgent'. India but also Latin America is another case in point where the harsher forms of counterinsurgency have proven their worth. David Lewis, looking at the case of Sri Lanka, speaks of a Sri Lankan model of counterinsurgency based on attrition. Zhukov concludes that these cases have not received the academic interest they deserve. He shows that regime type matters in counterinsurgency and authoritarian regimes are more likely to use repression. In fact, he argues, the harsher the repression, the greater are the chances of success.[1]

Abel Esterhuyse shows in his chapter on South African counterinsurgency that the South African Defense Forces, while not pursuing an all-out strategy of attrition in Angola, were able to successfully create a battlefield stalemate by using purely military means. This set the stage for an eventual political solution to the Angolan problem.

Other historical cases offer supportive evidence for the value of an 'enemy-centric' approach. Missing in this volume is a specific French perspective on counterinsurgency. Treated in other studies, great French thinkers, such as Lyautey, had traditionally an eye for the effectiveness of repression. It was widely practised in French colonial conflicts and to a certain extent quite successful in stabilizing French colonial presence. The case of Algeria provides a moot point. In recent years it seems that the French record of counterinsurgency is preferably forgotten or brushed over, with some exceptions such as the publication of the controversial memoirs by Paul Assaresses about his experiences in Algeria (2005).[2]

Even in the current operations in Afghanistan, the common front when it comes to the application of the hearts and minds strategy shows painful fissures. As Geraint Hughes discusses, there are important voices, including that of Vice President Biden, who try to promote a 'counter-terrorist strategy' in which enemy-centric and attrition aspects feature more prominently.

While the discussion about the validity and application of hearts and minds ideas and population-centric operations is important, David Betz also points in his contribution to the role of the hearts and minds of the domestic audience. Not only the risk of losing the hearts and minds of the local population, but also loss of support from the domestic audience, can undermine the chances of success. Betz writes in his contribution that the latter is the 'master narrative' or the 'Leitmotif' of operations in Afghanistan. We are losing the war at home, as we did in Vietnam and Somalia, rather than on the ground in the battle theatre. Similarly, Martin Wayne stresses in his contribution that an essential element in counterinsurgency is political will. It is 'a set of deep beliefs and preferences held by society', which was available in abundance in the case of China and contributed to its success to date in Xinjiang. These ideas point to the increasing recognition that narratives and strategic communications are playing crucial roles in counterinsurgency (Freedman 2006).

Apart from the prevalence in practice of the enemy-centric approach of counterinsurgency, as opposed to the population–centric one, an important mechanism manifests itself. Many of the cases studied in this volume describe a steep learning curve for the state in counterinsurgency operations. The state starts out by using repression deliberately or by default to only later consider alternatives. Thomas Mockaitis notes that hearts and minds policies are often instituted only after a highly violent phase of conflict (see also Hack 2009). Fidler and Ganguly conclude for the Indian case that in its counterinsurgency response the security services started out with a coercive approach, with little civil–military coordination. Only subsequently were thoughts devoted to alternatives. In the case of Pakistan, as Julian Schofield argues, there was a similar pendulum swinging between repression and conciliation. Martin Wayne argues that the Chinese state had a repressive approach at the outset but effectiveness increased with the introduction of more conciliatory measures. In the case of China, social policies affecting the fundaments of society were successful to curb insurgent violence. He analyses that the secret of the Chinese success was that 'the state countered the insurgent dream by creating a competing dream, one more plausible and tangible, achievable only through participation in the state's project'. It needs to be recognized that discriminate force requires not only reliable intelligence but also highly skilled forces, commodities not many states possess in the amount necessary to carry out a counterinsurgency.

One aspect of the counterinsurgency repertoire that seems to elicit widespread agreement between the enemy-centric and population-centric approaches is the fundamentally political nature of the counterinsurgency. It is common to find references to this idea. With insurgency, unlike conventional warfare, once the decision to go to war has been made by governments, operational decisions in war are often made by senior military commanders. Counterinsurgent warfare is warfare where, as David Galula has pointed out, 'politics becomes an active instrument of operation' (Galula 2006: 5). However, by stressing the political nature of war, it is as if the author aims to stress that insurgency is somehow more political than conventional warfare. Famously Galula, who is often quoted, stated that insurgency is 80 per cent political and 20 per cent military. In this volume David Ucko argues that 'US military thinking now reflects *greater* awareness of war's political essence' (emphasis added). David Kilcullen and Warren Chin argue among similar lines in their contributions.

This discussion, however, is highly misleading. It is based on a limited understanding of the essence of war and, frankly, dangerous. If one understands war in the Clausewitzean sense, all wars are 100 per cent political. It is only the 'admixture' of other means that may vary. It is the responsibility of the politician to make available the optimum means to conduct the war, using the correct strategy to deal with the political challenge. Regarding the political nature of armed conflict, the case of Malaya comes to the fore time and again. Chin, in his contribution about British counterinsurgency, starts out by pointing to the success in Malaya but also in other conflicts of the dissolution of empire. He argues that '[l]acking sufficient force to impose its will resulted in the British understanding that success depended on dealing with the political roots of a conflict rather than prosecuting a campaign to annihilate the threat'. A political solution in the shape of independence underpinned the success of the British model of counterinsurgency in the era of decolonization.

Catignani points, in the case of Israel, to the absence of a feasible political strategy and political will, which has led to the military filling the policy void. This situation has been remarkably consistent since the late 1960s. He sees this as the ultimate weak point of this state's approach; the substitution of a military strategy for the lack of a political idea to deal with the insurgency. This conclusion finds confirmation in the chapter by Harik and Johannsen, dissecting the cases of Hezbollah and Hamas. As noted in the introduction, today also in places like Afghanistan, counterinsurgency ideas and the operational level of war tend to be a substitute for clear policy and strategy (Strachan 2010).

While it might be one thing to have uncovered the key to success to counter an insurgency, it is quite another to disseminate this wisdom to those who matter. The British were effective during the period of decolonization through the fact that many officers involved in these conflicts were posted in one conflict zone after the other; Palestine, Kenya, Malaya, etc. In the case of India, the problem of dissemination of counterinsurgency knowledge surfaced. As Fidler and Ganguly argue, it was not passed on in a formal fashion but based on the insights of participation from the civilian and military agencies involved. This led to a repetition of mistakes. Thomas Mockaitis draws the same conclusion about the Philippine insurrection and the neglect of the lessons of that conflict for US armed forces. However, Mockaitis is hopeful that this time around, based on experiences in Iraq and Afghanistan, the United States will retain the lessons and pass them on to the next generation. For the case of South Africa, Esterhuyse concludes that the South African experiences with counterinsurgency belong to a period in the past that is preferably forgotten. In this case, institutional retention of the counterinsurgency past is nonexistent mainly due to political correctness.

These divergent perspectives question the apparent existence of a universal set of counterinsurgency principles. One cannot help but observe that there are few uncontested elements in what has been considered the state of the art. The current debate about existing insights and wisdom in this area is lively. There seem to be areas of convergence around the importance of history and historical studies (cf. Peters 2007; van Creveld 2006) and about the political and social dimensions of insurgency. Dividing lines in the discipline revolve around the role of force and hearts and minds and their measure. The counterinsurgency repertoire of what to do and when is highly ideological and prescriptive, the success of coercion is preferably brushed aside and the lack of counterinsurgency learning remains a problem. It is striking that the more theoretical treatises of counterinsurgency are dominated by the Anglo-Saxon contributions. In fact, the non-Western world has largely been absent in the discussion, save as producers of insurgencies. This is illustrated by the conclusion in the chapter by Fidler and Ganguly that India, since its inception, has been subject of a large number of insurgencies. Its counterinsurgency record, however, hardly features in any serious discussions about the subject. We now turn to the topics that the contributors to this volume have identified as subject of important debate.

The topics of debate

Despite its long historic roots and attempts at a more or less consistent delimitation of insurgency, there have been efforts to question the overall validity of the concepts. This debate has already been touched upon and the contributions in this volume further underline its importance. As Robert Bunker writes in his contribution, private warfare of warlords and militias and privatized warfare by mercenary companies push the boundaries of the concept of insurgency. Furthermore, he argues that narco-insurgency might warrant inclusion into the category of insurgency. Piracy does not fit because of its purely criminal nature rather than a link with politico-military agendas. We should not forget, however, that many early modern states in Europe started out as criminal outfits or overly successful protection rackets. Economic success can enable political action and vice versa. Riches creates power and power creates riches. Warren Chin adds to this discussion with the idea of hybrid wars, the fashionable buzzword of the day, to describe what was previously known as insurgency. Chin argues that recently it has been 'recognised that insurgency was mutating and becoming more hybrid in nature, meaning that past distinctions between high and low intensity combat were becoming increasingly blurred'.

Furthermore, conceptual misunderstanding is also increasing in the case of counterinsurgency. First, what is counterinsurgency but an intention, if one reads the American Field Manual, according to David Ucko? Second, what is the exact role of counterinsurgency in relation to the popular comprehensive approach concept and the previously popular peacekeeping discourse? Without acknowledging it, at the end of the Cold War many techniques of counterinsurgency were re-invented to conduct the peace operations (Mackinlay 2009). As Chin writes in this volume, 'many of the tactics, techniques and procedures used by the British in past counterinsurgency campaigns were used to good effect in ... peacekeeping mission[s], which probably served to reinforce the impression that existing counterinsurgency doctrine remained "fit for purpose"'. Furthermore, elsewhere James Pritchard and M.L.R. Smith have argued that 'it would seem that much of what comprises the so-called five principles [of Thompson] can be seen in the "Comprehensive Approach", which is the modern British incarnation of COIN theory' (Pritchard and Smith 2010: 68). Thijs Brocades Zaalberg tries to create some more clarity in this rather muddled debate by identifying the distinguishing factors. He argues that the concepts are not interchangeable. At its core, he writes, '[p]eacekeeping was by definition an outsider's job, while counterinsurgency was essentially about the local government'. The conceptual quagmire was largely the result of misuse of the term peacekeeping. In the case of Afghanistan, '[a]s long as the armed opposition against the Western-backed Karzai government was minimal and the job of the average NATO "peacekeeper" on patrol in Kabul differed little from that in Kosovo, the misuse of the term went largely unnoticed'. He argues that the term peacekeeping should be exclusively reserved for missions deployed at the request of formerly warring parties to monitor a ceasefire they have agreed to.

Not only do we face important conceptual challenges, practical interpretations of (counter) insurgent agendas pose serious problems. In the case studies of Hezbollah and Hamas, Harik and Johannsen conclude that for both organizations the issues of contention for the insurgents are the subject of debate among scholars. The existence of the state of Israel, the pathways towards peace and the role of regional states supporting the organizations has led to divergent interpretations of the actions and intentions of both these groups. For the case of Iraq, Ahmed Hashim notes a similar lack of unity among the vision of the insurgents. The diverse groups espouse different and sometimes conflicting agendas. Giustozzi notes the same about the groups in the Afghanistan insurgency. Beyond the aim of getting rid of the foreigners on Afghani soil, the agreement between experts ends. Is the insurgency merely a response to outside presence, or are the fighters involved in a communal clash or tribal uprising? Similarly, what are the ideas informing the counterinsurgent agenda in Afghanistan; removing the Taliban regime, fighting terrorism, state-building, keeping NATO alive and pleasing the Americans? These ideas seem to be continually evolving. Also David Spencer engages in this discussion about the confusion over strategic agendas in his treatment of the FARC and Sendero Luminiso in Latin America.

Conceptual issues and interpretations of agendas of the actors are the two main topics of debate that the authors in this volume have identified. These, of course, give rise to research challenges.

The challenges and pressing questions

The contributors to this volume have raised several important challenges for the research agenda. First, the conceptual debate about the essence of (counter)insurgency deserves more of a research effort. As Thomas Mockaitis has noted in his description of American counterinsurgency thinking, it has for a long time been considered the bastard child of the military profession. After the Vietnam War the concept was hidden deep within supposedly new categories of Operations Other Than War or Low Intensity Conflict. Counterinsurgency ideas were not revived in the decade of peacekeeping in the 1990s. But as Thijs Brocades Zaalberg writes the commonalities were often much more prominent than the differences.

A second important challenge forms the question of the proper application of counterinsurgency ideas in light of the changing circumstances under which they are applied (Pritchard and Smith 2010; Marshall 2010; Egnell 2010). There are those who see counterinsurgency in different guises being applied in Afghanistan. Thomas Mockaitis for example writes in his contribution that the Americans in Afghanistan have been largely engaged in the capture, if not the killing, of terrorists and insurgents rather than in a proper counterinsurgency campaign. Only since the arrival of General McChrystal in Afghanistan in 2009 have efforts been made to apply a full-blown counterinsurgency approach. While a comprehensive campaign plan was developed, its application has been hampered by a coalition, rather than a unitary actor carrying it out, with each participant adhering to diverging outlooks and caveats. These observations have been echoed by the work of Rudra Chaudhuri and Theo Farrell as well as Pritchard and Smith that a counterinsurgency strategy is really being employed in the Afghan and Pakistan context

(Chaudhuri and Farrell 2011; Pritchard and Smith 2010). Their arguments diverge over the degree of success of this application. Others do not recognize a counterinsurgency strategy in current operations in Afghanistan. David Kilcullen is most adamant in his contribution to this volume that in fact COIN should not be a guide to operations at all. What is being applied in Afghanistan he calls accelerated counterinsurgency; 'combining extremely intensive counter-network targeting with intensified efforts at reconciliation (of senior Taliban leaders) and reintegration (of lower-level foot-soldiers)'.

One of the obstacles for carrying out a counterinsurgency, is the fact that a coalition is carrying it out at present. Chin notes that despite the wealth of British experience of counterinsurgency and doctrinal adaptability, British counterinsurgency awaits an uncertain future because of the coalition and resources necessary to conduct it at this point in time. In these circumstances, is it at all possible to conduct counterinsurgency as a coalition? The past offers few guidelines and this pressing question still awaits an answer.

Not only has the application formed a challenge, the role awarded to the local allies seems to have changed. Only a few years ago, the 'Afghan model of war' was highly celebrated, i.e. indigenous forces together with special forces were used to do most of the fighting (Biddle 2007). Now Geraint Hughes writes of the recognition that proxy forces bring a host of unforeseen problems:

> In cases where elite military units engage local surrogates to help them fight irregular adversaries, the consequences for state stability can be grave. US and allied special forces weakened Karzai's government in Afghanistan by using militias against al-Qaeda, thereby empowering warlords involved in destabilizing and unsavoury activities such as drugs trafficking. Furthermore, surrogate forces may prove unreliable.

There are many examples where NATO troops have become victims of local power feuds.

Third, in her chapter on the role of policing, Alice Hills points out a glaring paradox in the existing literature and practice of counterinsurgency. On the one hand, policing is seen as crucial in conducting any kind of counterinsurgency. Police men and women are the individuals with a most direct finger on the pulse of local dynamics and the best sources for intelligence. In the case study of Indian counterinsurgency, the role of the police forces has been awarded crucial importance. On the other hand, few studies exist that do justice to this crucial role. Also in practice, not only is a solid police strategy lacking, but also many policing missions are under-resourced. In fact, she laments 'international and local militaries alike regard policing – and police – as in some way inferior, and this is reflected in the political attention and resources policing receives'.

Fourth, the information revolution and consequences for fighting insurgency and counter-insurgency are only starting to be recognized. Coker provokingly claims that 'we use technology as a substitute for risk'. This of course provides the opponent a strategic chance to try and raise the cost of war in human lives by attacking civilians via terrorist attacks. Being able to take large-scale losses in human lives might provide strategic weight to the insurgents. This disparity breaks what Coker terms the 'community of fate' opponents in war usually share and it negates the recognition of the humanity of the enemy. Thereby we enter a slippery slope towards a moral and ethical quagmire. Glimpses of this are available in the discussion about the use of drones by Geraint Hughes. Also on the topic of the information revolution David Betz notes that cyber-insurgency is still the domain of science fiction but the use of cyberspace does give current insurgencies new dimensions, in particular with respect to narrative and transmission of ideas.

Fifth, there are few studies, and this present one is no exception, which deal with the distinction between counterinsurgency at home and abroad.[3] It remains unclear what the differences are, if any. Fidler and Ganguly offer the internal nature of Indian counterinsurgency as one of the reasons why these experiences have not been not part of the wider counterinsurgency debate. Furthermore, they argue that the domestic counterinsurgency campaigns, as waged in India, are subject of a different form of appraisal than international campaigns. For instance, as they state 'there is no "exit strategy"'. Steven Metz calls the external counterinsurgency practices 'counterinsurgency support', with the most important effort being local. What is often neglected is the possibility that there are important in-group out-group dynamics at play, which might influence the applicability and effectiveness of counterinsurgency ideas. Acting against a domestic political opponent who has taken up arms might require a different mix of measures, compared to acting against a political opponent on the territory of an incumbent, allied state. In the latter case the staying power of the counterinsurgent can be fundamentally questioned. As Thomas Mockaitis writes in his overview of American counterinsurgency experiences, 'How long will you stay, and what will happen to us when you leave? [This] [u]ncertainty over America's long-term commitment made recruiting locals difficult'. This situation makes it inherently questionable whether trust and legitimacy can be awarded to an outsider. Can the outsiders credibly commit and possess staying power necessary for building up a fragile state?

So having drawn this research and argument together where does this leave work on insurgency and counterinsurgency in the decades to come? At the time of completing this volume in the early months of 2011 it is becoming increasingly evident that we might be living through major political transformations in international politics. A number of militant popular insurrections have challenged the authority of several Middle East dictatorships with the downfall of the regimes in Tunisia and Egypt. Osama Bin Laden, the West's number one 'bogeyman' as the titular head of al-Qaeda and the mastermind of the 9/11 attacks, has been killed by a US Navy Seal team in a safe house in Pakistan. Further insurrections look likely to continue to destabilize the Middle East in the following few years, presenting, to some analysts at least, the serious possibility for the partial neutralization of Islamist and jihadist challenges to the West by a range of low intensity democratic structures.

We may therefore be living through a watershed period in which the older debates around insurgency and counterinsurgency structured around a 'war on terror' in the aftermath of 9/11 become increasingly redundant. What they will be replaced with of course is an open-ended question. It is possible that a new democratization agenda will begin to emerge in the politics of the Middle East and the Islamic world more generally after decades in which scholars have often pondered on the possibilities of this (see for example Salame 1994). Such a process is likely to heighten, at least in the short term, social conflict and actually escalate in some areas insurgent conflicts (Mansfield and Snyder 2005). However in the longer term it promises to provide political mechanisms for the internal resolution of social and ethnic and regional disputes and the avoidance of a resort to insurgent warfare.

In a more general historical perspective this shift towards a more open political arena should not be seen as too surprising – though academic analysts of international politics have on occasions been prone (as with the failure in the 1980s to foresee the end of the Cold War) to being caught out by the sudden emergence of unforeseen events. Insurgency and counterinsurgency from at least the second half of the twentieth century can be seen as part of the response to the rapid modernization of societies that had formerly been under Western imperial control. What emerged by the 1950s and 1960s as 'third world modernisation' often led to a situation where post-colonial regimes were under the domination of small bourgeois elites keen to push through programmes of modernization and 'development' on the basis of Enlightenment ideas of progress. These programmes have broadly ranged from market orientated capitalist ones to state controlled socialist efforts at centralized planning though the downfall of communism in Eastern Europe and the USSR in the late 1980s has ensured the demise of almost all of these.

Most of the regimes have been authoritarian in nature and this has been the cause for a number of anti-state insurgencies, especially when the regime has been seen to be marginalizing or discriminating against minority groups – the chapters in the volume on Sri Lanka and China, for example, exemplify this. However, as Michael Howard has pointed out in a cogent examination of the concept of peace, the alternative to this authoritarianism has often not been a simple shift towards Western style representative democracy but a more anarchic collapse into state failure (Howard 2001: 110–11). This has been the roots for a number of insurgencies in sub-Saharan Africa in the post-Cold War period as the chapter by William Reno illustrates. In turn the response by some counterinsurgencies such as those in Iraq and Afghanistan (though not significantly in China and Russia) has been to move these societies some way towards the establishment of some form of democratic political system that is capable, to some degree, of reflecting popular demands.

It is still too early to say whether the Middle East is on the brink of experiencing something like a 'fourth wave' of democratization following the formulation of Samuel Huntington (Huntington 2002). However if such a process does occur over the next few years it will radically transform the political context in which insurgencies are being fought in the region. Even limited forms of democratization offer the prospect for the inclusion of radical Islamist groups such as the Muslim Brotherhood in Egypt into the political process and to a considerable degree undermining the appeal of insurgency and terrorism.

The popular democratically-inclined insurrections currently under way in the Middle East may of course extend beyond this region to a wider swathe of states in the less developed world. On the hand, they may just be contained within a few Middle East states with the rest remaining in some form of authoritarian control. Whatever the case, they do promise to transform the current axis of global insurgencies over the next few decades further into the sphere of failed or failing states.

This is not the place to get involved in the extensive and wide-ranging debate in International Relations on the various possible futures of the international system beyond the nation state. It clearly impacts in a general manner though on the way work on insurgency and counterinsurgency is formulated. As many of the chapters in this volume illustrate much of this work is orientated still around the centrality of the state despite the interesting recent debate on the possible emergence of a globalized Islamic insurgency against the West (Kilcullen 2005; Mackinlay 2009; Rich 2010). In a broad sense this debate relates to a wider discussion about the future of war itself in global politics with a range of possible scenarios being suggested to replace those of a system anchored in the territorial state. Hirst has suggested in particular four such scenarios of:

1 a 'borderless world' of liberal capitalism;
2 a 'new Middle Ages' with a collapse of centralized authority into competing plural powers operating within and beyond the territorial state;
3 a 'network society' in which power is diffused along a range of networks of wealth, power, information and images; and
4 a new 'cosmopolitan' global order where the relative decline of the state leads to the emergence of a new series of global power centres that regulate and order the international system (Hirst 2001: 112–14).

These four new scenarios offer the potential for a range of important new questions to emerge over the form and nature of insurgency in the international system. The first scenario of a world without borders perhaps suggests an increased possibility for the emergence of global insurgent movements – but then it is precisely this possibility which will in turn limit the feasibility of the scenario emerging in the next few decades as states seek increasingly to cooperate in defeating such insurgent challenges. Likewise the 'new Middle Ages' resembles in some respects the doomsday scenario of collapsing states outlined in Robert Kaplan's thesis and which might be increasingly nullified by the democratic advances being made in the Middle East (Kaplan 2000). The third scenario of a network society does indicate a fertile area for increasingly salient forms of networked 'terrorism' by both state and sub-state movements; as we have previously noted, the research on networked forms of insurgency may well prove to be one of the most important and fruitful areas for analysts in the years ahead.

Finally there is the last scenario of a 'cosmopolitan' world order that has become associated with the work of both radical liberal internationalists and some neo-Marxists in IR. This scenario offers, perhaps, the most fruitful avenue for advanced cooperation on a global basis to confront insurgencies with the increasing enforcement of human rights norms and international law against local and regional insurgent and warlord leaders. It presumes some form of global police force and counterinsurgency body capable of enforcing these norms – though how this might be constructed and on what basis remains as vague. This is an area for much future research since if there is growing evidence for an increasingly powerful 'globalized insurgency' then in turn this presumes a growing international cooperation in meeting this threat on a global basis. Much might grow out of existing international as well as regional bodies. However the experience of bodies such as the UN, NATO and the European Union since the end of the Cold War suggests that the lead will still be taken by a small number of key states with continuing difficulties over free-riding by some states, problems in forging a commonly agreed military doctrine and political resistance by democratic electorates to the expense and commitment to long-term cooperation.

Given these general dynamics at work within the international system it is clear that we can expect a lively debate on the changing shapes of insurgency and counterinsurgency in the years ahead. It is especially important though that 'non-Western' perspectives, outside the traditional arc of the North Atlantic and Australasia, are brought to bear within an increasingly globalizing field of insurgency and counterinsurgency studies. This would need to include the stories and experiences of insurgency groups through detailed field work, which needs to award a far greater role to regional specialists and anthropologists, as David Ucko also concludes in his contribution.

A further important consideration, based on the material in this volume, is that we can no longer escape the politically inconvenient truth that coercive and repressive counterinsurgency has in a large number of cases achieved the desired effect of pacification and stabilization (Merom 2003). As others have stated 'coercion was the reality – "hearts and minds" the myth' (Jackson 2006: 17). Our preferred views on how to deal with political violence in the shape of hearts and minds policies has led to us to distorting and misreading history (Duyvesteyn 2011). In fact, Robert Egnell has recently suggested that the causal relationship between hearts and minds policies and successful counterinsurgency might actually be make-believe. He argues that 'a highly restrictive approach should be adopted until the causal relations between aid, security and legitimacy are established' (2010: 300).

A third consideration is that counterinsurgency ideas are by no means wedded to existing state-building theory (though see the various analyses in Rich and Stubbs 1997). Counterinsurgency thinking, fundamentally, still lacks an understanding of state building theory, failing states and role of regime type. Metz, Reno and Hashim have noted in their contributions the close links between patronage politics and insurgency. Cline, in his case studies of Thailand, the Philippines and Burma, but also Qazi in his study of the Pakistani insurgents, point out that insurgency is often founded on pragmatism and exploitation of the lack of delivery of coveted social goods by the central state (Kilcullen 2009). It remains unquestioned whether it is at all possible for an outside force to exert positive influence on state building. As Alex Marshall writes '[t]he advocates of liberal peace theory have ... emphasised a state-building strategy of "institutionalisation before liberalisation", involving the imposition upon subject societies of a coercive modernisation process, framed by tightly externally policed economic and political conditionalities' (2010: 244). Existing state-building theory, which is largely based on the formation of states in early modern Europe, shows that it is importantly also a bottom-up process. Our efforts today are based heavily on a top-down process and on exogenous influences rather than endogenous development. This is an area that requires urgent elucidation because it forms the fundament of the currently dominant counterinsurgency thinking.

Fourth, a largely neglected area forms the role of insurgents in international law and a human rights perspective on the application of counterinsurgency. During colonial times, the British government had declared the Geneva Conventions, article 3 as not applicable to the empire (Marshall 2010). As Christopher Coker concludes there is a moral hiatus in the fact that insurgent movements have not signed up to the Geneva Conventions. In fact, most international humanitarian law is based on a state-based perspective on international affairs. The whole development of the prohibitions and limitations on warfare and their implementation and adherance are mainly focused on states. Today there seems to be little recognition of this state of affairs and much more could be done. A notable exception is the work of the Geneva Call NGO which aims to make insurgent movements sign up to the Geneva Conventions with the argument that it will make it harder for them to be tried for human rights abuses, if cases were to be brought to the attention of the International Criminal Court in The Hague (Sassòli 2006).

The aim of this volume has been to demonstrate the rich thinking in the study of insurgency and counterinsurgency. Despite important advances in recent years, as we have tried to show, a whole exciting research agenda remains open.

Notes

1 Corroborative evidence is that military victories offer stable peace (Licklider 1995; Toft 2006).
2 This impression was further confirmed at the Conference on Insurgency and Counterinsurgency of the Commission Internationale d'Histoire Militaire, 29 August–3 September 2010 in Amsterdam.
3 One exception might be Beckett, who distinguishes offensive insurgency aimed at disposing a national government from defensive insurgency focused on expelling an occupational power (2005).

References

Assaresses, Paul (2005) *The Battle of the Casbah; Terrorism and Counter-terrorism in Algeria 1955–1957.* London: Enigma.
Beckett, Ian F.W. (2005) *Insurgency in Iraq: An Historical Perspective.* Carlisle, PA: Strategic Studies Institute.
Bennett, Huw (2009) '"A Very Salutary Effect": The Counter-Terror Strategy in the Early Malayan Emergency, June 1948–December 1949', *Journal of Strategic Studies*, 32 (3): 415–44.
Biddle, Stephen (2007) 'Toppling the Taliban in Afghanistan', in Jan Angstrom and Isabelle Duyvesteyn (eds), *Understanding Victory and Defeat in Contemporary War.* London: Frank Cass, pp. 187–205.
Chaudhuri, Rudra and Theo Farrell (2011) 'Campaign Disconnect: Operational Progress and Strategic Obstacles in Afghanistan 2009–2011', *International Affairs*, 87 (2): 271–96.
Creveld, Martin van (2006) *The Changing Face of War; Lessons of Combat from the Marne to Iraq.* New York: Ballantine.

Dixon, Paul (2009) '"Hearts and Minds"? British Counterinsurgency from Malaya to Iraq', *Journal of Strategic Studies*, 32 (3) 353–81.

Duyvesteyn, Isabelle (2011) 'Hearts and Minds, Cultural Awareness and Good Intelligence: The Blue Print for Successful Counterinsurgency?', *Intelligence and National Security*, 26 (4): 445–59.

Duyvesteyn, Isabelle and Mario Fumerton (2009) 'Insurgency and Terrorism: Is there a Difference?', in Caroline Holmqvist-Jonsater and Christopher Coker (eds), *The Character of War in the 21st Century*. London: Routledge, pp. 27–41.

Egnell, Robert (2010) 'Winning "Hearts and Minds"? A Critical Analysis of Counterinsurgency Operations in Afghanistan', *Civil Wars*, 12 (3): 282–303.

Freedman, Lawrence (2006) *The Transformation of Strategic Affairs*, Adelphi Paper 379. London: Routledge.

Galula, Philip (2006) *Counterinsurgency Warfare: Theory and Practice*. New York: Praeger.

Hack, Karl (2009) 'The Malayan Emergency as Counterinsurgency Paradigm', *Journal of Strategic Studies*, 32 (3): 383–414.

Hirst, Paul (2001) *War and Power in the 21st Century*. London: Polity.

Howard, Michael (2001) *The Invention of Peace*. London: Profile Books.

Huntington, Samuel (2002) *The Third Wave: Democratization in the Late Twentieth Century*. University of Oklahoma Press.

Jackson, Ashley (2006) 'British Counterinsurgency in History; A Useful Precedent?', *British Army Review*, 139: 14–20.

Kaplan, Robert (2000) *The Coming Anarchy*. New York: Vintage Books.

Kilcullen, David (2005) 'Countering Global Insurgency', *Journal of Strategic Studies*, 28 (4): 597–617.

Kilcullen, David (2009) *The Accidental Guerrilla*. London: Hurst.

Licklider, Roy (1995) 'The Consequences of Political Settlement in Civil Wars 1945–1993', *American Political Science Review*, 89 (3): 681–90.

Mackinlay, J. (2009) *The Insurgent Archipelago*. London: Hurst.

Mansfield, Edward and Jack Snyder (2005) *Electing to Fight: Why Emerging Democracies Go to War*. Cambridge, MA: MIT Press.

Marshall, Alex (2010) 'Imperial Nostalgia, the Liberal Lie, and the Perils of Postmodern Counterinsurgency', *Small Wars and Insurgencies*, 21 (2): 233–58.

Merom, Gil (2003) *How Democracies Lose Small Wars*. Cambridge: Cambridge University Press.

Peters, Ralph (2007) 'Progress and Peril; New Counterinsurgency Manual Cheats on the History Exam', *Armed Forces Journal International*, 144.

Pritchard, James and M.L.R. Smith (2010) 'Thompson in Helmand: Comparing Theory to Practice in British Counterinsurgency Operations in Afghanistan', *Civil Wars*, 12 (1): 65–90.

Record, Jeffrey (2007) *Beating Goliath; Why Insurgencies Win*. Washington, DC: Potomac Books.

Rich, Paul B. (2010) 'Counterinsurgency or War on Terror? The War in Afghanistan and the Debate on Western Strategy', *Small Wars and Insurgencies*, 21 (2): 414–28.

Rich, Paul B. and Richard Stubbs (eds) (1997) *The Counter insurgent State*. London and Basingstoke: The Macmillan Press.

Salame, Ghassan (ed.) (1994) *Democracy without Democrats: The Renewal of Politics in the Muslim World*. London: I.B. Tauris.

Sassòli, Marco (2006) *Transnational Armed Groups and International Humanitarian Law*, Program on Humanitarian and Conflict Research, Occasional Paper Series, 6, Cambridge, MA: Harvard University.

Staniland, Paul (2005–6) 'Defeating Transnational Insurgencies: The Best Offense is a Good Fence', *Washington Quarterly*, 29 (1): 21–40.

Strachan, Hew (2010) 'Strategy or Alibi? Obama, McChrystal and the Operational Level of War', *Survival*, 52 (5): 157–82.

Toft, Monica (2006) *Peace Through Security: Making Negotiated Settlements Stick*, Working Paper 23, McGill University: Research Group in International Security.

INDEX

Page numbers in *italics* denote tables, those in **bold** denote figures.